BRITAIN'S ARMY

IN THE TWENTIETH CENTURY

Michael Carver, born in 1915, was commissioned into the Royal Tank Corps in January 1935 and was serving with 1st Royal Tank Regiment in Egypt at the outbreak of the Second World War. Thereafter he served in armoured formations throughout the desert campaign in North Africa, towards the end of which he assumed command of the regiment, which he continued to do in Italy in 1943 and in the landings of Normandy in 1944. There, at the age of twenty-nine, he was promoted to command 4th Armoured Brigade, finishing the war with them on the shores of the Baltic.

Since then he has held important command and staff appointments, at home and abroad, culminating in the posts of Chief of the General Staff and, as Field Marshal in 1973, Chief of the Defence Staff. He was created a life peer in 1977.

He has written twelve books and edited two others, mostly of twentieth-century military history, as well as numerous articles and book reviews.

BRITAIN'S ARMY

IN THE TWENTIETH CENTURY

FIELD MARSHAL LORD CARVER

GCB, CBE, DSO, MC

PAN GRAND STRATEGY SERIES

PAN BOOKS

in association with

The Imperial War Museum

First published 1998 by Macmillan

This edition published 1999 by Pan Books
an imprint of Macmillan Publishers Ltd
25 Eccleston Place, London SW1W 9NF
Basingstoke and Oxford
Associated companies throughout the world
www.macmillan.co.uk

ISBN 0 330 37200 9

Copyright © Michael Carver 1998

The right of Michael Carver to be identified as the
author of this work has been asserted by him in accordance
with the Copyright, Designs and Patents Act 1988.

All rights reserved. No part of this publication may be
reproduced, stored in or introduced into a retrieval system, or
transmitted, in any form, or by any means (electronic, mechanical,
photocopying, recording or otherwise) without the prior written
permission of the publisher. Any person who does any unauthorized
act in relation to this publication may be liable to criminal
prosecution and civil claims for damages.

1 3 5 7 9 8 6 4 2

A CIP catalogue record for this book is available from
the British Library.

Typeset by SetSystems Ltd, Saffron Walden, Essex
Printed and bound in Great Britain by
Mackays of Chatham plc, Chatham, Kent

This book is sold subject to the condition that it shall not,
by way of trade or otherwise, be lent, re-sold, hired out,
or otherwise circulated without the publisher's prior consent
in any form of binding or cover other than that in which
it is published and without a similar condition including this
condition being imposed on the subsequent purchaser.

ACKNOWLEDGEMENTS

I wish to express my thanks to the following: to William Armstrong, of the publishers, for having thought of the book and suggested that I should write it, and to Nicholas Blake, who copy-edited it with such diligence and expertise; to all those in the Imperial War Museum, who have been so welcoming and helpful to me, to Dr Christopher Dowling, Keeper of Museum Services, Roderick Suddaby, Nigel Steel, Simon Robbins and Stephen Walton of the Department of Documents; Gwyn Bayliss and Alan Jeffreys of the Department of Printed Books; David Parry and John Delaney of the Photographic Archive; and Angela Weight, Pauline Allwright and Jan Bourne of the Department of Art: to Miss Alex Ward of the Army Historical Branch, Ministry of Defence, and Brigadier Mark Strudwick, Director of Infantry, and all the Infantry Regimental Secretaries for help in tracing which units served in which campaigns between 1945 and 1997: to the following for permission to quote from their books; General Sir Cecil Blacker from his memoirs *Monkey Business*, General Sir Frank Kitson from *Gangs and Counter-Gangs*, and Major-General J. P. W. Friedberger and the Trustees of the King's Royal Hussars Regimental Fund from *Emperor's Chambermaids: The story of the 14th/20th King's Hussars* by Lieutenant-Colonel L. B. Oatts: to Lieutenant-General Sir Anthony Mullens, Colonel of the Royal Dragoon Guards, for permission to quote from the 4th/7th Dragoon Guards Regimental Magazine, and Major-General C. A. Ramsay to quote from that of the Royal Scots Dragoon Guards and the Regimental History of the Royal Scots Greys: to David Fletcher, Librarian of the Tank Museum, for his help and permission to quote the report by Lieutenant G. C. Hopkinson on the Shahur Tangi ambush: to the Secretary of the Institution of the Royal Engineers, and to the Regimental Secretaries or Editors for permission to quote from their Journals, which are listed in the Bibliography: to the copyright holders of documents held by the Imperial War Museum, listed in the Index of Contributors: as on so many occasions before, to the staff of the Prince Consort's Army Library, Aldershot, for their unfailing help and courtesy, and to my agent, Bruce Hunter, for help and encouragement; last, and certainly not least, to my daughter Alice and son Andrew and his children for passing on the computer/word processor which Alice, having found it too unsophisticated for her, handed over to Andrew for his younger children to play with, who, having found it too simple for them, passed it on to their octogenarian grandfather, who, without it, could never have undertaken the project and certainly not finished it within the tight timetable he was given.

PREFACE

There is no lack of literature describing in various forms both the operations in which the British army has been engaged during this century and also every aspect of life in its ranks, whether in operations or not; but, as far as I know, there is no single volume covering its history during this period. As the century draws to a close, it seemed appropriate to try and produce one, both for the sake of the army itself and for all those who are, or should be, interested in it. To compress the history into one volume inevitably involves omission of many facets and much detail. The course I have chosen, with the help of the Imperial War Museum, has been to record a brief narrative of the major themes, both of operations and of organization, and to illustrate them with personal accounts of those who, particularly in battle, experienced what these themes entailed for the soldier at the sharp end. I have concentrated on that to the almost total exclusion of non-operational life, for active service on operations is the fundamental purpose for which soldiers serve, and success in which is how armies should be judged. To know what his predecessors have experienced and achieved helps a soldier to face the challenge of his duty.

Throughout the century, as in previous ones, the army has been faced with having to reconcile the conflicting demands of three tasks: the direct defence of the home country, including its internal security; contribution to a European alliance designed to ensure that no power inimical to our interests dominates the Continent; and the security of our worldwide interests, connected with our trade. Within the limited resources which governments have been prepared to provide, and of manpower which could be recruited, the army has had to try to achieve the optimum balance between these tasks in the training, equipment, organization and location of its soldiers. Using the experience of the past as a guide to the balance required to meet future demands has, as subsequent pages reveal, often proved unreliable; but imaginative visions of how to meet them have also been, if not false, at least premature. The army has generally been distrustful of and slow to change, except under the stress of a major war, although change in the form of reduction in its size has been forced upon it.

In the case of personal accounts, I have, wherever possible, made use of the wealth of material held by the Documents Department of the Imperial War Museum. It is rich for the First and Second World Wars, but scanty for other periods. For the half-century since 1945 I have relied very largely on Regimental and Corps Journals, of which the Museum's Department of Printed Books holds an almost complete set, with, fortunately, a computerized index of articles within them. The Museum and I agreed that, wherever possible, we should avoid quoting papers or extracts which had been published before either in their own books, of which they have published several, or by other authors who have made use of them. The same principle has been applied to illustrations, which have been taken from the Museum's Department of Art or the Photographic Archive. Our method was for me to decide what operations or subjects should be covered and for them to produce the papers for me which they considered likely to meet my needs. I would scan through them and select extracts, which I would then sieve further until I had made a final choice. In the case of Journals, I identified which ones were likely to prove fruitful, having discovered which units had served in which campaigns at different periods, thanks to the help of the Army Historical Branch and the Director of Infantry. The Department of Printed Books then produced them for me to scan through. I have recorded under Acknowledgements where I have used other sources.

My choices were determined first by what was available covering the operations concerned; secondly by quality in terms of interest, dramatic impact and style; and thirdly by trying to achieve an appropriate balance between different campaigns, arms of the service and experiences. I have preferred comparatively long extracts, which are complete in themselves, to a larger number of short ones.

The title 'Britain's army' requires definition. I have taken it in its narrow sense of the army recruited within the United Kingdom of Great Britain and Ireland – from 1922, Northern Ireland, although for some time after that date a significant number came from south of the border. This book therefore does not record the history in this period of the Indian Army or the armies of the Dominions and Colonies of the Empire and its successor, the Commonwealth; nor of the Royal Marines, although they fought as part of the army in many places at many times. The Royal Navy and the Royal Air Force are only occasionally mentioned. It is not therefore a truly balanced account of operations.

CONTENTS

LIST OF ILLUSTRATIONS

All the illustrations are taken from the collections of the Imperial War Museum, the black and white from the Photographic Archive and the colour plates from that of the Department of Art. The numbers following the descriptions are the negative numbers of the former and the catalogue numbers of the latter.

Section One

Section Two

Section Three

Section Four

Colour Plates

1

FROM THE BOER WAR TO THE GREAT WAR
1900–1914

The dawn of the century was not an auspicious moment for the British army. It came only a fortnight after what was known as its Black Week, that of the defeat at the hands of the Boers in South Africa of Lord Methuen, attempting to relieve Kimberley, at Magersfontein on 11 December 1899, and of Sir Redvers Buller, attempting to relieve Lady-smith, at Colenso on the 15th. Ever since the abortive Jameson Raid over the New Year 1896, tension between Paul Kruger's Transvaal Republic, generally supported by Mathinus Steyn's Orange Free State, and the British Cape and Natal colonies had been growing. It was intensified when Sir Alfred Milner was appointed High Commissioner in 1897. The principal point at issue was the voting and representational rights of Europeans, who were not Afrikaners, in the Transvaal, where the discovery of diamonds and gold had led to an influx of them. Kruger was determined that his Afrikaner *Volk* should retain control, while Milner's grand aim was to establish a British South African dominion, which would incorporate the Transvaal and the Orange Free State with the colonies. In this he was supported by the Colonial Secretary, Joseph Chamberlain, but only partially by the Prime Minister, Lord Salisbury, and his Government. The garrison of the two colonies totalled 10,000 men, and as Kruger built up his military strength with purchases of arms from Germany and France Milner appealed to London for another 10,000, arguing that reinforcement, far from provoking war, would prevent it, and that a strong military presence in South Africa would persuade Kruger to give way.

Salisbury's Government dithered, principally for financial reasons. The mobilization of Lieutenant-General Sir Redvers Buller's army corps at Aldershot, by calling up reservists, was considered as a remote deterrent. It was not until September 1899 that the Government finally agreed to send 10,000 men, to be drawn from India and garrisons in the Mediterranean, as well as from Britain. The sixty-four-year-old Quarter-master-General at the War Office, Lieutenant-General Sir George White, was sent to assume command. Kruger decided to act before further reinforcements could arrive, and, on 9 October, two days after White had reached Durban, he issued an unacceptable ultimatum. Two days later his commandos, under General Joubert, crossed the frontier between the Transvaal and Natal near Majuba, where he had inflicted a humiliating defeat on the British in 1881.

This shocked the British Government into ordering the dispatch of Buller's corps. Meanwhile White's force, which was fatally divided, allowed itself to be surrounded and besieged in Ladysmith, north of the Tugela River, as Joubert pressed on towards Durban. But he had not reached the coast by the time that the first of Buller's troops, Lieutenant-General Sir Francis Clery's 2nd Division, began disembarking there on 12 November. He then withdrew to the Tugela, where he prepared strong defences on the river line. The rest of Buller's corps, Lord Methuen's 1st Division and Sir John French's Cavalry Division, landed at the Cape and were sent up the western railway to relieve Kimberley, where Cecil Rhodes himself was besieged by General Cronje. After a fierce battle on the Modder River, twenty miles south of Kimberley, on 28 November, Cronje withdrew a few miles to the hills round Magersfontein, where Methuen delivered his unsuccessful attack on 11 December.

Buller had decided to take command in Natal himself, when Clery's division had been brought up by rail to south of the Tugela. Botha, who had succeeded Joubert, was holding strong positions covering the one bridge at Colenso and the few fords upstream. They overlooked the plain to the south, making it difficult for Buller to reconnoitre approaches. That and a number of fatal errors in execution led to the failure of Buller's frontal attack on 15 December.

Black Week shook Britain to the core. The Government's immediate response was to send its two most prestigious military figures (other than Lord Wolseley, who was Commander-in-Chief) to the rescue. The sixty-seven-year-old Field Marshal Lord Roberts, hero of Kabul and Kandahar, Wolseley's great rival, was extracted from command in Ireland as he learned that his only son had been killed at Colenso. He was given the forty-nine-year-old Major-General Lord Kitchener, hero of Omdurman, as his chief of staff, although he actually acted as a deputy commander.

More reinforcements were promised, an assurance easier to make than to execute. The total strength of the regular army based in the United Kingdom was 130,000, to which, on call-up, could be added 78,000 regular reservists and 30,000 of the Militia Reserve. The 65,000-strong Militia could be called on, if they volunteered, but the 10,000 Yeomanry, a force of volunteer cavalry, and 230,000 Volunteers could not legally be sent abroad.

The Militia was a body of ancient origin which could be raised by Lords Lieutenant of counties in times of emergency, originally by compulsion. This was changed to compulsorily by ballot, and that remained the legal position for a long time; but by the middle of the nineteenth century this proved so unpopular that its ranks were filled solely by volunteers. They remained liable for call-up and served for six years, unless they re-engaged, and carried out twenty-eight days' annual training at the depot of their affiliated regular regiment. They received an annual bounty of £1, receiving their first one at the end of their initial six weeks' recruit training. For an annual bounty of another pound, they could volunteer for the Militia Reserve, which could be called up under the same conditions as the regular reserve. It had become a popular method of entry into the regular army, as if the recruit found he did not like army life, he could resign from it much more easily than by buying himself out of the regulars. Its soldiers were either very young or rather old, generally unskilled labourers. The officers were on the old side and the whole force was considered to be a support to the traditional landowning class, as was the Yeomanry, whose officers and men, landowners and farmers, were of a better standing. The Yeomanry's task, certainly until police forces had become properly organized, had been internal security, Peterloo having been one of their less glorious operations. The Volunteers were largely a product of the invasion scares. They were locally raised patriotic bodies, prepared to defend their own area. They did little training other than drill and rifle shooting, of which they were generally keen addicts. They provided much of their needs out of their own pockets, but received a capitation grant for every man present at their annual inspection, a temptation to keep as many men as possible on the books, whether or not they turned up on other occasions. The House of Lords tended to be the champion of the Militia; the Commons of the Volunteers. Some Militia units did volunteer for service in South Africa and were used as line of communication troops; but Volunteers and Yeomanry could not do so as units until the passage of the Volunteer Act in 1900. Instead, enthusiastic gentlemen were encouraged to raise special Volunteer and Yeomanry units, the City Imperial Volunteers and the Imperial Yeomanry being formed for that purpose. When, after 1900, the war turned into a monotonous campaign of occupation and suppression, enthusiasm waned and provision of manpower became a major problem.

Roberts's plan was simple: to give priority to a direct advance up the central railway to the capital cities of the two Boer states, first to Bloemfontein, and then on to Pretoria. With those occupied, he expected both states to accept defeat and sue for terms. Buller, meanwhile, at lower priority, should pull himself together, cross the Tugela, and relieve Ladysmith. But this simple 'master plan', as Montgomery would have called it, had to give way to the political importance of relieving both Rhodes, kicking up a fuss in Kimberley, and White, gloomily despondent in Ladysmith. Kimberley was relieved by French's cavalry on 15 February 1900, and a few days later Cronje's force, trying to escape eastwards, was surrounded and defeated in a messy battle, directed by Kitchener, at Paardeberg. A week later, on 28 February, Ladysmith was finally relieved. Buller had launched a further attack on Botha's defences after Lieutenant-General Sir Charles Warren's 5th Division had joined him in January. Having crossed the Tugela upstream of Colenso, Warren's division met with disaster at Spion Kop on 24 January, and, after a further unsuccessful attempt to break through at Vaal Krantz on 7 February, Buller withdrew south of the river. He now realized he must try another direction and different tactics, changing to a methodical step by step attack, each step supported by all the artillery that could be brought to bear. He launched this on 12 February at and downstream of Colenso and it broke Botha's defences open, the latter making off to the north, leaving the way to Ladysmith open.

Roberts's main problems were now logistic. He entered Bloemfontein on 13 March, but did not resume his advance to Pretoria until 3 May, entering Johannesburg at the end of the month and Pretoria on 5 June, as Kruger slipped away towards Portuguese East Africa. Meanwhile Buller drove Botha from the Drakensberg mountains and, for the first time in their lives, he and Roberts met in Pretoria on 7 July. Both left South Africa in November, Roberts, who was to succeed Wolseley as Commander-in-Chief, having handed over to Kitchener as the euphoria raised by the hope that the war was over began to fade.

It was not over, but had changed its form. At the instigation of Generals De Wet, for the Orange Free State, and De la Rey and Smuts, for the Transvaal, it was transformed into a mobile war of harassment and raids, executed by mounted commandos, each about 1,000 strong. They could concentrate against points on Kitchener's long and vulnerable rail lines of communication and against isolated garrisons or convoys, depending for their supplies on farms in the remote countryside and for concealment on the huge expanse over which they operated. Kitchener's answer was one which colonial regimes were to follow against similar threats in the rest of the century: to combine cutting off commandos from their supplies, by removing their families and concentrating them in camps near the railway, with trying to bring the commandos to action with columns of his own, gradually restricting their freedom of movement by the erection of an immense network of fences and blockhouses. His method gradually worked, causing much misery in the process, until both Boer states finally gave in and signed the Treaty of Vereeniging on 31 May 1902.

At the time that Roberts handed over to Kitchener the army's strength in South Africa totalled about 200,000, of which a high proportion was engaged in static guards and garrisons. A total of 448,895 white soldiers had served there, of whom 256,340 were regulars or regular reservists, 45,556 Militia, 36,553 Yeomanry, and 19,856 Volunteers. 29,395 had been recruited from the colonies (as they were then called), other than South Africa, over 16,000 from Australia, about 6,400 from New Zealand and 6,000 from Canada. 52,414 had been raised in South Africa itself, mostly Mounted Infantry and Light Horse. In addition a Constabulary had been raised to take over guard duties with 7,723 coming from Britain and 1,258 from Canada. Deaths had totalled 20,721, of which 7,582 had been killed in action or died of their wounds, and 13,139 from disease. The total of casualties from all causes, including wounded, was 52,156: of them, 1,400 had been Australian, 507 Canadian, 421 New Zealanders and 8,187 South Africans.

It had been a disappointing war in many ways. In the early stages the

British had enjoyed no significant superiority. The Boers could put more men into the field, their German and French artillery and rifles were superior in range and the fire of the latter, using smokeless powder, was difficult to detect. Their tactical mobility was superior, almost all their soldiers being mounted on hardy small horses, though generally fighting dismounted. But at Magersfontein and Colenso it was not Boer mobility which won the day, but superior firepower from well-prepared and concealed defences combined with superior tactical skill which prevailed, helped by the significant tactical blunders of their opponents. All the British army's operations since the Crimean War had been against opponents less well equipped, many primitively so. Lessons were learned the hard way, Buller's final attack over the Tugela at Colenso providing a model which unfortunately was seldom followed in the First World War. In spite of justified criticism of his conduct of the previous battles, Buller deserves more credit as a commander than he has generally received. Methuen appears as a steady, reliable plodder: French as unreliable. Neither Roberts nor Kitchener deserve further laurels for their contributions. Many of the column commanders were to achieve prominence in the Great War: Haig, Rawlinson, Plumer, Byng, Allenby, Gough and the wayward Ian Hamilton. Hamilton was to be an official observer in the Russo-Japanese War of 1904–5, where he witnessed the importance of machine-guns. Although both sides in the Boer War possessed the Maxim gun, they were so few in number that they did not play the significant part against both infantry and cavalry that they were to do just over a decade later. The importance of mobility, especially in the second phase of the war, had the unfortunate effect of making the commanders of that conflict too optimistic about the value of cavalry.

As soon as the war was over, Lord Salisbury instituted enquiries into what had happened and how to improve matters. It was clear that the general organization of the army and the way in which it was controlled had failed to cope adequately. Both of these had been the subject of reforms when Edward Cardwell was Secretary of State for War from 1868 to 1874. Cardwell had done his best to bring the army out of the eighteenth-century pattern in which successive Commanders-in-Chief had done their best to keep it (the Duke of Wellington 1827–8 and 1842–52; Lord Hardinge 1852–5; the Duke of Cambridge 1855–95). Starting at the top, he made the Commander-in-Chief subordinate to the Secretary of State for War and the Quartermaster-General to the Adjutant-General, who became Chief of Staff and deputy to the C-in-C, who was forced to move his headquarters from his elegant office above the Horse Guards arch into the War Office in Pall Mall, where all departments were made firmly subordinate to the Secretary of State, that of the Commander-in-Chief for everything to do with manpower, that of the Surveyor-General of the Ordnance, a civilian, for both armaments and stores and also for supplies and transport, and the Financial Secretary for all financial matters, expressed simply as Men, Material and Money. The ancient post of Master-General of the Ordnance, which had been abolished in 1861, splitting his responsibilities between the Secretary for War and the Commander-in-Chief, was restored in 1904.

The Crimean War had shown that there was an urgent need for reserves to bring units up to strength, replace casualties and meet needs that were not provided for in peacetime. Cardwell therefore changed the terms of enlistment from twelve years with the colours to six years with the colours and six on the reserve. In order to meet the problem of keeping units overseas up to strength and avoid them being left overseas for excessively long periods (the 72nd Highlanders were at the Cape of Good Hope from 1827 to 1840), he linked together different regiments which had only one battalion, and gave them a county territorial affiliation for recruitment, providing a depot in the county, which also served the Militia and Volunteers. The battalion at home trained the young soldiers and recruits, who were posted to the linked battalion abroad. His successor, Hugh Childers, went further, and in 1881 amalgamated the linked battalions into one regiment. In associating the Militia and Volunteers with the Regular Army depot he brought them under the control of the War Office, the Home Office having exercised a loose form of control over them previously.

But Cardwell's reforms had not by any means solved all the army's problems. At the top there was friction between the Secretary of State and the Commander-in-Chief, who now, ironically, exercised more authority over the various departments than he had before, and between the latter, the ultra-conservative Royal Duke, and his ambitious, modernizing Adjutant-General, General 'All Sir Garnet' Lord Wolseley.

As a result there was a general feeling that the army was badly run and that money could be saved if it was better organized at the top. The

Hartington Commission reported on this in 1889, recommending aboli-
tion of the post of Commander-in-Chief and the establishment of an
Army Board, of which the senior member would be a Chief of Staff.
However Lord Salisbury's Government did not dare to try to remove the
Duke of Cambridge. When he was with difficulty persuaded to retire, at
the age of seventy-six, in 1895, Queen Victoria wanted her son Arthur,
Duke of Connaught, to succeed him, but the Prime Minister, Lord
Rosebery, jibbed at this. The post was not abolished, but given to Lord
Wolseley, who was succeeded in 1900 by his old rival Lord Roberts, on
the latter's return from South Africa, although Queen Victoria again
proposed the Duke of Connaught.

Before he succeeded the Duke of Cambridge, Wolseley had told his
staff to 'prepare a scheme for the mobilization of two Army Corps and
the necessary lines of communication troops for war outside Great
Britain and Ireland'; but this coincided with another invasion scare.
In 1889 the Secretary of State for War, Edward Stanhope, announced
that fortifications were being built on the approaches to London,
which would need 120,000 Volunteers to man their 233 guns, while
the Regular Army manoeuvred to defeat the invaders, a task for which it
had neither the organization nor the means to move or sustain it in the
field.

This led to argument about what the army was for. Stanhope
presented a memorandum on the subject to the Cabinet in December
1888, which was not made public until June 1891. It read:

Her Majesty's Government have carefully considered the question of
the general objects for which our Army is maintained. It has been
considered in connection with the programme of the Admiralty, and
with the knowledge of the assistance which the Navy is capable of
rendering in the various contingencies which appear to be probable,
and they decide that the general basis of the requirements from our
Army may be correctly laid down by stating that the objects of our
military organization are:

(a) The effective support of the civil power in all parts of the
United Kingdom.

(b) To find the number of men for India, which has been fixed
by arrangement with the Government of India.

(c) To find garrisons for all our fortresses and coaling stations, at
home and abroad, according to a scale now laid down, and so

maintain these garrisons at all times at the strength required for a peace or war footing.

(d) After providing for these requirements, to be able to mobilize rapidly for home defence two Army Corps of Regular troops and one partly composed of Regulars and partly composed of militia, and to organize the Auxiliary Forces, not allotted to Army corps or garrisons, for the defence of London and for the defensible positions in advance, and for the mercantile ports.

(e) Subject to the foregoing considerations and to their financial obligations, to aim at being able, in case of necessity, to send abroad two complete Army Corps, with Cavalry Division and Line of Communication. But it will be distinctly understood that the probability of employment of an Army Corps in the field in any European war is sufficiently improbable to make it the primary duty of the military authorities to organize our forces efficiently for the defence of the country.

The Boer War had not conformed to any of these categories, and Lord Salisbury decided that further reforms were needed. He established two Royal Commissions, one, chaired by Lord Elgin, to examine and report on what had actually happened in the Boer War, the other, chaired by the Duke of Norfolk, to report on the auxiliary forces, the Yeomanry, Militia and Volunteers, and how they could be maintained 'in a condition of military efficiency and at an adequate strength'. But before this, in 1901, the new Secretary of State for War, the Hon. St John Brodrick, had proposed major reforms. The army in the United Kingdom would be organized into six Army Corps, each of which would contain troops of all arms and be organized as a field formation, while also being responsible for all the troops, regular and reserve, in its district. Its peacetime commanders would be the ones expected to lead their troops in war. The First Corps would be based in Aldershot, the Second on Salisbury Plain, which had recently been acquired as a training area, and the Third in Ireland. These would be almost all regular and capable of deployment overseas, accompanied by a cavalry division. The remaining three, the Fourth at Colchester, about half regular and half auxiliary, the Fifth at York, and the Sixth in Scotland, almost entirely auxiliary, would have home defence as their task. For the first time, except for the Honourable Artillery Company of the City of London, the Militia and Volunteers were to man some field artillery.

The auxiliary units destined to join these corps were to be specially selected from the total. This ambitious plan ran into various forms of opposition, and could not in any case be implemented as long as so much of the army was deployed in South Africa. It would have involved a significant increase in both the regular army and in the voluntary reserves, especially in the artillery, the number of batteries on the home establishment being increased from 55 to 131, some of them to be found from the Militia and Volunteers. However, two significant changes were made. At the suggestion of Lord Roberts, in the hope of improving recruiting, terms of service were changed to three years with the colours and nine with the reserve, and in future soldiers were to wear the same uniform in peace and war, khaki, not scarlet, green or blue; the helmet was at first replaced by a round peakless cap, which proved unpopular and was replaced in 1904 by the peaked cap which survives to this day, although largely replaced in the Second World War by the beret, originally adopted by the Royal Tank Corps from Roedean girls' school. There were also significant improvements in the army's equipment. The antiquated Armstrong field gun was replaced by the 18-pounder, with the 13-pounder for the horse artillery, and the short Lee-Enfield replaced its long predecessor as the standard rifle for the whole army, weapons which were still in service at the beginning of the Second World War.

One of the principal objectors to the Brodrick proposals was the Admiralty. The Boer War had revealed that Britain had no friends and several potential enemies. Russia and France were two, and, up to 1898, the navy's plans had been based on having to face both of their fleets; but from 1898 onwards the expansion of the German fleet, combined with Kaiser Wilhelm II's aggressive anti-British behaviour, was forcing the Royal Navy towards a Three Power Standard fleet, which would be astronomically expensive. It was also doubtful if sufficient volunteers could be recruited to man it. Brodrick's proposals would demand money and manpower, which the Admiralty argued were more urgently needed for the navy. They saw no need for the army to provide for home defence. Either the navy was strong enough to prevent an invasion, or if it were not priority should be given to making it so.

The Elgin Commission reported in July 1903. The two principal recommendations were to implement the Hartington Commission's proposal that the army should be headed by an Army Board, similar to the Board of Admiralty, abolishing the post of Commander-in-Chief; and that the army should be organized so that in time of need it could be expanded by the vast reserve of manpower which existed throughout the Empire.

In September there was a major Cabinet reshuffle, in which Brodrick was moved to the India Office and succeeded by Hugh Arnold-Forster, the post having first been offered to Lord Esher, a prominent member of the Elgin Commission, who declined. He did not want a ministerial post, but agreed to head the three-man War Office (Reconstitution) Committee to make recommendations about its organization. Esher took with him the highly intelligent and efficient Secretary of the Elgin Commission, Lieutenant-Colonel Gerald Ellison, who was to make an outstanding contribution in subsequent years to all the bodies involved in reorganizing the army.* The other members were Admiral of the Fleet Sir John (Jacky) Fisher and Sir George Clarke, who had been Secretary of the Hartington Commission. They worked with great speed, took no evidence and produced their report in February 1904.

They recommended a proper Defence Committee of the Cabinet, headed by the Prime Minister, with its own staff, and an Army Council, chaired by the Secretary of State for War, with four military members, the Chief of the General Staff (replacing the Commander-in-Chief), Adjutant-General, Quartermaster-General and Master-General of the Ordnance, and three civil members, an organization which, although recently renamed the Army Board, survives to this day. The Committee also recommended a decentralization of authority and responsibility to the military members and, through them, to their subordinates in the field, a concept which it has taken a long time to implement to the degree which they envisaged. They went on to draw up detailed organizations for the directorates within the different departments, including that for a properly trained General Staff, an organization which lasted until very recently, some of the names of the directorates being retained long after they described their function accurately. It was a remarkable achievement, and their recommendations were fully accepted by the Government, the Defence Committee being converted into the

---

* He finished his career as Lieutenant-General Sir Gerald Ellison.

Committee of Imperial Defence in 1905, the Chief of the General Staff at the same time being named Chief of the Imperial General Staff.

Arnold-Forster had ideas of his own about how the army should be organized, and insisted on proposing them, rejecting Esher's advice to wait until the War Office could come up with its own suggestions. He accepted much of the navy's case, suggesting that the only form of invasion that the army need cater for was 'raids'. He proposed to divide the army into two, a General Service Army and a Home Service Army, and Cardwell's linking of infantry battalions into pairs, with one overseas and one at home, would cease. At home the infantry would consist of ten Guards battalions, twenty-six General Service and seventy-one Home Service battalions, while overseas there would be seventy-eight General Service ones. The General Service battalions would be at a strength of 900 men each, the Home Service ones 500, enlisted for two years with the colours and six on the reserve. They would serve permanently in their own territorial districts. He was vague about the Militia, deploring its depressed state and promising consultation, but proposed major reductions in the Volunteers, which would be divided into two classes with different rates of bounty, the higher being associated with General Service field formations.

Soon after Arnold-Forster had presented his proposals to Parliament, the Norfolk Commission reported in May 1904. It had become entangled in the argument about the danger of invasion, and, disregarding the advice of the Committee of Imperial Defence in August 1903 that 'an effective force of 100,000 Militia and 200,000 Volunteers would meet with requirements of the mobilization scheme for Home Defence', concluded that: 'If the purpose is to produce a force which, without substantial help from the Regular Army, can be relied upon to defeat an invader, then improvements in the Militia and Volunteer Forces will not be enough . . . but that a Home Defence Army capable, in the absence of the whole or a greater part of the regular forces, of protecting the country against invasion can be raised and maintained only on the principle that it is the duty of every citizen of military age and sound physique to be trained for the national defence, and to take part in it should emergency arise.' Arthur Balfour, who had succeeded his uncle Lord Salisbury as Prime Minister in July 1902, had already accepted the navy's argument and immediately rejected any idea of conscription.

The international scene and a change of government to a Liberal administration were now to influence the matter. On 31 March 1905 Kaiser Wilhelm II landed at Tangier and, mounted on a white charger, rode to the German Legation and told the German colony to 'uphold the interests of the Fatherland in a free country' and stated that his visit was 'the recognition' of Morocco's independence, the country being regarded by the French as virtually their protectorate since the signature of the Anglo-French Entente in April 1904. The Kaiser's behaviour greatly alarmed the French Government, already concerned that its ally, Russia, was on the verge of being soundly defeated by Japan in Manchuria. The attitude of Germany and the feeling that Russia was a broken reed encouraged France to patch up her differences, mostly colonial issues, with Britain, leading to the Anglo-French Entente.

The French Foreign Minister, Paul Cambon, was anxious to be certain of British support at the conference on the future of Morocco to be held at Algeciras from January 1906. A British General Election at the beginning of that month brought a Liberal Government, under Henry Campbell-Bannerman, to power, and Cambon immediately approached Sir Edward Grey, the new Foreign Secretary, to seek an indication of what Britain's attitude would be if the Algeciras conference failed and serious tension arose between France and Germany. Grey's response was to confirm the assurance of general support, without any firm commitment, which their predecessors, Lord Lansdowne and Théophile Delcassé, had given to each other. But of far greater significance was the approval of talks on military cooperation between Major-General James Grierson, the Director of Military Operations at the War Office, and the French Military Attaché in London, Colonel Victor Huguet, started at the instigation of the military correspondent of *The Times*, Lieutenant-Colonel Charles Repington. Similar talks were offered to the Belgians, who gave a lukewarm response. The Prime Minister approved of these talks provided that 'it could be made clear that the conversations were purely for military General Staff purposes and were not to prejudice the complete freedom of the two Governments should the situation the French dreaded arise'.

This turn of events had a decisive influence on Richard Haldane when Campbell-Bannerman appointed him Secretary of State for War in the new Government. He was a successful barrister with a clear, objective intelligence and an interest in philosophy and education, some of it gained in Germany. He had no previous experience of military matters and had an open but penetrating and decisive mind. He was astute enough to ensure that he secured the services of the indispensable Colonel Ellison as a member of his staff. From the start he accepted the arguments of the Blue Water school and saw that first priority must be given to an Expeditionary Force. Both the Stanhope Memorandum and the Arnold-Forster plan were thrown out of the window. In his first speech on the Army Estimates, he said:

> We live on an island, and our coasts are completely defended by the fleet. Our Army is wanted for purposes abroad and overseas. It is necessarily a professional Army; we could not get such an Army by conscription. It must be of high quality; but because of the limited nature of its functions – to strike at a distance – it ought to be of strictly limited dimensions. Have we ever thought, scientifically and clearly, what those dimensions should be? I do not think so ... The striking force ... does not exist for the defence of these coasts – it does not exist merely for our own insular interests. This island is the centre of an Empire ... and we have to protect the distant shores of the Empire from the attacks of the invader ... We want therefore an Army which is very mobile and capable of rapid transport. For fighting which has to be at a distance and cannot be against large masses of men it ought to be on a strictly limited scale, and perfect rather in quality than in expanded quantity ... If the Army is something which is not wanted for Home Defence, then its size is something which is capable of being calculated. The size of the striking force is the principal ingredient in the present cost of the Army. I do not think you will ever satisfactorily reduce your striking force, even if you have solved the scientific problem [of] how much you require for action abroad, unless you provide some power of expansion behind it in the country.

That description of the army's *raison d'être* has a familiar ring and could have been applied to any century of its history. Haldane planned to please both his own party, by reducing the size and cost of the army, and the generals, by turning it into a more efficient force, readier for war. Major-General Douglas Haig, Director of Training at the War Office, became a strong supporter. The Cardwell system was to remain as the only sound basis for maintaining the large number of overseas garrisons, especially in India, and the Expeditionary Force had to be organized out of what that left in Britain. That would not run to seven infantry divisions, but it could form six, each of three brigades. Anything over that, other than the one cavalry division, was superfluous. Those six would incorporate a balance of all arms and adequate logistic support, and would total 150,000 men, of whom 50,000 would be men serving with the colours, 70,000 regular reservists and 30,000 from the Militia. The force was to be capable of mobilization and deployment within fifteen days. The short enlistment of three years with the colours had proved disastrous: too few men extended their service. Enlistment was restored to seven with the colours and five in the reserve, eight and four for some.

By 1907 the reorganization was complete. In Aldershot Command were the 1st Cavalry Brigade and the 1st and 2nd Divisions, the latter including the Guards Brigade in London: in Southern Command, the 3rd Division with two heavy artillery brigades; and in Ireland, the 3rd Cavalry Brigade with the 5th and 6th Divisions, one brigade of the latter being in Northern Command in England. The Yeomanry was to find the divisional cavalry regiments for these divisions. The reorganization was generally welcomed, although any reduction had its opponents, especially in the Guards.

That was not to be the case when Haldane turned his attention to the volunteer reserves, which he proposed should form a Territorial Force. A forty-five-strong Committee, nicknamed the Duma, was set up under the chairmanship of Lord Esher to try to reach agreement on its organization. In a memorandum of 25 February 1907 Haldane explained the purpose of the Territorial and Reserve Forces Bill which he was about to present to Parliament:

> Its ground plan is to divide the forces of the Crown into two categories and two only, any attempt to organize in three lines must, I am convinced, end in leaving us weak and ill organized everywhere. The National Army will, in future, consist of a Field Force and a Territorial or Home Force. The Field Force is to be so completely organized as to be ready in all respects for mobilization immediately on the outbreak of a great war. In that event the Territorial or Home Force would be mobilized also, but mobilized with a view to its undertaking, in the first instance, systematic training for war. The effect of such training, given a period of at least six months, would

be, in the opinion of all military experts, to add very materially to the efficiency of this force. The Territorial Force will, therefore, be one of support and expansion, to be at once embodied when danger threatens, but not likely to be called for till after the expiration of the preliminary period of six months.

The main problem was the Militia. The army now had its own regular reserve and the Militia Reserve had been abolished. The Militia faced a choice between becoming more closely linked to and under control of the regular army, or joining the Volunteers in Haldane's proposed Territorial Force. Their old and bold refused to do either, and the Militia ceased to exist. The Volunteers were to be converted into a Territorial or Home Force, into which the Yeomanry would be incorporated. A new reserve was created, known as the Special Reserve, by which volunteers could join the regular reserve without having served with the colours. Militia men, including members of the Militia Reserve, who did not wish to join the new Territorial Force, but wished to serve out the rest of their militia engagement, could join this reserve. 67,740, out of the Militia's establishment of 80,300, chose to do so, but by 1913 only 636 and 64 men of the Militia Reserve remained.

A significant feature of Haldane's proposals was the removal of the financial burden imposed on commanding officers of Volunteer units and to transfer it to County Territorial Associations, composed of local worthies, which would receive grants from the War Office and would be responsible for recruitment and administration of all units of the Territorial Force in the county, including both Yeomanry and former Volunteer units. They would not be involved in training or mobilization, which would be the responsibility of the regular army command in which the county lay. The Yeomanry and some Volunteers opposed the County Associations as removing much of the independence they had enjoyed, and they successfully resisted the idea that their members would be elected rather than appointed to represent various interests, including employers.

The Territorial Force was intended to form fourteen divisions and the same number of cavalry brigades with associated corps troops, for which it needed 302,199 men. By June 1908 it had 144,620, but by 1910 that had reached 276,618, falling by 1913 to about 250,000 of whom only about 20,000 had volunteered for overseas service on mobilization.

The Bill included the establishment of Officer Training Corps at schools and universities and of Cadet Corps, although the latter met opposition from the radical element of the Liberal Party. It became law before Parliament rose for the summer recess. The success of Haldane's creation was greatly helped by strong support from King Edward VII.

India

While these epoch-making decisions were being made at the highest level, the army got on with its everyday life. For many soldiers this involved service in India or Ireland. When the Boer War ended with General Horatio Kitchener's signature of the Peace of Vereeniging on 31 May 1902, Lord Curzon, who had been Viceroy of India since 1898, asked for his services as Commander-in-Chief in India. The army there was scattered all over the country, seeing internal security as its primary task. But Curzon's principal concern was the potential threat from Russia as she extended her power with the construction of railways into the area north of Afghanistan, which had proved so troublesome to the British in India in the nineteenth century. Curzon was later to regret his choice, when he and Kitchener quarrelled about who was really in control of military matters; but initially he welcomed the vigour with which Kitchener reorganized the army so that it provided nine divisions, each of three brigades, one British and two Indian, most of them stationed in the north-west, guarding the approaches to the Punjab from Afghanistan.

After the Pathan rebellion in 1897 there had been argument about the policy to be pursued in the tribal areas of the rugged North-West Frontier. Lord Roberts was a firm supporter of a Forward Policy: to keep the fierce Pathans under control and prevent them from coming under the control and influence of Afghanistan. This would involve stationing troops and building roads, and would be expensive. The British Government preferred a loose form of indirect rule, bribing the tribes with various forms of financial incentive. Curzon and Kitchener supported this, giving higher priority to being prepared to meet a Russian invasion.

In fact in Curzon's time (1898–1905) there was little trouble on the Frontier, although there was a Mahsud rebellion from 1900 to 1902. In a lecture to the Royal United Services Institute in 1905, Curzon boasted: 'For seven years we have not had a single frontier expedition, the only seven years of which this can be said since the frontier passed into British hands.' But after his departure the situation deteriorated, the Mohmands indulging in raids which penetrated almost to Peshawar itself, until, in 1908, it was decided to launch an expedition against the Zakha Khel tribe in the Bazar valley, south of the Khyber Pass.

One of those who took part, in charge of an ammunition column, was the future Field Marshal Archibald Wavell, then a lieutenant in the 2nd Battalion of the Black Watch, one of the units of a Highland Brigade based at Peshawar as part of one of Kitchener's new divisions. Since he had joined the battalion after its move from South Africa in 1903 it had taken no part in any operation. From the amusing account in John Connell's biography,* it seems that the battalion, under its lackadaisical commanding officer, 'Chumpy' Maxwell, would have been totally unfit to do so. The only aspect of British army life in India that most took seriously was sport. The burden of engaging in such fighting as there was during this period was borne by the various bodies of 'Scouts', raised from the frontier tribes themselves, with officers recruited from the Indian Army, whose units also took part, notably Sikh and Gurkha battalions.

Russia's defeat by Japan in 1905 resulted in an Anglo-Russian convention in 1907 which removed the Russian threat to India, taken so seriously by Curzon and Kitchener, who had called for plans to reinforce the army in India, if the threat became a reality. In 1909 he left India for Egypt.

* *Wavell: Scholar and Soldier*, London, 1964 (pp. 45–58).

Ireland

The army's other traditional trouble area was Ireland, but during this period it was not called upon to engage in any active operations against 'Fenians' or their successors, the Irish Republican Brotherhood, and, from 1905, Sinn Fein – Ourselves Alone. Their influence had been lessened by the prospect of achieving Home Rule by political means through John Redmond's Irish National Party, which after the 1910 General Election held eighty-two seats in the House of Commons. Reaction to this in the Protestant community of Northern Ireland led to the formation of an Ulster Unionist Council, led by Edward Carson, a Dublin-born Protestant lawyer and MP. The Council opened an armament fund and began drilling volunteers, both of which were legal at the time, the latter if approved by a Justice of the Peace, provided that 'the object was to help maintain the rights and liberties of the constitution of the United Kingdom'. When Asquith introduced the Home Rule Bill in the House of Commons in April 1912, Winston Churchill, First Lord of the Admiralty, made the rash statement that 'Rebellion, murder and dynamite, these have vanished from Ireland'. The Ulster Council's response was to organize a huge rally in Belfast, at which 218,206 men and 220,991 women signed a covenant, some in their own blood, that they would never accept Home Rule.

On 1 January 1913 Carson moved an amendment to the Bill to exclude the nine counties of Ulster, and at the same time the Ulster Council decided to form a 100,000-strong Ulster Volunteer Force of men between seventeen and sixty-five, recruiting through the Orange Lodges, and the eighty-one-year-old Field Marshal Lord Roberts provided a commander in the person of the retired Indian Army Lieutenant-General Sir George Richardson. Many retired British army officers joined the force, and one high-flying serving staff officer, Captain Wilfred Spender, achieved notoriety by resigning his commission to join Richardson's staff.

In reaction to this, a group in the South in November 1913 formed the Irish National Volunteers, which absorbed, in a loose coalition, a wide spectrum of supporters of Home Rule, from the extreme members of the IRB and Sinn Fein to followers of John Redmond's Irish National Party. As a result, in December, the Government banned imports of arms into Ireland. Between then and the second second reading in the House of Commons, after the first rejection by the Lords, Asquith tried to reach a compromise by which at least some of the counties of Ulster could be excluded from Home Rule. Anything but the total and permanent exclusion of all nine counties was unacceptable to Carson and his supporters, while any exclusion at all was anathema to almost all Irish Nationalists. Asquith's final compromise was that any county should have the right to opt out of Home Rule by plebiscite for six years. Unless, after that time (which must have included a General Election), the Westminster Parliament had decreed otherwise, they would come under Irish sovereignty.

On 9 March 1914 this was abruptly rejected by Carson, at a time when he was under pressure from Richardson to forestall any possible move by British troops to reinforce Ulster from elsewhere in Ireland or from England by occupying port and vital railway and telephone facilities, as well as depots of artillery, arms and other equipment. Threats were made that the Council would itself form an Ulster Provisional Government.

The Government decided that some precautionary measures were needed in case the Ulster Volunteers took action, and on 14 March the Army Council sent an instruction to Lieutenant-General Sir Arthur Paget, commanding the troops in Ireland, stating that as reports had been received that 'attempts might be made by evil-disposed persons to obtain possession of arms, ammunition and other government stores', he should take 'special precautions for safeguarding depots and other places where arms and stores are kept', mentioning that Armagh, Omagh, Carrickfergus and Enniskillen appeared to be 'insufficiently guarded' and 'specially liable to attack'. No mention of any other sort of action was even hinted at.

Paget replied on 17 March, detailing some minor steps to improve matters at the places mentioned, but stating that 'although it would be preferable from the point of view of safety' to move some troops from Mullingar (seventy miles west of Dublin) to Armagh and Omagh, 'in the present state of the country, any such move of troops would create intense excitement in Ulster and possibly precipitate a crisis'. He was summoned to London where a Cabinet meeting on 19 March decided that troops should be moved to reinforce Omagh, Armagh, Dundalk, Enniskillen and Carrickfergus; that troops in Belfast (1st Dorsets) should be moved out to join 1st Norfolks at Holywood and that Major-General Sir Nevil Macready should join the brigade headquarters at Holywood with an unannounced dormant commission as Military Governor of Belfast, with possible jurisdiction over the whole of Ulster, if any overt hostile act by the Ulster Volunteer Force occurred.

There was considerable discussion in the War Office between the Secretary of State, Colonel Seely, the Chief of the Imperial General Staff (CIGS), Sir John French, the Adjutant-General, Sir John Ewart, and Paget about what action to take if any officers hesitated to comply with these orders or threatened resignation. It was agreed that any officer who had 'direct family connection with the disturbed area of Ulster ... should be permitted to remain behind either on leave or with "details"' (men left behind for administrative reasons). At Paget's suggestion, it was also agreed that 'any officer who hesitated to comply with orders or threatened to resign should be removed', the Adjutant-General having rejected the CIGS' suggestion that they should be court-martialled, on grounds of the technical difficulties and delay that would be involved. Seely offered to put this agreement in writing, but Paget declined.

It was a day of high drama in the House of Commons, Carson departing for Belfast, implying that he was about to declare a Provisional Government there. Paget was undoubtedly affected by this atmosphere. The question of officers' attitude to the possible use of the army to enforce Home Rule on Ulster had been raised by King George V, prompted by Sir John French, back in September 1913. The King had asked Asquith: 'Will it be wise, will it be fair to the Sovereign as head of the Army, to subject the discipline, and indeed the loyalty of his troops, to such a strain?', and Asquith himself, in November of that year, trying to persuade Redmond that there were limits to what could be enforced on Ulster, had said: 'Anything up to 30 per cent resignations among army officers must be expected, if the army were ordered to put down insurrection in Ulster.' Behind the scenes, that flamboyant and influential figure Major-General Henry Wilson, the Director of Military Operations, was actively intriguing with Carson and leaders of the Conservative opposition to encourage these fears.

But at this stage all the army was being ordered to do was to move some troops north to reinforce those already in Ulster to strengthen guards against possible attempts by the Ulster Volunteer Force to seize army equipment. Nevertheless there was discussion in London about possible plans for more extensive action if Carson and company declared a Provisional Government and the Ulster Volunteer Force engaged in operations, even to the extent of attempting to march on Dublin. In that case, Paget's force of six brigades, including one of cavalry, was not considered to be large enough to control the whole country, and reinforcement from England would be needed.

Paget undoubtedly had this possibility in mind when on his return to Dublin he summoned his subordinates, Major-General Sir Charles Fergusson, commanding the 5th Division, and Brigadier-General Hubert Gough, commanding the 3rd Cavalry Brigade, both of them stationed at the Curragh, Ireland's equivalent of Aldershot, to confirm the signal he had sent from London. This was to state that 'In view of the possibility of active operations in Ulster, officers whose homes are actually in the province of Ulster who wish to do so may apply for permission to be absent from duty during the period of operations, and will be allowed to "disappear" from Ireland. Such officers will subsequently be reinstated and will suffer no loss in their careers. Any other officer who from conscientious or other motives is not prepared to carry out his duty as ordered, should say so at once. Such officers will at once be dismissed from the Service.' This extraordinary order, and the short time given within which a decision had to be made, not unnaturally caused general dismay. The reactions of the two principal commanders concerned were very different. Gough immediately visited his units and then on the same day wrote a letter to Command Headquarters, reporting that almost all the officers in his brigade opted for dismissal, as he did himself.

Fergusson did all he could by personal appeal to persuade officers not to make that choice, or to withdraw their application if they had submitted it. He argued that soldiers in the ranks might feel it unfair, for if they were called upon, in aid of the civil power, to open fire on strikers from their own community they would have no option but to obey. He also made considerable use of the argument that the order came from the War Office and must therefore have been approved of by the King. Paget had of course gone considerably further than the War Office by mention of 'the possibility of active operations in Ulster' and demanding an instant decision on that hypothetical basis. The King knew nothing about the matter.

A typical reaction of a young officer, serving with Fergusson's division, was that of Second Lieutenant Scott-Watson of the Royal Artillery. In a letter to his father he wrote:

80th Battery,
XV Brigade, RFA,
Kildare,
20 March 1914

This evening I and the other officers of our Regiment were called upon to make the most momentous decision of our lives.

We were all assembled in the Colonel's office, and he read out the following proclamation from the War Office.

In view of the possible active operations in Ulster, all officers *domiciled in Ulster* will be allowed to disappear from Ireland till the operations are over. Any officer, who from conscientious reasons, refuses to take part in these operations will send in an application by 10 a.m. tomorrow. Any officer doing so will be *dismissed the Service*. This we are all agreed is the greatest outrage that has ever been perpetrated on the Service. We have had to make this decision without any opportunity of discussing it with our people.

The words 'domiciled in Ulster' have been underlined, and under penalty of court-martial our Colonel has to state whether a man is domiciled in Ulster or not.

I had hardly time to write for your opinion, so I have decided to carry on. Seven in my Brigade have decided to refuse, and will probably be dismissed the Service either tomorrow or very shortly.

I have decided to stay on for the following reasons:

Although, as you know, my sympathies are absolutely with Ulster, I think that at a time like this the Army must stick together. If we once start to disintegrate the Service, then goodbye to the Empire and anything else that matters.

Moreover, in case of strike duty, the men whose sympathies are fairly obviously with the strikers have to carry on and do their duty, so that it is up to us to do the same.

I hope and pray that I have done the right thing, but anyway it is now too late for anything else, for if you don't avail yourself of this opportunity of quitting, and then you later on want to do so, it means a court-martial, with a possibility of being shot.

Altogether, it is the most diabolically ingenious thing that has ever been brought in. What we especially detest is being dismissed, and not allowed to resign.

Gough's letter caused consternation in London, whither he was summoned, confident of wide support, which his brother John, Chief of Staff to General Haig at Aldershot, was busy whipping up, helped by Henry Wilson, as news of what had happened appeared in the press. Pressure was put on Gough to withdraw his request to retire, and return to command his brigade. He finally agreed to do so and to persuade his officers to follow his example when presented with a memorandum, which had been cleared with the Prime Minister, but to which Seely had added two paragraphs of his own and French a postscript. The final text of the memorandum is reproduced below:

23 March 1914

You are authorized by the Army Council to inform the officers of the 3rd Cavalry Brigade that the Army Council are satisfied that the incident which has arisen in regard to their resignations has been due to a misunderstanding.

It is the duty of all soldiers to obey lawful commands given to them through the proper channel by the Army Council, either for the protection of public property and the support of the civil power in the event of disturbances, or for the protection of the lives and property of the inhabitants.

This is the only point it was intended to be put to the officers in the questions of the General Officer Commanding, and the Army Council have been glad to learn from you that there never has been and never will be in the Brigade any question of disobeying such lawful orders.

His Majesty's Government must retain the right to use all the forces of the Crown in Ireland, or elsewhere, to maintain law and order and to support the civil power in the ordinary execution of its duty.

But they have no intention whatever of taking advantage of this right to crush political opposition to the policy or principles of the Home Rule Bill.

(Initialled) J. S. [Seely]

J. F. [French]

J. S. E. [Ewart]

War Office. March 23rd 1914.

We understand the reading of the last paragraph to be that the troops under our command will not be called upon to enforce the present Home Rule Bill on Ulster, and that we can so assure our officers.

(Signed) H. P. Gough

This is how I read it. (Initialled) J. F.

C.I.G.S.

Gough immediately returned to his brigade and all resignations were withdrawn. Next day the newspapers, alerted by another officer who had been involved, announced that the army in Ireland had received a written assurance that it would not be used to coerce Ulster. Asquith did not learn the true contents of the Army Council letter to Gough until late on the 23rd, and, having explained to the King what had occurred, announced to the House of Commons on 25 March that the Government had given no such an assurance. Attempts were made to get the letter back from Gough, but he had prudently handed it over to his solicitor and placed it in trust for his daughter. Seely resigned, Asquith assuming responsibility for the War Office himself. Although strongly pressed not to do so, French and Ewart also resigned. To ensure that there was no repetition of this fiasco, the following Army Order was issued on 27 March.

1 No officer or soldier shall in future be questioned by his superior officer as to the attitude he will adopt, or as to his action, in the event of his being required to obey orders dependent upon future or hypothetical contingencies.

2 An officer or soldier is forbidden to ask for assurances as to the orders which he may be required to carry out.

3 In particular, it is the duty of every officer and soldier to obey all lawful commands given to them through the proper channels, either for the safe-guarding of public property or the support of the civil power in the ordinary execution of its duty, or for the protection of the lives and property of the inhabitants in the case of the disturbances of the peace.

Thus ended the Curragh incident, sometimes called a mutiny, although nobody at any time disobeyed an order.

Assurance or no assurance, both Asquith and Carson realized that a threat to use the army against the Ulster Volunteers was now hollow, a

situation reinforced by the latter's reception at the ports of Larne and
Bangor on 25 April of 24,600 rifles and 3,000,000 rounds of ammunition,
bought in Germany by a former army officer, Major Crawford, police and
customs officials being contemptuously pushed aside or turning a blind
eye. An unwelcome reaction to this was a rush of recruits to the ranks of
the Irish National Volunteers, brought up to a strength of about 100,000,
a third of them in Ulster. 900 rifles for them, also bought in Germany,
were brought into the port of Howth on 26 July by Roger Casement
in Erskine Childers's yacht *Asgard* after an adventurous voyage from
Hamburg, and 600 more by Conor O'Brien to Kilcoole on 1 August.

On 26 May 1914 the Home Rule Bill passed its final stage in the
House of Commons, to be followed by an amending bill including
Asquith's already rejected compromise. Efforts were made to find a new
one, Carson and Bonar Law accepting an exclusion of Ulster within
Northern Ireland's present (1997) boundaries, with an option to rejoin
the rest of Ireland by plebiscite at any time; but Redmond rejected it. In
desperation the King called a conference at Buckingham Palace from 21
to 24 July, attended by Asquith and Lloyd George for the Liberals, Bonar
Law and Lord Lansdowne for the Conservatives, Redmond and Dillon
for the Nationalists and Carson and Craig for the Unionists. No
agreement was reached.

Four weeks previously Gavrilo Princip, a Serbian Nationalist, had
murdered Archduke Franz Ferdinand of Austria in Sarajevo, the results of
which were to provide problems for the British army of a higher priority
than that of dealing with private armies in Ireland. That the latter were
taken seriously at the time is shown by the memorandum drafted by
Major-General Henry Wilson which the Military Members of the Army
Council addressed on 4 July to Asquith in his capacity as Secretary of State
for War, which he was far from pleased to receive. It pointed out that
there were now two unofficial private armies, of 100,000 men each, facing
each other in Ireland and that the Government and the army had no plan
to deal with the situation that would arise if they started fighting each
other. If this were to happen, and the army were called upon to restore
order, it would absorb the resources of the whole of the planned
Expeditionary Force. The army would then 'be inadequate security against
invasion; we shall be unable to give any assistance to either Egypt or India;
and finally, be unable to meet any of our obligations abroad'.

2

THE GREAT WAR
1914–1918

Henry Wilson's passion for intrigue and determination to ensure that events developed in the way that he thought best may have been troublesome in Irish affairs, but made a very significant contribution to seeing that the army was ready to take the field when war with Germany broke out on 4 August 1914. His dedication to ensuring that an effective British Expeditionary Force was deployed alongside the French army, if France was threatened by Germany, originated in December 1909, when as Commandant of the Staff College at Camberley he paid a visit to his French opposite number, Général de Division Ferdinand Foch, Commandant of the École Supérieure de Guerre, during which Foch explained the plans for the defence of France. It was either on that occasion or at a subsequent meeting that Wilson asked Foch what was the smallest British military force that would be of any practical assistance to the French, if war came, to which Foch is said to have replied: 'One single private soldier, and we would take good care that he was killed.'

When Wilson became Director of Military Operations at the War Office in August 1910 he threw himself with great vigour into examining British plans for the employment of the six regular divisions, stationed in the United Kingdom, which Haldane's reforms had created. At the time, plans for overseas deployment of only four divisions had been made, but there was no proper plan to mobilize horses and no plans for rail movement to ports. By March 1911 Wilson had persuaded the CIGS, General Sir William Nicholson, that he should plan to deploy all six divisions, embarking them on the fourth day after mobilization, to be followed by the cavalry division three days later and the artillery two days after that. The Agadir incident in July added urgency to this planning, Wilson going to Paris, accompanied by the indispensable

Colonel Huguet, to meet the Chief of Staff, General Dubail, and the War Minister, M. Messimy, and discuss where the BEF should be deployed and all the transport, supply and command problems involved.

Wilson explained the results of this to a meeting of the Committee of Imperial Defence on 23 August. The First Sea Lord, Admiral Sir Arthur Wilson, registered strong disapproval, suggesting instead a series of raids on the German coast in the North Sea and the Baltic. Henry Wilson's briefing was so thorough and persuasive and Arthur Wilson's so vague and ill thought out that the former prevailed. Behind the scenes he devoted considerable effort to persuading Lloyd George, Chancellor of the Exchequer, and Winston Churchill, President of the Board of Trade, but shortly to become First Lord of the Admiralty, of the need to involve Belgium and to mobilize on the same day as France. However, opposition to Henry Wilson's apparently bellicose attitude persisted, centring on plans to commit the BEF to France. At the time there was a tendency for the Conservative opposition, led by Arthur Balfour, to give priority to home defence. Both Sir John French, who became CIGS in March 1912, and Wilson lobbied against this. When the Admiralty withdrew eight battleships from the Mediterranean in 1912, arguing that without them the Grand Fleet could not guarantee control of the North Sea or be able to escort the army across the Channel, French and Wilson pressed for a formal alliance with France, without whose naval help troops could not be sent through the Mediterranean to Egypt or India. They were not successful, although detailed planning, with full naval cooperation, continued with the French authorities early in 1914. After the Curragh incident, it was based on only five divisions being sent initially.

The Western Front, 1914

As the international scene darkened at the end of July 1914, Wilson devoted all his energies to persuading Herbert Asquith, who was still both Prime Minister and Secretary of State for War, to order mobilization at the same time as the French, who mobilized at 3.40 p.m. on

1 August. Thereafter he pressed for a decision on the deployment of the BEF, urging this strongly on Haldane, who returned to the War Office on 3 August. Haig, commanding the 1st Corps (1st and 2nd Divisions), argued against this and suggested that there should be no deployment for two or three months, while 'the immense resources of the Empire could be developed'. Asquith summoned a Council of War at 4 p.m. on 5 August, attended by Sir Edward Grey (Foreign Secretary), Haldane and Churchill, Field Marshals Roberts, Kitchener and French (designated to command the BEF), all the military members of the Army Council, Prince Louis of Battenberg (the First Sea Lord), the two corps commanders, Lieutenant-Generals Haig and Grierson, and French's chief of staff, Lieutenant-General Sir Archibald Murray.

French thought it was too late to concentrate as far forward as planned, at Maubeuge, and proposed, to Wilson's horror, Antwerp. Kitchener suggested Amiens, which was agreed. Churchill and Roberts wanted all six divisions to go, which was provisionally accepted. When Kitchener took over as Secretary of State for War the following morning there were rumours of German landings on the east coast, and opposition to denuding the country of all its regular soldiers was voiced in influential circles. At a further War Council that day it was decided to send only four infantry divisions (1st, 2nd, 3rd and 5th) and the cavalry division immediately: to transfer the 6th from Ireland to England and to send the 4th later, Kitchener assuming Amiens to be the concentration area, although Wilson did nothing to change the prearranged plan. Embarkation started on 9 August, 80,000 troops with only 125 machine-guns, 30,000 horses and 315 field guns sailing at ten-minute intervals from Southampton and Portsmouth to Boulogne, Rouen and Le Havre. On 12 August the War Council met again to decide on the concentration area, French, Murray, Wilson, Huguet and two other French officers all arguing for sticking to Maubeuge, Kitchener finally giving way after three hours of argument.

From the moment at which he arrived in the War Office, Kitchener had behaved not just as the political head of the army, but, emphasizing his rank as a Field Marshal, as an autocratic Commander-in-Chief, paying little attention to the views of fellow members of either the Army Council or the Cabinet or of the General Staff, least of all to its self-effacing Chief, General Sir James Wolfe-Murray. His reluctance to allow the BEF to concentrate further forward than Amiens was due to his

distrust of the French addiction to the offensive and to his fear that
when it reached Maubeuge it might meet the Germans before it could
deploy properly, and that the army's first taste of Continental warfare
since the Crimea might take the form of an ignominious retreat, fatal to
its morale. His orders to Sir John French reflected these fears: 'The
special motive of the Force under your control is to support and
cooperate with the French Army ... and to assist the French in
preventing or repelling the invasion by Germany of French or Belgian
territory and eventually to restore the neutrality of Belgium'. As the
'numerical strength of the British force and its contingent reinforcement
is strictly limited' it would be necessary to exercise 'the greatest care
towards a minimum loss and wastage'. If he was asked to take part in
any 'forward movements' in which the French were not themselves
engaged in large numbers and in which the British might be 'unduly
exposed to attack', he was to consult the Government first and must
'distinctly understand that your command is an entirely independent
one and that you will in no case come under the orders of an Allied
general'.

Kitchener's fears came near to being justified. Sir John French's army
completed its concentration round Maubeuge on 20 August, with Haig's
1st Corps on the right and 2nd Corps on the left, commanded by
Lieutenant-General Sir Horace Smith-Dorrien, Grierson having died in
the train near Amiens two days before. French was intending to advance
towards von Kluck's German First Army which was approaching, but on
21 August he learned that all the French armies to his right were
withdrawing. Both corps therefore took up a defensive position along
the Mons–Condée canal, where they were attacked next day, putting up
a vigorous defence under intense artillery fire. The withdrawal of the
Fifth French Army exposed Haig's right flank, and on 25 August the
French Commander-in-Chief, General Joffre, ordered a general withdrawal to the River Marne.

The hot weather and constant pressure from the enemy's leading
forces imposed a severe strain on the troops trudging wearily back, the
two corps being separated by the forest of Mormal. Against French's
wishes, Smith-Dorrien decided that he must halt temporarily at Le
Cateau, where his corps suffered heavy casualties in holding up the
enemy, while the 4th Division, released from England, was beginning to
join French's army.

Sergeant John McIlwain of the 2nd Connaught Rangers in the 2nd Division describes his experience at Le Cateau on 26 August:

About 4 a.m. our officers, who were wearied as ourselves, and apparently without orders, and in doubt what to do, led us back to the position of the night before. After some consultation we took up various positions in a shallow valley. Told to keep a sharp look-out for Uhlans.* We appeared to be on some covering movement. No rations this day; seemed to be cut off from supplies. Slept again for an hour or so on a sloping road until 11 a.m. We retired to a field, were told we could 'drum up' as we had tea. I went to a nearby village to get bread. None to be had, but got a fine drink of milk and some pears. Upon the sound of heavy gunfire near at hand we w hastily formed up on the road. Then the Germans got the rar us, rained small shells, horse artillery apparently. I followed platoon officer, Lieut. Lentaigne, into a turnip field. When taking cover, Private Sweeney, an old Indian wallah, lying beside me was wounded. Had to cut our way through a hedge to help Sweeney on to the road. Formed up under our company commander, Major Alexander. Cut off from the remainder of battalion. Major at a loss. Met some French officers. Retreated again. I with eight men do advance guard. Fixed bayonets and a sharp look out each side of the road, but still no Germans. Germans mile or so behind us, burning the villages as they pass. The sky lit up. Then rain, rain! and I, in the stress of the retreat, like many others, who were trained by Kitchener always to travel light, had thrown away my great-coat.

I did not record at what time the remnants of our company were rejoined by others of the battalion, but it must have been at various times that afternoon after the confusion of the German shelling. By evening we mustered half-battalion strength. 'C' had about half a company. Over the whole Major Sarsfield took command, the Adjutant, Captain Yeldham, was also present. Colonel Abercrombie and 400 or so others, were captured by the Germans.

Continuing the march from the village where we had met the small party of Frenchmen, with the impression that we were surrounded by Germans, we became aware in the darkness of a large force close at hand. We were led cautiously off the road and waited. We had seen only small parties of French and concluded that the

* German cavalry.

troops on the road, making noise enough for an army, must be German. While the rain fell steadily, and the sky was lit by fires, the distant beat of troops of horse dominated all other sounds. Among them could be heard confused cries and shouting of orders: all heard faintly. It was like a whole cavalry division extended for miles. But through all other sounds, and unforgettable, was the shrill whinney-ing here and there of horses: calls and answering calls.

The prospect of being taken prisoner in our miserable condition – for we could never elude such an immense force, made the situation peculiarly tense and memorable. For all the years of the war after that time, and years after that, if, in the silence of night, I heard a horse calling, at once there would come to my mind again a picture of that waiting in uncertainty in the rain, while the clatter of a thousand hooves and the pathetic neighing of the horses came over the quiet fields under the lit-up sky.

But it was a French army. So we rejoined the road, passed through a town, the name of which I made no note of, and discovered the French force, now halted, arranging billets. But there was no room for us, nor for many of the French. We sought shelter in a wood by the roadside beyond the town. Now the tension was relaxed, while knowing we were comparatively safe, our situation was still most miserable. Wearied and hungry, we lay passively, shivering, with streams of rain falling on us from the trees.

To Joffre's dismay, Sir John French now decided that his troops needed to be withdrawn south-west of Paris for a rest, while his line of communication was switched from Le Havre to St Nazaire on the Atlantic coast. Kitchener realized that French's interpretation of his orders would bring about a crisis and travelled to Paris to confer with the French and tell Sir John to cooperate fully with Joffre. French, who was insisting on the need for his army to 'refit', was infuriated by the fact that Kitchener appeared in uniform and made him leave his headquarters to meet him at the British Embassy in Paris, leaving the impression that French was a mere military subordinate of his. On 3 September Haig and Smith-Dorrien's troops withdrew over the Marne and continued southward. However, French agreed on 5 September that his forces would participate in the counter-attack which Joffre ordered to start next day, advancing between Franchet d'Esperey's Fifth Army and Manoury's Sixth, which had been formed from the garrison of Paris and rushed to the front in taxis and buses. The blow was delivered in a gap between von Kluck's First and von Bulow's Second Army and pushed them back until the River Aisne was reached on 12 September.

Lieutenant the Hon. Lionel Tennyson had only just reached his battalion, 1st Rifle Brigade, at the start of the battle and found himself attached as an orderly officer to the brigade headquarters (11th) in the 4th Division. His diary for 9 September records:

At 2.30 a.m. I was awakened to go and inform our Colonel from the General* that we were going to have an attack at dawn on the opposite side of the river. By going down the hill from the château through LA FERTÉ half of the town the East Lancs had possession of on this side of the river, and the other half across the river the Germans held. We started descending the hill to LA FERTÉ about 3.20 a.m. and when we got to a square this side of the village, near the real LA FERTÉ château, it was decided for my battalion to go up the road to the right, up along the top of the hill, and try and effect a crossing on the right of the village of LA FERTÉ. The general and his staff took up a position on the top of this hill, where we would have a very good view of this village. We had been there about half an hour when the General sent me down on a bicycle with a message to Colonel Le Marchant of the East Lancs who was down in the village. As I was bicycling down this hill the German machine-guns from the opposite side of the river opened fire on me, but I kept close under a wall and so was fairly safe. I delivered my message to him and had some breakfast at the château with him, when I returned to the General. One minute after I left the Colonel of the East Lancs was no more, he was shot through the head by a German sniper.

About an hour after this I went down to the square in this village with the General, and the German machine guns opened on us again. The General is a particularly brave man, and while we were standing there the bullets from these machine guns were hitting the wall behind us only just above our heads, but he didn't seem to notice them. I must say I was very pleased when he moved as I had to stand with him. He had 3 horses killed under him at LIGNY the first day he came into action and still his nerve is wonderful, in fact he is

---

* Brigadier-General Aylmer Hunter-Weston.

much too brave for a general. As a man I do not like him much nor does anybody, he is very fussy, and has the reputation of rather losing his head, and being rather incompetent. I forgot to mention that the first thing I saw today before breakfast as we entered LA FERTÉ, was one English officer and four private soldiers, a white horse, and a dead German lying dead on the road. They must have been killed by a shell, though the German was probably shot before, as he would not have been so close to them. Jack Micklem of my battalion about midday did some good work it appears with his machine gun from the top of the hill near us, as we found their transport halted in a lane on the opposite side of the MARNE, and Micklem with his machine guns opened fire on them, and also our artillery, and I think did great damage. It was a wonderful sight to see our guns all day shelling the German snipers on the opposite bank, as we set many houses and farms on fire with our lyddite shells thus driving the Germans out. About 5 p.m. the General sent me to the château garden to get hold of the gardener and get some vegetables for his dinner. This I did, but coming back through a small wood, I came right upon 16 dead Englishmen including the Colonel of the East Lancs, Le Marchant by name, all lying side by side ready to be buried. There are awful sights like these one sees in war, but one has to get used to them. After a short quick dinner, the General sent me off three miles about 8.30 p.m. through some thick dark woods, all alone, to find the Hampshires. This was not at all a nice job, as he said I might come across a few Uhlans lurking about my way, but must have my revolver ready to shoot at a moment's notice. I walked I think quicker than I have ever walked three miles before, and the night was simply black as ink. All I met was a French labourer, who said goodnight, and I wasn't sorry when I eventually found the Hampshires, though I was nearly shot by their sentries who were very much on the 'qui vive' when I got there. I had a little more dinner, and a glass of claret, with the Hampshires, and then showed them the way down the hill to LA FERTÉ to where the general was. When we reached the general's château they were ordered to cross the MARNE in four boats as well as the East Lancs, during the night, which they did, though the Hampshires lost 2 men drowned in doing so. A rope was fixed to each bank of the river and about 8 men at a time pulled themselves across the river as the bridge across had been blown up by the Germans. The RE spent the night building a pontoon bridge which was to be ready by the early morning. I turned in to sleep in the château about 11 p.m.

Fierce fighting followed on the Aisne until 25 September, as the 6th Division started arriving to join the others. Casualties were heavy and it now became clear that a major effort would be needed to force the Germans further back. Each side then tried to outflank the other to the north, the French with the British achieving greater success. Hopes were raised that the Belgian army's hold on Antwerp could be exploited, but when that city fell to the Germans on 9 October those hopes were dashed and the Franco-British line stabilized a few miles over the Belgian border, the British having switched to the left of the French, with the Belgians between them and the coast. Sir John French did not abandon his attempt to advance in the north and launched an attack east of Ypres, which lasted from 12 to 21 October, but failed to push the Germans off the higher ground.

The future Field Marshal, Lieutenant Bernard Montgomery, of the 2nd Royal Warwicks in the 4th Division, was wounded on 13 October, winning the DSO for his bravery. Another participant was Gunner B. C. Myatt with the 23rd Brigade Royal Field Artillery in the 3rd Division. He describes events on 18 October:

We are still in the same position. Have strongly entrenched our guns. This is our battle day. We generally have a big fight on Sunday. There is a lot of prisoners passing us now, also hundreds of our fellows wounded. We are just going to give the Germans their breakfast. Well I think our guardian angel was with us this afternoon. It was about three o'clock and we were in the town of Obers through which we had driven the Germans yesterday and there had not been any shells over all day, and the people had started to flock back to their homes which had all been ruined by the drunken German beasts. Women were telling us of the German deeds and young girls who had been disgraced. Also old men who had been tied up and pricked with bayonets by the swine and the streets full of our troops and transports. When a fellow of a battery to the right of us was signalling to his battery with a white flag and he changed it to a blue one and I distinctly saw the hands on the clock move back, it was a signal to the Germans by a spy. Well they opened fire on the town. Well by God, they crashed their great shells, the terrible 'Jack Johnsons' into the town. The first one went right through the church, the next 12 in town and the next in front of my battery. By God it was fair terrifying. It killed dozens of infantry and the poor people and children fled terror stricken. I am not a coward by God no, but they terrify me. I was glad when this day was over, I said many a silent prayer, as I never dreamt of getting out of this lot alive, and by Lord we never got one man hit, and it flew all round us, but our fellows kept very cool. Our Major spoke and said 'keep calm and cool my men, be Britons, if they advance they are to come over our dead bodies.' Well it is not the shell but its awful explosion attached to the bursting. It is like a man dropping a thousand planks on a pavement, but more deadly. Well it fair shook my nerves up this day. The transport was flying all over the road without drivers and the hospital was hit. They were bringing the dead and wounded by us. It's a terrible sight and war is horrible. The poor people fled screaming for their lives. I shall never forget these poor women flying down the road. This war is getting beyond human endurance. This modern artillery is awful. Human beings cannot stand such shock. This kept up well into the night and they had a searchlight laid across and sending star shells up and what with the searchlight star shells rifle firing and shrapnel bursting in the air and two big villages ablaze in the front, it looked like hell on earth, proper 'dantes Inferno'. We laid down about midnight for a rest and a drop of tea. As we had been in action since 8 in the morning, firing all day and no grub.

From then until 11 November the Germans, supported by the artillery freed from Antwerp, attacked in their turn, but failed to overcome the stubborn British defence, and what is known as the First Battle of Ypres came to an end. Major the Hon. John Trefusis was serving with the Irish Guards in the 2nd Division at this time and describes their experience on 1 November:

Early this morning the enemy brought up a field gun, to within about 5 or 600 yards of our position, and proceeded to pound it all day. They blew in a trench killing six and wounding nine men. It became desperate about 1 p.m. because whenever the men were forced to leave their trenches, they got shot down by a machine gun, waiting for them. Nothing could be done, we seemed to get no artillery support of any sort. One company was forced to give way, and then the trouble began. Our reserve company was put to line the edge of the wood behind us, to cover the retirement of the company which withdrew. A perfect hail of bullets followed them, and many men were shot down. The C.O. and I tried to rally them, and had a certain amount of success, ably helped by Stepney. I was then sent to Brigade Headquarters to report what had occurred, but found they had moved on, as the Brigadier had taken command of 2nd Brigade as well. On my way back I came up with many stragglers, and got them back to the firing line. I also met the C.O. being brought down wounded, not badly, Teddy Mulholland very badly in the stomach, and Tom Vesey too. I then went up to Headquarters & reported what had happened. I got back only to be told that the Battalion was completely disorganized, so I wrote this to the Brigadier, and went off in search of some more of the Battalion who I was told had gone up a certain road. This proved not to be the case, but I met the G.O.C. 7th Division and told him what had happened and he put half a battalion at my disposal, but as they were so long coming, I went back, and found the Cavalry Brigade had arrived, and things were straightening out. It is a long story, and I can't write much now, but eventually we collected 300 men. In the last two days we have lost eleven officers, one missing and seven wounded. Maitland, who is missing, was last seen shooting a German, who was in the act of bayonetting a man in his trench, so I fear he must be dead too. At 7 p.m. we got the men something to drink, they having had no food or water for twenty-four hours, and took over a new line from the Cavalry who had helped us out. The French also we got to take over part of our line as we had so few men left. A draft with King Harman arrived tonight, which makes the Battalion up to 10 Officers and 350 men, but I hope a good many more will come in. I fear this is rather sketchy, but we live in times of stress, and I cannot collect my thoughts, nor have I time to say much. I can only be thankful that I am alive after these last two days.

*

As harsh winter conditions settled on the battlefield the trenches were dug which were to remain the grim home of countless British soldiers for the next four years. Casualties had been heavy. Between 14 October and 30 November, 614 British officers and 6,794 other ranks, and 552 Indian soldiers were killed, and 1,754, 43,735 and 4,075 were wounded or missing. Few of those who had confidently crossed the Channel in early August remained. By the end of the year the BEF's strength numbered 245,197: it had expanded into two armies, containing four infantry corps of eight divisions and a cavalry corps of three. These included twenty-three infantry battalions, fifteen engineer companies and seven Yeomanry regiments of the Territorial Force. In December they had been joined by one Indian infantry and one Indian cavalry corps. In addition to divisional field artillery, the BEF was supported by ninety-three heavy guns, few of them modern.

The war had now assumed the form which, at least as far as the Western Front was concerned, was to last until March 1918. Up to that time the Germans in the British sector were generally on the strategic defensive, their offensive effort, after the Second Battle of Ypres in April 1915, being directed against the French. Their defensive positions were well constructed and protected by the combination of barbed-wire entanglements and the firepower of machine-guns and artillery. Their foremost line was held in only sufficient strength to force the British to make a major effort to penetrate it. The latter's long and intense artillery preparation revealed where that effort was being applied, allowing the Germans to move reserves to counter any penetration that might succeed. It seldom did, partly from exhaustion of resources and spirit, partly because communication always broke down, prejudicing its exploitation. Neither the use of gas nor that of tanks, when they appeared in 1916, significantly altered the bloody stalemate which resulted. Meanwhile the cavalry hung about, still carrying sabres or lances as well as rifles, waiting for their day which never came. Artillery dominated the scene. The PBI, the poor bloody infantry, carried the main burden. When they were not being flung, wave after wave, into the attack, they lived, especially in the winter, in miserable conditions in their muddy rat-infested trenches, either on guard or taking part in raids which often proved fruitless and expensive in life and limb.

Manpower Problems

By the end of 1914 it had become clear that, as Kitchener had foreseen from the start, the war was going to be a long and expensive one, for which the army would have to be expanded far beyond the size for which the Haldane reforms had catered. In August 1914 the total strength, when mobilized, including the Territorial Force, was 733,514. Kitchener forecast that it would be 1917 before it could be strong enough to exert a decisive influence on the strategy of the war. Initially he did not propose to make the Territorial Force the basis of expansion, partly because he saw it as providing for home defence, partly because he knew little about it and held it in low esteem. His plan was to raise a series of New Armies, one after the other, each of six divisions of all arms and services, totalling 100,000 men each. As early as 7 August 1914 he obtained parliamentary authority to increase the army above its author- ized strength by 500,000 men, launching his appeal for the first 100,000 on that day for men between the ages of nineteen and thirty to enlist for three years or the duration of the war. Each regional command was to raise a division, recruiting to be organized through the regular army's machinery, not through Territorial Force Associations. However, if Territorial Army units volunteered en bloc for foreign service, they would be accepted, and by 25 August seventy of its infantry battalions had. A high proportion were sent to relieve regular battalions in overseas garrisons, so that the latter could be brought back to reinforce the BEF.

The immediate response was not remarkable: some 7,000 a day in the first week, rising to 10,000 a day in the second; but, when the retreat from Mons showed the seriousness of the situation, the rate shot up, reaching 30,000 a day at the beginning of September. However, it fell to 4,000 at the end of the month, by which time 761,000 had enlisted and Kitchener had launched an appeal for a second 100,000 and raised the upper age limit to thirty-five. The army's organization for recruiting, equipping and training this number was overwhelmed, and there was confusion and competition between it and the Territorial Army Associa- tions. However, it was helped by the increasing involvement of local civilian organizations, in particular in raising 'Pals' battalions. They were

locally raised units to which recruits were attracted by serving together
with their friends and workmates. In 1915, 145 battalions, 48 engineer
companies, 42 brigades of field and 28 of garrison artillery, and 11
divisional ammunition columns were raised in this way. Many of them
were to suffer heavy losses in 1916, with tragic effects on the commun-
ities from which they had been drawn. Recruiting varied considerably
across the country, the bulk coming from the industrial north. Lancashire, Yorkshire and Scotland produced over a third of the 250 battalions
in the first three New Armies, while Devon, Dorset, Cornwall and
Somerset provided only eleven, and they had often to be filled up with
recruits from other areas. Southern Ireland produced eight battalions for
the first New Army, seven for the second and none for the third. Up to
December 1915, recruits from Ireland represented about 11 per cent of
men between the ages of fifteen and forty-nine, compared with 26 per
cent from Scotland and 24 per cent from England and Wales.

This flow of men into the army took place initially in the absence of
any form of national manpower planning. One of the results of it was to
affect the output of munitions, which itself had not been centrally
planned, the assumption having been that the war would only last a few
months. In August 1914 only some 6,000 rifles and 30,000 rounds of
artillery ammunition were being produced a month, whereas in 1915 it
was to rise to an average of nearly 2,000,000 a month. This led to the
'Shells Scandal' of the spring of 1915, which, combined with the
resignation of Admiral of the Fleet 'Jacky' Fisher as First Sea Lord over
his disagreement with Churchill over the Dardanelles campaign, led in
turn to the formation of the Coalition Government and the appointment
of Lloyd George as Minister of Munitions in May and the passage of the
Munitions of War Act in July.

By that time voluntary enlistment was falling and failing to meet the
army's manpower needs, in spite of lowering the height standard back
to 5ft 3in – even in the case of 'Bantam' battalions to 5 feet. One of the
reasons was that there was no longer a pool of unemployed on which to
draw and that wages had risen as industry strove to meet the nation's
wartime needs. Conscription was seriously considered, particularly after
a National Register in August showed that 5,012,146 men of military age
were still not in the forces, and that of the 2,179,231 single men in that
total only 690,138 were in reserved occupations. In October 1915, after
the losses at the Battle of Loos, Kitchener estimated that 35,000 recruits

a week were needed just to keep units up to strength, while only 71,617 had been recruited in the whole of September. Lord Derby, appointed Director-General of Recruiting, introduced a scheme by which men between eighteen and forty-one who were not in reserved occupations were asked to state their willingness to serve: they would then be called up in succession, single men of nineteen first, older married men last. Objection to conscription weakened when analysis showed that half the available single men had failed to register.

In January 1916 the Military Service Act was passed, introducing conscription for single men between eighteen and forty-one, with exemptions on physical or compassionate grounds, genuine conscientious objection and essential war work: in May it was extended to married men. It was not applied to Ireland. Fears that it might be contributed to the Nationalist movement, which erupted in the Easter Rising in Dublin at the end of April. The army's manpower now had to support sixty-five divisions overseas, of which three were regular cavalry, two Territorial mounted, twelve regular infantry, thirty New Army, seventeen Territorial infantry and one a Royal Naval Division, for which the army had to provide all arms and services other than infantry. Although the Territorial divisions were very largely composed of men recruited into the Territorial Army, regular and New Army divisions consisted of units drawn from both.

With the high rate of casualties, conscription failed to solve the army's manning problem, partly because too many exemptions were made and partly because of inefficiencies in the use and allocation of manpower, both in the forces and in industry, at least until Brigadier-General Auckland Geddes' Ministry of National Service, originally formed under Neville Chamberlain, took over control of recruiting from the War Office in November 1917, when the army faced a severe manpower crisis with a 'wastage' level in the BEF of 76,000 a month. In April 1918 the upper age limit for conscription was raised to fifty, but this was too late to prevent the reduction in the number of infantry battalions in forty-eight divisions from twelve to nine, with further reductions in other divisions later in the year.

By the end of the war 5,704,416 men, slightly over 22 per cent of the male population of the United Kingdom, had served in the army, 4,970,902 having joined after its outbreak, of whom 2,446,719 were volunteers.

The Dardanelles Campaign, 1915

Facing the New Year of 1915, there was nothing that the British Government and Kitchener would have liked more than to mark time until the New Armies had been recruited, equipped and trained to take the field as a powerful British contribution to the strategy of the war, but political and military realities would not permit that. France was determined to eject the German army from her territory, while Russia, having suffered a severe defeat at Tannenberg in East Prussia at the end of August 1914, received a further setback when Turkey allied herself with Germany and Austria-Hungary in October and opened an offensive in the Caucasus. Early in January French asked for reinforcements to respond to pressure from Joffre to renew the offensive on the Belgian border in order to divert German forces from the attacks he himself planned further south. At the same time the Russian Grand Duke Nicholas appealed to Kitchener for action against Turkey to relieve pressure on the Caucasus. Kitchener saw little prospect of success in France. In a letter to French on 2 January he wrote: 'The German lines in France may be looked upon as a fortress that cannot be carried by assault and also that cannot be completely invested, with the result that the lines may be held by an investing force while operations proceed elsewhere.' In that view he was supported by Lloyd George, Churchill and Jacky Fisher.

Lloyd George proposed a transfer of most of the British army to the Balkans to support the Serbs: Kitchener suggested an expedition to land at Alexandretta (modern Iskanderun) and cut Turkish communications with Palestine, thus removing the threat to the Suez Canal: Churchill favoured forcing the Dardanelles in the hope that a subsequent bombardment of Istamboul would persuade Turkey to abandon her alliance with Germany and open the Bosphorus so that aid could be sent to Russia and the latter could export her grain. Fisher still hankered after the Admiralty's madcap scheme for a landing in the Baltic, but initially supported the Dardanelles project so long as only old ships were used.

These competing strategic fantasies were considered at a War Council meeting on 13 January, from which an uneasy compromise emerged.

French was allotted two more Territorial divisions with provisional approval for a renewed offensive, and authority was given for 'the Admiralty to prepare for a naval expedition in February to bombard and take the Gallipoli peninsula with Constantinople as its object'. Kitchener insisted that he could spare no troops to help the navy in that project, and Fisher was determined that it should not affect the navy's strength in the North Sea. The decision had been based on a plan made by Vice-Admiral Sackville Carden, commanding the Eastern Mediterranean Squadron, for a methodical step by step advance through the straits, as the coast artillery forts were reduced by naval bombardment. To Churchill's question: 'Do you consider the forcing of the Straits by ships alone a practicable operation?', he had replied: 'I do not consider the Dardanelles can be rushed. They might be forced by extended operations with a large number of ships.'

The operation began on 19 February with bombardment of the outer forts, but by then Fisher had cold feet about an operation which did not include the army landing on the peninsula. Kitchener's assertion that no troops could be made available was weakened when, on 9 February, he had offered the 29th Division as a contribution to an expedition to Salonika to help the Serbs against Bulgaria, which appeared to be about to join the Central Powers. However, he withdrew that offer and proposed instead some of the Australian and New Zealand troops who were in Egypt completing their training before joining the BEF. On 20 February he ordered Lieutenant-General Sir John Maxwell, commanding the troops in Egypt, to send as many Australians and New Zealanders as he could to the island of Lemnos, while their commander, the Indian Army Lieutenant-General Sir William Birdwood, went ahead to consult Carden and advise as to whether the naval operation was likely to be successful and whether troops would be needed to 'occupy the peninsula'. Privately he asked Birdwood to assess whether or not they might be needed to attack the forts from behind to ensure success.

Birdwood saw Carden on 2 March and in a telegram to Kitchener stated that army involvement could not be as limited as he had envisaged. Large numbers would be needed, which should land at Cape Helles at the southern end, with a diversion on the west side of the neck of the peninsula forty-five miles further north.

By now pressure for a major army operation was building up, both France and Greece being eager to participate, partly in order to persuade

Britain to join in an expedition through Salonika against Bulgaria. The naval operation was making slow progress, civilian-manned mine-sweepers, trying to clear the way for the bombarding ships, being both underpowered and vulnerable. The Turks, and their German advisers, were now thoroughly alerted and began to reinforce the peninsula. Kitchener reluctantly concluded that a major landing would be necessary, and, partly because of French involvement (the Greek offer had been turned down), he appointed a senior general, Sir Ian Hamilton, to overall command, to the disappointment of Birdwood, whose command was limited to the Australian and New Zealand Army Corps (ANZAC). A motive for the appointment may have been to make sure that the British commander clearly outranked the French. No detailed planning had been done in the War Office, and Kitchener's orders to Ian Hamilton, as he set off on 13 March, were limited to the terse statement: 'We are sending a military force to support the Fleet now at the Dardanelles and you are to have the command'.

On 17 March Hamilton reached the headquarters of Vice-Admiral de Robeck, who had the day before succeeded Carden, overwhelmed by strain, on the island of Tenedos. On the 18th de Robeck's ships failed in a renewed attempt to force the Straits, three out of the sixteen capital ships engaged being sunk and three put out of action for a long period. De Robeck and Hamilton agreed that no further progress could be made until the army had cleared the western side of the Straits. Hamilton informed London to that effect, telling Kitchener that the army operation would have to be 'more than mere landings of parties to destroy Forts: it must be a deliberate and progressive military operation carried out at full strength so as to open a passage for the Navy', to which Kitchener reluctantly replied: 'if large military operations on the Gallipoli Peninsula are necessary to clear the way, they must be undertaken, and must be carried through.' On 27 March Churchill reluctantly accepted the delay involved, as it was to be another month before the landings could take place, due to the need to reorganize the force and its transports, and improvise methods of landing from them. Meanwhile the Turkish Fifth Army, under the overall direction of the German General Liman von Sanders, reinforced and strengthened the defences of the peninsula.

On 25 April 1915 Major-General Hunter-Weston's 29th Division landed around Cape Helles, to be reinforced later by a naval brigade and a French division. Strong resistance was met and casualties were heavy, except on Y Beach, but inefficiencies in communication and command resulted in failure to exploit that, and the leading troops, after a gallant fight in which fifteen Victoria Crosses were gained, dug in a long way from their objectives. By the end of the day, 15,000 troops had been landed in the ANZAC sector and twelve and a half battalions at Helles.

At the latter Lieutenant James Blount-Dinwiddie, who had already served with the Transvaal Scottish in German South-West Africa, landed with the 1st Borders in the 29th Division and was wounded in the First Battle of Krithia on 28 April. He wrote to his girlfriend, Miss C. Croft, from the Cunard liner SS *Alaunia*, used as a hospital ship, on 1 May:

I have had a jolly old time since my birthday, last Sunday, when we landed on the end of the Peninsular, & when the British army has done as fine a thing as has been done yet. It was a perfectly glorious morning when our little performance started, everything quiet and still until suddenly as the sun rose the naval guns commenced, and then it was boom-boom-boom for the rest of the day. We got on to the little bay allotted to us [X beach] quite safely, but as soon as we were there the other side began sniping, & kept it up.

Then we had to rush forwards to cover the retirement of another regiment which had landed before us & pushed in, but had run up against rather more than it wanted. Anyway, the poor devils got badly messed up, & we pushed forward almost at once. We drove the beggars back a bit & then (about 12 a.m.) started to dig ourselves in & settle down. It was pretty hard work, but luckily we weren't interfered with much, & by night had got quite a good line – fortunately because they fairly come on after dark, but didn't do any good. Next day we had another slight attack before midday, but then all was quite [quiet?] round us, as the regts landing round the end of the peninsular got a good footing (This was one of the finest things done as they had absolute hell before most of the men even got on the beach from maxims* & guns concealed in the cliffs.) All Sunday & Monday we had not much to eat and practically nothing to drink as we were afraid of a shortage of water, & what there was was mostly half-condensed sea water. By Monday night we were more or less firmly fixed, but didn't have much rest, as another attack was made, though not in our part of the line. All Monday & Tuesday whenever

* Machine-guns.

anybody put their heads up, there was a quiet sizzle overhead as the snipers had shots at us. It was really quite soothing after a time and interesting. The blighters were all over the place, in trees and ruined cottages etc, while the beggar who gave us most trouble was actually firing from behind our line. They dropped a few shells on us, but they are absolutely nothing as you can hear them coming & duck. Once you hear the noise just above you, you are quite safe, as that means that they passed over & are meant for something else. Everybody was most interested with 'mark over' as a shell passed above us, or 'here comes Perceval' as a bullet sizzled gently past. All the time the navy were banging away, & knocking the earth about inland, but we couldn't see with what result. On Tuesday night, the whole of the right of the line moved forward stretching from sea to sea. We were on the left & commenced to push forward on Wed. morning & then we had our little bunder-buss & fairly got it in the neck. We marched for about 3 miles over heather & up & down steep ravines, with the regt on our right firing away merrily, until when we got to the top of a rise, we suddenly saw the blighters pouring over a hill about 1000 yds away, to stop us coming round their flank. They fairly swarmed over, & we got rid of our packs (no light weight to carry (20 lbs) on your back besides rifle, revolvers etc, etc etc) & got down into some trenches which were fortunately dug, though some of us were out in the open. My platoon with 2 others formed the firing line, as we had finished far ahead of the rest, too far for our comfort as we discovered afterwards. The enemy, who knew our range to a nicety, let us have it, & it was a perfect hail of bullets from then on. I was very lucky for some time, moving about trying to get the men to fire etc & watching the enemy through my glasses, and the bullets just didn't seem to want to hit me, but I was really too busy to worry much about them. Our men behaved very well especially as they had such a darned poor chance, & nearly all the wounded got back, as we couldn't risk leaving them in case we had to retire, as the Germans have a disgusting habit of sticking the wounded with their own bayonets – the devilish swine – excuse my language, but I have learnt a thing or two the last few days & one of them is that the Germans deserve pity from neither god nor man.

We had some ships close in shore who dropped a few visiting cards on the Turks etc as they advanced, but naturally they couldn't see much. After I was wounded I spent part of my time trying to direct the Queen Elizabeth on to the enemy – fancy an unimportant trifle like me sending messages to our latest battleship! but to continue, I was walking from the right to the left of my line when suddenly I felt what seemed like the whole earth hit me on a very delicate portion of my anatomy, & I fairly leapt in the air & swore, but as nothing else seemed to happen, I continued. It wasn't for some time afterwards that I discovered I had 4 holes in me, & I commenced to trek back & had to walk about 2 miles down a ravine to the shore, where they had a dressing station & then we were taken by one of the naval boats and shoved in here, where I am merry & bright & dashed annoyed to be away, as I don't know what happened to the other poor fellows & I feel I ought to be back, instead of lazing about with an absurd wound. I don't think it will be long before I am back.

Fifteen miles further north, where the peninsula was at its narrowest, the ANZAC troops met less difficulty in landing, but were faced with rough precipitous ravines and just failed to reach and hold the crest from which they could have cut off Turkish troops further south and overlooked the Straits. From then on, in conditions of great hardship and squalor, both the cause and the result of widespread sickness, a series of attempts were made to reach the original objectives; but all surprise had been lost, the ground favoured the defenders, and after a series of attacks in the first week of May it became clear that further efforts to develop the restricted areas captured would merely increase the casualty list, which had already risen to 60,000.

This, and arguments about whether or not the navy should make another attempt to force its way through the Straits, led to Fisher's resignation and the formation of a coalition Government, Arthur Balfour, the Conservative leader, replacing Churchill, who became Chancellor of the Duchy of Lancaster and continued to press for stronger action. The Dardanelles Committee, as a smaller War Council of the Cabinet was called, agreed and approved Kitchener's reinforcement of Hamilton with five divisions, two Territorial, 53rd (Welsh) and 54th (East Anglian), and three New Army ones, 10th (Irish), 11th (Northern) and 13th (Western). They were employed, as 9th Corps, to make a fresh landing in Suvla Bay, a few miles north of the ANZAC sector, on 6 August. The actual landings were made without difficulty, but the sixty-one-year-old corps commander, Lieutenant-General Sir Frederick Stopford, made no attempt to exploit this success by thrusting inland, with the result that the Turks rushed reinforcements to oppose him and the whole operation came to a grinding halt before a link-up with the ANZACs could be effected.

One of those taking part was the nineteen-year-old future field marshal Lieutenant Alan (John) Harding, commanding a platoon of the 1/11th Londons (The Finsbury Rifles) in 54th Division. Their brigade (the 162nd) had been switched to the 10th Division for an attack on 15 August along the Kiretch Tepe Ridge on the north flank of the landing area. Harding was the leading platoon commander of C Company. He and all his men were keen as mustard to prove their worth at last. They carried three days' rations – three tins of bully beef, a bag of biscuits and three tins of tea and sugar, packed in their mess tins. Their water-bottles were full, but these had to last all day in stifling heat, pestered by clouds of flies. As an officer, Harding carried a revolver and an alpenstock.

Late in the afternoon the brigade commander, who was shortly afterwards gravely wounded, called the company commander up to the head of the wadi in which the company was halted. Harding went with him and heard the orders: 'Take your company forward, carry the firing line with you and capture the position,' which was in fact the south-west slope of Kidney Hill. The ground in front was broken and covered with scrub up to knee height. His company commander, Major Windsor, told Harding to advance, whereupon he formed his platoon into line and went forward, having no idea where the Turkish position was. He soon came upon some frightened-looking soldiers from another battalion lying down, and asked them if they were the firing line. 'I suppose we are,' was the reply. 'Well, you've got to come forward with me,' said Harding. But they stayed where they were: so his platoon went on by itself, some men being hit as they advanced. He then halted his men and opened fire at what he thought was the Turkish position. More of his men were hit and a runner sent back to report the situation was shot dead. His platoon sergeant was the next to be hit.

Harding stayed there until it was dark and then picked up the wounded, left six of his men dead on the field and moved back a few hundred yards to the 'firing line' of 1/10th Londons and spent the night there. Next morning their position was shelled by the Turks and Harding was hit in the left leg by a piece of shrapnel. He was taken by stretcher to a casualty clearing station on A Beach and thence by boat to a hospital ship. Here he lay on a stretcher in the sun until a well-meaning sailor moved him into the shade. There he was forgotten about and went to sleep. Eventually, however, he was found, taken to a bunk and treated. This was not a proper hospital ship, but only a casualty carrier. It was grossly overcrowded and understaffed, the general impression being of a shambles reminiscent of the Crimea. The ship sailed for Alexandria and there, in a general hospital at Sidi Bishr, he was at last properly cared for.

On the day that Harding went into action Stopford was replaced by Major-General Beauvoir de Lisle, who had succeeded Hunter-Weston in command of 29th Division, which had been transferred to Suvla Bay, as had also the 2nd Mounted Division from Egypt, without its horses. A major attack was planned to capture the commanding height of Sari Bair Ridge on the extreme right, where 9th Corps would link up with the ANZACs. As before, it petered out in a confusing area of scrub-covered ravines, the soldiers suffering heavy casualties in conditions of extreme heat.

Corporal Colin Millis of the 2nd County of London Yeomanry (Westminster Dragoons) records his first time in action in the attack on Chocolate Hill on 21 August:

This day I shall always remember & not without a little pride. Of course the men as a rule are kept in ignorance of what preparations are being made for attacks etc, however after our morning swim we were given orders to pack, strike camp & to be ready directly after dinner. There was great excitement everywhere and punctual at 2.30 pm the first shot was fired from the ships, in all there were twelve, torpedo boats, monitors & cruisers they kept up a hellish fire until we were ready to move off at 3.30, the noise was terrific, for they were pounding in broadsides of 12″ & 6″ shells & through the glasses the havoc & destruction of the Turkish positions on the hills which the shells caused was marvellous to watch, huge great rocks seem to burst in two & go hurling down the hill side while most of the vegetation was wiped out [of] existence & fires quickly broke out, no time to see more for we hurriedly paraded. Our Colonel read a letter from Sir J. Maxwell wishing us good fortune & good luck etc & we marched off. Previous to this a number of Infantry Regiments had moved off so that the mounted division brought up the rear. Over the top of a hill, laughing & joking with a pick on our shoulder and our rifle slung ready for anything, our destination was to be

Chocolate Hill, which from where we started was two miles distant & across an open plain with the wide expanse of salt lake (now dry) on our left. The Turks with their guns soon spotted us, naturally, you can't hide a division of troops advancing in broad daylight – & they gave us a terrible welcome, as many as fifteen & sixteen shrapnel shells were bursting over our heads at once. I soon gulped down the lump in my throat, jammed my helmet on tighter and prepared to go through with it, after all I had quite prepared myself to go under, but I did not want 'agony' with it. There was no doubt, we were gun fodder – to draw fire until the Australians & N. Zealanders on the right were making a strong attack. It was not long before the Yeomanry came under that dreadful screen of fire & I saw very soon that the Herts were losing a good many, their Colonel dropped wounded and was burnt to death, while a high explosive shell demolished almost a troop (about 30 men), the men who had dropped wounded & killed were now seen in dozens every few yards, & it was this sight that unnerved me just for a minute or two. We had now advanced nearly a mile & had got the order to double. No confusion or shouting just a grim determination on everyone's face, dripping with sweat & not a few with streams of blood & now and again a hoarse shout from our officer to extend and not to get bunched up, although it made us farther to go, it was a wise thing and we were glad afterwards. The running with our pack was difficult. Across ploughed fields we went, jumping over ditches and trenches, almost falling exhausted on the other side amongst the dead & wounded. The shells and bullets were still raining fast & with wonderful luck I managed to dodge one which burst a few yards in front, the bullets from the shell even glanced off my helmet, while our sergeant just in front of me had his puttees torn to ribbons. Presently another horror, a long belt of gorse & scrub had caught alight with the shells & which very quickly spread, there was no help for it but to rush through & chance to luck which I did, but came out the other side like a nigger & almost choking with the smoke an awful death trap this was & it claimed many victims, the poor devils simply dropped in dozens & were speedily burnt with the flames, a sight that I shan't forget. Two hundred yards more & we had reached the base of Chocolate Hill & in comparative safety but we were pretty well 'done' & not a few had to have medical treatment, our Doctor was splendid, risking his life every minute to help the wounded in the advance, and our stretcher bearers, old men mostly, could not have been braver, two of the poor fellows found their graves on Chocolate Hill but we shall never forget that they gave their lives to help us, working day & night incessantly to bring in the wounded from the plain & to rescue those who were unlucky enough to fall in the burning scrub, now well alight. After a brief spell, during which the shells were still dropping & spent bullets whizzing over our heads, one of our Lieutenants, a fine looking chap, brought in a wounded officer, badly hit in the leg, for which act, calling for enormous strength, we gave him a rousing cheer. In fact there were many deeds done during that afternoon that earned the V.C. & it was really fascinating to watch the remnants of our troops, some limping, others crawling and not a few fainted with exhaustion, trying to reach our line.

A much more experienced soldier, Sergeant John McIlwain, took part in an attack on Sari Bair Ridge a few days later, 27 August. We last heard of him serving with the 2nd Connaught Rangers at Le Cateau. Now he was with their 5th Battalion in the 10th (Irish) Division. His diary recalls the day:

Attack begins at 4 p.m. Small parties of 'A' 'B' and 'C' Coys attack after heavy bombardment. We are in reserve. Our people have heavy casualties. Major Money commanding attack from sap where I am with him. After dark when fighting has slackened, and the trenches chock full of Irish and Turkish dead and dying, seem owned by no acting force. Capt. Webber takes up us the reserve (about 50 strong) to occupy the position. At bifurcation of trenches the Captain goes north and sends me to command right and occupy where practicable. I did not see him again. The dead being piled up quite to the parapet I take my party over the top in rear and with about 20 men occupy portion of trench nominally Australian as many wounded Anzacs are there. Not long there when Turks bomb us from front and left flank, also snipe us along the trench from left. My men with few exceptions panicstricken. By rapid musketry we keep down the bombing. My rifle red almost with firing. By using G.coats we save ourselves from bombs. Turks but ten yards away drive us back foot by foot. Have extraordinary escapes. Two men killed besides me follow[ing] me in the narrow trench and I am covered head to foot in blood. Casualties alarming and we should have fought to the very end but for the 18th

Australian Battalion a party of whom jumped in amongst us and held the position until reinforced. When able to look about me I find but two Rangers left with me. The rest killed, wounded or ran away before or after the Anzacs had come. Struggling all night, consolidating, firing, and looking out. Anzacs abusive for the Rangers having lost trench. The most awful night of my life. Weary and limp at sunrise I ask Lt. O'Donnell of the Anzacs 18th Australian Infantry for a certificate to take back to my C.O. Find a few skulkers of C Co. on my way back who join me. Learn that the Captain was wounded and the rest of D Co. beaten back almost to Reserve. I was reported killed of course. Receive congratulations but wish that I could change my bloody clothes.

28th August. Roll call. The Battalion is now 180 strong and 5 officers (Col. Jourdain, Maj. Money, R. Martin, Godber, Harvey). Have a long rest and sleep. Tom Duffy (R.S.M. since 21st August) tells me I am recommended.

*

Hamilton had asked for yet more reinforcements, but there was little enthusiasm for this in London, which was more concerned with the Bulgarian threat to Serbia, to counter which Hamilton was ordered to send one French and two British divisions to Salonika, only one of the latter actually leaving.

By October serious consideration was being given to abandoning the whole enterprise. It was clear to Vice-Admiral de Robeck that the navy could not get through the Straits until the army had firmly occupied the whole peninsula, which could not be achieved without massive reinforcement, although his chief of staff, Commodore Roger Keyes, continued to press for another attempt. When Kitchener asked Hamilton to estimate what losses would be involved in evacuation, his answer was: 'It would not be wise to reckon on getting out of Gallipoli with less loss than that of half the total force,' which at the time stood at 134,000 men, 50,000 of whom, in Hamilton's judgement, were physically unfit.

His estimate brought about his replacement by General Sir Charles Monro, who arrived on 28 October. Having visited all the corps and divisional commanders, he telegraphed to Kitchener on 30 October: '... another attempt to carry the Turkish lines would not offer any hope of success ... I recommend the evacuation of the peninsula'. This advice was not generally welcome in London, where Keyes had been energetically lobbying for his plan. The decision was taken to send Kitchener out to judge for himself, with the hope in some minds that he would take over command himself, thus shifting him personally and the responsibility for decision from Whitehall. Before leaving, he gave his support to a plan for a new landing at Bulair, while the navy forced the Straits and Birdwood replaced Monro, who would be switched to Salonika. This was frustrated both by the First Sea Lord, Admiral Sir Henry Jackson, and by Birdwood himself, who kept the decision secret, having a high regard for Monro; but it was with Birdwood that Kitchener toured the beachheads, as a result of which he came round to Monro's view, elevating the latter to overall command of all troops at Gallipoli and Salonika, Birdwood commanding the former and Lieutenant-General Sir Bryan Mahon the latter.

Kitchener recommended to London the evacuation of Suvla and the ANZAC sector, but retention of Helles 'for the foreseeable future', the War Committee replying that it preferred total evacuation. However a Cabinet meeting on 24 November failed to support that; the Foreign Secretary, Lord Curzon, concerned at the political consequences in India and elsewhere, painting a lurid picture of 'half crazy men, the swamping of craft, the nocturnal panic, the agony of the wounded, the hecatombs of the slain'. While others hesitated and prevaricated, and Keyes, backed by Admiral Wemyss (in de Robeck's absence on leave), continued to press for his plan, Monro stood firm as a rock, backed by his subordinates. On 7 December the Cabinet approved Kitchener's proposal, which was immediately put into effect, Suvla Bay and the ANZAC sector being evacuated without loss on the night of 18/19 December. On the 23rd Lieutenant-General Sir William Robertson succeeded Sir Archibald Murray as CIGS. Next day he told Monro to plan provisionally for the rapid evacuation of Helles also, which, having received Cabinet approval, he was able to confirm on 28 December. It was completed during the night of 8/9 January, again without loss.

Sapper J. K. Reynolds, a signaller of the 42nd Division Royal Engineers, attached to the 13th Division, describes how it was done:

Divisional Headquarters were about halfway between Firing line & the Base. My Control Station was more than half the distance between Div. Hdqtrs & the firing line. I was about 1 mile from firing line & 2 from Division. The station I was at was in the Eski Line on the extreme left of the British front which was semicircular trying to encircle the famous hill. 'Eski' is the Turkish word for last & Eski line was our last line of trenches. My wire reached back to Div Hdqtrs. My post had to be reached by passing through a series of communication trenches. It could be found easily by day but at night oh my! Out here, if it's cloudy at night it's as dark as pitch & one cannot have a light. But we were all sent out to find these places in the dark. Fortunately I had traversed the ground all round there so often that I found it easily. We each felt satisfied. All this time the army had been busy destroying everything of use to the enemy. Old carts were broken beyond repair. All foodstuffs and war material which could not be troubled about were made into huge piles & covered with petrol & tar & the inside of the piles made up of ammunition & bombs ready for burning. Trip mines were placed in front of the trenches & mines in every conceivable place. Tons of barbed-wire entanglements across the road & communication trenches with only space for our troops to finally pass thro' but to be closed after passage of last man. Special routes were marked off for the final retreat. Special roads were made & sandbags placed along the edges & sprinkled with flour so as they could be seen in the dark. Along the routes control stations were placed & reported passage of each body of troops as it returned. My job as telegraphist was at one of these & I had to remain with the controlling officer till I could report the last man as having passed through & then retire ourselves. At last we were pretty certain they meant to evacuate on Saturday night. On Friday morning I had instructions to proceed to Y Ravine (that's the place I was when I was at Brigade headqtrs for some time) it's a deep ravine the Signal Office being near the top & the sea, to meet my officer & shew him where our control post was situated. I started at 2. The Turks were bombarding furiously & our guns on land and ship pumping into them for all they were worth. It was no good go[ing] up the Gully to reach it. Far too many shells falling for safety's sake. This bombardment had been going on since 10 o/c & it was a bombardment too. I decided to take the beach route & up the new retiring trench. I set off quite early. I had just turned the corner when well up in front of me, about 300 yards a shell & a big 'un too – dropped and burst in the sea. Miss is as good as a mile. Still I walked on – puffing at the good old pipe. The cliffs were so high along the shore that one is perfectly safe. But I could still hear both sides bombarding furiously & could see the ships at sea blazing away. Everything went alright till I reached the mule Trench over the top of the cliff. Then I saw it was 'some' bombardment. The parapet had been knocked down & the trench strewn with pieces of shell & shrapnel. This was some distance from the firing line but our artillery was stationed about here & the Turks were after it. I had only gone a few yards when I heard the whizzing of a shell nose. It sounded too near to be pleasant so yours faithfully promptly ducked & it struck the ground about ten yards away. Ahead I could see great column[s] of black smoke rising from the Turks high explosive shells. 'I'm in for a good time.' This job must be got over as soon as possible. Finally I reached the ravine & saw the Signal Office up above. To get across was the next question. The Turks were enfilading the Ravine with as much shrapnel and high explosive as possible. I thought this was strange as during my sojourn in Y Ravine previously they had never shelled it. I was soon stopped musing by a shell too close to be pleasant. I retired round the corner of the ravine & sat down under a huge rock. From there I had a fine view of all the ships bombarding. Again I was interested. This time by a high explosive on the cliff above. The splinters flew down the cliff side and struck the ground with an unhealthy thud. They came down like rain & no mistake & have beautiful jagged edges. My word! I had a hot time there! 4 more of these beauties dropped very near, pieces falling about a yard away together with shrapnel. This position was far too unpleasant, with sudden sharp rushes I made my way back to the Naval Signal Station & took refuge in the dugout. The Turks were evidently feeling their way along the coast for the shells followed me up & they again commenced dropping shells about. Things were getting very serious & I had never known such a hot bombardment. Bang! Crash! A high explosive dropped 20 yds away. The force of the explosion drove the sandbag wall into my back & shifted me 6 inches further into the dugout. The 'coal boxes' were dropping at the rate of 1 a minute and the shrapnel at the rate of 6. Suddenly the Turks attacked & what a blaze of rifle fire! I arrived in this inferno about 2.30 & only at 5.0 did the artillery quieten down, after having to call on the assistance of more ships to drive the Turks back. Yet if Johnny Turk had pressed forward for all he was worth goodness knows where we should have been. Finally I ventured out again and reached the Signal

Office over a path strewn thickly with shell cases, shrapnel, ball, and jagged pieces of iron. Thank goodness I was safe. It was the hottest time I had ever had and I don't want another. The new division had been telling us of the 'Hell' they had at 'Suvla' but this was a 'super-hell' My word! it was too. I'm thankful to say Johnny Turk was drawn back. Orders came for me to stay at this brigade all night, my kit being sent up in the morning. They made me very comfortable. Saturday arrived and with it the final day of my stay in the peninsula. Everything was ready and I left for my post at 4. Fortunately Johnny Turk was very quiet owing to his severe gruelling the previous day. I arrived at my station & fitted up my instrument. There were about 50 men & The Control officer & myself. The officer was a brick and treated me very well too. I assisted all I could, wrote the message out for him & assisted generally. He had some eatables with him & insisted on my sharing them with him. Didn't the other Tommies stare and it was startling to see how they stared at my instrument. It was a portable one which I could sling over my shoulder. The communication link from the firing line to the beach passed through the trench at right angles. All trenches twist and turn so it was impossible to see more than about 10 yards along the trench. Presently footsteps were heard coming along the communication trench. It is the first lot leaving the support trench. They are halted, counted, & other particulars taken. The first batch are all here. At the stated time they are ordered to march and pass us on their way to embark. I signalled all particulars. Next a shuffling is heard. 'Who goes there?' 'RAMC stretchers & wounded'. Ah my! what an awful sight. The stretcher cases are awful. Men covered with blood whilst after them hobble the 'walking cases'. This batch was sent on immediately. It is getting dark now but all is going to time. At the stated intervals the batches arrive. Our post is very quiet. Suddenly the sentry calls 'Halt! Who goes there?' The answer comes 'So many Staffords' etc as the case may be. Thank God, the RAMC NCO now reports all wounded down. As each batch passes, so I assist in checking, make out the message & telegraph it. Ten o'clock arrives and things are critical. The firing line only is left and they are now being thinned out and only the rear guard left. They will not be here till about 11. Our men have been reduced to 20 all told. Eleven hears the sentry challenge. Reply comes – 'Worcesters, Staffs, Glosters & machine guns'. These are passed down. All this time we can hear the steady & consistent rifle fire going on up at the front. The British had been having 'periods of silence' that is they do not fire at all for about 3 or 4 hours. After the Suvla affair when we had been silent for 2 hours the Turks used to send out parties of 15 to see if our trenches were occupied. They were allowed to get near the wire & then our machine guns opened. The poor devils never got away. We had done this with a purpose so often that the Turks gave up sending out these parties. That was the very thing we wanted. From ten till 11 there were only 75 men in our left section of firing line & to make it appear as though everything was as usual these men had to keep running from one part to another of the trenches & firing making things to appear as normal. It was successful. At 11 o'clock the British fire was noticed to have ceased. Only the sharp & crisp crack of the Turkish rifle was heard. The question was would Johnny Turk take it for the usual silent period? The news came down. 'Last man has left firing line'. The sergt in charge of the men at the control station order[ed] Fix Bayonets! Well, thought I, here I am but I haven't a bayonet but here's for the next best thing so 5 cartridges went into my magazine promptly. This was now the most critical time of all. 'Would the Turks find out'. The weary hour dragged on. Two men from R.E. have joined us for joining up the mine in the communication trench & closing up the barbed wire gate. All seems normal. At about 12 o'clock hurried footsteps are heard. The sentry challenges. Reply. 'Rearguard' All's well. They pass through and with them go our guard of 20. The R.Es do their work & pass down to the next gate. There are only three at this post now, the rearguard officer, the control officer & myself. I signalled the final message of 'All clear' and immediately packed up. I had to guide the 2 officers along the retreat path. We overtook the rearguard near Div. Hdqs. & still brought up the rear to the place of embarkation. My lazy nature if I can term it so served me beautifully for I never worried a bit the whole time. It was the only thing to do to keep cool. What I should have been like if the Turks had come I can't say, but I do feel confident I should not have thrown down the rifle & hands up without firing a shot. Anyhow we arrived at pier and boarded the lighter in better order than the crowds go to picture palaces. The sea was very rough and we had a difficult job going up the ladders on to HMS Talbot which was specially waiting for the rearguard, the others having gone off on transports at the extremity of the peninsula. As soon as we got aboard a sailor grabbed us & trotted us below, took charge of our kit and gave us hot soup and tea – ad lib. They waited on us right & left & in fact could not do enough for us all the time we were aboard. They supplied us with Cigs – bath & books in fact everything we required. Later we went on deck & saw the old peninsula. When we boarded we could still hear the Turks firing away. They had not found out. We went on deck to see the dumps lighted. My word what a sight!

Major-General Stanley Maude, commanding the 13th Division, nearly got left behind. The lighter on which he was embarking went aground and he had to march some way to another, near an ammunition dump which had been prepared for demolition. He suddenly remembered that he had left his bedding-roll behind and sent back to fetch it. Lieutenant Lavell Leeson of the Royal Army Medical Corps, waiting to embark with him on the last lighter to leave at about 4 a.m., recalled:

In the darkness, we heard the approach of General Maude, his fellow officer, and a wheeled stretcher carrying his suitcase. Having been in a state of near panic over the idea of leaving a general behind, the embarkation officer had composed a little verse:

> 'Come into the lighter, Maude,
> For the fuse has long been lit,
> Hop into the lighter, Maude,
> And never mind your kit.'

*

Curzon's lurid forecast had been proved false. 118,000 men, 5,000 horses and mules, and over 300 guns were embarked without loss and transferred to Egypt. The British Empire casualties of the campaign totalled 205,000, of whom 43,000 British, Australian and New Zealand soldiers were killed, died of wounds or disease, or were taken prisoner, and 90,000 were evacuated sick.

Mesopotamia

Another eastern venture had fared little better: the expedition sent from India primarily to secure the oilfield terminal at Abadan at the head of the Persian Gulf. A subsidiary aim was to show the Arab sheikhs of the Gulf, who had treaties of protection with the Government of India, and their fellows in Mesopotamia (as Iraq was then called) that they would be assured of British support in throwing off the Turkish yoke of the Ottoman Empire.

In 1914 the Indian Army numbered 160,000 and the British army in India 75,000. The dispatch of the 6th Indian Division (Lieutenant-General Sir Arthur Barrett) from India in the first few months of the war to occupy the port of Basra was accompanied by preparations to make it a base for an advance inland, and the general administrative arrangements for the maintenance of the force in one of the hottest and unhealthiest ports in the world were reminiscent of the early months of the Crimean War. Once Basra had been occupied and a Turkish attempt to recapture it defeated, it was decided to advance up the Tigris and Euphrates in the vague hope of rallying the Arabs against the Turks and eventually occupying Baghdad. But instead of waiting, as Kitchener had done on the Nile in 1898, until the logistic arrangements to support such an advance had been made, a force under Sir John Nixon, after another division had arrived from India, began to move up the river by steamer at the hottest time of the year in 1915. Having reached Amara on 4 June, over 100 miles upstream from Basra, Nixon was all for continuing on to Kut, a further 150 miles, and to Baghdad itself, another 100 miles on. The Viceroy, Lord Hardinge, although initially doubtful, was carried away by the idea of the influence it would have on Moslem opinion, counteracting the failure to achieve anything at Gallipoli.

Major-General C. V. F. Townshend had replaced Barrett in command of 6th Indian Division, which was chosen to execute the advance. He was enthusiastic, and by the end of September had occupied Kut after inflicting severe losses on the Turks. From then on, everything began to go wrong. Shortage of transport of all kinds delayed any further advance and limited the force that could be supported beyond Kut to 12,000.

Lieutenant Harland Dean of the 2nd Dorsets was wounded in this fighting and wrote to his mother from hospital at Amara on 1 October:

There has been another big scrap, & I have got a bit of a smack this time, so am writing from hospital. We left the camp I last wrote you from early in the morning of Sunday 26th Sep & marched some miles up the right bank & halted behind a big double-banked ditch in sight of the Turkish position. They had evidently expected us about there, & had mined the crossing, so one of our sergeants unfortunately trod on a mine, & was killed.

After that, we carefully avoided all disturbed ground, & though a few more mines went off, no one was hurt. We entrenched behind the bank, which was fortunate, as in the evening they gave us some very accurate long range shelling, & our guns had a job to locate theirs and stop it. They shelled again at night, but didn't do any damage.

Next day we sat still. There was a lot of shelling in other parts, but we weren't worried much. I tried to get some sleep, as I hadn't really had any for three nights, owing to being on out-posts the two nights before we came on, & being kept awake by the shelling the night before. However, the flies were too much for me. We had some biscuit and bully-beef & tea about 5 o'clock, as it seemed the last chance of a meal for some time, & then advanced from our positions on the right bank, to make a demonstration on that flank, & to draw all the Turks across to that side (They were on both sides of the river, with a bridge of boats behind). We dug about, & made a dust almost till dark, then turned round & marched back 2 or 3 miles to our pontoon bridge & crossed the river. Then we marched all night with a halt from 11 p.m. to 1 a.m., out into the desert, to get on the left flank of the Turk's position. I was so sleepy, I kept dropping off on the march, & stumbling into people, & most of the men were much the same. Just before daybreak we halted, about 2000 yards away from the left work of the enemy's position, a big loopholed redoubt with wire netting all round, & absolutely open ground leading up to it. We were in general reserve with the guns, & halted & dug in here, as we expected to be shelled as soon as we were spotted.

The remainder of our column went on to attack, but we waited till about 9 o'clock. We were shelled a bit, but no damage was done. Then it was discovered that 6 battalions who had gone on, had

marched round miles too far, & were coming in behind the line,
but still some miles away. The redoubt in front appeared to be
deserted, & as time was getting on, & the enemy's people from the
other bank would be back soon, the half-battalion of native infantry
with us were sent on to it. As soon as they got close, a strong fire
was opened on them, & we were sent on too, & so 1½ battalions
attacked the position for which 6 were intended. It was rushed
through most extraordinarily quickly, as that was the only thing to
do, & the place was taken all right, but we lost a lot in doing it. I was
hit 500 or 600 yards from the wire, as I was walking forward. I felt a
tremendous smack in the left leg, & was rather surprised to find
myself sitting on the ground. I then noticed a man behind me with
blood oozing out of his leg, & thought I must be mistaken, & that I
had merely heard him hit, & thought it must be he. However, when
I next looked, there was blood coming through my shorts, so I knew
it was genuine. The bullet had gone clean through my thigh & broken
his shin-bone. I shoved my first field dressing on, as it was an easy
place to get at & found I could stand on the leg, so went on after the
company, which was lying down about 100 yards ahead. I had to
hobble, as my leg wouldn't bend & just as I caught them up again,
they rushed on again. I kept on and caught them on again, but was
again left behind, & my leg had got stiff & painful, so I had to lie
there.

This was very annoying, as I'd seen all my platoon's N.C.Os
wounded, & felt anxious about the platoon. However I put the oldest
soldiers in command before they left, & soon after saw they'd broken
through the wire further to the left. I then made my way back to try
& find the aid post, & it was rather a trying journey, as the enemy
plastered all the area where our wounded were being collected with
shrapnel, & how all the wounded weren't killed I don't know. Two
of our stretcher-bearers were wounded. The aid post had beeen
compelled to move, so we had to go about a mile before we found
another. We sat on the ground there about an hour, & were then put
in a transport pony cart to be taken back to the field ambulance. The
transport cart is a small springless two-wheeled vehicle, which
absorbs every possible bump and unevenness in the ground & it took
about three hours to reach the Field Ambulance. There we were
given tea & biscuits which were pretty welcome, & then came on for
another 2 hours to this place on the river bank, some miles or so

below the bridge we crossed by the night before. We were put into tents here & the wounds dressed properly.

Until I did that cart journey, I had no idea how far we'd walked the night before. It was pretty trying with a flesh wound, & must have been absolutely awful for those with broken bones & internal wounds. Fortunately the boat with our kits was here, so I got mine off & am fairly comfortable, but as this camp was only told to prepare for 150 wounded & there are 500 to 600 here, you can judge it's pretty crowded, & of course the supply of blankets etc was pretty low at first. The unfortunate doctors are worked off their legs. However they are sending a lot down river today & things should get better.

Meanwhile the Turks had strengthened their force at Ctesiphon, another eighty miles from Kut and only twenty from Baghdad. Townshend attacked them there on 22 November, and failed with heavy casualties, 4,300, about a third of his infantry. He decided that he must withdraw at least as far as Kut, where supplies had been built up by river-craft. Messages were being exchanged between London and Delhi, the latter being responsible for the campaign. London had at first been unenthusiastic about Nixon taking the offensive and then annoyed at feeling that they had been misled by over-optimistic estimates of Turkish weakness. The Viceroy rejected any idea of turning to the defensive on the grounds that it would have serious political effects in the whole area, as 'our success in Mesopotamia has been the main factor which has kept Persia, Afghanistan and India itself quiet'. He pressed for reinforcements to be sent, while pointing out his difficulty in providing any. On 2 December Townshend told Nixon that his forces were too exhausted to retire beyond Kut and that in any case it would take time to remove the supplies there. Nixon left the decision to him, saying that he intended to 'concentrate reinforcements as far forward as possible'. Townshend calculated that he had one month's rations for British and two for Indian soldiers, as well as ample ammunition. 'I have shut myself up here,' he signalled, 'reckoning with certainty on being relieved by large forces arriving at Basra.' Having sent away his cavalry, he was left with just over 10,000 men. However, when Nixon told him that it was unlikely that he could be relieved within two months, he changed his mind and proposed to withdraw a further thirty miles downstream, but Nixon vetoed it.

On 7 December the Turks surrounded Kut and the siege began, while London and Delhi each protested their inability to send reinforcements. On 24 December the Turks delivered their first, and, as it was to prove, their only major attack on Kut, which was driven off by the garrison, which inflicted heavy casualties on the enemy.

By this time Lieutenant-General Sir Fenton Aylmer, the Adjutant-General in India, had arrived to assume command of the force in the forward area, known as Tigris Corps, which consisted of two Indian divisions, recently arrived from India, the 3rd (Major-General H. d'U. Keary) and the 7th (Major-General Sir George Younghusband). The 12th Division had been split up and its brigades employed on a number of different tasks, the commander, Gorringe, becoming Aylmer's chief of staff. The War Committee in London decided that no further divisions would be sent to Mesopotamia and that once Kut had been relieved Nixon should adopt a defensive strategy. Early in January 1916 Aylmer advanced in very wet weather and turned the Turks out of their foremost position at Shaikh Saad, twenty miles as the crow flies from Kut. He continued his advance towards their main position at Hanna, eight miles upstream. On 21 January, two days after Lieutenant-General Sir Percy Lake had taken over from Nixon, Aylmer attacked them there without success, losing 2,741 men out of an assault force of some 8,000.

Inside Kut, Captain John Read of the 2nd Norfolks wrote in his diary that day:

21st Jan: 47th day [sic] of siege
At 6.30 a.m. the river now in flood, in conjunction with the sheet of rain water broke the bunds & flooded the 1st line trenches up to redoubt B. The 30th Bde in falling back to the middle line had several casualties from enemy's fire. The Gurkhas held on but had one man drowned at 8.30 a.m., the Turks had likewise left their trenches. We were ready for them & our Inf & gunfire cost them 300 casualties. Intermittent rain throughout the day, heavy at night. Orders read by O.C. Fort to remove all ammunition, shovels, picks etc out of the Fort preparatory to an intended evacuation, during the night. First fatigue party left at 6.30 p.m., under Bullock, & returned at 9.30 p.m. Second party, 150 men, under me, followed at 9.45 pm & returned at 1 pm. We had to carry out boxes of ammunition to the Middle Line & it can be well imagined what the state of the ground was when it took us over 3 hours to make the single trip there & back,

that is to walk some 3000 yds in all (under 1¾ miles). The surface
was so slippery that men fell into the puddle at every yard. The whole
ground was a quagmire on which one could only move at a snail's
pace. A firm footing had to be found for one foot before the other
could be moved & during this time the rain came down in torrents.
By the time we got back to our dugouts we felt like wet rags &
looked, owing to our numerous falls and besmirchings, like clay
figures. It was a night sans pareil.

After this trying ordeal, this 'Love's Labour Lost', the project of
evacuating the Fort was abandoned.

22nd Jan: 48th day of the siege.
General Aylmer's attack today on the Um-el-Harmah position failed
& he had another 4000 losses. He excused himself by saying: 'It was
only bad weather which prevented him breaking through. After this
check General Gorringe became Chief of Staff; his predecessor
General Offley B. Shore (the awfully sure), who had been Director of
Military Education, one of India's 'Deus ex Machina', after a brief
and inglorious flicker fades away now into the great gulf of oblivion.
A clear sunny day.

Aylmer tried again, after a night approach march, on 8 March 1916,
but again failed, his force suffering 3,474 casualties – 512 killed, 2,465
wounded and 497 missing. One of those killed was Captain Thomas
Watson, who had served with the 6th East Lancashires in the 13th
Division throughout the Gallipoli campaign and come with them to
Mesopotamia. He wrote to his mother on 10 February:

Many thanks for the congratulations from both contained in your
letters of the 27th December which arrived yesterday. Yes am so glad
John was decorated, but really personally cannot look upon it with
unmixed feelings of jubilation.

The more I see of this beastly show, the more it appears that
honours are out of place – and sometimes when I think of the
number of people I have seen through this Battn, many of them
twice through it, it seems almost unbearable, and this is the one
thing that makes carrying on so hard. Even this week we have lost 4
of the best possible officers including dear old Treadwell – who was
killed last Monday. Am afraid my feelings become so hardened in
this show that one cannot properly realize the various calamities we

suffer, and suppose this is one of the mercies of Providence – opposed to which she often seems strangely unreasonable – and the best of our people are killed it often seems in an entirely wanton and unnecessary fashion. Well it's no good being lugubrious about it – but we've been cut at fairly hard this week and try as I may I cannot find any solace in philosophy for the loss.

But one thing there is no doubt of and that is that this time Johnny Turk had had a most severe trouncing! – since Dec 14 we have never gone back more than momentarily – and the Turks have undoubtedly had extraordinarily heavy casualties compared with our own – which the papers and official wires are pleased to call inconsiderable. Inconsiderable of course they are – looked at from the proportion of the gains achieved but it always seems however few or however many we may lose, the inconsiderability or whatever it may be does not rest so much with the army or the nation but with the wretched folk who are left to mourn a loss which to them is the very extremely opposite of inconsiderable.

Am glad to be able to tell you Ball is doing well still and has now been moved to Amara. I want you to get *all* the photos done for him by degrees. The parcel containing picture [?] anchovy shortbread etc turned up safe and sound – but shortbread is the only thing consumed as yet. Very many thanks for them – and also for the birthday wishes from you both and the Chess board which has not yet had an opportunity of coming into action.

Well this is all this time. Heaps and heaps of love – and all the wishes in the world – and if ever am laid out as I feel by the law of averages I may be – I *know you* will do your best to consider the casualty inconsiderable and rest assured that *I* at any rate am perfectly content.

On 12 March Aylmer was replaced by Lieutenant-General Sir George Gorringe, who by 4 April had been reinforced to a strength of 30,000 men with 127 guns, facing about 18,000 Turks in their defences at and west of Hanna, while about 6,000 invested Kut. Between 15 and 23 April he delivered a series of attacks on the Turkish defences facing him, all of which failed with heavy loss. By this time the garrison of Kut was near starvation and in poor health, the Indian soldiers, who formed two-thirds of the garrison, being affected most. It was now clear that there was no hope of relieving them in the near future, and on 26 April Lake

ordered Townshend to begin negotiations with the Turks for surrender.
Those were concluded on 29 April when 13,309 men gave themselves
up, 3,248 of whom were non-combatant Indian camp followers.

Casualties in the siege had totalled 3,772 – 1,025 killed or died of
wounds, 1,954 others wounded, 721 died of disease and 72 missing. At
the time of the surrender 1,450 were in hospital, all but 314 of whom
were sent down river in exchange for sick Turkish prisoners of war.
About 12,000 men therefore went into prisoner of war camps, of whom
4,000 died there. Casualties of the force trying to relieve them during
1916 had totalled 23,000. It was a sad and humiliating event in the joint
history of the British and Indian armies. As at Gallipoli, the military
strength and toughness of the Turks had been underestimated.

The Western Front, 1915

While the results of the 'indirect approach' strategy of striking at the Ottoman Empire and hoping thereby to strengthen Russia's contribution to the
war had proved disappointing, operations on the Western Front had
fared no better. The BEF now consisted of two armies: on the right, the
First commanded by Haig, with Monro's 1st Corps, Rawlinson's 4th and
Willcocks's Indian Corps: on the left, Smith-Dorrien's Second Army,
with Pulteney's 3rd, Fergusson's 2nd and Plumer's 5th Corps. Allenby's
Cavalry Corps and Rimington's Indian Cavalry Corps were in GHQ reserve.

In March 1915 Sir John French, cooperating with Joffre in a general
offensive aimed to prevent the transfer of thirty-two German divisions
to the Russian front, ordered Haig to engage in a limited attack to
capture the village of Neuve Chapelle, north of the La Bassée canal, and
exploit it to secure the low Aubers Ridge, which overlooked the water-
logged British trenches. The attack was launched by the 4th and the
Indian Corps on 10 March. After a short, intense artillery bombardment,
the attack was successful in capturing the village; but as the frontage was
widened in an attempt to advance to the Aubers Ridge, the Germans
counter-attacked and impetus was lost, with a failure of coordination
between the two corps. Haig persisted with the attack as casualties

mounted, but after three days called it off, when they had reached 12,892.

Private Montague Goodban of the 4th Cameron Highlanders in the 7th Division was involved in the battle and his diary describes two of the days:

Thurs. 11th.

After a fairly quiet night last night the bombardment was again opened this morning. During the night however they have brought some Artillery up & start giving us a few back. About 11 o/c am it gets too hot for them & up go their 'White Flags' (Shirts on their rifles.) We get the order to cease fire & our Captain tells them to come over to us, which they do after a little hesitation, each holding his hands high above his head. We took about 300 prisoners, a great many of them wounded. We now take possession of their trench.

Fri 12th.

We have to change our position temporarily, a little further south, in order to do this we have to wade through trenches waist deep in water which is like soup and as cold as ice. We are however not much worried by our personal discomfort as the excitement is too great – this is our first glimpse of real warfare. What a sight! I cannot describe it. At about 4 o/c we return to our old positions things having now quietened down a bit. Hungry, wet and smothered in mud. At 7.30 pm we get the order to make a bayonet charge. We proceed to cross the fields which were behind the original German trenches. What a gruesome sight! Dead & wounded strewn everywhere, the latter groaning & moaning in a most heartbreaking manner, there are British & Germans all mixed up lying side by side, rifles & equipment everywhere. We eventually get the order to lie down and await orders, the 'Warwicks' are already in position on our left & the 'Grenadiers' in our rear in reserve. We are about 100 yds in front of the new German position, it is pitch dark, & we are lying in a field of rotten turnips. We are unobserved by the Germans & instead taking them by surprise. After waiting about ½ an hour, we are discovered & for reasons I am unable to find out we get the order to get back on to the road as quickly & as best we can, the road is about ½ a mile in our rear. As soon as the Huns discovered us they opened a terrific fire of Machine Guns, rifles, artillery, cries of chaps getting hit go up on all sides. Eventually myself & 3 pals get clear but we find we have lost touch with our Batt: & are mixed up with a bunch of 'Warwicks'. We decide we had better make for Head-quarters which we find after a good deal of tramping, and arrive there at 5.30 am Saturday morning, absolutely done up. All day odd chaps keep turning up who had got lost in a similar manner as ourselves.

Although Haig's artillery had fired 60,000 rounds, blame for failure was attributed by *The Times* military correspondent, Colonel Repington, to a shortage of them, provoking the 'Shells Scandal' already referred to.

On 22 April the Germans retaliated further north with an attack on the northern sector of the Ypres salient, held by two French divisions, one of them Algerian, on the left of Lieutenant-General Sir Herbert Plumer's 5th Corps, in which the use of gas caused panic. Although the Germans had used gas before, at the end of October 1914 near Neuve Chapelle and in January 1915 in Poland, it had not proved effective. On this occasion they had stocked large quantities of cylinders containing chloride gas in their front-line trenches, equipping their own soldiers with very primitive forms of mask. The initial result was a complete collapse of the French defences on a four-mile front. However the neighbouring 1st Canadian Division, helped by the 28th (Northumbrian) Division, managed to stabilize the situation which the Germans made no great effort to exploit in full.

Sergeant Wilfred Cotton of the 5th Northumberland Fusiliers in 50th Division describes a gas attack on Whit Monday, 24 May 1915:

I had been out with a night working party digging trenches in the left hand corner of the Ypres salient and had returned to our dugouts on the Ypres Canal bank – the night had been fairly quiet though at some cross roads the party, advancing in file, had been scattered by 3 small shrapnel shells but no one had been hit. It was about 1.30 a.m. when I had received my drop of rum and snugly ensconced myself in my dugout – Hardly had I closed my eyes (or so it seemed) when I was roughly awakened and told to 'stand-to' – When I did get my sleepy eyes opened and my senses aroused I noticed a peculiar white vapour floating about and each successive breath I drew seemed painful and caused a 'knife edge' feeling in my lungs. 'Gas' I thought and got out of my dugout very quickly – then I donned my respirator (which consisted of a piece of black crape and cotton wadding soaked in sodium-hypophosphate) and over the gag poured water out of my bottle. The flat country all around was covered to a height of from 5 to 7 feet with a greenish white vaporous cloud of Chlorine gas – I realised at once that the whole of the Ypres salient had been 'gassed' – Our guns and those of the Germans were thunderring out their deadly missiles – Many, many men were being carried or were staggering towards the Ypres Canal – they were all suffering from the effects of gas poisoning. We, the 5th NF 'A' Company were attached to the 5th S. Lancs for trench training, and the S. Lancs received orders to move forward and reinforce the front line. This was about 3.0 o'clock in the morning of Whit Monday – I was in No. 1 Platoon of the S.L. and we moved off in single file. On the way up we passed our own batteries, the artillery men were working like slaves and some were overcome with the gas – further on we passed a dressing station – propped up against a wall were a dozen men all gassed – their colour was black, green and blue, tongues hanging out and eyes staring. One or two were dead and others beyond human aid, some were coughing up green froth from their lungs. As we advanced we passed many more gassed men lying in the ditches and gutterways – shells were bursting all around – At La Brique we came under heavy artillery fire from the enemy and at some trenches beyond the 'Irish Farm' where we tumbled into rest the enemy sent over vitriol shells and played machine guns over us. These trenches were just behind our front line at Pilkem. At this point I could go no further and when the S.Ls advanced I was left lying in the trench with one other gassed man and various wounded beings and corpses. The gas which I breathed in my dugout had told on me – On the way up I was forced to spit and my respirator fell entirely to pieces with the continual removal and readjustment – the vitriol shells closed my eyes and filled them with matter and I could not see – I was forced to lie and spit, cough and gasp the whole of the day in that trench until the 4th NF could advance no further they took the wounded including myself and I was soon in a motor field ambulance on my way to hospital. That was a fearful day for the British – they sustained 3,000 'gas' cases alone not to mention the wounded and dead due to shell fire and rifle and machine gun bullets. The wounded lay on stretchers on each side of the few field dressing stations in the salient and awaited their turn for attention. Our own gunners used up all their ammunition at midday and could get no more up to the guns.

The horses, pulling the ammunition wagons, would not face the gas. Yet our infantry held on to the 2nd line of trenches, the 1st line being unhabitable, unsupported by artillery fire while the enemy shelled unmercifully and line after line of their infantry advanced only to be shot down.

Goodban was also in the thick of it, but apparently before the enemy started using gas. His diary for 17 May records:

Leave our reserve position at 4.30 am, having at last been called up. We make our way to the 1st line trenches under shrapnel fire all the way. Just before reaching the trenches 2 Lieutnts & several chaps are hit by a high explosive shell all rather badly wounded. On reaching the trenches we go right through them over to the 1st line German which have been taken by The Staffords yesterday. We still go on through these lines as well, out into the open, we are now extended out in skirmishing order and come under rifle as well as artillery fire & it is now about 9 o/c drizzling with rain. After advancing about 150 yds in the dark, we come across a big ditch about 6 ft across and 6 or 7 ft deep, full of muddy water, this presents rather an awkward obstacle, and we have to get across the best way we can, most of us tried to jump it, but with our heavy equipment it is impossible and the majority fell in including myself, thus getting soaked through to the skin & our rifles choked with mud. After we are all on the other side we go forward again & rush the German Communication trench in front of us, which we take and hold, but the two Batts who should have supported us, one on either flank, failed to come up, so we are now holding our position with Germans on three sides of us and the ditch previously mentioned on the 4th side. About 5 a.m. the Germans bring up reinforcements, with a large number of bombers who proceed to bomb us from all sides, the odds are too great for us, & our Colonel gives us the order to get back & join our main body the best way we can, while giving this order he is shot dead. During these operations we lost 228 men, & 13 officers. The remainder of us eventually got back to the trenches from which we started, soaking wet & covered in mud from head to foot.

Attempts to regain the ground lost proved expensive and were protested against by Smith-Dorrien, leading to his replacement by Plumer. However French then changed his mind, and in the teeth of protests from Foch, the French army commander in the north, he ordered Plumer to withdraw to a line some three miles east of Ypres, where his troops were to remain, overlooked by the Germans, for the next two years.

This Second Battle of Ypres came to an end officially on 25 May, by which time casualties totalled nearly 60,000. Fighting did not entirely die down thereafter. On 16 June the 9th Brigade in the 3rd Division was ordered to attack and capture three lines of enemy trenches near Hooge. The newly married Major Archibald Wavell, another future field marshal, was its brigade major. He lost his left eye, hit by a shell splinter, when he stepped outside the headquarters dugout for a breather.

No further British offensive was launched on the Western Front until September. Joffre's attacks earlier in the year had failed at high cost. He now planned a major offensive, which he optimistically declared would 'compel the Germans to retreat beyond the Meuse and possibly end the war'. He aimed to deliver two widely separated converging blows which would pinch out the German salient in northern France, the principal one in Artois in the area of Arras and Lens, the other in Champagne, to the east of Rheims. Haig's First Army was to play a major part in the former with an attack between Lens and the La Bassée canal.

Both Haig and the corps commander principally involved, Lieutenant-General Sir Henry Rawlinson, were opposed to it, as was Lieutenant-General Sir William Robertson, French's chief of staff. Haig maintained that he had insufficient heavy artillery and shortages of artillery ammunition generally, and argued that if he had to launch a major attack, it should be from the Ypres salient, aimed at cutting German rail links with the Belgian coast. Rawlinson was faced with attacking over open, flat ground with no cover, and he distrusted assurances that a strong effort by the French on his right would divert opposition from his front. Sir John French blew hot and cold, first cooperating with pressure from Foch and Joffre, then, as intelligence reported the strengthening of German defences on Haig's front, trying to whittle down British participation to artillery fire only. However, Kitchener, influenced by the serious situation on the Eastern Front, where the Russians were being driven out of Poland, and perhaps also by disappointment at Gallipoli, told French in August that 'We must act with all energy and do our utmost to help France in this offensive, even though by doing so we may suffer heavy losses'.

We did. The attack was launched on 25 September 1915, preceded by four days of artillery bombardment and supported by gas. Corporal Frank Cousins served with the Special Brigade, Royal Engineers, which delivered the gas. He describes the first day:

Rain was very heavy & the trenches a swamp. Our part of this operation was carried out N.W. of the Lens Road & S. of Vermelles thro' which we passed on our way to the Trenches. At 15 to 6 o/c we finished final preps, tho' the wind was very doubtful. We had quite given up all idea of using gas when word came to start in 5 minutes. The guns talked all night. At 5 o/c the guns were at it hammer & tongs. At 10 to 6 we threw over a smoke candle & the wind carried over the gas at an angle of 30°. At once the Germans sent up a red & a green light. At 6.30 the K.O.S.B's* went over. Our attack was hampered by the slowness & obliquity of the wind. Walker very soon gassed but I carried on. I was very busy and barely noticed the shrapnel & whizz bangs which came over in chunks. I fired off six cylinders having to stop because of the veering of the wind. A triple candle finished it. We wore a special brassard† of red green & white. Two companies of the K.O.S.B. followed by Camerons, Argyll & Sutherlands & Blk. Watch went over our parapet. I passed over many bombs. No sooner were the men over than our self imposed work began. One poor lad fainted at the parapet & then went over. In came a lad called Chestnut of 22 Drive Road Glasgow with a pierced vein which was turniqued. He was still there at 2 o/c. He too wanted to go over again. Then a fellow came in gassed. Then we got a man in who was shot thro' the stomach & gradually bled to death. Then came a man with a smashed leg. We helped all these. One Blk. Watch (?) officer came in with a shattered leg. We got him across our Trench & his remark was typical 'What a damned mess there is in this trench!'. We were busy in the trenches till 11.30. Then I went over the top & worked between the 2 trenches making men more comfortable & giving water.

The first day's attack was successful, but the Tenth French Army on Haig's right had failed to capture the vital Vimy Ridge, which overlooked the area over which further advance by his troops to Loos must take

* King's Own Scottish Borderers.
† Armband.

place. Two new divisions, the 21st and 24th, were in GHQ reserve, but
allotted to him. French had refused to place them under Haig's command beforehand. They arrived late and exhausted, to be flung into
battle on the 26th in the face of German reinforcement. They were
mown down, losing 8,229 men.

Private Frederick Billman of the 9th East Surreys was in the 24th
Division and describes this part of the battle:

By five o'clock we were going through Vermelles, a village with
scarcely one brick upon another. It was awfully muddy, & was very
difficult to get along, owing to wounded coming off the field. In a
few more minutes we were among our own trenches, which had held
our soldiers for months, & from which they made the charge. The
engineers had already built bridges over them for transports and
artillery, and soon we passed our old first line trench. Shells began to
drop around, and it was pitch dark and raining, not a very comfortable experience for troops quite new to war. But the rain was very
welcome, as we were awfully thirsty & we spread our waterproof
sheets out to get a few drops together. Several of us even sucked the
water out of our hats. Now the ground about was sprinkled with
dead and dying heroes, but we had no time to stop looking at them,
and soon got used to the ghastly faces, more so after midnight, as the
moon shone out brilliantly. Many lay as they fell, some in easy
positions, and one actually had a letter in his hand, as though he
managed to read it through before he died. Many a mother's son lay
on the wet cold ground at the time when perhaps that mother might
be writing to him or praying for his safety. Such are some of the
horrors of war. By this time we began to feel tired, and we were
already hungry, but had to keep alert, as it was easy to get lost, or to
get hit by a bullet or shell. Terrific rifle fire was going on, and on my
right was a big flare of light, & it was the flames of a burning village,
set alight by our artillery. At about ½ past 3 in the morning, a
corporal & I were sent back to Vermelles to try & find some of our
ammunition wagons, & it *was* a struggle, thro' mud and holes, & my
feet were sore & chafed, but we had to stick to it. At this time the
Germans were shelling the village, & every now & again, a terrific
explosion would take place, & someone would get it, as the place was
full of soldiers. The pair of us had a very narrow escape just then.
We heard the peculiar whistling that a shell makes going thro' the

air, & we dropped flat at once & it was lucky for us we did. The shell hit the foot of the wall very near to us, & for a minute the air was full of bits of wall. We got smothered with dust & half choked with the smoke of the shell, but otherwise we were untouched. The grey dawn was just breaking, & it began to feel chilly. We had found our mates again by the time it was light, & then we were forced to take a little rest, & some food. It was foggy, so we could not see the enemy, but it was still a bit dangerous, on account of the shells that kept flying about. I happened to stroll a little way from the rest of the party, & all at once I came upon a soldier, alive, but nearly dead with cold & exposure, and he was wounded. He had lain there since the previous morning, not a quarter of a mile from the dressing station, but somehow, in the rush, he had been missed by the stretcher bearers. So I went back & got help, & in a blanket, we carried him to the dressing station, & he was thankful, as he would have died where he fell, had we not seen him. He belonged to the Munster Fusiliers. I hope he got to 'Blighty' safely and got well.

About an hour after this our battalion was told it had to attack a village in front, at noon. That meant getting out of the trenches and advancing across a big stretch of open country, a very ticklish job, in the face of the German machine gun and rifle fire, besides the deadly shrapnel. But the boys did not hesitate, and in the lovely bright sunlight of a Sunday afternoon in September, they mounted the parapet, and started off to the attack. The air then began to whistle with shells & bullets, & the grass seemed alive with them, but still they went on. Of course many fell, but soon the rest reached the barbed wire entanglements of the enemy, where they had to stop, as by a mistake, it had not been blown up by the artillery, & without such a preparation, it was impossible to get through. In the meantime I ran up against a Scotch soldier, & I soon noticed he belonged to the Black Watch. Having at once Sonnie in my mind, I asked what Company he belonged to & to my joy he said 'B Coy'. Then I asked if he knew Thompson, & he did, too well, for he was his own pal. But imagine my dismay when he said 'He's dead.' For a minute I hardly knew where I was, till the bursting of the shells reminded me. I shook hands with this lad & we parted, & my attention was taken to the fact that the remains of our battalion were retiring, acting on an order to do so, as not one would have come back had they stayed to cut the wire in broad daylight. The Germans were very strong in numbers & had plenty of machine guns. In the retirement we lost heavily, but stuck in our trenches, till at night we were relieved by the Guards. We were absolutely done up and staggered back to the field, still well under shell fire, and there came the sad part of calling the roll. After the excitement of the fight wears down, its heart-rending to hear name after name of one's pals called out & no answer to it. Many & many a brave deed was done that day, & a fine battalion of men had been badly smashed. The fight was still raging but I slept on the grass as soundly as ever I've slept at home, & was only awakened in the morning as some hot tea was being served, and it was something delicious. I could have drunk a pail full, I believe. By daylight we could see only too well how we had suffered, & I went to Frank's regiment, & found he was missing, & believed killed.

Further attempts to gain ground proved fruitless, and the battle was brought to an end in the heavy rain of mid-October, Haig's army having suffered a total of 50,380 casualties in this battle, known as that of Loos.

Haig had never had confidence in French, and regarded the latter's failure to provide him with reserves under his own command, which could have exploited the success of the first day of the battle, and his attempt to lay the blame on Haig himself, as the last straw. He made his views known to King George V, who elicited them on a visit to France on 24 October. A month later, when he was on leave in England, Asquith invited him to lunch to seek his view about the higher command.

Haig recommended that Robertson should be appointed CIGS in place of Sir Archibald Murray, who had recently replaced Sir James Wolfe-Murray. Assisted by the Directors of Military Operations and Military Intelligence, it should be he and not Kitchener, the Secretary of State, who should give military advice to the Cabinet and orders to Commanders-in-Chief, while the Secretary of State should confine himself to administrative matters. Kitchener was visiting Gallipoli at the time, and on his return visited Haig and told him that he had recommended to Asquith that he should take over as C-in-C in France from French. This Haig did on 16 December, the suggestion about Robertson being adopted at the same time.

General dissatisfaction about the performance of French applied also to that of Kitchener, but the Government, itself under criticism, did not dare get rid of so prestigious a figure, although it was deeply dissatisfied at the way he tried to run the army almost single-handed, while keeping his colleagues completely in the dark as to his intentions or thoughts about events.

The Tank

1915 had not therefore been a good year for the army. Casualties in the BEF had totalled 285,107, of whom 44,158 had been killed, and there was little to show for it. Prospects for 1916, the year when Kitchener's New Armies should have come into their own, were not encouraging. With Haig as C-in-C in France and Robertson firmly in control in Whitehall, there was now no doubt that the Western Front would receive priority. Yet, out of a total British Empire strength of eighty-nine divisions, Haig had only thirty-eight, and they were 75,000 men under strength. The French, with ninety-five in France, were continually pressing Britain to assume a greater share of the burden of attacking the German army, thus contributing to keeping Russia in the war, even if the hope of driving the Germans from France was slender. Sideshows in the Middle East held out little hope of contributing much, nor did Italy, who had joined the Entente in April 1915. However, a tactical innovation to overcome the formidable combination of machine-guns and barbed wire showed promise. This was the 'tank', a code name adopted to maintain secrecy about the development of an armed and armoured tracked vehicle, which could crush wire and straddle trenches, while its crew were protected against small arms, shrapnel and shell splinters.

It originated in two minds at the same time. One was that of Lieutenant-Colonel Ernest Swinton, sent from Hankey's secretariat of the Committee of Imperial Defence to take charge of public relations at GHQ in France; the other, that of Admiral Bacon, responding to the needs of the Royal Naval Division and the Royal Naval Air Service in Belgium in 1914, both to move naval guns on land and to provide mobile bridges for the armoured cars of the RNAS. On 22 June 1915 Sir John French had forwarded Swinton's detailed proposal for such a vehicle to the War Office, commenting that 'it appeared to have considerable tactical value'. Swinton's return to Whitehall to replace

1. Field Marshal
Sir John French.

2. A company of the
4th Battalion Royal
Fusiliers, 7th Brigade,
3rd Division, resting in
Grand Place, Mons
before the battle of the
following day on the
canal bridge at Vimy,
two miles north of Mons,
during which the
battalion won two VCs
(Lieutenant Deare
and Private Godley),
22 August 1914.

3. British troops returning from the line after the Battle of Loos, September/October 1914.

4. 11th Hussars on the march northward from the Aisne to Flanders, in the Doullens district, 9 October 1914.

5. BE2A with a 70hp Renault engine. The first British aeroplane to land on the Continent after the outbreak of war, when it was flown by Major Harvey-Kelly of No. 2 Squadron.

6. Tea for wounded men on their way back from the fighting line. Mametz Wood, July 1916.

7. Battle of the Transloy Ridges. Moving a 60-pounder gun with a twelve-horsed team with men hauling on ropes. Bazentin-le-Petit, October 1916.

8. Royal Fusiliers resting near Albert, July 1916.

9. Vice-Admiral de Robeck and General Sir Ian Hamilton on board HMS *Triad*, on the afternoon of the general's departure for England, 17 October 1915.

10. Gallipoli: Lord Kitchener at Anzac, 13 November 1915, returning from Russell's Top and Bully Beef Sap, General Birdwood beside him.

11. A Faugh-a-Ballagh (Royal Irish Fusilier) of the 10th Division teases a Turkish sniper.

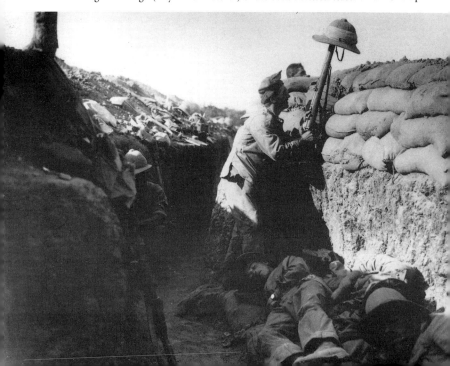

12. Battle of Morval. Supporting troops following the first line of attack near Morval, 25 September 1916.

13. A chaplain writing a field post card for a wounded man. Near Carnoy, 30 July 1916.

14. The King of Montenegro and Lieutenant-General Sir Edmund Allenby. Bryas, near St Pol, November 1916.

15. Battle of the Somme. The 39th Siege Battery RGA (8in. howitzers) in the Fricourt–Mametz valley, August 1916.

16. British troops entering Peronne, March 1917.

17. Royal Engineers building a pontoon bridge across the Somme at Peronne, 22 March 1917.

18. The Arras Offensive. A tank passing through Arras on its way into action, 10 April 1917.

19. Men of the York and Lancaster Regiment on the 62nd Division Front (Oppy–Gavrelle). Taking up wire for a night working party.

20. Third Battle of Ypres. Infantry wearing bandoliers of ammunition in a support trench at Wieltje, 19 August 1917.

21. Battle of Cambrai. Men of the 11th Leicestershire Regiment (6th Division) with machine-guns in captured second-line trench. Ribecourt, 20 November 1917.

22. 14th Hussars resting on their way back from the Third Action of Jabal Hemrin, Mesopotamia, December 1917.

23. Visit of the King of the Belgians to the British Western Front. At the entrance to an old German dugout with General Gough, near Ginchy, 16 May 1917.

24. First Battle of Bapaume. The CO of 15th Squadron RFC, Major H. U. Stammers, debriefing a pilot who had flown over the enemy's lines; near Albert, 25 March 1918. (The air mechanic is A. M. F. Jackson.)

25. WAACs attending to the engine of one of the staff cars. Abbeville, 15 September 1917.

26. Sir Douglas Haig with General Plumer and Lieutenant-General Sir Ronald Lawrence.

27. Field Marshal Sir Douglas Haig with Army Commanders and his Chief of Staff. Left to right: General Rawlinson, General Byng, Field Marshal Haig, General Horne, Generals Lawrence and Birdwood, Cambrai, October 1918.

28. Visit of the Army Council to the Rhine, December 1918. Field Marshal Sir William Robertson (centre) with the Rt. Hon. Winston Churchill, Field Marshal Sir Henry Wilson, and other members of the Army Council.

Hankey as Secretary of the Dardanelles Committee gave him the opportunity to urge action on his proposal at the highest level. Lloyd George at the Ministry of Munitions was enthusiastic, but at the successful demonstration of a prototype on 2 February 1916, Kitchener remained sceptical. Lloyd George took the decision to go ahead with the production of fifty tanks, and the War Office agreed to form an organization under Swinton to man them. The order was later increased to 150, but there was little hope of producing enough to have a major influence on the battlefield in 1916.

Haig asked for some for the Battle of the Somme and was promised 150 by 31 July, but only 49 were available to him by September.

The Western Front, 1916

Although an Allied conference at Chantilly in December 1915 had agreed that 'decisive results will only be obtained if the offensives of the armies of the coalition are made simultaneously' and that 'the general action should be launched as soon as possible', the British Cabinet was reluctant to give Haig its authority to commit himself to a firm plan, and did not finally do so until 7 April. He had grave reservations about a third paragraph of the Chantilly agreement, which said that 'Attrition of the enemy will henceforward be pursued intensively by means of local and partial offensives, particularly by the Powers which still have abundant reserves of men'. In an important meeting with Joffre on 14 February, he resisted attempts to make him take the offensive in April, when the French were not intending to do so until July. Haig would have preferred to make his main effort east of Ypres, but Joffre pressed for the area astride the Somme, where the British and French sectors joined. Although there was no clear objective there which if gained would have a significant effect on the German position, as there was in Flanders, Joffre seems to have chosen it in order to tie the British so firmly to the French action that they could not delay, evade or otherwise restrict their action. A week later the Germans launched a major offensive against Verdun, the first impact of which on Haig was to persuade him to agree to take over the sector of the Tenth French Army. However he resisted attempts to make him take the offensive before the agreed date. Nevertheless 'minor operations' between 19 December 1915 and 30 June 1916 cost him 125,141 casualties, many of them resulting from reaction to German initiatives.

Although called the Battle of the Somme, the British sector of the attack was to the north of the river, where the German Second Army's positions lay along a low ridge in open chalk-down country astride the small River Ancre and the main road from Albert to Bapaume. Haig's plan was to use Rawlinson's Fourth Army of eighteen infantry and three cavalry divisions in five corps (with two divisions also from Lieutenant-General Sir Edmund Allenby's Third Army) to assault the ridge after a long and intense artillery bombardment by 1,500 guns firing 200,000 rounds a day for five days. When Rawlinson had broken through the three successive lines of German defences, Haig would launch Lieutenant-General Sir Hubert Gough's Reserve Army of three cavalry and two infantry divisions through the open country near Bapaume to swing north behind the German lines as far as Arras, fourteen miles away.

Rawlinson's original plan, favoured by Foch, had been for an assault before dawn, so that his infantry could approach the German defences under cover of darkness, followed by a short, intense bombardment, hoping by this means to achieve surprise. He would then try to carry all three successive German lines in one attack. Joffre opposed this. Having plenty of ammunition, he wished to rely principally on prolonged artillery fire and a daylight attack. In order to conform to the French plan, Haig forced Rawlinson to change his. The result was disastrous. When the artillery barrage lifted at 7.30 a.m. on the clear sunny morning of 1 July 1916, the German machine-gunners came up out of their deep dugouts and mowed down the advancing infantry. In the first day Rawlinson lost 57,470 men, of whom 19,240 were killed. A fortnight later only a very short section of the German line had been breached and they had doubled the strength of their forces in the area.

Captain Wilfred House, who was commanding a company of the 7th East Lancashires in the 19th Division, gives his account of the battle:

Shortly before July 1st we moved up into the area of Havrincourt, and there we listened to the noise of the intensive bombardment which was going on before the offensive began. We were addressed

by the Divisional Commander, Sir Tom Bridges, on June 30th, who
told us that every strong point and machine gun would have been
knocked out! The Bn. Commander gave us a harangue, and foretold
a spectacular success. Then the Bn M.O. came and talked to us about
First Aid, and urged the officers to have their hair cut quite short by
the company barber, as long hair resulted so easily in scepticemia, if
we were hit in the head! We couldn't understand why the higher
command should be so optimistic after the disaster at Neuve Chapelle
and Loos, and our M.O. so pessimistic about casualties now and we
resented his claiming his jurisdiction over the length of our hair. We
had always been meticulous in C. Company about turnout etc., and
had long rebelled against Regimental short hair. Now I was told that
as Company Commander I must set the example and was sat down
first in the line of Officers on the soap box with the company barber
brandishing his implements. When he started to shear ruthlessly our
carefully groomed heads, one young subaltern said 'a sad day for the
long haired boys' to which the barber replied cheerfully 'wait till I've
finished with Captain House. He won't look like an officer any more
then!'

On the morning of July 1st we moved up into a reserve line of
trenches, from which we were to advance when our turn came, and
expected to move straight through to Poziers, on our way to
Bapaume. But we were not to move until all the Divisions who had
opened the attack had made their way through. We waited all day
for news, and nothing came except we eventually heard that the
attack 'had been held up'. We then side-stepped to the right into
Albert where we were to wait at least for the night. Our quarters, in
a rather ironical way, were in the cemetery, which had been got ready
for the casualties in the offensive. We were allotted dug graves to
spend the night in. It proved to be quite a cold night, so we were
very glad to have the cover and be out of the wind, but it was not
very comfortable or inspiring. Early in the morning I was woken with
an urgent message, and told that my Company and another were to
be detached from the Bn. and sent to a point where we should come
under the orders of another Division. We hurriedly got up and had
our breakfast, and in due course we paraded and were told where to
march to. The rendezvous was in a clearing in a wood not very far
behind the front line from which the attack on July 1st was to start.
There we were met by a Staff Officer who told us we were to attack

and capture a well-known German redoubt called Heligoland which our troops had failed to capture the day before. It was a bit alarming to find that we were expected to deal with a rather formidable portion of the front which we did not know, but we were assured that there was a newly dug communication trench from our original front line across 'No man's land' to within a short distance of Heligoland Redoubt. There was one corner in this new communication trench which I will always remember: there were the bodies of some of the men who had been killed in it on July 1st – i.e. the day before – and there was a great patch of red poppies and blue cornflowers and some kind of white cloth there – which made the most extraordinary 'memorial'. As soon as the Staff Officer had given us all the information he could, I called an Officers' Conference and we decided how we should set about the operation which was to clear Heligoland Redoubt and get in touch with a party of the Royal Scots who had established themselves a little South of the Redoubt the day before but were more or less isolated. I decided to send the Bombing Squad first, and then half my Company. The other company would be in reserve, with the other half of my company available for carrying up supplies of bombs, ammunition etc. I suppose it was some time in the afternoon when we were ready to start, and off we went. It all worked marvellously; the bombing squad was most efficient and they cleared the nearest German trenches and dragged out a number of prisoners from the deep dug-outs, which were wonderfully constructed in the chalk, with strong staircases, bunk beds etc. The Germans were obviously not expecting us to attack that afternoon. We took about 50 prisoners and we got rid of them down the communication trench, and they were glad to go! Luckily for them there was no shelling during this time.

Our men kept pushing forward and made contact with the party of the Royal Scots and got supplies of food and water up to them. They had had no contact with the rear since the day before. In due course we organized ourselves for the night, and did a certain amount of reconnoitering almost as far as La Boiselle which was on the far side of Heligoland. It was not too healthy to move about in the battered trenches or in the open, because one was quickly spotted by a sniper and shot at; but we escaped casualties. I did one fairly long reconaissance with my runner, and we were quite glad to get safely back to the rest of the Company. We settled down for the night with the necessary sentries etc, and had reassuring messages from the rear with a supply of rations and water. We gathered that we were likely to stay where we were for at least 24 hours. The next day (July 3rd) a Staff Officer arrived who said that we should be relieved by other troops in the Division that the Royal Scots belonged to. If I remember rightly everything went according to plan, and we were able to rejoin the Bn. who gave us a very warm welcome.

Within 24 hours we were sent into the line to relieve the King's Own in front of La Boiselle. We had a difficult time there. We were ordered to push forward, but when we tried to do so, we met with stiff opposition, and our efforts to advance with bombers down the communication trench at right angles to our front line were unsuccessful, and we made no progress. We held our line, but had quite heavy losses, including a nice young subaltern of mine called Webster, who was shot through the head while standing next to me. On our immediate left things went no better. The arrival of a contingent of Sherwood Foresters resulted in confusion; we lost heavily including some of our best officers, like Tyser and Lowe, who were trying to sort out the confusion, which involved their exposing themselves outside the trenches. It was decided not to try and press the advance further, and to get the Sherwood Foresters to withdraw and avoid jamming the trenches. It was a bad day and led to a lot of adverse criticism, largely, I am sure, owing to the fact that the King's Own had reported handing over to us a line which was some distance East of the line in which we had actually relieved them. The next morning we were ordered to renew the attack, and things at first went better and we made ground, but then we came up against stiff opposition from German bombers. It was then that we lost Hubert Corfield who was in charge of our bombers. He and some of his men leapt gaily on to the parapet and charged, but they were knocked down and died where they fell, and where we could not get help to them. The Germans tried to press home their resistance, and a group of my company and I were engaged in a long bombing duel, which we ultimately won, though I got a handful of small wounds in my back and side from a hand grenade thrown by a German, which exploded in our trench a couple of yards from me. It seemed nothing at the time, but was to give trouble a day or two later! After some time we were relieved by reinforcements which came up and went through our line, and we were ordered to move back, which we did very disconsolately as we had had bad losses. We were ordered to move back to Albert, to which we trudged our way.

Private Sidney Kemp, a signaller with the 6th Royal West Kents in the 12th Division, saw the battle from a different viewpoint:

That day [2 July] seemed very long and although it was Sunday the terrible shelling on both sides went on and on. Later in the afternoon we moved back to a support trench to break the monotony, where our D Coy already was. I met my brother and he told me that the parents of Captain Matthews had sent him out a bullet-proof waistcoat, but he didn't intend wearing it when he went over the top in the morning, which would be the 3rd of July. Captain Matthews told Fred that he was going to die tomorrow, waistcoat or no waistcoat, so why wear chain armour which was an encumbrance. Fred and I talked together for a few minutes. We then shook hands and wished each other good luck tomorrow. Much has been written about men saying good-bye to each other before going into battle, but we were brothers and the only sons of our parents and looking at what happened to the 8th Division our chances of survival looked slender. B Coy went back up to the front line. The guns never stopped shelling all the night. We were issued with a full days rations for tomorrow. Jack Webb and I and a new chap, whose name I didn't know, who had only recently joined us from a big draft of chaps, were to be B Coy's signallers, with me in charge. The Lance Corporal had been withdrawn by Sergeant Dale. It has always seemed very unfair, as happened on this occasion, to get big drafts of new chaps who have never been under fire and put them into battles such as this one was. Being old soldiers, now, Jack Webb and I found a dugout on top of the ground under the parapet, it was just off the trench. We lit a candle signallers had to use at night for message writing, got out our next day's rations and ate the lot and washed it down with water, feeling that at least if we are to die the rats, of which there are many everywhere, won't get our grub. We had to wait about another three hours, as it was about midnight when we had our meal. Our poor mate was petrified with fear and there was nothing we could do to help him. Well we had a smoke or two, talked about anything except what was happening later on today, and the time went. After we got back out of this we met another new chap from 7 Platoon who told us that while Jack Webb and I were eating and talking, he was lying petrified on his stomach on the bottom of the trench outside, too frightened to move, yet able to listen to our conversation and he thought us marvellous. We told him we had just got used to that sort of thing and that was the truth. You can get used to almost everything if you try.

The Germans had got quite a lot of captive balloons down this part of the line. We had a few but not so many. There were a few small aircraft flying on each side and our chaps of the Royal Flying Corps used to try and set the German balloons alight and make the occupants jump overboard and open up their parachutes, but this wasn't the real observation. I always felt the Germans knew how many yards each trench was away and they could have done that by ordinance maps for always they were so accurate with their shells on our positions. We signallers moved out of the dug-out just before 3 a.m. summertime for summertime had been introduced both in Britain and France at the end of April. We found that part of B Coy was already out in No Mans Land. We got up over the parapet and went towards the German lines. I saw a lot of fellows lying dead of the 8th Division who died on the 1st. I went over to the German trench and there wasn't anyone else about and it wasn't yet quite light. I went back a bit looking for Webb and the other signaller, when suddenly the German machine guns went into action. You see they had been hiding in deep dug-outs with their machine guns in safety. As soon as our shelling lifted to their reserve trenches, up came the Germans with their guns being pulled up on ropes like a lift. They already had the emplacements ready for the guns to pivot into. It was then only for them to let fly and send the murderous waves of bullets which were mowing everybody down. I was suddenly standing alone out in No Mans Land, with everyone else either killed, wounded or the few that were left, down on the ground and I could feel the bullets going past me and yet I didn't get hit by any. I then got down on the ground, still having the telephone and my rifle. Webb had the wire. I saw Captain Harris get up as he was going to advance again and he toppled over dead. I crawled to where Webb was and together we crawled nearer to the German trench, and there we stayed with a few of D Coy who hadn't gone over into the second line of German trenches with Captain Matthews. He was killed, as well as Captain Barnett of A Coy and the Captains of both the other Coys. When daylight really broke there we were, Webb and I and those few chaps from D Coy, tucked up right under the German trench against the wire. I was lying on the outside, trying with Webb's help to grub a bit of soil from under me, when suddenly a German sniper saw me moving and aimed two shots, one behind and the other at my head. They hit my tin hat a bit too high up and glanced off into the air and I laid still and let him think he had killed me. On my left lay a chap badly wounded I should think; who begged me to help him. I told him I couldn't save myself and said be quiet. But being in pain he continued to move about and was soon killed by a sniper's bullet.

We stayed under that German trench all that day and wasn't it a long, long day too. The sun blazed down and yet we couldn't move off. The evening came along and it was getting towards dusk and we had whispered that as soon as it got dark enough we would make a dash for our lines, when suddenly about fifteen yards from where we were a chap who was lying facing the German lines got up in a kneeling position and put his rifle up to his shoulder and fired over me. I looked round and just behind me was a German soldier coming through their wire, but our chap had toppled him, so we then got up and bolted, as we thought towards our lines. Instead we ran parallel with the German line. When we came to a deep shell hole we got into it. There was the Sergeant of D Coy with us and he said it was our wire. I told him it was German wire, and if you wait as soon as some more very [Verey] lights of ours go up I will take you to our lines. I did this, but not until the chap who shot the German was himself shot when he got tangled on our barbed wire, in trying to race forward to join the East Surreys who were holding the line which we had left earlier that morning. Well we got in safely and were recognized by the East Surreys, and soon were going down to our transport lines, when we met a ration party from the Buffs with Ian Bush in charge. He was pleased to see me as it had been the Queen's Royal West Surreys and us who went into action that morning to take Ovillers, and we could do no better than the 8th Division had done. Our casualties that morning were about 400 out of 600 who went into action. Some fellows were left back at the transport line. One of our signallers, Corporal Buss of Smarden, told me that he had seen Fred sitting in an ambulance going down with the wounded. Fred went up to Nottingham to hospital with leg wounds and so was out of it for a while, but his boss Captain

Matthews was killed and we the Royal West Kents had lost not only a fine officer, but a gentleman when Captain Matthews was killed that day in action on the Somme.

Kitchener's New Army had received a bloody baptism of fire. One of the divisions to suffer most was the 36th (Ulster), formed from the illegal Ulster Volunteer Force. Serving with them was Willie Nicol of the 10th Royal Inniskilling Fusiliers, also a signaller. He wrote to his mother on 5 July:

You will likely have heard by the time you receive this letter about the big battle our division took part in & in which we suffered severely.

There is no need for me to write you about the action as doubtless it will be graphically described in the papers. The attack on the huns was made in broad daylight preceded by a strong bombardment. Our battalion was the first to cross the parapet & make the attack & I am proud to say we reached our objective & were only kept from going further by the action of the divisions on our right & left in not giving us the support on which we counted. I don't know yet the total casualties for the division but – when the casualties for our battalion amount to over four hundred men and twelve officers wounded killed & missing – you can judge for yourselves what they will likely be. Two of our companys came back when it was all over in charge of a corporal all the officers & sergeants had been killed & wounded. It was pure hell & it lasted all day and night, but although our losses were great, the enemy's losses were far greater & we took an awful quantity of prisoners. The scenes all around us were awful with the dead & dying. Men with limbs torn off kept firing away until they pegged out. I am sure the North of Ireland will be in an awful state when the news is all known, but it has to be done & I would not be surprised if the war were to be finished this summer, as I can't see how the enemy can hold out on so many fronts. We are now away down the line, so don't be at all anxious about us for the next 3 months or so. I am glad to say that I got off very lucky, just a slight wound in the right arm. Capt. Knox was out at midnight in advance of our lines to see some of his wounded & I went with him. We got out alright but when coming back six of the germans attacked the two of us & threw a bomb right between us. The force of the explosion threw me down on the ground & I felt the sting in the arm but managed to get up again & we made off as I had my rifle & there were too many of them. We managed to get to our own lines alright & found that the flags I wore on my arm had saved it. They are all blown to bits & but for them I might have had a worse wound. The Capt was also struck by the same bomb & got off just as lucky as I did. I want you to keep this letter to yourselves & don't show it to any outsiders.*

I am still with the battalion as I did not go to hospital & I got my name taken off the list of wounded as I knew if it was published & you had no word from me that you would be anxious, so do not be at all worried.

Urged to maintain pressure on the Germans in order to relieve that which they were exerting with great effect on the French at Verdun, Haig battled on until 18 November, by which time the firm chalky ground had been reduced, in the words of the *Official History*, to a place where 'in a wilderness of mud, holding water-logged trenches or shell-hole posts, accessible only by night, the infantry abode in conditions which might be likened to those of earth-worms, rather than of human-kind'. Four and a half months of this grim struggle had advanced the Allied lines by an average of five miles on a front of fourteen, two-thirds of it within the British sector, at a cost of 419,654 British and 204,253 French casualties. Estimates of German casualties over the same period vary from 465,000 to 680,000.

At the end of August there had been a major change in the German High Command. Falkenhayn was replaced as Chief of the German General Staff, in reality Commander-in-Chief, by Hindenburg, who brought with him from the Eastern to the Western Front his faithful supporter, Ludendorff, who was given the new title of First Quarter-master-General. In fact he exercised command on the Western Front as Hindenburg's deputy.

---

* Perhaps he had evaded the field censor somehow.

1917

1916 had been a bad year at sea also. Although the Battle of Jutland on 31 May was hailed as a victory, it did nothing to compensate for the continuing loss of ships at sea from submarine attack. This led Jellicoe, who became First Sea Lord in November, to attach great importance to the capture of the German-occupied Belgian ports from which he believed, erroneously, that the submarines operated. Pressure for this fitted in with Haig's own preference for Flanders as the scene of any offensive in 1917.

Another conference was held at Chantilly in November, which could think of nothing better than to repeat the formula for 1916. Haig said he would be prepared to renew the offensive in February, but would prefer May. Joffre favoured the earlier date, fearing that the Germans would strike first, as they had in 1916. Haig sensed two things. First, that no major effort could be expected from the French army, which had suffered 1,675,000 casualties since the start of the war; and, secondly, that the French Government had lost confidence in Joffre. He was right on both counts, Joffre being replaced on 26 December 1916 by the sixty-one-year-old General Robert Nivelle, the day before Haig received a letter from King George V promoting him Field Marshal.

At Verdun in October and December 1916, Nivelle's French Second Army had carried out two remarkably successful limited offensives, which had impressed the French Prime Minister, Briand. Nivelle seemed to hold the secret which eluded Joffre and Haig, limited as the objectives of his attacks had been. He was also persuasive, with the advantage that he was fluent in English, the language of his mother. Lloyd George, who had become Secretary of State for War when Kitchener was drowned on 5 June 1916 on the way to Russia, initially resisted Haig's intention to renew the offensive in 1917 in conformity with Joffre's plan, but was won over by Nivelle.

Haig's first impressions were also favourable, but changed when Nivelle explained his plan. The French army would form a '*masse de manœuvre*' of twenty-seven divisions to effect a breakthrough, which would immediately be exploited. To make it possible both to create this force and to produce conditions on the French front favourable to success, the British should not only take over part of the French line, but also carry out a series of attacks to pin the enemy down in the Arras– Bapaume sector, while other French forces would do the same between the Somme and the Oise. His plan 'did not exclude the possibility, if the need arises, of an operation for the conquest of Ostend and Zeebrugge', but assumed that Nivelle's offensive would force the German armies in the north to withdraw, making it unnecessary. 'If our attack fails', he wrote, 'it will always be possible to carry out the projected Flanders operations in the good weather.' Haig did not like this. In reply he pointed out that although he nominally had fifty-six divisions, for one reason or another they were really only the equivalent of fifty. He would need thirty-six to carry out a significant offensive, which limited his ability to take over more of the front from the French.

Lloyd George's replacement of Asquith as Prime Minister on 7 December 1916 was viewed with concern by Robertson and Haig, having experienced his opposition to giving priority to the Western Front. At a conference in Rome in January 1917, he surprised everyone by suggesting a major Allied offensive from Italy to knock Austria out of the war. To Robertson's relief the Italian Commander-in-Chief, General Cadorna, turned it down. On his way back Lloyd George met Nivelle and was completely won over to his ambitious plan, about which Haig was in the process of establishing a number of pre-conditions. He was principally concerned to ensure that the British were not committed to another Somme, which could drag on until Nivelle's offensive had either broken through or failed, and that the operations which the British did undertake as part of his plan should not prejudice Haig's ability to launch an offensive to clear the Belgian coast in the summer.

Haig's doubts and his reluctance to take over more of the French line unless he was reinforced from Britain, where a large force was still kept for home defence, antagonized Lloyd George, who took the opportunity of the need to do something about the French railways' failure to meet Haig's requirements, to arrange a conference with Briand and their military advisers at Calais on 28 February. Under its cover a proposal was made by the French, which Lloyd George supported, that the British armies should come under Nivelle's command, Haig's responsibility being reduced to administration and logistic support. Robertson exploded, while Haig's reaction, naturally adverse, was more phlegmatic.

Hankey, now Secretary to the Cabinet, saved the day with a formula which left Haig firmly in command, but subordinated him to Nivelle for the duration of the planned offensive, while retaining the right of appeal to the British Government, if he thought that Nivelle's orders imperilled his armies. From that day forward any feelings of confidence or trust there may have been between the Prime Minister on the one hand and Robertson and Haig on the other were dispelled. Haig's suspicions were not removed by the appointment of the Francophile intriguer, Henry Wilson, as his representative at Nivelle's headquarters. In the event Wilson was totally loyal to Haig and the interests of the BEF. Argument between Haig and Nivelle continued, until the procedure for Nivelle's exercise of command was settled at a conference in London on 12 March.

Five days later the Germans withdrew from the salient astride the Somme and Oise to a shorter line, known by the Allies as the Hindenburg Line and by the Germans as the Siegfried Line. It ran from just south-east of Arras, west of St Quentin, to the Aisne east of Soissons. Haig's reaction was that this would free German reserves for a major German offensive; that Nivelle's plan should be scrapped and that he should keep his army in hand, prepared to deal with whatever surprise Ludendorff might have up his sleeve. Nivelle's was to maintain that the German withdrawal called for no change. Their new line would be outflanked, the French attacking at its southern end on the Aisne and the British at the northern end near Arras. While attempts to reconcile these differing views were being made, the Russian Revolution began and the French Government changed hands, the aged Ribot replacing Briand, and Painlevé, who was not favourably disposed towards Nivelle, becoming Minister for War. Nivelle had his way, and in April Haig's forces were launched into the Battle of Arras, three days after the United States of America, incensed at German attempts to subvert Mexico to her cause and her resumption of unrestricted submarine warfare, joined the Entente.

Haig's plan was for Lieutenant-General H. S. Horne's First Army with thirteen divisions to capture Vimy Ridge north of Arras and Allenby's Third Army with eighteen to advance astride the Arras–Cambrai road to high ground five miles beyond Arras, while Gough's Fifth Army with six divisions carried out a subsidiary attack near Bullecourt on the right. The Cavalry Corps was to exploit any success.

Sixty tanks were available, more or less equally distributed among the
attacking corps. Haig, with nearly 5,000 guns, had a four to one
superiority in artillery over the Germans facing him, and insisted on a
preliminary bombardment lasting five days, although Allenby wished to
restrict it to two. Initial results were encouraging: by 14 April the
infantry of the First and Third Armies had reached their objectives and
captured over 11,000 prisoners. The Canadians were on Vimy Ridge, but
the cavalry had not been able to move forward, and Gough on the right
had made no progress against the northern end of the Hindenburg Line.

Lance Corporal Sydney Abbott of 86 Company of the Machine Gun
Corps, who had originally enlisted in the Royal West Kent cadets,
describes his part in the battle:

> The night before the attack was due, the teams were told to send up
> men to dig forward positions for the morning's barrage. I was sent
> up among the others. We entered the village of Monchy just at dusk
> and then plainly saw the effect that the continuous shelling was
> having on it. The pretty little town was rapidly being smashed up.
> We had continuously to clamber over piles of masonry from the
> fallen houses and every street was paved with dead horses. The reason
> for this is, that, when the cavalry first captured Monchy they rode
> into it, dismounted, leaving their horses in the village, and continued
> their advance on foot. When the Germans found that they had lost
> the village, they turned every available gun on it and thus massacred
> the waiting horses. Thousands of them must have lain dead in the
> streets but fortunately not many cavalrymen. At the same time, the
> powerful system of trenches on each side of Monchy had held up the
> other wings of the attack, so that without horses and reinforcement
> the cavalry were compelled to retire. They actually left Monchy and
> it was not properly captured until our division [the 29th] advanced
> through it. They were just in time for the Hun began to push into it
> again. Since this the Germans had rained shell on the village. He
> commenced another bombardment just as we reached the square
> and we had to take cover in the buildings for nearly an hour before
> he stopped. We then moved forward to a cellar where the section
> H.Q. were. Here we were given tools and told to follow the guide.
> We entered the street again and followed on till we reached a high
> wall. We entered the enclosed ground through a gap and keeping
> close to the wall followed it round until we passed through a large

gateway out into some wooded grounds. Cautiously moving now, for
the Hun was only a short way outside the wood, we reached the edge
and commenced to dig a position. It was terribly difficult for the tree
roots made a network beneath the ground which was impossible to
clear properly. We did our best anyway, and about half-past one a
messenger crept up and told us to withdraw. We got to the gateway
safely though every now and then the Hun would loose a 'whiz-bang'
into the trees from a gun which could not have been more than a
thousand yards away, if that. Here we found Sergt Everhard and
some more working party who were waiting to be guided back.
Everyone else had gone and we still waited, so at last, although I did
not know the way any better than the others, I volunteered to lead
them back. We went round by the wall, whilst the fitful glare of the
occasional verry [Verey] light threw long shadows on the ground,
and had nearly reached the gap leading to the road when, with a
loud 'bang', a vivid flash leapt up right in my face. I started back,
almost falling into the arms of Everhard who was behind me, and
felt the warm blood rushing down my face. I was quite blinded by
the flash for the shell had exploded only yards from me, and called
out to the Sergeant to lead on as I couldn't see. I told where to find
the gap. He said 'What's the matter? Are you wounded?' I said 'I
believe I'm blinded!' I put my hand on his shoulder and he led on. I
could now feel a vague burning in my right shoulder and knew I was
hit there too, but my greatest fear was for my eyes. The left one was
very painful but I opened the right one and saw a red light floating
up in the air. I said 'There's a red light going up isn't it?' Someone
said 'No, it's a white one,' but I didn't care what colour it looked as
long as I could see it! We got safely to the cellar and there the others
bandaged me up. They couldn't do anything with my head, but when
they took off my tunic I could see that I had got a piece of shell in
my shoulder. It had gone through my leather gun-jacket, jerkin,
tunic, cardigan and two shirts and almost out to the other side! I felt
very dizzy and although I repeatedly asked, they would not let me lie
down. I believe the reason was, to prevent excessive bleeding, anyway
I only sat on a chair. I intended to make for the dressing station as
soon as it was light, but the Hun put such a heavy barrage on the
village that it was suicide [to] move out. The attack was commenced
and soon after, the news came in. All was not going well evidently
for casualties were reported to be heavy. About 11 a.m. three of Nr.

4 section men were brought in, one badly wounded, and soon after one of my Royal West Kent comrades was carried down moaning. His arm was nearly severed at the shoulder and he was obviously dying. He knew it too, for I said to him 'Cheer up, Jock! You'll soon be in Blighty with me.' He said 'It's no use saying that Abbott lad, I'll never see Blighty again!' He died the same day. In the afternoon I was very much upset to hear that our brave and kind officer Mr Street had been killed whilst leading the advancing teams. The cellar was now about half full of wounded, and nearly all fit men had left it. The air became heavy with the stench of blood and I began to feel very bad. I must have got lightheaded or else sleepy for I don't remember what happened until I found myself walking through the streets of Monchy next morning. I was quite alone and the cool morning air made me feel a lot stronger. I got to the Arras side and following the signposts 'Walking wounded this way' got safely to the dressing station. Here I was well received and soon made comfortable.

Nivelle's offensive on the Aisne, although leading to the capture of 20,000 prisoners and 175 guns, gained hardly any ground, incurred 96,125 casualties and sparked off widespread mutinies in the French army. This failure, combined with gloomy news from Russia and prospects of future American participation, made the French Government reluctant to continue the offensive, although Nivelle assured Haig that he would do so. Haig thought that the results of Arras had been promising and that if he did not make a further effort there, 'the enemy would be left free to recover and reorganize and seize the initiative in this theatre or another'. At the beginning of May he resumed the attack, intending to secure 'a good defensive line' east of Arras. Two further weeks of fighting resulted in nothing but more casualties, bringing the total since 9 April to 158,660, of whom 29,505 were killed. By that time Nivelle had been replaced by Pétain, who was determined to put a stop to further French offensive action.

Haig's principal interest all along had been his plan for an offensive in Flanders, aimed at the rail junction of Roulers twelve miles north-east of Ypres, the capture of which he believed would force the Germans to withdraw from the Belgian coast. As a preliminary to his main offensive, he ordered Plumer's Second Army to capture the Messines–Wytschaete Ridge at the southern end of the Ypres salient, under which twenty-four mines were dug, into which a total of 350 tons of explosive was packed. After a bombardment by 2,266 guns, 756 of which were 'heavies', lasting two weeks, in the second of which 3,500,000 shells were fired and nineteen of the twenty-four mines erupted beneath the German defences, which were assaulted by nine divisions in three corps (one ANZAC), supported by seventy-two tanks, forty-eight of which were bogged down and eleven knocked out, the ridge was captured in thirty-five minutes and over 7,000 prisoners taken for a loss of 21,000 men.

This success did not, however, persuade Lloyd George, nor even Robertson, that Haig should go ahead with his plans for a major offensive to clear the whole ridge from Wytschaete ten miles north-east to Passchendaele. They considered that his chief intelligence officer, Charteris, was painting too optimistic a picture of the difficulties facing the Germans. Lloyd George had his eyes on Italy again and wanted to send some of Haig's artillery to support an offensive there. Precious summer weather was lost in argument and, still without formal approval, Haig, who gave the principal task to Gough's Fifth Army, ordered the preliminary bombardment to start on 16 July. He received formal approval on the 25th, the day the assault was planned; but, as the First French Army on Gough's left was not ready, it was postponed until the 31st, by which time heavy rain, lasting four days, had started to fall. Gough's army of four corps had ten infantry divisions with two cavalry divisions in reserve west of Ypres. They were supported by 2,174 guns (752 heavy or medium) and 136 tanks, most of which became bogged down. In one of these, belonging to A Battalion The Tank Corps, Private Ernest Beall was a member of the crew. He describes what happened:

And now we are on our way over the trenches to the unknown. How far we had to go depended on the country after reaching points gained by the second wave. But Zonnebeke ought to be reached that day. So that is where we were now heading. It was some time before we reached that point where the second wave had concluded their task. Now we were on entirely new ground. The engine was overheated now our faulty radiator wasn't functioning at all well. The two-inch exhaust pipes were encircled by five-inch sleeves: these sleeves were getting dull red in places.

'Wow!' Mud – Mud – Mud! This was an nth column against our progress. It came in every hole in the tank's armour. It was like

sausage meat of fantastic shapes and sizes – round and rectangular
dollops to get about our feet and legs. We slipped and slid about,
and more and more came in the farther we went.

Then a dreadful thing happened – we stuck and stuck fast! The
tracks were slipping, but the white hot engine kept up revving. Vic
B. frantically called upon his tricks as though it was a light car he
was inducing to move. The expected order: 'Fix unditching beam!'
wasn't given as I had expected. This was my job. There was consultation with our section commander of the 'Lioness'. I was given an
order to attach our hawser to that vehicle which had followed in our
tracks.

No sooner said than done, I had the hawser strung between the
two tanks. No sooner said than done, the 'Lioness' started taking the
strain. It snapped as if it had been cotton. Then I was ordered to
attach the one carried by 'Lioness'. This was given the same treatment
– with the same result.

What a nerve! Why couldn't they have sent one of their crew to
help me? I was out there alone running from tank to tank in front of
everything. The section commander bawled another order to me
from his seat in the cabin of 'Lioness': 'Tell Lieutenant B. to abandon
tank. Bring back compass and machine-guns.'

How are we going to get back in that mud? And eight machine-
guns to manhandle!

'The order is, Sir, Bring back compass and machine-guns and
abandon tank'. Officer and corporal query this instruction. 'Shall we
try and get the bus back?' 'We could have a good try, Sir.' So a good
try it was going to be.

A contrivance called the unditching beam was carried by all tanks
and needed bolting to the tracks on each side. I waited for the order
to be given to me. I knew they had to try it. From the inside of the
tank I could see our officer and corporal placing cans of petrol (full
cans) into the mud so they could get a more solid foothold. They
were fixing the chains of the D.B. on their side. Without any more
to do, I was out my side and fastening the chains whilst hanging on
to whatever I could with my other hand. Frantic signals from both
the officer and corporal indicated that I could be sniped at made me
withdraw into the 'safe' bowels of the 'Lion'. But I had done what I
set myself. I had fixed the fastenings on my track.

As soon as the tracks began to move they pulled the beam

forward so that it fell off the front of the tank. Then the steel-faced lump of timber gripped the ground good and proper. It gripped all right. The beam held but the clutch slipped and slipped and slipped. It was suggested to our 1st driver that he tightened the clutch springs. The clutch readjusted, he climbed back into the driver's seat and tried it out. Was it going to bite the better for that attention? It bit, and what's more it stopped the engine this time. We started and started and started. The clutch held, but the engine just petered out every time.

Eventually the ingenuity of Private Beall and other members of the crew got 'Lion' going again, and they reached Zollebeke about 5 p.m., having been over their own lines for eight hours and forty minutes.

Anthoine's First French Army of six divisions and Plumer's Second Army, using five, attacked on Gough's left and right respectively. In the first four days little progress was made at a cost of 31,850 British casualties. Major Cecil Barton commanded C Company of the 1st Worcesters in the 8th Division at the start of the battle, which he describes:

Soon after 3.30 a.m. we began waking the men up – the order to fix bayonets was passed along. A faint streak of greenish gold light showed up in the East to our right front. I looked at my watch and thought of a saying of the men: 'Another minute And we'll be in it.' It is almost time, then one big gun speaks, and almost immediately hundreds of them were at it. It sounds very funny – a sort of rushing in the air – then we see the line of explosions in front. We are moving slowly now towards that reddish line. I suddenly see some wicker rivettments sticking up from amidst the jumbled earth – it is the Boche front line. We are almost in our own barrage now – a shell burst just in front of me (I don't know whether it was one of Fritz's but probably our own). I expect at any minute to see a Boche aiming at me and keep wondering if I shall be quicker than he. For some reason or other the men are sheering off to the left: it may be the lie of the ground or the knowledge that there is no one on our right. At all events I soon find that I am the right-hand man, with my servant who has stuck to me all the time. I remember shouting and waving to the men to come to the right, but of course they could not hear. We are now on the second line but still no live and active Boche. One of my puttees comes undone in the wire in front of the

parapet – my servant immediately rips it off. By now we are over the
ridge and going down the slope. Machine gun and rifle fire has
started in front but they seem to be firing rather too high. Our guns
are firing some shells which burst about 70 feet in the air in big
flaming drops of burning oil. By their light I see a small lake in front
of us and realize we are about 500 yards too much to our left. Just
about this point my servant scrambled up into a shell hole – I wonder
what is up until he says – 'I'm hit, Sir.'

We have had a certain amount of casualties and the Company is
jumbled up hopelessly, so I collected some men and started off to
the right in an endeavour to strike the Menin Road. At this moment
A Company comes up, led by O'Brien and Collins. I tell them they
are on the wrong track and start them off in what I thought the right
direction. (Both these officers were killed soon after while rushing a
trench). By this time the barrage is a long way ahead. The machine
gun and rifle fire is getting more intense. Suddenly I see a Hun just
in front in the remains of a wood. I remember shooting him and
seing him fall. As I was doing this, six Huns ran out from somewhere
and went into a pill-box shelter behind me. I got a couple of bombs
from a bomber and went up to the entrance and put a bomb in. It
was rather awkward as the entrance was so constructed that one had
to throw the bomb round a corner, which meant exposing oneself a
bit, but luckily they were a tame lot of Huns and did not do anything
vindictive. The first bomb did not seem to have much effect, so I put
another one in. After that, four of them came running out all
wounded – the other two must have been either killed or too hurt to
come out. One of the four was an officer with an iron cross. He was
slightly wounded in two or three places. He had an empty automatic
holster. I wanted the pistol and got quite angry with him. He got
annoyed and kept trying to make me understand that he had thrown
it away in his fright. I remember this very distinctly, especially how
angry I got. I sent these prisoners to the rear. We then went on. I
had just about twenty men with me. A Sergeant next to me suddenly
yelled out and I saw blood pouring from his chin, but it must have
only been a graze as I saw him looking quite alright later on.

We still went along to the right, putting bombs into overturned
pill-boxes in case there might be more Boches in them. We now
came to some Manchesters and Kings lying in front of a half
breastwork, half trench system of trench. These men belonged to the

division which ought to have been on our right at the beginning, but had come up later. They told us it was a strong point of Huns. I did not see an officer in charge of these men. I went forward to the slight rise in front (one other man came with me) and threw a bomb over. I waited a bit but nothing happened, so I went and looked over the place; it was absolutely deserted. After that we went on until we came to a few more men of the Manchesters. By now of course it was quite light and I saw we had come to the Menin Road. The fire was very hot at this place. We could get no further, and as I had passed my objective, I decided to consolidate. Here I was joined by an officer of the Manchesters.

By the end of the month the casualty total had risen to 68,010, of whom 10,266 had been killed. On 20 September the offensive was resumed, Plumer's army taking over the main task of trying to clear the ridge from south-west to north-east. Haig plodded doggedly on, his troops sinking deeper and deeper into the mud, partly because Gough's army would be in a very awkward situation if it stayed where it was stuck. Haig persevered until the ridge up to Passchendaele had been captured, and on 10 November, when the whole area had been reduced to a sea of mud, he called it off.

Private Albert Conn of the 8th Devons in the 7th Division, who had been wounded on the Somme and was to be wounded again in this battle, describes the later stages:

The weather & conditions were now at their worst, we had advanced towards the Passchendaele Ridge, there was a series of wooden tracks leading up to the front, used only at night. Guns had sunk down to their axles in the mud, & the badly wounded who could not help themselves died in the mud, we used to start off from Abraham Heights in the evening laden with our ammunition & picks & spades on to the old track & trudge several miles to be met finally by guides from the regiment we were due to relieve. We would then flounder through the mud to the shell holes half filled with water occupied by two or three men facing the Germans. The conditions were so bad that men were only kept there forty eight hours then relieved. The wide tracks were a nightmare, they were continually under fire & we stumbled over objects underfoot awash in the mud. Sometimes the track got a direct hit & we would run past screaming men & plunging mules. The artillery used pack mules to carry the ammunition up to the gun positions, dead mules were dragged off the track into the mud surrounding it. Isolated pill boxes stood out like islands in a sea of mud.

It was the month of November & we were wearing sheepskin coats over our own greatcoats also our boots and legs were encased in sandbags, but we were still very cold. We had our bully & biscuits & one of our party carried a small bottle of rum issued out to us. During the night we noticed at intervals single Germans running along the Ridge directly to our front. We thought this rather strange because they moved at incredible speed & always seemed to drop down on the same place & disappear. This must have been observed by others because after a while we had orders to leave our shell holes & advance. We did so & on approaching the enemy several of them jumped out of a large shell hole in a panic, number one on the gun [a Lewis machine-gun] fired a panniard into them as they ran. Now the German S.O.S. shot up into the sky but not before we found out that it was actually a ration dump in the shell hole & the Germans we had seen running had been sent from various shell holes to collect rations for a certain number of men. Needless to say we cleared the rations up ourselves. The German artillery were now answering the S.O.S. from the infantry & we were getting the lot, on top of all this somebody sent up our own S.O.S., two reds & a green, this with the German golden streamers made a fair firework display. Unfortunately our artillery had not been notified of our advance so they shelled us instead of the Germans, things got too hot for us, dragging our wounded and leaving our dead behind, we fell back to our original positions. Later two Germans wandered into our shell hole. I don't know whether they intended to give themselves up or not, but they carried no arms & we took them prisoner & sent them back to the rear after they had recovered from their fright. Dawn broke over this terrible place & as the light grew stronger we could see inverted rifles stuck in the mud marking the places where the dead had fallen. Then a curious thing happened, it was my turn to keep watch, which I did by clambering up to the edge of the shell hole & using a box periscope I could observe any movement from the enemy. I was startled to see a German officer about fifty yards in front stand up in full view holding a red cross flag above his head. I called the other two & they stared in amazement, the officer remained standing there for several minutes & nobody fired, he was then joined by two stretcher bearers & they proceeded to carrry away several wounded men lying about in various places, meanwhile a sort of truce was observed, coal scuttle helmets popped up in unexpected places & sitting on the edge of our respective shell holes we shouted greetings to one another. I remember one in particular who beckoned me over. I suppose this was all too free & easy for somebody for a shot rang out from the right and the officer clasping his stomach fell backwards. I think he was a very brave man & I hope he lived. Needless to say we all disappeared from sight and things became normal again. I didn't see any more movement & I could not see the officer although I strained my eyes through the periscope, I knew where he had fallen & wondered if he had managed to crawl away, perhaps he was dying in the mud he deserved a better fate than that.

British casualties since 31 July in this Third Battle of Ypres reached a total of 244,897. The British Official History estimates German casualties at 400,000, but some experts think that figure high.

The tank enthusiasts had viewed with dismay the prolonged effort in Flanders, where most of their vehicles became bogged down before they could even reach the front line. They sought an area for the employment of tanks en masse which had not already been ploughed into a morass by the prolonged artillery bombardments of both sides. Brigadier-General Hugh Elles, commander of the Tank Corps, finally selected the area between Bapaume and Cambrai in General Sir Julian Byng's Third Army sector as a suitable one in which to propose a 'raid' by six battalions of tanks, supported by two infantry or cavalry divisions. It was originally seen as an operation lasting only twelve hours, which would destroy enemy guns, sow confusion and then withdraw. By the time that Haig, seeing his Flanders offensive petering out in October, authorized it, Byng had developed it into a more ambitious plan, expecting it to lead to a major breakthrough and allotting to it six infantry and five cavalry divisions, supported by 1,000 guns. There were 375 tanks available, of which 54 were in reserve. The Battle of Cambrai, as it became known, was launched on 20 November and initial success was dramatic. By noon of the first day the German first and second defence lines had been captured and church bells in Britain were rung to celebrate victory.

Private Beall welcomed the absence of mud and describes the first day of the battle:

When we made off to get under cover it was obvious that the country hereabouts was green grass in abundance. There was an absence of any hint of war – no guns or dumps or shell holes. But the Tanks and their dumps of petrol and ammunition for this special 'do'. It was really staggering the amount of these essentials that each tank took on board. That is, if they all got issued with a like amount to ours. We had trebled up for this Cambrai attack. It struck us as being too much by long chalks. The extra .303 ammunition was left in the original boxes. The extra 6-pdr ammunition was loose. Petrol in 2-gallon cans was stacked anywhere it could be stacked. There was precious little room for the gunners to operate their guns when it was finally arranged in some sort of makeshift order. We weren't at all a happy band. Somebody was expecting too much. One redeeming feature was that we had left the rain behind. That was going to be a tremendous help if it lasted.

We arrived at the place allocated for us to do the usual greasing-up, checking guns, engine etc: it was called Dessart Wood. We each set about our various tasks as though we were driven to do it! There was a lack of any sort of liking for our jobs. This depressing attitude was eventually subdued after about three hours. One of the gunners gave vent to his feelings: 'What the hell's the matter with us? Have we *all* got the wind-up?' 'Seems as though we have had all the luck that was going. I have a feeling that this time will prove too much for us:' was the first reply. My reply came after a few minutes of the other comments, all of a like nature: 'I have a sort of presentiment that we are in for a surprise: on paper it looks too easy!'

With the remark: 'Well, I feel like that myself. But what's the use of talking about it. Let's forget it:' the matter was accepted by the crew as now closed. Two of the crew would not hear of any untoward happening. Try and catch some sleep with your brain turning over such problems as: How do we manage to cross that canal? Will the Hindenburg Line give us much trouble? It was impossible to sleep. All the covering we had was the tarpaulin slung over the front of the tank.

We moved off with the dawn over some real felt-like land that might have been a park, so beautiful was the turf and countryside in general. Then we came to a halt at what proved to be our second-line trenches. The sight was breath-taking, unbelievable! It couldn't be real!

In perfect symmetry the sandbags looked as precision laid as a brick wall. No sign whatever of any disarrangement by any shells or bullets. It just blended into nature. Yet it didn't! That fellow sitting on the fire-top with his eyes open wasn't moving. He was dead! How? Everything was so unwarlike.

'Puff!' fancy that! Just a single burst of shrapnel about fifty yards to the right. Nothing like the Ypres Front though. There was a delightful signpost at the junction of that second-line trench and the communicating trench which led to the front line. It had been painted a brown colour – it would never do to have it white. On it was painted in black letters: Villers Plouich. But that was one finger, I couldn't see where the other one was directing you. Everything was so strange! Our crew had even got out of the tank in the manner of getting out of a car to obtain a better view of the area which confronted us. Probably we were ahead of schedule!

Then off we sallied into another phase. What would it prove to be? There was some trouble with barbed wire. Our driver and officer were weighing up a new problem. A decision had been reached and we could tell that we were amongst barbed wire with a difference. It caused unusual noises inside the tank, It screeched, it lifted up the tracks even, to let them down again with a sound which I can only say compares to the buckets of a dredger.

Snapping and scraping, snapping and grating, it eventually fizzled out and we had got through. That wire defies description. Fantastic it nevertheless was. One might hazard a guess as to its real height. It could be compared to the height of hop-poles in a Kentish hop field. The depth could have been in places as much as sixty yards. How it got there was real mystery. The Germans could feel confident that no human beings could cross it on foot alone. That's why it was considered rest for the troops who had to hold.

Then the Hindenburg Line was contacted. Each section had its own fascine and we all crossed it to form up in the diamond formation of the Plan. That was, one tank formed a point of a diamond and and all advancing in that manner.

Now we had about seven miles to travel to get to Cambrai: it seemed to me that at the rate of progress we were now making down a sloping bit of land we would make it by lunch. I hoped so: that tank was travelling faster than any other that I had been in. It was inspiring a new enthusiasm. Our officer was letting himself go: 'Mind, no flirting with the girls when we get to Cambrai: our instructions are to go through the town and as far as possible on the other side!'. Two sections rolled down that slope to a bridge over the canal at Masnière. We were to the right of that diamond and our section was the right-hand section. Their first task was to try a crossing of that bridge.

The despondency of Dessart Wood was still very much with our crew. Our officer wasn't aware of the discussion of the night before. Yet he himself had all the gaiety of a schoolboy filled with a spirit of adventure. It had been intended that we could get to Cambrai all right. That was why we were so loaded up with ammo and petrol. But those extra tins of petrol were a damned nuisance to all of us. It was obstructing the escape door at the back besides making it very difficult for the gunners to move about. It seemed odd that we hadn't encountered any machine-gun fire and we had been travelling for some time. Then we came to a halt. When we moved off again it was in a new direction. It transpired that we struck the canal about half a mile from the bridge. So we travelled for a very short time. Then the excitement grew in intensity.

Machine-gun fire striking right in front of my eyes gave me the knowledge that we were fast getting to a point of resistance. But the most puzzling thing to me was that the machine-gun was firing from behind us. Because of my position as 3rd driver the canal should be at my back or to my right. But this fire was coming from my left. Let me qualify that for the sake of clarity: when the outside of the tank's armour is struck by machine-gun bullets, it causes the hardened steel on the inside to flake off. In the process of the flaking off a spark is created. So, when the succession of machine-gun bullets strikes the tank you get a display of sparks just like a catherine wheel. It was thus that we knew from whence the bullets came. The outside of the door was on my side. It then occurred to me it might have rivetted the safety catch. If this was so, we would be in a jam in an emergency. I tried that catch at the first opportunity. My fears were completely justified, it would not budge! If any signals had been made on my lights while this was happening the distraction thus made it possible that I had missed an order. This confused my thinking. But I did get out the oil-can and a hammer to try and free that catch at the first possible opportunity.

Events were moving so fast now that it began to bewilder me. Our 6-pdr gun was beginning to speak on one side. The machine-guns in front and at the side were blazing away. So it was sparks, sparks and more sparks all round us. Then the horrible thought of having so much petrol on board – and the two sealed doors – caused me to think back to those blazing tanks in the Third Battle of Ypres.

Then I must have blacked out! Everybody was excited and shouting became the order from then on. This shouting only penetrated my clouded mind in small doses. Then the horrible truth began to unfold itself to me. I asked myself: How long was I unconscious? Something pretty dreadful must have happened. I must have blacked out once more. A voice was shouting for someone to open the door. He replied: 'I canna, mon!' It was near me. I knew he couldn't open it. My head was giving me intense pain: Why? I put my hand to the back of my head and got the answer to my pain and the reason for the black-outs.

When I had regained consciousness the first time my head had been jammed down between my knees. Everything had taken on a grey appearance. And through the greyness I had seen at my feet a steel helmet with a hole in it near the rim. Now I decided that the steel helmet was mine and that we had received a direct hit. So I thought to try and open the door on the other side – it seemed to be needed pretty badly. To my amazement it opened.

After I dropped to the ground I laid on my side facing the tank. Some machine-gun was firing over my body. The bullets were striking about two feet above me. In spite of my condition I found myself noticing that these bullets didn't bounce off like marbles. They were staying where they struck for a mere fraction of time, then slowly dropping earthwards as though in slow-motion films. They were of course flattened circles of metal, nearly the size of a shilling. If I was in a mess, at least I was still alive. But I daren't stand up. My instinct more than alertness set my legs to the task of propelling my body along on its side. Being so near to the tank it was quite simple. I got to the rear end of the tank and got in between the tails.

Captain John Wilson was in another tank which met the same fate. He tells his story:

When at zero 6.10 a.m. November 20th 1917 the tank engines began to warm up and the heaviest barrage in history thundered its way across a seven mile front, and tanks looking like giant toads in the mist, began to crawl towards the starting point. There were four tanks to a section, one being kept back to form a battalion reserve, so that only three went over with the first wave, in each section. They were disposed in formation: one the pointer in front, the other two about fifty yards to the flanks and in rear of.

Although we got to the starting point without trouble, we ran into one of the unforeseeables that for ever seem to crop up in battle and what happened was this: when filling up with petrol before the start, one driver came to me in trouble, one petrol tin containing water (the petrol having been flogged) had been poured into the tank. In reply to my question 'How do you know' he answered that he was 'suspicious of the sound' and tasting the last few drops was sure it was water. (The whole tank was hurriedy emptied and even at that late hour we had taken the precaution of syphoning out the low lying drains before refilling.[)] Having got to the enemy front line the engine conked out with water in the jets. This was the pivot tank in which I was travelling. I had to make a quick decision and ran the gauntlet to the left rear tank commanded by Lt. Parsons which became the pivot. The stranded tank was remedied and followed on in due course.

We successfully silenced any enemy machine-guns that were plastering our look-out slits paving the way for the infantry following in our wake to mop up and take the village of La Vacquerie on our right flank almost without cost.

Having flattened out the wire of the two front line trenches, which enabled the infantry to amble peacefully along some of them enjoying a gasper, we made for what was considered by the enemy the impregnable Hindenburg Line. The isolated machine-gun nests that were left behind to impede our progress were easily disposed of by our six pounders and I remember thinking to myself that these men were much too brave to have to die like that. The Hindenburg Lines proved no serious obstacle. The unditching gear or fascine which each tank carried enabled the three lines to be crossed in file, one fascine being used for each trench. The enemy infantry which had manned them seemed to have vanished. Climbing the slight slope to the ridge beyond was a piece of cake, but a rod was in pickle for us when we showed our noses over the top, which makes one wonder if the enemy had not got more than an inkling after all and had we run into an ambush.

With hindsight, it is fairly obvious that the tanks having penetrated so far should have halted this side of the ridge, but our sights were on Cambrai and without putting out feelers in the way of scouts and a 'recce', we went I fear blythly and rather blindly on with the unhappy result that quite a number of tanks sustained direct hits from a battery, direct laying in the valley below. We were unlucky in getting two in as many minutes, the first smashing the left track causing us to swing to the right to receive a broadside from the second. We had a drill for 'evacuating tank' if hit, which we had put into action successfully, leaving only the driver and myself to receive the second one from which I escaped, but the driver, a young Scots man regrettably perished. Badly wounded in the face, I succeeded in crawling into a shell hole and plastering my field dressing on the wound, and, although I should not say this in public, fortifying myself with a swig of rum from my water bottle. I remember no more until finding myself in a field dressing station well behind the line.

Major Hugh Boxer had been temporarily transferred from the 14th Durham Light Infantry to command their 2nd Battalion in the 6th Division for the battle. He described the part he played in a letter to his mother, written on 7 December:

I have been meaning to write to you for some time, but have not had much opportunity as things have been very strenuous of late. I however have fired off whizz-bang postcards at you at intervals, which I hope have found their mark. I expect you have guessed that I have been engaged in the Cambrai show. As a second-in-command I was condemned to remain with the transport out of the show, but a few days before, the C.O. of the 2nd Battalion went sick & they put me in in his place, so I took the battalion 'over the top'. The advance on the 20th was a most interesting one. The objective was the farthest one, on the Premy Ridge, so we did not follow immediately behind the tanks, but went over the heads of those people who took the 1st and 2nd objectives, and then forward to our own objectives. The show went like clock work except that Flesquières village was not taken, and as I had been informed that this village had to be taken by the Brigade on my left before I could advance to the Premy Ridge, I naturally thought it was so, when it hove into sight, but I was speedily undeceived by a hail of Machine Gun bullets from it, but the shooting was high & they did not hit anybody, & we got our objective in spite of it, capturing 11 Hun guns & killing or capturing all the gunners. The remark about the fine work of the Durhams in the paper referred to this exploit. The 14th battalion also did jolly well, and on the 21st went forward on their own at the request of the Cavalry and took Cautaing Village & held it until relieved by the Jocks who got the credit of taking the village! We have been spending our time since the 20th in consolidating and beating off Hun counterattacks. The fourteenth were involved in competing against a very large counter-attack & pushed it back but were nearly annihilated themselves. The poor old battalion is now only a skeleton. I was not with them being still with the 2nd, or I might well be na-poo by now. Col. Rosher I am glad to say got through safely, and likewise the adjutant, but many fine officers are gone, including poor little Gold, who did such fine work in the show in April last. The C.O. of the second battalion has returned & I went back to the fourteenth for a day, when I was pushed off to Divisional Headquarters to act as 'Liaison Officer' between Division and my Brigade, so I am more or less in clover now as hanger-on on the Staff, and shall probably remain here as long as the Division remains here. I hope to get my leave in due course but of course things are very uncertain as you can imagine. I got the British Warm and blanket safely for which many thanks. As soon as I got here I had a bath, the first for 3 weeks! I was actually lousy which is a horrible thought, but fortunately was so busy that I had not much time to think about it.

On that first day, 179 tanks had fallen out, 65 from direct hits, 71 from mechanical troubles and 43 by ditching or other causes. Such swift success had not been catered for, and Byng's reserves, especially the cavalry, could not be moved forward quickly enough to support it, so that momentum was lost. Haig had said that he would call off the operation if it did not succeed after the first forty-eight hours, but for various reasons he did not. By the end of the month all progress had come to an end and Byng's army was thinly spread and vulnerable to counter-attacks on its flanks. The Germans launched these on 30 November and soon regained all that they had lost. But the victory of

Cambrai lay in the proof of what the tank could achieve, if properly used, and from then on it was established as a major weapon on the battlefield.

The Middle East

In 1917 the tide turned in the war against Turkey in Mesopotamia and Palestine. Sir Stanley Maude, the former commander of the 13th Division at Gallipoli, promoted Lieutenant-General, took over command in Mesopotamia from Lieutenant-General Sir Percy Lake in August 1916, and spent the rest of the year in improving the resources and organization of the base at Basra and the lines of communication forward from there towards Kut. He had been reinforced by the 13th Division from Egypt and the 14th and 15th Indian Divisions from India, before he concentrated to attack the Turkish defences covering Kut. On the north (or left) bank of the Tigris, they were still at Sanna-i-yal, thirty miles downstream of the town. On the south bank they extended for thirty-five miles, their centre point being five miles to the south of the town on a tributary called the Shatt-el-Hai. Maude's plan was that Lieutenant-General Sir Alexander Cobbe's 1st Indian Corps, with the 3rd and 7th Indian Divisions, the latter now commanded by Major-General V. B. Fane, should threaten the defences at Sanna-i-yal, while Major-General Marshall's 3rd Corps, with 13th and the 14th Indian Division, should tackle the principal defences on the south bank in a series of deliberate attacks. The operation began on 13 December, and, in spite of heavy rain in January, was successful. With Maude's troops already across the Tigris behind Kut, the Turks withdrew on 24 February, having lost several thousand men as prisoners of war.

They offered no serious resistance between Kut and Baghdad, which Maude and his troops entered on 11 March. He continued his advance against growing opposition up the Tigris, until capturing Samarra, seventy miles upstream, on 24 April. He then turned his attention to the Euphrates. A combination of Turkish resistance and hot weather forced the abandonment of an attempt to reach Ramadie, seventy miles up the river, in July; but a renewed attempt at the end of September was successful, 3,454 Turks surrendering as they abandoned the town. Thereafter there was no further Turkish resistance. On 18 November General Maude died of cholera (thought to have been caused by taking local milk in his coffee at a performance of *Hamlet* by the Jewish School in Baghdad), Lieutenant-General Sir William Marshall taking his place. The total of casualties in the campaign from start to finish was 92,501: killed or died of wounds, 14,814; died of disease, 12,807; wounded, 51,386; missing or captured, 13,494. The great majority were Indian.

Turkish weakness in Mesopotamia was largely due to events in Palestine. In January 1917 Lieutenant-General Sir Archibald Murray, the Army Commander in Egypt, at last began to turn to the offensive against the Turks in Sinai. Towards the end of the month Major-General H. G. Chauvel's Australian and New Zealand Mounted Division advanced from the Suez Canal to El Arish, a hundred miles up the coast, followed by the 53rd (Welsh) Division (Major-General A. G. Dallas). Both were under the command of Lieutenant-General Sir Philip Chetwode, commanding the Desert Column. He himself was subordinate to Eastern Force, commanded by Lieutenant-General Sir Charles Dobell. The Turkish garrison withdrew as they approached on 21 January. Having established a forward base at Rafa, thirty miles on, Dobell prepared to attack the main Turkish defences at Gaza, a further thirty miles to the north. He entrusted the task to Chetwode to accomplish with the 53rd Division, the Australian and New Zealand Mounted and the Imperial Mounted (Major-General H. W. Hodgson) Divisions, keeping the 52nd (Lowland) (Major-General W. B. Smith) and the 54th (East Anglian) (Major-General S. W. Hare), with the Imperial Camel Brigade, in reserve under his own hand. The attack was launched on 26 March, and at first appeared to be successful; but at a crucial stage, when the infantry were in some difficulties, the cavalry on their right flank was withdrawn, partly in response to the advance of a Turkish force from the direction of Beersheba, which threatened their rear, and partly because the horses had had nothing to drink all day. All impetus was lost and Dobell ordered a general withdrawal.

Another attempt was made on 17 April, this time with a full-scale frontal infantry assault by 52nd and 54th Divisions and the 53rd along the coast; but, although some gas and a few tanks were used, artillery support was inadequate and the operation failed to dislodge the Turks, commanded by the German General Kress von Kressenstein. Dobell's troops dug in on the line they had reached. They had suffered 3,800 killed and wounded in the first and 6,400 in the second attack. Dobell was sent away a sick man.

Trooper Arthur Fletcher of the Lincolnshire Yeomanry had survived the torpedoing of the troopship the *Ivernia* in the eastern Mediterranean and joined his regiment in time to take part in the first attack. He describes the part they played:

On Feb. 22nd the regiment was ordered to advance. Marching in the early morning we reached Ela-Rish on the coast where we pitched our camp for the night. The Turk continuing to withdraw it was essential for us to keep on the move so on the 29th we advanced nearly 12 miles north this time camping at the small oasis of Sheik-Houaid. After a day's halt we proceeded to the coast where my troop became attached to our Divisional H.Q. which was the Anzac Division. Our duties here lasted seven days consisting of telephone orderlies and as orderlies to the Divisional C.O. General Chevall [Chauvel].

At the end of the week the advance continued and we found ourselves advanced as far as Rafa. The Turks had now concentrated their forces at Gaza some thirty miles due north. This information having reached our I.D. the cavalry pushed forward leaving Rafa at midnight on March 24th the advance being taken along the coast. In the morning we proceeded inland having encountered very feeble resistance, as far as Belah where we halted to feed and water.

The latter by the way was extremely scarce, the only hope was to dig. During the day our duties were to reconnoiter carefully the outlying villages which was successfully accomplished before dusk. We soon made ourselves comfortable for a night's rest, but we were disappointed. At midnight all were quietly aroused and ordered to saddle up ready to move off in 20 minutes. We received instructions to move rapidly and cautiously as we were about to make an attack on GAZA. At 12.30 a.m. on March 24th [25th] we commenced our forced march losing no time as darkness afforded us the finest cover. Unfortunately with day break came an awful black fog which hindered our advance for something like 5 hours for it was past midday of the 25th before it lifted and it was, we found later, the greatest drawback to our splendid efforts. Reaching Friar's Ridge (by the way named after our Brig. General Friar) about 2.30 p.m. we halted for a little while before making the final onslaught. The ridge lay on our left some three miles N.E. of Gaza and two miles inland from the sea. Between the ridge and the sea stretched a plain as far as the outskirts of the town, then rising up immediately on the coast were the sand dunes. Crossing the ridge at 2.45 p.m. we found ourselves drawn up directly two miles north of the town with a plain directly in front. The cavalry attacked from the rear and the infantry in a frontal attack. At 3 p.m. the order 'Right wheel gallop' was given, and we steered dead straight for our objective which lay where the plain vanished into small hills. The charge was in every way a splendid achievement, but owing to the failure of the infantry we were forced to retire at dusk as large reinforcements were expected from Beersheba to assist the Turk at any moment. This left us absolutely at their mercy so to delay was ridiculous as one Division (tired out by the forced marches) was hopeless against the garrison in Gaza and for a few thousand fresh troops coming up. The retirement was as orderly as possible arriving back at our starting point Belah at 8 a.m. on the morning of the 27th bitterly disappointed at our failure. Suffering from the scarcity of water imagine our feelings on discovering a well not many yards away. After the horses had been attended to, the men took full advantage of it drinking larger quantities than people at home would believe. Naturally all were preparing for a rest which we found to be wrong as ere we had been settled half-an-hour, at 8.30 a.m. orders were received to saddle up although the horses were just about beaten, and march towards the left flank of Gaza, directly on the coast, to relieve the Imperial Division who had been badly cut up attacking the reinforcements from Beersheba. After a very cautious march we took over their position on the sand dunes shortly after dusk.

At midnight the Turkish reinforcements joined their garrison at Gaza and with their assistance made it so unhealthy for us that we were forced to retire this time as best we could. This was without order, so when daylight broke we had to sort ourselves out, getting together again about 9 a.m. we retired a few miles south before making a halt for food etc. The first halt proved unsatisfactory, Jacko easily pushing us a little farther back with his 5.9s until we reached the Wadi guzzle where we eventually watered and fed. At mid-day we were ordered to thoroughly scout the Wadi, also the old Turkish front line trenches on the N.E. Unfortunately for us Jacko had succeeded in making an advance to his early March line, and gave us quite an unexpected reception. However we were able to accomplish our mission returning to our HQ with a good report and few casualties.

Murray's failure led to his supersession in June by General Sir Edmund Allenby, fresh from command of the Third Army in France. He inspired new vigour into the command, while (as Maude had done in Mesopotamia) developing the resources of his base and forward lines of communication. Lack of water had imposed severe limitations on Dobell's force, especially on operations any distance from the coast. Allenby began the construction of a pipeline to carry it forward into Sinai from the Sweet Water Canal which brought Nile water to Ismailia on the Suez Canal. By October he was ready, his force organized into three corps, Chetwode's 20th with the 10th (Irish) (Major W. B. Emery) Division, the 52nd and the 53rd (now Major-General S. J. Mott); Lieutenant-General Sir Edward Bulfin's 21st Corps, with the 54th, the 60th (London) (Major-General J. S. M. Shea), the 74th (Yeomanry – dismounted) (Major-General E. S. Girdwood) and the 75th (Major-General P. C. Palin); and the Desert Mounted Corps, commanded by Lieutenant-General Chauvel, with the 4th Cavalry Division (Major-General G. de S. Barrow), the Australian Mounted Division (now commanded by Hodgson) and the New Zealand Mounted Division (Major-General E. W. C. Chaytor).

Allenby devoted considerable effort to a deception plan designed to persuade von Kressenstein that his main effort would be another frontal attack on Gaza, whereas his real plan was for Bulfin to draw the enemy's attention there while striking first at Beersheba, nearly thirty miles south-east of Gaza, where there were supplies of water, and from there outflank the defences of Gaza with Chetwode's 20th and the Desert Mounted Corps. The operation was mounted on 31 October and was successful after a week's battle. Allenby immediately pushed forward, reaching Jaffa on 16 November. From there he thrust into the hills to Jerusalem, the defences of which were attacked on 8 December. On the following day the Turkish Governor, Izzet Bey, gave the Mayor a letter of surrender to hand to the British, and left with the last Turkish troops. Allenby entered the city ceremonially on foot on the 11th.

1918

If 1916 had been a bad year for the Entente, 1917 had been worse. The French army was recuperating, the Russian had ceased to exist, the Italian had suffered a severe defeat at Caporetto in October, the British was running out of manpower. The Allies had not been able to do anything to help Romania, whose forces were totally defeated and her capital, Bucharest, occupied by the Germans in December. These set-backs were only partially offset by the turn of the tide in the submarine war, brought about by Lloyd George's insistence, against Jellicoe's advice, on the introduction of the convoy system, the capture of Baghdad by Maude in March, and Allenby's success against the Turks in Palestine.

Lloyd George was determined to prevent men being swallowed up in further offensives in France and Belgium. However, Haig's problem was not planning a new series of attacks, but having enough men to hold his front, which had been extended by taking over a further twenty-eight miles from the French in September. He now faced the likelihood of a German offensive, as they no longer had to worry about the Eastern Front. He had been forced to send Plumer with five divisions to support the Italians, reducing his strength to forty-seven British, ten Dominion and two Portuguese divisions. Lloyd George's strategy, which also appealed to the French, even to the pugnacious seventy-six-year-old Clemenceau, who had succeeded Painlevé as Prime Minister in November, was to remain on the defensive on the Western Front while trying to eliminate Germany's allies – Austria-Hungary, Bulgaria and Turkey – from the war by operations in Italy and further east. An offensive on the Western Front would have to wait until the Americans had deployed enough divisions to counteract the transfer of German divisions from the east. This could not be until 1919, by which time a major programme of tank production should have produced several thousands of them.

Haig and Robertson were opposed to this, seeing that it handed the initiative to the Germans, particularly as they were continually being pressed to send troops to Italy and take over more front from the French, while Haig's actual fighting strength was falling. Lloyd George would have liked to get rid of them both, and found one way of clipping their wings in the establishment of a Supreme War Council in November; the French military representative to the Council was Foch and the British Wilson. The Council recommended the formation of a general reserve for the Western and Italian Fronts, a proposal Lloyd George welcomed as effectively preventing Haig from carrying out any attacks. A further recommendation that an executive committee of the Council should be formed to determine the employment of the reserve was hotly opposed by Robertson and less strongly by Haig.

Lloyd George saw this as his opportunity to be rid of them both, and sent Smuts and Hankey on a tour of France to detect a potential successor to Haig. They could not find one. Haig had a strong supporter in King George V, with whom he kept in close touch, and in spite of all the casualties suffered under his command his subordinates and the troops under their command had confidence in him. To sack him would cause a major row. To get rid of Robertson was easier, and he played into the Prime Minister's hand. He stuck to the line that to hand over responsibility for British troops in France to a committee presided over by a French general was unconstitutional and undermined his own position. Haig was more subtle. He raised no objection to the formation of a general reserve, not even to its control by an Allied committee, provided that he did not have to contribute to it; and he judged that he had a cast-iron case for not doing so.

Lloyd George turned the tables on Robertson by deciding that Robertson himself would be appointed the British military representative, changing places with Wilson. Robertson refused and was replaced as CIGS by Wilson, whose place on the Council was taken by Rawlinson. Robertson was relegated to Britain's Eastern Command until June 1918, when he took over as C-in-C Great Britain from Sir John French, when he went to Ireland as Viceroy. Haig did nothing to help Robertson in this crisis, relations between them having cooled as Haig considered that Robertson did not fight hard enough for his cause in Whitehall.

The major battle was over manpower. Haig's divisions were all seriously under strength in infantry. Instead of stripping the United Kingdom, which could no longer realistically be thought to need troops for home defence, and filling the gaps in Haig's ranks, the Government decided to reduce the number of battalions in each brigade from four to three and to maintain a general reserve of 120,000 men in Britain. Haig viewed this with dismay, as his intelligence staff noted the progressive increase in the number of German divisions. In mid-February 1918, eighty-one German divisions faced Haig's fifty-nine on a front of 126 miles, while seventy-one faced ninety-nine French and one American division on their 324-mile front. In addition, the Germans had twenty-five divisions in reserve. This figure of 177 increased steadily over the following four weeks, reaching a total of 201.

For the first time since 1914 the British army had to think in terms of defence. Haig could not afford to yield ground in the northern sector of his front, nearest to the Channel coast. Further south, down to the junction with the Sixth French Army at Barisis, the actual line held was less critical. His allotment of divisions to armies reflected this. Plumer's Second, round Ypres, had fourteen divisions for twenty-three miles of front; Horne's First, between Armentières and Arras, sixteen for thirty-three; Byng's Third, from Arras to the Cambrai battlefield, sixteen for twenty-eight; and Gough's Fifth, for the forty-two miles from there to Barisis, fourteen with three cavalry divisions in reserve behind him. Gough was understandably concerned, particularly as a significant stretch of his line had recently been taken over from the French and was in a poor state.

At 4.40 a.m. on 21 March an intense bombardment, incorporating large quantities of gas shell, opened up on the whole front of Byng's and Gough's armies. Five hours later, in a thick mist, the infantry of three German armies (sixty-five divisions supported by 6,608 guns) attacked, using new tactics of infiltration, by-passing any posts which held out, and overran the whole of Gough's defensive system. By the evening of the 23rd Gough's army had been driven back twelve miles. Byng's left held, but his right wing swung back in line with Gough. Ludendorff's plan was for this first blow to break through at the junction of the British and the French and swing north behind the former: a second blow in Flanders would then turn Haig's left flank, and the whole British army would be cut off from the sea. While his only reserve of eight infantry and three cavalry divisions was thrown into the battle to hold the Germans off Amiens, Haig appealed to Pétain for help in seeing that their two armies were not separated. Pétain expressed sympathy, but was more concerned with fears that the next blow would fall on his front in Champagne.

Major Joe Rice of the 82nd Brigade Royal Field Artillery with the 18th Division in the Fifth Army wrote frequently to his parents:

> *22.3.18.*
> By now you know what has been happening. Once again I have been most fortunately placed through no action of my own. So has Walter.
>
> As I told you I have been reconnoitring all the reserve artillery positions for this corps [the 3rd], & the Boche attack came off the day before I thought it was finished, so I was not with the battery. My captain who was running the battery for me was killed; another major, who was attached to divisional artillery headquarters, & I & 2 others are the surviving battery commanders out of 8. But all the batteries did magnificent work, fairly mowing the Boche down frequently with direct laying, & with rifles as well. Walter was fortunate in that he was at his battery's rear position which was not captured. The batteries all had their guns arranged in depth in two or three positions, & it was generally the front two that succumbed after doing great work.
>
> Of course I have been worried about Walter & it will have been a trying experience for him, but we both have cause to be thankful.
>
> My work here was found to be so useful that they will not let me go for two or three days, although the colonel is trying hard to get me. I am quite close to the battery and visit them nearly every day to keep in touch with things. The Boche had had to pay for his advance, & as we were holding our lines thinly our losses per mile of front have been light. The division was outnumbered four to one. We have withdrawn into decent country, & the Boche has advanced into country which he carefully flattened out before his retreat a year ago! Rather funny!
>
> Don't worry about us. I'll try to send F.S.P.Cs* pretty often but may easily forget sometimes.
>
> *1.4.18*
> We are safely out of the big show now, none the worse, except that I have just developed my third boil since my return from leave & this time it has caused a gland in my groin to swell rather uncomfortably.

---

* Field Service Post Cards.

I took over command of the battery on 23rd & we occupied 4 different positions in the next 24 hours. Our last acquaintance with the Boche was on the 25th when most of the troops in the district had to retire across a certain bridge. Three roads converged on to this bridge and each one was blocked to a standstill with traffic, & the bridge was being mildly shelled at long range by a Boche 10.5cm howitzer battery. He was only sending over a salvo of three shells every three minutes: I can't imagine why he didn't turn on many more guns because if he had broken that bridge there would have been some trouble for us. As I said, the road was blocked with transport of all sorts & I was just thinking the battery would never be able to get a move on when a general came along & said all artillery was to get over first. My battery was the last in the brigade to cross. Three shells arrived just as we were crossing but did no damage, and a complete team not far behind the tail of my column was knocked out by the next salvo.

After that we found ourselves in the French area & marched for six days, sometimes at very short notice. For three of these days we were quite cut off from our A.S.C.,* & men & horses went a bit short, but we managed to requisition or pick up quite a lot of forage etc. Sleep none too plentiful that week!

*

On 26 March the Supreme War Council was convened at Doullens. Haig realized that alone among the French generals Foch had the determination, backed by Clemenceau, to grip the situation. He willingly accepted the agreement that 'General Foch is charged by the British and French Governments with coordinating the action of the Allied Armies on the Western Front'. Ludendorff's southern thrust ran out of steam by 5 April, when his forward troops were ten miles from Amiens. By that time Haig's casualties amounted to 177,739, of whom 14,823 were killed, and Fifth Army had lost 500 guns. German casualties were over 250,000, and, as a result, Ludendorff had to reduce the strength of his northern thrust.

This was delivered on 9 April by eight divisions with six in reserve on a front of twelve miles, held by Horne's First Army on the La Bassée canal with three British divisions and one Portuguese. It was extended

* Army Service Corps' ammunition supply wagons or trucks.

next day to the Messines Ridge in Second Army's sector. Both armies were driven back, but the Messines Ridge on the left was held. The important rail junction of Hazebrouck was threatened and Haig called on his troops for a supreme effort with his famous 'Backs to the Wall' message on 11 April.

The straits to which Haig was reduced in order to get troops into the line are illustrated by the experience of Lieutenant Gilbert Flemming of the 7th Rifle Brigade in the 14th Division, who was on his way back from leave when the crisis broke:

We were now a party of 5 officers, myself, Major Thornton and three others who had joined like myself but later from leave and courses (only finding us by great luck!). Of Thornton's original 3 companions, one had been wounded on the 23rd, and the other two were so weary, that he had decided to leave them with the transport. We had hoped for a rest the next day – Easter Sunday* – but we were warned to 'Alert' 2 Coys of an 'Entrenching Battalion' i.e. troops rendered surplus by the reduction of battalions in January and employed since then in digging work behind the line. This battalion had been attached to the 14th Div. for all the last week's fighting, and were as weary as our own men. We were then joined by about 260 men, 5 officers and an American doctor, and proceeded at once to reorganise in case we had to move. I received command of the new 'C' Coy, just over a hundred strong. I had one officer under me from the 'entrenchers' – quite useless as it turned out – one sergeant and about 8 men from the old 'C' Coy, about 10 old oddments, 25 of the new draft and the rest entrenchers – mostly men of the K.O.Y.L.I.† Some of them looked quite good, but I had no N.C.O.'s to speak of: my old sergeant acted as Coy Sgt Major, and my four platoon sergeants were (1) The Brigade Batln Sergeant – a very old man who had not been in the line for over two years (2) a 'boy' fresh from England (he seemed likely to be better than my old private rifleman) (3) a useful looking Sergeant of the K.O.Y.L.I. (4) a pioneer sgt. of the same – very inexperienced in combat duties. I spent Sunday afternoon doing my best to make a company out of this material, though I hoped to have longer to do it in. But the very next morning' at the bottom of the page. In fact Easter Sunday 1918 was 31 March.

* The author puts 31 March in the margin against this line and 1 April against 'but the very next morning' at the bottom of the page. In fact Easter Sunday 1918 was 31 March.
† King's Own Yorkshire Light Infantry.

next morning we marched off, drew rations from the roadside and
got into lorries about 2 miles from Baconel and travelled by Amiens
(now looking very strange and deserted and somewhat damaged
by bombs) to Boves, S.E. of it. Two battalions per Brigade had
been made up over 400 strong, the third had only about 100 men,
but we were going to hold a piece of line at once. We spent the
afternoon in a wooded slope S. of the Bois de Gentelles and moved
up at night along the Roye road through Domart to hold the line
between Hangard (river Luce) and the main road. We took over all
sorts of weary oddments: there were of course no trenches – only
rifle pits and holes in the road-side banks. I was support Coy. – H.Q.
was in a barn of the water mill. I had a long night disposing of the
men, and learning the lie of the land. French troops were holding
Hangard itself but North of them again was a British battalion, with
whom I made touch in the morning. The enemy was some way away
and at first quite quiet: later, when an attack was attempted by our
troops in the north, they shelled us somewhat, and inflicted a few
casualties with M. Gun fire – wounding 'D' Coy's commander.
(Gooch who had been with us through 1917). But it did not last
long. We found a calf in the village, which an expert killed and
dressed – which with potatoes and leeks from a chateau garden made
a very good dinner.

We were to be relieved at night by the French, and I was told off
as the best (!) speaker available to transact the business. I discussed it
first with the commander of the troops holding Hangard discovered
the organization and probable numbers of the incoming battalion
and laid my plans for the relief, which would not be by any means a
simple one. When they arrived I had another long discussion with
the commander and his officers in the French H.Q. in the chateau
and we at last reached complete decision. Meanwhile the whole
battalion had come up and halted on the roadside just behind the
front line: However my guides carried off their respective 'Sections'
without arousing the attention of the enemy and we got away at last.
We had a long march back through Gentelles to Bois de Blangy, just
S. of the Amiens–Villers Bretonneux road and railway. We arrived
about 3 a.m. and lay down as we were in the wood to sleep.

Foch sent reinforcements, and the position was held until the German
attacks ceased at the end of the month. Haig's casualties between 9 and

30 April amounted to 82,040, of whom 7,918 were killed: the Germans suffered another 98,300.

Foch and Haig were united in their resolve to exploit the situation created by these German losses and the existence of two large German salients on ground not previously reduced to a quagmire; but they had to battle against the politicians and generals in both countries who shrank from a return to the offensive until the full strength of the Americans could be deployed in 1919. However, they won the argument. On 18 July Pétain and the Americans under Pershing launched attacks all round the major salient which extended from Villers Cotterets south of the Aisne to west of Epernay on the Marne, and on 8 August Rawlinson, who had returned from Versailles to relieve Gough, made the scapegoat for the withdrawal in March, and had renumbered the latter's Fifth Army the Fourth, launched an attack east of Amiens with Monash's Australian Corps of five and Currie's Canadian of four divisions, supported by 324 Mark V heavy tanks. On his right Debeney's First French Army, under Haig's command, attacked at the same time. Rawlinson also had Kavanagh's Cavalry Corps of three cavalry divisions and 96 medium (14-ton) Whippet tanks for exploitation. Rawlinson attacked at dawn, and by midday all objectives had been captured: the Germans suffered heavy losses and Ludendorff described it as 'The black day of the German army'.

Major Cyril Ommaney's battery in the 83rd Brigade RFA was supporting the 18th Division in the attack. He himself was in temporary command of the brigade. His diary records the first day:

> *Thursday Aug 8.*
> Zero hour 4.20 am. Everything very quiet up to then. The whole country quickly covered with dense smoke & mist – can see nothing – just like a thick London fog. Up to 7 am we had no news of anything, though by that time we should have reached our final objective. 6.45 am came news of that. Hayville of C, now commanding A, Hopkins & Currie of B and nine men have been gassed. Since then a good many horses killed and wounded last night. So far not a shell near us.
>
> At 11 am get the first definite news – from a gunner of course. All objectives gained except in extreme left, the scene of the past two days' fighting when the Boche was of course very strong & alert. The battle fluctuated a good deal during the day, but finally we ended up

just this side of our final objective. We were firing pretty continuously all day, the enemy not replying much.

Hayville, Hopkins, 4 other officers and about 60 other ranks of A and B Batteries suffering so badly from gas that they had to be evacuated. The D.A.C.* came nobly to the rescue & sent on every officer they could spare.

In the afternoon I walked round the forward area & 55 Inf Bde HQ. – Saw the beginning of a Bosch counterattack, which I don't think achieved anything, and visited some of the batteries on my way back.

The night was quiet.

Col. Seagram returned in the evening but will stay at DA.†

News from the South very good. 7000 prisoners & 100 guns. Canadian cavalry corps through and the whole front moving forward rapidly.

On 15 August Haig halted this thrust and ordered Byng to attack near Arras on 21 August, when he advanced two miles and took 5,000 prisoners. Major Richard Foot, who was commanding another RFA battery, D Battery of the 310th Brigade, normally with the 62nd Division, gives his account:

The 23rd of August was a heavy day of fighting, this time in support of another Division, 37th. That day is memorable for me for two reasons. D/310 was in action behind the sharp slope of a hill, with two other 4.5 [inch] Howitzer Batteries on either side of us. Once the attack, and our barrage, started, we were busy at the guns, when, with a roar and a cloud of dust, the adjoining howitzer of the battery on our left blew up, one of its own shells bursting within the gun. A few minutes later the same thing happened to the adjoining howitzer of the battery on our right: in both cases the whole gun detachment was either killed or wounded. Consequently, we all had the jitters, expecting a similar premature burst in one of our howitzers. Behind us, across the valley a line of 18-pdr batteries was firing over our heads, and, at intervals, one of their guns would have a premature shrapnel burst, peppering us with a hail of whirring bullets; and this did not add to our composure in D/310.

* Divisional Artillery Centre.
† Divisional Artillery.

As the rate of fire slackened, I withdrew three gunners from each detachment, and made them settle down in shell holes behind the guns, relieving the others at their own gun after a quarter of an hour of shelter and a smoke. Just after another of these 18-pdr premature bursts had come from behind, I looked for one of my subalterns, Jack Massy-Beresford, who should have been somehere close behind his section of two howitzers, arranging these reliefs. I called him; no answer; went to look for him, and found him lying on his face, stone dead; the shell case of an 18-pdr shrapnel had hit him fair on the back of his steel helmet. Jack was a splendid youngster, and his death depressed us all even further. We were glad, when the barrage was done, to get orders to move to join our own Division; and when the teams came up, we carried Jack's body with us, wrapped in a blanket, on the trail of the leading gun.

On the march, I was called to the head of the Battery, to find no less a person than the C-in-C himself, Sir Douglas Haig, by the roadside. He was alone, except for a Sergeant of 7th Hussars carrying his Union Flag as a lance pennon. I had known Haig in pre-war days at my home, he was a contemporary of my Father's at Royal Military College, Sandhurst; and when I reported, as was customary, my name, rank, and unit, he at once remembered me. He was a very taciturn man; but, as the battery filed by on the road and saluted him, he asked about the body on the leading gun, and I told him about Jack's death, complaining, rather bitterly and brashly no doubt, about our day's troubles with faulty ammunition. After the Battery had passed, he fell in behind them on the road with me, got out a notebook and made a note of Jack's name; later I heard that he had indeed taken the trouble to write a personal note of condolence in his own hand to Jack's family. This was the only time, in more than three years on the front in France, that I ever saw the Commander-in-Chief; and his kindly sympathy, communicated later to the Battery, did a lot to cheer us up after a horrid day.

Three days later Rawlinson resumed his attacks, and by the end of the month Haig was approaching the formidable defences of the Hindenburg Line. Wilson warned him that the Government would not view favourably an attack with heavy losses which did not succeed in breaching it. Haig was furious. He pointed out that he had captured 77,000 prisoners and 800 guns in the last month, and insisted that the pressure had to be maintained. Foch was of the same mind, and planned coordinated attacks over the whole Allied front at the end of September. They brought the war to an end, by which time Haig's armies had suffered a further 180,000 casualties.

Bulgaria surrendered on 29 September, and Turkey on 31 October after Allenby had defeated Liman von Sanders's Eighth Turkish Army in an attack with four divisions on 19 September, known as the Battle of Megiddo, and occupied Damascus on 1 October. Austria-Hungary sued for peace on 3 November. Tentative negotiations with the Germans had started when the American President, Woodrow Wilson, received a message from Chancellor von Herzling on 4 October. He had replied with a reiteration of his fourteen points. On 12 October they replied, accepting them, provided that all the Allies did so. In that case they agreed to withdraw from all occupied territories; but on 10 October 520 lives had been lost when the Irish passenger ship the SS *Leinster* was torpedoed by a German submarine, which had then proceeded to sink it by gunfire before the passengers could be saved. Lloyd George and Clemenceau asked Wilson for clarification of his intentions before committing them. On 14 October he replied to the Germans, saying that the terms of an armistice were a matter for the military authorities and that none of the Allied governments would deal with authorities whose armed forces behaved as badly as the Germans had done. On 20 October the Germans replied, rejecting his accusation and saying that they could not accept terms 'irreconcilable with the honour of the German people and with paving the way to a peace of justice'. Wilson sent a stern reply on 23 October, saying that the only armistice terms Germany would be offered were those which would leave her militarily defenceless. On 26 October the Kaiser dismissed Ludendorff and on 6 November a delegation, headed by Count Oberndorff, met Foch and asked him for 'conditions of an armistice'. 'I have no conditions to give you', was the reply, forcing them to ask formally for an armistice. 11 a.m. on 11 November was fixed for it to come into force, but it was not until a message from the new German Chancellor, Prince Max of Baden, to the delegation was intercepted by the Admiralty at 8 p.m. on 10 November that it was known that the Germans had decided to surrender. In a letter to his wife on 1 November, Haig wrote: 'I am afraid the Allied Statesmen mean to exact humiliating terms from Germany. I think this is a mistake, because it is merely laying up trouble for the future, and may encourage the wish for revenge.' He was right.

*

The Great War army was unlike any British army that had preceded it. It was the nation in arms. Over five million men had served in it. Assembling, maintaining and operating this huge military machine turned the army into a vast industrial complex, employing all the skills of civilian life; and the need to create and sustain it wrought profound changes in the life of the nation, especially in the expanding field of Government activity. It was a railwayman's war. The huge volume of supplies was transported by rail almost to the front line, and major troop movements were executed by the same method, although the use of motor vehicles increased steadily as the war progressed.

The one traditional arm which had proved almost useless was horsed cavalry; but its success in Allenby's campaign in Palestine, both at the Third Battle of Gaza and, notably, at Megiddo, obscured the reality that its day was done: the machine-gun, combined with barbed-wire entanglements, rendered it useless, and was the chief enemy of the infantry. The hand-grenade and the mortar were the principal close-quarter weapons. The trench and its 'dugout' shelters enabled infantry-men to survive the intensity of artillery fire, which was deadly to men, and even more so to horses, in the open. The tank was the answer to the combination of obstacles and firepower, but had not been developed to a sufficient degree of reliability nor produced in adequate numbers to prove its real potential. Artillery remained dominant up to that time.

The principal innovation was the aeroplane. Its effect as an offensive weapon was slight, even by 1918, but its main value was to make it possible to see 'the other side of the hill', both to provide information and to direct artillery fire. In 1911 an Air Battalion had been formed from the Balloon Factory of the Royal Engineers at Farnborough, with an establishment of 14 officers and 150 men. On 13 April of the following year the Royal Flying Corps was formed, intended to serve both the army and the navy, each having its own Wing. It was not long before the Wings became independent, the naval one becoming the Royal Naval Air Service, and the Corps becoming part of the army. In the Army Wing, the operational unit was to be the squadron of three flights, each of four aircraft. By the beginning of 1914 there were six squadrons, No. 1 of balloons, 2, 3, 4 and 5 with aircraft and 6 in the process of forming. On the outbreak of war almost the whole of the Army Wing accompanied the BEF to France: 105 officers and 755 men with 63 aircraft. By the time of the Battle of the Somme in July 1916, Major-General H. M. Trenchard, the commander of the RFC with the BEF, had four brigades with a total of nine wings, in which he had twenty-seven squadrons of aircraft, a total of 407 aircraft, and four of kite-balloons. In the second Battle of Arras in April 1917 the RFC's 365 aircraft faced 195 German, and lost 75 in combat and 56 in accidents. Two months later German Gotha aircraft bombed Liverpool Street station in London, killing 162 people and wounding 432, and in another raid on 7 July killed 54 and injured 190. The air defence of Britain was the responsibility of the Royal Navy, but it had not taken the task seriously. These raids lent urgency to the inquiry which the Government had set up under the chairmanship of Jan Smuts, the former Boer commando leader, now a British general after his successful campaign against the German Lieutenant-General P. von Lettow-Vorbeck in East Africa. Dissatisfaction over confusion in reconciling the differing requirements of the navy and the army in both the design and the production of aircraft had already led to the creation of a Joint Air Committee and then an Air Board under Lord Cowdray; but the air raids on London provoked the Government to go further and accept Smuts's recommendation that an air force, separate from both the navy and the army, should be formed, as had been originally intended for the RFC. One of the factors which influenced Smuts was the information, which was not correct, that existing plans would result in the production of many more aircraft than the army and navy would need in 1918. 14,168 were produced in 1917 and it was expected that 1,800 to 2,000 a month would be produced in 1918.

On 18 January 1918 Trenchard was appointed the first Chief of Staff of the new service and the Royal Air Force formally established on 1 April. But shortly before that, on 19 March, Trenchard proffered his resignation. He, like Haig, had opposed the abolition of the RFC and the formation of an entirely separate service. Lieutenant-General Sir David Henderson, another member of the Air Council, and the real father of the RFC, also resigned. Major-General F. H. Sykes took the place of Trenchard, who was posted to command the Independent Force in

France, Major-General Sir John Salmond having replaced him as Commander of the RFC with the BEF.

The Independent Force was the brainchild of those who put their faith in bombing far behind the enemy lines, and it had been agreed that the force would operate under the orders of the Supreme Allied Commander, Foch. This concept had been supported by Smuts, who had written in his report: 'And the day may not be far off when aerial operations with their devastation of enemy lands and destruction of industrial and populous centres on a vast scale may become the principal operations of war to which the older forces of military and naval operations may become secondary and subordinate.' At that time it consisted only of ten squadrons with very limited range and payload, but the appointment was to convert Trenchard eventually into a passionate supporter both of an independent air force and of an independent bombing role.

A further innovation, which could have had a significant effect if it had been more fully developed, was that of wireless (radio). Even when reserves were available to exploit success in attack, and had sufficient mobility to do so, they were seldom used in time, because the higher commanders had no idea what the situation was. Communication relied either on field telephones or on a man on his feet, carrying a written message. The enemy's artillery fire invariably cut all telephone lines and killed many of the runners. Plans had to be rigid, both because the information on which to change them could not be obtained and because the orders to effect the changes could not be transmitted.

One of the gruesome aspects of the war had been the execution by firing squad of soldiers convicted by court martial; a total of 245 for desertion and 37 for cowardice or similar offences. James Wolfe, when he commanded the 20th Foot in 1755, issued a regimental order that 'A soldier who quits his rank, or offers to flag, is instantly to be put to death by the officer or sergeant in rear of that platoon: a soldier does not deserve to live who will not fight for his King and country'; but between 1803 and 1901, when Kitchener confirmed a death sentence in the Boer War, no soldier had suffered this fate, fear of the lash having been considered a sufficient deterrent up to 1881, when flogging was abolished. The trials were generally perfunctory. The medical evidence, not asked for until after conviction, was generally restricted to whether the culprit was of sound mind or suffering from some recognized malady. In a very large number of cases the court and the intermediate authorities – the brigade, division and, occasionally, the corps commanders – made a recommendation for mercy, but almost invariably the army commanders and the Commander-in-Chief took the line followed by one army commander in the case of a private sentenced to death for cowardice in the Battle of the Somme, who wrote on the proceedings: 'If toleration be shown to private soldiers who deliberately decline to face danger, all the qualities which we desire would be debased and degraded.'

Private W. A. Quinton of the 2nd Bedfords in the 30th Division records his dismay at finding himself detailed as a member of such a firing squad:

It was at the village that I had an experience of army discipline forced home to the uttermost. It stands out as well in my memory that I relate it in every detail. Twelve of us were detailed off to parade in fighting order (arms, ammunition, and haversack etc) at three o'clock the following morning, at the village square. No further information was forthcoming. Why at three o'clock in the morning? Why only twelve of us? And why in fighting order? Why? we asked ourselves and each other. We twelve were made to sleep together that night and I lay awake a long time wondering what it was all about. It was the query that I have placed first that worried me. 'Three o'clock in the morning'. And whenever I hear it sung or played it reminds me of that fateful morning in October 1915.

Yes the time above all worried me. And twelve of us. I began to see daylight. I tried to convince myself that I was wrong. I hoped I was. But subsequent events proved only too well how right I was in my reasonings. About two o'clock one of the guards from outside roused us. A quick wash under the pump in the farmyard and we were soon dressed for parade. We fell in and were told to empty our ammunition pouches, putting the contents into a sandbag. The sergeant in charge then walked around us, feeling our pouches to make sure that no ball cartridges remained. We then marched off to the village square, halted and stood at ease. We were still wondering what it was all about. After a few moments a private car drew up followed shortly afterwards by an army lorry. Several officers alighted from the car and had a short consultation with our sergeant. We received our orders and clambered aboard the lorry.

Off we went through the village, the car containing the officers going on somewhere ahead. We passed several villages, and it was not yet daylight when we at length drew in beside the roadway and were ordered to dismount. Marching a short distance along the road we turned left into a field. Two whitish objects in the far corner arrested my attention and I was just able to discern them as bell-tents. We filed into one of them and were told to be ready to fall-in outside in a few moments. We squatted on the ground and lit our cigarettes. Then one of our number spoke of the business in hand. 'Something funny about this!' Nobody answered. 'Why don't they tell us what we are supposed to be doing?' he went on again. 'Strikes me we're a blinking firing party, and there's a chap here as don't care about it.'

He was right! I had had my suspicions all along, and I knew his solution was right the moment I had spotted the bell-tents. We were not left in doubt very long, for a second or two after the sergeant poked his head round the tent door, with instructions that when called upon, we were to file out and enter the adjoining tent, each man to pick hold of one of the dozen rifles lying there (our own rifles had been taken from us) with strict orders to take them as they came, and not to pick & choose. We were strangely silent after having received those last instructions. Five minutes passed, and then in single file we proceeded towards the tent wherein lay our rifles. I was third man as we passed into the tent. There were now ten rifles laying neatly in a row. Two had been taken up, and I took possession of the third one. In less than a minute we were all outside again and marching two deep towards a corner of the field.

'Halt! Left turn! single file! Stand at ease!'

And we stood within a few [feet? yards?] of a hedge, & facing it, our backs to the tents & the small group of officers. For some minutes we stood there, when the sound of a car from somewhere behind made us feel inclined to turn our heads in that direction, but the watchful eyes of the sergeant were upon us & we keep our faces to our front. The car stopped. We heard voices, & then silence. Footsteps from behind us, & in a moment an officer, a lieutenant by rank, was addressing us. He looked very serious & his face seemed rather white.

'Men! You know the first duty of a soldier! Obedience! In a few moments you will be called upon to fire at a given target. You will obey all orders, & remember this, if you wish to show mercy, show it by taking careful aim, & hit the bull's eye, which will be a small round white disc.'

My rifle seemed to have suddenly grown heavy. I felt sick at heart. I stole a glance at the man next to me. His eyes were staring straight ahead and his eyelids flicking queerly.

'Squad!' The cautionary word of command made me jump, and brought me back to my senses.

'Shun! About . . . turn!'

What I saw at one glance takes much longer to describe in writing. Straight in front of us at a distance of about twenty-five yards was our target. A lone figure in khaki, his arms pinioned behind him around the trunk of a young tree, his legs fastened just above the ankles. His tunic was fastened by a piece of string, the brass buttons having been cut off. He wore no hat, & around his eyes was a white bandage. He hung limp the tree supporting him. On his left breast pocket was pinned a white disc, about three inches in diameter.

Sharply following the order to about-turn, came the command: 'At your target, take aim'.

Twelve rifles came up to the aiming position.

'Fire!'

I just had time to see that helpless figure shudder & then hang very still, when

'About turn!'

We again stood facing the hedge. We heard movements and voices behind us.

'Form two-deep! To the lorry in the roadway, quick march!'

A little group around the tree hid the victim from a view; but a few yards away two men were busily digging a grave.

Such is army discipline in time of war. We were back in our billets in a very short time & were excused duty till midday. Naturally it was some time before we could dismiss the happenings from our minds, but I had the satisfaction of knowing this; that no bullet from my rifle hit the target. For as soon as I fired, I knew by the absence of any recoil of my rifle, that I had merely fired a blank cartridge.

Captain L. Gameson of the Royal Army Medical Corps was the medical officer of the 71st Brigade RFA and relates his first experience of a court martial, on 10 June 1917:

I attended a Court Martial on the morning of my all-night sitting with poor Burton. Here too I appeared as a medical witness, and I think I had pressed to be called. It was my first experience of such a judicial assembly; and not indeed the happiest case as an introduction, for the prisoner (one of our gunners) was up against the capital charge of cowardice in the face of the enemy.

The Court was held at a little farmhouse in a low-ceiled room with a stone floor. Apart from the prisoner, the only person present I can distinctly remember is the Prisoner's Friend, a competent officer in his late thirties who was normally somewhat aggressive but not so this morning. I recall that an air of constrained embarrassment seemed to affect those who were taking part; amateurish embarrassment, so to say, in the case of a few. This I remember with certainty while forgetting ranks, names and faces. It is probable that the anxious, sleepless night which preceded the hearing had made me unimpressionable as regards detail.

In a bell-tent for guard-room I had spent several hours with the prisoner before his trial. He had laughed much and had been unmoved by the very possible later prospect of being shot at dawn. I have forgotten the circumstances of his alleged cowardice, but there was no question of his having deserted while actually under fire. I took the line that his failure should be imputed to those who had passed him fit to serve in the Field Artillery, contending quite seriously that his instability made him less fitted for such active service than a man who was deaf or had flat feet. My contention had the advantage of being patently true, and I had not gone to the Court without full data and a formidable case-history. I was also prepared to be asked why the boy's instability had not been detected and reported to me before the break came. As far as I can remember no questions were put to me. My evidence though taken down in detail was (as far as I can remember) received in silence without comment. I could not wait until the end of the hearing, but was told later that cowardice had been established and a verdict of guilty found.

There must have been a strong recommendation for mercy attached to the findings before they went from the Court to some high final authority, because the boy was not shot.

I felt that the machinery for dealing with such cases was inadequate. As an ordinary M.O., with no experience whatever outside hospital, I was inexpert in both the thorny matter of mental states and the technique of presenting a case. In theory at any rate, it was the Court's job to dig out the truth. Were the truth handed to it intelligently the job was made easier. No other medical evidence than mine was offered and I am almost certain that I had had to shove myself into the picture, as I did later in at least one similar case. Which is not to say that medical evidence with all its demerits was useless, only that it was not sought as a matter of routine. This was typical of the period. Here, I fancy, it may have been useful, for without mitigating evidence – to the best of my knowledge and I put it no stronger than that – the boy would have been shot; as a whole lot more were shot. Opinion was divided on this question of the firing-squad. Some, by no means necessarily blimps, would have no quarter at any price. They would shoot every deserter mitigating circumstances or none. To men of this stamp, medical officers were intruders.

*

In the light of history, the war appears to have been a terrible waste of life and effort. On the Allied side, 5,200,000 men died, of whom 2,300,000 were Russians, while Central Powers' deaths were 3,450,000. European civilization and the balance of power were fundamentally affected, and the seeds sown of the totalitarian regimes that developed in Russia and, later, in Germany. Casualties of the British army recruited from Great Britain and Ireland amounted to 513,093 who were killed in action or died of their wounds, 188,317 dead from other causes or missing who were never traced, 1,662,625 wounded and 170,389 taken prisoner, some of whom died while prisoners, and may therefore be included in the total of dead.

Post-war judgement of the principal commanders, particularly of Haig, strongly influenced by Lloyd George's memoirs, was harsh. There is no doubt that Haig was rigid in outlook, convinced that he had the support of a very Scottish deity. In spite of the appalling losses and miserable conditions that the soldiers endured under his command, he retained to the end the confidence of his subordinates at almost every level. His main fault was to persist in pressing attacks long after all hope of any success had faded, trusting in attrition to bring eventual victory. In his final dispatch he wrote:

In the stage of the wearing-out struggle losses will necessarily be heavy on both sides, for in it the price of victory is paid. If the opposing forces are approximately equal in numbers, in courage, in morale and in equipment, there is no way of avoiding payment of the price or of eliminating this phase of the struggle.

Of the other principal figures, Rawlinson, Plumer, Monro and the Australian Monash, as well as Allenby after he had been transferred to Egypt, earned creditable reputations.

3

BETWEEN THE WARS
1919–1939

As euphoria over victory and the end of the war began to die down, the one thought that united everyone in all walks of life was *never again*. Attempts to fulfil that wish took many forms, from pacifism to determination to find ways of waging war that took less time and cost fewer lives, at least for one's own side. The navalist school of sailors insisted that we must never again commit ourselves to fighting a land campaign on the Continent: we should stick to 'The British Way in Warfare', favoured by Basil Liddell Hart – a limited commitment, delivered by sea, to a subsidiary target. The strategic airmen, also backed by Liddell Hart, argued that a decisive blow against the enemy's capital, probably using chemical bombs, could break his will to fight and avoid long drawn-out and expensive naval or land campaigns.

In the army it took different forms. One, aligned to the navalist school, was that the Western Front experience was a freak, which should not and would not be repeated. Methods developed for it, such as the tank, would no longer be needed, and the army should concentrate on its primary and traditional task of 'Imperial Policing'. That was music to the ears of the traditional arms, cavalry and infantry. The airmen had a partial ally in the enthusiasts for 'mechanical warfare': those who saw the tank as the principal weapon for a new form of mobile, mechanized land warfare, aimed primarily at the enemy's command system rather than the destruction of his armed forces. This mechanized army would act in close cooperation with aircraft. Lieutenant-Colonel J. F. C. Fuller, on the staff of Tank Corps Headquarters in France, was the leading prophet of this school. Finally there were those who believed that the methods used in the last 'Hundred Days' offensive on the Western Front, in infantry tactics, in their support by tanks and in the application of artillery, should form the basis of the army's organization, training and equipment. Lieutenant-Colonel Bernard Montgomery, who had been chief of staff of the 47th (London) Division in these operations, was one of those.

Meanwhile the army had to face practical tasks while being reduced in size, although not as rapidly as some serving in its ranks hoped: the initial plan for demobilization, which gave priority to the needs of industry for skilled men and for former employees, led to trouble, and was changed for one based on age and length of service. Some of these tasks were the aftermath of the war. A British Army of the Rhine, 45,000 strong, was deployed in Germany to enforce the terms first of the armistice and, later, of the Treaty of Versailles, remaining there until 1930. Troops were also deployed to support anti-Bolshevik forces in Russia: the future Field Marshal, Edmund Ironside, commanded a thousand-strong expedition sent to Archangel to support General Yudenich, who was trying to recapture St Petersburg in cooperation with the Finnish General Mannerheim, and another future Field Marshal, the twenty-seven-year-old Lieutenant-Colonel Harold Alexander, a member of General Gough's Allied Mission to the Baltic States, found himself in command of the local Baltic German Landeswehr.

The largest, and most permanent, addition to the army's responsibilities was that imposed by the collapse of the Ottoman Empire and British determination to control as much of it as possible. Allied occupation of Istamboul, to command which Ironside had been transferred, was followed by the 'Young Turk' rebellion against the Sultan, led by the hero of Gallipoli, Mustafa Kemal, later known as Atatürk, who was based on the Asiatic mainland. After his defeat of the Greek troops, who rashly tried to advance to Ankara, and his capture of Izmir in September 1922, Lloyd George's championship of the Greek cause nearly led to open war between Kemal's forces and the British occupying troops at Chanak. It was averted by the good sense of the two generals on the spot, Sir Charles Harington and Ismet (later Inönü). Lloyd George received no support for his bellicose stand either from the dominions or from the allies, France and Italy. The incident forced his resignation as Prime Minister and he never held office again.

An earlier clash between Kemal's forces and British troops, in July 1920, had seen the last charge on horseback by a regular British cavalry regiment, the 20th Hussars. Their regimental history tells the tale:

> The 20th Hussars left Egypt to join the 'Army of the Black Sea' on
> the 28th June, at a strength of 13 officers and 523 rank and file,

commanded by Lieut. Colonel M. C. Richardson, and joined Ironside at Deringe on the 20th July. The Turks had meanwhile advanced along the coast of the [Ismid] peninsula and occupied the village of Gebze where they blew the bridge. It being urgently necessary to throw them out and repair the bridge, Ironside sent a detachment consisting of the 20th Hussars, 2/39th Royal Garhwal Rifles, a Field Battery and some Royal Engineers to take the necessary action.

This resulted on the 13th July, 1920, in the 20th Hussars being drawn up in a mass on the Turkish right flank watching the Garhwalis make a frontal attack. As this developed the Turks moved forward and occupied prepared positions in front of Gebze. The distance from the 20th Hussars was about 1,000 yards, across very reasonable and open ground. The enemy were in full view and the glorious opportunity was not lost on Colonel Richardson.

An officer of the Garhwalis who witnessed the operation wrote:

'Our artillery opened fire and I could see the shells falling on the enemy position. Suddenly, as I watched, I saw movement on the ridge to the north. Over the crest of the ridge came the whole of the 20th Hussars, two squadrons abreast in columns of troops with the third squadron in depth, nearly three hundred men in all. Their sabres were drawn and glistened in the early morning sunlight, their trumpets sounded as they moved, slowly at first, but gathering speed as they approached the enemy's flank. Our artillery stopped firing. The Turks huddled together as best they could in small groups facing the oncoming horsemen. Some lay down and fired, some knelt, a few fired standing. All stood their ground, though lamentably positioned and with little hope of checking the cavalry. The Turk was always a dour fighter.

'Now the Hussars reached the Turkish flank. We could see their sabres flashing in the sun as they struck, withdrew, and struck again. All the time the trumpets echoed, fierce and thrilling, lifting one's spirits in some sort of savage exultation. The charge swept clean through the Nationalists' line. Beyond it the Squadrons rallied, regrouped, turned and charged back through the bewildered Turks, now making off for the cover of the vineyards round the village itself. Not more than thirty minutes after appearing over the ridge the Hussars had vanished whence they came, leaving huddled bodies on the plain to bear testimony to their passage.

'The last of the Nationalists disappeared into the thick country

behind Gebze and it was time for me to advance with my company
to take possession and to complete the job begun so competently by
the cavalry.' The only casualty to the 20th Hussars was Lieutenant
Groves who was badly wounded in the knee and several horses were
wounded.

*

But more significant than the clash with Atatürk was the continued
occupation of Mesopotamia and Palestine. Cyprus and Egypt, occupied
by Britain since 1878 and 1882 respectively, had been formally recognized as still part of the Ottoman Empire until Turkey joined the Central
Powers in 1914. The former was then annexed as a colony and the latter
declared a British protectorate. The status of Cyprus was confirmed by
the Treaty of Lausanne in 1923, which established peace between Greece
and Turkey, and Britain recognized Egypt as an independent sovereign
state in 1922, the Khedive Fuad becoming King; but British troops
continued to be garrisoned there, although that was not recognized by
treaty until 1935. Six infantry battalions and a cavalry brigade were
stationed there in 1923. Palestine and Iraq, as Mesopotamia became
called, were declared League of Nations mandates, and as such allotted
to Britain. The burden on the army of their occupation was reduced in
1921 when Churchill moved from the War Office (with responsibility
also for the Air Ministry) to the Colonial Office and handed over the
task to the Royal Air Force to exercise through 'air control' – bombing,
after warning, the villages of recalcitrant tribal leaders.

However, it was not these new tasks which would prove the army's
main burden, but the resurrection of trouble in two traditional areas,
Ireland and India. The British army in India was reduced to 60,000
(forty-five infantry battalions, five cavalry regiments, eight armoured car
companies and sixty-nine artillery batteries) and the Indian Army to
190,000 (a hundred infantry battalions, twenty-one cavalry regiments
and eighteen mountain artillery batteries). The need to maintain the
British army establishment in India and elsewhere overseas through the
Cardwell system of duplicating it with units based in Britain imposed
an inflexible pattern on the army's organization, which encouraged
conservatism.

Faced with this confused amalgam of imperial responsibilities, the
army struggled, as it always has, with the attempt to establish a rational

justification of its organization. A committee set up for this purpose in
1919 recommended a field army of twenty divisions, each of which
would throw off another division on mobilization, the Brigade of Guards
being expanded also into a division. This would entail either compulsory
home service in peacetime or an annual intake of 150,000 volunteer
recruits. Even if either of these had been practicable, an end was put to
any possibility of an organization on that scale by the drastic reduction
in defence expenditure called for in 1919 by the Treasury: from £502
million to £135 million, of which £75 million was to be shared between
the army and the RAF. This was accompanied by the famous Ten Year
Rule, which was to remain in force, renewed every year, until 1932, the
year before Hitler came to power in Germany. It stated:

> It should be assumed that the British Empire will not be engaged in
> any great war during the next ten years, and that no Expeditionary
> Force is required for this purpose ... The principal function of the
> Military and Air Forces is to provide garrisons for India, Egypt, the
> new mandated territory and all territories (other than self-governing)
> under British control, as well as to provide the necessary support to
> the civil power at home ...

Ireland, 1916–1923

While the victorious wartime leaders were struggling with the problems
of a peace treaty and how to enforce it, that desirable state of affairs did
not apply to the army's traditional stamping ground and recruiting area
of Ireland.

All those who had been concerned in the dramatic events surrounding the Home Rule Bill in 1914 thought then that the affairs of Ireland
had been more or less satisfactorily settled. The Bill, granting Home
Rule, was now the law of the land and no amending bill had started its
passage through Parliament. John Redmond and his Irish National Party
were satisfied with that. The agreement that the Bill would not come
into force for twelve months or until the end of the war also satisfied

Redmond, for few people thought that it would last much longer than that. Carson and company were also satisfied, as they relied on Lloyd George's secret assurance that the six Ulster counties would be excluded, knowing also that, if the Conservatives came to power, that assurance would rest on even firmer ground. The Government was content, as it put the problem on the back burner while the war was on the front one, particularly in view of the line which Redmond proceeded to take.

He calculated that the more that Ireland showed itself a firm and loyal supporter of Britain in the fight against Germany, the stronger would be the case against any resurrection of an amending bill to exclude Ulster from Home Rule. When the British Government accepted the Ulster Volunteer Force almost unchanged into the British army as the 36th (Ulster) Division he hoped that the same recognition would be given to the Irish National Volunteers, and was deeply disappointed when it was not. Nevertheless he encouraged the Irish, including members of the Volunteers, to join the British forces, with the result that by the autumn of 1915 there were 132,454 Irishmen in the forces, 79,511 of whom were Catholics. Of these only some 22,000 had been serving before the outbreak of war and 30,000 had been called up as reservists. Since then 81,408 had volunteered, 27,412 having been Ulster Volunteers and 27,054 National Volunteers.

Many of the reservists had held key posts as instructors and low-level commanders in the National Volunteers, and with their departure, and that of those whom Redmond encouraged to enlist, the less extreme element of the National Volunteers was gravely weakened and the movement became increasingly under the influence of those who, following the Fenian tradition, saw Britain's difficulty as Ireland's opportunity and Britain's enemies as Ireland's potential friends. The longer the war went on, the greater was this shift of emphasis, especially after the coalition Government was formed in 1915, with Bonar Law and Carson in the Cabinet. Casement had left Ireland for America before the war, and then had gone to Germany, where he tried to raise an Irish brigade from prisoners of war; he could only enlist fifty-five men, of whom only twelve, he told the Germans, could be relied on. In Ireland itself the leader and inspirer of the anti-British Sinn Fein element within the Volunteers was Patrick Pearse, who was determined that an armed insurrection should take place, however slender its chances of success. He saw more clearly than Casement that as long as Irish patriots were seen to be shedding their blood, while being suppressed by the British, they would be acclaimed as martyrs in the cause of Irish freedom by a far wider proportion of the population than those who would otherwise look favourably on their cause.

This was exactly the result of the fiasco of the Easter Rebellion, which lasted from 24 April to 3 May 1916, made doubly sure by the grave error committed by General Sir John Maxwell, the Commander-in-Chief, of approving the execution by firing squad of fifteen ringleaders, after the most summary of trials by military courts. Redmond appealed to Asquith to prevent this cardinal political error, but he took no effective action, although making an appeal to Maxwell to cease. For a time this extreme element appeared subdued, and the hopes of Nationalists began to be based on an appeal to whatever International Peace Conference was established after the war was over. But support for all elements of Sinn Fein was restored by fears that conscription would be applied to Ireland, fears realized by the announcement on 9 April 1918, after the losses in Ludendorff's March offensive, that the decision had been taken to do so, although it was never implemented. It was supposed to be balanced by an offer to bring the Home Rule Bill into effect, but with the exclusion of the six Ulster counties. Both measures served to unite every element of the Nationalist community and the Catholic hierarchy in opposition.

On 12 May Field Marshal Sir John French replaced Lord Wimborne as Viceroy, and on the pretext of their support of a fictitious German plot arrested seventy-three leading Sinn Fein figures, including Arthur Griffith and de Valera, while three significant hardliners, Michael Collins, Harry Boland and Cathal Brugha, went underground. In the General Election held in December 1918, after the armistice, Sinn Fein won 73 out of the 105 Irish seats, but they refused to take their seats in Westminster and, on 21 January 1919, declared that they had formed an assembly, which they called Dáil Éireann.

That month, in which Winston Churchill became Secretary of State for War, saw the first shooting by the IRA of members of the Royal Irish Constabulary, led by Collins and Brugha, a campaign which escalated through the year and in January 1920 led to the imposition of military control of the worst affected districts, of which Cork, Limerick and Tipperary were the principal ones.

In November 1919 Irish Command, headed by Lieutenant-General Sir Frederick Shaw at a strength of 37,259 men, had thirty-four infantry battalions, six of which were due to disband. The three military districts were reorganized into two divisions, the 5th at the Curragh, with four brigades (two in Dublin and one in Belfast), commanded by Major-General Sir Hugh Jeudwine, and the 6th at Cork, with three brigades (Major-General Sir Peter Strickland). A vicious circle was now created that would become familiar to British soldiers in their colonial struggles after the Second World War. The rebels (or terrorists) would murder a member of the security forces. The security forces would impose restrictions on freedom of movement and activity, unpopular with the local population, to which, in time, might be added reprisals, unofficial or even official, the harshness or brutality of which would attract much wider attention and condemnation, locally or further afield, than the original rebel or terrorist action, including more attacks on the security forces.

Collins deliberately set out to exploit this, as brutality was answered with brutality on both sides. By the end of 1919 his men had killed eighteen officers of the Royal Irish Constabulary and wounded twenty others. It became worse when in 1920, in order to offset resignations from the RIC, a recruiting campaign aimed at ex-servicemen raised 7,000 men, two-thirds from Great Britain and most of the rest from Ulster. As there were not enough green RIC uniforms for them, they wore army uniform below the waist and were nicknamed 'Black and Tans' after a famous pack of foxhounds. They were supplemented by another specially raised force, the Auxiliary RIC, which formed mobile columns. These forces bore the brunt of active operations against the IRA and gained an unsavoury reputation in doing so.

The army's principal task was to impose restrictions of various kinds on the population, especially control of movement, and to carry out raids and searches for wanted men and arms, few of which achieved much success, as intelligence was almost totally lacking. It depended on information from police scattered about the country in small posts. Their vulnerability led to concentration, and sources of intelligence dried up. By the end of 1920, 182 police and 50 soldiers had been killed and 387 wounded: the strength of the RIC, including Black and Tans and Auxiliaries, stood at 10,000; there were 50,000 troops in Ireland, and courts martial had taken over much of the work of the normal courts, although martial law had not been declared and internment, although legally authorized, had not been introduced.

That year saw the appointment of a new Chief Secretary, Sir Harmar Greenwood, a new Commander-in-Chief, General Sir Nevil Macready, a new Commandant of the RIC, Major-General H. H. Tudor, and a new commander of the Auxiliaries, all dedicated to the pursuit of a tough line. It was reciprocated by the IRA, which began to form its own 'flying columns', of thirty-five men each, on full-time active service for limited periods. Out of a total strength of 112,000, these were allotted 3,000. At the same time steps were taken to weed out the less desirable elements of the Black and Tans and Auxiliaries. Cooperation between the army, the police and the Secretariat at Dublin Castle was abysmal. There was constant friction over the question of responsibility for police action in areas which were under 'military control' and between civil and military courts. It was no better in the intelligence field, although it was headed by an army officer, Colonel Winter. He did little to organize methodical collection and assessment of information, preferring to rely on secret agents.

The situation deteriorated towards the end of the year, after Lloyd George was so ill advised as to claim that he had 'murder by the throat'. Macready had started by trying to reduce repressive measures and increase reliance on mobility; but motorized patrols were too obvious and too vulnerable to roadblocks and ambushes to be effective. There was a serious lack of expertise in fieldcraft and marksmanship, skills which had not featured much in the Great War. On 21 November 1920, known as Bloody Sunday, Collins had twelve British officers, all but one of whom were involved in intelligence directed against the IRA, shot in their hotel or other bedrooms in Dublin. Among them was Hugh Montgomery, first cousin of Bernard, the future field marshal, who was posted as brigade-major to the 17th Brigade at Cork in January 1921. On the same day the RIC opened fire on a crowd at a Gaelic football match, killing twelve civilians, and two IRA prisoners were shot out of hand in the guardroom of Dublin Castle in retaliation for the shooting of two Auxiliaries that day. A week later seventeen Auxiliaries were shot in an ambush in West Cork.

These incidents led to the proclamation on 11 December of martial law. French and Macready had been pressing for it for some time, but Greenwood opposed it. In August the Restoration of Order in Ireland Act, replacing reliance on the wartime Defence of the Realm Act, brought most offences and coroners' inquests within the jurisdiction of military courts. French and Macready assumed that martial law would apply to the whole island and envisaged that the army would exercise authority over almost everything everywhere, certainly over the police and the law. But it was only applied to four counties in the south-west (later to another four), and the police never came fully under army command, with the result that there was constant confusion about the relationship between courts martial and the civil law, the appeal court overturning court-martial convictions for murder.

Fusilier J. P. Swindlehurst of the Lancashire Fusiliers returned from service with their 2nd Battalion in India in December 1920 and found himself posted to the 1st Battalion in Dublin for the last few months of his service. His diary describes the scene:

January 8th Dublin

We arrived at Arrans Quay on the Liffy at 9 this morning. All Dublin seemed to be out in fete to see us arrive. I bet they got a shock, we looked and felt terrible, cold, hungry and fed up to the teeth.

Stewed bully [beef] and dried bread didn't improve our spirits, but the tea has been better. The C.O. of the 1st Bn of the Lancashire Fusiliers gave us a welcome, told us what we had come for, and said we would all feel better when we had had good sleep and a general clean up, he never said a truer word. We have come over here to finish our time, doing guards, curfew patrols, street patrols, and heaven knows what else. Ship Street Barracks, Great Dame Street is the new address, and its raining, what a life!

The men stationed here have regaled our ears with some lurid things that take place daily. The Black and Tans seem to do a lot of bloodthirsty deeds, but the Sinn Feiners dont seem far behind. I thought of chucking this, it might not be possible to get time to write my experiences, but I'll see later. On the backs down is the best place just now, Gilby at the moment has started to drive the pigs home so I'm going to do the same.

January 9th

Gilby and I have just arrived back from the city. After we had cleaned up etc, passed the doctor, had a lecture at the same time, that the 'Colleens' are likely to put in our way, and a hundred and one little formalities to go through, not forgetting the tin hat, to stop the empty bottles of 'Guinness', we were given a pass out until 9.30. The time is now 8.45, we thought it better to get back, after what happened to us. We were along Sackville Street admiring some 'civvy boots', when someone came up behind us, and told us to 'stick your hands up' at the same time we both felt two hard things sticking into our backs. The voice spoke Irish alright, but we never saw a face, we were told to look to the front and answer politely, and no harm would come. It seemed to be a long while before he finished questioning us, of all the questions – were we married – where had we come from – how long were we going to be here – and I don't know what else. To say we were alarmed is putting it mildly, there seemed to be a general hold up around us, all seemed to become very quiet. Our pockets were tapped from behind and after explaining what the contents were, the voice said 'Away wid yer Tommy down the road a bit and you don't look back at all, now go.' We didn't stop it would have been foolish to look back, so we made our way back to barracks. We have since heard that a sergeant out of the 1st Batt has been brought in shot in the stomach, he showed fight, silly chap, it's no use when the odds are against you. I felt the situation keenly at the time, but what's the use. We must have given the Sinn Fein element something to think about, it appears, quite a lot of us have been held up in different parts of the city. Dublin seems to be on our first acquaintance a rotten place to be in, people hurry along the streets, armoured cars dash up and down, bristling with machine guns. We have two extremely fast cars, with Rolls Royce engines, we had a talk to the drivers this morning, and were told they are kept in readiness to catch the elusive Michael Collins when news of his whereabouts comes to hand. He must be famous £500 is being offered dead or alive for his capture, but all the Black and Tans (who by the way seem to be all the out of work demobbed officers and men who can't settle down) and C.I.D. men from Scotland Yard can't get hold of him. The men who stile themselves as Black and Tans walk about like miniature arsenals, a brace of revolvers on each hip, bandoliers of ammunition slung around and a short musket to finish the ensemble. They dash about in cars with wirenetting covers at all hours of the day and night, bent on some raid, reprisal, or the capture of some Sinn Feiners. The wirenetting on the cars is to prevent bombs being thrown in amongst the occupants, an occurrence which seems to have been frequently done quite recently. The C.O. has said a few words about being on active service, and being liable to be called out at any moment – what a coincidence, a sergeant has just been round and collared twenty men to hold up the centre of Dublin, along with a lot more, six lorries, with twenty men in each are just about to leave, Gilby has clicked. I have been detailed to mount guard at the City Hall for 48 hours at 12 noon tomorrow, so I must finish for tonight, things are happening sooner than we expected.

January 12th

The time is six in the evening, we have just had tea, the first guard is over, I feel a bit tired, it will be nice to undress, and sleep right through till morning. How time drags, we do two hours on and four off, it feels the other way about, you hardly seem to have closed your eyes when it's time to go on again. It's a fine big building we have been in, but badly knocked about, bullet marks all over the place, rooms ransacked, mirrors and furniture smashed to bits. The central hall had a statue of Parnell taking up a prominent place in the centre, some of the attackers or defenders, I don't know which, appear to have bled rather profusely around it, the marble base and floor was badly bloodstained. The sergeant in charge told us seven men were shot down near Parnell's statue, so things have been bad about ten days ago. The first night passed quietly, just a few distant shots to be heard, all the city goes still at curfew which is ten o'clock. Once we heard hurrying footsteps dodging the curfew lorries, but little else happened. Not so last night, opposite our place is the newspaper office of the 'Dublin Times.' At about two o'clock when the presses were going full speed ahead with the morning news, two open cars drew up, and out jumped a dozen Sinn Feiners, who began to shoot the place up. In about two minutes all the windows had gone, we overlooked them and could see the workmen hiding behind the machines, out of the way of the flying bullets, The place is only five minutes from barracks, and the noise of their firing brought a party of Black and Tans on the scene, the result of the fight was two killed and three wounded one Sinn Feiner deceased, and two wounded, the rest were from the Black & Tans. We had them laid out in our place while the ambulances came and cleared them to mortuary and hospital respectively. The wounded Sinn Feiners came in for a lot of questioning from the C.I.D. They were only young men, but typically Irish. The 'Virgin Mary' stood witness ten thousand times to the truthfulness of the answers, no amount of threats to shoot them brought any further news to what the C.I.D. men wanted, so they carted them off. I have since thought if we hadn't been there, that the Black and Tans would have done them in, they seemed very bitter, especially since their confederates lay stiffening on the floor. It does seem awful that there are men who will stoop to such dastardly actions as taking their own countrymen out of their beds at dead of night, and shoot them down out of hand, just because they have a different view to theirs on how the country should be governed. The rest of the day until we were relieved passed peaceably enough, hundreds of sightseers came to look at the shattered windows. But the police took charge and kept the crowds moving, and life goes on as if nothing has happened, although one can sense the undercurrent of alarm and anxiety in most of the faces of the passers by. The constant shootings, hold ups and raids are leaving their marks, one can tell by the earnest whispered conversations, the darting furtive glances, and the ever on the alert look, that many don't know what will happen next. We were on the main street when a lorry backfired, and instinctively people dodged into doorways, some stood still, but it just shows, that the greater part of the population are living in a reign of terror. If their sympathies are with the Sinn Feiners the moment may come when the Black & Tans appear and take them off for a grilling or worse. On the other hand their own countrymen may come and extract vengeance for lack of sympathy to their cause. Even if they are strictly neutral and are content to let things alone, they may be shot down at any moment by a stray bullet from rival factions when ever they meet. Taken in the whole Dublin is the last place on earth I would like to live, if I had a choice, but then I aren't Irish, that accounts for a lot.

*

In the first nine months of 1920 the security force casualties were 125 killed and 235 wounded: for the next nine and a half months, to 11 July 1921, they were 400 and 700 respectively. IRA casualties could not be calculated, but in 1920, 41 civilians had been killed and 43 wounded when failing to halt when challenged by soldiers. In 1921, between 1 January and 11 July, 707 civilians were killed from all causes and 756 wounded. Over a hundred of these were almost certainly shot by the IRA as suspected informers. 1921 therefore saw a marked deterioration in the situation as violence escalated on both sides and areas in the south passed virtually out of control of the Government and into that of Sinn Fein, which set up rival institutions and the services they provided, including courts, in spite of the introduction of internment and the declaration of martial law in the south-west.

Major-General George Wood recalled his service as a subaltern with 1st Dorsets in Londonderry in this period:

> Eventually I could claim to know every alley cat and ash can in the Bogside. Our procedure of challenge was strictly laid down: a quiet 'Halt' was almost always enough, but any indication of flight brought a warning shot from the officer's pistol. Then if desperation or panic made a man run for it, he was in no great danger; it was accepted that no officer ever hit anything with his personal weapon, the monstrous .45 calibre of that period, until one very young subaltern proudly brought in a wounded fugitive. He claimed a range of two lamp-posts, and thereafter visited his victim in hospital daily bearing the rich gifts appropriate. Captives spent the night in the dismal basement of the Old Court House, to be brought before a magistrate next morning. The standard award for a simple breach of the curfew order was forty-two days.
>
> Patrol duty also included house visits and searches, either on our own observation or advice from the military intelligence people or the police. We were more quiet and polite than the Gestapo, but equally effective and the hurried exit from backdoor or bedroom window ended in a brawny pair of Dorset arms – 'No, my dear, you'll bide along of me.' Wanted men, against whom adequate evidence could be brought, appeared before special military tribunals observing the full process of the law. Finally it must be said that we imposed the curfew impartially. The order covered the whole city and occasionally we left our usual haunts to enforce discipline on the loyalists. A concerted weekend drive would produce a good haul of bright boys, loudly proclaiming their 'true-blue' sentiments as they went down to spend the night in our horrid basement. Naturally nothing could give greater pleasure to the Bogside.
>
> Two personal episodes of patrol duty remain vivid. For the first I was woken (we slept by day) by a message that a woman was demanding to speak to me and would not be denied. She was of a decent type and in great distress, telling me that her husband,

returned from a cattle-droving trip with pockets full of money, was now permanently mad-drunk and violent. She was in fear for her young daughter and herself. Remembering that the police were no longer on their beats, I reluctantly promised to look in at her cottage in the Bogside that night. The street door opened straight into the living room and I found a girl crouched on the floor with a man standing over her brandishing a boot in each hand. He was much smaller than me and after a short scuffle I slung him out into the street, where my sergeant promptly arrested him for breach of the curfew. He was still without his boots in court next morning, to go down for a salutary six weeks cure. I can only excuse my own conduct by pleading that I had never heard of sociology, but to make a story-book ending, the battered daughter married one of our drummers and apparently lived happy ever after. My second memory is of slipping into the Bogside by sinister Fahan Street, and hearing my name called softly through the crack of a door. 'Sir, sir, our old gentleman has passed away and we're waking him this night. He knew you right well and he'd have liked fine for your honour to take a glass with us to his memory.' It was not only the dram of good Bushmills that warmed me on that cold night.

It was about this time that the senseless violence of the Black and Tans in the South and especially in the city of Cork shocked us all, Military, Orangemen and Sinn Fein alike. Fortunately Derry had a man to trust, 'Our colonel won't have those rascals here.' He had made no such pronouncement, but an irregular gendarmerie, whether Black and Tans or the Ulster 'B' Specials, would have been as welcome in his bailiwick as poachers on his family estate on the Isle of Wight. Then I had my own experience to report. I went down to Dublin with our boxing team for the Command championship meeting, and after one evening session was walking back to my hotel, in plain clothes as ordered. The quiet street was suddenly alive with vehicles and running men and I found myself roughly seized by both arms and dragged towards a truck. By great good luck I recognised one of my captors as a young corporal in the Coldstream in my company of an Officer Cadet Battalion in 1918. By the time I had finished addressing him by name he was standing to 'Attention' as a guardsman once more.

On 23 December 1920 the Government of Ireland Act, which established separate parliaments for the six counties of the North and the twenty-six of the South, became law, with the intention that elections for them would be held between January 1921 and March 1922. The army was asked to say when, between these dates, the security situation would make it safe to hold them. Macready assured the Cabinet that application of martial law to all twenty-six counties would do the trick, the CIGS, Sir Henry Wilson, prophesying that after six months of it 80 to 90 per cent of the people would side with the Government. General Strickland was more optimistic, thinking four months would suffice, a forecast welcome to the Cabinet which decided that elections would be held in May 1921.

By June 1921 the army's strength had been increased to fifty-one infantry battalions. 1st Division, in Ulster, had ten in two brigades; 5th Division, in the centre, nine in three brigades; 6th Division, in the south-west, twenty in four brigades; and Dublin District twelve in two brigades. Tactics were now extended to the execution of sweeps through the countryside, combined with cordon and search in towns. These began to exert greater pressure on the IRA, particularly after some effective searches in Dublin resulted in a significant haul of arms and disruption to Collins's command organization.

The elections on 25 May in the North returned forty Unionists and twelve Nationalists. In the 128 constituencies of the South, Trinity College returned four Unionists and all the rest went to Sinn Fein. There was an immediate upsurge in IRA activity. Incidents rose from an average of 300 a week to 500, and security force casualties from 55 a week to 67. It was envisaged that if the Southern Parliament refused to meet, the twenty-six counties would have to be ruled as a Crown Colony under unrestricted martial law. Macready talked of a hundred shootings a week and of taking the offensive with three cavalry brigades. Plans were being considered for raising British army strength to 250,000 and even for instituting a blockade, but it was clear that, apart from the problem of finding the numbers, the British public was not prepared to devote resources of that nature to such an unpopular task, the final result of which could not be regarded with confidence. Nevertheless seventeen extra infantry battalions and two regiments of mounted infantry, formed from the Royal Artillery, were sent over in early June.

King George V opened the Northern Parliament on 22 June and expressed the hope that the South would follow suit and accept 'dominion status'. His speech received a wide welcome and Lloyd George felt able to offer negotiations without conditions to Sinn Fein. Tentative negotiations had been going on with Arthur Griffith and de Valera (who had returned from eighteen months in the USA at the end of 1920) in Mountjoy Jail in Dublin, the Australian Roman Catholic Archbishop of Perth acting as an intermediary. Lloyd George's offer was hesitantly accepted by de Valera and agreement was reached with the IRA on 9 July 1921 to a truce which became effective after two days of shooting in Cork, where four unarmed British soldiers were kidnapped, three of whom were killed, and a justice of the peace who sympathized with the Nationalists was shot by the Black and Tans. In Belfast sixteen Catholics were killed and a thousand driven from their homes. In all 264 people, of whom 171 were Catholic, had been killed in the six counties in the year, and many had fled either to the South or to Glasgow.

After long and difficult negotiations with the Sinn Fein leaders, the Anglo-Irish Treaty was signed on 6 December. The principal issues were continued allegiance to the Crown and the exclusion of the six counties. Argument and emotion about the former tended to take priority over the latter, which was confused by Lloyd George's proposal of a Boundary Commission to recommend adjustments to the border, so that principally Catholic areas could join the South and Protestant ones the North. As before, he gave different assurances to the two sides. He assuaged the fears of the Unionists by assuring them that adjustments would be minor, and those of the Nationalists by telling them that they would so reduce the areas of the six counties that the North would not be able to survive as a viable economic unit separate from the South. The whole process split the IRA down the middle and led to a vicious civil war between the pro- and anti-Treaty factions which lasted until May 1923. By that time the Free State Government of the South, of which Arthur Griffith was the Prime Minister and Michael Collins the Commander-in-Chief of the Army, had executed by shooting seventy-seven of their former colleagues, three times as many as the British had executed over two and a half years, and they had imprisoned 13,600 of their supporters. Griffith died in August 1922, Collins being killed in an ambush on the 22nd, and his principal opponent, Liam Lynch, in a firefight with Free State troops on 10 April 1923. Another casualty was Field Marshal Sir Henry Wilson, shot by the IRA on the steps of his London home on 22 June 1922. At the end of his four-year term as CIGS in February of that year, he had been returned unopposed as MP for North Down. The IRA correctly regarded him as one of its most implacable enemies.

In this unhappy atmosphere the British army's centuries-old involvement in the twenty-six counties came to an end, although it continued to recruit there. Many assumed, wrongly as time was to show, that the army would never be involved in operations in Ireland again. One of the sad results was the disbandment of regiments with battle honours of great distinction: the Royal Irish Regiment, the 18th Foot, the Connaught Rangers, the 88th and 94th Foot of Peninsular War fame, and the Leinster Regiment, the Royal Munster Fusiliers and the Royal Dublin Fusiliers, the last three having originated in European regiments of the East India Company's army.

India

Soon after the war ended, the Emir of Afghanistan, Habibullah, became the target of those who thought that he had followed too submissive a policy towards the British. On 19 February 1919 he was murdered by a colonel in his army, but it was generally suspected that his third son, Amanullah, had instigated it. A power struggle ensued between Amanullah and the second son, which Amanullah won, seizing power on 3 May. He tried to persuade the frontier tribes to rise against the British, at the same time encouraging anti-British nationalist feeling in the Punjab, which he would exploit by crossing the frontier. March saw rioting break out in the principal towns of the Punjab, including Amritsar, where, on 13 April, Gurkha troops under Brigadier-General Dyer opened fire on a crowd, in ten minutes killing 379 men and boys and wounding a further 1,500. Rioting thereafter ceased throughout the Punjab, but the slaughter horrified both the Indian public and much of the British. On 4 May Afghan troops crossed the frontier at Bagh near the Khyber Pass, and the Indian Government declared war on Afghanistan. By 20 May the penetration at Bagh had been defeated by troops of the 1st Division, based at Landi Kotal. By then a further threat had developed through the Kurram valley, which in its turn was defeated by troops from the 16th Division, commanded by Dyer, who returned from his victory to face investigation into the events at Amritsar and dismissal. He died a few years later.

Although the Afghan invasion was quickly and effectively dealt with, it was the precursor of unrest among the frontier tribes which was to continue up to the outbreak of the Second World War. Curzon's policy was partially reversed and a Modified Forward Policy pursued with the establishment of garrisons at Razmak and Wana in Waziristan to prevent Afghan raids across the border and keep the Wazirs and Mahsuds in order. One of the principal troublemakers was Abdul Ghaffar Khan, who combined all the Afghan love of fighting with a passion for self-determination whether from British-ruled India or from a Hindu-controlled one. His Red Shirt 'Servants of God' were a constant source of trouble between 1929 and 1931, leading to riots in and around Peshawar, and fighting in the area between it and the frontier, in which armoured cars of the Royal Tank Corps and aircraft of the Royal Air Force supported the infantry.

In 1935 the Mohmands, north of the Khyber Pass, were the trouble-makers, and an expedition was mounted in July to advance into their territory and suppress them, the two brigades involved being commanded by rival future field marshals, Auchinleck and Alexander, the former, as the senior, in overall command in the absence of their general on leave. It was a slow, methodical campaign, laboriously driving a road into the mountains, and was brought to a successful conclusion at the end of October, one of the Indian Army battalions having suffered heavy casualties in an ambush. Two years later the Fakir of Ipi stirred up trouble in Waziristan, over 30,000 troops being sent into the field to deal with him and the trouble he caused. It was suppressed but not eliminated before events elsewhere pushed frontier troubles into the background. The Fakir himself was never caught and died in Pakistan in 1960.

An example of a typical operation was that at Shahur Tangi, a narrow and precipitous gorge on the Wana road in Waziristan. The road was cut into the cliff on the north bank of the gorge and so narrow that vehicles could hardly pass. On one side the rock rises sheer and unclimbable and on the other falls steeply to the *nullah* bed. On 8 April 1937 a convoy of forty-seven lorries was escorted by a section of four armoured cars of the 8th Light Tank Company, Royal Tank Corps, with about sixty men of the 4/16th Punjabs and drivers of the Royal Indian

Army Service Corps. The column was about two miles long and the four armoured cars of the section were spread along the column. All was quiet until 7.35 a.m., when the whole column was within the gorge and the escorting aircraft had seen nothing. At that hour the leading vehicles came under a devastating fire at point-blank range, which killed or wounded not only the vehicle drivers but also many of the escorting infantry. The convoy halted and the survivors were forced to take cover in the roadside ditch, where they were pinned down by accurate rifle fire. The leading armoured car, commanded by Lieutenant Gerald Hopkinson, and the three lorries behind him, cleared the defile, after which he returned to the head of the column and opened fire on enemy on both sides of the road, which the other armoured cars were also engaging. Another section, stationed at Sarwekai Fort further up the road, commanded by Lieutenant F. I. C. Wetherell, arrived at the head of the column at 9.15 a.m. just in time to prevent the tribesmen blocking the exit from the gorge with boulders. Hopkinson's report on the action describes what happened next:

> Lieutenant Wetherell and No. 3 Section arrived and I put him in the picture and we decided what was to be done. It was decided that the lorries must somehow be moved. However at this moment the enemy tried to move down the East spur to the road and we engaged them with heavy fire from our cars. I should imagine their strength was approximately 5,* some of which were armed with knives. Targets were very fleeting and at a range of approximately 400 yards, although the enemy were only 50 yards from the second block of lorries.
>
> Lieutenant Wetherell and I decided to try and move the lorries. I placed my car on the North side of the lorry giving it protection by armoured car. I then dismounted and joined the infantry in the ditch and ordered them to give covering fire and ordered the drivers to start up their lorries. In the meantime Lieut. Wetherell had turned his car round and backed on to the front of the Bagai lorry, where he dismounted and jumped into the lorry starting it up. Fire from the enemy was fairly heavy at this period. The driver of the Bagai was lying under the rear wheels and to remove him Private Grundy of

---

* 50? The section commander, Captain Crouch, estimated the total enemy strength to be about a hundred.

my car and a Naik* of 4/16th Punjab Regiment removed him and Lieut. Wetherell managed to drive the lorry away. In the meantime the second lorry a 3-ton R.I.A.S.C.† refused to start and unfortunately the driver was wounded in the attempt. It was afterwards discovered that the lorry had been shot through the induction manifold.

1045 hrs.

I again mounted my car and decided that we must tow the lorry away. Reversing out of the way, I instructed Lance-Corporal Gordon in armoured car BADAJOZ to turn round, reverse onto the front of the lorry, and fix the tow rope. In the meantime we silenced heavy enemy fire. The tow rope was fixed on by the Naik of 4/16th who then removed the driver from under the lorry. I should like to praise the action of this Naik. I do not know his name but could recognise him easily. Throughout the day he displayed great daring and initiative and in my opinion put up a very good show. The tow rope having been fixed a driver got into the seat and the lorry was successfully towed away.

While this had been going on I had ordered the lorries to be started up and they managed to move a short distance sufficient to move into the left of the road. Unfortunately the then leading lorry was shot through the petrol tank and then stopped what might have resulted in an early clearance of the first block of lorries. The lorry after about 5 minutes burst into flames and unfortunately the driver and others were badly burnt. A horse and syce‡ were in the back of the lorry, the syce having failed to dismount remained with the horse up to now. However he now jumped out and ran down the South side of the road, unfortunately unseen by our infantry; the horse then burst its way out and ran down the road East obviously badly burnt. At this stage the tribesmen again became very active and we engaged them with heavy fire. The infantry escort in the meantime had to move further down the road and had fixed bayonets as it appeared that the enemy might now try to rush the Convoy.

11.45 hrs.

An unfortunate incident now occurred. The lorry fire having subsided

* Corporal in the Indian Army.
† Royal Indian Army Service Corps.
‡ Groom.

a little, the infantry returned to their original position and started to remove some of the burnt superstructure which had fallen across the road. Suddenly the syce jumped up from the South side of the road towards the infantry who thinking they were being rushed shot and bayonetted him. This was very regrettable, but no blame can be attached to them. I moved down the road past the lorries to the next block to see if I could give any support to the Infantry from the East flank, as they had then decided to try and move up the hill, but we discovered that this was not feasible as the enemy were stuck directly above this and there would have been no hope of success.

By nightfall some twenty lorries had been moved away to the west with the survivors and dead from them. All through the night attempts to clear the rest of the column continued under accurate sniping fire. The leading lorry was found to have a damaged engine and to be too heavy to tow, so that eventually, after beating off a knife attack by tribesmen, efforts were confined to extricating the remaining survivors and frustrating all attempts to loot the convoy. Soon after dawn reinforcements arrived to secure the high ground and drive the enemy out of range.

The action had lasted twenty-two hours. The casualties were seven British officers, two British other ranks and twenty-seven Indians killed; five British officers, one British other rank, two Viceroy's Commissioned Officers and forty-two Indian soldiers wounded.

Mechanization

The greatest challenge facing the army in the twenty years between the wars was replacement of the horse by the internal combustion engine and all the changes, technical and organizational, which went with that. A central issue was the part to be played by the tank. Was it to remain, and if so for what purpose and in what form? Was it to remain a supporting arm to infantry, like artillery, or to take the place of cavalry in its traditional roles, or to introduce an entirely new form of land warfare? Each of these functions had its advocates.

In many quarters, especially among the tank enthusiasts, the army's inferiority in both the quantity and quality of its tanks in the early years of the Second World War, and the failures on the battlefield which they attributed to that, is believed to have stemmed from the conservatism, prejudice and obstruction of the army hierarchy, based on its traditional arms, against the tank pioneers. That is a distortion of the truth. There was indeed resistance to change, but the factors that led to the army's unpreparedness for modern war in 1939 were many and various, most of them originating in the policy laid down in the Ten Year Rule and the financial stringency which accompanied it. The future of horsed cavalry was clearly in doubt, but there was strong resistance to its abolition. In 1922 the three Household Cavalry regiments were reduced to two, and the twenty-eight cavalry regiments by amalgamations to nineteen, two of them, the 11th Hussars and 12th Lancers, being converted to armoured cars in 1928. In 1923 the Tank Corps was given Royal status, becoming a permanent part of the army, with four battalions, one for each regular division. In addition it was to maintain twelve (later reduced to ten) armoured car companies overseas. Fuller, ensconced in the Staff Duties directorate of the War Office, had fought hard for its retention against those who wished to abolish it altogether, to absorb it into the infantry or the Royal Engineers, or to keep it, as it had been, a corps into which officers and men were seconded from their parent regiment or corps.

In 1918 Fuller had produced a highly ambitious and unrealistic *Plan 1919* for a force of 5,000 tanks, which would operate almost on its own. It was partly based on a paper written in November 1916 by Major Martel, a Royal Engineer at Tank Corps Headquarters, entitled 'A Tank Army', which envisaged tank warfare very much in naval terms, with 'destroyer', 'battle' and 'torpedo' tanks. Fuller added to this his concept that the target should be the enemy's command system. Once that had been put out of action, the enemy army would be thrown into confusion and its resistance would collapse. He won the Gold Medal of the Royal United Services Institute in 1920 for an essay on these lines and developed his ideas further in his book *The Reformation of War* in 1923. By then he had extended the target from the enemy's military command system to its national Government, predicting that 'A fleet of 500 aeroplanes, each carrying 500 ten-pound bombs of, let us suppose, mustard gas' would cause such panic that the war might 'be won in 48 hours and the losses of the winning side be actually nil'. As a supplement to this, he envisaged 'A force of submarines which would carry and discharge six tanks each. Large numbers would not be needed. The tanks, secretly conveyed across the sea, would land to coordinate their appearance with that of the gas-delivering aircraft, which also might be able to carry small tanks. On landing, whether from submarine or aircraft, the tanks would dispense incapacitating gases which would reduce the population to helpless tears or laughter.'

That could well have been the reaction, and in some cases was, of other military men, particularly when, as an instructor at the Staff College, he proceeded to elaborate abstruse strategic theories, based on a variety of principles expressed in trinities. In spite of this, in 1926 (as a colonel) he was appointed Military Assistant to the CIGS, General Sir George Milne, with prime responsibility for setting up an Experimental Mechanized Force. This was brought together in 1927, consisting of two battalions of the Royal Tank Corps, one of medium tanks, the other a mixture of tanks, armoured cars and machine-gun carriers, an infantry machine-gun battalion, carried partly in half-tracks and partly in trucks, a field artillery regiment (18-pounders) and a light battery (3.7″ howitzers), all mechanized in one form or another, and an engineer field company, commanded by Major Martel. Fuller was appointed to command, but refused, as it was combined with command of an ordinary infantry brigade and the garrison of Tidworth. Although he was later promoted major-general, it was effectively the end of his career and of his influence on the future of mechanization of the army. The trouble with the Experimental Force was that, apart from the variety of vehicles, it was not at all clear what its military function was intended to be, and it was disbanded in 1928.

Fuller's influence was superseded by that of Basil Liddell Hart. Having cut short his study of history at Cambridge to be commissioned into the King's Own Yorkshire Light Infantry in 1914, he was gassed at the Battle of the Somme, and, after recuperation, put in charge of training a Volunteer home defence battalion. This led to the production of an infantry training manual, which brought him to the attention of General Ivor Maxse, Inspector-General of Training with the BEF. After the war, having read Fuller's prize essay, Liddell Hart contacted him and largely adopted his general ideas, which chimed in with two strategic studies he was engaged in, Genghis Khan's Mongol cavalry hordes and Sherman's campaign in Georgia in the American Civil War. They led him to his theory of indirect approach, complementing Fuller's emphasis that the target was the enemy's nerve system rather than his forces. In his book *The British Way in Warfare*, published in 1932, he wrote:

> An examination of military history ... points to the fact that in all decisive campaigns the dislocation of the enemy's psychological and physical balance has been the prelude to a successful attempt at his overthrow. This dislocation has been produced by a strategic indirect approach, intentional or fortuitous ... we can ... crystallize ... two simple maxims, one negative, the other positive. The first is that in face of the overwhelming evidence of history no general is justified in launching his troops to a direct attack upon an enemy firmly in position. The second, that instead of seeking to upset the enemy's equilibrium by one's attack, it must be upset before a real attack is, or can be successfully launched.

In fact it is difficult to find evidence to support this. In most campaigns the dislocation of the enemy's balance has resulted from, rather than preceded, the defeat of his forces in battle, although a successful outflanking movement or envelopment has generally upset the enemy's equilibrium.

The collapse of the Experimental Force revealed the divergences of the aims of mechanization, the most fundamental one being whether to concentrate what effort and resources could be made available on mechanizing the traditional arms to carry out, with the help of wheeled or tracked vehicles, the functions they had previously performed with horses or on foot, or on the creation of an entirely new force, based primarily on a more mobile and longer range tank, in close cooperation with aircraft, to perform the sort of role which Fuller, Martel, and now also Liddell Hart, were proposing. The influential figures in the Royal Tank Corps, whose views differed to a certain degree, were Brigadier George Lindsay, formerly of the Rifle Brigade and the Machine Gun Corps, Lieutenant-Colonels Charles Broad and Frederick (Tim) Pile, both ex-Royal Artillery, and Percy (Patrick) Hobart from the Royal Engineers. None of them had actually served with tanks during the war. Lindsay was the most realistic of these, the one who realized that, while tanks should not be relegated to siege weapons in support of infantry, they must work together with other arms as part of a general plan both on the strategic and the tactical level. Hobart was the most extreme. He envisaged at least an all-tracked, if not an all-armoured army, and wanted to avoid association with other arms who, he suspected, not without reason, would impose a degree of conservatism which would obstruct the development of a force of the type and for the purpose envisaged by Fuller and Liddell Hart.

However all four were united in their desire to see the production in sufficient quantity of a tank with improved armament, better protection and greater mobility (in terms of speed, cross-country capability and range), than the Vickers Medium then in service. At the time of its first production in 1923, it was a significant improvement on its predecessors, particularly in mobility, but it was underpowered, gave poor protection and presented a large target. Martel had other ideas. He favoured a very small two-man tank, little more than a mobile armoured machine-gun, to accompany the infantry. It would in no way be suitable for the sort of independent mobile operations which he, originally, and the others envisaged.

The basic problem lay in resources. The finance provided for the army was reduced every year from 1923 to 1932, as its strength fell from 231,000 to 207,000, only about £2m being allotted to new equipment. Money for mechanization generally, let alone that for the provision of new tanks, had to compete with the demands of imperial garrisons, especially that of India and of the army at home needed to maintain it. One of the major expenses of mechanization was the unglamorous one of replacing the horse as a method of transport and traction. Capability for tank design and production existed only in the Royal Ordnance factories, centred on Woolwich Arsenal, and Vickers, the latter employing a gifted designer in Sir John Carden. Hopes were focused on a development of the Vickers Medium, the 16-tonner, but the financial crisis of 1931 put paid to that. Unfortunately a coalition of interests led to the development of a light tank, armed only with a machine-gun, at the expense of concentration on that of an effective medium tank for general purposes. The light tank was cheap to produce and it could provide the basis for mechanization of the cavalry in its traditional role, both on the battlefield and for imperial policing, replacing or in addition to armoured cars. As developed in that role, initially as a two-man tank and later with a crew of three, it was too lightly armoured to meet

Martel's requirement, for which a heavily armoured, very slow machine was developed.

In spite of these problems and the restrictive conditions of the Ten Year Rule, which offered no prospect of Continental warfare, the disciples of Fuller, encouraged by Liddell Hart in the columns first of the *Daily Telegraph* and later of *The Times*, were supported by Milne's successor, General Sir Archibald Montgomery-Massingberd, the tradition-oriented gunner who became CIGS in 1933. In that year he confirmed the 1st Tank Brigade as an official formation and Hobart as its commander. For the previous two years three of the Royal Tank Corps's battalions, the 2nd, 3rd and 5th, had been drawn together for training under Broad to practise the independent role on Salisbury Plain. The 4th, stationed at Catterick, was to concentrate on preserving the technique of infantry support, and, a year later, the 1st was resurrected from the depot and training schools at Bovington in Dorset as a reconnaissance unit for the brigade, equipped entirely with light tanks.

Contrary to the impression given by Liddell Hart in his memoirs, Montgomery-Massingberd gave Hobart full support. He went further. In 1934 he decided to form a Mobile Division. The development of this idea was to reveal deep divisions about the way forward for mechanized and armoured formations. Many orthodox soldiers thought of it as a mechanized cavalry division, carrying out the traditional tasks of reconnaissance, flank protection and pursuit. Lindsay, whose idea it was, would probably have commanded it if he had not fallen out of favour as a result of a disappointing performance in an exercise, partly the fault of Hobart. He had conceived it as a balanced force, the main element of which should be the Tank Brigade, capable of restoring mobility to the battlefield in all types of operations. Hobart viewed the addition of other arms to the Tank Brigade as unnecessary and likely to restrict its mobility and effectiveness. It was not in fact formed until 1937. Leslie Hore-Belisha, who became Secretary of State for War in Neville Chamberlain's Conservative administration in that year, advised by Liddell Hart, wanted Hobart to command it, but the CIGS, General Sir Cyril Deverell, was strongly opposed and wanted a cavalryman. A compromise was reached in the person of Major-General Alan Brooke, a highly respected horse-gunner. Hobart, promoted major-general, took his place as Director of Military Training. When Brooke left on promotion eight months later, he was succeeded by a cavalryman, Major-General Roger Evans.

In the intervening years, and after its formation, there was a great deal of discussion about the role of cavalry when mechanized. They rejected conversion into mounted infantry, in spite of that having been the original role of dragoons. Eventually, with the exception of the Household Cavalry, the Royal Scots Greys and the Royal Dragoons, they were converted to light tanks or armoured cars as light armoured brigades or infantry divisional cavalry regiments.* Eight Yeomanry regiments, out of the fifty-five existing at the time, had been converted to armoured car companies and associated with the Royal Tank Corps in the 1920s. Twenty others were converted into artillery. In 1939 fifteen were still horsed cavalry. With the four regular regiments still horsed, they formed the 1st Cavalry Division, which was sent to Palestine in May 1940 to relieve infantry on internal security duties. It was eventually mechanized in 1941 and formed the 10th Armoured Division. There was also argument about whether or not the Tank Brigade should be included in the Mobile Division. It eventually was, in addition to two light armoured cavalry brigades. At the same time the Royal Tank Corps was being expanded in order to provide more battalions for the direct support of infantry, several infantry battalions in the Territorial Army being converted also to battalions of the RTC in that role.

The relationship between the RTC and the cavalry came under scrutiny. Recruiting for the former was good, for the latter poor, as potential recruits assumed that it was still horsed. The cavalry had no central training organization and for conversion to its new role was wholly dependent on the RTC, both on its Central Schools and on individuals as instructors. A committee headed by a senior Guards officer, Lieutenant-General Sir Bertram Sergison-Brooke, examined the matter and recommended that the mechanized cavalry and the RTC should be incorporated into one Royal Armoured Corps, the Royal Tank Corps changing its name to Royal Tank Regiment, adopting cavalry nomenclature so that battalions confusingly became regiments and private soldiers troopers. The recommendation was adopted in April 1939: this forced marriage was never an easy one, the relationship becoming severely strained at times.

General Sir Cecil Blacker was a subaltern in the 5th Inniskilling

---

* These were the reconnaissance regiments of infantry divisions.

Dragoon Guards at this time and describes their attitude to mechan-ization:

The best of the rank and file, old-style cavalrymen, were readily adaptable to mechanisation. They had the sense to realise that the tactics of a mechanised regiment would be much the same as those of the cavalry, with horses replaced by machines about which they now had to learn. They were regular cavalrymen of many years service, for whom the regiment was their life. Their devotion and loyalty rendered all doubt superfluous; their regiment wanted them to make this change in their lives; it was the best cavalry regiment in the army and now they would make it the best mechanised regiment.

They had the authority and personality to instil the same feeling into the new arrivals, militia men – for the government had at last nerved itself to introduce National Service – and reservists. All over the British army the same example was doubtless being set by its non-commissioned officers. In my regiment I particularly recall Jack Clayton, Corporal Clayton in the first troop I commanded. Loyal, tough and brave, humorous and compassionate, he earned a Military Medal and became regimental sergeant major. Men like him won us the war.

As officers our relationship with the men was a good deal more formal and distant than it could ever be now because we lived very different lives. The men did not expect any other attitude from us, and we were shocked if an officer became too familiar – but they had very definite ways of indicating that their officer was not finding favour with them. They soon divined whether an officer was up to the job and was interested in looking after them and if he passed the test the prevailing atmosphere was a joy to experience – team spirit at its best, lightened by much leg-pulling and joking and often resulting in friendships that endured.

The word man-management was not in our dictionary. If care for our men was not an automatic impulse, the lesson was soon learnt from our superiors. There is no reason to feel particularly smug about this. The officer/man relationship of the 1930s simply reflected the prevailing social attitudes. But at least in our regiment, and doubtless elsewhere in the army, we tried to display these attitudes at their best.

Just over 15 months after we had paraded for the last time on horses we paraded again as a mechanised regiment, this time for formation training with the 4th Division at Shorncliffe. After two days at camp the news of the Hitler/Stalin pact broke and we returned to mobilise for war. Reservists – old dogs not all capable of learning new tricks but in surprisingly high good humour – poured into the barracks.

*

By 1939 the production of light tanks with which to equip the cavalry was proceeding satisfactorily, the three-man Vickers Carden-Lloyd Mark V having succeeded the two-man version. It was lively and reliable and proved valuable as a means of introducing horsemen to tracked vehicles, but on the battlefield it was useful only for reconnaissance, and even for that its short track-base limited its cross-country capability.

The position of medium tanks was highly unsatisfactory. A Vickers design, the A9, was regarded as inadequate in all its characteristics, an up-armoured version, A10, being produced for infantry support. Dissatisfaction with its design and limitations of finance restricted its production, which started in a limited fashion in 1937. By then Martel, as Director of Mechanization, had been impressed on a visit to Russia in 1936 by their BT* tank, using a suspension designed by an American, John Christie, from whom he obtained a prototype. Lord Nuffield agreed to produce a design based on it, which became the A13, first produced in November 1937. It was to become the principal 'cruiser' tank of the army in the first half of the Second World War, praised for its speed and low silhouette, but condemned for its inadequate armour and armament and unreliability. (The 'cruiser' tank was intended to be the principal fighting vehicle of armoured divisions, whereas the 'I' or 'Infantry' tank provided the equipment of army tank brigades for the support of infantry.)

Largely owing to pressure from General Hugh Elles, who was Master-General of the Ordnance from 1934 to 1937, a separate tank was produced for infantry support. The first, the Infantry Tank Mark I, was a development of Martel's tankette, but heavily armoured. With only a machine-gun, a crew of two and a top speed of 8 m.p.h., it was of limited value. It was succeeded by the Mark II (A12), a development

* Bystrochodyi (fast) Tank.

of an earlier attempt by Woolwich Arsenal to design a medium tank, and was later known as the Matilda. Heavily armoured, with a 2-pounder gun and a machine-gun, it proved highly successful in its particular role, but only two had been produced when war broke out in 1939.

The tank situation, as war clouds gathered, was therefore highly unsatisfactory. The great majority were light tanks, virtually useless on the battlefield. The few medium tanks available were unsatisfactory. This was partly due to lack of finance both to develop and produce them, but it was partly the fault of the army itself in having no clear idea of what their function was to be, and with the designers in not making provision in their design for further improvements to meet possible enemy developments. These failings can be traced to the Government's determination, backed by some expert advice, not to become involved again in a military commitment on the Continent and to the high priority given to defence against air attack on Britain, the scale and effects of which were greatly exaggerated. Although later the armament of these tanks came in for much criticism, the 2-pounder gun fitted to all the medium tanks and the Matilda, which in a towed version was also the anti-tank gun of the artillery and some infantry, was perfectly adequate for the conditions of 1939 to mid-1941. The German equivalent, the 37mm, was no better. But the concept of operations in which Hobart had trained the Tank Brigade, inherited from Fuller and encouraged by Liddell Hart, laid too much emphasis on speed and not enough on armament and armour and the cooperation of all arms on the battlefield.

Conditions of Service

The mechanization programme had become possible as a result of the rearmament embarked upon in the late 1930s in reaction to Hitler's increasingly aggressive attitude, although the major share of finance made available went to the navy and the air force, and a high proportion of the army's allotment to anti-aircraft defence. It was still by no means clear that the army's future battleground would be on the continent of Europe. Hore-Belisha, faithful to Chamberlain's views, was not in favour of that and was supported by Liddell Hart. Whatever is thought of Hore-Belisha, and he had many critics, he did a great deal in a short time to improve the lot of the soldier. He built new and much better barracks: he improved conditions of service, at last introducing professionalism into the army's cooking and feeding arrangements; he improved pay; introduced clothing more appropriate both to the daily and the fighting tasks of the soldier; and he generally created an impression that the dead hand of tradition was being swept away and the army brought into the twentieth century. Recruitment improved dramatically, but it was too much to expect that such a radical new look would not meet opposition. By the conservative, Hore-Belisha was regarded as a bounder, and he antagonized the top brass of the War Office, not so much by promoting younger and promising generals like Wavell and Gort to replace the Old Guard, but by introducing Liddell Hart into the War Office as his personal adviser.

Army pay had remained virtually static from the eighteenth century to 1914. In that year a captain received 12s 6d a day, a lieutenant 8s 6d and a private soldier still 1s. A married soldier over the age of thirty also received a marriage allowance of 1s a day. By 1919, largely owing to discontent in the navy, the soldier's rate of pay had been almost doubled, the basic rate for a private going up to 2s 9d a day. Comparison with wages paid in civil life was complicated by the fact that soldiers, living in barracks or married quarters, paid no rent and nothing for the principal items of their military uniform, although its upkeep cost them a certain amount. In 1925 the Anderson Committee assessed the value of the benefits the soldier received in kind at 23s a week on top of his pay of 19s 3d, and comparing the total with the average wage of an agricultural labourer of 27s 11d, an engineering labourer's of 40s 4d and a building labourer's of 53s 4d, concluded that the soldier was being paid too much, and the basic pay of privates joining after the report was accepted by the Government in 1925 was reduced to 2s a day. In 1937 Hore-Belisha raised the pay of the private soldier to 3s a day after three years' service, and that of a second lieutenant (which the author then was) from 9s 10d to 10s a day. At that time the weekly cost of feeding a soldier was 9s, and the average weekly earnings of equivalent civilians had risen: the agricultural labourer to 34s, the postman to 42s 6d, the general labourer to 60s, the bricklayer to 77s and the bus driver to between 82s and 90s.

The small sum that a soldier would actually receive in cash on joining was not the only factor discouraging men from enlisting in the army either as officers or in the ranks. The 1920s saw a general revulsion against the experiences of 1914–18. In many cases this took the form of anti-militarism, pacifism and a belief that war could be prevented by international organizations and disarmament. The army, driven in upon itself and not entirely unhappy in the cosy seclusion of its regimental life, appeared to be, as in many ways it was, antiquated, philistine and set in its old ways, more appropriate to the eighteenth than to the twentieth century. The cartoonist David Low's caricature of Colonel Blimp epitomized the popular view. The Great War had effected radical changes in society, from which the Royal Navy and the army seemed immune. Only the Royal Air Force, and, in the army, the Royal Tank Corps and the Royal Army Service Corps, and in the navy, the Fleet Air Arm and the submariner seemed to have moved with the times. An army that in 1933 still had a hundred and thirty-six infantry battalions and seventeen horsed cavalry regiments, but only four tank battalions and two regiments of armoured cars, certainly gave that impression. Even by 1938 little had changed. At that time there were forty-seven infantry battalions as a British garrison of 55,498 men in India, eighteen battalions as a garrison of 21,187 in the Middle East and Mediterranean, one as a garrison of 1,800 in the West Indies, and eight as one of 12,143 in the Far East: a total of 90,628 men overseas, balanced by 106,704, including sixty-four infantry battalions, in the United Kingdom.

The Middle East

The garrison in the Middle East had been increased partly as a result of the threat to Egypt from the Italians in Libya and from Abyssinia (Ethiopia) after the Italian invasion of the latter in 1935, and partly to deal with the growing trouble from the Arabs in Palestine, who opposed the increase in Jewish immigration resulting from the persecution of the Jews in Germany and Austria, as well as in other countries of Eastern Europe, including the Soviet Union. Between 1933 and 1936 the Jewish population of Palestine had increased from 230,000 to 400,000 – a third of the Arab population. Widespread rioting and attacks on Jewish settlements initiated a full-scale rebellion. In 1921 the RAF had assumed responsibility for military support to the police, as it had in Iraq and Aden. One squadron of aircraft and two of armoured cars were supposed to look after the external and internal security of Palestine and Transjordan; but bombing villages to keep the people in order could clearly not be applied to Palestine, and the army had to take over. By 1938 two divisions were deployed there, Major-General Richard O'Connor commanding the 7th and Montgomery assuming that of the 8th in December of that year.

Italy's invasion and occupation of Abyssinia, her involvement with Germany in the Spanish Civil War and her generally hostile attitude as she aligned herself with Germany in the 'Pact of Steel' raised fears about the safety of the Suez Canal and the defence of Egypt. These were shared by the Egyptian Government, headed by Nahas Pasha, with the result that a treaty was signed in 1936 under which British troops would over a period of four years be withdrawn into the area of the canal, retaining rights to train there and in Sinai, and in time of war to return to Cairo and Alexandria. Britain would help to train and equip the Egyptian forces, which would be responsible for static air defence, while Egypt undertook to improve infrastructure and communications and to co-operate in wartime. The British garrison was reinforced in 1938 and the cavalry brigade stationed there mechanized, augmented by the light tank battalion from the Tank Brigade in England. In October, following the Munich crisis, Major-General Hobart was sent out to expand this into a mobile division, which was later renamed 7th Armoured Division. With his dynamic energy he set about training it intensively and creating, out of almost nothing, the means to command it and provide it with logistic support in the unique conditions of the Western Desert, facing Libya. However, in January 1940, five months before Italy joined in the war, his unorthodox tactical ideas and his refusal to obey restrictions imposed on training and movement in order to preserve engines and tracks in case of war led to his dismissal and subsequent retirement, in March, to the ranks of the Home Guard, until his resurrection by Churchill in November of that year to raise another armoured division, the 11th.

Pre-War Strategy

It is impossible to understand why the British army was so much less
well prepared to fight the German army on the Continent in 1939 than
it had been in 1914 unless one realizes that the Government's policy, up
until almost the last moment, had been that it should not do so. After
Hitler had defied the verdict of Versailles by marching into the Rhineland
in 1936, while Britain and France did nothing, there was talk of providing
an Expeditionary Force of two infantry divisions, which would be sent
to Belgium as a reserve to bolster the resolution of its army and thereby
prevent the Germans from occupying Belgian airfields. But Belgium's
subsequent declaration of neutrality in that year put paid to the plan.
The Francophile Duff Cooper, then Secretary of State for War, pressed
his colleagues in Baldwin's Cabinet to agree to the provision of full war
equipment for five regular (four infantry and one mobile) and twelve
Territorial Army divisions; but this was hotly contested by Neville
Chamberlain, Chancellor of the Exchequer, who, supported by the
Cabinet, would not even consider a modified proposal to equip five
regular and four TA divisions, the remaining eight of the latter to be
equipped after mobilization.

When Chamberlain became Prime Minister in 1937 the combination
of Hore-Belisha and Liddell Hart did nothing to clarify the army's task.
Liddell Hart's suggestion was the formation of an Imperial Strategic
Reserve of four regular and two Territorial armoured divisions and eight
regular and eight Territorial slimmed-down infantry divisions. Nor was
there any support for a Continental commitment from Sir Thomas
Inskip, who had been appointed Minister for Coordination of Defence
in 1936. A Cabinet meeting in December 1937 nearly abolished consideration of such a commitment on the grounds that, as the French had
completed the Maginot Line, it would not be needed. The priorities then
laid down for defence were: first, the security of the United Kingdom,
especially from air attack; second, the protection of imperial communications; third, defence of British imperial possessions; and finally 'cooperation in defence of the territories of any allies Britain might have in
war'. No money was to be spent on providing for the last if it prejudiced

the other three. Liddell Hart, in common with almost all the politicians and many of the military, was obsessed by the fear that an army commitment to cooperate with France would mean that Britain would be dragged into an offensive similar to those of 1915–18. If anything was to be sent, Liddell Hart suggested that two armoured divisions would be the best contribution Britain could make, as the French had plenty of infantry divisions. The immediate effect of the Cabinet's priorities was to establish a heavy demand on the army to man anti-aircraft guns and searchlights for the air defence of Great Britain.

In spite of the Cabinet's decision, talks with the French began in May 1938 and continued up to and beyond the Munich crisis in September. The army's representatives were rigidly restricted to discussing the embarkation and movement of up to two divisions within sixteen days of the outbreak of war, but with no promise that they would actually be sent. Not surprisingly this did not impress the French. Although the result of Munich was to remove the threat of thirty-five Czechoslovak divisions from Germany's eastern flank, the conclusion was not drawn that France would now need a larger British army contribution. At the time of the Munich crisis the Chiefs of Staff emphasized that the first priority for the army was 'to secure the home base': it was thought that the army, as well as manning anti-aircraft defences, would be needed to maintain order in the aftermath of heavy German air attacks, while the next priority would be to ensure the security of Egypt and the Middle East against threats from Italy and Japan.

Returning from a visit to Paris in November, Chamberlain is said to have remarked that as the British army was so small it was hardly worth worrying about whether it was ready to go to war or not. Discussions were still based on the provision of two divisions within sixteen days. The General Staff, now headed by Lord Gort, took the more realistic view that once the army was committed to the support of France the liability could not be limited, and began to press for authority and finance to equip four regular infantry and one mobile division, and as many of the twelve Territorial Army divisions as possible, for war on the Continent. The Chief of the Air Staff, Air Chief Marshal Sir Cyril Newall, strongly opposed it. He did not believe that even with a British contribution the Low Countries could be held, and thought that equipping the Territorial Army divisions for war would lead to 'the unlimited expansion of land warfare'. But the First Sea Lord, Admiral Sir Roger

Backhouse, concerned at the possibility of German occupation of the Channel ports, swung to the support of the army. The French continued to press for a concrete demonstration of British support (conscription being the only one they recognized as meaningful), and the Foreign Office became anxious that unless something were done to meet her demands France might opt for a settlement with Germany at British expense. The whole weight of the German armed forces, particularly that of the dreaded Luftwaffe, could then be directed against Britain.

Early in 1939 the Chiefs of Staff supported the army's demand, Hore-Belisha's fall-back position being that of the Territorial divisions, other than the five anti-aircraft, four should be fully equipped for war and the remainder provided with full training equipment at a cost of £82m. Chamberlain and his Chancellor of the Exchequer, Sir John Simon, opposed it; but in February the Cabinet agreed to full equipment and reserves for the five regular divisions and war equipment for four Territorial, but stipulated that the second contingent of the Field Force (one mobile and two infantry divisions) need not arrive in France until forty to sixty days after mobilization and the four Territorial not until four to six months after it. Conscription was rejected, as was Hore-Belisha's request for the establishment of a Ministry of Supply to organize procurement.

Three weeks later Hitler occupied Prague and absorbed Slovakia. This had a dramatic effect on Chamberlain's attitude. Suddenly he went from one extreme to the other. At the end of March, without consultation with the Chiefs of Staff, he announced a hundred per cent increase in the Territorial Army and, three days later, 31 March, a guarantee of the defence of Poland, followed a week later by further guarantees to Romania and Greece. Both announcements were meaningless. Nothing effective could be done about either, and they certainly did not have the desired political effect of deterring Hitler. On 3 April he told his generals to start planning to attack Poland in September. The Chiefs of Staff had opposed the guarantees, which left the decision as to peace or war in the hands of governments over whom Britain had no control and little influence. As France had no intention of launching an offensive against Germany, the guarantees could only make military sense if Russia could be associated with them, which was not acceptable either to the countries concerned or to the Conservative Chamberlain and his Foreign Secretary, Lord Halifax.

The French continued to press for conscription, to which the Trades Union Congress was strongly opposed. However, it was introduced on 20 April, largely because it was impossible to provide an effective anti-aircraft defence without it, and staff talks with the French were resumed. They were still based on only two infantry divisions being dispatched to reach their assembly areas within a month of mobilization, the third to embark after three months, the fourth, the mobile division, and the Territorial divisions even later. It was assumed that the neutrality of Belgium and Holland would be respected, and, as the French had no intention of launching an offensive against the German Siegfried Line, reliance was placed on forming an eastern front, based on Poland, Romania, Greece and Turkey, and the possibility considered of an offensive against Italy and her colony of Libya. It was made clear to the Poles that they could expect no direct help: even air attacks on Germany were ruled out for fear of retaliation. Ironside, then Commander-in-Chief at Gibraltar, assuming that he would command what was known as the Field Force, urged that it should not be sent to France, but to the Middle East. A further bone of contention was that of its air support. Newall was reluctant to provide any, classing direct air support of land forces as 'a gross misuse of airpower'. Gort requested that seven bomber and five fighter squadrons should be provided, but the actual 'Air Component' that accompanied the force to France in September 1939 consisted of only two bomber and two fighter squadrons, with two flights of light communication aircraft. By May 1940 this had been increased to four Blenheim bomber/long-range reconnaissance and four fighter squadrons, and five Lysander close-reconnaissance and liaison flights.

On 21 August the bombshell exploded in the form of the Soviet–German non-aggression pact, which Ribbentrop signed in Moscow on the 23rd. Two days later the Anglo-Polish treaty of mutual assistance was signed. On 31 August Hitler gave the order for his troops to cross the Polish frontier next day. Two days after that Britain and France were at war with Germany.

4

THE HARD ROAD
TO ALAMEIN
1939–1942

The BEF

In contrast to 1914 and to the strategic arguments about a Continental commitment which had hamstrung defence policy over the previous decade, there was no hesitation about sending a British Expeditionary Force of four regular divisions to France or planning for its reinforcement. The decision was accompanied by the surprising one to appoint Viscount Gort, then CIGS, as its Commander-in-Chief, and to replace him by General Sir Edmund Ironside, who, as Inspector-General of the Army, everybody, including himself, had assumed would take command. The reason for the change was an increasing antipathy between General Gort and Hore-Belisha; each was equally glad to get away from the other: but Ironside was wholly unsuited to the assumption of such a vitally important post at such a critical period. He was essentially a traditional, bluff commander of imposing presence; but he had never served in the War Office and did not have the clarity of mind and combination of strength and flexibility of character and judgement which the post demanded and which Alan Brooke was to display in later years. One who had those qualities was Lieutenant-General Sir John Dill at Aldershot Command; but if he had replaced General Gort, the problem would have been to find a post for Ironside. General Wavell had already been appointed to a new Middle East Command.

Gort's subordinates in the BEF were Dill, commanding the 1st Corps (1st and 2nd Divisions), and Lieutenant-General Alan Brooke, commanding the 2nd (3rd and 4th Divisions). For fear of German air attack, ports in the eastern Channel were not used either to embark or to disembark them and their supplies, which were routed through Cherbourg, St Nazaire and Nantes. By 12 October they were in the line facing Belgium, in an area round Lille only too familiar to veterans of the Great War, sandwiched between General Blanchard's First French Army on the right and General Giraud's Seventh on the left. Command arrangements were unsatisfactory. Gort was operationally subordinate to General Georges, commander of 'The Armies of the North-east', that is all the armies, nine French and one British, between the Alps and the Channel. Above him, General Gamelin commanded the whole French army, including that in North Africa. It was not until the Germans attacked in May 1940 that an army group commander, General Billotte, was appointed to coordinate the actions of Gort with those of his neighbouring French armies, and when national political issues were involved Gamelin tended to deal with Gort direct.

The overall plan was entirely defensive. In spite of Belgium's declared neutrality, the French plan assumed that, if Belgium was imminently threatened or actually attacked, its Government would cooperate and welcome British and French troops to enter the country and adopt with them a defensive position on the line of the River Dyle, east of Brussels, while Giraud's Seventh French Army advanced north into southern Holland. This would shorten the general line of defence north of the Maginot Line, while adding the resources of the Belgian army.

As the Germans, having completed the destruction of Poland before the BEF had finished deployment, did nothing, the British troops spent their time digging defences in Flanders and training, which most of them badly needed, even the thirty-six regular infantry battalions, the ranks of which had been filled out with reservists who had done no training since they left the colours and were not familiar with the little modern equipment that was supplied. In fact the BEF was not equipped for modern war and therefore not trained for it. Artillery of all types, medium, field, anti-tank and anti-aircraft, was woefully inadequate both in quantity and, in many cases, in quality also. The same applied to the infantry's own anti-armour and anti-aircraft weapons. The only tanks with the force were the light tanks of the divisional cavalry regiments and one regiment (4th Royal Tank Regiment) of Mark I infantry tanks. Not until the first week of May 1940 was it joined by a second (7th RTR) with twenty-seven Mark I and twenty-three Mark II Matildas. The

Mobile Division, renamed 1st Armoured Division, was not considered to be yet adequately equipped and trained to join the BEF. Air support from the Royal Air Force was minimal. One of the main deficiencies was in radio-telephonic communications. Transmitter/receiver sets were unreliable, and apart from the Royal Armoured Corps and the Royal Artillery few commanders at any level were trained to use them.

In December 1939, 5th Division, all regular, joined 2nd Corps, followed in the next two months by three Territorial Army divisions, 48th (South Midland), 50th (Northumbrian) and 51st (Highland). In April 1940 3rd Corps was formed (Lieutenant-General Sir Ronald Adam) with the 42nd (Lancashire) and 44th (London) Divisions. Finally, three more divisions, 12th, 23rd and 46th, were sent over with no artillery, little equipment and less training, to act as labour and 'complete their training'.

Norway

By then the army had become involved in the first of those strategic mismanagements and tactical failures which were to dog its path and tarnish its reputation in the first three years of the war, the campaign in Norway. This originated in the British and French desire to deprive Germany of iron ore from the mines in northern Sweden, which was exported partly through Lulea in the Baltic, partly through Narvik in northern Norway, from which it could be shipped all the way to the Baltic entrance through the 'Leads', the Norwegian territorial waters inside a string of offshore islands: in winter that was the only route. Churchill, who had become First Lord of the Admiralty on the outbreak of war, wanted to mine the 'Leads'. Action was precipitated by the Russian invasion of Finland and her appeal to the League of Nations on 14 December 1939. Support to Finland, with both supplies and troops, could justify landing at Narvik and an advance up the railway which led to the iron ore mines. The unrealistic hope was indulged in that Sweden and Norway would cooperate.

A plan was concocted to deploy 24th Guards Brigade and two

29. British troops in the Kenmare District of south-west Ireland in 1921.
A Rolls-Royce armoured car at Kenmare.

30. Indian North-West Frontier, 1930s. Crossley armoured cars of the Royal Tank Corps.

31. Vickers medium tanks Mark II.

32. Light tank Mark VIa.

33. 0.55in. Boyes anti-tank rifle.

34. Machine-gun carrier No. 2, with Vickers machine-gun.

35. Bren gun on anti-aircraft mounting (Scots Guards).

36. 2-pounder anti-tank gun ready for action.

37. Bofors 40mm light anti-aircraft gun.

38. 3.7in. anti-aircraft gun (1st Anti-Aircraft Division).

39. Major-General Sir Percy Hobart.

40. Lord Gort and General Sir Edmund Ironside at the War Office, September 1939.

41. Evacuation from Dunkirk.

42. Generals O'Connor and Maitland-Wilson with Brigadier Selby, Mersa Matruh, Egypt, 27 October 1940.

43. Matilda tank of 7th Royal Tank Regiment on the battlefield of Sidi Barrani, 19 December 1940.

44. With an Indian Brigade in Eritrea, January 1941.
Signal posts in communication with observation posts and guns.

45. Artillery shelling the defences of Derna, January 1941.

46. Withdrawal in Greece, April 1941.

47. A soldier sleeping during the withdrawal from Greece, 3 May.

48. Dead German soldiers near a crashed glider, Crete, May 1941.

49. Generals Auchinleck and Wavell, Cairo, September 1941.

50. A British soldier being searched by Japanese troops, Malaya, 1941.

51. A Stuart tank of 7th Armoured Brigade in Burma, 1942.

52. Guns on the move in Malaya, 1941.

53. Generals Norrie, Ritchie and Gott, near Tobruk, 31 May 1942.

54. A Grant tank and crew, 8 June 1942.

55. A Stuart
tank near
Himeimat,
El Alamein Line,
26 August 1942.

56. Crusader tanks moving up to the battle area.

57. Infantry in the Alamein area.

Territorial Army divisions, due to go to France, to land at Narvik, and also at some other ports, to prevent the Germans using them. Before this could be put into effect, the Finns capitulated on 12 March 1940, and the justification was thus undermined. Before that, a British destroyer had entered the 'Leads' to intercept the German ship the *Altmark*, which had been supplying the German commerce raider, the *Admiral Graf Spee*, in the South Atlantic, and was carrying the survivors of the nine ships the *Spee* had sunk. Norway reacted sharply to this infringement of her waters. With the strong support of the French, Churchill persuaded a reluctant Chamberlain and Halifax to approve a new plan: to mine the 'Leads' and to occupy Narvik and other ports in order to pre-empt any German reaction, under the protection of a strong fleet action.

Mining was to start on 8 April. Unbeknown to the Allies, Hitler was also making plans. His naval Commander-in-Chief, Grand Admiral Raeder, had for some time been trying to persuade him to occupy Norway. The *Altmark* incident seemed to show that Britain was prepared to infringe Norway's neutrality, and on 2 April he approved plans to invade Norway, which also involved the occupation of Denmark. 9 April was fixed as the launching date. When the British Admiralty realized that the German navy had put to sea, actually carrying troops to Narvik, the British troops destined to go there were disembarked in Scotland in order to free the fleet for a naval action in the North Sea. The fleet failed to intercept the Germans, but caught several of their ships on their way back. The plan for unopposed landings of a brigade at Narvik, and one battalion each at Trondheim, Bergen and Stavanger, was no longer appropriate. The decision was taken to capture Narvik with the 24th Guards Brigade, Major-General P. J. Mackesy, commander of the 49th Division, being charged with the task, while two of his brigades were to land, one (146th) north of Trondheim, and one (148th) to the south. The former was under the command of the sixty-year-old Major-General A. Carton de Wiart VC, a colourful one-eyed, one-armed friend of Churchill's of Belgian origin, who had a legendary record of gallantry, gained in Somaliland, and in both the Boer War and the Great War. He had recently been the British liaison officer with the Polish army. The other was under its own commander, Brigadier H. de R. Morgan. Mackesy, Carton de Wiart and Morgan reported separately to Ironside in London.

The Trondheim brigades were intended to exploit a direct assault on the port by the third brigade of the division, the 147th, and 15th Brigade, withdrawn from the 5th Division in France, both under yet another commander, Major-General B. Paget, who would report direct to Ironside also, although the operation was to be primarily a naval one. The aim, although never entirely clear, was to give support to the Norwegian forces, which, accompanied by the King, were withdrawing from Oslo, the Germans having already captured it by a combination of airborne and amphibious assault. In the event, the direct assault was cancelled as too hazardous, and Paget's force joined Morgan. With total supremacy in the air, and with well-trained and equipped troops, the Germans had no difficulty in driving both forces back to the sea, all being evacuated, the southern from Andalsnes, the northern from Namsos, by 2 May.

Corporal Charles Lane, of the 4th Lincolns, describes his part in the withdrawal to Andalsnes:

There was no cover to conceal oneself so, as the long station platform was built of railway sleepers, we started to rip them up to make our own barricades. There was nothing you could do about the camouflage against aircraft but the main concern was for protection from bullets and mortars. The position my platoon took up was in a small trench that the Norwegian troops had dug. They made an attempt at camouflage with some white linen. There was snow up to a depth of four feet and even deeper in places. The trouble with it was that it was not possible to cross it except on skis. We fortified our position with sleepers. We also made a dugout of sleepers using snow to camouflage it from the air. In the distance was the town of Steinkeger. On the Friday we saw German planes over there dropping leaflets telling the population to get out. About three hours later they were over in force dropping incendiaries on the town, with an occasional high-explosive bomb. From our positions we watched that little town burning for two days. A spotter plane came over our positions continually on the Sunday morning and about 11 a.m. the action started. Some of C and D Companies were dispatched down the road to contact the enemy. We had received information that they had got further down the Fjord than our people in Whitehall thought possible. They had penetrated by breaking the ice with one of their pocket battleships. There was soon a fierce battle raging and the first casualty was a young Grimsby lad of C Company. Tragically enough, he was twenty-one that day. He was turning to give the 'enemy in sight' signal when he was immediately shot and killed. After that there was a persistent firing and the superior firepower of the enemy took its toll, and they were pinned down, eventually having to take cover in a barn. This proved a bad move as it became a mass of flames. How many escaped from it we never knew. The men of D Company who had been in the engagement got out under the cover of smoke from the burning barn. After this engagement was broken off the enemy turned its attention to the remainder of D Company holding the farmhouse, and my own section holding the trench in front of the railway, and Company Headquarters holding the farmhouse. We were being heavily mortared with their multiple mortars, this being a new experience for all of us. We had to listen intently because you could hear the bombs as they spun in the air. They made this peculiar whistling sound entirely different from ordinary shells. We were having to hit the ground every few seconds, but through all this the young soldiers never wavered, although hungry and tired as we were still only getting the odd pack of hard biscuits and very, very little sleep, and we hadn't had a hot drink in seven days since we landed. We were under heavy mortar fire for over three hours and luckily we had suffered no casualties, although they had found the range on the railway. Our little trench and dugout was standing up to the bombardment well. Company Headquarters in the farmhouse was hit and was burning so the Company Headquarters was moved to our position. We had two Brens and seven men with rifles and three boxes of ammo. The mortars giving us all the bother were in a wood about 800 yards away. We had sent patrols out the night before the enemy landed with orders to pace the distance to the woods. All our fire was directed at the area of the woods. We had seven men refilling Bren magazines for all of three hours while the two Bren gunners pumped their bullets into that area. What the result of all that was we never knew.

About 3 p.m. the Company Commander gave orders to evacuate our positions. It would have been only a matter of time before we were dispatched to oblivion. Miraculously we had sustained all the heavy mortaring for three hours or more, but Gerry was succeeding in hitting the railway behind our position only a matter of about 15 feet. Our troubles started as soon as each man crawled out of our little dugout. Three of the first men out were caught by a mortar bomb. One private, Cutler, was very badly hit, one stretcher bearer got it too, and the Company Commander had a very severe wound below his private parts, but he carried on despite his terrible wounds. We had no medical personnel so it was a case of patching them up as best we could. The Company Commander directed us to join C Company in a wood behind our positions. We had to go along the railway and down the roads which were being well mortared. We reached them but sustained another casualty. An old reservist, Geordie Cray, had one wrist just hanging on by the skin and the young militia lad, Cutler, had to be left for the enemy to pick up, as that was the only chance he had of surviving. We had no transport of any kind and I never saw an ambulance in the whole campaign. After reaching the woods we found it was coming under heavy small arms fire. We stayed in there only a short time as the danger seemed to be from ricochets hitting the large fir trees, so we had orders to leave there under the leadership of an officer. We proceeded down the road for a few miles and as we were the last ones to leave Vist, we headed for Steinkeger, the town that we had watched three days previously being burned to the ground. What a sight met our eyes. I'd never seen a town devastated like that. The only building standing was the barrack block, which had been occupied by us for about three hours. The town looked like a giant cemetery full of large tombstones but they were not that, but the brick chimney stacks, standing tall and gaunt against the sky. All the houses had burnt down around them leaving only the stacks, the only part of the houses which were built of bricks. It looked so grotesque you could hardly believe what you were seeing. It was like something from a science fiction film.

Operations further north, designed to capture Narvik, fared little better, although the German garrison, which had arrived there by sea, was now completely cut off. The original plan had been for Mackesy's 49th Division, reinforced by 24th Guards Brigade, to land at the nearest harbour at which ships could be unloaded, and when complete to make its way to Narvik, reinforced by troops withdrawn from France. It was thought that it would be several weeks before an assault could be made. Nevertheless Mackesy was told by Ironside: 'You may have a chance of taking advantage of naval action, and you should do so if you can. Boldness is required.' The diversion of the whole of his division to the Trondheim operation put paid to any thought of rapid action, quite apart from the practical difficulties caused by the logistic chaos at the small port of Harstad on the island of Hinnoy and the lack of any means of transport forward from there.

Churchill, now Chairman of a Cabinet Committee trying to coordinate operations in Norway as well as being First Lord of the Admiralty, appointed the fiery, red-headed Admiral of the Fleet the Earl of Cork and Orrery to coordinate operations at Narvik, pressing for urgent action. Cork tried to persuade Mackesy to make a direct landing at Narvik, supported by naval gunfire, promising to destroy the place and its defenders by bombardment. Mackesy turned this down both as impractical (the only landing craft were ships' boats) and on the grounds of the physical and psychological effect on the Norwegians, with whom he had been urged to cooperate. However, he agreed to reconsider the operation if bombardment of military targets near Narvik on 24 April proved effective. It did not; and an attempt to land west of the town on 28 April was driven back.

On that day three battalions of French Chasseurs Alpins arrived, to be followed by two of the Foreign Legion and a Polish brigade. In addition, it was agreed in London on 1 May that when shipping could be made available the 5th Division would be withdrawn from the BEF and sent to Narvik.

By now, with the Allies withdrawing from around Trondheim, the Germans were sending troops by sea and air further north. In an attempt to hold them off and help the Norwegians to do so one of the battalions of 24th Guards Brigade was sent by sea to Mo, 200 miles south of Narvik, detaching a company to Bodo, halfway there, where the rest of the brigade was to join them; but one of the ships carrying 200 men of one battalion, including all its senior officers, was bombed and sunk, and one carrying part of the other battalion ran aground. The brigade was finally withdrawn at the end of May, as Norwegian, French and Polish troops entered Narvik. However, by then events in France had intervened and the decision was taken to withdraw all the troops, evacuation being completed by 8 June. It had been a sorry story, and ironic that the man who more than any other individual must be held responsible for it, Winston Churchill, had by then been acclaimed by all as the country's inspired war leader.

The Fall of France

It was the long-awaited German onslaught on France and the Low Countries, launched at dawn on 10 May 1940, which persuaded Neville Chamberlain that his Conservative administration must be converted into a National Coalition. He had hoped to head it, but it soon became clear that Churchill was the only leader whom all parties would accept. As he, with no reluctance, gathered up the reins of power, the BEF moved forward without incident to its planned deployment area on the River Dyle, covering Brussels, arriving on 11 May, with the Belgian army on the left of Alan Brooke's 2nd Corps and the First French Army on the right of 1st Corps, now commanded by Lieutenant-General M. G. H. Barker, Dill having left to become Vice-CIGS. Adams's 3rd Corps (42nd and 44th Divisions) was in reserve on the line of the River Escaut, while the three 'labour' divisions remained with GHQ in the area of Arras. 51st (Highland) Division was detached 'gaining experience with the French' in the Maginot Line defences of the Saar.

It was not until 14 May that the BEF was seriously attacked, the fighting intensifying next day, but the line being held. On that day, however, General Bock's German Army Group B (twenty-eight divisions, including three armoured) had driven far into Blanchard's positions, while von Rundstedt's Army Group A (forty-four divisions, including seven armoured) had penetrated even further across the Meuse in the French Ninth Army's sector west of the Ardennes. General Billotte therefore ordered a phased withdrawal of all the armies, British, Belgian and French in his First Army Group, first to the River Senne, through Brussels, then to the Dendre, about ten miles further west, and finally to the Escaut, where he expected to be able to stand. But over the next five days von Rundstedt's lightning advance, which brought his tanks to the sea near Abbeville at the mouth of the Somme, undermined his plan. Billotte's four armies were surrounded with their backs to the Channel and subjected to repeated assaults from Bock's armies to the east and north and von Rundstedt's from the south and west.

On the night of 17/18 May the BEF withdrew from the Senne to the Dendre and on the following night to the Escaut, while the 'labour' divisions formed 'Petreforce' under the commander of the 12th Division, Major-General R. L. Petre, to garrison Arras and nearby towns on the Canal du Nord, as well as Doullens, and Amiens and Abbeville on the Somme. All these were attacked on 20 May by von Rundstedt's leading troops. On that day Ironside visited Gort and gave him the totally unrealistic order 'to move southwards upon Amiens, attacking all enemy forces encountered and to take station on the left of the French Army'. Fortunately Gort ignored it. He had already ordered a counter-attack near Arras by his two reserve divisions, the 5th and the 50th, both denuded of some of their troops, which had been sent to Norway. The attack was intended to relieve pressure on 'Petreforce', which was being attacked by the SS Totenkopf Division and Major-General Rommel's 7th Panzer Division. In the event, it was made by only two battalions, supported by all the remaining infantry tanks, fifty-eight Mark Is, armed only with a machine-gun, and sixteen Mark II Matildas of the 4th and 7th Royal Tank Regiments of 1st Army Tank Brigade.

On that day also General Maxime Weygand replaced Gamelin as French Commander-in-Chief. He decided to fly up north to see Billotte and King Leopold of Belgium at Ypres. His plan was for the BEF and the First French Army, their rear protected by the Belgians, to attack south-eastward and cut off the German penetration along the Somme, conjuring up the prospect of a new French Army of some twenty divisions, drawn from the Maginot Line and North Africa, which would attack from the south to form the other arm of a pincer. This was reinforced next day by an order to Gort on the same lines from Churchill, who was visiting Paris. By then the Arras counter-attack, although it had provoked a disproportionate degree of alarm within Army Group A, had petered out, and the BEF's main position on the Escaut was severely threatened, causing it to be withdrawn to its original position on the Franco-Belgian frontier on the night of 22/23 May.

Lieutenant Gregory Blaxland of the 2nd Buffs describes the 1st Division's stand on Marlborough's old battlefield of Oudenarde:

A great rumpus broke out on our right flank, as if in defiance of the expectation of an attack from the left. Although the noise was muffled by distance and by the convex slope betwen us and the river, it appeared that D Company (extreme right) or A or both were coming under attack. We could hear bursts of very rapid fire and could see tracer bullets soaring in gleaming streams against the darkening sky, thus proving that the Germans were in breach of the Geneva Convention, under which we had conscientiously confined our tracer bullets to Bren magazines required for anti-aircraft action, at a density of only one tracer to every eight bullets. I had an awful sinking feeling that we just could not compete with these demons who had put so much thought and practice into the brutality of war. All the firing appeared to be coming from their side. They seemed to have hundreds of Tommy guns (against our none), making quick, brief, staccato bursts, and long, vibrating, solid bursts came from machine-guns I had yet to know by the dread name of Spandaus. The occasional short, deliberate burst, easily identifiable as the response of a Bren, seemed inoffensive by comparison. I assumed the distant crashes I could hear were made by mortar bombs, and I knew that the mortars in a German battalion, of calibre around 3-inches, outnumbered those in a British one by six to two. There were frequent conflagrations as Very lights went up, most of them dazzling white and slow to fade, intermixed with green and red ones. I wondered who was illuminating whom.

A lance-corporal came running over from the other entrenchment and breathlessly told me that Cpl Pilling said the signal for a withdrawal had been given. I hauled myself out of our trench and doubled across to investigate. It was Cocky Pilling who had made the great discovery. Red followed by green always meant withdraw he assured me.

'*Withdraw*, Corporal Pilling?'. I was proud of the scorn with which I put the question.

'Standing Orders, Sir; always used to be at Aldershot.'

'Corporal Pilling, we are at Oudenarde, not Aldershot, and the Buffs do *not* withdraw from Oudenarde.'

I was quite surprised to find that I could make so powerful a riposte, but it did not put Pilling to rout. He now wanted to know whether there was anything about withdrawing in the operational order, and all I could say to this was that if there had been I was sure I would have been notified of it. Melancholy Pilling then pointed out that as all the other troops had fallen back through us it must now be our turn to fall back through them; they would not have fallen back through us if this had been meant to be a permanent line. I replied that it was a permanent line as far as I was concerned and that they were to put any ideas they might have to the contrary right out of their minds – unless of course the order to withdraw should be delivered to me by runner, in which case I should pass it on to them by giving three blasts on my whistle.

One thing about living in a trench is that it instils the notion that there must be great danger in being above ground. I felt very dashing as I climbed out of the Pillings' trench, nipped back across the 70 or so yards of turf that separated us, and made a spectacular leap to the bottom of my particular hole. I had put the Pillings well and truly in their place, I reflected. Yet the truth was that they had well and truly converted me to their expectation. I thought of Jimmy's description of our frontage as a whopper, well over double that decreed as a battalion's capability in the official manual. Surely we could not be expected to hold it permanently, and surely the Pillings were right in supposing that the troops who had withdrawn through our position had done so with the object of holding a position through which we would in turn withdraw. I wished that I had had a chat with Jimmy about it when he paid his early morning visit. Obviously I could not leave my post to do so now, and I had no link with him either by telephone or wireless. It would have been absurd to send off a runner on such a vague mission. The mere thought of doing so made me suddenly, chillingly aware that all I knew about the location of Company Headquarters was that it was somewhere in the vicinity of Petegem, far away.

As I was pondering this matter, there came a very brief whistle, an orange flash, and a gigantic crash. It was quickly followed by another, and even after the warning, the brevity of the whistle scarcely gave me time to duck before the crash. Down came yet more, drawing from Sgt Skippings a plea for mercy from the Mother of Jesus. We were being mortared, and the odd thing is that, perhaps because I supposed the enemy to be far distant, I felt convinced that the bombs were arriving from our side. Again I hauled myself out of the trench, and I ran down the road past the Carrier Sergeant's house yelling, 'Stop those bloody mortars!'

This was sheer lunacy. I had no idea where our mortars were, and they had no reason whatever to be lobbing their bombs in our direction when the enemy was attacking from the other. Yet, amazingly, my intervention appeared to have done the trick. The mortar bombs ceased to fall, and I returned to our trench, bringing with me three or four men who had followed my foolish lead. The trouble about mortar bombs was that they just fell from the sky without giving any warning of their coming or clue to their starting point. The danger was the same whether they came from east or west, and a trench offered the best protection either way. It was odd that such simple matters of logic had to be learned from experience. Anyway we had all escaped physical hurt, even though the arm of Cpl French's greatcoat, which had been lying on the parapet, had received a great tear. He displayed it with cheerful, almost triumphant, pride.

Later – I had little idea how much later, but the war diary indicates that it was around 4 a.m. – I heard two or three men coming down the lateral road from Petegem. One of them was limping. They went righthanded down the road away from my platoon, towards the enemy, and soon afterwards I heard a conversation between Trucky and Stiffy. Their voices were clear and calm. Trucky was saying that he would try and work his way forward in rushes, and Stiffy said he had a platoon ready to make a converging movement along the path. Neither sounded in the least excited. I felt a coward for not dashing forward and offering to join in the attack.

Trucky must have taken his men much further forward than the place from which I heard him speak, for the sound of firing was muted when I heard it break out. Once again the German weapons seemed to be in the ascendancy. I could hear the crump of grenades and sensed that Trucky was among the hurlers. Obviously things had gone badly to require him to lead a counterattack through the lefthand company when his own should have been holding the centre.

Dawn began to break, and since we had been standing-to all through the night, I did not have to order a stand-to now. Then suddenly they sprang to life in the misty half-light – a party of Germans running towards us from our right flank. We all fired, myself and Froggy French with rifles and almost barging each other over in the process. The Germans went smartly to ground, out of sight, in some dead ground just on their side of the lateral road. We waited for their heads to reappear. They did not do so. I began to wonder whether they really had been Germans. Then it struck me that they were engaged in the infiltration tactics for which they were famed, probing for gaps betwen posts, and I am sure in retrospect that this was the correct interpretation. It was clear that they were as scared of us as we of them.

*

Gort's most vulnerable area was now in the south, where Bock's Army Group B was pressing westward between Lille and Arras, while Army Group A threatened to turn north to the west of Arras and penetrate into his rear area, cutting him off from the Channel ports of Boulogne, Calais and Dunkirk. He therefore switched the 2nd and 48th Divisions to that area and ordered the withdrawal of 'Petreforce', still gallantly holding out at Arras. In an attempt to comply with Weygand's and Churchill's orders, he planned another southward attack by 5th and 50th Divisions and three divisions of the First French Army on the 26th. But when he discovered from Blanchard (who had replaced Billotte, killed in a traffic accident) that the French attack from the south had been cancelled, and learned from intelligence that Bock was preparing to launch a major thrust near Ypres to separate the BEF from the Belgians, he cancelled it and switched the two divisions to his left flank, a decision made on his own authority which undoubtedly saved the BEF.

Blanchard now realized also that the First Army Group's only hope was to form a bridgehead covering Dunkirk, and he gave orders on 26 May for a withdrawal to effect it, while the British Government decided to implement Operation DYNAMO, the evacuation of the BEF through Dunkirk. Before that, it had in vain sent troops from England to Boulogne and Calais, both being overwhelmed by the Germans on 25 May. Learning of the British decision, King Leopold capitulated on 27 May, making necessary some rapid redeployment, particularly in Brooke's 2nd Corps, in which Montgomery's 3rd Division was expertly transferred from right to left, when the 5th Division was under intense pressure. Two divisions were withdrawn from the old frontier defences to the River Lys, while Adams's 3rd Corps Headquarters, with the 1st Division, was withdrawn to Dunkirk to plan with the French the immediate defence of the port.

The Lys position was strongly attacked by Bock's troops all through the day of 28 May, and the troops there were withdrawn with difficulty during the night to the Yser, under the protection of the 50th and 3rd Divisions. Evacuation was now in full swing, pounded from the air by the Luftwaffe and under heavy artillery fire from the guns of General

Kuchler's Eighteenth Army. By 31 May 126,160 men had been evacuated, and the remaining troops were placed under the command of Lieutenant-General Sir Harold Alexander, who had been commanding the 1st Division. German attacks on the perimeter intensified every day until evacuation was complete at the end of 3 June, those French troops who remained surrendering next day. 224,320 British troops and 113,906 others, almost all French, were evacuated from Dunkirk harbour and the surrounding beaches, a remarkable achievement. There was undoubtedly some panic, and breakdown of discipline and morale, but in the vast majority of cases the withdrawal and evacuation were orderly, in spite of traffic chaos under frequent air attack and artillery bombardment. Much of the credit must go to the troops who were holding off the German attacks at every stage, many fighting to the last man and round.

Driver Samuel Gresty of the 3rd Division Supply Column, Royal Army Service Corps describes how he left:

It was not long before I got to the beach. I could see the black smoke at Dunkirk. I was never in the actual town of Dunkirk. I walked along the beach with the other soldiers till we got more or less opposite a fleet of a few ships, boats and two small motor boats.

It looked to me the smaller the boats the closer to the beach they came. That was only common sense, it was no good getting stuck on the bottom. These 2 little motor boats were doing a great job of work. I think they ferried most of the evacuated off the beach that day. I know there would have been a lot left on the beach had it not been for them. Thanks to the RAF, after taking a full load to one of the ships they came back again to where we were. Some of the soldiers were getting on. I had the small valise with 200 cigarettes in. I tied it as high as I could get it on my chest. I walked to the first motor boat. The one in charge said 'Will some of you go to the other boat, I can't get you all in here'. A few of us went wading to the other boat in about 4' to 4'6" of water. Some of the men had not the energy to climb over the back of the boat. I went to give one a helping hand. As soon as the one in charge could see my rifle he said, 'You will have to throw the rifle away, as we can only take personnel. We are short of space.' At that I pulled the bolt out and let the bolt and rifle drop into the sea. I gave one or two a lift up on the boat and then got in myself.

The young man in charge said 'You look a fit man,' I said 'Not too bad for a lad'. He had a look around and said 'It looks as if you are the last for a while'. He asked me if I would give him a helping hand to pull on the rope to take the slack when the other boat started off for the ship. He said it would not be such a dead drag on the motor boat that was towing this one. I said 'Of course, I will be glad to help you'. He said he had been out of petrol all day. He then showed me his hands. They were red raw caused by pulling on the rope all day. They must have felt like fire.

The other boat started away. I said 'Tell me what I have to do as we go along, you have a rest'. We got to the rope ladder on the ship. I said to the young man in charge 'I was the last on. I'll be the last off'. I was last up the rope ladder. On deck I was standing at the side of the ship looking down on the motor boat, I was close by the naval officer when he said to the one in charge of the little boat 'There are a few more just arrived on the beach. I can just about find a space for them if you care to go and pick them up', he said, 'it's up to you'.

The man in charge of the boat looked at me. I knew what he was going to say before he said it. I said 'Yes, I will come with you and pull on the rope'. They shortened the rope between the two boats then off towards the beach. The man in charge asked me 'Do you know who we are with these motor boats?'. I said 'I don't, should I?'. He said 'We are some of the RAF motor boat rescue squad'. We had a chat about the war and became good pals in less than half-an-hour.

Everyone that had been on the beach were now on the boats, they waited a few minutes to see if there were any more, then went to the ship. Some of the men were soon up the rope ladder on deck. The others were a bit slower, tired out. As the last soldier got on the ship my new pal and I wished each other good luck and a safe passage home.

But Dunkirk was not the end of the BEF. There were still 140,000 British soldiers in France, west of the German penetration along the Somme. Many were in rear area units, but there were two operational formations, 51st (Highland) Division (Major-General Victor Fortune), which had been recalled from the Saar and at the end of May was under the command of the 9th Corps of the French Tenth Army, facing Abbeville across the Somme, and 1st Armoured Division (Major-General Roger Evans), which started landing at Cherbourg on 21 May without its artillery or its infantry, which had been diverted to Calais. It too was moved up to the Abbeville area under the French Seventh Army.

With the fall of Dunkirk, all Bock's and von Rundstedt's forces were free to turn south. They now began to outflank from the east the French between the Somme and the Seine and to drive down the right bank of the latter to entrap them. When at last Fortune was allowed to leave his position on the River Bresle on 8 June he was too late to be able to reach Le Havre, and he was surrounded at the little port of St Valery-en-Caux, where the French started surrendering as the German tanks, on the cliffs overlooking the harbour, made evacuation impossible.

Captain Basil Brooke of the 1st Gordons recorded the events of the final day, 12 June, in his diary:

> *0100*
> Still having received no orders to withdraw, the Col sent Hutchy into St VALERY to contact DIV. H.Q. & find out the situation.
>
> *0145*
> Hutchy returned having failed to find DIV. HQ, but stated everyone was going back.
>
> *0200*
> Hutchy and the I.O. returned to St VALERY & eventually met with the DIV staff beside the quay. Apparently the withdrawal zero hour had been 2200 hrs on 11th. They then returned to Bn H.Q.
>
> *0230*
> VICTOR CAMPBELL (Bde Maj 152), who had come out from St VALERY alone, arrived to confirm our withdrawal, he then went on alone to inform the 2 SEAFORTHS. Pte Carle our best M.C. D/R* had been waiting all night at Bde H.Q. to bring us the message!
>
> The Col ordered Capt Colville to take back C Coy (in his efforts to do so he was killed) and Capt Christie to take back H.Q. personnel & Hutchie took Taylor, R.S.M. TITLEY, & 2 Lt Dunlop in his P.U.† – Dunlop had been badly shot through the ankle while on a bicycle trying to get through to the Coys. There had been three previous attempts.
>
> A fighting patrol of P.S.M.‡ Dingwall & 12 men tried to contact the Coys but failed – Meanwhile the Col was alone at Bn H.Q.

* Motor cycle dispatch rider.
† Pick-up.
‡ Platoon Sergeant-Major.

Capt Hector Christie, Lt Campbell (QM*) myself & about 20 men of H.Q. left about 0230 for St VALERY. On reaching the junction of the main road I insisted on going by cross-country believing the roads to be under M.G. fire. A thrilling adventure. We got soaked, I carried a rifle; as each verey light went up we fell flat. We crossed a road & railway & entered St VALERY from a SW direction.

0330

P.S.M. Dingwall & his 12 men returned. The Col saw it was impossible to contact the Coys & that they had no doubt been rounded up and captured during the 2200 hrs attack.

0340

The Col, Dingwall & 12 men were captured by tanks having come under fire while on the road, this diverted them into the tanks.

0400

Hector, Campbell & I reached St VALERY only to find the place stiff with men. Thousands – Here we met up with Hutchy & his lot & we tried to find out the possibility of getting a boat! NONE WHATSO-EVER! the tide was also out. Hutchie had reached St VALERY at about 0315 & had also met some of our Jocks.

0630

2Lt Rhodes visited Bn H.Q. to find it deserted and returned to D Coy in the Col's car.

A, B and D Coy R. NORFOLKS tried to withdraw to St VALERY. They were all captured by tanks.

0700

These Coys passed Bn H.Q. 2Lt Rhodes & a few men in the Col's car with LMG pointing in all directions made a dash & reached St VALERY.

Meanwhile we had taken shelter in a wood SW of St VALERY here I returned carrying a double carrier tarpaulin & 3 blankets to keep some of us dry & warm. I was certainly very fit. Hutchie & Taylor went off to try & get orders etc.

Later we were informed that it might be possible to hold off the Germans till nightfall & then get off on ships we therefore set about to defend St VALERY. I tried to cooperate with some Bn, but our

* Quartermaster.

small force was not needed. We started to dig in, but later occupied a Gendarmerie.

Hutchy had been informed by Div Comdr of hopeless situation & told that organized parties could do their best to get away providing an officer was left with the remainder.

Hutchy tried to contact the navy to take us off from VEULES, however in the middle of this the Div order was countermanded & we were to take up a defensive position EAST of the town. This is when I liaised with some Bn. We started to dig in but later fortified the Gendarmerie.

I cleared the house of all flammable material, each room with 2 buckets of water and each window with a L.M.G.

0930

We sat down & had some sardines bread & hard tack from the town. I had collected food & for myself a pack out of the gutter & the better stuff from an officer's & man's pack I kept (& was I to prove glad of it!). Retired for short sleep & to dry clothes.

1030

AUS! AUS! CAPTURED.

We learnt afterwards that the French had capitulated by putting a white flag on the church steeple & at the same time allowed enemy to enter the harbour; while the DIV Comdr was out on a recce for the defence of St VALERY – as a result the DIV Comdr had no alternative but to surrender and end the campaign.

1st Armoured Division, having lost most of its tanks in fruitless attacks ordered by the French, managed to escape the trap and cross the Seine on 8 June. Churchill still hoped that the situation in France could be saved and planned to send the 52nd (Lowland) Division and the 1st Canadian to Cherbourg, appointing Alan Brooke to command all the troops in France. He arrived on 13 June, and when he saw Weygand next day he realized that the latter had no plan which offered any hope of success. With considerable difficulty he persuaded Churchill by telephone to stop all reinforcement and authorize the withdrawal of all British troops from France. Except for the unfortunate 51st Highlanders, it had been accomplished when Marshal Pétain, on 17 June, announced the French surrender. By then, after Dunkirk and Cherbourg, 39,251 men had been left in enemy hands as prisoners of war, with 2,472 guns and 63,874 vehicles of all kinds. Casualties had been 4,438 killed, 14,127 wounded and 10,923 missing.

It was an almost disarmed and a dispirited army, suffering from deep shock, as was the nation itself, that was rallied by Winston Churchill's stirring rhetoric to the defence of the home country. It was all very well to call on it to 'fight on the beaches', but there was hardly anything to fight with.

*

Although the BEF had been ill equipped and ill trained to meet the threat posed by the German armies, spearheaded by tanks and closely supported by dive-bombing aircraft, that was not the reason why it had to retreat to the coast, abandon all its equipment and escape across the Channel, the unlucky ones trudging off into prisoner of war camps. However well it might have been equipped and trained and however bravely it might have fought, it was the collapse of the French armies on its right and the Belgian on its left flank which sealed its fate. The German tanks at the time were not qualitatively superior to the British, but there were many more of them and they were handled, in cooperation with other arms, with imaginative skill and great boldness, as were the aircraft supporting them, the effect of which on morale was more significant than the actual damage their weapons inflicted.

The Middle East

Fortunately the army did not immediately have to 'fight on the beaches, on the landing grounds, in the fields and in the streets, and in the hills' as Churchill had predicted in his famous broadcast speech on 4 June; but it was immediately faced with fighting Hitler's ally Italy, when Mussolini, having waited carefully to see who was winning, jumped on Hitler's bandwagon and declared war on France and Britain on 10 June.

With 215,000 troops in Libya and 290,000 in Abyssinia, Eritrea and Italian Somaliland, Italy posed a clear threat to the mere 86,000 soldiers in General Sir Archibald Wavell's Middle East Command, covering Palestine, Egypt, the Sudan, British Somaliland and East Africa. Before his arrival in August 1939, the army in all these places had been separately subordinate to the War Office, Lieutenant-General Sir Henry Maitland Wilson commanding the army in Egypt. Tension between Britain and Italy in the area, first aroused by Italy's invasion of Abyssinia in 1935, was intensified by her invasion of Albania in April 1939. This led to the move of the Mediterranean Fleet from Malta, where the anti-aircraft defences were as woefully inadequate as those of the fleet itself, to Alexandria. Guarantees of support if attacked were given to Greece and Romania, and talks about future cooperation were initiated with the French authorities in the region and with Turkey.

When war with Germany broke out in September 1939, Wilson had some 40,000 men in Egypt, including one ill-equipped armoured division (the 7th), two infantry brigades with a few extra battalions, and an Indian infantry brigade under training. Further reinforcements from India, Australia and New Zealand were on their way. Wavell and his French colleague in Syria, General Weygand, were all for planning offensive action, but the policy of not doing anything to provoke Italy into joining in the war was continued, and nobody thought Weygand's idea of an expedition to Salonika a practical proposition. However, as German victory in Norway was followed by bad news from France and Belgium, the likelihood of Italian intervention increased. Major-General Richard O'Connor, with the headquarters of his 6th Division, was sent from Palestine to command the forces in the Western Desert, facing Marshal Balbo's Tenth Italian Army of 70,000 men in Libya. The only force immediately available was 7th Armoured Division (Major-General M. O'Moore Creagh) with only one of its two armoured brigades, and that had only two regiments of tanks. One was equipped solely with light tanks, the other with a mixed collection of 'cruisers', some of which were awaiting delivery of their guns.

When Mussolini declared war on 10 June 1940 his troops on the Libyan frontier were taken by surprise, and for several months 7th Armoured Division dominated the area; but constant activity began to impose a strain on the mechanical state of vehicles and logistic resources. When there were signs that Italian forces (now reinforced under Balbo's successor, Marshal Graziani) were bestirring themselves for action, the frontier was left to light forces, while O'Connor's main force was concentrated near Mersa Matruh, 120 miles to the east, where it was intended that any Italian invasion would be stopped.

Meanwhile Churchill was pressing Wavell and his colleagues, Admiral

Sir Andrew Cunningham and Air Chief Marshal Sir Arthur Longmore, for offensive action, including attacks on the Italians in Abyssinia from the Sudan and Kenya. Wavell was summoned to London, where his taciturn realism annoyed Churchill. Anthony Eden, Secretary of State for War, and the CIGS, Dill, did their best to defend him, with the result that his request for three regiments of tanks to be sent out to him was agreed. It did not help matters that greatly superior Italian forces invaded British Somaliland, defended by only five infantry battalions, on 3 August, the day that Wavell left for London. While he was there, Churchill accepted reluctantly the inevitable loss of the colony and evacuation of the troops; but, when he learnt, after Wavell's return to Cairo, that the British casualties were only 38 killed and 222 wounded, he was furious and demanded the dismissal of the commander, Major-General A. R. Godwin-Austen. Wavell refused, replying: 'A big butcher's bill is not necessarily evidence of good tactics,' which added fuel to the flames. Wavell's stock with Churchill fell even lower still a month later when the Italian Tenth Army advanced ponderously from the Libyan frontier fifty miles into the Western Desert of Egypt and settled down into a string of scattered defences.

Wavell was a firm believer in the value of surprise, and he restricted to a very small number of senior officers and members of his staff knowledge of plans to take the offensive both against the incursion from Libya and against Italian East Africa from the Sudan and Kenya, to which South African forces had been sent. Ignorant of these plans, Churchill sent Eden, accompanied by Dill, to urge Wavell into action as soon as the reinforcement of tanks arrived at the end of September. Wavell revealed to Eden that he planned 'a short and swift operation lasting four or five days at most' to eliminate the Italian forces that had entered Egypt and drive the remnants back across the frontier. He then intended to switch 4th Indian Division (Major-General N. M. de la P. Beresford-Pierse), O'Connor's infantry, to the Sudan, replacing them with the newly arrived 6th Australian Division, although he did not tell O'Connor of that intention. On 9 December 4th Indian and 7th Armoured Divisions attacked the Italian positions south of Sidi Barrani, and within three days had totally defeated them. To his fury, O'Connor had to pause, while the Australians replaced the Indians, before he could attack Bardia, just across the frontier. That fell to the Australians on 5 January 1941, followed by Tobruk on the 22nd.

O'Connor's logistics were now stretched to breaking point and another factor had intervened. On 28 October 1940 Italy had invaded Greece from Albania and Churchill was anxious to honour Britain's guarantee of help. However the Greek dictator, General Metaxas, was reluctant to accept for fear that it would provoke the intervention of Germany, which was already showing signs of an intention to move into the Balkans. Eden, who had succeeded Lord Halifax as Foreign Secretary at the turn of the year, was extremely keen to involve Turkey on our side and believed that British intervention in Greece was essential to that. The result was a decision on 9 January, firmly opposed by Wavell and his colleagues, that help to Greece was to take priority over all operations in the Middle East, once Tobruk had been taken. However, when the port fell, intelligence showed that German moves towards the Balkans were not as imminent as had appeared, and Wavell was allowed to let O'Connor advance as far as Benghazi 'provided that the move would not prejudice the formation of a strategic reserve for employment in Greece or Turkey'.

Signs that the Italians were preparing to withdraw from Benghazi towards Tripolitania sparked O'Connor to move rapidly to cut them off, which he succeeded in completing on 7 February at Beda Fomm, his small force capturing 25,000 prisoners, 100 tanks and 100 guns. In two months O'Connor's force of basically two divisions, one armoured and one infantry, had captured 130,000 prisoners, 380 tanks and 845 guns at a cost of 2,000 casualties, a quarter of them killed. O'Connor wanted to push on the 500 miles to Tripoli, but London would not agree, and it would have been very difficult, if not impossible, to have provided air, naval and logistic support to him there. Had he been allowed to do so, and had he reached Tripoli within four days, he would have forestalled the arrival of Lieutenant-General Erwin Rommel and the first troops of the German 5th Light Division, with all the consequences that might have had for the course of the war in the Mediterranean.

The Germans had first considered joining the Italians in North Africa in October 1940. If there was a chance that Graziani might reach the Nile they wanted to be in on the act, and sent General von Thoma to investigate. He advised against, unless at least four German divisions were employed; and as logistics would not support them in addition to Graziani's nine, four of the Italians would have to be withdrawn. The Italians would not agree to that. When Hitler and Mussolini met on 19

January it was a very different kettle of fish: now it was a question of the minimum to save the Italians from total collapse and the danger that they might pull out of the war. It was therefore agreed that two German divisions, a normal armoured one (15th Panzer) and a light one (5th Light, later renamed 21st Panzer), should be sent, 5th Light immediately, to be complete in Libya by mid-April, and 15th by mid-May.

Rommel had no inkling that he was destined to command the Afrika Korps, and was at home on leave when he was summoned to see Hitler and told to go immediately via Rome to Tripoli, where he would be under the command of Graziani. When he reached Tripoli on 12 February Graziani had left, handing over to his chief of staff, General Gariboldi. The Italians were planning to defend Tripoli in the hilly country fifty miles east of the town, but Rommel persuaded them to move 350 miles further east to the south-east corner of the Gulf of Sirte. There he sent his reconnaissance troops as soon as they arrived, reinforcing them with Italians and taking operational command himself.

Wavell learned of the arrival of German troops at Tripoli on 22 February, the day that Rommel's reconnaissance units first met their British counterparts, but he was not unduly worried. O'Connor was not well and had been replaced in Cyrenaica by Lieutenant-General Sir Philip Neame, who with a VC and DSO from the First World War had a high reputation. His experienced troops, 7th Armoured and 6th Australian Divisions, had been replaced by the inexperienced and ill-equipped 2nd Armoured (Major-General M. D. Gambier-Parry) and 9th Australian (Major-General Leslie Morshead), and his logistic support was precarious, priority having been switched to Maitland Wilson's Expeditionary Force to Greece, which landed there on 8 March. Wavell told Neame that the enemy would not be in a position to take the offensive until May, by which time the campaign against the Italians in Abyssinia, which was going well, should be over, and troops from there could be transferred to reinforce him. Meanwhile the preservation of his force was more important than holding ground: Benghazi was 'of little importance and it is certainly not worth risking defeat to retain it'.

Rommel's orders were that he could undertake limited operations up to fifty miles from where he was in contact, but that he must wait until 15th Panzer Division had arrived in May before embarking on an offensive to regain Benghazi. However, when he found that his attempts to improve his position led to a withdrawal of the British troops facing him, he moved rapidly to exploit the situation and soon threw 2nd Armoured Division into utter confusion, aggravated by constant changes of orders from Wavell downwards, made worse by failure in communication. Wavell sent O'Connor up to 'advise' Neame, both of them being captured as the Australians withdrew to the defences of Tobruk, and the armoured division disintegrated. Wavell flew to Tobruk, reinforcing the stalwart Morshead's 9th Australian Division with another brigade. On 11 April, however, Rommel had invested the garrison, driving away a hastily organized mobile force back to the Egyptian frontier, from which he dislodged them towards the end of the month, as the evacuation of Wilson's force from Greece was in train.

Abyssinia

Failure in Greece and Crete had overshadowed the success of the campaign in Abyssinia, in which forces from the Sudan (4th and 5th Indian Divisions, under the command of Lieutenant-General Sir William Platt), attacked from the north and those from Kenya (1st South African and 11th and 12th African Divisions, under Lieutenant-General Sir Alan Cunningham), from the south. Platt's forces advanced into Eritrea on 19 January, capturing Agordat by the end of the month. He then faced the formidable natural defences of Keren. Meanwhile Cunningham was advancing against much weaker opposition, capturing the port of Mogadishu in Somaliland at the end of February and reaching Jijiga in Abyssinia on 20 March, five days after Platt had launched his attack on Keren, which ended in total victory on the 26th. Cunningham entered the capital, Addis Ababa, on 6 April, while a force from Aden reoccupied British Somaliland. 5th Indian Division then advanced on Amba Alagi from the north, while 1st South African did so from the south and Orde Wingate's Gideon Force, bringing the Emperor Haile Selassie with it, made its way through the mountains to join them. Amba Alagi was successfully assaulted on 15 May, the Duke of Aosta, the commander-in-chief, opening negotiations the next day for an armistice, which took effect on the 19th, when the five-thousand-strong garrison marched past a guard of honour and was disarmed. However it was not until the end of June that the last Italian resistance at Gondar was overcome.

The 1/6th Battalion of the King's African Rifles was involved in these operations and Lieutenant John Pitt describes the crossing of the Billate River near Colito on 19 May:

Soon we were told that we were to go through the Nigerians and attack the Italians across the river. I little realised as we went forward I was to be involved in or witness several incidents which were to remain for ever on my mind.

D Company was to do a frontal attack, while two other companies were to swing off to our right. We soon came under artillery fire; this time, profiting from our experience on the Little Dababa, we all went to earth and there was no semblance of any panic. After a while our own artillery came into action, the enemy firing ceased and we were able to pull back a little. We were then told to move round to our left and launch an attack on the enemy's right flank while the two other companies were to try and across the river higher up and attack the Italian left flank.

Usually Nos 17 and 18 (mine) platoons were in front, but as we had already been under shellfire, Nos 19 and 20 moved off and 17 and 18 fell into reserve. When 19 and 20 came out of the bush they were held down by light machine-gun fire and so 17 and 18 were told to come up on the left and see what they could do. We too came under fire and both my machine-gun sections took cover behind large antheaps. At this stage I took one gun forward and got it into action; the team at once joined me, so I handed over and went back for the other gun which I also got into action. I had to stop firing after each burst or two, as the enemy fire was, very fortunately, a bit low and the dust from the bullets obscured my targets. By now the company commander and more of our own askaris* had come up and the other gun section took over. Under cover of their fire we then prepared to launch a bayonet attack. Two of my men had been wounded so I took one rifle and off we charged down the slope to the river. The sight of the cold steel was too much for the Italians who started waving white handkerchiefs. We certainly had the blood lust up and I had to draw my revolver to stop some of my men from

---

* African soldiers.

taking pot shots at the surrendering enemy, who were coming out of the small gulleys on the other bank. I asked myself later 'Would I have used the bayonet?' The answer was 'Yes, after all it was war, though I might have used my revolver instead.' Thanks to some timbers from the blown bridge I was able to get my men across the river and round up our prisoners, some of whom were wounded. I do not remember what I did with them, but presumably left a few men to guard them.

By this time, judging from the sounds from our right, it was evident that the encircling companies were mopping up the enemy's left flank. I took stock of our resources and found that most of my platoon, some of No. 17 and the Forward Observation Officer (FOO) of our gunners were across and learnt that a medium machine-gun section from 3 KAR was about to join us.

We then heard enemy tanks, so I put my men into the heads of the little gulleys back from the river bank, thanking God for the erosion which had caused them. We were quite safe there as only grenades lobbed from a tank could reach us and from our experience at Afmadu we knew that there was little danger in them.

After a while we heard the tanks withdraw, so we went cautiously up the bank on to the flatter ground beyond. We found two abandoned 65 mm guns; we turned them round to face a possible further counter-attack, the FOO having shown us how to load and fire the guns. The medium machine-guns I put out on our flanks and covered these guns with my own LMGs further out and some riflemen. We then sat back with some confidence, waiting for the anticipated counter-attack to develop further. This was not to be, thanks to the gallantry of Sergeant Nigel Leakey, one of the battalion's 3" mortar sergeants. He had gone round with the two companies who had crossed the river higher up and then attacked the enemy's left flank. His section had run out of mortar bombs, so he had joined the forward troops when the tanks came in. He was seen to leap on to the back of a tank, open the turret and shoot the occupants; he then went off after another tank, revolver in hand, and was never seen again. It transpired that he had shot the tank commander; this was too much for the others who turned and fled to Soddu. For this single handed action, which halted the Italian counter-attack, Nigel Leakey was in due course awarded a posthumous Victoria Cross.

Greece and Crete

The campaign in Greece had not had such a happy result. In January 1941 there were increasing signs of German intentions to push through the Balkans, having already moved troops into Hungary and Romania with the cooperation of their rulers. Churchill, Eden and the whole Defence Committee agreed on 9 January to 'do everything possible, by hook and crook, to send at once to Greece the fullest support within our power'. The principal purpose was not just to honour Britain's guarantee of support to Greece, made at the time of the Italian invasion of Albania, but to try to persuade Turkey to join the British in resisting German aggression in the area, and to demonstrate to the USA that the British were prepared to fight the Germans and not just confine their efforts to the Italians. Wavell and his colleagues were told that 'assistance to Greece must now take priority over all operations in the Middle East once Tobruk is taken, because help for Greece must, in the first instance, at least, came almost entirely from you'. The curt reply was: 'With our present resources we can give no direct assistance to Greece and Turkey', which brought a sharp rejoinder from Churchill: 'We expect and require prompt and active compliance with our decision for which we bear full responsibility.'

From then on Churchill and the Chiefs-of-Staff in London, the Commanders-in-Chief in the Middle East and the Greek authorities wavered to and fro in their enthusiasm for the venture. The one voice constantly urging the dispatch of an Expeditionary Force was that of Eden. His main aim was to persuade Turkey to join the Allied ranks; but he was also concerned to impress the United States, where President Roosevelt's Lend-Lease Act was facing a difficult passage through Congress. Wavell's naval and air colleagues were sceptical, but if he was prepared to accept it as a viable operation they were prepared to support him. Wavell's own attitude was crucial to the decision to dispatch the force, but remains enigmatic. There is no doubt that Eden, who was in the Middle East at the time with Dill, brought great pressure to bear on him, but he was not a man who normally gave way to pressure. After a crucial meeting in Cairo on 21 February, following discussion in Greece and Turkey, Eden signalled Churchill: 'We are agreed we should do everything in our power to bring the fullest measure of help to Greeks at earliest possible moment.' But the previous day Churchill had told the War Cabinet: 'It is unlikely that it would be possible for a large British force to get [to Greece] before the Germans.' In tune with that pessimism, he signalled Eden: 'Do not consider yourself obligated to a Greek enterprise if in your hearts you feel it will only be another Norwegian fiasco. If no good plan can be made, please say so', but he qualified that by adding: 'But of course you know how valuable success would be.'

Eden's reply, based on his meetings with the Commanders-in-Chief, admitted that the dispatch of troops would be a gamble. He reminded Churchill that before he left London they had been prepared to 'run the risk of failure, thinking it is better to suffer with the Greeks than to make no attempt to help them. That is the conviction we all hold here . . . we are not without hope that it might succeed to the extent of halting the Germans before they overrun all Greece'. Next day Eden, Dill, Wavell and Longmore flew to Athens, where Wavell took the lead in persuading the Greeks to accept the force and to agree that it would be deployed on the line of the River Aliakhmon, just north of Mount Olympus, to which Greek divisions further north in Macedonia would be withdrawn.

In London the Chiefs-of-Staff showed no enthusiasm for approving the dispatch of the force to Greece, but they advised the Defence Committee that as the Middle East Commanders-in-Chief 'evidently think there is a reasonable chance of successfully holding a German advance, we feel we must accept their opinion'. Nevertheless, the Director of Military Intelligence in the War Office advised the Vice-CIGS (Lieutenant-General Sir Albert Haining, acting for Dill in his absence) that 'We must be prepared to face the loss of all forces sent to Greece'. Eden's signal had restored the confidence of Churchill, who more or less bulldozed the War Cabinet into agreeing on 23 February and then signalled Eden: 'Decision was unanimous in the sense you desire. Therefore, while being under no illusions, we all send you the order "Full Steam Ahead".'

That was not the end of the matter. After a visit to Turkey, Eden and Dill returned to Athens on 2 March, three days before the force was due to sail from Alexandria, to find that the Greeks showed no sign of uncovering Salonika by withdrawing to the Aliakhmon as agreed, Bulgaria having joined the Axis on 1 March and invited German troops into the country. Even before then, in the light of the ULTRA* information, Churchill was again getting cold feet, and Eden's party in Athens found themselves having to prove once more to London that the chances of success still justified implementing the previous decision. Cunningham and Longmore were certainly not optimistic. Wavell insisted that given the uncertainty of the Yugoslav position only the Aliakhmon line offered a reasonable chance for a successful defence. Dill took the lead in discussion and negotiated with General Papagos, the Greek Commander-in-Chief, an agreement that the equivalent of three Greek divisions would join the British on the Aliakhmon. They returned to Cairo, where Wavell briefed the Australian and New Zealand commanders, Lieutenant-General Sir Thomas Blamey and Major-General Bernard Freyberg. After reconsidering the matter, Eden signalled Churchill: 'We are unanimously agreed that, despite the heavy commitments and grave risks which are undoubtedly involved, especially in view of our limited naval and air resources, the right decision was taken in Athens.' The War Cabinet gave its blessing next day, 7 March, the day before the first troops, acting on the decision taken on 23 February, were due to disembark in Greece.

The troops involved were the 2nd New Zealand (Freyberg) and the 6th Australian Division (Major-General Sir Ivan Mackay), formed into an ANZAC Corps commanded by Lieutenant-General Blamey, and the British 1st Armoured Brigade, detached from the 2nd Armoured Division, which had replaced the 7th in Libya. The first troops began landing at Piraeus on 7 March, and except for part of the Australian Division were in position on the Aliakhmon line when on 6 April Germany declared war simultaneously on Yugoslavia and Greece, invading both. One corps of Field Marshal List's Twelfth German Army swept through southern Yugoslavia; the other two crossed the Greek frontier with Bulgaria and entered Salonika on 9 April, while 1st Armoured Brigade withdrew from Thrace to the left of the Aliakhmon line.

Greek plans had assumed that Yugoslavia would remain neutral. They could not provide forces to hold a German thrust from that direction. Wilson therefore decided that the Aliakhmon line was in danger of being

---

* ULTRA was the codename for intelligence obtained by the interception and decryption of German signal traffic encoded by the machine named ENIGMA. It was only available to commanders at a high level.

outflanked and that he must withdraw. By 15 April the Germans were pressing hard on his troops as they stepped back from position to position, constantly harried from the air. He met General Papagos, who suggested that British troops should leave the country, and he realized that evacuation was the only sensible course. His aim was to conduct an effective delaying action to make that possible, the next stand to be on the line of the famous pass of Thermopylae. Wavell came to Athens on 19 April, reaching agreement on evacuation with the King and his Government, the Prime Minister, Mr Koryzis, having committed suicide. Greek forces capitulated on the 21st. Evacuation was to take place from ports and beaches in Attica, as long as that was possible, and from those in the Peloponnese (Morea), further away from airfields the Germans were using. The only route lay by the one bridge over the Corinth Canal, which was blown before two German parachute battalions dropped to seize it on 26 April. By 1 May the evacuation was complete, 50,732* men being embarked out of the 60,000 sent to Greece; 7,000 (of whom 2,000 were Cypriots or Palestinians) were captured as they were about to embark at Kalamata. All equipment that could not be carried personally was left behind.

Just over half went to Crete, principally in order to provide a quicker turnround of ships, and the question of Crete's future became an immediate issue. Wilson arrived there on 27 April and asked for orders. Wavell had just learned from ULTRA that the Germans were planning an airborne assault on the island, possibly as a stepping stone to Cyprus or Syria, or to Iraq, where a political adventurer, Rashid Ali, had staged a successful coup against the Government of the Regent, who had fled to British protection. Wavell told Wilson that Crete was to be denied to the enemy, who, according to London's intelligence estimate, would probably combine an airborne with a seaborne attack, and was unlikely to attempt the former without the latter. Based on this, Churchill signalled Wavell that the island must be stubbornly defended and said that it ought to be 'a fine opportunity for killing parachute troops'.

The trouble was that the 6,000 British troops already on the island had been sent there solely for the close defence of the temporary naval base at Suda Bay. No preparations had been made for a major defence of the island, which would not have been threatened if the expedition to

---

* This figure included an uncertain number of Greeks and Yugoslavs.

Greece had succeeded in its aim. The 21,000 troops that arrived from Greece had no transport and no heavy weapons. They had expected to move on back to Egypt. Freyberg was far from pleased when on 30 April he was told by Wavell, who had flown to Crete, that on orders from London his troops were to stay there and he himself was to be placed in command of the defence of the island. Next day, after Freyberg had studied London's estimate of the scale of enemy attack, he signalled Wavell that unless air and naval support was increased to reduce the estimated threat his forces were 'totally inadequate to meet attack envisaged' and urged that the decision to hold Crete should be reconsidered. He sent a similar message to the New Zealand Prime Minister, Peter Fraser, saying that there was no evidence that naval support would be capable of guaranteeing him against seaborne attack and that the air forces available on the island were hopelessly inadequate.

Wavell, backed by Admiral Cunningham, replied that the navy would support him, and that even if it was decided to reverse the decision to hold Crete there was little time to evacuate the troops. Churchill followed up with reassuring messages to the New Zealand Prime Minister, who had decided to fly to London, and to Freyberg himself, saying that he was confident that his 'fine troops will destroy parachutists man to man at close quarters'.

Freyberg's moods were as changeable as Churchill's. On 5 May he replied:

> Cannot understand nervousness: am not in the least anxious about airborne attack; have made my dispositions and feel can cope adequately with troops at my disposal. Combination of seaborne and airborne attack is different. If that comes before I can get guns and transport here the situation will be difficult. Even so, provided Navy can help, trust all will be well. When we get equipment and transport, and with a few extra fighter aircraft, it should be possible to hold Crete. Meanwhile there will be a period here during which we shall be vulnerable. Everybody in great form and most anxious to renew battle with an enemy, whom we hammered every time we met him in Greece.

Most of the troops on the island were from Freyberg's division, but a regular British brigade, the 14th, was already there with a number of Royal Marine and Royal Artillery air and coast defence units, the anti-aircraft having thirty-eight heavy and thirty-six light guns. Nine Matilda Mark II infantry and six light tanks provided the only armour available. The troops brought there from Greece included a large number of artillery units without their guns, as well as administrative units of all kinds. There were ten Greek battalions. Freyberg's defence plan was dictated by the topography of the island and what he knew, from ULTRA, of German plans. It was clear that the key points to be defended were the airfields at Maleme in the west, Retimo, fifty miles further east, and Heraklion another fifty miles beyond; Maleme was the most important, both on account of its position and because it was the only one from which combat or transport aircraft could be operated without further development. Suda Bay was also of considerable importance. The fact that only one single road joined these areas, that Freyberg had very few vehicles and that movement in daylight was hazardous in the face of total German air supremacy meant that he had to distribute his forces widely and that he could not rely on one area reinforcing another. His own division, command of which he handed over to Brigadier E. Puttick, was in the western sector, covering Maleme. East of it, the Suda Bay–Canea area was held by a composite force under the command of the Royal Marine Major-General E. C. Weston, who had been in command of troops in the island before Wilson's arrival. The Retimo area was the responsibility of Brigadier G. A. Vasey's 19th Australian Brigade and Heraklion of Brigadier B. H. Chappel's 14th British Brigade.

On 25 April Hitler directed the Luftwaffe, with General Student's Fliegerkorps XI, flying from airfields in Greece, to capture Crete 'as a base for air warfare against Great Britain in the eastern Mediterranean'. Student planned to attack all three airfields with his parachute troops, and then fly in the 5th and 6th Mountain Divisions to land at whichever one or ones he had captured. A seaborne expedition, including part of the 5th Panzer Division, would follow up. Intense air attacks in preparation for this started on 14 May, and the assault itself, preceded by devastating air attacks by the 430 bombers and 230 fighters of Fliegerkorps VIII, was made at dawn on 20 May. The parachutists, many of whom landed directly over the defending troops, suffered very heavy casualties; but by first light on 21 May the Germans had secured Maleme airfield. Failure to deliver an effective counter-attack to regain it that day proved fatal, and by the end of the day German transport aircraft were landing there.

Fighting was fierce between Maleme and Suda over the next few days, as the Germans flew in more and more troops and pounded the New Zealand and other areas mercilessly from the air. The total German air supremacy, reinforced by the occupation of Maleme, meant that the Royal Navy would have increasing difficulty in reaching the north of the island, where the only usable ports were, and in preventing further attempts by the Germans to reinforce their forces by sea. On 26 May Freyberg signalled to Wavell that the fall of Crete could only be a matter of time and next day Wavell ordered evacuation. The New Zealanders, with all the British and Australian troops at Suda and Georgopolis, were to make their way by the narrow road through the mountains to the little port of Sphakia on the south coast. The Australians at Retimo were intended to make their way south to Plaka Bay, but never received the order to do so and were eventually forced to surrender. 14th Brigade was embarked from Heraklion itself, but 800 of its 4,000 men were lost when the ships carrying them were attacked and sunk by German aircraft. The final embarkation from Sphakia took place on 1 June. By then 18,000 men, including 1,500 wounded, had been evacuated. 1,742 were killed, of whom 797 were British, 671 New Zealand and 274 Australian; 1,737 wounded, of whom 1,467 were Australian and New Zealand; and 11,835 taken prisoner, of whom 3,079 were Australian and 2,180 New Zealand. The navy lost 1,828 killed and 183 wounded: one aircraft carrier, three battleships, six cruisers and seven destroyers were damaged, while three cruisers and six destroyers had been sunk.

Gunner James Brooks of 64th Medium Regiment, Royal Artillery, was one of the fortunate ones who had come through unscathed. His account, in a letter home, starts with his arrival in Greece:

We managed to spend a couple of hours in Athens and found it a very interesting place. We soon moved from there, and started on our trek towards the border, we passed through a lot of towns, the name of one of them sticks in my memory, Larissa, a town devastated by earthquakes and bombed by the Italians. We arrived at our position near a village called Kelly, dug our pits, and made ourselves as comfortable as was possible, incidentally this is where I received my first batch of mail from home. While we were there Mr Eden and Sir John Dill paid us a flying visit and chatted with some of the boys. On the 6th of April Germany declared war on Yugoslavia and started moving towards Greece. On the 8th we moved out of the position without firing a round, the Germans had started to get round us, we had rather a job getting out, as it had been raining for days and the lorries and guns were bogged. We moved a few miles down the road & took up a position near a village called Vivy. We fired our first rounds at the Gerry on the afternoon of the tenth, we were told to stop at the position for 48 hours we managed to carry on for 72 hrs, the Germans made many attacks, but were pushed back each time, and we inflicted many casualties, all the time we were at Vivy it was raining and snowing, we couldn't get any sleep and we were soaked through, we only got out by the skin of our teeth, only a handful of infantry and a couple of anti-tank guns was all that was between us and the Gerry, and the anti-tank guns were firing at tanks which we could see coming over the hills as we were going down the road, one of the guns toppled over into a ditch and had to be blown up, but we were very lucky not to lose any men. From there we went to a position on the Serbian frontier. The Greeks held a line here and we had come up to give them a hand. But the next day the Greeks had to throw the towel in, they were streaming along the road, most of them walking, some of them in stockinged feet, they were very poorly equipped, and no match for the Germans. We had to get out of there in a hurry, and the lorrys and guns were stuck in the mud again. We travelled all the next day across a plain and were bombed and machinegunned the whole way, the road was packed tight with our vehicles and made a marvellous target for the Gerry pilots, it was here that our Colonel was killed by a bomb splinter, it was a tragic loss to us, as he was a good chap, we lost several other chaps as well.

We stopped under some trees for a couple of days for a rest, and it was here that Mr Churchill had promised us Air Support. From there we moved up to a position near the town of Molass and dug our pits, we had a Parade there and the Major told us that the Greeks had capitulated and we had to get out, but we were going to go up and have another crack at him. We moved up under cover of darkness, and fired all the next day, we made such a nuisance of ourselves the Germans sent waves of Dive bombers after us, and as they failed to stop us firing, shelled us from all sides, you can imagine how much we looked forward to nightfall, when we knew that we were getting out for good. A truck loaded with fags tried to get to us, but was shot up by aircraft, so bang went our fag issue. When the sun did go down, we put all the guns out of action, and the whole troop, or what was left of them, boarded the one lorry, which was ours, and set off for Athens. I don't remember much of the journey as I was asleep most of the time, but I was told afterwards that behind could be seen the headlights of the German column coming up the road. We passed through Athens on our way, and the population cheered us again, eventually we arrived at the coast, and hid the lorry under some trees, where it was put out of action, we rested all day, and in the evening marched down to the beach, we had to leave all our kit behind except our small packs and the clothes we wore. After waiting for several hours a lighter pulled in, and we climbed aboard, we transferred from there to a destroyer. We have often used the term 'thank God we've got a Navy' but we used it there, they gave us a wonderful welcome, we sat down to a swell tea, and were given cigarettes. We started moving in the early hours of the morning, and kept going till the afternoon, we had a few bombing raids and one ship was sunk. On the 27th of April we landed on Crete, when I was walking up the road towards the reception camp I got talking to a chap in the Mercantile Navy, I thought I recognised him and he turned out to be a chap named Harris who used to live in Duncan Terrace, he [used] to work down the Initial yard remember him?

After hanging about for a few hours we marched to an area under some olive trees and settled down. We were quite near a town called Canea and went there several times there was a NAFFI there and I met a chap who used to belong to my Cycling Club he was in the RAF. We also went swimming a few times. After a few days rest we started to do Parachute Patrol, every day the Gerry planes came over and Dive bombed Suda Bay. Every day troops were leaving the Island en route for Egypt and we began to wonder when our turn would come. After about a fortnight we collected some 105 M.M. Italian Guns and set out for the other end of the Island, on arrival we manhandled the guns into position and dug ourselves in. We were told to expect a lot of enemy air activity and we got it, at all times of the day single planes used to come over, poodle around dropping bombs and machine gunning and nobody to stop them, we had one old Gladiator and that used to go up and have a go, but that was soon written off. This went on for a couple of days, and in between air raids we dug slit trenches, and stacked the ammunition. On the

20th of April [May], we sent a couple of chaps on a days leave to
Heraklion or Candia, the capital of Crete, it's known by both names,
a fairly big town, in the afternoon, the usual bombing and strafing
increased until the sky was full of planes of all sizes with dirty black
crosses on them, needless to say we were down our holes, and
although cramped not worrying much, as they didn't pay much
attention to us, at about 4-30 the bombing stopped and only the
drone of the planes could be heard, and then somebody pointed out
to sea, and we could see big troop carriers coming in skimming the
water, they were upon us in know time and parachutists were
dropping in all directions, those of us who had rifles started to let go,
and everybody was out of their holes, either firing or cheering, a
solitary Bofors gun which had kept silent all through the afternoon
started firing, and the troop carriers, being very slow, made a perfect
target for its shells. I saw four burst into flames and other chaps said
they saw six, we could see the Germans trying frantically to get out
of the burning planes, some jumping with their chutes in flames, one
of the Gerrys landed in a cornfield near our position, and I and a
few more of our troop went after him, we soon finished him off, but
not before he had hit one of our chaps with a burst from his tommy
gun. We couldn't go into action with our guns as the telephone wire
had been cut by the bombing, but by evening it had been fixed up
and we started firing, but by then a good proportion of the Germans
had been accounted for. We fired during the night, and when
morning came, we had time to look around, all around us were
tattered and torn parachutes, some with bodies still hanging on them,
over on a hill opposite was a troop plane crash landed and near it a
couple of burnt out wrecks. About 7 o'clock we were told to stand to
as more troop carriers had been sighted, and we could see them
approaching but they avoided our side of the island and landed out
of reach of our troops. This went on for days, we were firing night
and day and we also had to do patrol duty at night we didn't get
much chance to sleep, and ammo was running low. One morning
some fighters circled overhead, and we recognised them as Hurri-
canes, they landed on the airdrome, but they didn't come up anymore
as some Gerry planes machine gunned them on the ground. Another
time some more planes were circling overhead and instead of
dropping bombs they dropped leaflets, telling us to give in or be
blasted off the earth. Our cookhouse was some distance from the

guns, and to get to it we had to cross an open field, we always made a dash across here, and sometimes a Gerry sniper would take a pot at us and we would finish up by crawling on our guts with our mess tins to get our grub. On the 28th May, the air raids seemed a bit heavier, bombs dropping quite near to our position, and we prepared for more parachutists, but they didn't come, after the raid we were told to be prepared to evacuate the island. We smashed the guns up, dumped what kit we had, and as soon as it was dark marched down to Heraklion harbour, where we boarded a destroyer without much hanging about, As soon as it was light, and we were on the move, the Luftwaffe was after us, and right until we were only a few miles from Alex [Alexandria], we were continually bombed and machine gunned.

Many boats were hit and a lot of chaps were killed, we were very lucky only one sailor was killed, hit by a cannon shell. The Navy saved us again, and we got out just in time, they treated us the usual way tea directly we were on board, and as much grub to eat as we wanted. We arrived in Alex on the night of the 29th, and lorries took us to a camp in the town, where we got some well earned sleep, even the Ack Ack* guns banging away didn't keep us awake, and they were right next door.

Iraq and Syria

Between the evacuation from Greece and the German attack on Crete Wavell had a major row with Churchill over Iraq. Auchinleck, the Commander-in-Chief in India, held responsibility for army matters there, although the only British forces stationed in the country, the Royal Air Force, came under Longmore. In response to Rashid Ali's rebellion, 20th Indian Brigade, sailing from India, started disembarking at Basra on 30 April, Major-General W. A. Fraser assuming command with the headquarters of 10th Indian Division. Rashid Ali's reaction was to surround the RAF base at Habbaniya, fifty miles west of Baghdad, and

* Anti-aircraft.

to start shelling it on 2 May. To the consternation of Wavell, who justifiably felt that he had enough on his hands already, the Defence Committee in London on that day transferred responsibility for Iraq to him and told him to send troops to relieve the siege of Habbaniya. Wavell, who had just returned from visiting the troops facing Rommel on the Libyan–Egyptian frontier, flashed back: 'I have consistently warned you that no assistance could be given to Iraq from Palestine in present circumstances . . . My forces are stretched to the limit everywhere and I simply cannot afford to risk part of forces on what cannot produce any effect.' The Chiefs of Staff replied that it was essential to restore the situation at Habbaniya and control the oil pipeline from northern Iraq to Haifa, adding: 'Positive action as soon as forces can be made available will be necessary.' Wavell aggravated matters by starting his response: 'Your [signal] takes little account of reality. You must face facts.' He went on to list the small force he felt able to send, adding: 'Very doubtful whether above force strong enough to relieve Habbaniya or whether Habbaniya can prolong resistance till its arrival. I am afraid I can only regard it as an outside chance. I feel it my duty to warn you in gravest possible terms that I consider prolongation of fighting in Iraq will seriously endanger defence of Palestine and Egypt. Apart from the weakening of our strength by detachments such as above, political repercussions will be incalculable and may result in what I have spent two years trying to avoid, serious internal trouble in our bases.'

Wavell was quite wrong. The spirited action of the garrison of Habbaniya and the arrival of the small force – a brigade improvised from the cavalry division in Palestine in the process of being converted from horses to trucks – resulted in the collapse of Rashid Ali's revolt. His protest critically undermined the little confidence which Churchill had in him.

Iraq was not the only source of Churchill's dissatisfaction. General Charles de Gaulle had arrived in Egypt in April and tried to persuade Wavell to support with tanks and aircraft an attempt by Free French forces to enter Syria, then held by French forces loyal to Vichy, in the hope that after token resistance they would change sides. Wavell refused. On 14 May it was confirmed that German aircraft were using Syrian airfields en route to Iraq to help Rashid Ali, and Wavell was pressed to reverse his decision. He replied that he was fully committed and that such an expedition 'would be painfully reminiscent of the Jameson Raid and might suffer the same fate'. The signal was sent on the day after the failure of an attempt to dislodge Rommel's forces from the Libyan frontier area. It was the final straw that caused Churchill to tell Dill on 19 May, the day before the German attack on Crete, that he had decided to replace Wavell by Auchinleck. He was persuaded to hold his hand; but, as the attack on Crete was launched, Wavell was told to undertake an operation against Syria, Churchill's signal ending with the words: 'We of course take full responsibility for this decision and should you find yourself unwilling to give effect to it, arrangements will be made to meet any wish you may express to be relieved of your command.'

Wavell was forced to comply. The task was given to the 7th Australian Division (Major-General J. D. Laverack) with some troops also from the 6th and from the 1st British Cavalry Division. A Free French force of about six battalions under Brigadier-General Legentilhomme also took part. It proved to be a slow and expensive campaign, ending with the capitulation of General Dentz's Vichy French forces on 12 July. British (mostly Australian) casualties of all kinds totalled 3,300, those of the Free French 1,300. Vichy French losses are thought to have been about 6,000, of whom 1,000 were killed.

The Western Desert

Wavell's fate was sealed by the failure of Operation BATTLEAXE to drive the German–Italian forces back from the Libyan–Egyptian frontier and relieve the besieged garrison of Tobruk. Since Rommel had invested the fortress on 11 April he had made several unsuccessful attempts to penetrate the defences of the 9th Australian Division, supported by a number of British artillery units and a small number of tanks, organized from several different units into one composite regiment. Towards the end of April Rommel's forces on the frontier drove back Brigadier Gott's mobile columns, based on 22nd Guards Brigade, and forced them to withdraw below the escarpment near Sollum, a few days before Rommel launched a major attack on Tobruk on 30 April, which failed with heavy loss.

The investment of Tobruk had provoked Churchill to respond to an urgent request from Wavell by sending a convoy, named Tiger, carrying 295 tanks and 53 modern Hurricane aircraft, through the Mediterranean rather than all the way round the Cape. One ship, carrying 57 tanks and 10 aircraft, was sunk on the way, but the rest arrived safely in Alexandria on 12 May. Churchill was anxious to see them in action against Rommel without delay, and kept on pressing Wavell for early action, but they were not all unloaded for another two weeks and then needed workshop attention and modification for desert conditions. Before the convoy arrived, Wavell ordered Beresford-Pierse, who was now commanding Western Desert Force, to recapture the escarpment at Halfaya and Sollum and the defences round Fort Capuzzo, and, if possible, relieve Tobruk before the German 15th Panzer Division, which was on its way from Italy, could reinforce Rommel. The force employed to do this on 15 May was too weak and could do no more than recapture Halfaya Pass, which the Germans took back again at the end of the month with a strong force of 160 tanks.

The loss of Halfaya complicated the plan for the next attempt to make the pendulum swing the other way, known as Operation BAT-TLEAXE. Unfortunately security was not what it had been for the Battle of Sidi Barrani, and Rommel made good use of wireless intercept to lay his plans. Beresford-Pierse's force consisted of two divisions. On the coast was 4th Indian Division (Major-General F. W. Messervy). Its 11th Indian Brigade, on the coast road, was to recapture Halfaya Pass, while 22nd Guards Brigade and 4th Armoured Brigade, with most of the hundred Matilda tanks, above the escarpment, were to advance to recapture the oft-disputed area of Capuzzo. 7th Armoured Division, still commanded by Creagh, was to move round the western flank by Sidi Omar, 7th Armoured Brigade with about a hundred cruiser tanks leading, while the Support Group formed a screen towards Sidi Omar. It was hoped that 4th Armoured Brigade would join the division, if this move led to a clash with the German armour.

Rommel had entrusted the defence of the frontier to the newly arrived 15th Panzer Division, who were fortunate to have some of the new 50mm anti-tank guns as well as their 88mms. Their eighty tanks were held just to the north, those of 5th Light Division being kept partly to watch Tobruk and partly near Gambut, halfway in between.

The attack was launched on 15 June. By the end of the day 4th

Armoured Brigade had penetrated to the north of Capuzzo, but had not been followed by the Guards Brigade; 7th Armoured Brigade had run up against 88mm guns on the left, and with casualties and breakdowns was reduced to forty-eight tanks. On the right 11th Indian Brigade had failed to recapture Halfaya. Rommel had moved up 5th Light Division and gave it the task for 16 June of carrying out a wide sweep round the flank and rear of 7th Armoured Division, while 15th Panzer's tanks counter-attacked at Capuzzo.

Beresford-Pierse's plan was to leave the task of clearing up the Capuzzo–Halfaya area and pressing on to Bardia to 4th Indian Division, while 4th Armoured Brigade passed to Creagh to help him against the German armour. But 15th Panzer's counter-attack to Capuzzo led to such fierce fighting that the brigade could not be released, and 7th Armoured Brigade's cruisers had to face the German tanks with the help only of Gott's Support Group. Their battle lasted all day, as they were forced back to Sidi Omar. The plan for the 17th was much the same. Gatehouse's 4th Armoured Brigade was to leave the Guards to secure Capuzzo by themselves, and to pass to Creagh for a joint effort to defeat the German tanks. Rommel's plan, based again on what he had learned from intercepting British radio conversations, was much more ambitious: two enveloping hooks were to squeeze the British in a pincer, one side of which was the beleaguered garrison of Halfaya, the other being provided by both his panzer divisions, starting from south of Capuzzo at dawn. Gatehouse managed to hold his ground for a time, but was reduced in strength to seventeen Matildas. Creagh's cruisers, down to only twenty-eight, could not hold the wider thrust on his left flank, and it appeared that the whole force above the escarpment might be cut off. Retreat was the only answer, and back they went, leaving sixty-four of the hundred Matildas and twenty-seven of the cruiser tanks knocked out or broken down on the battlefield.

The defeat came as a bitter blow to Churchill, who had expected much to result from the risks he had taken in sending the Tiger convoy through the Mediterranean. It was not long before heads began to roll, and the first to go was Wavell. The order for him to change places with Auchinleck in India left Whitehall on 21 June, the day before Hitler invaded Russia. Beresford-Pierse and Creagh left also, while Messervy remained, as did the brigadiers, of whom Gott and Gatehouse were to play prominent parts in many of the desert battles to follow. The impressions left by this battle, on participants and onlookers alike, were to have a profound influence on the plan for and the conduct of Operation CRUSADER, the next attempt to swing the pendulum. Direct assault on the fixed defences of the Capuzzo area had led to heavy losses, particularly among the Matildas, accustomed hitherto to being almost invulnerable on the battlefield. It was certainly not realized by the British, as it was by the Germans, that the 88mm guns, and perhaps the new 50mm anti-tank guns also, had been the principal cause of their defeat. Yet there were no more than thirteen 88mms in the battle. The impression left, both on the Matildas and on the cruisers, was that they were no match for the German tanks, and the same lack of confidence affected the crews of the Royal Artillery's 2-pounder anti-tank guns.

O'Connor's campaign against the Italians alone had been too easy. The Western Desert Force now faced a much more formidable foe, to defeat whom needed rigorous training of all arms to fight together under decisive professional command. That had not applied before Operation BATTLEAXE and was not to be very evident in the battles which followed later that year and in the next. It must be appreciated that nobody in the British army, at any level, had had previous experience of mobile mechanized warfare of this nature. Experience with tanks in the First World War had been limited to the close support of infantry. That was still useful with the Matildas, but of no value in the more mobile role of the 'cruisers'. Pre-war training in that role by Hobart both in the Tank Brigade and 'Mobile Division Egypt' should have helped, but he had emphasized avoiding rather than fighting the enemy, had shunned cooperation with infantry and artillery, and encouraged a dispersion, which was practised to a high degree in the desert as a protection against air attack.

Wavell's departure was inevitable. It is very difficult to make a confident judgement about the performance of that enigmatic character, especially as his personal papers have never been released. He deserves praise for planning the victories over the Italians in the Western Desert and Abyssinia, but the principal credit must go to the executors of those plans, O'Connor and Platt. His judgement in the orders he gave to Neame when faced with Rommel, in his advice to Eden over Greece, and in his outburst over Iraq, is certainly open to criticism; but he carried a tremendous burden of responsibility, was subjected to great pressure by his political masters, and clearly had inadequate resources with which to carry it.

*

General Auchinleck assumed the reins of what Churchill called 'Your Great Command' on 2 July, and almost immediately found himself urged to consider an early renewal of activity in the desert, at the same time as finishing things off in Syria. The Prime Minister was keen to take advantage of 'the temporary German preoccupation in their invasion of Russia'. The first of the many damping replies which Auchinleck was impelled to send was signalled on 4 July: 'No further offensive Western Desert should be contemplated until base is secure.'

Churchill was prompt to reply that the desert remained the decisive theatre for that year. More tanks were already on their way round the Cape and would have arrived by the end of July. Thereafter few more could arrive until October. Auchinleck was supported by his fellow Commanders-in-Chief, among whom Air Marshal A. W. Tedder had replaced Longmore, in resisting pressure to renew the offensive before at least mid-November, by which time he considered that one armoured division, an additional armoured brigade and an army tank brigade would be ready to take the field. Two armoured divisions could not be ready until the new year, and he concluded his reply with the words: 'We still consider two, preferably three armoured divisions necessary for offensive operations to retake whole Cyrenaica.' He was sent for to London, where he succeeded in resisting pressure and in getting agreement to the appointment of Lieutenant-General Sir Alan Cunningham to command the Eighth Army, as the enlarged Western Desert Force was to be called, instead of Churchill's preference, Wilson. But the seeds of mutual distrust were unfortunately sown at the meeting which were to grow and bear fruit in the dismissal of Auchinleck a year later. Matters were further complicated by the demand of the Australian Government that its 9th Division should be relieved in Tobruk so that all the Australians in the Middle East could serve together. At considerable cost to the navy, they were replaced by sea by the 70th (the former 6th) Division, a Polish brigade and a further regiment of tanks.

Auchinleck now set about building up a force with the aim not only of relieving Tobruk but of recapturing the whole of Cyrenaica, so that from its airfields the RAF could give air cover to ships sailing to and from Malta. Cunningham's Eighth Army was to have two corps, the 13th (Lieutenant-General A. R. Godwin-Austen), with 4th Indian and 2nd New Zealand Divisions, supported by 1st Army Tank Brigade's 201 infantry tanks, and the newly created 30th, with 7th Armoured Division, enlarged by the addition of 22nd Armoured Brigade, which arrived ahead of its parent division, the 1st, to a strength of 523 tanks. The corps was to be commanded by Lieutenant-General Vyvyan Pope, but he was killed in an air crash soon after arriving from England, and his place was taken by Lieutenant-General C. W. M. Norrie, who was on his way out by sea as commander of 1st Armoured Division. The corps also included 1st South African Infantry Division, in the process of being completely motorized, and 22nd Guards Brigade. This force was ready to take the offensive on 18 November.

Rommel had also been building up his forces, planning to attack Tobruk between 15 and 20 November, while still holding the defences near the frontier which he had occupied since BATTLEAXE. He had 174 German and 146 Italian tanks, the former technically superior to the British cruisers, and he had a significant superiority in anti-tank and heavy artillery.

Cunningham's plan for this Operation CRUSADER was an uneasy compromise between ensuring that 13th Corps was not vulnerable to tank attack, while dealing with the frontier defences, and concentrating the effort of 30th Corps to join up with the garrison of Tobruk as rapidly as possible. The initial advance took Rommel by surprise, but a combination of Cunningham's hesitancy with tactical failures and slow reaction in 30th Corps allowed Rommel to recover and embark on a rash counterstroke to regain contact with the frontier defences. This caused confusion and concern in the rear areas and led Cunningham to seek Auchinleck's agreement to a temporary withdrawal. The latter took the field himself, appointing one of his senior staff officers, Major-General Neil Ritchie, promoting him Lieutenant-General, to replace Cunningham. After confused and tough fighting, in which the New Zealanders played a prominent part, Tobruk was finally relieved on 8 December.

Captain Ben Thomas of the 1st Bedfords was involved in 70th Division's part in the breakout:

About midday the shelling eased and later my colonel sent me forward to find some troops of another unit who were operating somewhere on the left flank, with whom we were to join when it became dark. No information of exactly where they really were was available. Everything gets totally blind under these circumstances but off I had to go, choosing a compass bearing and counting the paces taken. This proved a ghastly episode as after about 500 yards a terrific barrage of shells came down and seemed to be directed solely on me as no other troops were there. This was just a blanketting and hope effort by the Italian gunners. I didn't know what to do – it was just as dangerous to turn back as to go on – so on I went trying to keep the same compass bearing and counting my paces. One shell landed almost at my feet knocking me flat on the ground but it was so close that all the shot went over my head umbrella-wise leaving me unharmed. Then an incident occurred that leaves me somewhat ashamed to this day but I record it. I stumbled across a solitary 'bod'. He could only have been 19 or 20 years old. He was lost from some other unit and was immobile and quite terrified – me too – but to bolster myself I tore into him for deserting or something near it and told him to get busy and catch up with his unit, which, of course, he could not possibly have done. Having plucked up courage from his plight I told him not to bother to try and find his unit saying he would be quite useless to them anyway but to get busy and walk back to where I had come from, give himself into someone's hands and mention only that he had got lost and was anxious to join his unit. But how I used him to bolster myself.

On I went and found a small body of troops, who were not our mob but after deciding that they would have to do I returned on the reverse bearing to base. So after dark following the same bearing we moved up – this must have been over a mile of ground – I praying that the compass bearing and paces were approximately OK. We hit some troops latish that night not the same ones I had found earlier but that didn't matter. They were not enemy so we joined them. There were about 40 of us in a small low circle of stones and we were shelled nearly all night but not one landed in amongst us. Before dawn the bombardment ceased and everyone went into a sleep of stupefaction but of that I was incapable. As dawn broke I had my first glance of enemy moving some way away and in a panic I woke everyone up wondering if we were to be attacked, but they moved across our front and into the distance. During the night an ambulance had moved up behind us and stuck itself unwittingly on the sky line. We got it to move back as quickly as possible but it was too late and had been spotted and once again down came the shelling. However, this soon stopped and we saw some of our own troops moving across the front on an attack in daylight. To look at they were just walking slowly forwards towards, we supposed, the enemy troops who had passed in front of us earlier. What a target they appeared to be crossing such open ground. We could hear firing being exchanged and feared for them. All then disappeared into the haze, however, we later heard that this was one of our companys. How they got to that position nobody knows but David was with them and said it was easy the opposition fading away and our casualties were few, I wonder? By now the breakout battle was getting fully engaged on all the sectors of the front and we seemed to be pushing out further away from Tobruk, no big counter attack materialised against us but we were getting stretched out both laterally and in depth with no sign of the 8th Army arriving to relieve us. The main defence line of TOBRUK was now very much depleted and we were advancing on an even deeper and widening front so there was plenty room for anxiety.

Our main objective then became 'TUGUN', where a stronghold lay on our flank which had been pretty quiet and not harassed us directly but it was unquestionably watching every move we made from our first breakout and was able from this observation post to direct all that shelling which we endured from the start.

It became absolutely vital to remove this menace so a company attack was launched in the evening but was unsuccessful. Next morning I went up there to find out all about it and things were unhappy not so much from the point of view of casualties but because a number of men were pinned down in the open and unable to move forward or backward in daylight. The main thing then appeared to be to get them off the ground. Luckily we found quite near an anti-tank gun detachment but though they were not under our orders they agreed to fit in with what we wanted without bothering to ask for permission from their bosses. A bold decision from a very junior commander to act on his own initiative. More and more of this individuality developed throughout all operations which, of course, was of infinite value in such a fluid and messed up situation.

So a ten minute blitz of anti-tank guns, machine guns mortar and rifle fire descended on 'TUGUN' and though perhaps none of the enemy were killed, by God they kept their heads down.

The men lying in the open triggered what was on and after a slight delay one, then two, then all stood up and made for home and no one from 'TUGUN' fired a single shot at them. The anti-tank guns had to up sticks and shift positions as quickly as possible for their flashes had given away their position so down came the shellings. They got away in time but unfortunately our ground troops, in the excitement of getting their men back were a little slow in moving and suffered several casualties but at least thirty or forty men had been extricated from an uncertain future.

So 'TUGUN' still remained and an attack was launched later by another company in broad daylight which set off over about a thousand yards of open ground without any tank or air support. There were only about 45 of them led by Teddy, a second lieutenant of about 21 and he must be mentioned. He was a rosy faced good looking boy of a P. G. Woodhouse character who loved girls and had gone out of his way in the past to tell everyone how frightened he was and perfectly sure he couldn't make it when the time came.

I was upside this attack about half way between their starting line and 'TUGUN' and could see the whole episode from start to finish and is as clear to me now as it was then. These 45 men just walked slowly on towards 'TUGUN' armed only with rifles a Bren gun or two and some hand grenades. 100 yards, 200 onwards up to about 300 yards from the enemy before they let loose. Here and there a man went down, hit or taking temporary cover. But Teddy strode on and Sergeant Major Kemp with him until they hit the defence wire which they bashed down or found a gap. They disappeared from sight and it seemed that about 8 or 9 men followed in and all disappeared from sight. Then there seemed an interminable lull when one couldn't tell what had happened, but all firing ceased on both sides. Then suddenly figures appeared signalling success – then more and more figures and some 80 Italians had given themselves up and were straggling back over the ground covered in the attack to surrender. In fact, they gave in when face to face with the first few of our men to get in. Then as soon as it was realised that we had taken 'TUGUN', down came the enemy shelling which was kept up the rest of the day and it was impossible to get ammunition or supplies up to them till night fall, or get the wounded

out. Luckily there were few of these, unfortunately Teddy, first man
in, had a hand to hand struggle for a moment or two and lost an eye
in the process, neither he or anyone else knows quite how. Anyway,
he was in good form when he got back and on to hospital and that
was the last we saw of him until years later we heard that he had
captured and married a rich American girl – good for him – well
deserved and he was awarded the Military Cross for the attack – not
the girl!

After a major row with General Bastico, who had succeeded Gariboldi
as his official superior, Rommel insisted on a withdrawal of the whole
Italo-German force out of Cyrenaica to Mersa Brega, from where he had
started his lightning dash at the end of March, and they were back there
in the first days of 1942. But he was not to stay there long. Additional
supplies and equipment soon reached him through Tripoli, Admiral
Cunningham's fleet having suffered several setbacks and the strength of
the German air force in the Mediterranean having been increased.
Meanwhile Godwin-Austen's corps in Cyrenaica, which now included
1st Armoured Division (Major-General H. Lumsden),* was in logistic
difficulties. On 21 January 1942 Rommel struck and repeated almost
exactly his exploit of the previous year, although this time he switched
towards Benghazi. As before, order and counterorder from above added
to confusion, and by 6 February 13th Corps was back on the line Gazala–
Bir Hacheim, covering Tobruk in an arc fifty miles west and south of
the harbour.

The Battle of Gazala, the Fall of Tobruk

Eighth Army was to stay there for three and a half months, while
acrimonious signals passed between London and Cairo. Churchill was
deeply concerned about the fate of Malta, now isolated and contributing
little towards the interference of Rommel's supply. After the fall of

---

* He was wounded in an air attack soon after arrival and replaced temporarily by Major-
General F. W. Messervy.

Singapore and the escape of the German battlecruisers the *Scharnhorst* and the *Gneisenau* up the Channel, both in mid-February, he could not afford another disaster, and pressed Auchinleck for an early reconquest of Cyrenaica. Having lost troops to the Far East, the latter was concerned at the possibility of the Germans in Russia reaching the Caucasus in the spring, and with his Indian background felt that the security of the Indian Ocean and Persian Gulf ranked higher in priority than the relief of Malta. He refused to visit London and insisted that he needed a superiority of three to two in tanks in the desert before he could launch an offensive. After much argument, Churchill reluctantly accepted that this could not take place before June.

In May it became clear that Rommel was planning an offensive himself to retake Tobruk, and Ritchie was allowed to adopt a defensive stance; but his dispositions, and particularly the location of his huge forward logistic base outside the defences of Tobruk, were designed as a start-line for the proposed offensive, and could not be significantly changed at short notice. By mid-May Ritchie had five infantry divisions, two of which were Indian and two South African, supported by 276 infantry tanks, and two armoured divisions equipped with 573 tanks, of which 167 were the American Grant tanks, with a 75mm gun, and the rest cruisers. To face them, Rommel had 332 German and 228 Italian tanks, his German ones retaining a technical superiority over Ritchie's cruisers.

ULTRA gave accurate warning of the timing of Rommel's attack on 26 May, but none of its direction. Auchinleck tried to persuade Ritchie that the main blow would come against his centre, and to modify his dispositions accordingly; but Ritchie guessed, correctly, that Rommel's main effort would be to outflank the minefields, which stretched as far south as Bir Hacheim, occupied by the Free French. Nevertheless Rommel's thrust south of the French caught Messervy's 7th Armoured Division unprepared, and, by the end of 27 May, Norrie's 30th Corps, although much of it intact, was in a state of confusion.

But Rommel was in more desperate straits. His two panzer divisions were widely separated and one of them was out of fuel. His situation, behind Ritchie's defences, remained precarious for several days; but a combination of slow and hesitant reaction with local tactical failures on the part of Norrie and his subordinates allowed Rommel to recover, and, as Norrie's tank strength fell, to turn the tables on him.

Major Jock McGinlay of the 7th Royal Tank Regiment took part in 32nd Army Tank Brigade's unsuccessful attack on 5 and 6 June:

After one particularly nasty night, when we had taken rather more damage than usual, I was told by the Colonel to go into reserve with my squadron, on a move along the edge of the famous cauldron, where most of Rommel's armour was. I was grateful for the rest, and tagged along behind the rest of the battalion.

Suddenly over the brigade line flashed a message: 'Enemy armoured division advancing towards you from the south, on the top of the escarpment'.

We couldn't see them, but my squadron was immediately taken out of reserve, and told to protect the battalion's right flank.

We halted, and took full advantage of the small breathing space we had before they were on us from over the high ground to our south. I ordered my tanks to take up as good hull-down positions as they could manage in the featureless desert. I even found time to take my tank south of them a bit, and advise them the better as to how much of their tanks were exposed. Fingers were very much on the triggers as we waited, knowing full well what we were probably in for.

Suddenly, the enemy appeared over the crest. Hundreds of tanks. We waited, and watched. Then suddenly, it dawned on us. They weren't Germans, they were the Ariete Italian Armoured Division. The result was quite astonishing. Immediately every Matilda opened up the turrets and waved. Some braver types even got out and started to brew up. The relief was tremendous. The Italians took a long hard look at our Matildas, and withdrew. Such was the morale of the Italians.

On one attack, together with Major Tony Gardner, I went for an O group (Officers' conference) to the Colonel's tank. We were briefly told the enemy position we were to hit, told that the R.A.F. were to bomb it just before we hit it, that another force was to attack it from the other side, and that we would attack, two squadrons up, Tony on the right, my squadron on the left.

Running back to my troop leaders, I was just able to pass this quickly, mount, and drive off in the direction of the enemy, when all hell broke loose. The R.A.F. did not materialise; the attack from the other side did not materialise either. The shelling we were now under immediately showed that the enemy were strong in 88 mm guns.

Now real tragedy struck. Tony Gardner had only been able to give the order over the tank radio to his squadron 'Advance and follow me', no doubt meaning to continue his orders as they went along. Unfortunately, an 88mm hit him, killing him instantly, at over 2000 yards from the enemy. His crew, or what was left of them, veered away to the right, with the whole squadron naturally following.

This left my squadron going into the attack alone, completely without protection on my right. We copped the lot. Out of 17 tanks, I was lucky to get out with three, including my own, when ordered to rally. I dare say we did some damage to the enemy, who withdrew immediately after, but he definitely won that round.

I saw one of my sergeant's tank, a few yards from me, with the sergeant about to close down his cupola after receiving some verbal instructions from me (we were to go straight for the 88mms under smoke, I told him), when he was hit at about 300 yards range. The entire gunmounting, containing the two-pounder gun and the Besa machine gun, was blown clean through into the turret, cutting him clean in half. I can still see his arm flung into the air as he was hit.

I tried to recover some of my burning tanks under cover of smoke, but it took the reserve squadron, under Major Tom Hepple, to rescue any of us alive.

Some of my crews were pretty badly cut up, but counted themselves lucky to be alive after that lot. One Scot, a driver, had both legs off, and when I went to see him in the Forward Casualty Station next day, he was grinning up at me, and said 'That's my bloody war over, anyway'. Unfortunately he died within hours.

The turning point came on 12 June, after the French had been withdrawn from Bir Hacheim, when, in a badly handled tank battle west of El Adem, Norrie's tank strength fell to around 50, while Rommel still had some 200. The infantry in the forward defences, 1st South African and 50th (Northumbrian) Divisions, were in danger of being cut off, and Ritchie ordered their withdrawal to the frontier area in accordance with a contingency plan dating back to February, when the Commanders-in-Chief had insisted that they could not again face an investment of Tobruk. The latter was held by 2nd South African Division, which

Ritchie reinforced with 201st (former 22nd) Guards and 11th Indian Brigades. When Churchill got to hear that plans for evacuation were being made, he sent a strong protest to Auchinleck, who gave equivocal orders to Ritchie, which the latter had no confidence that he could carry out successfully. The result was a disaster, Tobruk falling to Rommel on 21 June, 32,220 men being taken prisoner with 2,000 tons of petrol, 5,000 tons of food, large quantities of ammunition and 2,000 serviceable vehicles.

The Italo-German plan had been that once Tobruk had been taken effort should switch to an airborne attack on Malta, and that Rommel would not advance into Egypt; but, as usual, he took no notice of his superiors and crossed the frontier on 23 June with only forty-three German and fourteen Italian tanks, while Ritchie was withdrawing another 150 miles to Mersa Matruh. Hitler had never liked the Malta plan and Mussolini was only too pleased to cash in on Rommel's success, which would, he expected, bring him to the Nile after all.

Auchinleck ordered Ritchie to stand at Matruh, having sent Freyberg's New Zealanders from Syria to join 50th Division in its defence; but on 25 June he flew up from Cairo and himself replaced Ritchie in command of Eighth Army. At the same time, he abandoned the defence of Matruh in favour of keeping 'all troops fluid and mobile', giving 'no hostage to fortune in shape of immobile troops holding localities which can easily be isolated' and fighting the enemy in 'the large area between the meridian of Matruh and the El Alamein gap'. The result, predictably, was confusion, followed by a helter-skelter withdrawal to the El Alamein line, where defences were hurriedly being prepared only fifty miles from Alexandria.

In the month that followed, a series of ding-dong battles left both sides exhausted. Rommel was operating on a logistic shoestring, while Auchinleck was close to his base. He was well supplied with intercepted intelligence about Rommel's intentions and moves, but his demands for instant action to exploit it, often impractical, met with a disappointing response from his weary and disillusioned troops. When he reported to London at the end of July that offensive operations could not be resumed before mid-September, Churchill, with the support of Alan Brooke, who had succeeded Dill as CIGS on Christmas Day 1941, was determined to replace him and flew to Cairo for that purpose.

Just as it was inevitable that Wavell should leave after Operation

BATTLEAXE, so there could be no doubt that Auchinleck should go after the withdrawal to El Alamein. He and Ritchie must share responsibility for the failures which led to that, but Ritchie's subordinates cannot escape blame either. A great many factors contributed to failure, but there is no doubt that one significant one was that the Germans proved more effective in attack. The reasons for that were varied, but chief among them was that they had standard tactical methods which combined the action of all arms, notably the offensive use of anti-tank guns. The British army tended to let every commander devise his own tactics, and the same lack of firm grip infected the whole command structure. As the author has written elsewhere:*

> The British commanders were not supermen. They were neither better nor worse than those who succeeded them. They were faced with a form of warfare completely novel to all, for which their experience and training was of little value. As one who saw almost all of them at first hand and served under their successors (and under Ritchie again in North-west Europe), I am convinced that few of their successors would have achieved results much different. In the latter half of the war, intricate as the problems of planning might be, there was seldom, if ever, any danger of one's plans being completely disrupted by surprise enemy action. When mistakes were made, their results were less disastrous and far less obvious. If Montgomery had been appointed to command Eighth Army earlier, he would undoubtedly have refused to accept the anomalies of the situation in May 1942. Whether he would have solved them better, or been removed for protesting against them, is pure conjecture.

Although Churchill's first choice, Gott, was greatly admired by those who had served in the desert with him from the start, there is little doubt that, tragic as it was for him and all those who loved and respected him, it was fortunate for Eighth Army that he did not assume command. Not only was he exhausted, but he shrank from anything that resembled the battles of the First World War, and defeat of Rommel at El Alamein was bound to involve something like that. Montgomery had no such inhibition. Ritchie never recovered from starting off on the wrong foot with Auchinleck. His opportunity to remedy that came after the clash

* *Tobruk*, London, 1964 (p. 254).

with Godwin-Austen over the withdrawal from Benghazi in February 1942. It was Auchinleck's intervention then which caused the counter-order leading to disorder. Ritchie should have demanded that he be either allowed to command his army in his own way or replaced. But he was too decent, loyal and traditional a soldier to put his superior, whom he liked and admired, in such a difficult position. He was to suffer for it. High command in war demands tougher and more ruthless qualities: Montgomery knew this well and had no hesitation in employing them.

The Far East

Although the situation which Churchill faced in Cairo at the beginning of August 1942 was critical, that further east was worse. Hong Kong, Malaya, Singapore and Burma had all been lost to the Japanese, who were now threatening India. Given the course of events in Europe and the Middle East, and the general shortage of resources with which to wage war, it is understandable that Churchill's Government took the risk of relying on American naval power in the Pacific to deter Japan from extending her war with China into a wider conflict to include British- and Dutch-controlled territories in the area. However, when Japan extended her occupation to the whole of French Indo-China in July 1941, having forcibly obtained military facilities in Tonkin after the fall of France, the threat to Malaya had to be taken seriously.

Churchill's reaction was to send out the battlecruisers the *Prince of Wales* and the *Repulse*, and the aircraft carrier the *Indomitable*. The battleships reached Singapore on 2 December without the aircraft carrier, which had run aground off Jamaica before it could join them. The Commander-in-Chief Far East, who coordinated planning and operations of the army and air force in the region, Air Chief Marshal Sir Robert Brooke-Popham, had assumed that a combination of naval and air forces would suffice to defend Singapore, provided that aircraft were based on airfields far enough north in Malaya. He saw the army's task as primarily to provide defence of those airfields. Churchill had taken much the same view. When, in September 1940, it had been suggested that the

7th Australian Division should be sent to Malaya instead of the Middle East, he had minuted his chief of staff, General Ismay:

1 The prime defence of Singapore is the Fleet. The protective effect of the Fleet is exercised to a large extent whether it is on the spot or not. For instance, the present Middle Eastern Fleet, which we have just powerfully reinforced, could in a very short time, if ordered, reach Singapore. It could, if necessary, fight an action before reaching Singapore, because it could find in the fortress fuel, ammunition and repair facilities. The fact that the Japanese had made landings in Malaya and even begun the siege of the fortress would not deprive a superior relieving fleet of its power. On the contrary, the plight of the besiegers, cut off from home while installing themselves in the swamps and jungle, would be all the more forlorn.

2 The defence of Singapore must therefore be based upon a strong *local* garrison and the general potentialities of sea-power. The idea of trying to defend the Malay peninsula and of holding the whole of Malaya, a large country four hundred by two hundred miles at its widest part, cannot be entertained. A single division, however well supplied with signals etc, could make no impression upon such a task. What could a single division do for the defence of a country nearly as large as England?

3 The danger of a rupture with Japan is no worse than it was. The probabilities of the Japanese undertaking an attack upon Singapore, which would involve so large a proportion of their fleet far outside the Yellow Sea, are remote; in fact, nothing could be more foolish from their point of view. Far more attractive to them are the Dutch East Indies. The presence of the United States Fleet in the Pacific must always be a main preoccupation to Japan. They are not at all likely to gamble. They are usually most cautious, and now have real need to be, since they are involved in China so deeply.

However, when Lieutenant-General A. E. Percival arrived in April 1941 to command the army in Malaya and Singapore, the threat of a Japanese invasion from Siam (modern Thailand), and probably also from the sea on the east coast of Malaya, was taken more seriously. Percival estimated that he needed five divisions to meet it. He got significantly less – about two-thirds. From Australia he received their 8th

Division (Major-General H. Gordon Bennett) of only two brigades: from India, the 9th and 11th Indian Divisions (Major-Generals A. E. Barstow and D. M. Murray-Lyon), each of only two brigades (in one of which there were two British battalions), two independent Indian brigades and a number of Indian battalions for airfield defence. He also had two Malayan brigades, a total of thirty-one infantry battalions including three British, supported by seven regiments of field artillery, two of anti-tank and five of anti-aircraft; and by eight field companies of engineers. Some of these came from the British, some from the Indian Army. The two Indian divisions and one independent brigade formed the 3rd Corps (Lieutenant-General Sir Lewis Heath), the 11th on the west coast, covering the roads from Siam, the 9th to the east, covering the roads (and one railway) which led from the widely separated ports, where there were also airfields, towards the more populated west. The Australians and one Indian brigade were in reserve in the southern state of Johore, and the Malayan brigades in Singapore. The state of training of all these troops, at every level, was generally low, and equipment was poor in quality and sparse in quantity, particularly in the case of radio communications. They were ill prepared in almost every way to face the experienced, tough Japanese army, well supported by its own air force.

*

The first attack was made on Hong Kong on 8 December 1941, a few hours after the American Pacific Fleet had suffered a crippling blow in Pearl Harbor. The colony was defended by two brigades, consisting of two British, two Canadian and two Indian battalions, under Major-General C. M. Maltby. One brigade was in the New Territories, facing a possible land attack, the other on the island to repel a seaborne one. The Japanese 58th Division took four days to clear the New Territories and completed the conquest of the island on Christmas Day. The result was a foregone conclusion. The garrison had fought hard, suffering 4,000 casualties, including 675 killed, and inflicting 3,000.

The attack on Malaya was also launched on 8 December. Two landings by the Japanese 5th Division took place on the east coast of the Kra Isthmus inside Siam at Singora and Patani. The division was then to advance to the border, fifty and eighty miles away respectively, and then down the roads which led from there to converge north of Butterworth on the west coast opposite Penang. A third force of 5,000 men landed at

Khota Bharu on Malaya's east coast, just south of the border, with orders to capture the airfields on that coast, as it advanced towards the southern port of Kuantan. This area was defended by 8th Indian Brigade, which, by 11 December, was driven from the airfields, from which the few aircraft that had survived Japanese air attacks had flown off. This was the day after the *Prince of Wales* and *Repulse* had been sunk by Japanese aircraft not far offshore from there. The brigade then began to withdraw down the railway towards Kuala Lipis.

11th Indian Division failed to hold the Japanese advance on the roads from Singora and Patani. Position after position was overcome by a rapid combination of frontal attack and encirclement, the morale of the division's inexperienced troops sinking lower and lower as days of fighting were followed by nights of withdrawal in an atmosphere of increasing confusion. Even though it was reinforced by an additional brigade from Percival's reserve, the division was back on the Perak River, sixty miles south of Butterworth, on 23 December. But Heath decided not to risk being outflanked there, and withdrew another eighty miles to the Slim River, where a bold Japanese attack penetrated the defences on 7 January, virtually destroying 11th Indian in the process. Its commander, Murray-Lyon, was replaced by one of his brigadiers, A. C. M. Paris. 9th Division on the east coast had not been under such pressure, but, as a result of a muddle typical of this campaign, 22nd Indian Brigade was withdrawn from Kuantan airfield before it was attacked.

By this time the Chiefs of Staff in London had decided to reinforce Percival with 17th Indian Division (Major-General J. G. Smyth VC), about to start training for service in the Middle East, and the 18th British (Major-General M. L. Beckwith-Smith), which was at sea on its way there, and sending from Auchinleck's command 7th Armoured Brigade with two regiments of the American light cruiser Stuart tank. The first brigade (45th) of 17th Division arrived on 3 January and the first of the 18th (53rd) on 13 January. The tanks never came, but were diverted to Burma, as was most of 17th Division.

Percival now decided to base his plan on holding Johore, the Japanese harrying Heath's troops as they withdrew. As a result of intervention by Wavell, who had been appointed by Churchill and Roosevelt to the phantom ABDA Command (American, British, Dutch, Australian), covering everything from Burma to the Philippines, 3rd Corps Headquarters was withdrawn into reserve with 11th Indian Division and one

Australian brigade, while the Australian Major-General Bennett assumed command of 'Westforce', which included 9th Indian Division and his own division, less its two brigades, one of which was held by Percival in reserve and the other allotted to 'Eastforce'. The latter consisted of 22nd Australian Brigade and some other units, looking after the east coast. Johore was more plentifully supplied with roads and generally easier to move about in than the mountainous, jungle-covered country further north, and it was not long before the Japanese managed to penetrate between Bennett's widely strung out four brigades and forced a general withdrawal. On 1 February those troops which had escaped their clutches withdrew into Singapore.

Percival was told to hold the island to the last, although it was unprepared to face a siege, let alone an attack. It depended for water on a pipeline from Johore, and practically nothing had been done about civil defence, or active defence either, apart from coast defence artillery, designed to engage a seaborne expedition. Its defence was complicated by its topography, mangrove-lined creeks restricting lateral movement. Percival now had twelve brigades, totalling thirty-eight battalions, including local volunteers. He divided the island into three sectors, giving the northern to 3rd Corps, with 11th Indian Division and the recently arrived British 18th. The southern was held by the two Malayan brigades and one of volunteers, under Major-General Keith Simmons. The key western sector was allotted to Bennett, with his own division and the recently landed 44th Indian Brigade. 12th Indian Brigade was in central reserve.

General Yamashita's Twenty-Fifth Army employed twenty-one battalions in three divisions for the attack, concentrated in the north-west, during the night of 8 February. Bennett had no chance of being able to hold such a concentration, backed by greatly superior artillery fire. After twenty-four hours, his troops had been pushed back to a line running north from Jurong, only eight miles from the city itself. Percival had prepared a contingency plan for a further withdrawal to the edge of the city, which unfortunately was interpreted by some as an executive order for withdrawal, so that the Jurong line was needlessly abandoned during the night of 10 February, all troops being withdrawn to the city perimeter by the morning of the 13th. Attempts to counter-attack failed, and Percival and his subordinate commanders considered surrender to be the only possible choice, if only to spare the civil population. On the

12th he asked Wavell, who had visited Singapore himself two days before, for discretionary power to negotiate, saying: 'There must come a stage when in the interests of the troops and civil population further bloodshed will serve no useful purpose.' Wavell continued to order him to fight on, while reporting to Churchill that he feared that resistance was not likely to be prolonged, to which he received the reply: 'You are of course sole judge of moment when no further results can be gained in Singapore and should instruct Percival accordingly.' On 15 February Wavell signalled Percival: 'So long as you are in a position to inflict loss and damage to enemy and your troops are physically capable of doing so, you must fight on ... When you are fully satisfied that this is no longer possible, I give you discretion to cease resistance.' Percival replied: 'Owing to losses from enemy action, water, petrol, food and ammunition practically finished. Unable therefore continue fight any longer. All ranks have done their best and grateful your help.'

Private Robert Hamond was with the 2nd Norfolks in the unfortunate 18th Division. He describes the penultimate day, 14 February:

Bombs were falling all around us, the noise was terrible my already taut nerves were nearly broken, I could have screamed. Small arms fire could be heard between the explosions of the falling bombs. Well the Japs had landed on the island, desperate bloody battles were going on all around us. A runner came up and spoke to our Sergeant. He told us that we were pulling out to reform with the main body of troops near the centre of the island. We pulled ourselves from the monsoon drains. The bombing had stopped. We proceeded to fall back at a steady run. Shots rang out, three of our platoon dropped to the ground without ever moving again. I glanced down at one of them, a neat hole was dead centre in his forehead. That could mean only one thing, snipers. More shots rang out from a different angle this time. The bastards were in the trees around us, we threw ourselves down on the ground. We were pinned down with practically no cover. What seemed like hours was probably no more than a few minutes, it was hell having to lie down not daring to move a muscle for fear of being shot. Our Sergeant (whose name I cannot mention) suddenly jumped to his feet and aimed his automatic at the surrounding palm trees. Firing from the hip, he walked towards those trees. He shouted to us telling us to make a run for it, we did so, glancing back I saw him drop to the ground riddled through and through, but his brave action saved us. We ran like hell and dropped thankfully into another monsoon drain. Recovering my breath, I took a look around our temporary haven of rest. We were no more than 16 men now with just a Corporal in charge. We all realised that our Sergeant had sacrificed his life to save us. All over the island similar actions were taking place. Hardly the action of beaten men, more like men determined to give their all in the face of the enemy.

We had to get out of this monsoon drain, no one was foolhardy enough to poke his head over the top, so removing my steel helmet, I placed it on the end of my rifle and cautiously shoved it upwards to the top of the drain. Nothing happened. Pulling it down again, I waited a few seconds, so we decided to risk it. Pulling ourselves out of the drain, we proceeded once more to our rendezvous. No further incidents occurred and we reached our destination.

Our Corporal reported to an Officer of the 2nd Cambridgeshires who happened to be the nearest troops to us. We were put into a position facing the Bukit Timah road down which was proceeding a large formation of Jap tanks and troops. Our batteries of 25 pounders were at our rear and stripped to their waists, they were all ready for action.

The noise of the battle was getting very close now, the guns suddenly opened up, firing at will, the 3.7 [inch] bofors* were adding their noise to the din. I shall never in my life forget that scene. We learned afterwards that the havoc they caused to the advancing Japs on the Bukit Timah road was terrible. Thousands of Japs died in that holocaust never knowing what hit them.

The day wore on, by now the whole island was a terrible mess. Dead and dying troops and civilians littered the streets everywhere the smell of death and cordite from the guns was overpowering.

In seventy days three Japanese divisions had totally defeated a British imperial force of comparable size, occupying one of the Empire's richest territories and its most important overseas naval base, taking more prisoners of war, 130,000, than they had men in their own ranks. It was a deeply humiliating disaster. Nobody can escape blame. The general plan for the defence of Malaya and Singapore was fundamentally unsound, and the resources needed to implement it effectively were not

* Bofors anti-aircraft guns.

provided. Nevertheless, it need not have been the chaotic muddle it proved to be. The inexperienced formations, largely Indian Army, were not effectively trained to fight a modern opponent of the calibre of the Japanese. There were many incidents of gallant and stubborn defensive fighting, but the instinctive reaction to withdraw at the first sign of any form of encirclement proved fatal, and continuous withdrawal imposed increasing physical and psychological strain, until fighting spirit dissolved. Higher command was weak and vacillating, and the whole command system vitiated by gravely inadequate communications.

Burma

These faults recurred in the second defeat which the Japanese inflicted on the British and Indian troops. The threat to Burma arose as soon as the Japanese landed on the Kra Isthmus on 8 December to invade Malaya. At that time they occupied one of the airfields at the southern tip of Burma near Tenasserim, while they concentrated two divisions of their Fifteenth Army at Rabeng in Siam, east of the Burmese port of Moulmein. At the end of December Lieutenant-General T. J. Hutton, Wavell's Chief of Staff in India, was appointed to command the troops in Burma, which consisted of 1st Burma Division (Major-General J. Bruce-Scott) and 17th Indian. The former had two brigades of Burma Rifles, but few supporting arms: the latter had two of its own brigades, and two independent Indian brigades replacing the one that had gone to Singapore. Hutton gave Bruce-Scott responsibility for Central Burma with one of his own brigades and an Indian one, and Smyth responsibility for the south with three Indian and one of the Burma Rifles.

The Japanese advance towards Moulmein started on 20 January 1942, opposed by the 16th Indian Brigade, the pattern of their advance in Malaya being repeated. Hutton had intended that Smyth should stand on the Salween River for as long as possible, but he was threatened there with encirclement, and having been outmanoeuvred on the Bilin River he obtained Hutton's agreement to withdrawal to the Sittang, the last river obstacle east of Rangoon, over which there was only one bridge.

There was confusion over its defence, and it was demolished before a significant body of Smyth's troops had been able to cross it. Only 4,000 men, carrying 1,400 rifles, from his division could be assembled west of the river at Pegu, eighty miles north of Rangoon.

If Rangoon could not be held, no reinforcements or supply could arrive, except for the Japanese, and the troops remaining in the country would have no alternative but to withdraw up country, and eventually, as they were forced to do, make their way through roadless jungle-covered mountains to India. Hutton decided that an attempt to hang on to Rangoon would risk the encirclement of all the troops in the south. He took steps to move stores up country and told Wavell, who was back in India, ABDA Command having folded up, that he proposed to abandon Rangoon and move north. Wavell disagreed and told him to hold the port until 63rd Brigade, on its way by sea, had arrived, which it did on 1 March. 7th Armoured Brigade landed on 27 February. Wavell also decided to replace Smyth, who was not well, by Major-General D. T. Cowan, and asked for, and got, from England Lieutenant-General Sir Harold Alexander to replace Hutton. He arrived on 5 March, the day on which the Japanese 33rd Division crossed the Pegu River, while the 55th was directed on Pegu itself. Rangoon was now seriously threatened with encirclement. The day after his arrival Alexander realized that his immediate decision to cancel orders for the abandonment of Rangoon had been a mistake, and, just in time, he ordered a withdrawal north to Prome. It was by pure luck that he succeeded in getting his force away, as the Japanese 33rd Division had already moved west of the Pegu–Prome road, allowing Alexander to escape between it and the 55th.

Alexander not only exercised command of the British, Indian and Burmese forces, which by now were all in the valley of the Irrawaddy, but he had also been given a general authority to coordinate operations with the Chinese forces under the American Lieutenant-General Joseph Stilwell, which were trying to defend the lower reaches of the Burma Road, which led to Chiang Kai-shek's capital and base at Chungking. He therefore asked for a corps commander to take control of the Irrawaddy valley and was fortunate to be given Lieutenant-General W. J. Slim.

Thereafter it was a slow, painful withdrawal northwards, as the Japanese were able to build up their forces by sea through Rangoon. The depressing atmosphere of continual retreat was made worse by the hot weather, and after crossing the Chindwin, where all vehicles had to be abandoned, the lack of a road and any form of civilized amenity.

Lieutenant Patrick Cleere of the 7th Hussars in 7th Armoured Brigade describes an action during the retreat:

On the 28th April I was ordered to go south in my Honey* tank to establish whether a bridge had been blown, so I took my Troop Sergeant, Kilty, with me to give covering fire if necessary. Kilty and I arrived at the bridge to find it intact and we decided that although we had no explosives, we could burn the bridge if we had some petrol. Sergeant Kilty was sent back to HQ to pick up a 40 gallon drum of petrol which was placed on the back of the Honey tank over the engine. When Kilty got back I led him down to the bridge and I pulled up my tank on the right of the road as close to the bridge as I thought would be safe. I told Kilty over the radio to turn his tank around and I would get out and back him up on to the centre of the bridge.

The bridge was situated on a straight road, well out in the open about 500 yards from the nearest tree. As I got out of my tank, four Japanese fighter bombers arrived, machine gunning us. I jumped back into my tank and told Kilty to follow me to the nearest bit of cover; we were machine gunned and bombed all the way. We overshot a track covered with a line of trees up to a farmhouse on the right of the road, I pulled up under a tree on the right of the road and Kilty did the same on the left of the road. The Japanese bombed and machine gunned us very heavily and I engaged them with my Browning Ack Ack machine gun.

I told Kilty over the radio that I would move back and go up the track for more cover as soon as the first lot of bombing was over and that he should follow and Kilty followed. I got up the track where Captain Allen and another tank, which took no part in the action, had already taken cover. Before Kilty's tank got off the road at the entrance of the track, the planes returned and the machine gunners caught the petrol drum which went up in flames on Kilty's tank setting the whole tank on fire.

As soon as I saw what was happening, I got out of my tank and ran back to try and rescue the crew. I saw Trooper Shirt who was the operator. He was naked but his socks and boots were still smouldering.

* Stuart light tank.

I took his boots and socks off and carried him back to my tank. On the way I was knocked off my feet several times by the bomb blasts which were sinking in the soft paddy fields. I rolled Trooper Shirt up in a blanket and passed him into my tank via the driver.

I then went back and found Sergeant Kilty. His head was split open but he was still alive. Again, I managed to get him back to my tank and passed him into the crew to be bandaged via the turret. Then I went back to the tank to try and find the driver. On the way I saw Trooper Britt who was the gunner, he seemed OK, just a bit dazed. I directed him up the track to Captain Allen's tank.

When I got back to Sergeant Kilty's tank, which was burnt out by now, it was too hot to touch, however I looked into where the driver should have been but there was no sign of him. By now the planes were back with heavy bombing and machine gunning. I had to dive under the tree on the left of the road when I saw the driver. He was naked, lying in the paddy field. I ran and picked him up. His socks and boots were smouldering and when I removed them I noticed that his leg was broken above the ankle. I got him back to the side of the road opposite the entrance to the track but by now the bombs had broken some big branches off the trees across the entrance. Somehow or other I got the strength to pull the branches to one side and, still under heavy fire, I ran to my tank and told my driver to follow me. I led him to the side of the road where I had left the injured driver, Trooper Roache.

I wrapped Roache in a blanket and somehow managed to lift him on to the back of my tank, I told the driver that I would get on the back of my tank and hold Roache in my arms, and soon as I was ready I would tell him to go and he should drive north along the road until he came to Major Congreve at Squadron Headquarters. When I arrived back at Squadron HQ there was a medical team there ready to take over. Major Congreve asked me if I was alright and although I was exhausted, I said yes. He then said he would give me a composite troop and I would have to go back to Kyankse on patrol which I did and I stayed there until we were called in to leaguer that night.

On 12 May the monsoon broke, and a week later the last rain-sodden troops reached Assam. They had retreated 1,000 miles and had suffered 13,000 casualties, of whom 4,000 had died or been killed.

*

Wavell now turned his mind to how to reverse this situation, which posed a threat to India itself. He saw a need for three separate operations: an advance past Imphal, to which there was a road, to cross the Chindwin and regain Mandalay, in cooperation with Chinese forces advancing south-westwards from Yunnan; an advance in Arakan to seize the Japanese air base on the island of Akyab; and finally an amphibious expedition to recapture Rangoon. The resources for these did not then exist. He had nine infantry divisions, of which two were British (2nd and 70th), and three armoured divisions, three independent armoured brigades and a parachute brigade, all Indian. But the main restricting factor was the capability of the road and rail system to and in Assam for their logistic support. The route to Imphal could never support more than three divisions. In practice, therefore, for the campaigning season from November 1942 to May 1943, Wavell had to limit his operations to Arakan.

Command in the area was exercised by Lieutenant-General N. M. S. Irwin at HQ Eastern Army. Under him the 14th Indian Division (Major-General H. L. Lloyd) was given the task of pushing south from Chittagong towards Maungelaw, fifty miles north of Akyab. When he reached the coast opposite the island, an amphibious assault would be launched. Although Wavell was forced to cancel this for lack of air support, he ordered Lloyd to continue his advance beyond Maungelaw to launch an assault on Akyab himself. This came to a halt short of the objective at the end of February, leaving 14th Division vulnerable to a counter-attack from east of the Mayu River. That was launched by the Japanese 55th Division in April, threatening to cut off the division from its supply route to Chittagong. Wavell and Irwin told Lloyd to hold fast, sending Slim there to take a grip. He quickly realized that the situation was hopeless, and in May withdrew the division all the way back to where it had started south of Chittagong six months before.

None of the commanders involved in this double debacle comes well out of it, except perhaps Alexander and Slim. They managed to maintain the morale of their men and the cohesiveness of their force as it withdrew in conditions which severely tested both. Wavell's contribution is difficult to assess. His interventions in Malaya do not appear to have been of much help. Once again he was burdened with a huge load of responsibility without the resources with which to carry it. Whatever the faults of Percival's exercise of command, it is doubtful if any other result could have been achieved. Would the outcome have been different if, say, Slim had been in command? If Singapore and southern Johore had been successfully defended, the force there could not have been reinforced or supplied for long, given Japanese naval and air superiority in the area. Tragic as it was for those who were left there in prisoner of war camps, it was, as in the case of Crete, strategically advantageous that we were not faced with trying to keep a force there. Even more casualties would have been suffered.

5

FROM LOW EBB
TO HIGH TIDE
1942–1945

Eighth Army's Victory

By May 1943 the situation in the Middle East was completely transformed. On his visit to Cairo at the beginning of August 1942 Churchill's choice had fallen on Lieutenant-General W. H. E. ('Strafer') Gott, then commander of 13th Corps, to command Eighth Army and General Alexander to replace Auchinleck as Commander-in-Chief; but Gott was killed when the aircraft bringing him from the desert to Cairo was shot down, and Lieutenant-General B. L. Montgomery, who was to have replaced Alexander in command of First Army for the projected Anglo-American landings in French North Africa, was sent for instead.

On arrival on 12 August Montgomery, supremely self-confident as always, set about immediately cancelling all contingency plans for further withdrawal or 'fluid and mobile' defence, realizing that if one of the recently arrived divisions, the 44th (Major-General I. T. P. Hughes), held back in the Egyptian delta to meet such a contingency, were sent up to him, an effective defence could be established on the thirty-mile front of the El Alamein line, the left flank of which was protected by the practically impassable Qattara depression.

His first test came at the end of the month, when Rommel attacked in an almost exact repetition of his Gazala operation; but he was delayed by having to tackle minefields defended by 7th Armoured Division (Major-General J. M. L. Renton) and then came up against a resolute and skilful defence by 22nd Armoured Brigade, while all the time being pounded from the air. Suffering also from fuel shortage, he decided, after three days of this, to withdraw. Montgomery ordered a counter-stroke to cut him off, but Freyberg, whose heart was not in it, gave the task to an inexperienced British brigade, and it failed. This battle of Alam Halfa was in fact the turning point of the campaign. After it, Rommel had no hope of advancing further. His eventual defeat if he did not withdraw was inevitable, given the resources now being made available to Montgomery and in his support.

As usual, Churchill pressed for an early return to the offensive, but Montgomery was not going to be rushed. Alam Halfa had shown him that much needed to be done in the field of training and organization. Every week that passed meant that the mined defences he had to tackle – they could not be outflanked – grew more formidable. By this time the anti-tank mine had become a dominant factor in restricting the employment of tanks, especially where the minefields were covered by fire from infantry and artillery, which made clearance of gaps through them a dangerous task, made more hazardous by mixing anti-tank and anti-personnel mines. Nevertheless he was confident of success. Some of his subordinates did not share his optimism.

His first plan envisaged an infantry attack by 30th Corps (Lieutenant-General Sir Oliver Leese), the principal parts played, from right to left, by Morshead's 9th Australian, Major-General D. M. Wimberley's 51st (Highland) and Freyberg's 2nd New Zealand Divisions, which would capture the enemy minefields in one night. Lumsden's 10th Corps, with Major-General R. Briggs's 1st and Gatehouse's 10th Armoured Divisions, the latter with two armoured brigades, would then pass through gaps made in the minefields and, swinging round in an arc southwards, hinged on the New Zealanders, who would return to Lumsden's command, cut Rommel's supply routes and destroy his encircled armour, while the infantry 'crumbled' his static defences.

Neither the armoured nor the infantry commanders thought this plan practicable, and Montgomery changed it on 6 October to a less ambitious one. The 30th Corps would destroy the enemy infantry, while the 10th, having passed through the minefields, would hold off the enemy armour, which Rommel would have to commit to an attack in order to save his infantry. In thus modifying his plan, he created a fatal ambiguity about the relative tasks of the infantry and the armoured divisions which was to have serious consequences during the battle, aggravated by the superimposition of the mainly armoured 10th Corps on the infantry 30th. In the south, 13th Corps (Lieutenant-General B. G. Horrocks), with 7th Armoured Division (Major-General A. F. Harding) and Hughes's 44th Infantry Division, would attempt to break through the minefields north of Himeimat and, if possible, thrust round Rommel's southern flank. Horrocks was not to incur heavy losses, his principal task being to keep 21st Panzer Division tied down in the south, which an extensive deception plan had been designed to convince the enemy was to be the area of the main attack.

Rommel himself had gone on sick leave on 19 September, handing over command to General Stumme, fresh from the Russian front, who could see few reasons for optimism in the situation. The build-up of his German and Italian forces had been slight in comparison with that of the Eighth Army; his logistic position was precarious, and the British were masters of the skies. He had 220 German and 278 Italian tanks to face Montgomery's 1,029, of which 631 were the US Shermans or Grants with the 75mm gun. The latter's artillery had also been greatly increased. He had 52 medium and 832 field guns, and anti-tank guns totalled 602 2-pounders and 849 of the very effective new 6-pounders. His army had 195,000 men to Stumme's probable 104,000.

Montgomery's artillery bombardment opened at 9.40 p.m. (Cairo Summer Time) on 23 October, the infantry and engineers following closely behind it to enter the minefields. All seemed to be going well, but in the later stages, particularly in the Highland Division's sector, which widened as it advanced, some enemy defences held out and caused delays and confusion. The Australians had reached almost all their objectives, but their sector was not one through which 10th Corps was to move its tanks. In both the Highland Division and the New Zealand sector Lumsden's tanks maintained that they could not move through, as the minefield gaps were not clear or were dominated by enemy anti-tank guns.

Lieutenant Charles Potts took part in these attempts with 1st Buffs, the motor infantry battalion of 8th Armoured Brigade in 10th Armoured Division. Potts had started the war as an army chaplain. Posted to Palestine, he found himself with nothing to do and felt guilty at not taking a more active part in the war. Overcoming strong episcopal opposition, he escaped from his holy orders and joined the infantry. He wrote every few days to his fiancée, Pamela Stubbs, whom he later married.

27th Oct. 1942.

Just a short letter to tell you that I am fit and well. The last few days have been pretty exciting as you can imagine from the news on the wireless. As to our part in the show, I am afraid I am not allowed to give you any details. I can only say that I have never been so frightened in my life, but I'd rather have been here than back in a base camp. It was a great experience. I brought back 10 wounded during one day, one or two at a time in my little Bantam car. There were 2 Germans amongst them, one of whom was an officer. I have been miraculously lucky so far. One shell bounced over a shallow trench that I was in & burst just beyond, another grazed my cap & made a groove in the sand on the parapet. One shell burst in a trench about a minute after I had left the spot. Another officer sitting with me in a trench & sharing a tin of cold sausages was wounded in the hand as he put it out to take the tin from me. The noise has been frightful. It was my first time in real action & I am glad I have got through it all right without losing my nerve. I find that one's feelings vary. At one minute I just don't give a damn for all their bombs and shells, machine gun bullets etc, at another minute I am almost paralysed with fright & just sweat blood with terror. The best thing to do is to keep busy & keep talking. I talked an awful lot of nonsense to keep the men amused. One night I had a busy time collecting in some abandoned vehicles under a terrific hail of fire. My company commander, the Mole, has been wounded & gone back to hospital. He has lost a few fingers. Capt Matson is now commanding the company & I am 2nd in command, This morning I hear that one or two have been 'mentioned' for good work in the battle. From our company 2 names have been sent in, a corporal and myself (you may be pleased to hear). I did try to put up a good show because I know that you expect it of me.

A renewed attempt the following night was no more successful, in spite of pressure applied to Lumsden by Montgomery, who then decided to abandon the attempt to get out through Freyberg's sector. He told the Australians to start 'crumbling' in the north and Lumsden to get Briggs's 1st Armoured Division, reinforced by a brigade from Gatehouse, out through the Highlanders. Rommel had returned on 25 October, Stumme having died, and he flung all his available tanks into a violent counter-attack in the south. They suffered heavy losses, but Briggs made little

westward progress in spite of the gallant action of one of his motor
battalions, 2nd Rifle Brigade, after it had captured the 'Snipe' position
during the night of 26 October.

Rifleman R. L. Crimp, a company signaller, starts his account on the
morning of the 27th.

Nobody feels like stirring far, so we just wait. Our hopes are naturally
pinned on the armour putting in an early appearance. Some essential
articles of wireless kit have gone astray in the night's alarums, and with
no truck on hand from which to replace them, Rusty and I must
abandon our scheme for a ground station. Not that it matters, anyway,
as with the Battalion concentrated together, wireless isn't necessary.

Out on the southern side are the two tanks, whacked last night,
still smoking. Several more – live 'uns – are lurking further back, out
of effective A/T range, and they soon start shelling us, with maybe a
few 88mms mixed in as well. We're getting a bit impatient over the
non-appearance of our promised armoured support, but after a while
half a dozen Shermans become visible on the ridge behind us to the
northeast. The Jerry guns, however, must have the range worked out
to an inch, for two of the tanks are immediately hit and set on fire,
and the rest retire hastily from sight.

Half an hour later our tanks appear again, and seem to be making
a more determined effort. Quite a number charge straight over the
ridge into the open desert north of our position. Some Jerry panzers
have meanwhile filtered round our western flank, skirting it at a safe
distance, and a shooting match ensues betwen them and the recklessly
advancing Shermans. In the resulting respite on our area we can keep
our heads up for a perfect view of the battle. One by one the charging
Shermans, pennants flying and guns blazing, are brought to a halt as
they receive hits. Out of some their crews leap or crawl but others
show no sign of life. Our six-pounders crash away with all the
support they can muster and an equal number of Jerry tanks and a
large recovery vehicle, which boldly comes to whisk their casualties
from further harm, are likewise brought to a standstill. But the result
of this forlorn yet courageous attempt at relief is stalemate, and our
situation looks like getting a bit precarious. Jerry, of course, under-
stands and switches his whole weight on us. He reinforces his panzers
to the northwest and they're now on three of our flanks, still however
keeping a respectful distance.

For the next half hour we get a concentrated dose. It's most unpleasant crouching in the bottom of the pit, packed tight with even more chaps now whose single object is to keep their nuts down as low as possible, silently braced and wondering whether the next one's coming our way. The shells scream down in inexorable succession, and all around us is the driving, rending crash of high explosive. Several times my tin-hat is crushed on to my head by the impact of nearby detonations, and once my lungs seem filled by a rush of sand. Everyone lies still; you can't do a thing – it just has to happen. If one lands in the trench – well, we shan't know much about it. Llewellyn keeps very calm, though there's a strained look in his eyes, and often when the sand and grit from a near one sweep in he mutters encouragingly and is almost friendly; but as soon as a moment of respite comes he squashes passionately, scorpion-like, all hopes of getting out alive. When at last the inferno does slacken our rather capricious Company Commander, a white handkerchief bandaged on his biceps, runs round to warn all sections to meet an attack. With Jerry unwilling to risk more tanks against our six-pounders, it looks as though he's thinking of using his infantry – the barrage, no doubt, being intended to soften us up.

It's difficult to estimate the actual extent of the damage. But all our carriers, without exception, have been hit and are blazing fiercely. Their crews, who were lying in hastily clawed-out slit 'uns nearby, have come creeping back for a share of our more substantial, yet already overcrowded, cover. Casualties are being brought in too. And when our Company HQ dug-out is full of them, it's decided to park the rest of them in our trench – so we have to clear out. Slithering on my belly up to the slope behind Coy. HQ, I scoop a hole in the soft sand and the first thing I find is a pool of squitters – some poor sod's guts must have turned to water.

Very soon the barrage starts up again, but most of it falls a short way ahead towards the enemy. The shells, however, are coming from behind us, so they're obviously from our own artillery, a couple of miles back, to keep the enemy off our position and break up his suspected infantry assault. Many of them fall close enough, all the same.

About mid-day.
No attack has yet materialised. Perhaps the barrage is too discourag-

ing. Now we can see what it's like on the sharp end of our 25-pounders, and it's pretty murderous. No doubt the gunners back behind the ridge are sweating hard to help us in our plight. For there's no question about it, we're well and truly marooned out here. Half an hour ago our armour made another attempt to get through. But as soon as they appeared on the ridge, the 88 mms began picking them off. Great turgid growths of black and yellow smoke rose on the summit, stayed static, then rolled away; more tanks were hit, and the rest had to scarper. But Jerry losses have also been high. Our position is ringed round with derelict and burning panzers. The six-pounders have whacked everything within range. And now the situation is fairly quiet. Our people can't relieve, and Jerry can't mount an attack, or doesn't appear to like the prospect. But one factor begins to look ominous for us: A/T ammo is running low. Already orders have been given to use the remainder very sparingly, only on certain knockouts.

By mid-afternoon ammo-stocks are almost exhausted, and the panzers, as though suspecting it, have begun creeping in again. They come in groups of two or three, still very cautiously, from various directions, feinting and probing. Our chaps have to let them in pretty close, and this gives the Jerries a chance with their machine-guns, which they use to spray the six-pounder sites and keep the crews lying doggo. They also fire their 75mms point-blank at the guns, in the hope of blowing them to bits. Nevertheless a few more panzers, venturing too near, are knocked out. The Colonel* and the Adjutant – I can see them from their waists up as they stand in their trench down at Battalion HQ – are having grand sport with borrowed rifles, picking off the crews climbing out of the stricken panzers. They vie with each other in choosing their targets, take careful aim, and chalk up their respective 'bags' with mock-emulative gusto. You'd think they were out shooting grouse.

An hour later.
Several guns are now completely out of ammo. The situation's so bad that two officers of S Company try to effect a re-distribution of what remains by jeep. They travel slowly over the dunes (four-wheel drive carrying them on) quite heedless of the M/G bullets

* Lieutenant-Colonel Victor Turner, who was awarded the Victoria Cross for his gallantry that day.

slashing the air around them and panzers potting straight at them, collecting odd rounds from knocked-out guns or the guns of knocked-out crews, and taking them to guns that can still strike back. One bullet among the ammo on board and the lot would go sky-high.

This day seems to be going on for ever. The sun's still high.

About four o'clock.

The enemy tanks, convinced of our weakness, resume their attack. This time they make a more determined approach, well dispersed and working in concert, from S., S.W., and W. with other arms in support. Quite a hubbub ensues: the brittle rasping and spitting of machine-guns; mortar bombs feeling over, whispering gently, and crashing suddenly; solids blasting by like express trains, leaving groaning, feverish turmoils of vacuum in their wake; and the mewing and squealing chorus of the 25-pounder shells as they arch over our heads. Our own six-pounders are mute. But the barrage saves us again. The panzers are forced to withdraw. Except one. He gets to within 50 yards on the western side and halts, as though undecided what to do next. None of our guns has a single round, otherwise he'd be a sitting bird. He lumbers forward, clumsily and warily, hosing a clear path with his machine-gun, right up to our perimeter trenches, where the chaps lie low (who wouldn't? What use are rifles against Mark IV panzers?) and on until he's almost up to Battalion HQ. The Colonel and Adjutant, heads and torsos protruding from the sand, look ludicrously inadequate as they brandish their bondooks at the oncoming monster.

Then he stops again. His gun veers slightly, till it's horizontal. And when he fires the atmosphere seems to sustain a stunning impact. My tin-hat hits my head with a hard jolt. But nothing near seems to get whacked. Then after some more waggling, as though adjusting aim, another terrific crash and blast. Yet still no damage. Maybe he can't sink his barrel on to a low enough plane – thank heaven for that!

However, just as some of us are thinking This Is It, one of the A/T chaps crawls from his trench and with bullets ripping into the sand around him, runs stooping over to a six-pounder fronting north, extracts a shell already in the breech and creeps back with it to his own gun which faces the panzer. It's amazing how the M/G stream misses him, but he calmly puts the shell in, takes steady aim, and fires.* Immediately there's an explosion from the panzer – whether the Jerry has fired again or the six-pounder found its mark, we can't tell. But the M/G cuts out, and the tank stays still. A strand of smoke issues from the turret, and minutes later it starts to blaze.

The rest of the evening passes without much incident: Jerry seems to have had enough for the time being. The island is now ringed round with derelict tanks, some blackened and burnt out, others still smouldering redly in the failing light.

At about eight o'clock a sergeant brings orders from the Company Commander. As soon as it's dark, the whole position is to be evacuated. When word comes, the Company, in small groups well dispersed, will proceed eastwards, back to the minefields, on foot. All portable equipment will have to be carried, and all casualties that can be moved will have to be helped along. The six-pounders, with breech-blocks taken out and securely buried, will be left behind.

The minutes crawl to last light. Obviously another attempt at a tanks-and-infantry attack is expected shortly, which for us in our present state and under night conditions would be hard to repel. So we hope it doesn't start too soon, before the great trek back gets going.

Eventually, when it's almost dark, we notice signs of a general exodus, and, although no signal has been received, we sling our kit and join in. About a dozen of us travel together. The sensation of being able to move freely again after being pinned down on our bellies all day is a delicious relief. We march as quietly as possible, but before we've covered a quarter-mile, machine-gun bullets come spraying after us. Nobody minds, though, as they're obviously being fired at random and most of them fall short. One of the chaps in the party turns out to be an Italian prisoner, a lean bedraggled urchin of about eighteen. The fellows don't want the bother of looking after him, and tell him to scram back to his own lines. But he implores to be taken with us. 'Io prigionero, Io prigoniero!' he keeps asserting ardently; and with dramatic gestures of disgust and horror: 'Tedeschi no bono. Mussolini no bono. Ma Inglesi molto bono!' Whenever the following M/G bullets rip at all near, he darts about as though scorpion-stung. Once we stumble on the bulk of a tank in the darkness, and with eyes wide with dread he immediately identifies it

* This may refer to Sergeant Calistan, who was awarded the Distinguished Conduct Medal. Lieutenant-Colonel Turner helped to serve the gun with ammunition and was wounded while doing so.

as 'tedesco', beseeching us to keep away. He's right too, but it's stone cold and a 'dead 'un'.

We hit the minefield after an hour's tramp, and the straggling groups amalgamate into a company again. The chaps, pretty tired though quietly jubilant at having got out of the 'show' intact, lie on the ground in their overcoats, but the night is too cold for sleeping.

Montgomery now called off the thrust in the centre, intending to switch the main effort to the north to exploit the Australian success. He was persuaded, however, to make his next major thrust south of the Australians, led by Freyberg with three British brigades – 9th Armoured, 151st from the 50th Division and 152nd from the 51st Division. This attack, launched on the night of 1 November, almost broke right through, and Rommel decided to withdraw. He was in the process of doing so when a final attack by 1st Armoured Division, through the salient created by Freyberg, led to the collapse of Rommel's attempts at resistance. Montgomery tried to get all three of his armoured divisions – the 7th had been brought up from the south several days before – as well as the New Zealanders out into the open to cut off Rommel's retreat. The result was confused, and although large numbers of the enemy were rounded up – 30,000, a third of them German, were taken prisoner – Rommel managed to get away what was left of the Afrika Korps, which now had only 20 tanks, leaving 1,000 guns and 450 of his approximately 500 tanks on the battlefield. Eighth Army's casualties had been 13,500, seven per cent of the force engaged. 500 tanks had been put out of action, but only 150 beyond repair.

Montgomery's determination, realism and flexibility to change his plan, although he would never admit that he had, made a decisive contribution to victory, and victory was all important at that time, especially for Churchill.

However he did not handle the pursuit well, having tried to get too many different formations forward at the same time. Failing to cut off the remnants of Rommel's forces, his follow-up was cautious. Rommel did not make a serious stand until he reached Buerat, 200 miles east of Tripoli, early in January 1943, having briefly held Montgomery up at Christmas time near his old stopping place at Mersa Brega. But the dice were loaded against him. Four days after the end of the Battle of El Alamein, Eisenhower's forces, including Lieutenant-General Sir Kenneth

Anderson's First British Army, landed in Morocco and Algeria. Rommel realized that his only hope was to conduct an orderly withdrawal until he had joined hands with the German forces hurriedly dispatched to Tunis. He did not therefore put up a prolonged fight for Tripoli, which 7th Armoured and 51st (Highland) Divisions entered simultaneously on 23 January 1943, to much rejoicing.

Tunisia

Considerable argument had preceded the decision, taken in July 1942, to mount an Anglo-American expedition to occupy French North Africa with the main aim of preventing the Axis, perhaps helped by Spain, from doing so. The American Chiefs of Staff were wedded to the concept that the quickest way to defeat the Germans was by the shortest route, that is from Britain across the Channel, and that everything should be concentrated on that. But by July 1942 it had become clear that it was not possible to launch an effective cross-Channel expedition which could then be exploited in that year. Churchill and Roosevelt, for their separate reasons, did not want to see the newly raised American armies doing nothing until the summer of 1943: both feared that that would play into the hands of the Pacific-first lobby.

In August the American Dwight D. Eisenhower was appointed overall commander. His plan was for three landings: one in Morocco, the force for which would sail direct from the USA, commanded by Major-General George S. Patton: one, wholly American, sailing from Britain to land near Oran in Algeria under the command of Major-General Lloyd R. Fredendall; and the third near Algiers, half American and half British, under the American Major-General Charles W. Ryder. After landing, Patton's and Fredendall's forces would be formed into the Fifth US Army, commanded by Eisenhower's deputy, Major-General Mark W. Clark. It would be prepared to face a Spanish threat from Spanish Morocco or Spain itself. The force landed at Algiers would be transformed into the First British Army, commanded by Lieutenant-General Sir Kenneth Anderson. Its task would be to secure Algiers and nearby airfields and move eastward as rapidly as possible to capture Bone and Tunis, hopefully occupying the whole of Tunisia. Its ability to do this would largely depend on the attitude of the French forces in the country, hitherto loyal to Vichy. It was thought that they would be more amenable if the landings were represented as almost wholly American.

The British element of the landings near Algiers on 8 November 1942 consisted of two commandos, some of their members being American, and 11th and 36th Brigade Groups, which with 1st Guards Brigade and divisional troops would thereafter form 78th Division (Major-General V. Evelegh). In the event, except initially at Algiers harbour, there was only token resistance from the French forces, which was transformed into cooperation when Admiral Darlan, Commander-in-Chief of all the French armed forces, who happened to be in Algiers, ordered them to cease opposition on 11 November, the day after the Germans entered the unoccupied zone of France. On the 10th, 36th Brigade had re-embarked and was on its way to Bougie, a hundred miles to the east, where it landed unopposed on the 11th. The next step forward, of fifty miles to Bône, was made next day by 6th Commando by sea and two companies of the 3rd Parachute Battalion in the first operational drop of British parachute troops other than in commando raids. Both were unopposed.

By this time the forward troops and airfields were receiving sharp blows from the Luftwaffe. The Germans and Italians had reacted swiftly to the landings by sending reinforcements, originally intended for Rommel, to Tunis, another 150 miles beyond Bône. The leading troops of 78th Division met them about fifty miles west of Tunis on 17 November. They fought their way forward, 11th Brigade getting within fifteen miles of Tunis before the end of the month, before being severely counter-attacked and forced back a few miles to Tebourba. A further attempt to advance was made in December, by which time the 6th Armoured Division (Major-General C. F. Keightley) had joined the 78th in the forward area, both under 5th Corps (Lieutenant-General C. W. Allfrey); but a combination of sharp German counter-attacks and the onset of wet winter weather halted it.

As no threat from Spanish Morocco or Spain materialized, the American troops which had landed at Oran and in Morocco were moved east and came under Anderson's command. He now had three corps: in the north the British 5th, which had been joined by 46th Division (Major-General H. A. S. Freeman-Attwood); in the centre the French 19th (Lieutenant-General L. M. Goetz); and in the south the US 2nd (Lieutenant-General Fredendall). Anderson lacked the flexibility to cope with such a variegated command, and in order to improve matters, but also in anticipation of the entry of the Eighth Army into Tunisia, General Alexander handed over the Middle East Command to Wilson and arrived on 19 February to form the 18th Army Group, responsible to Eisenhower for all land operations in Tunisia.

Five days before that, Rommel had withdrawn 15th Panzer Division's fifty tanks from the Mareth Line, the defences which the French had built to face the Italians in Libya, and at Gafsa had attacked the Americans, whom Anderson ordered to withdraw. Joining up with the 140 tanks of 10th and 21st Panzer Divisions from von Arnim's Tunisia command, Rommel struck Fredendall's troops a fierce blow and drove them back from the Kasserine Pass. But he could not afford to exploit it by advancing north and cutting off the Allied forces facing Tunis, as he had been ordered, because his rear was threatened by the arrival of the British 7th Armoured Division at Médenine, fifteen miles from the Mareth Line, on that day.

Montgomery had held back in the area of Tripoli the whole of Eighth Army except for the 7th Armoured Division, which had followed up Rommel after he withdrew, making skilful use of demolitions, mines and booby traps. He was intent on building up logistic supplies which would free him from having to pause, once he had tackled the Mareth Line. A major road transport exercise all the way from Egypt had been needed to supplement supplies by sea to Tripoli, the harbour of which required a great deal of clearance and repair before it could handle much cargo. Rommel now thought he could give Montgomery a bloody nose before he could build up his army in the forward area. Taking all the panzer divisions, totalling 141 tanks, he planned to attack 7th Armoured Division at Médenine on 6 March. From ULTRA Montgomery got wind of what was afoot and sent the New Zealand Division, equipped with the new 17-pounder anti-tank gun, and 201st Guards Brigade up to join 7th Armoured and 51st (Highland), which was between them and the coast. All were in Leese's 30th Corps. The bloody nose was Rommel's, not Montgomery's. He lost fifty-two tanks, almost entirely to anti-tank guns, while 30th Corps's losses were negligible.

Lieutenant John Weir of the 2nd Scots Guards in 201st Guards
Brigade described the battle in a letter home:

At Medenine we were in the front line at last and we took up a
position below some hills with a wide plain between ourselves and
the Boche in the hills five miles away. Although from our lines the
plain looked flat enough, it was a mass of Wadis giving us welcome
cover from the all too vigilant Hun. I am allowed to tell you now
that I was looking after a platoon of carriers, and as their job is
scouting ahead and generally looking for information and trouble I
got to know that plain pretty well. We used to go out to some house
or olive grove for 24 hours and watch his positions, hoping he didn't
spot us and start shelling us. In this way we lost three carriers (not
any of mine) one morning when some German tanks crept up at
dawn. That was the day of the big tank battle which you probably
read about, when we knocked out 52 in a day.

I had a grand view of everything that day, though not without
excitement. The tanks chose our positions to attack, but as we were
in a hollow at the foot of the hill, they couldn't see us till they were
right on top of us. They could however see me for I was half way up
the hillside in an olive grove, and when their first few tanks had been
knocked out by our anti-tank guns in the hollow, the others put
the blame on me (who hadn't fired a shot) and opened up with
everything they had. We were lucky to have no casualties considering
the amount of rubbish that was thrown at us, and our only grievance
was that our view of the battle a few hundred yards below was for
ever being interrupted by the necessity of playing musical bumps to
the tune of countless shells and a few bullets. How I hate shells! I
have seen strong, courageous men reduced to whimpering wrecks,
crying like children. Some arrive with a long screeching crescendo
giving one time to take cover; others come faster than sound and
burst without warning. And when one has nothing to do, the fumes
and dust and echoed cries of 'stretcher-bearer' strain ones nerves
almost to breaking point. Yet if one goes to ground how incredibly
hard it is to get out into the open again to do a job of work! I would
sooner have a thousand bullets or even dive bombers than a day's
shelling. Still lets forget about shells: they are best forgotten.

At the end of that day the Huns had left 52 blazing wrecks on the
field, and a dozen more had been towed away more dead than alive.

That night I had to take out a patrol to blow up four wounded tanks before the enemy recovered them. It was raining hard, the Boche were very close and I was dead tired (and very frightened). Having laid two of the charges we were about to lay the third when one of the Sappers lost his nerve and ignited a charge thirty yards from where we were standing. The subsequent explosion was staggering as the whole magazine blew up, breaking a huge tank into fragments one of which was larger than a card table! How any of us escaped I just don't know but the only casualty was my sergeant who was standing next to me and had four ribs broken by a chunk of tank. There being no Sappers left after the explosion, we had to drag our weary, sodden bodies back. It was then 2 a.m. and to my horror I was told to go out on a reconnaissance patrol with one N.C.O. at 3.30 to find out whether the enemy was withdrawing. So an hour later in even heavier rain I set out feeling that Death would be a pleasant relief! However we reached the enemy positions safely, finding him about to depart, but as we crouched there listening to sergeants shouting and vehicles starting up, our own guns decided to open up. So in a few seconds we found ourselves sitting on the edge of a Wadi that had grown a crop of flaming mushrooms. We did the return journey in record time, for once completely unappreciative of our gunners' accuracy. By then I was more than convinced that I had done enough for 24 hours, but not a bit of it; I was promptly sent out on a 24 hour patrol to find out how far the enemy had withdrawn! What a life!

After this setback, Rommel withdrew behind the Mareth Line and left Africa for good three days later, handing over to von Arnim. Before that, the latter had also launched an unsuccessful attack on the British 5th Corps, using seventy-four tanks, fourteen of them the huge new Tiger with an 88mm gun. 46th Division bore the brunt of it on the approaches to Beja, while 78th Division successfully beat off attacks on Medjez el Bab. Fighting continued there until 1 March, when the Germans, with only five tanks left, called it off.

Montgomery's plan for the battle of Mareth was for Leese's 30th Corps to deliver a frontal attack with 50th Division across a waterlogged wadi, intended to draw in German reserves, while Freyberg's New Zealanders, reinforced by 8th Armoured Brigade, made a wide outflanking movement through the hills to cut off the Germans and Italians manning the Mareth defences. 50th Division's attack was an expensive failure, as had been a preliminary attack by 201st Guards Brigade. Montgomery thereupon decided to switch his main effort to the out-flanking movement, adding 1st Armoured Division to it and sending along also the commander of 10th Corps, Lieutenant-General B. G. Horrocks, with an undefined authority over Freyberg. Brilliantly supported by bold and unorthodox air attacks devised by Air Vice-Marshal Harry Broadhurst, the recently appointed commander of the Desert Air Force, it was successful in forcing the enemy's withdrawal from the Mareth line, but not in cutting him off.

Charles Potts had taken an active part in this, as he told his fiancée in a letter written on 23 March:

The battle which will probably be known as the Battle of Mareth is at its height. Showers of shells are landing all round the place. Planes keep swooping over, ours and Jerry's, I don't know which are worse. We have been bombed & strafed by our own planes nearly as often as by the enemy. Cyril Matson our company second in command was hit by machine gun fire from a Hurricane yesterday – smashed his ankle – so I am once more second in command of the company, a job I don't like. I've just pinched this writing paper from an Italian dug out. I am enclosing a photo which was found amongst some German kit. It looks just like the well I sheltered behind on January 25th and the well got a direct hit – well, well, well. I am sitting leaning against my vehicle – sitting on my wee camp stool. The sun is shining & it is warm. I always prefer enemy shelling to cold winds. Some shrapnel has gone through one of my petrol tanks &, worse still, through the tin containing our sugar ration. Lots of other bits of bomb and shell all over the place. One finds shrapnel in one's haversack & one's bedding & various other odd places. This morning I took one or two wounded fellows back in my Jeep. I also buried a Major, a Sergeant & a Lance-bombardier. I used some ready-dug Italian slit trenches as graves & filled them in & stuck a wooden cross up. Hell! I suppose one gets casual about death. I suppose it is because we realise that the blokes that get killed or wounded are well out of this hell, – & yet it is not altogether hell. We are having fun. I was driving along cheerfully in my Jeep just now when a shell burst right in front of me. Fortunately – against orders – I had my windscreen up & a shower of earth and little bits of shrapnel spattered onto it. The big bits went over me – one through the hood of the car. I roared with laughter – until I found that it had also punctured one of the wheels. One of my trucks has had a bit right through its engine – another is smashed to pieces – four more have shrapnel through the radiator. I am mighty sorry not to be still commanding the machine-gunners, as I was until yesterday when 'Mat' got wounded & I took his place. They have just gone off on an exciting party now – & I should have been with them.

A further attack was needed on the Wadi Akarit before Eighth Army was free to advance north and join hands with the First. In the latter, an attempt by the British 9th Corps (Lieutenant-General J. T. Crocker) to cut off the German and Italian forces withdrawing in front of Montgomery failed, as did an attack by the latter to drive them back near Enfidaville at the end of April, in which the 56th (London) Division (Major-General E. G. Miles), which had only recently arrived from Iraq, had an unfortunate introduction to battle.

Alexander now decided, with Montgomery's agreement, that Eighth Army should no longer play a major part and that 4th Indian Division, 7th Armoured Division and 201st Guards Brigade should be transferred to 9th Corps, Horrocks going with them to command the corps, Crocker having been wounded at a weapon demonstration. Alexander moved 2nd US Corps, of which Major-General Omar Bradley was now in command, to the left of the line, aimed at Bizerte, next to 5th Corps, with 1st (Major-General W. E. Clutterbuck), 4th (Major-General J. L. I. Hawkesworth) and 78th Divisions. To their right, and due to pass through their right sector, was 9th Corps, with 4th Indian and 6th and 7th Armoured Divisions on the left, and 46th Infantry and 1st Armoured Divisions on the right. The French 19th Corps was to advance through the hilly country between them and the Eighth Army. 9th Corps met some fierce resistance before it reached the start line for this attack.

The Reverend Geoffrey Druitt was with the 16th/5th Lancers in 6th Armoured Division. His diary describes Easter Saturday, 24 April 1943:

It's been one hell of a day!

As usual we had harboured with the tanks & at 4.30 am had dispersed while the tanks had moved into hull down positions. The enemy were thick in all the hills facing [us] – well concealed & well dug in, with innumerable guns commanding the whole plain over which we had advanced. Our job now was to knock them off the high range of hills – chief among them JEBEL KORNINE. During the night our guns had come up & taken their positions among the low foothills approaching the Jebel i.e. behind us & to our right.

We started to dig slit trenches at once – while others prepared breakfast. I had started ours – it was good ground & I had progressed well. 'Come on Horace' I called 'have a go at this' – he was toddling about as usual achieving nothing except boring everyone with his 'funny' stories (very hard to endure before breakfast). I remember he dug for a few minutes and then said 'That will be deep enough. So long as you are covered, Sir. I don't mind about myself.' If I had been a layman I could have made the correct response & told him not to be 'bloody silly'. As it was I told him not to be dramatic so early in the morning. I couldn't bear it!! The upshot of it all was that we had a larger and deeper trench than we have ever had before. Thank God for the mulish perversity of the Druitt family! Horace's dramatic statement of unselfish care for my bodily welfare had been the cause of a protection which was to save our lives.

It was shortly after breakfast that a few ranging shells started to fall among the echelon, 100 yards away. 'If they are trying for the guns', I said, 'I hope they soon find out their mistake!!' gazing anxiously around. Renewed activity was to be seen on slit trenches! Then those shells started coming over thick & fast – landing up to 40 yds from our RAP* which was slightly withdrawn from the rest of the vehicles. Two wounded chaps were brought up & David took them into his slit trench to be dealt with. Shortly afterwards, another man was brought up with nerves – cringing & crying at every shell-burst, tears streaming down his cheeks & shaking in every limb. I took him into our slit trench where he sat cowering & trembling but becoming quieter as Horace & I attempted to restore his confidence. Finally I left him to Horace who is pretty good at mentally holding such men to his ample bosom!

Shortly afterwards, his range changed & Jerry lobbed over his shells in salvoes of eight shells which landed all round us. Again & again they came & the earth shook & shrapnel whistled viciously across our trenches. It was becoming most unpleasant. Then to my

---

* Regimental Aid Post.

horror I saw two men doubling over to us – one was obviously wounded in the chest – then another was seen coming from another direction, also accompanied by a comrade. I prayed that nothing would drop – the first one arrived at David's trench & the wounded chap was squeezed in. Just as the second one arrived at my trench I heard Jerry let go another salvo – I yanked the lad in on top of me – shells landed very close as he fell in on our heads and he cried out that he had been hit again. I yelled to those who had come with him to get back again while they could. Then I started plugging the wounds of the latest arrival. I had finished my morphia & called out to David for some more – he threw a tube over. We squeezed the lad in but it made congestion frightful. Horace's foot was giving him pain which became excruciating – due to cramp – but shells were landing so thick & fast now that it would have been death to raise a head. It was very 'jolly' in our trench just about this time, I remember – the wounded man was groaning, Horace was half-sobbing with the pain of his foot, & the 'nerve' case was squealing in a sort of falsetto voice & shaking like an aspen. I was endeavouring to get my head below ground level, which meant scraping my head against earth which seemed particularly hard. Some shells fell so near to the trench that the shock of the earth bruised my head – a bruise which remained for several days. During a brief lull, I raised my head – both men who had accompanied their friends were lying dead close by; all our trucks had been hit but not directly – other vehicles were burning & the smell & smoke of explosives hung in the air. David poked his head up too & we grinned somewhat wanly at each other. Then down we bobbed again. Horace had relieved the position of his foot meanwhile, but now he was in further trouble. 'I want to go to the lavatory, Sir', he said. 'You can't now, old lad' I said, 'hold it.' 'But I *must*' he replied urgently. 'Then do it where you are – you can't get out'. Silence, except for a few more shells, then 'I *must* go, Sir' weakly. 'Don't be a fool – do it where you are – we can take it' I said with a grin – he did look so funny. Another short lull & David & I exchanged a few words. I turned round & there was Horace, lying at full length on the parapet, struggling to pull down his pants! He succeeded – a short, gasping pause & then he came tumbling in again – *not* having adjusted his clothes before leaving.

*

The attack on Tunis was launched on 6 May with massive air and artillery support, and the leading troops of the 6th and 7th Armoured Divisions entered the city next day, while those of the US 1st Armoured Division entered Bizerte; but it was not until the 12th that, hemmed in with their backs to the sea, over which neither by air nor by sea could they escape, the troops of von Arnim and of the Italian General Messe and the generals themselves surrendered – 101,000 Germans, 90,000 Italians and 47,000 others. First Army's British casualties since landing had been 25,742, of whom 4,094 had been killed: Eighth Army's, since entering Tunisia on 9 February, 12,618, of whom 2,139 had been killed. The three-year North African campaign, with all its ups and downs, had come to a triumphant end.

Montgomery was rightly hailed, by the British at least, as the hero of the North African campaign, and his two favourite corps commanders, Leese and Horrocks, shared his glory, as did Alexander, who never sought the limelight, but made a vital contribution by not interfering and seeing that Montgomery received all the support of every kind that he needed. Lumsden, who had clashed with Montgomery at El Alamein over the performance of his largely armoured 10th Corps, had been relegated to limbo after the battle. Anderson in Tunisia had not had an easy task and had not shone as a commander. Many of his subordinates later gained laurels in Italy, but he himself disappeared out of sight, although initially selected to command the Second Army for the landings in France. However he was replaced by Montgomery's favourite, Lieutenant-General Sir Miles Dempsey.

Sicily

The next step had been decided at the Allied conference at Casablanca in January. It was clear by then that Tunisia would not be fully occupied for some months and that a cross-Channel operation would not be practicable in 1943. The US Army Chief of Staff, General Marshall, strongly opposed any further operations in the Mediterranean, but the navy wanted to clear it to save shipping round the Cape and the air forces wanted to base bombers in southern Italy in order to be able to attack Germany from all directions. Both Sardinia and Corsica were considered, but agreement was reached that as soon as possible after Tunis was cleared, Sicily should be the target.

Eisenhower's plan was to use two armies, Montgomery's Eighth to the east and a US Seventh, commanded by Patton, to the west, both under a 15th Army Group, headed by Alexander. Eighth Army had two corps: on the right the 13th (Lieutenant-General M. C. Dempsey), comprising the 5th and 50th Divisions (Major-General H. P. M. Berney-Ficklin and Major-General S. C. Kirkman), supported by 4th Armoured Brigade, all sailing from Suez, and 1st Airborne Division, flying from El Djem in North Africa; and on the left Leese's 30th, comprising 51st Division, sailing from Tunisian ports and Malta, and 231st Infantry and 23rd Armoured Brigades sailing from Suez. 1st Canadian Division (Major-General G. G. Simonds) and 1st Canadian Armoured Brigade would join the corps, sailing direct from Britain.

Montgomery had raised strong objections to the original plan, which envisaged widely separated landing areas, including two in the west of the island. He wanted to concentrate in the south-east corner, and largely won the argument. The whole of Eighth Army was to land between Syracuse and the south-eastern tip at Pachino, while Patton's Seventh landed on the south coast, his right flank some fifty miles west of Montgomery's left. The enemy they had to contend with was General Guzzoni's Sixth Italian Army of four divisions, in addition to coast defence troops, which since the fall of Tunis had been reinforced by General Hube's 14th Panzer Corps, with the Hermann Goering Panzer and the 15th Panzer Grenadier Divisions, totalling 32,000 men with 160 tanks.

The assault before daylight on 10 July 1943 was everywhere successful, in spite of poor weather causing many mishaps to landing craft and severe losses in the 1st Airlanding Brigade, many of whose gliders were released prematurely by their towing aircraft and fell into the sea.

Sapper Richard Eke of 754 Field Company Royal Engineers describes their task of clearing the beaches:

> The alarming news that German Panzers were now facing the beach-head, spread a fatalistic concern among us that if the Germans broke through, we would be used as infantry.

We were roused from our despondency with a demand for volunteers to wade out to sea and blow up a sandbank that was grounding the incoming landing craft. Mad Corporal Pearson was obviously the first, he appeared to be afraid of nothing, and his enjoyment seemed to increase when in the greatest danger. He had come ashore early with the Commandos, and now was ready to lead us back into the sea again. There was no getting out of it, I was known as a strong swimmer, and with Norman Hopson and four others stripped off our boots and shorts.

The rest of the platoon grimly resumed work in the minefield, taping out another forty feet width, and with the other platoons further along were ordered to clear the whole of the beach by mid-day.

We had the idea of utilising the discarded lifebelts once again, but this time stuffed with 'ammonal' a cratering explosive to blow up the sandbank. They were rapidly collected and crammed with the grey powder like huge sausages, then wrapped around with 'cordtex' an explosive cord. We held the long snakes of explosive above our heads as we waded out in line through the warm water. It was a luxurious feeling after the sweat and dirt of the red hot beach to feel the water creeping up to our chest. The thought of another lightning air attack was uppermost in our minds, but we knew there would be no getting out of the water in a hurry this time.

The charges were pushed down through the water and held down with our feet whilst others lay sandbags on the long cushion of explosive. The preparation was almost complete, the skys remained clear, and we were able to relax in the cooling water. I was reluctant to return to the stifling heat of the beach, and waded over to Norman Hopson and suggested a swim before returning. Just further out as the water became deeper, the top of one of the crashed gliders was visible. We swam out to it and dived down. The sand-clouded water stung our eyes as we peered through the flickering green shadows towards the dark shape of the glider. A large gap in the side showed where the exit door had been discarded, and no doubt was where the two murdered paratroopers had escaped from. In the cockpit, white faces were pressed to the windows, their blank eyes staring as if surprised to see us. Their bodies were gently floating and rolling in the current, still dressed in full equipment and trapped in their flimsy tomb.

We broke the surface and gulped in mouthfuls of air. I was trembling with shock, and with the horror behind us, struck out for the sandbank. The glider was full of the bodies of our best fighting men, who through a miscalculation, together with most of the squadron, had all missed the island and plunged into the sea. They were all volunteers and, ready to lead the assault on the beaches, had not even been given the chance to fight for their country.

We waded back to the beach as the Beach Commander's hailers diverted all landing-craft away from the area. Our ingenious mine was detonated from the beach and surprisingly it worked perfectly, and the landing-craft were able to follow the new deeper channel through to the beach.

The Italians put up little resistance. Montgomery now planned that 13th Corps should advance to Catania and then up the narrow strip of coast east of Mount Etna to Messina to prevent German and Italian troops from escaping from there to the mainland. He directed 30th Corps west of Etna towards San Stefano on the north coast, halfway between Palermo and Messina, in order to cut off the enemy in the west of the island and to provide another route to Messina. He asked Alexander to get Patton to protect his left flank while he did this, requesting an adjustment of the boundary between them, so that he could use a road which had originally been allotted to Patton. Alexander obligingly agreed, infuriating Patton, who complained to Eisenhower. Alexander prevaricated, and Patton, in high dudgeon, drove fast for Palermo, where he turned east towards Messina.

Meanwhile the Germans, although reinforced with a parachute division landed near Catania, had decided to evacuate their forces from the island, seeing that the Italians were not prepared to fight. Hube conducted a skilful gradual withdrawal which prevented Montgomery and Patton from cutting off any of the German troops, and, as neither the navy under Cunningham, nor the air forces under Tedder, Eisenhower's naval and air commanders, did anything effective to prevent it, between 1st and 16th August he succeeded in transferring to the mainland 39,650 men, including casualties, 9,185 vehicles, which included all his heavy weapons, and 11,855 tons of stores.

Italy

The question of where to go next after Sicily had been discussed at the Anglo-American summit meeting, Trident, in Washington in May. The Americans had started with a demand that there should be no more Allied operations in the Mediterranean after Sicily; but after they had secured agreement to the definite target date of 1 May 1944 for the cross-Channel operation, and reluctant acceptance of their demand that seven veteran divisions, four American and three British,* together with most of the theatre's landing ships and craft, should be transferred to Britain by 1 November 1944, they agreed that with what he had left Eisenhower should 'plan such operations in exploitation of HUSKY† as are best calculated to eliminate Italy from the war and to contain the maximum number of German forces'.

Eisenhower looked again at Corsica and Sardinia and rejected both, as well as landings north of Naples. The decisive factor was fighter cover, which fixed the bay of Salerno as the northernmost landing site. He therefore decided that Fifth US Army, commanded by Mark Clark, with 6th US Corps (Lieutenant-General E. J. Dawley) on the right and 10th British Corps (Lieutenant-General R. L. McCreery) on the left, should land there on 9 September and advance north to capture Naples. Meanwhile Montgomery should have crossed the Straits of Messina and started moving north to join him.

The plan itself, and its execution, became complicated by events in Italy. On 25 July, while fighting in Sicily was still going on, Mussolini was deposed and a military Government, loyal to the King, established, headed by Marshal Badoglio. Contact with the Allies was established through Madrid and Lisbon, and surrender terms discussed. The aim of the Allies was for an Italian surrender to coincide with the Salerno landing, rather than precede it, which would give the Germans time to react and reinforce their presence in the country. The Italian aim was to try to ensure that the Allies had sufficient forces in the country at the

---

* They were to be the 50th and 51st and the 7th Armoured.
† The Sicily operation.

time of the surrender to protect them against the Germans. They proposed an unrealistic plan by which an Allied airborne division would be dropped near Rome, while an armoured division landed at the mouth of the Tiber. Serious consideration was given to the airdrop, but, fortunately, it was rejected late in the day as impractical. The surrender was actually announced on the evening before the Salerno landing took place at dawn on 9 September.

The Germans realized what their allies were up to, and took measures to strengthen their forces and prepare to face landings almost anywhere. The area of Naples, and from there to the east coast, was the responsibility of Hube, who had the 16th Panzer Division as well as those he had brought back from Sicily. He appreciated that Salerno was a likely landing place and did not propose to defend the 'toe' of Italy south of that. Montgomery therefore had an easy task when he crossed the straits with 1st Canadian and 5th British Divisions on 3 September, supported by a tremendous bombardment from air, sea and land, which proved unnecessary. His progress thereafter was slow, hindered by extensive demolitions on the narrow mountain roads.

10th Corps landed successfully with 46th Division on the left and 56th (Major-General D. A. H. Graham) on the right; but they soon came under heavy attack, as did the American 6th Corps to their south. A crisis arose on 19 September when General Herr's 76th Panzer Corps, reinforcing Hube, attacked the centre of the beachhead, threatening to split it in two. It was overcome partly by airdropping part of the US 82nd Airborne Division and partly because by that time Montgomery's leading troops were approaching from the south. Ten days before that, satisfied that the Italian fleet was surrendering, the navy had transported the 1st Airborne Division from Bizerte to Taranto, from where they advanced to Brindisi and then Bari, their commander, Major-General G. F. Hopkinson, being killed at Castellanata and succeeded by Major-General E. E. Down.

Fusilier Gilbert Allnutt was with the 8th Royal Fusiliers in 56th Division at Salerno, and describes his experiences:

Later in the day we moved up to our positions well in advance of a farmhouse at which Battalion H.Q. had been established. In position on the edge of a field we dug in. Machine gunners from the Middlesex Regiment were in front to support us. We were told that a German attack was expected at any time – and so, once again, we waited.

'It's quiet.' 'Too damned quiet.' In how many War plays or stories has that corny dialogue appeared? Yet those words were precisely what we all were thinking. The quiet was unbelievable – a sinister quiet – we could tell that an attack was imminent. The feeling was in the air; one could sense that the quiet would not last.

The attack came with a suddenness that shattered the peace and the morale of many who were in action for the first time. Shells fell all round and bullets were flying over head. Amidst the cries of the wounded some one was shouting 'get back' and the scene became one of utter confusion. Later we learnt that the order to withdraw to defensive positions at the farmhouse had been given by a Lance Corporal, another Fusilier and I had heard no order and for a while we remained where we were. Realizing that we were alone we crawled back along a ditch over which bullets were still flying. When the ditch ended we were stranded, for the open ground was being pounded by shells from both directions. We lay where we were with the earth shaking around us and all night long the battle raged. By dawn the fury seemed to have subsided and, not having heard the order to get back to the farmhouse, we feared that our Company had met with disaster. We decided to go back hoping that we might meet a British patrol and this in fact we did, later reaching the farmhouse H.Q. in safety. In the centre of things was Regimental Sergeant Major Murphy.

From the day, as a recruit, that I committed the cardinal army sin of saluting a Regimental Sergeant Major, I have had a built-in horror of R.S.M's. It was always my policy to keep as far away as possible from them. However, to see R.S.M. Murphy at Battalion Headquarters when the Battalion was in a tight spot helped me to see them in a different light. He was obviously pleased to see us back with our weapons and in reasonably good shape. He told us that the Battalion had fought off the attack but the position of W Company was not yet known. We were to stay at Headquarters until the Company location was known. His bearing and attitude towards us certainly boosted my morale. It had never occurred to me that an R.S.M. could be a comrade but that day, and later at Anzio, I saw Murphy as one and realised his value to the Battalion.

Later in the day a Fusilier appeared who knew where W Company was located. Together we set off but it soon transpired that he only thought he knew the way. As we reached a lane I suddenly heard the unforgettable sound of the Nebelwerfer 'winding up', automatically followed by the swish of the shells through the air. I looked despairingly to my left and in an orchard a few yards away I saw British steel helmets. In a Charlie Chaplinish flight from the descending shells I dived head first into a slit trench in the orchard just as the mortars exploded in the lane. Apart from some good humoured chaffing for bringing the 'stonking' so near them I was made most welcome. I was with the Royal Fusiliers but not W Company. The Platoon Sergeant put me in the picture – it was a grim one. The Company were on continual stand to because a German attack was expected. I heard of the intensive build up of forces only a short distance away. If the mortar attack had not interrupted us we would have walked right into the German positions. That evening, from our rear, a terrific bombardment was set up. In a trench behind me a signalman was in radio contact with a destroyer, for the Navy was playing its part in this effort to break up the forces mounted against us. Even with the thunder of all these guns, in our tiredness we could have dropped off to sleep. However, the Platoon Sergeant's voice kept everyone alert and ready for the attack which seemed inevitable.

The dawn came, the sun came up to warm us and quietness prevailed. Later the news came through that our bombardment had caused such havoc that the attack was abandoned and that the enemy had withdrawn. By mid-morning a patrol appeared who really did know W Company's position down by the canal and I went back with them.

W Company were well dug in and the section that I reached was about to partake of tea and a meal of 'M and V' (meat and vegetable stew) re-inforced with local tomatoes. Could any gourmet have enjoyed a meal as I did that evening? What accomodation could have seemed more inviting than a deep slit trench which I fondly hoped would give me my first sleep for days.

Initially Hitler had intended to evacuate southern Italy and hold the line of the mountains along the southern side of the valley of the Po; but he was persuaded by Kesselring that this would allow Allied bombers to establish airfields which would greatly increase the bombing threat to Germany, and agreed to a strategy of holding the Allies as far south as possible. Kesselring then decided to establish a succession of strongly defended lines across the country. The principal one, which he intended to hold throughout the winter, was the Gustav line, running from the mouth of the River Garigliano in the west, past Cassino, and then across the Apennines to the River Sangro, south of Pescara, in the east. Meanwhile his forces would fight a determined delaying action on a succession of lines back to the Gustav line.

On 21 September Alexander announced to his subordinates his plan of campaign: first, to secure the line Salerno–Bari: then to take Naples and the group of airfields round Foggia: after that to take Rome and the airfields and communication centres between it and Terni; and, in the more distant future, to secure Leghorn (Livorno), Florence and Arezzo. He hoped to be able to make considerable use of amphibious operations to land behind German defence lines. Eighth Army was to operate on the east coast, Fifth US on the west. His first two aims were soon achieved, as the Germans withdrew to the River Volturno on the west and to the Biferno on the east of the watershed. They were pushed out of that position by mid-October, but thereafter both armies faced strong opposition, the Fifth on the Garigliano, the Eighth on the Sangro. After fierce fighting by 46th and 56th (now Major-General G. W. R. Templer) Divisions for Monte Camino, the Fifth was up to the river by the end of the year, but not strong enough to force a crossing. Alexander hoped that Montgomery would reach Pescara, twenty-five miles beyond the Sangro, where he fought a particularly tough battle to cross, and then strike across the mountains by the Via Valeria to Rome, getting behind the Germans holding up Fifth Army, or forcing them to withdraw.

By this time Eighth Army had eight divisions, the 1st, 5th and 78th British, the 1st and 5th Canadian, the 4th and 8th Indian and the New Zealand; but in spite of this strength, a combination of determined and skilful German defence, rugged terrain and foul weather brought them to a halt in mid-December halfway between the Sangro and Pescara. At the end of the month Montgomery handed his army over to Leese and returned to England to assume command of 21st Army Group in preparation for Operation Overlord, the long-awaited Channel crossing. Eisenhower left Algiers to become Supreme Commander, his place there being taken by that great survivor, Maitland Wilson.

Montgomery was glad to go. He had found the campaign, in which he did not really believe, intensely frustrating, and it had not shown him at his best, although the operations were of the type in which he excelled, the carefully planned set-piece battle, in which infantry and artillery played the major part. The combination of German skill and toughness in defence with the weather and the nature of the country, heavily populated and broken up by mountains and ravines, meant that success on the battlefield was hard to achieve and expensive. There could have been no greater contrast with conditions in the desert. On top of that, he no longer enjoyed Alexander's undivided support. It had to be shared with Mark Clark, and he found Alexander indecisive about where priority lay.

The latter now decided that the main effort was to be made by Fifth Army, to which several divisions from Eighth Army would be transferred, and that it would include a strong amphibious landing at Anzio, sixty miles behind the German Gustav Line on the Garigliano. Eighth Army was left with 78th Division, the two Canadian divisions grouped into 1st Canadian Corps (Lieutenant-General H. D. G. Crerar), the two Indian divisions and the newly arrived 2nd Polish Corps (General W. Anders) with, at this stage, only its 3rd Carpathian Division (Major-General Duch). The divisions transferred were the 1st, to join Lieutenant-General J. P. Lucas's 6th US Corps for the Anzio operation, and the 5th, to join 10th Corps, while the New Zealand Division moved into army reserve in Fifth Army's area. Clark's plan was for an assault to be launched on 17 January 1944 by 10th Corps across the Garigliano and by 2nd US Corps across the Rapido. Five days later 6th Corps would land at Anzio and cut the German communications between Rome and the Liri valley. General Alphonse Juin's French Colonial Corps, with Moroccan and Algerian troops, would storm the mountains north of Cassino.

The operation was a disappointment, although the troops managed to cross the rivers and make several dents in the Gustav Line. The landing at Anzio, in fact on the 22nd, far from acting to loosen up the German defence, soon became a liability, as German reinforcements hemmed the cautious Lucas in. Several further attempts were made to break through the Gustav Line into the Liri valley, but, although more divisions were transferred from Eighth Army, including 4th and 8th Indian, little progress was made and casualties were high. A major renewed effort was made in mid-February, when the New Zealand and 4th Indian Divisions, under Freyberg's overall command, assaulted Cassino. At the request of Major-General F. W. Tuker, the commander of 4th Indian Division, the famous monastery was bombed into ruins; but all was to no avail, and this further attempt to reach the Liri valley was called off on 20 February. Meanwhile the 56th British Division had joined the 1st at Anzio in time to help defeat a major attempt by the Germans to throw 6th US Corps, now commanded by Lieutenant-General Lucian K. Truscott, back into the sea. Alexander's hopes of reaching Rome had received a severe setback; but one of the principal aims of the campaign was being achieved, that of containing German divisions which might otherwise be facing the Russians, or, more significantly, guarding the Channel coast. The human cost was, however, high.

On 15 March 1944 Alexander renewed the attack on Cassino with the same divisions, supported by a massive air bombardment of the town itself, but no progress was made through the rubble it left, and the third battle of Cassino ended on 26 March at a cost of 4,000 casualties. Planning for a renewed offensive was complicated by American pressure for Alexander to release troops and amphibious shipping for a landing in the south of France. After much argument, 11 May was set as the date for Operation DIADEM, yet another attempt to break into the Liri valley and join up with Anzio. For this Alexander brought Eighth Army over to the west, leaving only 5th Corps, with 4th and 10th Indian Divisions, east of the watershed. Leese was given the task of breaking into the valley through Cassino with 13th British and 1st Canadian Corps, while the Poles thrust through the mountains in the monastery sector on their right and 10th Corps, with only the New Zealand Division, moved forward higher up between them and 5th Corps. Fifth Army, with Juin's French Expeditionary Force of four divisions playing the principal part, would thrust through the mountains west of the valley, and the reinforced 6th US Corps at Anzio, where 5th Division replaced the 56th, struck out to cut off von Vietinghoff's Tenth Army from Rome.

Private Charlie Framp was serving in the 6th Black Watch, in 4th Division in 13th Corps. He describes their part in the attack:

We raced by a Bren carrier, it was on fire, its cargo of small arms ammunition exploded in all directions. We passed a number of bodies, their faces, where visible, were already taking on a waxen appearance. The bridge was hidden by smoke but the Germans knew, roughly, its whereabouts, they deluged the area with fire. We ran a gauntlet of bursting shells, then we were on the bridge. As we raced off, at the other end, we passed through a number of bodies lying scattered on the ground. One of the figures was still alive, he lay spread-eagled on his back, snoring frantically, blood bubbles formed and burst in rapid succession about his mouth. The din of battle reached new heights, we raced by a line of slit trenches, many only partially dug. The ground about them was torn by shell fire, a litter of abandoned and broken equipment surrounded the trenches. I saw Lt. Colonel Madden walking along through the fire, swinging his stick like he was out for a country stroll. Then we met our tanks, we had several hundred yards to go to our Company start line. Rounding a very sharp bend in the road, one of the tanks tippled into a ditch. Major Coates swore at the crew but they were unable to extricate their vehicle and we carried on without it. I felt an iron band of fear clamped itself tightly about my chest.

Our company objective was a group of farm buildings, or rather, what remained of them. It was a strong position, we'd been told, and the Germans were well dug in. I didn't know whether it represented blue line, red line or what, nor did I care. We couldn't see it but the fire from it ripped through the mist towards us. That morning the mist was our friend, as we moved steadily forward, through the shellfire, the strangest thing happened to me, the band of fear, which had clamped itself around my chest, suddenly relaxed its grip, I felt a tremendous upsurge of spirits, I felt something I'd never felt before, I can only describe it as an exhultation, perhaps the exhultation of battle. It may sound boastful but that's how I felt just then, I walked forward boldly and confidently, I amazed myself. The crackle of small arms fire and the repeated 'Br-r-r-r-p—Br-r-r-r-p' of spandaus before us grew louder. We took to the ditches, in order to deploy ourselves for the final assault across the two hundred yards or so of fire swept ground remaining between us and our objective.

Company H.Q. crawled single file along a ditch, bullets cracked and zipped above our heads. A constant hail of shells howled down and exploded around us, as the Germans, well aware of our coming, frantically mortared the area. I was struck forcibly on the head by a huge clod of earth thrown up by a near miss on the ditch. We'd come to a halt, I waited patiently for the man in front to move on. He didn't. After a minute or two I ventured to ask him 'What are we waiting for?' He didn't answer, something about his reluctance to answer aroused my suspicions. I crawled right up to him and repeated the question, he gestured towards the man before him, indicating that he was waiting for him to move first. I looked at the man in front, he lay still, too still, I crawled up to him, he was dead. I was certain the other man had guessed it but had decided not to make sure, in order to stay longer in the protection of the ditch, I cursed him soundly, he could have lost touch with the others of H.Q.

I took the lead and led the way forward once more. I quite surprised myself, for the second time that day, by this assumption of responsibility. That kind of thing, I'd always been more than content to leave to others. Nor had I been at the whisky bottle, such front line luxuries as that weren't for the likes of me. I'd never sought promotion, it had never ever occurred to me, nor, I think, did such a preposterous idea ever occur to my superiors. I was a born private, tailor-made for the rank, I knew it, they knew it. I was quite happy, confident in the final victory, to leave the actual conduct of the war in such capable hands as those of Lance-Corporal Smith, Sergeant Major Davison and, of course, Major Coates.

*

Success came at last, owing much to the brilliant exploits of Juin's Moroccans and Algerians, who levered open the western flank of the valley on 15 May, while the Poles raised their flag over the ruins of the monastery on the 18th. The breakout from Anzio started on the 23rd, as the Canadians passed through 13th Corps in the Liri valley, and it looked as if Truscott would reach the main German escape route through Valmontone in time to cut them off; but Mark Clark's eyes were on Rome and, to Alexander's intense annoyance, he switched his main effort in that direction and let the Germans escape. After a brief contest on the Caesar Line east of Rome, the Germans withdrew to their Gothic Line, based in the mountains north of Florence. The 88th US Division entered Rome on 4 June, two days before Montgomery's troops landed on the beaches of Normandy.

From then on, the campaign in Italy had to play second fiddle, but that did not lessen the difficulties and hardships of continuing the fight there, especially in the winter in the mountains. Alexander planned to turn the Gothic Line by transferring the Eighth Army back to the east and making the major effort on the Adriatic coast. This was done in

Norman Wilkinson. *Troops landing on C Beach Suvla Bay.*

John Nash. *Over the Top*.

Harold S. Williamson. *German Attack on a Wet Morning.*

Richard Eurich. *Dunkirk Beaches.*

Anthony Gross. *Three of Garret's Companions.*

Edward Ardizzone. *Soldiers and Transport in the Mountain Village of Castel del Rio.*

Barnett Freedman. *The Landing in Normandy, Arromanches,*
D-Day + 20, 26th June 1944.

John Devane. *The Look-out, Cyprus 1978.*

Ken Howard. *King Billy and the Brits, Belfast.*

Peter Howson. *MFU 1994, Bosnia.*

the second half of August, and Leese launched his attack on the 25th with the Canadian Corps (Lieutenant-General C. Foulkes) of two divisions, aimed at Rimini, and Keightley's 5th Corps, with the 4th, 46th, 56th, 4th Indian and 1st Armoured Divisions, directed to cut the Via Emilia between Rimini and Bologna. This posed a serious threat to the Germans, who reacted strongly, fighting back from ridge to ridge as Eighth Army fought its way doggedly forward, reaching Rimini by 21 September, while Fifth Army struggled through the mountains from Florence towards Bologna in driving rain. After Anzio, the 56th Division had been withdrawn to Egypt and reorganized, returning to Italy in July 1944.

Although there had been many changes, Gilbert Allnutt was still with the 8th Royal Fusiliers and describes their part in some of this fighting:

Major Chard's new team first tasted battle at Montefiore and then advanced on the village of Croce. It was a war of movement with Officers' skill at map reading being of prime importance. Inevitably units were never exactly where they were expected to be and on one occasion the men of X Company Headquarters found themselves well in advance of the fighting platoons!

Under orders to advance beyond Croce because the 'powers that be' believed that village to be in British hands the Company found themselves in positions of great peril. Early casualties had been caused mainly by machine gun fire. Later it was exceptionally intense shelling that led to losses. It was a testing time for every Officer and man.

I had the impression then that Major Chard was conscious of the fact that he was a professional soldier without actual battle experience who was now required to lead a Company of Fusiliers many of whom had considerable experience of battle conditions. He was out to 'win his spurs'. He certainly did so in these battles of the Gothic Line and this was officially recognised when he was mentioned in despatches. His technical knowledge and his inspiring leadership proved invaluable but he received more than full support from his Officers and N.C.O's.

Under ceaseless and terrifying shelling it would have been understandable if the Company had wavered. Indeed at one stage some men were reluctant to leave their positions to advance. Perhaps they were aware of the 'faulty appreciation'; perhaps the situation was too much for them for even Fusiliers are human. However a minor crisis was solved and the Company advanced to help make the first cracks in the Gothic Line.

The battle of Croce covered four unforgettable days for X Company. The fighting that followed was relatively easy but the Company still suffered casualties from machine gun, mortar and heavy artillery fire. On the night of 18/19th September, when the Company returned from Croce to the B Echelon area, they had a full share of the Battalion's casualties of ten Officers killed or wounded among the total of 193. By 21st September, after the battle of Mulazzano Ridge, the Battalion was finally relieved. By then both the 8th and 9th Battalions, rebuilt so painstakingly in Egypt, were drastically reduced in numbers.

Both armies kept up the pressure, until finally calling off the winter offensive at the end of the year, by which time Eighth Army had reached Ravenna and the Senio River beyond, and the Fifth was halted in the mountains only nine miles from Bologna. It had been the most costly period of fighting in the worst conditions that the army had faced anywhere since 1918.

Captain Ronald Coltman of the 52nd Field Regiment Royal Artillery, which was supporting the 8th Indian Division in 13th Corps, describes it:

The weather at this time was atrocious – rain – rain – rain. Eight and a half inches fell during one night in ten hours. I was engaged for the greater part of a duty night in mopping up pools of water formed by the rain dripping through the leaking roof. Drip, drip, drip, all through the night. Outside, the mud was appalling; it was knee deep in the lane that led by the church. Vehicles, using the lane, sank into the mud up to their axles.

The infantry were having a rough and gruelling time, the weather probably being their worst enemy. What accomodation there was in the way of cottages and farmhouses were on the lower mountain slopes and in the valley. The infantry were holding the line thinly and mainly by occupying positions on the heights and peaks where there was no accomodation whatever. They lived in slit-trenches half filled with mud, and were exposed to hours of incessant heavy rains as well as enemy mortar bombs and shells. The battery was still supporting the Mahrattas and the O.P. was on the forward slopes of Mount Ceco, and in a slit-trench. Because of complete lack of cover the O.P. had to be occupied under cover of darkness, just before first light in the morning, and at night after darkness had set in again. In between time the party were exposed to the worst elements of the weather, to damp and penetrating coldness, to hours of cramp and numbness, to say nothing of a hostile enemy. Conditions were so bad that O.P. parties were relieved every two days. They would depart for the O.P., ballooned out with an abundance of clothing in an effort to keep warm and dry, and waders reaching to the thighs kept the feet and legs clear of the mud. They would return to the gun position two days later, fatigued, dishevelled, and thickly plastered with mud. The infantry, in spite of the severe weather conditions, were undergoing long spells in the line without relief. It was customary for an infantry battalion to have a two weeks stretch in the line and then be relieved, but at this period, and enduring this most foul weather, the Mahrattas were in the line for an unbroken spell of five weeks before eventually being relieved.

By then also there had been changes in the higher command. Leese left Eighth Army on 1 October to command the land forces of South-East Asia Command under Mountbatten, and was succeeded by Mc-Creery. In November Wilson replaced Dill, who had died, as the Chiefs of Staffs' representative with their American colleagues, whose warm respect he had gained. In December Alexander replaced Wilson as Supreme Commander in the Mediterranean and Mark Clark took over 15th Army Group, in which Truscott took his place in command of Fifth Army.

The armies dug in where they were until April 1945, when the final offensive in Italy coincided with that in North-West Europe. Clark's plan was for Fifth Army to fight its way down into the Po valley west of Bologna and entrap the German divisions before they could withdraw across the river. Five days before that, on 9 April, Eighth Army launched its attack. While amphibious vehicles transported 56th Division across Lake Comacchio on the right, the main German position on the Senio River was attacked by 5th Corps on the right, with 8th Indian and the New Zealand Divisions, with the 78th in reserve, 13th Corps, with 10th Indian Division, in the centre and the Poles on the left, all with massive air and artillery support. The German positions broke one after another, and on 21 April the Poles entered Bologna. Two days later the leading troops of Fifth and Eighth Armies, encircling Bologna, met at a village aptly named Finale. On 28 April, five days before a similar deputation visited Montgomery on Lüneburg Heath, German emissaries arrived at Alexander's headquarters to discuss terms for an armistice, which became effective on 2 May 1945, to the great relief of every Allied soldier in Italy.

Few British commanders emerge from the Italian campaign with their reputations enhanced, certainly not at the highest level. It was hard pounding throughout and success was difficult to come by. Although Churchill greatly admired Alexander, there does not seem to be much real basis for it. Some commanders at divisional level undoubtedly shone, among whom Bernard Freyberg and Francis Tuker, with the New Zealand and 4th Indian Divisions, stand out. The conditions, especially in the winter, under which the soldiers lived and fought resembled those of the First World War more than in any other campaign. Although the results of operations were disappointing, the pressure they exerted on the German army made an essential contribution in limiting the effort which it could deploy against the forces under Eisenhower in North-West Europe.

North-West Europe

After Montgomery had left Eighth Army on 23 December 1943 he went to Algiers to see Eisenhower, who, three weeks before, had been told by President Roosevelt that he was to be appointed Supreme Commander of the Allied forces for Operation OVERLORD, the cross-Channel operation to liberate France and defeat the Germans. Together they considered the plan, which had been worked out by an Anglo-American staff under the British Lieutenant-General Sir Frederick Morgan, known as COSSAC (Chief of Staff to the Supreme Allied Commander). The Combined Chiefs of Staff had told Morgan to plan on the basis of nine assault divisions, five in the initial wave of landing craft, two as follow-up and two airborne, to be followed by twenty divisions which would be available in Britain by 1 May 1944. Morgan's plan was that the actual landings, by one British and two US corps, under the command of First

US Army, would be under the overall command of 21st Army Group. After the assault phase, First Canadian Army would take over command of all British and Canadian troops. At a later stage, another US Army would join the First, forming 12th Army Group, and Second British Army would join First Canadian in 21st Army Group, which at that stage would cease to command the Americans, Eisenhower assuming command of the two Army Groups as Land Force Commander as well as being Supreme Commander.

Neither Eisenhower nor Montgomery liked the plan, which they thought employed too few divisions on too narrow a front in the assault. Agreeing that Montgomery should command both the British (including the Canadian) and the US armies in the initial phases, Eisenhower asked Montgomery to get it sorted out in England, while he went for a few weeks to the USA. Montgomery, in consultation with the overall naval commander, Admiral Sir Bertram Ramsay, soon realized that landing craft were the restricting factor. After much argument, sufficient additional ones were made available by postponing the planned Franco-American landings in the south of France (Operation ANVIL) until after OVERLORD, which itself was postponed for a month, during which British shipyards could produce more craft.

The actual plan, which, after 24 hours' postponement due to bad weather, went into effect on D-Day 6 June 1944, gave separate sectors to US First Army (Bradley) on the right, landing on a twenty-five-mile front either side of the south-east corner of the Baie de la Seine, where the Cherbourg peninsula juts north from the Normandy coast, and British Second Army (Lieutenant-General Sir Miles Dempsey) on the left, stretching for the same distance to just east of the mouth of the River Orne, north of Caen.

The first of Dempsey's troops to land were 6th Airborne Division (Major-General R. N. Gale), who parachuted and glidered into the area on and east of the River Orne and its canal soon after midnight. By first light on the 6th they had secured their objectives, including the important bridges over the river and canal halfway between the coast and Caen. West of them, 3rd Division (Major-General T. G. Rennie), and a Commando Brigade, and 3rd Canadian (Major-General R. F. L. Keller), also with a Commando Brigade, landed under the command of 1st British Corps (Lieutenant-General J. T. Crocker) between Ouistreham and Courseulles. Lieutenant J. J. Moore describes the part his battalion,

the 8th King's (Liverpool), the Liverpool Irish, played as a Beach Group
for the 3rd Canadian Division:

> It was a very rough crossing and, before daylight, as we neared the
> Normandy coast, the shattering attack started, firstly from the
> bomber aircraft which saturated the area, and then with a terrific
> bombardment from the Navy behind us. The six Canadian self-
> propelled 105mm guns on our Landing Craft Tank, with several
> others, opened up, blasting targets on the beach area. Slowly, as the
> darkness gave way to light, the coast near Courseulles appeared as a
> dark grey line. Gradually the dim silhouettes of our landing-area at
> Graye-sur-Mer to the west of Courseulles became discernible, with
> the dull green countryside rising slightly beyond. The whole invasion
> was a miraculously impressive sight: there were hundreds of landing-
> craft firing at the coast, and to the rear of them the cruisers Belfast,
> Diadem, and others, together with their accompanying destroyers,
> were hammering the German fortresses on the almost impregnable
> Western wall. There were ships as far as the eye could see.
>
> We watched hundreds of five-inch diameter rockets (LCR) rising
> alongside us. Three of our 'Mustang' planes roared in toward the
> coast just at that moment, and the second one was accidentally hit
> by our own rockets and blew up, fragmenting into thousands of
> pieces. Well over to the East there was a huge explosion on a large
> ship, sending up a massive plume of smoke.
>
> The coast, its forts and its obstacles now seemed very close and
> well defined. A German reinforced-concrete pill-box fired some shells
> at the Landing-Craft just to our right, but this was an LCG* armed
> with two 4.7 inch guns, and having turned slowly around as if badly
> damaged, it fired a salvo, blasting the pill-box into rubble.
>
> Now slowly overtaking our Landing-Craft-Tank were the small
> Assault-Crafts that had been launched from the troop-carrying ships
> well to our rear, the Langriddy Castle, the H.M.C.S. Prince Henry,
> the Mecklenburg and others. These Assault Landing Crafts were
> carrying the heroes of the day on to our beach, the infantry men of
> the Royal Winnipeg Rifles and the two beach-companies of the
> Liverpool Irish: all of these had been cruelly tossed about in these
> lightweight, flat-bottomed landing crafts, packed tightly together,

* Landing Craft Gun.

thirty or more to each landing craft unable to see out and almost all violently sick because of the rough sea.

At this stage, just ahead of them, lay the fearsome beach obstacles, the massive iron structures, Element C, the concrete tetrahedra and the crude iron Hedgehogs, all with German 'Teller' mines and captured French explosive shells, all tar-coated and crudely wired on to the obstacles. Because of high winds and stormy weather the tide was much deeper than expected, with the result that bombs thrown at the obstacles by men from the special landing crafts (Hedgerow) were almost totally ineffective. We watched as the Assault Landing Crafts carrying the assault troops of the Winnepegs and the Liverpool Irish tried to manoeuvre through the gaps in the barrier of obstacles. Some had the bottom of their landing crafts torn off by the jagged obstacles: others were sunk or blown up by the exploding mines or shell. Almost one in three of the assault-landing crafts were sunk or badly damaged.

For the troops involved in a landing such as this, the greatest fears were of being hit or drowned while still in the water, and then in crossing under fire before reaching the relative safety of the minor sand-hills. Beyond these was a flat plain of some four-hundred yards width to the lateral road with no shelter from German machine-gun fire. It seemed incredible that the enemy had survived such a devastating barrage, but several of their reinforced-concrete gunposts, buried in the sand-dunes, were nevertheless intact, and the first troops of the Royal Winnipeg Rifles and one of the Regina Rifle Regiment, together with A and B Companies of the Liverpool Irish, were met with scything machine-gun fire. German gun and mortar fire now rained down on to the beach and an intense fusilade raked the entire length of the narrow shore, catching all the debarking troops in enfilade. Several men were killed or wounded while still in the water: others staggered limp, wet and seasick to the shore where thousands of bullets were kicking up spurts of sand.

On the Western end of the beach A Company of the Liverpool Irish landed with the leading company of the Royal Winnipegs. Major E. M. Morrison, the A Company [Commander] was the first out of his landing craft: heavily laden, he jumped unwittingly into nine feet of water but managed to stagger ashore. Others disembarking from the same landing craft, including the Second-in-Command of the Royal Winnipegs Company were killed struggling to the shore.

With a mere handful of his troops Major Morrison reached the limited protection of the sand-dunes and established a command post for the 'Mike Green' beach area.

His first task was to rescue the troops wounded on the shore and bring them up to the sand-dunes. More of his men reached him, and when he had gathered enough men, having spotted a nearby enemy defence post to the rear of the sand-dunes, he led a fierce frontal charge, killing or capturing several enemy troops. Almost at once, another German command post was seen and was immediately attacked with hand-grenades. A white flag appeared and the Germans surrendered with hands upraised. More enemy troops surrendered at various points around. Meanwhile heavy gun and mortar fire rained down on the beach and the dunes. There was a group of buildings inland from the beach from which mortars were firing: these were instantly charged by a patrol of twenty men led by Major Morrison, charging across the minefield and taking the Germans prisoners.

Between the 3rd Canadian and Arromanches, 50th Division (Major-General D. A. H. Graham), with a Royal Marine Commando, landed under 30th Corps (Lieutenant-General G. C. Bucknall). By the end of the day all were ashore and had penetrated up to five miles inland, but neither Caen nor Bayeux had been reached and there was a two-mile wide gap between 3rd British and 3rd Canadian Divisions, from which the Germans had not been evicted.

Private Lionel Roebuck was with the 2nd East Yorks in the 3rd Division, attacking a fortified German gun-position:

From the fringe of the wood, we could see the perimeter defences of pill-boxes and wire of the strongly fortified positions. From the relief models and maps in the briefing-tent, we knew that, behind the wire fence, there was a complex system of interlocking and overlapping cover of cross-fire machine-gun positions. A deep, open-trench network linked all the pill-boxes and, partly below ground level, blockhouses with a central domed shelter and ammunition store bunker. There the four 75-mm guns were housed, standing out on a large concrete base along with a stack of shells. Other guns were mounted in steel cupolas each capable of traversing in all directions on top of a concrete housing, their fire directed towards the beach and the vital crossings from it. This was until, of course, *strong?* attacking forces could knock them out. It was also believed that extensive mine-fields covered all the approaches to the strong-point's defence system.

All that were left from the original complement of C Company were assembled, plus a few from a Signals unit, and other non-infantry soldiers. There was no more than half of a full company, but all were needed to make up the numbers. Suddenly the guns from near the beach opened up, right on target, and although the promised artillery support from a cruiser was missing (*just as at SOLE*) the 76th Field Regiment's guns, the Self-Propelled Guns and the tanks of the 13th/18th Hussars more than made up for it as they bombarded the position with a good twenty minutes spell of heavy shelling.

As the guns laid down their high explosive shells to good effect, our small force of assault troops started to organise ready to be able to attack across the open field. We lightened our loads by stacking big packs and any surplus gear by the track, hopefully for picking up later, and crept forward, nearer to our goal, until we were about fifty yards from the wire fence and then waited for the end of our supporting fire. There was a wide sloping dug-out pit to the right of the track (a feature used frequently by the Germans to protect and house their vehicles) and, for a few of us, including myself, it made the ideal place in which to take temporary cover. Others stood nearby watching from a gateway, curiously tempting providence, as bits of the spent shrapnel from exploding shells, screaming and singing, winged over towards us. One piece hit an officer hard in the chest giving him quite a shock, slightly winding him. He quickly picked off the hot piece of metal and threw it down with no apparent harm done to him.

Bren gunners were positioned to give covering fire along each side of the line of attack and, as the shelling finished, the rest of us in the company, with rifles and fixed bayonets at the ready, started out on our advance towards the outer wire and pill-boxes. We were in a single line abreast in what could have been seen as rather a futile gesture, had fate decreed it so, for there was every possibility of the German machine-gunners opening up their fire from the pill-boxes even before the wire was reached. Miraculously, nothing happened and we reached the wire unscathed. It was a simple style of double-apron fence, which spread over a three to four foot base and at about the same height, and didn't appear to be a serious obstacle. Even so, in attempting to step through the wire my trouser leg was caught up on the barbs – not really the best spot to be caught up in, so close to the possibility of being blasted by the fire from German machine-guns. So, I quickly tore myself free and dashed straight for the nearest pill-box on my right with a Mills (36) grenade in my hand, pin out, and ready to throw it into the slotted opening. To my surprise, there was no need. The pill-box wasn't even manned and the machine-gun wasn't there either. We could never have expected such luck! It certainly never happened to us again in later clashes. For some reason, which was obviously associated with the heavy supporting stonking and later found to be correct, all the German defending forces had vacated their posts during the stonking to shelter in the main bunker by their 75-mm field guns and stack of death-dealing shells.

Over the next week, Bayeux was taken and the beachhead expanded, linking the two armies, while reinforcing divisions were landed; but no progress was made in attempts to secure the key area of Caen. Meanwhile German panzer and panzer-grenadier divisions were making their way, in the face of intense air attacks, to try to seal it off. Montgomery planned a pincer movement round Caen with 51st (Highland) Division (Major-General D. C. Bullen-Smith) from 6th Airborne's area to the east, while 7th Armoured Division (Major-General G. W. E. J. Erskine) and 50th Division swung round from Tilly in the west and 1st Airborne Division landed south of the city. But Air Chief Marshal Sir Trafford Leigh-Mallory, Commander-in-Chief of the Allied Expeditionary Air Forces, vetoed the airborne drop, and neither of the land thrusts developed successfully.

In the southern thrust by 7th Armoured Division Major Robert Belgrave, with the 5th Regiment Royal Horse Artillery, was supporting the 4th County of London Yeomanry when they were ambushed at Villers-Bocage by Tiger tanks of the German 501st Heavy Tank Battalion. He describes the scene:

> The column had stopped at the first shot and I gave 'Driver reverse' on the I.C.* and turned to signal Robert to go back. He looked puzzled, then backed fast. In front was smoke and flame. Every few seconds the smack of an 88; a section of the concrete disappeared,

---

* Internal communication.

and another tank flared. I ordered A.P.* Load and kicked Rowe into the gunner's seat. A Cromwell reverses at a maximum speed of 2 miles an hour. Robert's Sherman went faster. With a gasp I saw him ram the logs by the side of the road, ricochet off and hit a White half-track belonging to a medium Battery commander. He had a receding chin and his mouth gaped. They extricated themselves. Those seconds back to the corner were years. As I backed round it I saw the tank two in front of me go up, saw running figures. A pandemonium of shots broke out from the windows. A lot of rubble hit the tank.

Steering slowly through the melee came a Dingo Scout Car, Luny† standing upright on it. As he passed me he said 'Cover him back, use your gun, boy; we've got to stop this chap.' He was completely calm.

The turret was jammed.

I decided I would never make the next corner in reverse, and gave 'Driver right, right, right, OK. Halt. Advance left, flat out.' As we sped down the street something started firing straight down it. I saw a white tracer go past my left side; a tank in front burst into flames. I saw a turning to the right, a narrow right-angled side street and shouted 'Right, right up this street'. By a miracle of driving MacDowall got her round. The street narrowed, bent to the left. I hoped it was not a cul-de-sac. We turned a corner and the turret of a Cromwell 50 yards away traversed towards us. I stood up in the turret and hoped.

He was the leading tank of the second squadron. A captain with an MC was standing in the road. I stopped, jumped out. 'Do you know what's going on?' I said. 'No'. 'There's a Tiger coming down the main street. He's brewed up most of RHQ.'‡ 'I'll whistle up my Firefly.§ Thanks. 'Is this the way we came in? My turret is jammed.' 'Yes'.

I ran back to my tank, jumped on. As I did so something came round the corner to my left and there was an explosion which swept me off my feet into the road again. My tank started to back through

---

* Armour-piercing ammunition.

† Brigadier W. R. N. Hinde, commander of 22nd Armoured Brigade, whose nickname was 'Loony'.

‡ Regimental Headquarters.

§ A Sherman tank mounting a 17-pounder gun, which was effective against a Tiger.

the wall of the house. I jumped up, grabbed the I.C. 'Halt. Everyone OK? Advance right.' We squeezed round between the Firefly and the wall. The Firefly fired.

I slowed MacDowall down and began to look for the Squadron Leader. I came to a troop in an orchard just by a corner and stopped in the road there & got out & told their commander what had happened.

Montgomery's next major effort, Operation EPSOM, was an attempt to outflank Caen from the west, using the newly arrived 8th Corps, commanded by Lieutenant-General Sir Richard O'Connor, who with General Neame had escaped from his prisoner of war camp at the time of the Italian surrender, and with the help of Italian partisans had made his way through the German lines, finally by boat, to Eighth Army's sector, the day before Montgomery left it. O'Connor's attack, delayed by a storm raging in the Channel from 19 to 22 June which held up supply and reinforcement, was launched on 26 June, spearheaded by 15th Scottish Division (Major-General G. H. A. Macmillan) and 11th Armoured Division (Major-General G. P. B. Roberts), with 7th Armoured and 43rd Wessex Division (Major-General G. I. Thomas) in reserve. By this time the Germans had eight panzer divisions on Second Army's front, and their fierce opposition brought O'Connor's thrust to a halt just south of the River Odon, where his troops were counter-attacked without success by five panzer divisions in the first few days of July, the Germans losing heavily in the process. The next effort was a direct attack on Caen, coinciding with a major offensive by the Americans, who by now had cleared Cherbourg. Commanded by 1st Corps, and supported by a massive air attack by heavy bombers, 51st, 3rd, 59th (Major-General L. O. Lyne), 3rd Canadian and 43rd Divisions were launched against Caen itself, now largely reduced to rubble. After two days of heavy fighting, the area of the city north of the River Orne was secured, but south of the demolished bridges the Germans still held the suburb of Vaucelles. Another attempt was made between 10 and 18 July to thrust south between Caen and Tilly by 12th Corps (Lieutenant-General N. M. Ritchie) with 15th, 43rd, and 53rd Welsh Divisions (Major-General R. K. Ross), and 30th Corps with 49th West Riding Division (Major-General E. H. Barker) and 50th Division, but it made no significant progress.

By this time Montgomery's superiors, political and military, back in England under bombardment by V-1s, the first cruise missiles, were becoming impatient, and criticism was growing, particularly from Americans and airmen, the latter having their eyes on the construction of airfields in the open country south of Caen. There was also a degree of disillusionment among Montgomery's troops themselves, always being exhorted to make one more effort that would lead to a breakout, and then finding that it led nowhere. Casualties, particularly in the infantry, were mounting. Montgomery therefore decided that his next thrust should be east of Caen into the open country between the city and Falaise, and should be almost entirely an armoured affair, employing 11th, 7th and Guards Armoured Divisions (Major-General A. H. Adair). To ensure success, he demanded a major preliminary bombardment by heavy bombers, which was reluctantly agreed by the senior airmen, when Montgomery assured them that it would lead to the capture of the area they had set their eyes on for airfields.

Operation GOODWOOD was launched on 18 July. It lasted for two days and resulted only in the clearance of the southern suburbs of Caen and the expansion of the area between that and 6th Airborne's sector to a depth of six miles at the maximum.

Lieutenant W. Steel Brownlie was commanding a troop of the 2nd Fife and Forfar Yeomanry in 11th Armoured Division, which spearheaded the attack. He describes the first day:

The regiment assembled behind the start line, and the next tremendous sight was the crawling barrage in front of us, put down by some 1500 guns. There was simply a grey wall of shell-bursts, and we moved along a couple of hundred yards behind it as it advanced. It was difficult to believe that anything could live in this inferno, but at one point the barrage moved on, leaving a big grey horse tethered to a post, leaping about in fright yet apparently unhurt. We drove on in formation for about a mile.

Some opposition began to appear. There was some firing on my right, and I saw some Germans prisoner as they came out. We rolled on, firing at every bit of cover, and without much trouble crossed the first railway line. The barrage was thinning out, and two or three tanks were brewed up over to my left. I shot at some enemy infantry directly ahead, some of whom were running away. Some mortar shells landed among us, but it was impossible to know where they were coming from.

My squadron's immediate objective was the second railway line, and we got across this one way or another, there being embankments to negotiate. My troop and the Third-in-Command of the Squadron, Pinkie Hutchison, now had the task of looking left and covering that flank, while the rest of the regiment went on, down into the valley in front. We had no cover, except for the shape of the ground, and simply sat in the corn.

As soon as I was in position I was fired on by what appeared to be a self-propelled gun in the valley ahead. Two tanks to the right of me went up in smoke. My recollections of the next few hours are confused, but I am clear about the following. Burnt and injured men came back through the corn, and we gave them a drink of water and told them to keep going. A Panther tank came at full pelt on our left front, and into the village on our left. It stopped at the edge of the village, and one of its crew got out and started to camouflage it with branches. My Charlie tank brewed it up with its 17 pdr. Various targets were engaged, so that by midday my troop had run out of ammunition. There seemed to be no hope of the Echelon coming up with supplies, so I replenished from a knocked-out tank that had not brewed, and we were able to continue firing. By the middle of the afternoon, the barrels of my two Browning machine-guns were worn out, and these were replaced from knocked-out tanks nearby. This was a hazardous business, because we were frequently shelled or mortared, and anyone outside his tank was exposed.

About dusk we were relieved by other troops, and given a map reference at which to rendezvous, a few hundred yards back. My troop was intact, except for one tank that had been attached to me about midday, for want of a troop-leader to command him. He had been brewed up beside me.

Our bag for the day, in addition to the Panther already mentioned, was one SP* and three Panthers to our front, and three guns on our left front that were firing on our troops as they went into the valley ahead; plus numerous infantry. There was also a field-car at extreme range on the ridge beyond the valley. It was moving over the fields, and I bracketed it with HE until it stopped and a figure ran

* SPG, self-propelled gun.

away from it. I later had the horrible feeling that it might have been civilian, but there was no way of telling. Our lack of casualties was of course due to the good luck of having been hived off to watch the left flank, while the others went on.*

GOODWOOD was a public relations disaster for Montgomery, who not only beforehand but during its execution claimed results for it far in excess of actuality. It infuriated his inveterate enemies, the Americans and the airmen, but its failure to achieve a breakout did not in fact matter. It had drawn the bulk of the German armoured forces to the east: while Dempsey had 645 German tanks facing him, Bradley had 190, paving the way for him to break through at last south of St Lô on 25 July. Montgomery switched Second Army's effort to cooperate with this, 8th Corps thrusting south from Caumont towards Vire with 11th Armoured and 3rd British Divisions (Major-General L. G. Whistler). On their left, 30th Corps made only a limited advance to Mont Pinçon, leading to the replacement of its commander, Bucknall, by Lieutenant-General B. G. Horrocks, recovered from wounds received in an air attack on Algiers the year before. First Canadian Army (Lieutenant-General H. D. G. Crerar) now entered the fray, taking over the eastern sector with 1st British and 2nd Canadian Corps (Lieutenant-General G. G. Simonds) under command.

By this time the Third US Army (Lieutenant-General George S. Patton) had been formed, and, as had been planned from the start, Bradley handed over the First to Lieutenant-General Courtney H. Hodges and assumed command of 12th Army Group. Montgomery continued to exercise overall command of both army groups until 1 September, when Eisenhower, who had established a headquarters in France at Granville, took over, Montgomery's command thereafter being limited to 21st Army Group. Before then, Field Marshal Kluge, who had replaced von Rundstedt as German Commander-in-Chief in France at the end of June, was forced by Hitler to launch a major counter-attack westward to try and cut off Patton's Third Army as it burst out into Brittany through a narrow corridor near Avranches. While he did so, Montgomery exerted pressure by both his armies on Kluge's northern flank, 2nd Canadian Corps thrusting south from Caen towards Falaise; but they did not reach it until 16 August.

* 11th Armoured Division lost 126 tanks that day.

Three days before that, Patton's leading troops had reached Argentan, twenty-five miles to the south, Bradley ordering them not to move further north for fear of confusion with the Canadians. This 'Falaise Gap' was not finally closed until 21 August, when the 1st Polish Armoured Division (Major-General S. Maczek) in 2nd Canadian Corps had beaten off a series of attacks made by the Germans as they fought desperately to keep their escape route open. They left behind them over 700 armoured fighting vehicles, nearly 1,000 guns and 7,500 other vehicles. It is estimated that the Germans lost 10,000 men killed. Some 50,000 were captured and it is thought that about 20,000 escaped eastward. Of their fifty divisions in action in June in Normandy, only ten remained in any recognizable form. The remnants of the German Army Group B that escaped across the Seine took only 120 armoured fighting vehicles with them.

The Battle of Normandy was over. It had cost 21st Army Group's British, Canadian and Polish forces 83,000 casualties, of whom 16,000 had been killed, principally from the British infantry divisions, for most of whom it had been their first experience of battle. Although the Allied forces reached the Seine almost exactly according to the timetable (D+90) originally estimated, the campaign had not followed the pattern that had been expected. Montgomery had hoped to avoid being hemmed into a restricted beachhead, and had envisaged more mobile operations, as the two Allied army groups gradually forced a German withdrawal eastwards, the Americans occupying Brittany and basing themselves on its ports while freeing Cherbourg for use by the British. Hitler put paid to that by forcing Rommel and von Rundstedt to fight the battle forward in Normandy, in the hope of driving the Allies back into the sea. It was a decision which was fatal to his army. Although it caused frustration in the Allied camp, it helped their cause by facing them with virtually no opposition, when the Normandy battle was over, in the rest of France and in Belgium.

*

21st Army Group's race from the Seine towards the Rhine was led, on the right, by 30th Corps with the Guards Armoured Division, heading for Brussels, which they liberated on 3 September, and 11th Armoured Division, which reached Antwerp the following day, but was unable to clear the docks in the northern part of the city. First Canadian Army had the unenviable task of forcing the Germans, who had remained in strength in the Pas de Calais awaiting a second landing, gradually back along the coast. Between them and 30th Corps, 12th Corps, led by 7th Armoured Division (Major-General G. L. Verney) advanced to Ghent.

Montgomery now made a major strategic error. Uncharacteristically carried away by the prevalent state of euphoria, he conceived the unrealistic plan of dashing across the Meuse and the Rhine and encircling the Ruhr from the north. He did recognize that the key to further advance was logistics, but his answer to that was not, as it should have been, to make a major effort to clear the River Scheldt to the sea, so that the port of Antwerp could be used, but to demand from Eisenhower that overriding priority for supplies should be given to 21st Army Group, halting Patton short of Metz, so that, at a strength of forty divisions (at least half of which would have to have been American), he could execute his ambitious plan.

Eisenhower compromised by giving priority to 21st Army Group, and to First US Army on its right, directed to Aachen and Cologne, at least until Montgomery was beyond Antwerp; but he did not emphasize that clearing the Scheldt estuary should have priority until he met Montgomery in Brussels on 10 September. In the week since 11th Armoured Division had reached Antwerp, Montgomery had decided to use the 1st Airborne Corps (Lieutenant-General F. M. Browning) to help him cross the Meuse and Rhine by seizing the bridges at Venlo and Wesel with 1st Airborne Division (Major-General R. H. Urquhart) and the Polish Airborne Brigade; but the RAF and Browning himself thought the risk from anti-aircraft fire was too great, and the latter proposed using the whole Airborne Army, including the US 82nd and 101st Airborne Divisions, to open up the route to Arnhem, capturing the bridges there and at Eindhoven, thus providing an alternative route to the Ruhr, albeit a longer one which would involve Second Army's effort diverging from that of the First American.

Montgomery leaped at the idea and obtained Eisenhower's support for it, both of them hoping that the operation, code named MARKET GARDEN, would help to force the Germans to leave Holland, and would thus open up the Scheldt estuary. The operation, commanded by 30th Corps, succeeded in opening the route to Eindhoven and beyond, the Guards Armoured Division moving up to join the US airborne divisions; but 1st Airborne Division, dropping a considerable distance from its main objective, the bridge at Arnhem, was fiercely attacked by the German divisions reorganizing in the area, and, after a gallant fight, the remnants were evacuated south of the river on 25 September.

Sergeant Richard Ennis of the Glider Pilot Regiment was the second pilot of one of the gliders which landed on 17 September. He relates his experiences:

My 1st Pilot gripped the release knob and pulled – We were now in free flight. Immediately there was a terrific explosion. A shell had burst close on to our Port Wing tip. The Kite rocked and heeled. The 1st Pilot was slumped in his seat: his blood stained the perspex close to his head. Beyond him I could see our smashed wing tip with fragments of it clawing at the air. My one thought was to get down. I tugged on the Flap control; but nothing happened. We still had too much height to make the Landing Zone without flap, but it was a case of try or nothing. I pulled the kite into a steep turn. Out of the corner of my eye I could see parts of our wing breaking loose into the slip stream. I stuck the nose down and headed for a patch of the field. I found that I was overshooting without enough height left to turn in. Straight ahead was the wood at the far boundary of the field. I pulled back on the stick in an effort to pancake on top of the trees, but the damaged kite was slow to respond. We hit the trees head-on with well over a 100 on the clock – I should have been killed. However, I went straight through the perspex instead. I ploughed along the ground and finished up among the trees about 20 yards from the glider.

I have no recollection of being knocked out, but I must have been out for a couple of minutes or so, as when I struggled to my feet a Dutch lady was handing me a glass of wine. It may have been Port or Sherry – or even cocoa. I don't know, but it did pull me together a little. The seat of the Glider was still strapped to me. I pulled it off and dashed back to the Kite. It had a couple of trees lying across it, and the fuselage was smashed to matchwood practic-ally up to the tail piece. – Everything was deadly quiet. – I called out . my 1st Pilot's name 'Allan; Allan; where are you?' – No answer. I screamed his name again in a fit of hysteria. Looking round I saw that the Dutch lady was still there and now nodding her head and 'tut-tutting'. I pulled myself together and made for the tail. The tail door was jammed, but I could hear movements inside. I hammered on the door and forced it open. Our two passengers alighted, very shaken, but quite safe and sound. The three of us then returned to the front of the Kite and started to pull away the debris. We found Allan lying with a Jeep and trailer on top of him – quite dead. I don't know, of course, but in all probability he was killed in the air before we crashed.

We jacked up the Jeep with three branches and pulled him away. I removed his identity disc. I also took a photograph of a family group and one also of his girl friend, from his smock pocket. We then buried him quietly beside the Glider.

Ennis takes up the tale two days later:

After what seemed an endless night, the first ray of daylight glimmered through the trees and with it came our order to 'Stand to'. We 'stood to' and we did not have long to wait before it started. In the distance we heard a series of whistling moans coming nearer. A veteran of previous ops nearby said one word 'Mortars' and we all got down. The first salvo landed some distance away, with the second one following immediately behind and landing a bit closer. These were Jerries 'moaning minnies' – his multi-barrelled mortar, and they were quite accurate. He had our position well in range and well taped. The mortar shells came over thick and heavy. There were two of us to each foxhole. One of each pair had always to be on the lookout in case of an infantry attack. While the mortaring was going on we took it in turn to look out – one keeping his eyes open as to what was going on while the other crouched down in the trench to avoid shrapnel.

A mortar shell only penetrates the ground a few inches before exploding. The main use of this is to spread shrapnel over quite a large area. This shrapnel can be quite deadly and did, in fact, cause us quite a number of casualties. After 20 minutes or thereabouts the mortar barrage stopped as abruptly as it had started.

The sound of the last shell had not died away, however, before the attack proper was put in. They did not come in an extended line as on the previous day. This was a closely grouped frontal assault. We saw what appeared to be a continuous line of field grey advancing straight upon us. As on the previous day we gave them our all – bullets zipped all ways. Our mortars in the rear got the range and shells whistled over our heads towards the enemy. Phrases learnt at battle-school were running through my head – 'You will kill the Boche. You will kill the Boche'.

We killed the Boche . . .

They were now close enough for us to exchange grenades. The air was thick with curses, bullets and smoke. 'Will they break, will they break?'. 'Ah: yes – they are faltering, now we have them.' Slowly, still firing, the enemy pulled back. We had taken a fairly heavy hammering.

There was a lull, just long enough for the enemy to regroup, and then they were on us again with an assault as furious as their first attack.

I honestly don't know how any of us survived that second attack. At one point it developed into hand to hand fighting, but slowly – very slowly, the enemy once more withdrew.

We had suffered heavily in these two attacks, so heavily that we knew we would be unable to survive another one in our present condition. We were ordered to fall back to what was our second line of defence. These lines were now to become the extreme edge of the perimeter. We moved our wounded back under cover of fire, and then, just as the rest of us prepared to move, Jerry attacked again. We knew our position was hopeless, so we immediately put into operation a very speedy withdrawal. The enemy literally chased us into our new defences and was firing into our backs as we ran. We reached our line and jumped into foxholes which were already occupied. Now that we were out of the way, the occupiers of these foxholes had a clear view before them. They now knew that every one in front of them was a German and they set to in tremendous style to repel this attack. Everything went well for us.

In spite of this setback to his hopes of crossing the Rhine, Montgomery continued to give priority to Dempsey's eastward advance over Crerar's approach to the Scheldt, and a major row erupted between him and Eisenhower, Montgomery blaming his inability to advance further on Eisenhower's failure to give 21st Army Group and First US Army the logistic priority he had promised, and Eisenhower, and his staff, blaming Montgomery for failing to give priority to opening Antwerp.

Towards the end of October Montgomery at last did so, giving the task to Crerar with 1st British and 2nd Canadian Corps, the latter reinforced by 49th Division. The Scheldt estuary was guarded by the island of Walcheren; it was taken by the 52nd Lowland (Major-General E. Hakewell-Smith), ironically trained as a mountain division, after an RAF attack flooded it. Antwerp was opened to shipping on 28 November. Crerar's army had already cleared Le Havre, Boulogne, Calais and Ostend, all of which had held out until attacked. The rest of the year was spent in deliberate operations by both First Canadian and Second British Armies to clear the area of Holland and Belgium up to and beyond the River Meuse (or Maas as it is called in Holland), shortage of manpower causing the disbandment of 50th and 59th Divisions, the commander of the latter succeeding Verney in command of 7th Armoured. At the same time O'Connor was succeeded in command of 8th Corps by Major-General E. H. Barker.

Montgomery's plan for the new year was for First Canadian Army, reinforced by 30th Corps, to attack south-eastwards from Eindhoven to clear the Reichswald forest and the area between the Meuse and the Rhine as far south as Wesel, so that Dempsey could attack across the Rhine north of the town, the operation to be named VERITABLE; but before it could be launched, on 16 December the Germans began a major offensive against the Americans in the Ardennes, which entailed diverting some of 30th Corps (51st and 3rd Divisions with three armoured brigades) to support them south of Liège. The postponed VERITABLE was launched on 8 February 1945, 30th Corps leading with 15th (Major-General C. M. Barber), 43rd, 51st (Major-General T. G. Rennie) and 53rd Divisions and 2nd and 3rd Canadian, the last two being joined by 4th Canadian Armoured Division (Major-General H. W. Foster) in 2nd Canadian Corps, when the latter came into the line in the second phase, having 49th and Guards Armoured Divisions also under command, 11th Armoured Division joining 30th Corps at the same time.

It was tough fighting in filthy weather. Corporal David Evans of the 6th Royal Welch Fusiliers in 53rd (Welsh) Division, describes it:

> Climbing a steep slope out of the valley we came upon a lane that crossed our line of attack; it lay upon a slight embankment with a rise of perhaps four or five feet facing our side. The first men there began to cross only to come under fire from a Spandau about four hundred yards away, the tracers skipping and whining off the tarmacadam. Across the road lay 'our' wood, but the machine-gunner wasn't going to let us into it lightly.

Jack [the platoon commander] looked enquiringly at Tom [the platoon sergeant], it was his first time under fire and he had to give his first orders under these conditions. Tom had already worked out where the Spandau was firing from and quietly told Jack to get two sections to fire at the distant hedge where the machine-gun seemed to be while the other section crossed, then to repeat this for each section in turn – the classic 'fire and movement' manoeuvre, in fact. Taking his cue from Tom, Jack called to Colin and Fred to use their sections as fire cover while Harry took his section over then, when Harry was established and firing, Fred could follow and so on. We shook out into position, using the embankment as cover, and firing while Harry and his men crossed, followed by Fred's section. Thus far a text-book operation as the machine-gun ceased to fire after the first volleys from us. Once Fred was settled and adding his section's fire to that of Harry's, Colin called on us to line up at the foot of the embankment.

The machine-gunner was no fool. When he saw he was rumbled he had obviously moved position so that when our section rose to cross he fired a long burst which bowled two lads over, killing one and wounding the other. Colin screamed to us to drop down behind the cover of the embankment again; Tom bawling for us to stay there; meanwhile – as I later found out – the company to our right, in whose path the machine-gun nest lay, had spotted them and wiped them out so that we could cross our lane in safety while Jimmy gave attention to the wounded man before stretchering him back. The dead man was checked, as usual, to make sure he was so, then a note made as to where he lay so that the clearing squads could pick him up.

Moving cautiously through the trees of the wood we advanced without further incident almost to its further edge where we dug in so as to command the rising ground to our front. Frank, who I had kicked out of my trench in the Reichswald, was the odd man out in my section as, now that Jack was with us, Tom had reverted to his job as Platoon Sergeant and Colin was back in charge of our section, with me being relegated once more to the command of the Bren-gun team. I therefore had Dave again as my trench mate. No one elected to dig-in with Frank and he had to dig a trench for himself, but, as he was in a state of partial sulk, he was careless for once, digging merely a virtual scrape in the ground. I remonstrated with him, urging him to dig in more deeply but he wasn't to be advised by me or anyone else. After being told we were there for the night, and after the cleaning of weapons and replenishment of ammunition, we spent the hours of darkness at 50 per cent stand-to.

I was asleep as dawn broke but was rudely awakened by a sudden storm of mortar bombs which crashed and cracked onto the wood. For a quarter of an hour the very air was thick with flying branches, earth, roots and steel splinters. We could do no more than cower in our trenches and sweat it out, praying that a bomb wouldn't drop in with us. Screams and shouts for stretcher-bearers rent the air as men were hit. (I heard later that Jimmy, our kindly and brave Jimmy, was about in the middle of the stonk giving help where he could.)

The deluge stopped and Tom bawled for everyone to pop up their heads and be on the alert in case a German counter-attack was following through. Staring about, I saw Frank standing in his shallow trench, exposed from the ankles up. He stood there in a dazed manner – looking almost stunned, so, as wounded men in a state of shock often appear like that, I feared that he had been hurt. Calling out to him I said, 'What's up Frank, have you been hit?' He brought his eyes to focus on me but seemed not to have understood my question, so I rose from my trench and, with others who were concerned, ran over to him. 'Have you been hit, Frank?' I repeated.

He looked at me, swallowed and said, 'No, I've shit myself.' And he most certainly had.

By 10 March the area between the rivers was cleared and contact made with Lieutenant-General W. H. Simpson's US Ninth Army, also under Montgomery's command. By this time there were no German troops left west of the Rhine. British and Canadian casualties in VERIT-ABLE totalled 15,500.

It was now Dempsey's turn. During the night of the 23rd and early hours of the 24th, the river was crossed by amphibious tanks and infantry in tracked amphibious vehicles (Buffalos), 1st Commando Brigade near Wesel, 15th Division under 12th Corps north of Xanten, and 51st under 30th Corps near Rees. At 10 a.m. 6th Airborne Division parachuted and glidered in to land just beyond them.

Rifleman Patrick Devlin was with the 1st Royal Ulster Rifles, which was one of the glider-borne battalions of the division. He was from County Galway in the Irish Republic and had first volunteered to join the British army in 1939. In 1942 he responded to an appeal from General Sir Hubert Gough for Irishmen in the army to join the airborne forces and found himself posted to the Royal Ulster Rifles, having expected to join the Parachute Regiment. When he was on leave at home, after having taken part in 6th Airborne's landing in Normandy, his mother tried to persuade him not to return, calling on a local priest to help; but, to use his own words: 'I never wavered in my intention to return to the Army, even though I could have obtained Medical certificates to delay my return until the landing was over. Such an option wasn't open to those on leave in the UK, and N. Ireland.' He describes his part in the Rhine crossing:

About 10.30 a.m. we were cast off from the aircraft tug and we were on our own and committed to land, the glider could only fly a mile, fully loaded, for every thousand feet in height. I sat alert and ready, gripping my machine gun, intent on getting out fast as soon as the glider landed and stopped. The two lads on either side of the door stood up and slid into the roof and before anyone could move I was first out that door like a jack rabbit, jumped to the ground and ran to the tail of the glider to cover the rear as I had often done in training. As I ran I saw German soldiers in the 2-storied farm house about 50 or 60 yards away, and one of them was firing a Schmeisser submachine gun and brought it into the aim, at the same time releasing the safety catch. This only took seconds but the German nipped smartly back into the house and the beam. I put a few quick bursts after them through the door and windows to keep them pinned inside and not in a position to shoot us up at the glider as the platoon got out and unloaded our spares. They say that only one in five gliders landed undamaged of the 400 or so used by our division, I was in one of the undamaged, how is that for luck?

I continued firing short bursts through the windows and doors, and as I was changing a magazine there was a shout that the Germans were running for the village (HAMMINKELN). I looked up and saw about a dozen of them from the house were legging it for cover behind a tall hedge away from us. In my excitement I fired before I was properly into the aim and my burst hit the ground in front of me, I had to wait a few seconds before I could aim and fire again. This time I sprayed them as they were reaching the cover of the hedge and I could not say if I had hit any of them. Looking back from this distance in time, I hope not, but that morning the adrenalin was up and I was determined to shoot any of them that got in my way. As I looked about me at the platoon lying beside the glider everybody was flat on the ground, a ploughed field, taking cover, I seemed to be the only one firing. Then there was a shout that 2 German tanks were coming up the road. This road ran North/South and bounded the landing zone, it was about 70 yards or so away. I repositioned my gun so that I could fire at them as they came opposite the glider, I would only have fired if the tank commander had his head exposed from his turret. In the event they weren't tanks but armoured personnel half track vehicles. The first one, the Germans were standing up, shoulder to shoulder, they had obviously packed it as much as possible to get back to their own troops on the other side of the River ISSEL via the village of Hamminkeln. As they came opposite I let them have a burst and they all collapsed behind the armoured sides, I couldn't have hit them all but there was an amount of shouting and screaming. The troops in the second vehicle were concealed behind the armour, having no doubt seen what happened to the first vehicle, they were travelling about 50 yards behind but I sprayed it with a burst anyway hoping to hit the driver. Both vehicles continued towards Hamminkeln. I was highly elated, my attitude was I'd got some of the bastards before they got me. It now became quiet by the glider. The only incoming fire since we landed had been rifle bullets fired from a distance as I had contained the nearest Germans in the farmhouse before they fled for the village. I don't think we had taken any casualties as the rifle fire had been at the gliders and not the platoon lying flat on the ground.

It must have been 20 minutes since we had landed and no move had been made to get to our objective, a 'T' road junction south of the village, which we had to occupy and deny passage to the enemy. It was now on the far side of the landing zone four or five hundred yards away as we had landed on the wrong side of the ploughed field. I might add that there were only a few gliders on this field although the main supporting troops of the battalion were supposed to land here, they had all landed in the wrong place. Now that we were on the ground the temptation was to lie doggo but I knew it was time we got a move on. I did not notice the platoon commander so I called out to our platoon sergeant (Sgt. Geordie Redpath, a regular soldier, a Belfast Protestant and a good fellow) 'Geordie, let's get to the objective.' He immediately shouted, 'No. 2 Section get to the objective,' at that they picked themselves up and away they went at the double and I following. As I ran I was carrying my Bren gun with my right hand by the carrying handle on the barrel which was hot to hold, the gun itself was jammed by overheating. Under my left arm I was carrying a pile of empty magazines which I intended to reload at the objective. When we were about half way there and still in the ploughed field, the empty magazines slipped from my arm and fell on the ground so I stopped to pick them up. As I ran on again I realized I was now running alone and I passed a couple of dead airborne which made me decide to alter my direction and make directly for the ditch at the side of the road, under cover of which I could make my way to the road junction. As I ran I suddenly noticed 2 Germans working on a Spandau (MG34) machine gun, they were at the edge of the wood on the far side of the road, the gun I expect was jammed, I knew I had to get to the ditch before they repaired it. Whilst still about 20 yards from the ditch and possibly 80 yards from the Germans they got behind the gun and started to feed the belt magazine into it. As I was the only one in view, up and running directly towards them I was their target. It flashed through my mind to zig-zag, I didn't have time, but I must have turned to zig when I was hit. Instead of getting a burst in the stomach I had turned out of the line of fire and was hit in the right fore arm below my elbow breaking the bone, along my right side and across the small of my back, right side only. The gun and magazines must have dropped as I was hit as I was thrown forward in a kind of jump, letting [out] a shout of 'Oh' and fell flat on my face with my arms in front of me to protect my head as I fell. It all happened automatically and I lay there for some seconds before I knew I was hit and did not move. They did not fire again as they thought they had killed me. I found I could not move which was just as well for me as I might have attracted more fire from them and I had a small anti-tank mine tied on the strap of my small pack on my back, if they hit it I'd be blown to pieces so I kept still. I have been asked what it felt like to be hit by bullets, in my case it was as though somebody had hit me a severe blow across the small of my back with a big stick. The pain wasn't too bad, like a nagging toothache, but I could feel what I thought was my blood pouring along my right thigh and I thought I would bleed to death. I discovered later it was the 2 tins of Carnation evaporated milk I had in my side pack which had been ripped open by the burst as well. I also had tea and sugar in that pack which I had purloined with the aid of the cook and these supplies would have been used by me and my pals for a brew of tea when the chance arose.

Other divisions of both corps soon passed through 6th Airborne and drove further into Germany, while Montgomery learned to his dismay that Ninth US Army was to pass to Bradley's command, and that 21st Army Group was to be directed northwards towards Bremen and Hamburg, and not east towards Berlin, on which his eyes were set. Although there were a few tough actions in different places as his armies surged forward, there was no serious hold up. Bremen fell on 25 April and Hamburg surrendered on 2 May, the day before the arrival at Montgomery's tactical headquarters on Lüneburg Heath of representatives of Grand Admiral Dönitz, who, on Hitler's suicide on 30 April, had assumed the office of German head of state.

On 2 May also, at 9 p.m., the Royal Scots Greys, detached to 6th Airborne Division from their parent brigade, 4th Armoured, met Russian troops at Wismar on the Baltic coast. Their regimental history describes the scene:

By now the leading light tanks were well on their way to Wismar. They had long since run out of all large scale maps, but all the roads were well and accurately signposted, and a steady speed of about twenty-five miles an hour was being maintained. Germans in all types of vehicles, walking, on horseback and riding bicycles, continued to stream southwards against the direction of the regiment's advance. Some were in parties, some by themselves: their different reactions to the sight of allied tanks were amusing to watch: some, when they saw a 'Honey' come round the corner, would leap into the nearest ditch, lying there with a puzzled expression on their faces, as if wondering why they were not shot. Others had already recovered, and were standing by the side of the road with a bewildered grin on their faces. Others again seemed totally oblivious of the fact that those were British tanks and, as the tanks went up one side of the road, they were busily pedalling down the other side, their rifles slung over their backs with never a glance to the other side of the road. About eight miles short of Wismar Sergeant Randall, in the leading tank, came up on the air to say that he had reached a level-crossing, but could not get across as there was a train passing over. There indeed was the train, loaded with German soldiers and equipment, including three self-propelled guns. It could not be stopped except by shooting at it: it was therefore allowed to proceed unmolested in case it 'brewed up' on the level-crossing and blocked the road. B Squadron, coming behind, managed to stop the next five trains, a 'bag' which can have fallen to few tank squadrons. At this time also several German fighter aircraft flew down the road very low. They did not attack, and nobody quite knew what they were going to do: possibly they realized that they could not do much, as there was certainly more German traffic going one way down the road than there was British going the other. At one o'clock the leading light tanks reached the outskirts of Wismar, while the Shermans of C Squadron were still some twenty minutes away, coming along at the best speed they could make. A few bazooka-men did appear among the outlying houses, but after a look appeared to change their minds and go away. The problem was how to attack a large town with eleven light tanks. Was it perhaps better to wait until the Shermans and the infantry arrived? As there were two important bridges northeast of the town, carrying the road which ran east and west along the coast, it was decided to try and reach these, and then wait for the remainder of the force to come along. Getting through the town was a difficulty as there were no large-scale maps, but by trial and error and the help of an obliging German officer, the 'Honeys' eventually found their way through to the eastern outskirts, where a road-block was found to be down. The road beyond was packed for miles with civilian refugees mostly in carts, while inside the town there was a seething mass of German soldiers, each with his rifle or bazooka under his arm. However there were no incidents, except that somebody dropped the road-block on the southern outskirts of the town behind the Reconnaissance Troop, thereby holding up C Squadron for a short time when it arrived; but with the help of some German soldiers the road was soon clear again. C Squadron joined the Reconnaissance Troop and the airborne infantry, having dismounted rapidly, soon took up positions all round the town.

It was at this time that a German threw a hand-grenade at the Commanding Officer*: he missed, but the Commanding Officer did

---

* Lieutenant-Colonel Douglas Stewart.

not miss with his pistol in reply. Odd German aircraft still continued to fly low over the housetops, and it was obvious that there was an aerodrome close at hand, although there was none marked on any of the maps. The Reconnaissance Troop therefore set off to search with one troop of C Squadron, and soon discovered it northeast of the town on the seashore. A large number of men were seen running about in the hangars, and some shooting took place on both sides. Eventually, however, a German officer came up to say that they were very sorry: they had not realized that these were British tanks and, if the firing would cease for a few minutes, they would come out and surrender. Five minutes later two hundred Germans marched out in threes in perfect step; they were told to go back and fetch their transport, which they did, and the whole convoy set off back for the town. At nine o'clock in the evening the first Russian troops arrived from the east. They consisted of two White scout cars and two motor-cycle combinations, each carrying seven men and one female soldier. Half-an-hour was spent in frantic handshaking and Vodka drinking before the party returned eastwards again, and the 'Iron Curtain', in the shape of a monster road-block, went down. Towards evening the remainder of the Regiment arrived, and all squadrons found themselves billets in a large farm a few miles southwest of the town. Thus ended a day which must ever remain vivid in the memories of those who witnessed it. No dream, however wild, could imagine meeting a whole German army, as indeed this was, going west at an estimated rate of 5,000 men an hour on the same road as the British spearhead was advancing eastwards. This was indeed the end of the Axis.

*

The year's campaign from the Normandy beaches to those of the Baltic was the British army's largest-scale involvement in the Second World War, of which it had every reason to be proud. Excluding the Canadian and Polish troops, fifteen divisions had been involved, of which four were armoured and two airborne. In addition there were five Army Groups Royal Artillery, with five heavy, twenty-one medium and seven field regiments, and five Army Groups Royal Engineers, with sixteen regiments, as well as a very large number of supporting troops of all kinds. Most of them had spent four years, frustratedly and often boringly, training in Britain, waiting for the day when they would take the field; but some had been in action almost continuously since 1940. Among them, although not with all its original units, was 7th Armoured Division, which had fought throughout the North African campaign and in Italy from Salerno to the Garigliano, before being brought to England to re-equip and land on D+1 in Normandy, finishing the war in Hamburg. One of its original brigades, but independent since 1943, 4th Armoured (which the author commanded from Normandy to the Baltic), went one better, having fought in Sicily also. The toughest fighting in the North-West Europe campaign had been in the *bocage* of Normandy and in the approach to the Rhine. Both had involved fierce battles at close range against a well-armed, determined and skilful enemy. Only the closest cooperation between all arms in the use of their different forms of firepower made advance by tanks and men on their feet possible, and it was expensive for both. The use of aircraft in close support was valuable, especially when operations became more mobile. It was essential for interdiction, that is restricting the enemy's movement behind the front line. The value of heavy bomber support, as in Operation GOODWOOD and, in Italy, at Cassino is doubtful. The campaign showed both the value and the limitations of airborne forces. Their contribution to the initial landings in Normandy was a key factor in success; but the difficulty in finding suitable tasks for them thereafter was demonstrated by the story of Arnhem. 6th Airborne Division played an important part in the crossing of the Rhine, but it could undoubtedly have been successful without an airdrop. The clear lesson was that airborne operations succeed when they can be rapidly joined by formations with heavier equipment.

Montgomery was rightly the hero of the hour. His greatest contribution was his clear-headed and firm grip of the planning of the landings and the confidence he instilled in all those taking part in them. The same applied to subsequent operations, especially when success seemed long in coming in Normandy. His soldiers were ignorant of and unaffected by his arguments with Eisenhower over strategy thereafter, and he continued to inspire them to persist in the struggle for victory in spite of the disappointments of the last winter of the war. In this he totally overshadowed Dempsey, whose contribution is difficult to assess; but there is no doubt that Montgomery owed a great deal to his brilliant chief of staff, who had been with him since he assumed command of Eighth Army at El Alamein, Francis de Guingand.

Victory in Burma

The war with Germany was over, but that with Japan was not, and relief at victory in Europe was tempered for some by the knowledge that they were earmarked for transfer to the Far East, although the Japanese army had just been forced out of Burma by Slim's Fourteenth Army, Rangoon being entered on 4 May. In the two years that had passed since the failure of Wavell's offensive in Arakan, the scene in the Burma theatre had undergone a total transformation, beginning with a major change in the command structure. In June 1943 Wavell succeeded Lord Linlithgow as Viceroy of India, and was replaced as Commander-in-Chief by Auchinleck; but he was not to exercise operational command. That passed to a new Anglo-American South-East Asia Command, established at the Quebec summit conference in August. Vice-Admiral Lord Louis Mountbatten, the Chief of Combined Operations, was appointed its Supreme Commander. General Sir George Giffard, who had succeeded Irwin as Commander Eastern Army, became Commander of the Land Forces, known as 11th Army Group: under him, two corps, 15th (Lieutenant-General A. F. P. Christison) and 4th (Lieutenant-General G. A. P. Scoones), were formed into Fourteenth Army (Lieutenant-General W. J. Slim). A further change was the formation of a Special Force, or Chindit, brigade (77th), commanded by Brigadier Orde Wingate, designed to form company-sized columns from a British and a Gurkha battalion for a deep penetration role. In February 1943 they left Imphal to cross the Chindwin, penetrate to the Irrawaddy and harass the Japanese. They marched between 1,000 and 1,500 miles over four months, losing 800 men and causing some minor damage to Japanese communications. Their significance was the experience they gained and their demonstration that jungle defences could be penetrated.

In spite of their limited success, Churchill took Wingate with him to the Quebec Conference and persuaded the Americans that provision of air support for the deployment and supply of such forces was a promising military alternative to more conventional operations. The Americans were primarily interested in getting supplies to and helping Chiang Kai-shek's forces in Yunnan, and were prepared to support

Wingate if his operations were aimed in that direction. They were not interested in liberating southern Burma. Moreover, Churchill and the British Chiefs of Staff viewed with distaste the prospect of a major long-drawn-out land campaign to re-enter Burma through the Imphal plain and Arakan. They preferred the concept of an amphibious operation to land at Rangoon. The resources for that, however, would not be available in the campaigning season from November 1943 to May 1944. Mountbatten's plan for that period, therefore, was for offensives in Arakan, with the same objectives as before, and from Imphal towards the Chindwin, while Wingate, promoted Major-General, deployed four brigades of Chindits, three by air and one on foot, to the area of Indaw to disrupt the rear of the Japanese Thirty-Third Army, facing an advance by the Chinese under Stilwell from Ledo towards Myitkyina.

Christison started to move south into Arakan late in January, while Wingate began his operation with the march of 16th Brigade (Brigadier Bernard Fergusson) into the jungle in mid-February. Scoones was not to start his operations until March. Meanwhile Lieutenant-General Kawabe, commander of the Japanese Burma Area Army, was also planning offensives in that period. Christison had forestalled the offensive by their Twenty-Eighth Army in Arakan. 5th Indian Division (Major-General H. R. Briggs) had reached its first objective at Maungdaw, and the 7th (Major-General F. W. Messervy) was about to attack his at Butidaung, when the Japanese 55th Division launched its attack behind them and cut their communications with Chittagong, scattering Messervy's headquarters in the process, an unpleasant reminder of his experience in command of 7th Armoured Division south of Tobruk in May 1942. Slim reacted quickly and robustly, ordering Christison to stand his ground, while he arranged supply by air and reinforced him with 36th Indian Division (Major-General F. W. Festing) to back up the 26th (Major-General C. E. M. Lomax), which Christison had already sent south to relieve Messervy. The crisis passed, and by 12 March both Briggs and Messervy had reached their objectives and the Japanese offensive in Arakan had been defeated.

Slim now realized Japanese intentions and gave permission to Scoones to abandon his planned offensive and withdraw his widely separated divisions back to an area nearer Imphal, the 17th (Major-General D. T. Cowan) from Tiddim, a hundred miles to the south, and the 20th (Major-General D. D. Gracey) from Tamu, fifty miles south-east, while the 23rd (Major-General O. L. Roberts), near Imphal, pulled in its horns to form a defensible area. It was a prudent move, executed just in time, which was to prove the foundation of victory. By 4 April all three divisions, after fighting fierce rearguard actions, were back in a ninety-mile arc round Imphal, joined by 5th Indian Division, flown up from Arakan, and 50th Indian Parachute Brigade.

By this time Imphal had been stocked by road with supplies to last a month; but on 29 March Lieutenant-General Sato's 31st Japanese Division, advancing on foot through the jungle-covered mountains all the way from the Chindwin, cut the road from the army's main base at the railhead at Dimapur to Imphal a few miles south of Kohima, seventy miles north of Imphal and only forty from Dimapur. Slim ordered 161st Brigade, the first of the brigades of 5th Indian Division to arrive, to Kohima to reinforce the 1st Assam Regiment there; but when he handed over responsibility for Kohima, Dimapur and the whole line of communication area to 33rd Corps, its commander, Lieutenant-General M. G. N. Stopford, ordered the brigade back to Dimapur, thinking that the Japanese might bypass Kohima and make straight for the railhead. Stopford's fears being allayed by the imminent arrival of the 2nd British Division (Major-General J. M. L. Grover), 161st Brigade was ordered back to Kohima, but only one battalion, 4th Royal West Kent, reached the town itself before the Japanese cut the road to the west, isolating them from the rest of the brigade. Over the next month a fierce battle raged around the little hill-town, where the garrison fought with the greatest gallantry.

Private H. F. Norman of the 4th Royal West Kents kept a diary and records the critical day, Sunday 9 April 1944:

At 0030 hrs. we heard digging and we couldn't think what it was, but we soon knew because at 0200 hrs. a 3-ins. mortar commenced firing from where the Japs were digging and for 15 minutes they fired plenty of H.E. bombs at us and also the Japs were firing a 75 M.M. gun on 'open sights' straight at our pits, as this gun was on ground higher than our feature, no sooner did we hear the bang than the shells exploded all around us. He plastered us 'like hell' and it was terrible, Lieut. PHYTHIAN's pit was hit and Pte. WALTERS, his batman, was killed and it was reckoned he saved Mr PHYTHIAN's life by falling on him. Mr PHYTHIAN had only slight leg wounds.

At 0245 hrs. the barrage 'lifted' and the Japs started another attack. We immediately started firing our .37 [inch] guns but unfortunately one of the .37 shells landed on Cpl. REES' pit killing poor old Ted WELLS and burying Cpl. REES and Pte. SKINGSLEY. These two managed to dig themselves out, and came back to our pit, in which were Cpl. BEAMES' section (Ptes. LOVELL, SHIPP, one of the convalescent lads (1/1st Devons[]) and another lad from 14 Platoon. At 0300 hrs. 'Butch' came running up a little hysterically saying that he had been hit in the behind. I pulled him into our pit because there were shells, mortars and grenades exploding everywhere near us. Previously Pte. HILLS had come up to us with a hand injury and him and 'Butch' were evacuated to Battalion H.Q. Poor old ALL-CHIN had 2 grenades thrown into his pit which collapsed on top of him, killing him. There was again 200 Japs attacking and again they were 'mowed down like flies'. When Cpl. REES had to evacuate his pit and ALLCHIN was killed the other positions were in danger as there was insufficient fire-power to keep the Japs away so the pits had to be evacuated. The attack finished at 0400 hrs. the Japs having gained a foothold on the bottom of our feature and they commenced 'digging in'. 15 Platoon's Bren Group halfway up the feature, level with us, had suffered no casualties and had a Bren Gun covering the entrance to our pit so that if the Japs attacked us it could have been costly for them but this was necessary because we were pinned in our pit unable to move or put out our heads in the daylight because we were now surrounded by thousands of Japs who were occupying the big feature in front of us which overlooked us and their snipers could see our every movement. I had no breakfast or tiffin today. We were sitting in our pit when a sniper started shooting along our trench and hit poor Pte. 'Nobby' HALL in the hand and as nobody could get to us because of the Jap sniping we did the best we could for 'Nobby' but after a few hours he died in our pit. We then left our pit and went to Cpl. BEAMES' pit which was attached to ours so we didn't have to leave our pit really. As the position was very serious as far as we were concerned we heard that L/Cpl. HARMAN, the son of the millionaire owner of LUNDY ISLAND, had volunteered to go on a one man bayonet attack past our pit to clear the Japs off of our feature. He went down past our pit and killed some Japs. He was covered by Sgt. TACON who was in a pit well behind us and could move about. He killed a Jap who was just going to throw a grenade at HARMAN. HARMAN killed the rest of the Japs but instead of running back as we were shouting for him to do he walked back calmly and the inevitable happened. He was shot in the spine by a Jap machine gun and was killed (Later we heard that he had been awarded the V.C. for this action.). REES who was sitting next to me in the pit when L/Cpl. HARMAN ran past wouldn't stay in the pit but stood on top of it. I tried to pull him back into the pit because the Japs had 'fixed lines' on our pit but he wouldn't let me and whilst HARMAN was engaged in his action 'Taffy' REES was hit twice in the side. Sgt. TACON shouted out. 'Hang on, Taffy, I'm coming', but when he crawled towards 'Taffy' he was hit in the arm and leg (fracturing his leg) and just managed to roll out of the danger area. Although we couldn't help 'Taffy' we did start talking to him because he was only about 2 yds. from us down in a dip, but when he told us that he was paralysed we didn't think that there was much hope. He was soon delirious and for eight hours he was screaming, shouting and calling for his Mum and Dad and praying, until he died. While he was lying there the Coy. Commander tried to get a smoke screen laid down so that 'Taffy' could be evacuated by the stretcher bearers but this proved unsuccessful. It was really nerve racking for the 14 of us left because we couldn't defend ourselves if we were attacked and would die 'like rats in a trap'. We kept on asking if we could take a chance and evacuate this pit for one a bit further up the feature which we had a reasonable chance of defending. We kept pleading to the Coy. Commander that our nerves were all 'shot to pieces' (so they were, what with poor 'Taffy' shouting, poor old 'Nobby' Hall dying in our arms, and the continuous mortaring, shelling and sniping) and L/Cpl. HANKINSON told the Coy. Commander (Capt. COUTH) that he did not know what we had been through, and then Capt. COUTH told us that he realised what conditions were like (we also had had nothing to eat or drink since breakfast the day before) and that if we could stay here until 1900 hrs. we would be relieved by a Relief Brigade. (The times we had heard that). At 1700 hrs. we were told that 'B' Coy were going to attack the positions that 'Japie' held at the bottom of our feature and take over our positions from us. At 1900 hrs. when it was dark, one Platoon of 'B' Coy. was sent down to take those positions. One of the positions fell but the others held out so that one had to be evacuated. 'B' Coy. withdrew and 15 minutes later L/Cpl. HANKINSON gave us the order to evacuate so we did. Capt. COUTH was wild but he could do nothing. We were sent to re-inforce 16 Platoon (Sgt. STAMMERS) and were put in a defence pit with Cpl. GUEST. We did guard duty (50% manning. 2 hrs. on 2 hrs. off) Some of our section went with Cpl. GUEST to attack and try to recapture our old pit but Pte. SHIPP was wounded in the leg and the attack failed. Weather. Rainy. Windy and Cold. I've had a 'hell of a headache' all day as well as a nasty cold.

The garrison was relieved on 18 April by the 2nd Division, which then began to push the Japanese back in bitter fighting from every position to the next. This lasted until 1 June, by which time a brigade from 7th Indian Division, which had also been flown up from Arakan, joined them.

During this period Imphal, supplied by air, had been under continuous attack, the casualties of Lieutenant-General Mutaguchi's Fifteenth Japanese Army mounting with every week that passed, until the tide began to turn, as the monsoon broke, in June. But it was not until 22 June that the road was finally open, and Mutaguchi did not finally abandon his attempts to reach Imphal until 4 July, when he withdrew to the Chindwin, abandoning all his guns and tanks, every second soldier in his army having become a casualty to wounds, fatal or other, or sickness.

Meanwhile Wingate had started deploying his brigades into the area astride the railway south of Myitkyina, which provoked a fierce reaction from the Japanese. Wingate had intended one of them to move south to disrupt the rear area of the forces attacking Imphal, but that was cancelled when he was killed as his aircraft flew into a mountain west of Imphal on 24 March. His brigades suffered severe casualties and endured great hardship, being finally rewarded by the capture on 24 June of Mogaung, thirty miles west of Myitkyina, which fell to the Chinese in August.

The 1st South Staffordshires was one of the battalions of the 77th Chindit Brigade. Captain Norman Durant was with them and describes the attack towards Mogaung:

We moved off early and took a line through thick jungle with the object of coming out well on the flank, so that progress was very slow due to all the cutting that had to be done. Eventually we came out in open ground with clumps of trees and bushes providing adequate cover within sight of the village and about 800 yds. short of the river. One coy remained here and two others moved off to clear the ground to the river. Archie Wavell's coy,* with whom I moved was on the left and in contact on his right was the other one. We pushed on about 400 yds, until we came to a cart track running East into the village and we stayed there waiting for the coy. on our right to clear their area and swing round to join us. We heard firing break out on the right and after some time a runner came up to say that they had run into a number of Jap snipers who they couldn't see and from whom they were suffering heavy casualties. A Pl. commander who had been flown in as a reinforcement the day before had been killed and the coy. 2-in-C had been hit in the leg, besides which there were several O.R.† casualties. They could make no headway and to save casualties were withdrawing. This left us in a very nasty salient. Archie had one Pl. on the right facing out towards these reported snipers, one Pl. 40 yds. away on the left facing the village which was our objective, and one Pl. in the centre facing the river, and we knew it was only a question of time before the snipers turned their attention to us. The first we knew was when Archie's 2-in-C (a motherly married and family character who should never have been in) was shot through the head and killed instantly as he fussed about getting people under cover. At the same time everything opened up on the left as the Jap tried to push out the Pl. facing the village and things got so serious there that the centre Pl. had to be moved over to give support. The sniping on the right became heavier and still it was impossible to see where the fire was coming from. I had a Vickers mounted as if for AA and sprayed all the large trees, but it was entirely blind shooting. A Pl. came up to reinforce us and was sent round to the right to clear what they could, but they hadn't gone 15 yds. before 4 men were down and the rest pinned down. The Jap then began, quite successfully, to grenade the wounded and when we tried to bring them in two more men were hit. Archie Wavell trying a new line set off with a section but within a few seconds was back holding his left hand which was hanging by a shred of muscle, having been hit by a sniper at 20 yds. range. He was astonishingly calm, gave out orders and then walked back unassisted

* Wavell was the son of the field marshal.
† Other Rank, i.e., not officers.

to the R.A.P. Meanwhile on the left casualties were equally heavy and as it was getting dusk we were none of us feeling too happy, and even when the order came for us to withdraw we knew that somehow we had to get the wounded in. They seemed to be covered by two snipers so David Wilcox stationed himself where he might be able to get a shot and someone else began rustling the bushes nearby. The Jap moved and standing up David shot him at the same time getting a graze under his chin from the second sniper's bullet. But he saw him as well and having a beeline was able to fire quickly enough to get him; it was a very courageous action, well deserving of a decoration which I hope he will get. After that it was just a matter of holding on until the wounded had got back and then moving ourselves to join the rest of the Bn. It had been a disappointing day and our casualties had not been light, but at least we had gleaned a great deal of information.

These were the last operations the Chindits were involved in. After them, they were flown out to India and disbanded. For all their gallantry and wonderful example of endurance and fighting skill, it is doubtful if the effect they had on operations justified the resources, human and material, especially in air effort, devoted to them.

The Chiefs of Staff were no keener than before on a campaign to clear Burma from north to south, preferring an amphibious operation aimed directly at Rangoon, code named DRACULA; but the resources for it could not be made available until March 1945. Before then, as soon as the monsoon ended, Fourteenth Army would cross the Chindwin and advance to Mandalay, the starting point of the Burma Road to China. Slim's first plan was for Stopford's 33rd Corps to lead the advance, while 4th Corps was airlifted, preceded by a paradrop, to the area of Shwebo, fifty miles north-west of Mandalay; but the 50th Indian Parachute Brigade could not be ready to paradrop before February. 4th Corps's move to Shwebo would have to be by land, 19th Indian Division (Major-General T. W. Rees) on the left linking up with Festing's 36th, which had been moved to Stilwell's command. This they did in mid-December, by which time a bridge over the Chindwin had been opened at Kalewa, as the Japanese withdrew to the Irrawaddy. Slim's new plan was for 33rd Corps to relieve the 4th and advance to Shwebo with 2nd British and 19th and 20th (Major-General C. G. G. Nicholson) Indian Divisions. 4th Corps, now commanded by Messervy, with 7th (Major-General G. C.

Evans) and 17th Indian Divisions, would slip secretly south, west of the Chindwin, and cross the river at Pakokku, below its confluence with the Irrawaddy. From there they would thrust east to Meiktila, seventy miles south of Mandalay, cutting off the Thirty-Third Japanese Army and what was left of the Fifteenth to the north, whose eyes would be fixed on Stopford's advance.

The plan worked perfectly. Stopford's leading division, the 20th, crossed the Irrawaddy on 12 February, and Messervy's, the 7th, two days later, the 17th passing through and completing the clearance of Meiktila on 5 March, three days before Stopford attacked Mandalay, which the Japanese abandoned two weeks later. Meiktila now became the centre of the storm, which continued there until the end of the month, when both corps joined hands and the Japanese withdrew.

Lieutenant Peter Collister was commanding a platoon of the 1st Gloucesters attached to the 2nd Dorsets in the 2nd Division. He describes a night attack on a hill held by the Japanese:

As we approached the top the machine guns opened up horrendously close but we kept on going upwards, all my efforts straining to ensure that we did not lose touch; we were more closed up than usual with the flank man of each section having to be in physical contact with his opposite number of the next one. We stumbled upwards out of breath and cursing heavily as we tripped occasionally. The heavy Japanese mortars opened up as we reached the top and threw ourselves down. I crawled over to company H.Q. which was hard to locate in the dark, to get fresh orders from Pag, and with my runner crawled back again as the whine and crump of the bomb and the pulsating earth hugged to the chest. Every nerve of my body ordered me to claw my way deep into the earth or, better still, run for dear life and it took a great effort of will to crawl back to the platoon where sections had anticipated the order to dig in where they were. It was pitch dark, the hillside was rocky and it was difficult to wield a pick in these conditions, especially when work had to stop every time a crump was heard as we huddled into the shallow recesses we were able to make. We never got down below a foot or so, but it was enough to give a slight feeling of protection. We gave no answering fire as our training was never to disclose a position at night – even though, as in this case, its general outline was already known – and never waste ammunition except on a visible target so all we could do was sit it out throughout the long dragging night which seemed endless. There was sporadic rifle fire and answering machine gun fire from somewhere near at hand, but we never saw anyone. The Japs had done just as they had at Shwedaung. They had withdrawn, allowing us to get to the top, and then, closing in again, opened up on us. The vicious whistle of shrapnel flying past my face seemed perilously familiar to that day three years before.

The night was dark, illuminated only by the flash of explosions. We held our fire and squeezed as low as possible in our shallow trenches, peering into the black void for creeping figures and straining to hear the rustle of movements over the banging of mortar bombs, the whistle of bullets and the occasional swish of shrapnel. At last a few faint green streaks began to finger the horizon but the coming of dawn brought no relief. We could now see the rest of the company dotted about the slope, but we must still have been pinned down as there were no orders for movement. As the sun rose the dust of battle thickened and sandpapered throats and cracking lips demanded liquid but by now water bottles had been emptied. The excitement of battle, the noise, the stench of cordite and blood added to the usual warmth, even at night, had forced recourse to water bottles during the dragging hours. We were also hungry, not having eaten since five o'clock the previous evening. As the sun's rays began to burn more fiercely, all the irritation increased: the stones of the shallow trenches became intensely uncomfortable, equipment chafed and when we spoke our voices were hoarse and cracked. Then hours dragged by and nothing seemed to be happening. Firing had by now died away in our immediate vicinity and it sounded as if the enemy had withdrawn, but we had no orders to move and there was no sign of food or water. When Paget Fretts was called away to get his orders from the C.O., I learnt that Roger Johnson had been killed, and a brief visit to his platoon showed him lying, ashen grey, with his head covered in a sodden scarlet field dressing. I was saddened by the sight as he had become a good friend. Miraculously, we learnt later that despite a very severe head wound he was in fact just alive and had been restored to complete recovery. There were other casualties and the hill was dotted with little groups of stretcher bearers and walking wounded making their way down to the Regimental Aid Post, where Joe and Gus were ready for them. Other men, unshaven and grimy, walked behind stunted bushes to relieve themselves and some squatted on the edge of the trenches smoking, although sentries in each section were still alert.

Meanwhile Christison's 15th Corps, under the direct command of Leese (who had succeeded Giffard as Land Force Commander), had launched an offensive in Arakan, which secured airfields in the south, essential to the support of Operation DRACULA. It was now a race between that operation's 26th Indian Division (Major-General H. M. Chambers) and Slim as to who would reach Rangoon first, as Stopford pressed down the Irrawaddy valley and Messervy down that of the Sittang, the latter reaching Pegu on 29 April and the former Prome on 3 May, the day after 26th Division landed unopposed and the monsoon broke. Rangoon, from which the Japanese had fled, was occupied on 4 May.

The war was in fact over, although Fourteenth Army was due to take part in a further operation which Mountbatten was planning to liberate Malaya and Singapore; but the explosion of the atomic bombs on Hiroshima and Nagasaki in August turned that into a peaceful occupation. Fourteenth Army's Burma campaign had been a masterpiece of generalship, supported by the skill, endurance and gallantry of its soldiers, most of whom were Indian, although one must remember that British soldiers served in many different capacities in Indian formations; nor must one forget the service of the airmen, British, Indian and American, without whose support, in combat and transport aircraft, Fourteenth Army's operations would not have been possible.

The transformation of Fourteenth Army from the force that had withdrawn from Burma and fought in the Arakan in 1942 was truly remarkable, and it is not easy to be confident in attributing credit for it fairly. Some must undoubtedly go to Auchinleck as Commander-in-Chief in India, responsible for training, especially that of the Indian Army formations: some clearly to Mountbatten for obtaining the resources of all kinds and developing an atmosphere of confidence; but there is no doubt that Slim, in his handling of operations and of the men of every rank who had to execute them, was the architect of victory. It is difficult to judge what contribution was made by his immediate superiors, first Giffard and then Leese. The conditions in which Fourteenth Army fought were as challenging as any in other campaigns, as the personal accounts quoted show, and the difference between performance in Malaya in 1941 and Burma in 1945 illustrates what excellence in command, training and morale can achieve. The human material was the same.

The Home Front

No account of the British army in the Second World War would be complete without mention of Anti-Aircraft Command, which, under the operational control of the Royal Air Force, played a vital part in the defence of the United Kingdom. Formed initially from five Territorial Army divisions, it was organized into seven regional divisions, each commanded by a major-general, under the overall command of Lieutenant-General Sir Frederick Pile, who held the post throughout the war. At its peak it had a strength of 330,000 men and 170,000 women, a sizeable slice of army manpower. In May 1940 Pile estimated his requirement for effective defence of the United Kingdom at 3,774 heavy and 4,410 light guns, supported by 8,500 searchlights; but at the height of the Battle of Britain in September 1940 he could only deploy 1,311 heavy and 698 light guns.

Manpower posed a serious problem for the army throughout the war. There were many more demands on it for other purposes, particularly for the Royal Air Force, than in the Great War, and within the army itself there were many demands, particularly in supporting services, other than that for combat units in the field; and in the field itself there were new ones, such as anti-tank and anti-aircraft artillery. In September 1939 the army's male strength was 892,697: 224,188 serving regular, 219,613 regular reserves and 448,896 in the Territorial Army; female strength was 22,801: 17,614 in the Auxiliary Territorial Service, 711 nurses in Queen Alexandra's Imperial Military Nursing Service and 4,476 in the Territorial Army, including nurses. 3,643,000 men and 300,000 women were enlisted during the war, and at its end the army's strength was 2,920,000 men and 196,800 women in the Auxiliary Territorial Service, a reduction from a peak of 212,475 in September 1943, and 8,000 nurses in the Queen Alexandra's Imperial Military and the Territorial Army Nursing Services.

A total of forty-eight divisions (eleven armoured, thirty-five infantry and two airborne) were raised during the war, a significant number being disbanded before they ever left Britain's shores and some after. The army could not have manned as many as it did had not a large proportion remained in the United Kingdom from Dunkirk to D-Day. From then on, 21st Army Group was given priority over everything else; but, in spite of that, was forced to reduce the number of its divisions. The army's total casualties were 569,501, of whom 144,079 were killed and 152,076 prisoners of war. There were 2,267 still missing in 1946. These figures include some men from overseas, in particular from Newfoundland and Southern Rhodesia, but not those recruited locally in overseas theatres.

6

BEATING RETREAT
1945–1960

With the war finally over, the principal aim of almost all soldiers, although not necessarily that of pre-war regulars, was to get out of uniform and back home as soon as possible; but, as was the case in 1918, the army found itself saddled with tasks that demanded more men in the ranks than could be provided if there were a rapid return to voluntary service. Many members of the Labour Party, which formed the Government that came to power as a result of the General Election of July 1945, hoped that that would be possible; but the Prime Minister, Clement Attlee, and his senior ministers, who had served in Churchill's wartime coalition Government, were bound to take a more responsible view of the tasks to which Britain found herself committed. A formidable list of these was set out in the June 1946 Defence White Paper. It was:

a. Our share of forces to ensure the execution by Germany and Japan of the terms of surrender;

b. Our share of the forces of occupation of Austria;

c. Provision of forces to assist the Greek nation in its recovery;

d. Provision of forces to carry out our responsibilities in Palestine;

e. Liquidation of Japanese occupation in Allied territories in South East Asia;

f. Maintenance of internal security and settled conditions throughout the Empire;

g. Safeguarding of our communications and the upkeep of our bases.

Wartime conscription, based on the 1939 Act, as extended in 1940, could not be prolonged indefinitely. When Montgomery succeeded Brooke, now Viscount Alanbrooke, as CIGS in July 1946, he proposed that the situation should be regularized by legal action to establish

National Service for a period of eighteen months. As a result, a bill to bring that into effect in 1949 was introduced into Parliament in November 1946. It met with considerable opposition from Liberal and Labour MPs, but with the help of the Conservative opposition it was passed through the House of Commons on 1 April 1947. However, as a sop to its opponents, the length of service was immediately reduced to one year. This was designed to produce an army of 305,000, which Montgomery planned as a replica of the 1939 army, the ranks of the Territorial Army being filled by ex-National Servicemen, who had a six-year reserve liability.

It was to prove inadequate to meet the demands on army manpower. Denys Whatmore, aged eighteen, was called up for his National Service in 1949 and to his surprise, as he lived in Kent and had started work at the Admiralty, was sent for his recruit training to Fort George near Inverness. He describes his initiation:

We were divorced from the old world. Civilian clothes were parcelled up into pathetic brown paper bundles and sent home. We were confined to barracks. We worked in denim fatigues, battle dress being kept for special occasions. We were marched to meals, to training classes, everywhere; individualism disappeared, except for one brief moment in the afternoon of the first day when we were documented. We followed in line along a row of trestle tables set up on the chilly parade ground, and filled in forms and answered personal questions presented by a team of clerks. One form asked 'What do you want to join, the BW, the HLI or the Argylls?' I guessed Argylls meant the Argyll and Sutherland Highlanders, but who or what were the BW and HLI? None too patiently I was made aware that these acronyms stood for the Black Watch and the Highland Light Infantry, and I opted to join the latter because the KRRC* whom I had hoped to join were light infantry. I left those tables a properly inducted soldier – 22168881 Private Whatmore D. E. HLI.

The first few days and nights went by in a whirl, in which I can distinguish much uncertainty. My room mates came from all walks of life, from Scottish city slums to English public schools. Only a few of us put on pyjamas at night and were the butt of much ribaldry as a result. But fellowship developed out of our common trials and

* King's Royal Rifle Corps.

tribulations, and within forty-eight hours we worked together without rancour or even comment. We learned how to strip and lay out our beds for inspection each morning. These were the days when, every morning, beds were laid bare and blankets and sheets were folded precisely – So!; when vests and pants and shirts, with cardboard strips one inch wide folded inside to give a crisp and uniform outline, were piled one upon the other and presented exactly in lockers – So! Webbing belts were blancoed and brass buckles were buffed until they shone. Boots were given a glass-like surface by arcane processes; an old soldier (he had been 'in' for at least three months!) showed us how to reduce the roughness of the leather by 'ironing' it with the red hot handle of a spoon, and then how to spit and polish until a patina developed. The patina cracked when the boots were worn and, at Fort George, I was to see a Corporal of the Guard carried on to parade by his mates so that his boots were in a pristine state for inspection! The rest of us simply got down to more spitting and polishing. Every effort we made was closely inspected by our NCOs and punishments awarded for failures. Most time consuming were preparations for inspections by officers, for which special – sometimes all night – efforts were made, not least by our NCOs upon whom poor results would reflect. I do not recall ever being resentful of the regime, despite the pettiness of some of its minutiae. Once the pattern was established, some of it – even drill parades and the interminable physical training – was fun.

Within a few days, we were required to take Personnel Selection Officer (PSO) tests and interviews. The tests involved Progressive Matrices and other intelligence tests, including mechanical aptitude tests. I failed to assemble a bicycle pump in the given time! On a more positive note I was able at the interview to get off my chest my disappointment at failing to get to the KRRC.

Life settled into the routine of a training programme, broken again by a reshuffle of men into new training Platoons with resulting Nissen hut changes. I found myself in a group of Other Ranks Grade 1 (OR1s), i.e. potential officers. Morale improved, we had something to aim for, and an excellent Sergeant Instructor soon had us working hard for him, not through coercion but because we wanted to, in order to live up to the high standards he clearly expected of us. Friends were made; three of us went into Inverness when, after about ten days, we were allowed out of barracks, self conscious in our

battledress (I never did get to wear the HLI kilt): we made straight
for a hotel and enjoyed the luxury of hot baths for the first time
since joining at the Fort.

We drilled, we ran cross country races, we became fit and, being
young, we began to enjoy it all. We fired our weapons for the first
time, on the 30 yards range built into the dry moat around the keep.
Then, for me, came a surprise. On 31 August I was called to the
Training Office, to be told that I was to be transferred to the KRRC
at Winchester. I left the Fort the next day with genuine regret at
parting from my new friends.

Having continued his training as a rifleman at the Light Infantry
Training Unit, run by the 1st KRRC, he was transferred to the Depot of
the Wiltshires for his officer training, and then commissioned into the
Royal Hampshires. So much for the army's devotion to its regimental
system!

India

One of the first of the commitments which Attlee faced up to was that
of India, to which he was determined to grant independence, hoping to
be able to do so through some form of federation, agreed both by the
Congress Party, led by Nehru, and by Jinnah's Muslim League. In March
1946 he dispatched a mission of three senior Cabinet Ministers to try to
effect this, but without success. Rejection of the mission's proposal led
to serious rioting in which British and Gurkha troops found themselves
involved in their traditional task of attempting to quell inter-communal
violence. As the deadlock continued, Wavell, the Viceroy, suggested that
from March 1947 power should be handed over to Congress in those
provinces in which it had a majority, while he continued to exercise
authority in those with a Muslim majority, as well as in the two
important ones with a Hindu majority in the north-west, bordering on
what would become Pakistan. A year later Britain would withdraw
altogether. He told the Cabinet that the only alternative to this so-called

Breakdown Plan was to reinforce the Indian Army with four or five British divisions and try to hang on to power for another fifteen years.

Neither choice was acceptable to Attlee, who turned to Mountbatten to replace him, in the hope that he could find a way out of the impasse. Having extracted from the Prime Minister an agreement that Britain would transfer power 'not later than July 1948', Mountbatten arrived at the end of March 1947 to find inter-communal tension high almost everywhere. After two months of fruitless negotiation, he concluded that partition was the only possible solution. The difficult question as to whether all British officers serving in the Indian Army or other services of the Indian Government would have to leave on the transfer of power was overcome by the agreement of both Nehru and Jinnah that as Dominions of the Commonwealth each would have a governor-general, representing the Crown, but he would be the same person for both, assuming that Mountbatten himself would fill the post. Auchinleck was to preside over the Commission which would divide the Indian Army between the two.

260,000 went to India and 140,000 to Pakistan. It was agreed that the Brigade of Gurkhas would be split between India and the British army, a total of 15,000 men to the former and 10,000 to the latter, the actual numbers transferred at the time being higher. Both battalions of each of the four regiments which joined the British army (2nd, 6th, 7th and 10th) were sent to Malaya. Of the thirty British combat units left in India at the end of 1946, only fourteen remained by Independence Day, 15 August 1947. The last to leave were the 2nd Battalion The Black Watch from Karachi on 26 February 1948 and the 1st Battalion The Somerset Light Infantry from Bombay two days later. The British troops that were still in the country after Independence Day played no part in the unsuccessful attempt by the 55,000-strong Punjab Boundary Force, formed from reliable mixed regiments of the Indian Army and led by the commander of 4th Indian Division, Major-General T. W. Rees, to bring under control the appalling outbreaks of inter-communal violence in the Punjab, in which at least 200,000 people were killed and which led to a vast refugee problem. Auchinleck insisted that British troops should be confined to protecting British lives.

NATO

It was a sad end to the British army's long association with India; but at least a commitment had been shed which could have imposed an impossible burden on it. But there were other heavy ones.

In December 1947 negotiations between Britain, the USA and the Soviet Union over the future of Germany finally broke down, and fears were raised that the Russians would try to impose their solution by force. Ernest Bevin, the Foreign Secretary, backed by his French colleague, Georges Bidault, took the lead in trying to establish a military alliance, backed by the USA, and, as he hoped, by the 'White' British Dominions also, to prevent this. As a first step, primarily to convince the Americans that the nations of Western Europe were prepared to make an effort to cooperate in their own defence, the Brussels Treaty was signed in March 1948 by Britain, France, Belgium, the Netherlands and Luxemburg, forming a Western European Union, for which a military command structure was created, headed by a Commanders-in-Chief Committee, established at Fontainebleau in France. With sighs of relief on all sides, Montgomery left Whitehall to assume the post of Chairman of the Committee, in which he clashed with the French Commander-in-Chief of the Land Forces, Marshal de Lattre de Tassigny, as sharply as he had with his colleagues in London, where he was replaced by Slim. A series of events persuaded the Americans to agree not only to a binding North Atlantic Alliance, but also to the establishment of an integrated military command organization, the principal posts of which were to be held by them. When discussion about the North Atlantic Alliance started, neither the Americans nor the British imagined that they were committing themselves to the permanent presence of their armies on the Continent. Both hoped that they could limit their contribution to naval and air support once the Continental European members of the alliance had been built up by US military aid, while their economies were supported by the Marshall Plan. The events that prompted the Americans to commit themselves to a greater degree were the Communist coup in Czechoslovakia in February 1948, the crisis over Berlin, culminating in the Soviet blockade in July, which, relieved

by the airlift, continued until May 1949; the crude pressure which the
Soviet Union applied to Norway to try and prevent her from joining any
Western European grouping; the explosion of the first Soviet nuclear
device on 23 September 1949, and, coinciding with it, Mao Tse-tung's
victory over Chiang Kai-shek and the latter's departure to Taiwan.
Eisenhower returned from retirement to become the first Supreme Allied
Commander Europe (SACEUR) with his headquarters near Paris, and
the Western Union command organization was absorbed as a subordinate headquarters covering what was known as the Central Front, that is
from the Alps to the Kiel Canal, Montgomery leaving it to join Eisenhower as his deputy. Although the North Atlantic Treaty was signed in
April 1949, it was not until June 1950, after the Korean War had started,
that Eisenhower's headquarters, SHAPE, was set up.

The most significant effect of this on the British army was the need
to convert the British Army of the Rhine (BAOR) from an occupation
force, equivalent to two divisions and relying on supplies through
Hamburg, into a field force of at least four (seven were promised but
never produced), with all that was needed to fight the Russian army at
short notice, including a supply line back through Antwerp. This was
to become a permanent commitment which, at its height, amounted to
77,000 men.

Palestine

The other major demand on the army at this time was the situation in
Palestine.

Before the war, the army's operations there had been directed against
Arab militant organizations which opposed Jewish immigration and
settlement. In fact, Orde Wingate's 'Special Night Squads' had cooperated with the Jewish Agency's unofficial defence force, Haganah, led by
David Ben-Gurion. In deference to Arab opposition, the British Government in 1939 proposed a limit on Jewish immigration of 75,000 over
the following five years, after which no further immigration would
be allowed without Arab consent. This was hotly opposed by all Jewish

organizations; but as long as there were fears that Hitler's Germany might be victorious, active protest ceased, and Jewish contingents from Palestine joined the British army, a brigade being deployed to Italy.

However, when by 1943 it had become clear that Britain and the USA would win, the organization known as Irgun Zvai Leumi (National Military Organization) became active again. Originally formed by a Russian Jew, Vladimir Jabotinsky, as the militant arm of the Union of Revisionist Zionists, it had always been opposed to the policy of cooperation with the British followed by the Jewish Agency, headed by Chaim Weizmann. Irgun threw off an even more militant branch, Lohamey Heruth Israel (Fighters for the Freedom of Israel), known as LHI or, by the British, as the Stern Gang. It never altogether ceased activity and Stern himself was killed in a clash with the police in February 1942. Later that year Menachem Begin arrived from Poland and began to make Irgun more active. In January 1944 he agreed an uneasy alliance with LHI and issued a formal and uncompromising declaration of revolt against the British administration, which was followed by attacks on the immigration department and the police. He tried, but failed, to gain the cooperation of Haganah, which in October agreed to cooperate with the administration against Irgun. A fortnight later LHI, without warning Irgun, murdered Lord Moyne, the British Minister of State in the Middle East, an act which cemented the support of Haganah and the Jewish Agency for the administration.

That alliance was fatally undermined by their disillusionment with the policy of Attlee's Government, heavily influenced by Bevin. The British Labour Party had always favoured the Zionist cause, but the Foreign Office and the Chiefs of Staff were extremely sensitive to Arab opinion in the Middle East as a whole, fearing that a policy which departed from the 1939 immigration proposal would cause an upsurge of trouble in the whole area, affecting the security of the Suez Canal and oil supplies from Iraq and the Persian Gulf. As a result, in August 1945, Ben-Gurion's Haganah changed sides and cooperated with Irgun and LHI in an alliance known as Tenuat Humeri (United Resistance Movement). Its formation was closely followed by the dispatch of 6th Airborne Division (Major-General E. L. Bols) to join 1st Division in Palestine. At this time Haganah was thought to have about 50,000 members, but most of them were tied to the static defence of settlements, only some 1,900 in the elite Palmach under Yigel Allon being available as a mobile striking force. Irgun probably had about 1,500 and LHI under 1,000. None of the organizations had arms for all their members or any heavy weapons.

October 1945 saw a series of explosions, Haganah alone setting off over 500, mostly aimed at the railway system. In November General Sir Alan Cunningham, last heard of when he was sacked by Auchinleck from command of Eighth Army in the desert four years before, replaced Lord Gort as High Commissioner, and Bevin announced his policy in Parliament, including the maintenance of the immigration quota to be determined after consultation with the Arabs, for the interim not to exceed the then monthly rate of 1,500. This was followed by a serious riot in Tel Aviv, which involved the deployment of the whole of 3rd Parachute Brigade, a curfew being imposed which lasted for five days. In November there were attacks on police and coastguard stations and an arms raid on an RAF camp. It was now clear that Haganah, supported by the Jewish Agency, was involved and the British were getting little or no cooperation from any Jewish authority. This led to a series of massive cordon and search operations, almost the only result of which was to antagonize the whole Jewish population and range them behind the men of violence. December 1945 and January 1946 saw the situation deteriorate, although British army strength had risen to 80,000 in addition to the police, who were bearing the brunt of the attacks, and the Arab Legion from Transjordan. The country was turned into a form of military camp, the police barricaded into their Tegart fortresses, the army and the administration surrounded by barbed wire, the country almost under military rule, members of the resistance forces, when caught, being tried by military courts. Arms raids continued, including a spectacular one on the RAF base at Aqir near Gaza at the end of January. This was followed in February by attacks on RAF bases in which several aircraft were destroyed.

In April 1946 the railway was a target for Irgun, a third of the hundred-man force involved being killed or captured; a success for the new Army Commander, Lieutenant-General Sir Evelyn Barker.* However it was followed by a number of setbacks, including an LHI attack on 6th Airborne Division's car park for recreational transport in Tel Aviv, in which seven paratroopers were deliberately killed. Up till then

---

* He succeeded Lieutenant-General G. H. A. MacMillan.

soldiers had not considered themselves to be direct targets of attack, especially off duty.

For the British soldier it was a frustrating sort of war. His principal activity consisted of cordon and search operations. The aim of these was to help the police find suspected terrorists or their active supporters. The police having selected their target area, probably from clues arising from some terrorist incident, the army would try to surround it, usually in the early hours of the morning, so that nobody could move in or out. A separate body of troops, accompanied by the police, would then search either selected or all houses both for wanted persons and for arms and documents. All those who might be suspect would then be brought before a special police screening team, perhaps assisted by hooded informers. Those marked out by this process were then removed to a detention centre for further interrogation. On some occasions these operations, for instance in Tel Aviv, were executed on a colossal scale involving a prolonged curfew. This raised major practical problems for the continuation of normal life, such as the distribution of food and milk, and coping with such natural events as births and deaths. The soldier seldom saw any result for his effort, occasionally an arms find if he was lucky. The active and interesting detection work was in the hands of the police. The soldier received insults for his pains and often found his tasks, such as that of dealing with illegal immigrants, distasteful. They arrived crammed in overcrowded hulks in filthy conditions and then had to be searched and moved, usually protesting, into other ships to be transported to Cyprus. When he was not engaged on these tasks, he was probably on guard or patrolling the railway. There was hardly ever a real military operation as such, involving active action or military skills, although he was always liable to be a target for a mine, an explosion or shot. Most of the soldiers were National Servicemen. They accepted the task with resignation, but had no great enthusiasm for it.

In June 1946 a new turn was given to the vendetta between Irgun and the security forces. Two Irgun men, captured in a raid on the army camp at Sarafand in March, were tried and sentenced to death. In retaliation Irgun kidnapped six British officers in three incidents. One escaped; two were released when the Jewish Agency voiced its disapproval of the act; the three others were released only when the High Commissioner commuted the death sentences to life imprisonment. Once more Irgun had succeeded in humiliating the administration. The reaction was to carry out a massive cordon and search operation, called AGATHA, designed to pick up leading members of the Jewish Agency, Haganah, Palmach and, if possible, Irgun and LHI. Nearly 3,000 people were arrested, of whom 600, including 135 suspected Palmach men, were detained. But on 22 July Irgun went too far. A huge explosion blew up the wing of the King David Hotel in Jerusalem in which the administration's secretariat and the army headquarters were housed. Ninety-one people were killed and forty-five injured. The British reaction was to publicize the involvement of Haganah and the Jewish Agency in these acts of terrorism. Although Irgun had carried out the operation, the United Resistance Organization had authorized it; but general worldwide revulsion made Haganah decide to opt out. Unfortunately the British failed to exploit this opportunity and imposed even stricter repressive measures on the population as a whole, including another vast cordon and search operation, which, although it screened 100,000 people, nearly 800 of whom were detained, produced very meagre results.

However, violent incidents did decline while political activity increased; yet more partition plans were aired and a meeting between Britain and the Arabs held in September. Nothing came of these, and towards the end of the year Irgun stepped up its activity, mostly by the use of more sophisticated electrically detonated mines on roads and railways. The British clocked up one notable success in frustrating an attempt to blow up Jerusalem railway station. In December Irgun again resorted to kidnapping, this time in retaliation for the imposition by a military court of a sentence of eighteen strokes of the cat on top of eighteen years of imprisonment on two Irgun members, caught when taking part in a bank robbery in Jaffa. Irgun announced that if the sentence were carried out, 'every officer of the British occupation army will be liable to be punished in the same way'. A Parachute Regiment major and two sergeants were abducted, given eighteen lashes and then released, following which one of the Irgun men, who had received the sentence but was out of the country, and sixteen Arabs were granted an amnesty. This fooled nobody, the administration was humiliated again and the sentence of flogging was never subsequently imposed. Incidents continued. In January 1947 Cunningham discussed future policy with Bevin, Montgomery and Creech-Jones, the Colonial Secretary, following which another division, the 3rd, due to relieve the 1st, was sent out, bringing the total army strength to about 100,000. Another conference ended in deadlock, and in February the Government announced it had decided to refer the problem to the United Nations General Assembly in September.

If they thought that this would ease tension in Palestine, they were to be disappointed. Irgun and LHI carried out further kidnappings in retaliation for death sentences and attacks on army personnel and installations. Martial law was introduced, civil courts suspended and stricter curfews imposed. Two huge cordon and search operations, one in Jerusalem and one in Tel Aviv, were carried out. In spite of this Irgun and LHI attacks continued, including one on the oil refinery at Haifa on 31 March, starting a fire which lasted for three weeks. In May Irgun staged a dramatic breakout from the prison at Acre, in which over 100 Jewish prisoners, including 50 important Irgun and LHI men, and 171 Arabs escaped. Following this, there were a number of incidents of kidnapping, culminating in LHI hanging two British sergeants, whose bodies they then booby-trapped, in retaliation for the execution of three of their members on the day on which the refugee ship *Exodus 1947*, which had sailed from France with 4,500 illegal immigrants and been intercepted at sea, arrived back at its port of embarkation.

On 29 November 1947 the UN General Assembly voted to establish a Jewish state, whittled down from the UN Partition Committee's recommendation of 6,000 square miles to 5,500 by the exclusion of part of the Negev and the city of Jaffa. On 15 May 1948 Britain gave up her mandate as the two successor states immediately began to fight each other.

The heavy demands on army manpower caused grave concern to the Army Council when it was faced, in March 1948, with a defence budget envisaging a reduction from 534,000 to 345,000 men, and a threat from the Minister of Defence, A. V. Alexander, of a further reduction, while he refused to accept proposals designed to encourage the recruitment of more regulars. This forced Montgomery to insist that when the National Service Act came into effect in 1949 the period of service should be for at least eighteen months, as originally intended, and preferably for two years. He threatened his resignation and that of his colleagues on the Army Council if this was not accepted. He handed over to Slim before the issue reached Prime Ministerial level; but Slim, immediately on taking office, persuaded Attlee to approve eighteen months, having no need to pull out of his pocket the letter of resignation, which was backed

not only by the military members of the Army Council but also by his
fellow Chiefs of Staff.

Malaya

No sooner had the Palestine commitment been discarded than a new
one arose in Malaya. Japanese occupation during the war had undermined the slight authority which Britain had exercised there. Penang,
Malacca and Singapore had been colonies, known as the Straits Settlements. All the rest of the peninsula formed the Federation of Malay
States, each of the eight ruled by its own Sultan, advised by a British
Resident, under the overall supervision of a British High Commissioner
to the Federation. During the war Force 136, the South-East Asia branch
of the Special Operations Executive, had encouraged a resistance movement known as the Malayan Peoples' Anti-Japanese Army (MPAJA),
which was based on the Malayan Communist Party (MCP) and recruited
almost entirely from the Chinese population. One of its principal leaders
was Chin Peng, who was rewarded for his services by the award of an
OBE and a place in the Victory parade in London. This development
was not helpful to the return of colonial rule, and it was aggravated by
the Labour Government's proposal for a much more direct form of
administration, bringing the Federation into line with the Straits Settlements, with which it would be merged, and under which all races would
have equal rights. This was highly unpopular with all Malays, and in
particular with the Sultans. Chin Peng, under the banner of the Old
Comrades' Association of the MPAJA, exploited this and embarked on a
policy of violent militant action, working through the trade unions.

British authority was exercised in an indirect fashion. In 1946, when
Mountbatten's South-East Asia Command was wound up, Lord Killearn,
who had been Ambassador to Egypt throughout the war, was appointed
Special Commissioner for South-East Asia, responsible for the coordination of British Government policy in all fields in the area, and Malcolm
MacDonald, who had been Secretary of State for both the Dominions
and the Colonies in his father's National Government before the war,

became Governor-General of Malaya (including Penang and Malacca), Singapore and North Borneo. In 1948 Killearn left and MacDonald replaced him, but thereafter exercised no direct authority over the individual colonial Governors in the area, including Sir Edward Gent, the High Commissioner, but de facto Governor-General, of Malaya. The military set-up consisted of a British Defence Coordinating Committee in Singapore, a triumvirate of the Commanders-in-Chief of the Far East Fleet and the Far East Land and Air Forces. In 1948 the army Commander-in-Chief was General Sir Neil Ritchie.

The spark which set off the declaration of a state of emergency on 16 June 1948 was the murder of three European rubber estate managers near Sungei Supit, a hard Communist area in the state of Perak in northwest Malaya, shortly after the deployment of Gurkha troops in the area. The reaction of the MCP, probably with foreknowledge that it was about to be banned, was to go underground, mobilize its armed forces out of the MPAJA Old Comrades' Association, renamed the Malayan Races' Liberation Army (MRLA), and move them into the jungle, where secret camps had already been prepared near Chinese squatter villages, from which they could be supplied.

Gent was in the middle of a row with MacDonald, who, alarmed at what he regarded as Gent's complacent attitude towards the threat to British authority and economic interests, had recommended his dismissal. Gent flew back to Britain on 28 June and was killed when the RAF aircraft in which he was travelling collided with another as it approached London. His successor, Sir Henry Gurney, who had been Chief Secretary in Palestine, did not arrive until October. The Commissioner of Police, Mr Langworthy, who had been in ill health for some time, resigned as soon as the emergency was declared and his successor, Colonel Gray, also from Palestine, did not take over until August. The army commander, Major-General C. H. Boucher, had only assumed command a few weeks before, and both the officials holding the posts of Attorney-General and Financial Secretary were only temporary appointments. It is not surprising therefore that there was a lack of drive and direction on the part of the administration.

The general attitude was that the prosecution of the emergency and dealing with violence was the responsibility of the police, and it was for the army and the administration to provide them with whatever support they requested; but when the police asked for the support of the army in providing guards the army firmly opposed what it regarded as a misuse of its limited resources. At that time Boucher had eleven infantry battalions available in Malaya, of which six were Gurkha, two Malay and three British, supported by one British field artillery regiment. There was another infantry brigade in Singapore. The Gurkha battalions had an abnormally high proportion of new recruits and the British battalions were composed largely of National Servicemen, who were continually changing over.

Boucher's line was that his troops should be used for offensive operations against terrorist gangs or formed units, acting on information provided by the police. The trouble was that this intelligence was almost non-existent, responsibility for it being split between the police and an independent organization known as the Malayan Security Service, the head of which was unfortunately obsessed with the threat from Malay nationalist organizations with links to Indonesia. One of Malcolm MacDonald's main criticisms was of the paucity of intelligence: his other chief demand was for priority to be given to guarding mines and plantations and their managers in order to keep the economy of the country going. With the army unwilling or unable to help in this and the police gravely overstretched at a strength of only 10,000 for the whole country, the decision was taken to raise a force of Special Constables for this purpose. The initial target was for a force of 15,000: this was soon raised, and 24,000 men, almost all Malays, were enrolled in the first three months. At its peak, in late 1952 and early 1943, the strength of the force rose to 41,000.

The police were undoubtedly faced with a major problem both in rapid expansion and in adapting themselves to an entirely new and unfamiliar role of combating terrorism. At first, at the higher level, the army adopted a somewhat aloof attitude. It took the view that its main task was to defend the Far East against a major military invasion of the Second World War type, probably originating from an alliance between Russia and the Chinese Communists; and that in any case the defence of the base in Singapore took priority over support to the police and administration in Malaya. Unless the latter could provide information about the enemy, there was little the army could do. However, Boucher did his best to tackle the problem on somewhat conventional military lines. He explained his plan at the end of July 1948 as being to break up the insurgent concentrations; to bring them to battle before they were ready; to drive them underground or into the jungle, and then to follow them there with soldiers, and with the police accompanied by soldiers and supported by the RAF. His aim was to keep them permanently on the move in order to deprive them of both supplies and recruits.

While Boucher was putting this plan into operation, Chin Peng and his colleagues were primarily concerned with forming and training their units and attempting to establish them in areas which could become the basis of their proposed alternative Government. They undertook little in the way of offensive action, which lulled the administration into a complacent attitude. This appeared to be supported by the figures of terrorist incidents, which having averaged 200 a month from the beginning of the emergency to the end of 1948 fell to 100 in the first half of 1949.

However, this was the lull before the storm. With Chin Peng's reorganization complete, the groundwork of his support organization laid and the heady optimism of the early days – that the economy and administration would soon collapse – dispelled, there was a steady increase in the number of terrorist incidents, until by mid-1950 they were running at an average of 400 a month. These included attacks on police stations by gangs over a hundred strong, as well as frequent ambushes on roads and railways, all serving the combined purpose of discrediting the Government, intimidating the population and providing a source of arms and ammunition. In addition they drove the authorities to impose restrictions and repressive measures on the Chinese population, especially on squatters and plantation labour, which tended to weld them into an alliance with the Communists. By the end of 1949 it was clear that the forecasts made early in the year had been much too optimistic. General Sir John Harding, who had succeeded Ritchie as Army Commander-in-Chief in the Far East in July 1949, realized that neither the resources available to Gurney nor the methods employed by him and his administration were capable of improving the situation unless the army was prepared to take over more direct responsibility and commit itself more to static tasks. To do so, more troops would be needed over and above the seventeen battalions to which Boucher's force had now been increased. Above all there was a need for a better organization to direct the whole machinery of Government and of operations as a whole, in contrast to one which merely did its best to coordinate a series of conflicting demands of varying priority, leaving it primarily to the police to take the initiative in countering the activities of the bandits, guerrillas, terrorists or whatever label was attached to the Communist perpetrators of violence.

In March 1950 an additional Gurkha brigade was transferred from Hong Kong in partial response to an assessment by Boucher that he needed six more battalions in order to provide a framework of army presence all over the country to ensure that the effect of army operations, concentrated in a particular area, was not dissipated as soon as the soldiers moved on to operate elsewhere, and to provide a reserve of three battalions, permitting an opportunity for rest and retraining in rotation. This was especially necessary for the British battalions, which received a continuous trickle of partially trained National Servicemen to replace those who had just learnt the skills of their trade and had to make the long journey back home before the date of their release. Both Boucher and Harding felt frustrated at the waste of military effort involved in what Harding described as 'will-o'-the-wisp patrolling and jungle bashing', based on the slenderest of intelligence, which produced very meagre results for an immense effort on the part of a large number of soldiers. Even when there was intelligence and it was correct, the type of jungle sweep the army employed gave their opponents ample warning to slip away and await the end of that particular operation before returning, re-establishing their contacts and resuming their activities.

In July Boucher's full demands were met by the transfer of another brigade from Hong Kong, 3rd Commando Brigade Royal Marines. By this time he had left and been succeeded by Major-General R. E. Urquhart, who had commanded 1st Airborne Division at Arnhem. The army was now keenly aware that the problem was not going to be solved by military operations alone, nor primarily by them. The key lay in weaning the Chinese population away from the Communists, and the best way of doing that must be by demonstrating that their stake in the country was a prime interest of the administration, which had the will and the power to provide for the security of all. While the army concentrated on dealing with the armed forces of the MCP, based largely in the fringes of the jungle, the civil administration and the police had to create a political, administrative and security climate which would cut off the MCP's support in the population at large.

In April 1950 the pressures from MacDonald and Harding, as well as from the European community, led Gurney and the British Government to agree to the appointment of a Director of Operations to act under the High Commissioner, not just to coordinate but to direct all measures, civil and military, to prosecute the campaign against the MRLA and its supporters, known as the Min Yuen. The man chosen was Lieutenant-General Sir Harold Briggs, recently retired from the Indian Army, his last appointment having been command of the troops in Burma before it became independent in 1948. His path was not smooth, his arrival in April 1950 involving treading on a good many toes. He moved swiftly, taking a week to analyse the situation and produce his famous Briggs Plan. This was to clear up the country systematically working from south to north, making certain that once the process had been completed in one area a firm framework of sound administration and security could thereafter be maintained there. He would deal with the Min Yuen in the populated areas first, isolating the armed terrorist gangs, who would then be forced to come into the open to keep themselves supplied. On top of a basic framework deployment of soldiers to support the police all over the country, the army would provide a striking force which would deploy to each area in turn as the clearing up process developed. Its task would be to establish itself in the populated areas and from them dominate the jungle for a distance of about five hours' travel on foot, relying principally on ambushing the routes between terrorist camps and areas of potential supply.

Operations under the Briggs Plan started on 1 June in the southern states of Johore, Negri Sembilan and southern Pahang, but results were disappointing, largely because the army started its intensive operations before the administrative measures had begun to take effect. Most of the army's operations were undertaken on the basis of little or no intelligence and were still 'will-o'-the-wisp' patrolling. There were also difficulties in cooperation with the police, who resented losing control of the direction of operations to Briggs's triumvirates of police, army and administration. However, the more active the terrorists were, the greater the number of contacts between them and the security forces, and the higher their casualties. In 1950, 650 guerrillas were killed, while the security forces lost under 400 men: in 1951, 1,100 guerrillas were killed and some 300 surrendered, while security force casualties rose only by about 100.

Lieutenant Greville Charrington of the 1st Suffolks describes a successful ambush carried out by the battalion in Johore in August 1950:

As the sun sinks slowly into darkness and the beetles buzz past your head the men of the Suffolk Regiment in Malaya go out for their nightly task; some go on foot from the Company base in the rubber estate and others go in trucks – they appear to the onlooker to be feeling the cold because they are muffled up with netting scarves, sleeves rolled down, with some carrying and others wearing sweaters; hats are pulled low over the eyes and each man seems to have an automatic weapon of some sort. They are on their way in parties of five or six to ambush the bandits who may attempt to come in under the cover of darkness to the local labour lines to collect food and money or to meet their girl friends. The extra clothing is not to keep out the cold but to defeat the extra long probosces of the mosquitoes which make ambush after dark a most disliked operation.

Each party of five has an Officer or N.C.O. in charge of it and has about three automatic weapons. In addition, the ambush commander has a Verey pistol with some illuminating cartridges, also a trip flare. The orders are strict and uncompromising; no smoking, talking, moving about or fidgeting. No one will open fire until the commander does; that alone will be the signal.

The Platoon Commander of 10 Platoon 'D' Company had been given a patrol through the swamps of the bandit-named 'Hanging Bridge Area', finishing up near a timber workers' kongsi (lodging house) and saw mills at the 91st milestone on the main north–south road between Singapore and Segamat. Major L. Field M.C. believed, quite rightly as it turned out, that the bandits came in to this place fairly often to obtain supplies for their notorious bugle blowing gang which operated in a district known as Labis.

The Platoon found the going very hard indeed through this very thick swamp. At one time the jungle had been cut about by woodcutters and it had grown up again as secondary jungle, twice as thick as it had originally been, and difficult to get through. For this reason the patrol took much longer than it should have done. However, at about 5 p.m. the Platoon made base on the River Labis, about half-an-hour's walk to the main road and the place where the ambush would have to be laid.

The Platoon Commander left his Sergeant (Sgt. Harry Aldridge) to make base and took two Bren-gunners and two riflemen to do the ambush. He himself had a rifle and a trip flare.

The small party set off for the road, having had a very quick brew of tea and some bully and biscuits. The Platoon Commander marched due east on his compass and at about 5.45 p.m. they reached the jungle edge, which at this place was about 300 yards from the main road. Having quietly pushed through this unpleasant area of elephant grass, dense secondary jungle and fern, the party could see its objective, the kongsi about half-a-mile to their right.

Time was now a vital factor as the group had to get on to the track behind the kongsi unobserved, and the Platoon Commander had to have time to select a good position and put his men in before 7 p.m., from which time the bandits would most likely appear if they came at all. He had about half-an-hour to play with.

To go straight through the thick stuff directly towards the place would have taken far too long, so he decided to cross the road into an oil palm estate and then to go through it parallel to the main road under cover of the palms until he came to a place near to his objective, where he could slip back across the road, make his way through the thick stuff to the track which went into the jungle from the timber workers' bunkhouse.

Crossing the main road in broad daylight was accomplished by a short concerted rush as soon as a party of Chinese on bicycles had passed. At this place the road was dead straight for about a mile and even as they crossed they were afraid that they might have been seen from a distance. However, it was a risk that had to be taken and as it turned out they accomplished it without being seen by anyone.

Time spent waiting for a suitable opportunity to cross the road had considerably cut down the time for them to get into position, so they had to hurry through the oil palms at top speed. They soon came back on to the road about 200 yards from the saw mill and after again having a long wait they dashed silently across in a short line and flopped into the thick lalang grass* the other side of the road.

Making a fairly wide detour they moved in behind the kongsi just as the alarm clock beetle was signalling ten minutes to seven.

Instead of a footpath or road the Platoon Commander found himself confronted with a narrow gauge railway, used for bringing logs from the jungle to the sawmill. It appeared to be the only track of any kind so he walked down to pick a spot where his Bren guns

* Elephant grass.

could fire down the track; unable to find a bend he discovered that 100 yards behind the building the railway divided into two, one branch going to the sawmill, the other to the living quarters. Between the junction and the sawmill, about 40 yards away from the ambush, was a small derelict, though fairly weather-proof basha, which he decided to make his base.

Summoning his party with a low whistle he made his way to the hut. Quickly he briefed them and again reminded them of their orders. They cocked their automatic weapons and put their packs down in the hut and made their way to the junction.

The ambush covered some 30 yards, one Bren was nicely sited, firing straight down the branch line to the labourers' quarters. The other fired across the track further down. Each man was in the ideal night ambush position – one yard off the track with no cover to his front.

The Officer quickly walked down the ambush position to check and then sat down himself looking down the track towards the kongsi. He rested his rifle across his knees and took his trip flare and grenades out of his pouch, loosened the pins on them and put them in a place where they could be found quickly in the dark.

At that moment someone walked past him going towards the kongsi; exceedingly annoyed, as he thought it was one of his own men walking about, he stuck his head out for a good look. It was ten past seven and very nearly dark, but he could see another man coming towards him down the track carrying a rifle over his shoulder and dressed in a pale coloured shirt and a pork pie hat. His stomach felt empty with intense excitement as he realised they were bandits. He could see one more, making a total of three.

Waiting until the last bandit was opposite the end Bren-gunner he fired at the middle bandit, bringing him down on to the track, twitching somewhat. At the moment he fired the ambush opened up with an appalling din – he threw the trip flare in the general direction of the first bandit, whom he could not see, but it failed to go off, so he flung a grenade after it into the grass. The firing stopped abruptly on his command. The night was very dark and quiet except for the groans of the dying bandit in front of him, who had also his bandolier set on fire by a supplementary burst of Bren. There was no movement, so he left two men with a Bren in position and went to investigate. He found two bodies, the leading man having apparently escaped. The search for the leading man immediately commenced with the party sweeping down the blind side of the ambush. They found nothing, but going down the railway a bit the Officer saw a heavily bloodstained track leading off into the lalang, which he followed with his torch. He came across a rifle and a little later, where the bandit had entered the baluka (tree covered bracken) on his belly, he found a one star bandit cap covered in blood.

The Officer immediately threw his two grenades and ordered the other men to do the same so that a pattern of grenade bursts was formed like a naval vessel searching for a submarine with a pattern of depth charges. They then spread out and tried to sweep through. The blackness of the night and the denseness of the undergrowth soon made it apparent that they were not getting anywhere. The Officer spread his men out round the edge of the bracken and crawled down the bandit's track, following it by the light of his torch on the blood stains. It was eerie in this tunnel in the bracken with the possibility that the bandit might be waiting for him round every bend. Pig tracks, mere tunnels in the almost solid undergrowth, ran parallel to and across his bandit track, but he was able to keep to the wounded Chinese by the blood which coated the stems of the bracken on three sides of the narrow pig-run. As he went he passed two places where his grenades had exploded. After a bit the blood trail started to diminish and it became more and more difficult to follow the track which was only marked every two yards by just a spot of blood. Ten yards after this even these slight signs gave out. The Officer pushed on hoping that by now he might have caught the wounded man up – he went on the old line for ten minutes and then came back and went in a complete circle round the place where the track had given out. It was no good, however, and he crawled out into the open again, hot, tired and with bits of dry fern down his neck. His feelings were mixed; he was annoyed that he had been unable to find the bandit and finish him off, but at the same time he was relieved to get out of the bracken with the attendant strain of waiting for a possible pistol bullet directed his way at point blank range.

He immediately searched the kongsi itself, finding a considerable quantity of food, gym shoes and Chinese medicines all nicely done up ready to take away. He aroused the timber workers, who had been lying there like so many schoolboys pretending to be asleep when the headmaster comes round, and marched them up the track to his ambush base to remain under guard for the remainder of the night.

A soldier was sent to hitch a lift on the main road 50 yards away, up to Labis Police Station and inform Major Field of the success of the ambush.

In the morning after a weary night guarding the timber workers, 9 and 12 Platoons, under Lts. Kelly and Moffit, turned up together with Company H.Q., a Platoon of 'B' Company, under Lt. Ponsonby, with a corps of Iban trackers (Dyacks) to join in a follow-up search for bigger game in the shape of the main camp from which the dead bandits had come. C/Sgt.* Alfie Mayhew also arrived with some very welcome eggs and bacon and some dry socks. The char-wallah was also there so 10 Platoon, who had just come in, were able to stock up for the follow-up along the logging railway.

Although the missing bandit was not found by 10 Platoon, he gave himself up that day to a police vehicle going down the main road. He had been shot through the jaw and through the wrist and had lost a considerable amount of blood.

About three weeks later, under the name of 'Judas' and the influence of benzedrine, he was very useful to us in showing us the camps and tracks of his former friends.

The result of the ambush was three rifles and a pistol captured, two bandits killed and one surrendered through fear of succumbing to the wound inflicted by us. The sawmill and kongsi were later closed down for assisting the Communists.

Growing dissatisfaction at the lack of progress led Harding, who had handed over to General Sir Charles Keightley in May, to recommend to Slim that Gurney should be replaced by a general who should have responsibility for all aspects of Government. Two events led to this recommendation being accepted: the return of a Conservative Government in the General Election in July and the tragic death of Gurney in a terrorist ambush in October. General Sir Gerald Templer was appointed to combine the posts of High Commissioner and Director of Operations, Briggs retiring in December and Templer arriving in February 1952. At the same time Gray was replaced as Commissioner of Police by Arthur

* Colour sergeant.

Young from the City of London force and a new head of intelligence was appointed. Templer delegated much of his day-to-day responsibilities to his deputies, to Lieutenant-General Sir Robert Lockhart for operations and to Sir Donald MacGillivray for administration, while he himself toured the country, enthusing all and sundry with his dynamic energy and determination.

By this time the army had learned to operate more effectively in the jungle in pursuit of smaller bodies of men. In order to enlist the help of its aboriginal tribesmen, a force had been raised from ex-members of Force 136, who used Dyak trackers from Borneo. A development of this was the resurrection of the wartime Special Air Service (SAS). Another source of help was the introduction of the helicopter for casualty evacuation and supply. The RAF was slow in developing this form of support, partly because the few helicopters it had were seriously underpowered, but the Royal Navy, encouraged by the presence of the Royal Marines, showed the way. Training in jungle operations became a high priority, the Gurkhas proving themselves skilful at it.

Templer now had twenty-two battalions, a total strength of 45,000 men, of whom 25,000 came from Britain, the remainder Gurkha, Malay and East African, later to be joined by men from Australia, New Zealand and Fiji. Although major operations involving several units or even brigades continued to take place, the emphasis from now on was on thorough, systematic effort, area by area, lasting several months, at the end of which it was hoped that the area could be classified 'white', that is cleared of terrorists and one in which restrictions imposed on the population could be lifted and life return to normal. Quick results were not expected and not obtained; but by the end of 1953 the situation had clearly taken a turn for the better. The year had seen the total number of incidents drop from 3,727 in 1952 to 1,170: more significantly, major ones had fallen from 1,389 to 258. This compared with 2,333 major and 3,719 minor incidents in 1951. Yet the number of terrorists killed was still round the thousand mark and surrenders had risen to 372, while security force and civilian casualties had fallen to 209 and 143 respectively, from 1951 totals of 1,195 and 1,024, and, in 1952, 554 and 632.

In June 1954 1st Queens was operating on the slopes of Mount Ophir on the border of Johore and Pahang. 10 Platoon of its 'D' Company was sent out on a patrol to search for bandits there. Their regimental journal tells their story:

Mount Ophir rises to 4,107 feet, is extremely steep and is covered with primary jungle. There are many mountain streams strewn with huge boulders in steep valleys, vertical rock faces and the going is extremely difficult. The bandits and the security forces always make jungle camps near water for obvious reasons.

At 0300 hrs., 22nd June, 10 Platoon set off. We were inside the jungle by first light, 0600 hrs., and after a strenuous climb to 2,500 feet, dropped some 200 feet into the valley of our objective. We 'based-up' for the night 200 yards from the stream, and we were preparing for the night when L/Cpl. Pitchers came in very excited from his local security patrol; he said that he had come across signs of C.Ts.* In fact, these signs had been spotted by a surrendered bandit who was with us, and who noticed some shoots that had recently been cut from an unpleasantly thorny jungle bush; these shoots, he said, were cut by bandits for food.

We were certain that we were in striking distance of a bandit camp, and the next morning set off, leaving six men to guard our base. The plan was to move down to the stream and, if we could find definite tracks, continue as one patrol of fourteen under the Platoon Commander, 2/Lieut. Davidson. If we could not find any we should then split into two parties, the second party under 2/Lieut. Foster (who was on his first patrol) and patrol up-stream, one patrol on each bank.

We did find a definite track, so continued together. We moved very cautiously for about two hours parallel to the track in the hope that we would get into the camp without being spotted by the sentry. In this time we covered about 300 yards and suddenly came upon a camp that was deserted. It was a small camp for three men, and after searching it we found another camp for twelve, twenty yards away. While we were searching and destroying this, 2/Lieut. Foster and Pte. Morrison went to investigate a noise from the first camp. As the former clambered up a rock, a bandit put his head over the top and was instantly shot in the head by 2/Lieut. Foster, as he did so falling backwards into the stream. There were only three bandits in the camp and the other two attempted to fight; one fired one rifle shot which bounced harmlessly off a rock, and the other opened up with his tommy-gun or automatic; but, fortunately for 2/Lieut. Foster,

* Communist terrorists.

who was only seven yards away, the first round was a misfire. He didn't try any more and both bandits fled.

Meanwhile the remainder of the party, somewhat bewildered by the shooting, were just wondering whether we were attacking or being attacked when Pte. Vowles (now L/Cpl.) saw movement across our front on the steep slope above us; he fired but couldn't tell if he had hit. 'Cease fire' was called and we found one dead body with two packs in the middle of the first camp. The bandits must have come in just after us and they were starting to cook their lunch!

In order to find tracks of the escaped bandit, Pte. Vowles went back to his fire position and directed 2/Lieut. Davidson on to the spot; after a small search a footprint was found and also a drop of blood. Pte. Vowles had obviously scored a hit. With a small patrol we followed the footprints and blood trail, and after going 150 yards we heard a Chinese shouting in front of us. 2/Lieut. Davidson, seeing the outline of a man through the jungle, fired at him and we charged in. The CT was not dead and Pte. Vowles took the wise precaution of making a dive at his tommy-gun and grenade. He was very badly wounded; both his right ankle and left knee were shattered, and he also had a stomach and mild chest wound.

It took one and a half hours to patch him up and get him on to a stretcher. Meanwhile an Auster which flew over told us we were too high for a helicopter evacuation and so we decided to march him out. By the time we had packed up our base and were ready to move we had only one and a half hours of daylight left and 1,100 yards of precipitous and thick jungle to traverse. Apart from our own kit and weapons, we had two men, their kit and weapons to carry.

That evening we travelled 250 yards, and when it was too dark to move further we lay down for the night. It was a miserable night; it poured with rain and only by great care did we keep the wounded man dry. He was having regular morphine injections; even so, it was a miracle he was alive in the morning. It took us four hours to travel the remaining distance out of the jungle. We were still 800 feet up, but in open lallang (elephant grass) and as our captive had taken a turn for the worse, we decided to ask for a helicopter. He died before the helicopter arrived, and some ten minutes before the arrival of a carrying party from the Company. We had kept him alive for twenty-six hours, and all the Platoon had worked to their last ounce of energy to get him out. This was a very great disappointment:

captured bandits are most useful for the information they are prepared to give.

Before he died he told us that the man we killed was a State Committee member who had been sent after a high-powered meeting three days before to reorganize the Tangkak District and take command of it. His documents, which were many, proved to be of considerable value. He was the senior C.T. killed in that area for three years: the other man was his bodyguard.

The improved security situation created the conditions for a dramatic step forward in the political situation, with the possibility of independence looming nearer. Templer had been active in promoting cooperation between the different community political leaders, with independence as the carrot with which to bring them together. The result was the formation of the Alliance Party by an agreement between Tunku Abdul Rahman, leader of the United Malay National Organization (UMNO), and Tan Cheng Lock, leader of the Malay Chinese Association. An offer of amnesty to terrorists who surrendered was made to Chin Peng, but received no satisfactory reply. Early in 1955 it was announced that elections for a Federal Assembly would be held in July. They resulted in a sweeping victory for the Alliance Party. Towards the end of the year the Tunku held a fruitless meeting with Chin Peng, who then returned to the jungle.

From 1956 onwards the resources of the Government, both in security forces and in the administration, were fully and vigorously deployed on the pattern which Briggs had initiated and Templer improved. The army, with increasing support from the air force, became more skilled and sophisticated in exploiting intelligence and in the techniques of jungle warfare.

Operations by the 2nd Royal Welch Fusiliers in Negri Sembilan in September 1956 were an example of this. Major Conroy ('Cheshire') Hilditch was commanding their C Company and wrote an account of his company's part in them:

'C' Company was given an area more or less in the centre of the massif, and including the mountain known as Gunong Pasir (2,930 feet). Our specific area of search were the head-waters of a river called Sungei Surut Angin, which rose on the south-eastern slopes of Gunong Pasir, and a stream called the Sungei Klapi and its tributaries, further to the north-east. There had been an indefinite report from a surrendered terrorist that the headquarters camp of the Tampin/ Pedas A.W.F. was in the former area.

The whole fighting echelon of the Company, upwards of eighty strong, was lifted by three helicopters to a landing zone about 3,000 yards south of our search area by 1000 hours on Thursday 13th September 1956. On Saturday 12th September [15th September, after Nine Platoon had been sent off on a different task] I ordered full scale patrolling by Seven and Eight Platoons, mostly along the banks of the main stream and including the place at which the surrendered terrorist had said the Tampin/Pedas A.W.F. camp was situated. No information of importance resulted, although one patrol sighted a figure believed to be an aborigine. During the day, with C.S.M. Morton, I looked for a place to cut a Dropping Zone for our air re-supply, scheduled for Monday, and we decided on the southern slope of North Breast, as the best we could hope for in this mountainous terrain, though it was not by any means perfect.

On Sunday, 16th September, I allotted Eight Platoon entirely to the clearing of the Dropping Zone and only sent out one patrol from Seven Platoon. This was a fairly light programme designed to rest men who had had three hard days. I ordered the patrol to move downstream to its junction with the Sungei Surut Angin proper about 400 yards below our base, and then to move west upstream searching the banks of the Surut Angin and the tributaries nearest its source.

At about 1200 hours the patrol returned, and its commander, Cpl. Humphreys, reported that they had found a camp occupied by an estimated six to ten terrorists, about 600 yards upstream from the junction at which they had started their search. They had withdrawn, so he believed, without having been seen.

The force [Seven and Eight Platoons with some of Company Headquarters, organized into Assault, Search and Follow-up, and Cordon Parties] left the patrol base at 1305 hours and reached the Dispersal Point at 1440 hours. The stream beds were very rocky and boulder-strewn all the way, but by scrambling among the boulders we were able to avoid the thick vegetation. Our rubber-soled jungle boots were well suited to this sort of work, and any small sounds we might have made were drowned by the splashing of the streams.

At the Dispersal Point I decided to leave Fus. Williams, the leading scout of the patrol which had found the camp, with Sgt. O'Sullivan, so that he would have with him someone with knowledge of the actual position of the camp. The Assault Party and Search Party then moved off at right-angles, north up the steep hillside. The Cordon Party did in fact take about one hour to get into position. To the north and south they were about 30 yards away from the camp, to the east or at the downstream end about 60 yards.

On the move around the camp 2nd Lt. Jannetta navigated. I gave him the bearings to follow, told him when to change on to a new bearing, and checked with my own compass that we were moving accurately. The success of the operation depended on good navigation, as well as on silent movement and accurate shooting.

The first two legs of the move around the camp took about one hour. Going was thick and difficult and we were impeded by young attap palms except when we were near the top of the ridge. Attap grows sharp hooks for use in its struggle up to the light. Once it is hooked on you the only way to disengage yourself without making a deal of noise, is to step backwards and gently to pull out the hooks in the opposite direction from which they entered.

A colony of monkeys decided that they were on our side and created a diversion by holding a conference nearby, and by moving about in the tree-tops. Once or twice we heard the sound of talking from the terrorist camp and once the sound of timber being struck: the enemy were still in occupation!

After turning on to the third and southerly leg, we climbed down the ridge and crossed a number of gullies. I knew the camp was on a small ridge between the stream and a dry gully, but here were several ridges. Which one was the camp on? I eventually decided to turn east towards the camp, and as the going was more open, the Assault Party was able to move in line with the Search Party behind.

We had moved less than 50 yards when our left flank contacted L/Cpl. Vaughan, who proved to be the left-hand or end man of the southern section of the cordon. We had moved right across the open end of the cordon and had been about to move down altogether outside of it!

This meeting was a piece of very good fortune, and enabled us to correct our position, but in doing so we had to move again into very thick jungle, which made it necessary to revert to single file. After some casting about we found a cut path obviously of terrorist origin, leading through the thick stuff. We worked cautiously down this path, Fus. McLaughlin, one of the light machine gunners, leading, followed by 2nd Lt. Jannetta. I was moving at the rear of the Assault Party with Mr Tan* and the Seven Platoon Signaller, Fus. Jones, and the Search Party came behind us. It was now nearly 1730 hours, and, in the jungle, due to get dark in not much more than an hour: the move round the camp had taken nearly three hours.

Our advance down the path did not stop until the leading members of the party were actually looking into the camp: 2nd Lt. Jannetta found himself looking at a terrorist who was busy cleaning his carbine. There had been no sentry upstream of the camp, as I had expected there would be: in this deep jungle, perhaps never before visited by Security Forces, the terrorists must have felt completely secure.

Before further action could be taken, firing broke out from the northern area of the cordon. Afterwards we found out that a terrorist had crossed the stream by their water point, possibly to act as a sentry while the others washed, possibly to collect wood from the jungle, only to come face to face with Fus. Jones of the Cordon Party, who took correct action in shooting him dead, in preference to being shot himself.

All hell now broke out, and I, for one, thought that we were meeting determined resistance. During a lull I moved up to 2nd Lt. Jannetta and, after a brief word with him, decided to sweep the camp with a magazine from both light machine guns and then to get in as soon as possible. We were able to deploy a little, as the jungle on the right of the path in the vicinity of the camp was partially clear. At about this time some of the men further back started firing into the Camp, endangering those further forward. I was lucky in being able to stop this before any of us were hit.

As soon as the light machine guns had emptied their magazines, we entered the camp. It was empty except for the body of one female terrorist.

Heavy bursts of firing from the Cordon Party continued sporadically for some time. After it seemed to have finished, I decided to send out the Search Party to search the area between the camp and the cordon, but realized that I had not arranged a whistle signal to

* Julius Tan, Junior Civil Liaison Officer, a Straits Chinese.

warn the Cordon Party that a search was starting. I had arranged a cease-fire signal, but I did not want to use this in case any terrorists were still at large. However, I managed to shout (or rather Sgt. Mercer did for me) to the wings of the Cordon Party, warning them to pass it down the Cordon Line that the Search Party was going out, and that on no account were they to fire except at recognised enemy. Thereupon both the Assault and Search Parties started to search, leaving me with four sentries around the camp and with Fus. Jones, who had already begun to put up his wireless aerial (rod aerials were useless in the jungle).

Before conditions became impossible, I was able to send a signal to Battalion Headquarters saying that we had killed one terrorist and that we believed others had been killed by the Cordon Party; that we had had no casualties; and that we would have to remain where we were for the night. C.S.M. Morton also picked up this message, and, having heard the heavy firing, was much relieved to know that we were all unhurt.

By last light it was clear to me that no terrorist had escaped, though I was not sure until morning whether there had been five or six in the camp. I therefore ordered everyone to concentrate around the camp for the night, except for 2nd Lt. Jannetta and a few men, who stayed with the badly wounded female terrorist whom we had not been able to move before dark. A further two bodies had been brought into the camp, but the others had to be left. Including the wounded one, there were apparently three males and three females. They were variously armed with rifles, carbines and pistols, though it seems doubtful now if any were given a chance to fire a shot.

After sentries had been posted and areas of responsibility allotted, we said a short prayer of thanks for having all come through safely. After the amount of lead that had been flying about, it seemed pretty wonderful that all of us had done so. The problem of having a comrade hit while in such deep mountainous jungle did not bear thinking about.

The men curled up in twos and threes amongst the dead leaves, reminding me of the Babes in the Wood. Pretty dangerous babes, but a lot of them were under twenty years old. Some of them had the bright idea of sleeping in one of the terrorist shelters, but retreated hastily on finding three bodies laid out inside. Sgt.

O'Sullivan gave me the first cigarette I had smoked since being wounded at Kohima twelve years previously. I enjoyed it.

By about two o'clock we were bitterly cold and I gave permission for a fire to be lit. We sat around it till morning, burning the terrorists' stock of wood, dozing and chatting.

By this time the total security forces of all kinds, including all the variations of police and guard units, amounted to some 300,000, of which the great majority were Malay, although the Chinese were taking an increasing part, especially in the police Special Branch and in guarding the New Villages. The net gradually tightened, more and more of the populated areas were declared 'white' and the MRLA was forced back into the remote jungle. By the time of Independence (Merdeka) Day, 31 August 1957, the number of active terrorists had fallen to some 1,500. In that year they lost 540, of whom 209 surrendered, in addition to those who had died in the jungle and whose deaths were not recorded. There were only 40 major and 150 minor incidents. The security forces suffered forty-four casualties, of whom only eleven were killed, and civilian casualties attributable to the emergency were only thirty-one. The campaign was won, but not yet over. In an attempt to eliminate the MRLA, operations continued for another three years, by which time Chin Peng and the remaining members of his army had taken refuge in the jungle over the border in Thailand.

The Malayan emergency campaign has been regarded as the perfect example of counter-insurgency warfare. It certainly was a success story, of which those who participated in it and directed it have every reason to be proud. The greatest credit must go to the people of Malaya itself, who made great personal sacrifices, saw with sound sense where their real interests lay and employed considerable political skill, imagination and restraint in attaining their ends. To successive British Governments must go credit for their determination to accept their responsibilities and for taking the risk of bringing Malaya forward to independence while the war was still going on. Gerald Templer was the man of the hour. He arrived at the crucial moment, endowed with the qualities of intelligence, imagination, but above all determination and drive, which made it possible to implement the plan which had been so soundly formulated by Harold Briggs. A great deal of patience was needed by many different people, soldiers, police, administrators and, most of all, humble peasants and workers, over a period of twelve years. They were all fortunate that their opponents received very little help of any kind from outside the country.

Korea

Soon after trouble erupted in Malaya, an entirely different commitment arose elsewhere in the Far East – in Korea. At the end of the war against Japan, which had occupied Korea since 1910, the Soviet Union occupied the country as far south as latitude 38°, just north of Seoul, and the Americans the southern half. An attempt to reach agreement on democratic elections for the whole country broke down in 1948. Elections, held only in the South, resulted in victory for the aged Syngman Rhee, who became President of the Republic of Korea (ROK), to which the response of the Communists in the North was to proclaim a Democratic People's Republic of Korea (DPRK) and name Kim Il-sung as its first Prime Minister. At the end of the year the Russian forces withdrew from the North, having built up a strong army for it. US troops withdrew from the South in June 1949, the year in which Mao Tse-tung finally gained control of all of mainland China.

Official American statements led Kim Il-sung to believe that the USA would not intervene if, with his 90,000-strong army led by General Chai, he attacked the South, defended by an army of 65,000 men without tanks or aircraft. He crossed the 38th parallel on 25 June 1950, taking everyone by surprise, including General Douglas MacArthur, the US Supreme Commander in Japan. President Truman called a meeting of the UN Security Council, which passed a resolution calling on its members to 'furnish such assistance to the ROK as may be necessary to repel the armed attack and to restore international peace and security in the area'. At that time the Soviet Union was boycotting the Council and could not therefore exercise its veto. The first US troops landed at Pusan, at the southernmost tip of Korea, on 1 July and by 1 August three divisions were there, totalling 47,000 men, forming the US Eighth Army under Lieutenant-General Walton Walker.

The Security Council resolution not only provided a UN umbrella for the American action, but it also encouraged other members to contribute. The British Chiefs of Staff were not keen on doing so, but the Government thought that it must show more support for the USA than just a naval presence, and decided to dispatch 27th Infantry Brigade (Brigadier B. A. Coad) from Hong Kong with two battalions (1st Middlesex and 1st Argyll and Sutherland Highlanders), followed by the 29th (Brigadier T. Brodie) from Britain (1st Northumberland (Fifth) Fusiliers, 1st Gloucesters and 1st Royal Ulster Rifles), supported by 45th Field Regiment Royal Artillery and the Centurion tanks of the 8th Hussars, as well as the 41st Commando Royal Marines. To bring units up to strength, regular reservists were called up, generally to their intense indignation.

The Pusan perimeter being now secure, MacArthur decided to turn to the counter-offensive, for which purpose he had obtained the 1st US Marine Division. Against all professional advice, he made the bold decision to land the Marines at Inchon, where the physical conditions presented every sort of difficulty and risk. MacArthur overrode all objections and was triumphantly vindicated on 15 September, when the Marines struggled ashore with the support of a devastating naval bombardment and carrier-borne air attacks. A week later General Walker's troops broke out of the Pusan perimeter, in the course of which the Argylls, in a gallant attack on a hill, lost eighty-nine men, sixty from an air attack by the US Air Force, said to have been caused by the enemy using American recognition panels. On 28 September Seoul was recaptured and the decision had to be made as to whether MacArthur's forces should advance beyond the 38th parallel. In spite of great pressure brought by the Soviet Union, both in the Security Council and in the UN General Assembly, to convince the waverers like India that to do so would be overt aggression against North Korea, MacArthur was authorized by the US Chiefs of Staff on 27 September to move north of the dividing line 'to carry out the destruction of the North Korean Armed Forces'; but with the limitation that only ROK forces should be used, unless there were indications that Russian or Chinese forces were entering the country. On no account was he to cross the Yalu River into Manchuria, and, if he were to approach it, only ROK forces were to be used.

Rhee ordered his forces to move north of the parallel on 1 October;

MacArthur thought that this entitled him to move US forces also, although Chou En-lai, the Chinese Foreign Minister, announced on 2 October that, if they did so, Communist China would enter the war. The warning was repeated after the first US troops crossed the line on 7 October, the day after such action had received the approval of the UN General Assembly. It was not long after this that intelligence reports began to reach MacArthur and Walker that Chinese troops were moving towards the Yalu. When Truman met MacArthur on Wake Island on 15 October, ROK troops had already reached Wonsan, eighty miles north of the parallel on the east coast. On 21 October Pyongyang fell and the North Korean army began to surrender en masse. On 24 October the US 24th Division, with the British (Commonwealth) 27th Brigade, crossed the Chongchon River forty miles further north, heading for Sinuiju and the Suiho Dam on the Yalu, seventy-five miles further on. Two days later the 6th ROK Division reached the river to the east of them at Chosan, where they were sharply counter-attacked by the Chinese and fled in disorder. In spite of this, there was a general mood of great optimism and a confidence that although Chinese land and air forces were present in strength they were only concerned with defending the Manchurian border.

This complacency did not last long. MacArthur gave a warning that their presence was 'a matter of gravest international significance', and for three weeks nothing happened. MacArthur asked for permission to bomb the Yalu bridges and Chinese concentrations beyond the river, but was refused it, the Russians having stated that if the US Air Force attacked airfields in Manchuria they would retaliate. MacArthur was told by the Chiefs of Staff to clear the area up to the river and then organize elections throughout the country to be held under the auspices of the UN. In fact the Chinese General, Lin Piao, was preparing to attack all along the line with an army of 300,000. To face them, MacArthur had a total of 205,000 men. Walker's Eighth Army, in the centre and west, had four US and four ROK divisions, with one Turkish and two British brigades, facing sixteen Chinese divisions. In the east, separated by a gap of fifty miles, Lieutenant-General Edward M. Almond's 10th US Corps of three US and two ROK divisions, with the British Royal Marine Commando Group, faced fourteen.

On 27 November, four days after the American feast of Thanksgiving, when hopes of the American soldiers had been raised that they would be out of the country by Christmas, both these forces were fiercely attacked by the Chinese, who made their main effort along the hills in the centre, intending to swing round behind both Walker and Almond. After four days of fighting, Eighth Army and 10th Corps were retreating everywhere, as many of their formations were outflanked. MacArthur's hope of holding the line Pyongyang–Wonsan failed, the North Korean capital falling on 5 December, whereupon MacArthur decided to go right back to the 38th parallel; but by 13 December Eighth Army was already back to the Imjin River south of it. On 28 December General Walker was killed in a traffic accident and was succeeded by General Matthew B. Ridgway, wartime commander of the 82nd US Airborne Division. Ridgway found himself unable to hold the line under renewed Chinese pressure, especially on his western flank, and withdrew again. It was in the middle of this withdrawal that the British 29th Brigade arrived and, on New Year's Day, was deployed in support of the 1st ROK Division north of Seoul; but was soon withdrawing with the rest of Eighth Army, abandoning Seoul.

Ridgway finally formed a firm defensive line in mid-January 1951, running due east from Pyongtaek, seventy-five miles south of the 38th parallel in the west, to the east coast, forty miles south of it. To defend this line he had some 365,000 men in three US and three ROK corps. He faced Lin Piao's twenty-one Chinese and twelve North Korean divisions, which together had, at the start of their offensive, 485,000 men.

On 24 January Ridgway, who had taken a firm grip and done much to restore Eighth Army's weakened morale, launched a deliberate counter-offensive, which continued up to and through the spring thaw, as the country turned into a sea of mud. The last phase of this, Operation RIPPER, was launched on 7 March, the day MacArthur made public his disagreement with President Truman and the Joint Chiefs of Staff, whom he had failed to persuade to extend the war to China itself, including the use of nuclear weapons. By the end of March Ridgway's troops had pushed the Chinese, now led by Peng Teh-huai, back to the 38th parallel, and in some cases a few miles beyond, raising the issue of what to do next. MacArthur continued openly to press for full-scale war against China. As a result, on 10 April, Truman dismissed him, Ridgway taking his place, handing over Eighth Army to Lieutenant-General James Van Fleet on 14 April, eight days before the Chinese launched a counter-offensive.

Its strongest thrust, designed to encircle Seoul, struck hard at the
positions on the Imjin River, thirty miles north of the city, held by 29th
Brigade on a seven-and-a-half-mile front between the 1st ROK and 3rd
US Divisions, the latter on their right. The 63rd Chinese Army attacked
them with three divisions, and it was not long before they had penetrated
between the brigade's widely spaced defences. After two days and nights
of intense fighting, Brodie received orders from his American superior
to withdraw to a new position nearer Seoul. Of the three British
battalions of the brigade (there was also a Belgian one), the Northumberland Fusiliers managed to withdraw with fewest casualties. Many of
the Ulster Rifles did so on the tanks of the 8th Hussars, but others were
not so lucky and one company was surrounded, as was the position held
by the Gloucesters, who, after a gallant stand, were eventually forced to
surrender. Of the battalion's original strength of 850, 63 were killed and
only 169 escaped. The rest, including about 180 wounded, were taken
prisoner.

Twenty-five miles to the east, 27th Brigade, which now included
Australian and Canadian battalions and a New Zealand field artillery
regiment, fought a fierce action defeating attacks by the Chinese 118th
Division, which had caused the withdrawal of the 6th ROK Division.

Denys Whatmore, in yet another regimental migration, was commanding a platoon in D Company of the Gloucesters just south of the
Imjin. He describes their action:

> As the firing down at the river ceased and even the artillery fire
> slackened, the night took on an added darkness until our night vision
> was gradually restored. But the firing began again, over to our left, in
> the Castle Hill (A company) area. It became intense and continuous
> and it was possible roughly to gauge the rate of the enemy advance
> up the lower slopes of the hill by the flashes of their weapons. There
> was clearly a most tremendous fight going on. Then the Machine
> Gun Section sited immediately behind me joined in, sweeping fire
> towards the north eastern front of Castle Hill, the long, slow arcs of
> their fire beautiful in the night sky. I decided that the arching bullets
> seemed to travel so slowly because only one in every six or so was a
> visible tracer round, creating an illusion of a lazily moving firework
> display. Then return fire began to come in and nothing was lazy any
> more.
>
> It was obvious that we too were in for it. Soon – it must have

been about 0230 hours on 23 April – we heard the enemy directly to our front. He was blowing a bugle, a strange and frightening sound on the night air, raucous and menacing, something I had not expected but which, I was told later, was a standard and simple Chinese device for keeping their soldiers in touch with the Headquarters and leaders when advancing at night. More bugles joined in, then whistles, and they were coming closer all the time. Then we heard the movement of men through the scrub, men advancing up the ridge, and I ordered the 2-inch mortar man (as it happened, it was Private Andman) to fire an illuminating parachute flare. The mortar banged, but no flare; it was a dud, one of the several we had that night. Sensibly not waiting for orders, Andman fired another and this one worked. And there, about forty yards away, were the attacking infantry, the shapes of men almost white in the combined glare of the magnesium flare and the moon. The leading Sections needed no orders from me to open fire and enemy soldiers began to fall. Another flare or two were needed to continue the fire until that initial assault ran out of steam and the survivors went to ground. But they now knew precisely where we were.

So began a night and an early morning of repeated attacks, more parachute flares in the dark, fierce fire from the Sections, minutes of calm as the Chinese reorganised themselves, then again their rushes forward. There seemed to be hundreds of them, concentrated onto the ridge at the top of which we formed a barrier to their advance and from which we kept up a constant fire. I soon learned that they had infiltrated around our flanks as well, as the rear Section and then 12 Platoon began firing. Later, there was firing from the B Company area, a thousand yards behind us, as infiltrators round our right flank reached it.

Early in the engagement, I thought it was time to call for the 3-inch Mortar Section's defensive fire I had been advised about. I had no instructions about using the Battalion's 3-inch mortars but, as the MFC* was sitting in my trench with his radio, it seemed reasonable to make use of him; no one else could. The Corporal was all for it and made the necessary incantations into his radio mouthpiece. Soon, we heard the muffled thump in the rear which we took to be the mortars firing and down came the bombs – precisely on my

* Mortar Fire Controller.

Platoon position! The two bombs straddled us neatly, one near my
left Section, one near my right. The concussion made my ears sing,
but I heard the Corporal blaspheming and then, into his radio,
speaking tersely, seeking to correct the range so that the next bombs
would hit the enemy, not us. A cry from No. 2 Section informed me
that the bomb there had injured one man, not seriously, but he was
bleeding all over the place, our first casualty. I got him over to my
slit trench and used the 'phone to contact Company HQ, where the
Medical Sergeant agreed to come over and look at the wound. A few
minutes later, he jumped into the trench, breathless, and declared
the soldier – one of the latest National Service reinforcements, whose
name I hardly knew – not badly hurt; a bomb fragment had sliced
his ear and, like many ear wounds, the blood ran copiously but the
actual cut was not too bad. The soldier returned to his position with
a dressing on his ear but, just then, the Chinese made another frontal
attack on the Platoon position, and kept it up so that it was
impossible to get the Medical Sergeant back to Company HQ. He
remained with me. This attack brought a few of the Chinese into our
midst but we shot them out again without resorting to hand to hand
fighting. But when the Company Sergeant Major phoned through a
few moments later asking about our situation, I was able to tell him
'They are right in among us, but we are coping'.

We began to run out of the precious parachute flares but, using
the Company radio net this time – and, in the excitement, getting
my wireless procedures wrong, for which I was severely rebuked by
the broad Gloucestershire voice of the Private at the other end – I
asked 10 Platoon to fire some in our direction and they helped no
end. 10 Platoon was not seriously engaged in their location but 12
Platoon behind me was blazing away as the Chinese infantry outflanked me and pressed on towards the South, clearly with orders to
make as much progress into the UNO lines as they could. On our
front, however, we began to be seriously plagued by a Chinese
machine gun; I believe it was this gun that killed three or four of No.
1 Section and wounded others so that they had to be evacuated. I
yelled to Private Andman, drawing his attention to the gun's location,
about 100 yards out on the occasionally illuminated ridge, its muzzle
flashes giving it away. I wanted some 2-inch mortar high-explosive
bombs put down on it. Andman replied and within seconds had fired
his mortar; it was the most amazing shot, for the bomb fell with a

remarkably loud explosion exactly where the flashes had been seen, and the gun did not fire again. Fluke or skill, it did the job, and I yelled congratulations to Andman, into the din around us. It must have been soon after this that he was wounded.

The dawn came and we were so engaged in the fight that it was full daylight before we knew it. At about 0530 hours, the Chinese over-ran part of No. 1 Section, got into the slit trenches there and opened fire on the rest of us. I had a glimpse of a young Chinese in a steel helmet, mouth open, shouting, and then he threw a grenade at me. It flew towards my trench, the wooden handle gyrating in the air, and I just had time to yell 'Grenade' to warn the others, and to duck, when it fell on the breastwork on the lip of the trench. It teetered, dropped back outside the breastwork and exploded with an awful bang, showering us with stones; singing ears again but no injuries. I popped up and gave him a grenade in return; but mine was a phosphorous grenade, intended really to create an instantaneous smoke screen, but nasty because the ignited phosphorous burnt anything it touched. The grenade burst in the enemy soldier's face, he disappeared in a cloud of smoke and, when the air was clear, he had gone. So too had the others who had gained a toe hold.

Then disaster struck. A Chinese machine gun party had worked its way around to our right flank and began to spray us with very accurate fire. I put up my head to locate it and so did Private Binman, advancing his rifle at the same time to get a shot off. We were met by a burst of fire exactly at the height of our heads. Private Binman took a bullet in the eye, gave a gasp and fell over backwards at the feet of the crouching Medical Sergeant. The remainder of the burst went over my right shoulder and I hit the deck fast. Another burst scattered the stones above us and hit the MFC's radio, cutting us off from the mortar section. My batman lay on his back breathing stertoriously but quite unconscious; the Medical Sergeant, when I glanced at him, shook his head. And then the breathing stopped.

And still the attacks came on. We all fired our weapons – there were plenty of targets – until they were hot and uncomfortable to handle. Then my Sten gun jammed; that weapon had an infamous fault, in that occasionally it managed to feed two rounds into the chamber at once, causing an explosion which left jammed in the barrel the split brass casing of the first round. There was a clearing tool which could be used to get the casing out. In my case there was no time to fiddle with that, so I seized Private Binman's rifle and continued with that. I think someone else must have got the Chinese machine gun, for after a while it ceased to fire, at least in our direction.

By now it was about 0700 hours, broad daylight, sunny and warm. And we began to run out of ammunition. Even before dawn had broken, Corporal Norley had been calling for more ammunition and I had tossed over to him all the spare rounds we had. Now, from all sides, there were calls that ammunition was nearly exhausted. I myself ran out of rifle bullets and, soon after, pistol ammunition. In desperation, I loaded the Verey light pistol with a cartridge and aimed it at an advancing Chinese soldier who was firing a Burp gun;* the searing red flare missed him, but he had a nasty fright; the next red and the last green missed too, but he fell eventually to someone else's shot. I had one grenade left and no other ammunition of any kind.

I now had to decide what to do. 11 Platoon had been sited in that position to prevent the enemy capturing it and I was reluctant to leave. But to stay without ammunition was impossible; we had fought to pretty well the last round – to fight to the last man seemed pointless. The field telephone line had been cut long since so whatever decision was to be taken, it had to be mine, and it had to be quick. I made the decision; we would go. I yelled at the top of my voice to the Sections, ordering them to retire as soon as they saw the last 80 grenade burst. Then I threw the grenade to screen us from the nearest enemy, yelled 'Go' and joined the rush towards 12 Platoon's position. As we went, I saw the Sergeant commanding the Machine Gun Section on the ridge wave and shout to us urgently, warning us of his fire; it seems that for some time his guns had been firing over open sights at the Chinese around the D Company hill, and we were in danger of running into a stream of bullets from the Vickers guns. He held his fire until we had passed through his position while, behind him, 12 Platoon continued to fire at the enemy on their right front. I noticed that only one Vickers was in action. The other was on its side and the Sergeant said it had been put out of action by enemy fire. I looked back towards the position I had just evacuated but the enemy did not seem to be chasing us. I

* Sub-machine-gun or machine-pistol.

passed on through to Company HQ, where I informed Mike Harvey of the situation. He accepted the information calmly and sent what remained of the Platoon to a site along the ridge, behind 10 Platoon, to form a new reserve, however meagre. The Medical Sergeant was able to rejoin Company HQ. I counted the men of 11 Platoon; only 13 of us had made it, none of us wounded. We learned, however, that several wounded men from the Platoon (much later I learned that Private Andman, with a bullet through the arm, was with them) had been evacuated during the night, so I was able to hope that the death toll had not been so very bad.

During the rest of the day D Company was moved to join Support Company and the remains of A Company on Hill 235, where the commanding officer, Lieutenant-Colonel J. P. 'Fred' Carne, had his Headquarters. During the following night the Chinese attacked B and C Companies about half a mile away to the north-east, forcing them eventually also back to Hill 235. By this time the battalion was completely cut off. Two attempts to open a route to them and to resupply them by airdrop failed. The Chinese launched another attack during the night of the 24th, which was held. Whatmore picks up the tale on the morning of 25 April.

The battalion remained cut off, with many wounded, little ammunition, no food and water nearly exhausted. The unwounded were pretty worn down, but not yet quite exhausted. It was obvious, though, that we could not hold out much longer and soon, I was told that Colonel Carne had made this clear to Brigade HQ on the radio, now fading as the batteries ran down. It was on that radio that the message was finally received that the Glosters, having done the job they had been sent to do, could now retire from the position and extract themselves from their situation as best they could. At 1030 hours on 25 April, Colonel Carne gathered his Company Commanders to give his final orders. Mike Harvey attended this meeting and soon returned to brief his Platoon Commanders. He told us that the Commanding Officer had received permission to abandon his position; that there were many wounded who could not be moved and the Medical Officer, Bob Hickey, and his staff, and the Chaplain, Padre Sam Davies, intended to remain with them. He said that the Commanding Officer, too, had decided to remain behind; this last point was later shown to be erroneous, Colonel Carne making his way South, leading the rest of the Battalion towards safety. Starkly, Mike Harvey put it to us that we had only two choices – to remain and surrender, or to fight our way out. If we chose to fight, we should have to move fast; there would be no stopping on the way for anyone wounded. We Platoon Commanders (and Lieutenant Bob Martin, the Machine Gun Platoon Commander, who had joined us) did not discuss the matter; we did not even glance at one another. We all said together 'We fight', and so the decision was made. Mike Harvey then told us his plan. He proposed to avoid what must be the shortest way out, that is, due South, where he thought it was probable the enemy lay in strength. He would take the Company due North to start with, into ground from which the enemy were likely to have moved on, then West along the lower North-facing slopes of the hills and so South down a valley towards friendly lines.

It would be a long way round, but with luck we should meet fewer Chinese that way. He advised us to pair off the men so that each man could help another, and then gave us a few minutes to brief and organise the men. It took no time at all to tell my twelve soldiers what we were going to do and they prepared for the trek with a will. Sergeant Dee assigned them in pairs and made sure that each man had at least some ammunition. I discarded my battle dress blouse, for already it was warm and it was likely to get warmer, in more senses than one. And then we were off, D Company HQ, 10 and 12 Platoons which had received few casualties so far, the thirteen of 11 Platoon, and a miscellany of Support Company soldiers, mainly Machine Gunners; a total, I believe, of 90 men.

After a hazardous journey, which involved clashes with several groups of Chinese, Harvey and forty-six others, including Whatmore, out of the ninety-six who had started off, reached the front of a neighbouring ROK unit, but not before they had been shot at and suffered some casualties when fired at by an American tank. Eleven of the party were killed, the rest, some wounded, being captured. Colonel Carne and the other companies did not get far, stopped by strong Chinese machine-gun fire, and were forced to surrender.*

Fighting on and around the 38th parallel continued until the end of

---

* Lieutenant-Colonel Carne was awarded the Victoria Cross for his courage in this action.

June 1951, when feelers were put out for peace negotiations, both sides accepting that until they reached agreement fighting would continue. It was to do so for another two years in conditions reminiscent of the trench warfare of 1914–18, operations being limited to attempts by both sides to make their positions more suitable as semi-permanent ones or as bargaining chips.

A considerable effort was put into patrolling. Sergeant Tom Nowell, of the 1st Duke of Wellington's, tells of an eventful one in the winter of 1952–3. Its object was to provide information about a tunnel which the Chinese appeared to be digging opposite his battalion's sector:

Come late afternoon, I went down to the Company dug-out and joined up with Ian 'O'.* After a final conference with the Company Commander, Barry 'K', and had a final briefing, we were escorted down to the wire and mine-field gap. There we were bid a 'good patrol and the best of luck' and we were off.

Threading our way down the remainder of the hillside and negotiating the mine-field and extents of the wire, we made it to the first bound, or objective that we had set ourselves. It was the stream that some standing patrols used quite often for 'listening and obser-vation'. It was frozen over at this time of year but there was the little ricketty footbridge still there to effect a dry crossing in the event that it was thin ice or water to cross. The night was fairly dark and the moon had not yet broke through the cloud base. We wanted as much darkness as we could get, seeing that we were to be travelling a good way over and into enemy territory. The snow that was still down and the ice that glistened in the eerie night-light reflected what light there was and made it seemingly brighter than we would have liked. What a noise we seemed to be making. The ice underfoot crackling and the ground foliage 'swishing through' as we tried to step carefully as we went along. Picking out our landmarks and leaps and bounds. Making our way to those, often stopping and listening as we made progress to them. It was slow and nerve-wracking, the senses being acute all the time to try and pick up any old noises that would indicate to us the presence of other people, or enemy that may be about. We could hear the sounds of gun-fire and the occasional flare that went up made you freeze in your position until it finally died its

* Second Lieutenant Ian Orr.

death and left you in the relative dark again. This was a time when you wished that you could float, or soar across and not make any noise at all. Secrecy was to be the watchword and the least that anyone knew what we were up to, the better it would be for the two of us. The 'bunds' or banks of the broken down paddy fields occasionally giving way and making one lose his foothold and crash to the floor. It seemed an eternity, that travail across the valley. Not talking too much at all, keeping the speaking down to the minimum and making do with the odd sign, or grabbing the other's arm to attract their attention. Resting up a little on reaching each of the various objectives that we had set ourselves. Thanking our lucky stars that so far, so good. We both felt naked out there, having got past the point of no return. We concluded that it was now safer to go forward than to retrace and go back. Suddenly, a series of clicks and bangs went off and we were illuminated by a string of flares and tracer fire that lit the sky. What the hell was happening? We were supposed to be given the quietest of night time activity so as to get the best conditions that we could, to effect a crossing of the valley. There was obviously some disturbance further down the valley and for a short time there was quite a racket going on. Somebody must have won that exchange and asserted their authority, because it quietened down and we were able to then make our way across the last leg, or objective, to the foot of the opposing side's hill and trench emplacements. We did hear later that the 'ruckus' that was going on was one of our night patrols trying to do a 'snatch' and at the same time create a diversion for our efforts to get across into enemy territory and out of the bareness of the valley.

We paused for a while to look back and take stock of our bearings and land marks. The hills opposite now being our own friendly lines. Those idiots will insist on sending up flares. Another time, they would have been a welcome sight with the added attraction of being able to find one's way about, but not tonight. The temperatures were well below freezing and our clothing on the outside was beginning to go hard and getting hands into pockets to retrieve items of equipment was quite a feat of dexterity. We were both equipped with body warmers that went into your pockets and around other parts of your person, so at this time we were not too distressed with the weather conditions. We also carried an assortment of goodies to help sustain us for the period that we were to be out there with no food back-up.

Cutting down on the equipment as much as we could, we were travelling light. A couple of grenades and a Sten gun each forming the bulk of our armoury. No radio cover, we were not expected to be sending messages back throughout our stay over there, just to make notes or mentally take stock of the layout and the fortifications that were there.

We came to the foot of our objective and decided to go around and further into the enemy territory to come up on the hill from the rear. Approaching the suspected tunnel work site from the rear would not arouse undue suspicion if we were spotted at that close range. Climbing up the slopes at the rear then we made our way along the top, or ridge of the outcropping feature. Along the top of this way, we came across some large logs, or sawn down trees that were being used for the construction of the tunnel so we knew we were on the right track for the tunnel itself. Getting near to where we thought the tunnel entrance should be, we split up and were to make separate 'hides' or observation points that was to be our position for the rest of the next day and who knows. Ian 'O' stayed at that point, myself, I decided to go further towards where I thought that the tunnel entrance should be. Out with the jack-knife then and cut some small firs that were growing in the area and fashion them into something like a sort of cover from view, if not altogether cover from fire. This wasn't as easy as it sounds, particularly as we didn't know where the 'chinkies' might be and in what strength. After some agonising minutes doing this activity, I thought that my little hide was coming along quite nicely. I could hear Ian 'O' doing the same, that twenty yards or so further back and I thought God, what a noise he is making. I hope that I wasn't making as much noise as that. Later on, after the event, I asked Ian if he could hear me doing my thing and he said, 'Yes, I thought you were giving "chinky" a bit of a hand in your spare time!' It turned out later that some of the sounds that he could hear and put down to me were actually made by the two Chinese workers who were preparing an evening meal for themselves, and the patrol that came along a little later in the night.

Having made everything as ready as I could, then it was a case of settling in and making myself as comfy as I could. A cup of hot soup, the variety that is self heating would be nice, so out with the can and activate the striker. God! what a noise, the crack that it made sounded like a gun shot going off. As it warmed up, there was the inevitable sizzle as it got hotter and it sounded like a kettle when it was about to blow its whistle. I couldn't stop the thing and it seemed to be getting louder, the whole time I am trying to smother it to quieten it. Only to be showered with hot, steamy 'beef stew' in the process. After that episode of the exploding can's, I was to be a little more wary as to where I was before I let another one of those off. The stillness of the night exaggerating sound beyond normal daylight noises and senses.

Daylight wasn't too far away now and the streaks of dawn were appearing over the hill tops. There was some movement below me which I assumed to be 'big and little dusty' getting squared up for another day of digging and excavating. It turned out to be the night patrol going back across the little re-entrant to their day quarters, possibly to get a meal and to rest up, ready for another trip out on patrol. Strange how the thought of 'Chinky' doing the same as we did on the other side of the valley. We behaved like a set of moles, in fact. When daylight finally came, I found myself, with my little hide, just on the lip of the entrance to the tunnel that we had come all this way to see and report on. I had a grandstand view of what they were up to alright. In fact I considered myself too close for comfort but there wasn't anything that I could do about that now. It was a case of staying very still and try not to make any undue noise that would alert them and give the game away. What with the situation I found myself in, and the bitter cold temperatures, you could say that I was in a precarious position. Every move that I made to ease my position gave me the distinct feeling that I had given the game away and that I would be discovered and captured, or worse. However, it didn't appear that they had heard, or were too engrossed in what they were doing to be worried about any little noise that I may have made. Probably the sound of 'little dusty' singing, if that is what it was, would have drowned out any little noise that I made. He sounded terrible. More like a cat in agony would be more like it. The other fellow, the taller one, was content to grunt and spit. Whether it was in sympathy, or disgust, I wasn't too sure. Anyway, while 'little dusty' was prepared to work, his 'singing' didn't do anyone any harm. Good job the commissar wasn't around to rebuke him and exhort him to greater activity. I had a good view of all this 'work schedule' from where I was situated. A bit too close for comfort, as I said, but it was a case of make the most of it now that I was here.

My colleague, Ian 'O', a little further back thought I was having a whale of a time. He wasn't aware that I was just about sitting on the chinamen's laps. The temperatures never rose above freezing point and my limbs were beginning to play me up. I tried to revive them with a little light massage but it sounded too noisy for safety so I had to devise other methods of getting the circulation going. 'Little dusty' came away from the mouth of the tunnel and made to come in my direction, ostensibly for another tree log, or something. It turned out though that he wanted a 'pee', so I had the indignity of having my home-made hide 'peed on' by a chinese labourer. Apart from that, he splashed me in the process and the wonder of it all was that he didn't see me in the hide. How much of that was due to my efforts to camouflage the 'joint', and myself, or the fact that he hadn't washed or bathed for about a month and his eyes were caked up, I shall never know. More to the point, I think that I would have preferred to have been 'peed on' than have been caught out at that time.

All during this time on the enemy hillside, we continued to log as much as we could of the enemy tunnel and the size of the logs etc. It would appear that they were almost finished with what they had in mind and it wouldn't be too long before the enemy was going to use the tunnel emplacement in earnest upon our own defences.

Sergeant Nowell and his companion managed to extract themselves from their hides during the following night, while a group of Chinese was making a good deal of noise. They had an exciting journey back, taking a different route to the 'ricketty bridge', where they were challenged by one of their own patrols. Sergeant Nowell was awarded the Military Medal for this exploit and for leading a subsequent attack on the tunnel.

The unsatisfactory situation in which both 27th and 29th Brigades found themselves was remedied by the formation of a Commonwealth Division (Major-General A. J. H. Cassels), a Canadian brigade having now joined the other two, while the Canadian battalion in 27th Brigade was replaced by a second Australian one. Over the two years, the original units were replaced at intervals by others. By the time the armistice agreement was signed on 27 July 1953, British (UK) casualties had totalled 793 killed and 2,878 wounded and missing: American totals were 30,000 and 170,000.

The outbreak of the Korean War, coinciding with the formation of NATO, forced Attlee's Government to reverse its plans for continued reduction in defence expenditure. A three-year programme, costing £3,500 million, to strengthen the forces, including the extension of National Service to two years, was announced in September 1950. Attlee went to Washington in the spring of 1951 to try and get an assurance from President Truman that he would not authorize the use of nuclear weapons without British approval. He did not succeed, although he thought he had obtained one guaranteeing prior consultation. In return he was pressed to improve the strength of Britain's armed forces further by expanding his programme to one costing £6,000 million; but his colleagues would not accept more than one of £4,700 million, which doubled pre-Korean War expenditure at 14 per cent of national income. The army's share of this (35 per cent) was based on a plan for ten active divisions, of which four (three armoured) would be in Germany, and twelve (including one armoured and one airborne) from the Territorial Army, in addition to the latter manning anti-aircraft and coastal defences. A major re-equipment programme was involved, including the Centurion tank with its powerful new 105mm gun.

Although Labour had been returned to Government in the General Election of 1950, Attlee's difficulties in meeting the heavy commitment of this rearmament programme led him to go to the country again in October 1951, when he lost, Churchill and the Conservatives returning to power.

Kenya

Just as the situation in Malaya was taking a decisive turn for the better in the second half of 1952, Britain found herself faced with another unexpected colonial conflict, in Kenya. The Governor, Sir Philip Mitchell, retired in June, telling his successor, Sir Evelyn Baring: 'There really is a genuine feeling of desire to cooperate and be friendly at the present time.'

The situation in fact was that a movement, of which Jomo Kenyatta was the acknowledged head, had almost succeeded in completely subverting the Kikuyu tribe to reject the Government, the missions and everything European, with the eventual aim of getting rid of both Europeans and Asians from the country altogether. The movement operated through a number of organizations, the principal one being the Kenya African Union, a legal political body, control of which had by then passed into the hands of the banned Kikuyu Central Association. Mau-Mau was the strong-arm paramilitary organization, combining the functions of both warrior and witch doctor. The basic impetus behind the movement was varied, from the frustration of the mission-educated African at finding that neither the religion nor the education which he had received changed him into the equivalent of a European, to much more primitive fears, frustrations and resentments. Fundamental to these was the impact on a tribal society, based on strict conformity within the group, of contact with Western civilization, which had only reached the country in the late nineteenth century. The First World War had had a decisive effect. Large numbers of Kikuyu had been recruited, many virtually impressed, into the Carrier Corps as porters and labourers to take part in the campaign against the Germans, led by Lieutenant-General P. von Lettow Vorbeck, in Tanganyika, and many of them had died of disease. After the war there had been a considerable influx of Europeans and the question of land purchase or allotment, particularly in the southern part of the Kikuyu reserve bordering Nairobi, became a burning issue. It was an area which had been continuously in dispute, and, although the Carter Commission in 1922 made restitution of 110 square miles, the accusation that the Europeans had stolen their land was widely believed and readily exploited. The Kikuyu was the largest and the most intelligent and industrious tribe, occupying the key central area running north from Nairobi for about a hundred miles on the eastern side of the Aberdare Mountains.

Baring arrived on 29 September and immediately started a tour of the affected areas. He was shaken by all he heard and saw. Everywhere he went he was told by the Africans who were working with or for the Government that the situation was almost out of control and that unless he took immediate steps against Kenyatta and his principal supporters not only would their lives be at risk, but the Government would lose control of the Kikuyu altogether. Any inclination he might have had to hesitate was dispelled on 9 October by the cold-blooded murder of the

respected Chief Wariuku. On that day he sent a long telegram to
the Colonial Secretary, Oliver Lyttelton, in which he recommended the
declaration of a state of emergency and the arrest of Kenyatta and his
associates. He concluded by saying that if he did not do this:

(i) the chiefs, headmen, Government servants and missionaries
among the Kikuyu who still support us will cease their support
and may well be killed;

(ii) the trouble will spread to other tribes who are more warlike
than the Kikuyu and who provide the men for the Kenya Police;

(iii) there will be reprisals by Europeans.

His recommendations were accepted and, allowing time to make the
necessary preparations (including the dispatch of a British battalion by
air from the Suez Canal Zone), a state of emergency was declared on 20
October 1952 and orders were signed to detain 183 known leading
members of the Kikuyu Central Association, including Kenyatta.

The army in Kenya was totally unprepared for anything of this
nature. In 1950 an attempt had been made to set up a Joint Internal
Security Intelligence Committee to provide warning of such a situation,
but the army had soon opted out of it. The headquarters of East Africa
Command in Nairobi (Lieutenant-General Sir Alexander Cameron) was
subordinate to GHQ Middle East (General Sir Brian Robertson). The
command extended to all military units in Kenya, Uganda, Tanganyika
and Mauritius, and was still engaged in handing over those in Northern
Rhodesia and Nyasaland (now Zambia and Malawi) to the newly formed
Central African Federation. The only combat troops were African,
infantry battalions of the King's African Rifles (KAR) of which Kenya
normally had three, Uganda one and Tanganyika one, a company of
which was in Mauritius. Additional battalions from Kenya and Tanganyika had been raised for service in Malaya. The only other force was the
Kenya Regiment, a part-time volunteer infantry battalion of Europeans.
The pick-up operation on 20 October was carried out successfully
without any resistance at 5 a.m., two and a half hours before the 1st
Lancashire Fusiliers arrived in RAF aircraft, after which they drove round
Nairobi looking warlike, while the KAR supported the police.

Cameron took the lofty view that as the Governor was also Commander-in-Chief, the Brigadier of the KAR brigade in Nairobi should
advise him about military support and provide it, while he, Cameron,

attended to the affairs of his command as a whole. The Royal Navy chimed in with an opportune visit by HMS *Kenya* to Mombasa, 300 miles from the nearest Kikuyu. Settler morale was raised, but quickly dashed again by the murder within the first two weeks of one of the most respected Kikuyu chiefs, Senior Chief Nderi, and of Eric Bowyer, the first European settler to be killed. The first reaction of the Government was to concentrate on defensive security measures and to plan a major expansion of the police. It was also decided to raise a Kikuyu Home Guard to serve as both a local security force and a resistance movement around which Kikuyu could rally in opposition to Mau Mau. The army was to back up the police, the British battalion in the European settled area and the KAR in the reserve, where the Tribal Police operated under the orders of the Native Affairs administration, the Colony Police serving under the Commissioner in the towns and the European settled areas.

There was no real plan of campaign nor any offensively directed operations, for, as usual, there was little intelligence on which to base them. Baring realized this, and in November, as the situation deteriorated, he asked Lyttelton for expert advice on the organization of intelligence and for the appointment of a Director of Operations in the rank of Major-General. After flying to London and pleading with the Prime Minister, Churchill, Major-General W. R. N. Hinde was appointed, and very valuable he proved to be. Sir Percy Sillitoe, head of the Security Service, was sent out and recommended a concentration of all the separate bodies involved in intelligence, both in the police and in the administration, and measures to link their work with the security forces; but there was a long way to go before the organization began to work satisfactorily.

Hinde set about trying to establish a pattern of organization similar to that devised by Briggs in Malaya, but found himself up against many obstacles. Provincial Commissioners and District Officers, who had traditionally been left to run things their own way, were jealous of their authority and reluctant to share it with police, military or anybody else. Hinde himself, who at this stage only held the post of Chief Staff Officer to the Governor, exercised no authority except over the army until in April 1953 his appointment was changed to that of Director of Operations.

The organization which Hinde set up was headed by a Colony

Emergency Committee, presided over by the Governor: below it, Hinde had his own Director of Operations Committee, overseeing Provincial and District Emergency Committees. The defects of the organization lay in a diffusion of authority and responsibility for action. General Harding, now CIGS, visited the colony soon after Hinde had arrived and persuaded Churchill and Lyttelton to appoint a more senior general, Sir George Erskine, as Commander-in-Chief, with authority over the army and the RAF and over the police in respect of emergency operations. To Erskine's embarrassment Cameron stayed on for some months, concerning himself with the rest of the command. A further result of Harding's visit was the dispatch of a British infantry brigade, the 39th, with two battalions, 1st Buffs and 1st Devons. They arrived in April, but Erskine did not appear until June, by which time the situation had deteriorated further, one incident causing grave concern, the Lari massacre, in which the Mau Mau burnt down a Kikuyu village friendly to the Government, brutally killing eighty-four people, mostly women and children, and wounding another thirty-one. The incident led both to the decision to equip the Kikuyu Home Guard with firearms and to a fuller realization of the bestiality of Mau Mau methods, which rallied more Kikuyu to the Government side. However this was offset by a major exodus of Kikuyu from the settled areas back into the reserve, as a result partly of expulsion by their employers and partly of their own fears of retribution against them by Europeans. Landless, disgruntled and unemployed, they provided a fertile recruiting ground for the Mau Mau, more and more of whom were now based in the forests.

When Erskine arrived he realized that the major fault lay in the lack of any plan of campaign. The army available to him consisted of 39th Brigade, with three British battalions, and 70th (East African) Brigade with five KAR battalions, an armoured car company and a heavy anti-aircraft battery, as well as the Kenya Regiment, in all some 7,000 soldiers. He also had a flight of RAF Harvard training aircraft, which could drop 19lb bombs. Information about his Mau Mau opponents was very vague. The current estimate of the total organized in gangs, based in the forests but operating from them into the reserves and settled areas, was 8,000; but it was later found to have been nearer 12,000, of whom only about 1,500 had firearms, other than home-made ones which were more dangerous to the firer than to the target, although useful for intimidation. In general, they were organized in three groups: those recruited from the

58. El Alamein. 51st Highland Division, advanced dressing station, 28 October 1942. These men and their comrades reached their objectives. Most of them suffered leg wounds from enemy mortars.

59. El Alamein. A 25-pounder firing at enemy positions during the British attack.

60. El Alamein. British infantry advance at the double towards the ridge beyond the disabled enemy tank.

61. Victory in North Africa, 1943. The Prime Minister, Winston Churchill, with military leaders during his visit to Tripoli, 7 February 1943. Left to right: Generals Sir Oliver Leese, Sir Harold Alexander, Sir Alan Brooke and Sir Bernard Montgomery.

62. The 17-pounder Mk II anti-tank gun in action, February 1943.

63. First Army advance. Sherman tanks drive past one of their late targets, an 88mm gun. 6th Armoured Division, near Goubellat.

64. The final phase before the capture of Tunis. 1/4th Essex Regiment moving into action behind a Churchill tank.

65. The invasion of Sicily. Men of the 51st Highland Division wading ashore from landing craft.

66. Sicily, 3 August 1943. Centuripe falls to 78th Division after two days of heavy fighting. Bren-gun carriers move into the town.

67. Italy. Battle of the Cassino Plain. 214 Field Company, Royal Engineers (Staffordshire Territorial Company of 78th Division) working on a Bailey bridge and a track for tanks. This bridge had been built in two days under continuous fire, and was about 1,000 yards from the River Gari bridges.

68. Fifth Army. Anzio offensive. 7th Cheshires take cover in a German trench while they wait for reinforcements to come up and drive out three German snipers who are preventing them from establishing a machine-gun position.

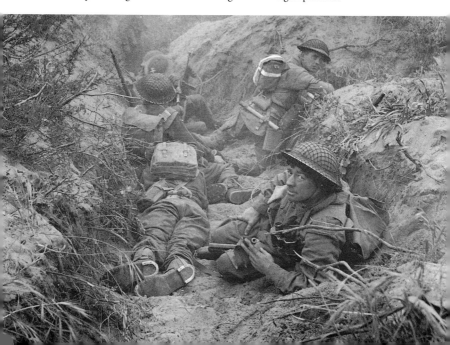

69. Italy. The Capture of Cassino. Men of S Company, Scots Guards on a mopping-up patrol through Cassino.

70. Heavy guns of the 75th Highland Heavy Regiment, Royal Artillery approaching and crossing the Bailey bridge at Borgo San Lorenzo.

71. Nurses of QAIMNS in Italy.

72. 6th Airborne Division troops at Ranville, D-Day, 6 June 1944.

73. Troops coming ashore from Tank Landing Craft, Normandy, 7 June 1944.

74. An Armoured Vehicle Royal Engineers, with petard, in Normandy.

75. A 105mm self-propelled field gun (Priest), Lion-sur-Mer, 6 June 1944.

76. Generals Crerar, Montgomery and Dempsey in Normandy.

77. A 6-pounder anti-tank gun of 7th Green Howards in Normandy.

78. Infantry in bocage south of Caumont, July 1944.

79. Regimental Aid Post (43rd Division) south of Caumont, 31 July 1944.

80. Advance towards Brussels after the Battle of the Falaise Gap, 21 August 1944. General Horrocks, GOC 30th Corps, in US sector near Argentan.

81. British paratroops (1st Airborne Division) landing on the outskirts of Arnhem, September 1944.

82. The Guards Armoured Division is welcomed in Brussels, 4 September 1944.

83. Infantry advancing with a Crocodile flame-throwing tank, St Joost, 21 January 1945.

84. Troops of 6th Airborne Division greeting a Soviet T34 crew near Wismar, 3 May 1945.

85. Duplex Drive tanks crossing the Rhine near Rees, 24 March 1945.

86. General Slim and CQMS Harold Milnes of the Worcestershire Regiment at Mandalay, 20 March 1945.

87. Major-General Orde Wingate, after the return of the first Chindit columns, July 1943.

88. Chindits of 16th Brigade carrying one of their wounded.

89. Allied troops clambering up a rough, precipitous hillside in a typical Arakan daylight attack, February 1944.

90. West Yorkshires advancing behind a tank. Imphal–Kohima road, May 1944.

Nyeri and Fort Hall districts and based in the Central and Northern Aberdares under Dedan Kimathi; those from the area south of them, surrounding Nairobi, under Stanley Mathenge; and a group based on Mount Kenya under 'General China'. The gangs were supported in the reserves, in Nairobi itself and in the settled areas by a passive wing of about 30,000 out of a total Kikuyu population of a million and a quarter. The European population, excluding British service personnel and their dependants, numbered 42,000. By the end of 1953, when a further British brigade, the 49th, had arrived with two more battalions and an engineer regiment, the strength of the security forces had risen to 10,000 soldiers, 21,000 police and 25,000 Kikuyu Home Guard. In prohibited areas, generally the forest, they could shoot at sight: in 'special' areas, generally the Kikuyu reserve, they had the right to fire only on those who did not stop when challenged; but they could question and search, and, if suspicious, hand over the suspect to the police. Up to this point, European civilian casualties had been very small, only 16 killed and 5 wounded, compared with 613 loyal Kikuyu killed and 359 wounded. Mau Mau had lost 3,064 killed and over a thousand captured, while the astonishing figure of 156,459 suspects had been arrested, of whom 64,000 had been brought to trial.

While major changes were being made in the top levels of the police, intelligence and administration, and in the method of conduct of the emergency by the introduction of a War Council, Erskine had decided that his next target area must be Nairobi itself. Operations in the reserve had shown that the Kikuyu population of the city was the main base of the Mau Mau's passive wing and source of supply for the gangs in the forest. A vast cordon and search operation, named ANVIL, was planned for April 1954, in preparation for which detention camps had been secretly constructed, the largest at Mackinnon Road, site of an abortive attempt to build a military stores base as an alternative to Egypt. While this was being planned, an attempt was made to detach 'General China' and the Mau Mau in the Mount Kenya area from their colleagues in the Aberdares, but it came to nothing. When the story became generally known, it led to severe criticism from the Europeans.

All the attention of the security forces was now directed on Operation ANVIL, which started on 24 April and lasted two weeks, with five battalions and large numbers of police employed. By 8 May 30,000 Africans out of an estimated Kikuyu population of Nairobi of 65,000 had been screened. Of them 16,538 were detained and 2,461 returned to the reserve. The first immediate evidence of its success came in a dramatic fall in the crime rate, but it was not long before it was realized that it had proved to be the turning point of the whole emergency, destroying the effectiveness of the passive wing both in supporting the gangs and in intimidating the rest of the Kikuyu population. From then on a very large proportion of the able-bodied male Kikuyu population which was not actively supporting the Government in the Home Guard and other organizations or in gangs in the forest was languishing in detention camps.

Erskine had intended to switch his effort into the forests in the latter half of 1954, but the need for troops and police to help the administration during and after ANVIL to impose a tighter control of the population forced him to postpone this until the beginning of January 1955, when in any case the weather would be more favourable. Until then, the RAF was given a free hand to bomb suspected Mau Mau hideouts in the forest, a squadron of Lincoln heavy bombers having arrived for that task. The principal sufferers were the large animals, elephant and rhino, who, wounded or frightened, became the main threat to soldiers patrolling there. The Mau Mau found no great difficulty in avoiding both the enraged animals and the British and African soldiers, who at this stage were not very skilled in jungle craft.

During this period the intelligence organization began to improve. Police and army intelligence had been brought together under the Head of Intelligence, John Prendergast, with army intelligence officers integrated into the Police Special Branch, both at the centre and at province and district level.

One of these was Major Frank Kitson of the Rifle Brigade. On Christmas Eve 1953 he was dining with General Erskine's ADC, dressed in his dinner jacket, when he received a message that a gang had been contacted near Thika and that the commander of the patrol which had found them had been killed. He rushed off, picked up his colleague, Eric Holyoake, and went to the scene, which he describes:

We learnt that the gang had first been reported in the afternoon and that a patrol of the Black Watch, together with a police mobile squad, had set off to chase it. The Black Watch company commander* had

* Major the Earl Wavell.

decided to lead the patrol himself and his second in command came with him. Apparently they had picked up tracks of the gang fairly quickly and had followed them up a shallow valley to the area in which we were now standing. Then quite unexpectedly there had been a shot and the company commander had dropped dead with a bullet through him. For the next few minutes business must have been brisk as two more of the patrol, this time policemen, were wounded. The second-in-command then took over but decided not to assault the enemy because he felt that to do so in the long grass and thick bush would result in further casualties. He also appreciated that it would be easy to surround the enemy by putting a cordon on the railway, the road and the path. Once in position he felt – with good reason – that the enemy would have to surrender.

By the time we arrived the cordon was in place but it had taken rather longer to organize than was at first hoped. Meanwhile the day had gone. The cordon was made up mainly of K.P.R.* officers who had flocked in on hearing of the need for their services. There were, in addition, some policemen from Thika and most of the Black Watch company. The command of the operation had devolved onto the District Commandant of the K.P.R., Peter Deane, who normally controlled any combined operations in the area because he was a natural leader and by far the best man to do so.

By this time it did not look as though the gang had much intention of surrendering, so the District Commandant decided to get a drum of petrol from Thika and pour it into the bush from the railway embankment. It was hoped that by setting the scrub on fire the terrorists would be forced into the open. They could then be shot down by the light of mortar flares. The petrol took some time to arrive and to make sure that the particular bit of bush was properly marked, Peter Deane drove his car over the edge of the track into the long grass so that its lights should mark the spot. Although he drove it within thirty yards of the gang he got back to the shelter of the cordon unscathed.

Soon after Eric and I appeared on the scene, the petrol arrived. We were on the path on one side of the triangle with Peter Deane and the petrol opposite us on the railway embankment. As it was poured down the hill someone in the cordon heard the terrorists

* Kenya Police Reserve.

move and fired a few rounds at the spot. This was the signal for the soldiers to put up their flares, and for thirty seconds we saw, for the first time, the whole area laid out before us. While the flare was alight distances shrunk to normal and we all seemed close together. The railway embankment opposite appeared to be only a few yards away and the men on it were easily recognizable. When the flare faded the people on the far side of the arena receded until the embankment itself was only faintly visible in the dark. Then another flare would go up and I should think that two or three flares burned out without showing any sign of the gang. Then, as another one burst into light, a number of shots were fired at the cordon from long grass. I think one or two of the terrorists fired in our direction because I heard the crack of bullets passing over not very far away. Undoubtedly most of the gangsters aimed at the group clustered round the petrol drum, nicely silhouetted against the sky on top of the railway embankment. For the next quarter of a minute until the flare burnt out, they fired as fast as they could into this group which was not more than thirty or forty yards from them. Meanwhile the men in the cordon shot back into the area in which the gangsters lay. Unfortunately we were firing at an area and they were firing at clearly defined targets. By the time that darkness returned four members of the cordon had fallen.

As soon as the firing stopped, Eric and I ran across to the other side to help with the casualties. One African policeman was dead and another was badly wounded. The Assistant Commandant of the K.P.R. had also been hit in the arm and the leg, but worse still, Peter Deane was shot through the stomach. We helped to carry the wounded out to an ambulance on the track. Later we heard that the African constable and the Assistant Commandant recovered, but Peter Deane died. Thika was to feel his loss severely in the next few months.

The attempt to burn them out failed, partly because it came on to rain. Later in the night the gang crept up to the cordon, shot two policemen and raced through the gap created. They seem to have been about twenty or thirty strong, all of whom escaped.

Another promising development was the use of captured terrorists, who were persuaded to turn against their former comrades, not merely as informers but as active infiltrators in pseudo-gangs. Led by Kikuyu-speaking Europeans disguised as Africans, most of them from the Kenya

Regiment, they formed teams masquerading as Mau Mau gangs in order both to contact the latter and to identify their suppliers and supporters. It was essential to avoid clashes between the security forces and pseudo-gangs, and, as this technique developed, a certain rivalry built up between the two, particularly as the operations of the one had to be restricted to permit freedom of movement to the other.

Kitson describes taking part in one of these operations in 1954:

There was some really good information as to where the Rift Valley committee's gang was staying for the night and we decided that we would try and catch them.

Soon the time came to prepare for the evening's work. We would go as a gang so as to make certain of getting past the sentries. First I had to change into a battered old mackintosh and sling a blanket round my shoulders. Then there would come the process of blacking face and hands. To complete the disguise I pulled on an old African bush hat to hide the fact that my hair is slightly different from the average African's. This was not an elaborate disguise because we were only going out for a short time and our purpose in dressing up at all was only to fool one sentry.

When we were all ready we piled into two Land-Rovers and drove to a suitable parking place about ten miles outside Nairobi. There were, with Derek Prophet and myself, two F.I.A.'s,* the ex-terrorist guide, and two or three of the Nairobi team.

Once we moved away from the vehicles, Derek was in charge of the party. My inefficiency at the language made it too risky for me to take tactical command of a patrol and anyhow the men belonged to Derek. It was a fine light night and we made good time over the open country. We were moving through coffee and then down a track past some disused huts and along the side of some maize. I did not know quite where we were going but Derek was navigating so I was happy to soak up the surroundings and forget that our expedition might well land us in trouble within a couple of minutes. As time went by I gradually got more nervous. My recipe for avoiding the ill effects of fright has always been to refuse to face up to the reality of a situation until it forces itself on me. Thus by carefully keeping my thoughts off the gang I was able to enjoy my walk to some extent.

* Field Intelligence Assistants.

All too soon I was jerked back into the present. The patrol had stopped and I heard our African guide whispering in the shadow of a stone hut about three yards ahead. I looked carefully and saw the man talking to two more Africans who were evidently members of the gang. It was no doubt a good thing that we had not drawn blank but as usual when looking at Mau Mau from close quarters I was frightened. My heart was beating quickly and I was conscious of being cold.

As I watched, the two Mau Mau and our men walked into the hut. The ruse had worked and the sentries were not suspicious. We had a fraction of a second at least in which to be sure of surprising the enemy. There was no point in waiting any longer. With a yell Derek and I pushed into the hut and shone our torches on the occupants. I remember shouting as hard as I could to keep them frightened for long enough to get them properly covered. We all piled into the hut and pinned the gang up against the far wall. There were nine of them, that is to say about twice as many as there were of us.

Poor creatures! they were more frightened than I had been. Not one tried to get away, which was just as well from their point of view because we had our fire-power handy. Then with one of us covering the terrorists with a sterling gun* the other two would select one of the line and throw him on the floor where we tied him up with straps, ropes or handkerchiefs and bundled him outside.

After about twenty minutes they were all secured. It was as well that we had taken those precautions which we had. Our prisoners consisted of the gang leader of the Rift Valley gang with six of his men, plus the leader and second-in-command of the Fort Hall gang, They were a pretty rough bunch and proved it later by their obstinacy when interrogated and by their repeated attempts at escape. We had pulled off one of the best successes of my experience as a result of the surprise effect of our appearance.

When Erskine began to consider his plan to switch effort to the forests he realized that major sweeps by large numbers of soldiers, crashing through the forest, were not likely to be effective. His general plan was to allot sectors of the forest to units, within which they would

---

* Sterling sub-machine-gun.

combine static and patrol operations to find and eliminate the gangs, who would be kept permanently on the move. If they attempted to escape from the forest into the reserve or the settled area, they would be intercepted at the forest edge by Kikuyu Home Guard or Tribal Police, manning a ditch full of bamboo spikes. Units were reorganized to select and train their best soldiers to form Forest Operating Companies, each of three tracker/combat teams. In addition each battalion was to produce a 'Trojan' team of five soldiers, led by a Swahili-speaking NCO from the Kenya Regiment, to follow up at short notice hot information provided by the local intelligence officer.

This organization was introduced for Operation HAMMER, which began in January 1955 under Hinde's direction in the Aberdare Mountains. The results were disappointing, only 161 Mau Mau being accounted for. The Northumberland Fusiliers were involved in this, and their journal describes the part that their X Company played:

Whilst the other Companies were preparing for their arduous parts in the high forest of the Northern Aberdares, X Company was operating in the lowland forest (up to 8,000 ft.), which extended for about 50 miles north-west from the Aberdares. At first the Company operated in the Murijo Forest, which lies up to five miles wide of the south of Thompson's Falls and in the adjacent farm land in the immediate vicinity of the Company camp. Later 5 Platoon, under Mr Middlemas and Sgt. Lowes, set up their camp in the Marmanet Forest, which extends for about 25 miles north of Thompson's Falls and is about 10 to 15 miles broad – a dense block of primeval cedar and olive forest, a few plantations and thick scrub.

The object of our patrolling was to assist the police to drive the Mau Mau gangs which were lying in these outlying forest areas back into the Aberdares and into the area where the main operation was to take place.

The operations of 4 Platoon, under Mr Seidl and Sgt. Peters, in the most southerly part of this great area, were undoubtedly successful in driving the gangs which were known to be in those parts back into the main forest. Only one Mau Mau was known to have been killed, however, in spite of all their efforts. The energetic operations of 4 and 6 Platoons, the latter under Sgt. Million, in the Murijo Forest led to no noteworthy results. Before Christmas, however, Mau Mau gangs were reported in the Marmanet Forest, and two police

patrols inflicted some casualties upon them. 5 Platoon then transferred their attention there for three days from the unproductive
operating in the Murijo Forest with notable success. The Platoon
arrived in their new area early on the morning following the police
action. Whilst one patrol pitched camp the other two patrols set off
immediately to work up into the hills. Their efforts that day were
unsuccessful. The following day two trackers were obtained from a
Masai village. They were both active old savages, one of them the
village headman. Two patrols again set out the following day at first
light. They moved along opposite sides of a deep thickly wooded
valley, leading to the escarpment of the great Rift Valley which
stretches from the Dead Sea to the Drakensburg Mountains in Natal.
Mr Middlemas and L/Cpl. Carman were leading one patrol and Sgt.
Lowes the other. L/Cpl. Carman sighted a scout as he moved away
ahead of the patrol. The patrol followed quickly, and the Masai found
tracks which led down to a gang of five who had been carrying food.
One of the gang was killed immediately. The rest made off before
they could be seen. A home-made rifle and a large stock of maize
was found in the area. On hearing the shots, Sgt. Lowes' patrol,
which had been moving on a parallel course, hurried into fire
positions and waited in ambush. Shortly afterwards part of the
remains of the gang ran into them, and another was killed and a
second rifle taken. In this action a slight casualty was caused by one
of the Mau Mau, who fired his home-made rifle. The bullet hit Fus.
Robinson's rifle magazine, breaking it open, and cut his neck slightly.

Whilst these patrols were in progress, Cpl. Tyler took the third
patrol to a hide where two warm fires had been found the previous
day. He and three others stayed behind in ambush, whilst the rest,
acting as a decoy party, returned to camp. At about 2000 hrs, five
Mau Mau came right into the hide. One was killed instantly, and two
others seriously wounded – their groans were heard for some time in
the thick bush. It was pitch dark, however, and the patrol could not
search properly, due mostly to the steep broken ground which was
itself dangerous unless known most intimately, and secondly to the
danger, once they moved, of presenting a sitting target against the
sky line to any Mau Mau left in the place. In the morning, neither of
those bodies could be found, but a very superior home-made rifle
was found, with bolt action and spring trigger, ingeniously adapted
to fire either rifle or shot gun ammunition. By this time this gang,

which was originally reported to be 30 strong, had suffered seven killed and several wounded. Whilst these patrols were still in progress a leader of part of the same gang, which had evidently fled back to the Aberdares after it had been shot up, was found by native farm guards asleep beneath a tree not far from the Company camp. Cpl. Wildman and a patrol went and took him prisoner, together with a beautiful Portuguese 9 mm. sporting rifle and ammunition. He had an up to date diary of events written in Kikuyu, which was of great intelligence interest. On interrogation, he said that various actions had reduced the gang's strength from about 30 to nine. This includes various desertions and men wounded, in addition to those already known to have been hit. The man promised to show us the hide which he believed was occupied by the residue of his part of the gang, and the place where he had hidden a book containing the names of his gang members, and food carriers, together with details.

This book was found and one empty hide was discovered on the edge of the Aberdare Forest. He also led Cpl. Wildman and his patrol to a second unoccupied hide further from the edge of the forest, in very thick country. Shortly afterwards, when heading the patrol through very thick forest, the man bolted, and was shot through the head by one of the patrol, probably Fus. Cunningham.

5 platoon returned from the Marmanet Forest to the Company camp in time for Christmas, very pleased with themselves and all having fallen in love with the extremely charming daughter of the local Scots saw mill manager, who lived near the Platoon camp.

The only other notable occurrence before Christmas was an ambush on a herd of cattle which had frequent visitations from Mau Mau in search of food. This ambush had been placed on these cattle every night for 16 nights. Finally on the night before Christmas Eve, the gang at last arrived, but the patrol failed to kill any of them. They may have wounded one of them. However, they didn't get any cattle, and they have not been back again.

After Operation HAMMER, effort was switched to Mount Kenya in Operation FIRST FLUTE, where more systematic operations in slower time produced better results. At the same time Erskine was persuaded by Prendergast to try to negotiate a surrender through pseudo-gang contacts. This began in February, aimed at detaching Stanley Mathenge and his followers from Dedan Kimathi. It nearly succeeded, but Kimathi got wind of it and threatened reprisals against Mathenge's group. It failed in its main aim, but it sowed the seeds of a permanent rift between the two.

Erskine left in April 1955, handing over to Lieutenant-General Sir Gerald Lathbury. Over 5,500 Mau Mau had been accounted for in the previous twelve months, reducing the number in active gangs to 5,000. The back of the rebellion had been broken, but the cost had been high in terms of the restrictions imposed on every section of the population, not just the Kikuyu themselves. Lathbury appreciated that the task of eliminating the smaller and more scattered gangs required more skilled and sophisticated methods, and if they were to succeed the restrictions had to be maintained. His plan was to leave the task of finding the gangs and pursuing them in the forest more and more to specialized teams, like the pseudo-gangs, and to give the soldiers the task of operating on and from the forest edge, the KAR in the reserves and the British in the settled areas. He himself devoted a considerable effort to improving relations with the Europeans in order to persuade them to continue to accept restrictions which were unpopular and which they might think no longer necessary.

One more major operation on the HAMMER–FIRST FLUTE pattern was launched in July, named DANTE, the immediate results of which were not impressive; but the toll of terrorist casualties continued. By the end of the year twenty-four out of the fifty-one principal gang leaders had been killed, most of them in pseudo-gang operations, and the total gang strength reduced to about 2,000. By this time the Kikuyu could see that the Government was clearly winning, and they were prepared to turn out in large numbers to sweep the forest edge to find terrorists who lay up there in order to obtain food. Success snowballed in 1956 and by the second half of the year the terrorists were split up into small gangs almost permanently on the move within the forest, while life outside it was returning to normal. The climax came when Dedan Kimathi himself, wounded in a clash with a pseudo-gang, was found by a Tribal Policeman at the forest edge on 17 October 1956. Stanley Mathenge was never traced. In the following month the army was withdrawn from operations, four years after the emergency had started, and although the emergency was not formally brought to an end until 1960 the active war against Mau Mau was over.

During this war 10,527 of them had been killed, 2,633 captured,

26,625 arrested and 2,714 had surrendered. Some 50,000 of their supporters had been detained. Mau Mau had themselves killed 1,826 and wounded 919 African civilians, killed 32 and wounded 63 Europeans, and killed 26 and wounded 36 Asians. Casualties inflicted on the security forces were 63 Europeans, 3 Asians and 534 Africans killed, 102 Europeans, 12 Asians and 465 Africans wounded. It had taken 10,000 British and African soldiers, 21,000 police and 25,000 Home Guard four years to defeat a rebellion limited to one tribe, which had no support of any kind from outside and a very limited supply of firearms. The cost of the emergency was assessed at £55 million, borne equally by the British and Kenyan Governments. Although in terms of the resources devoted to it by the British Government it could have been regarded as little more than a sideshow, it had a profound effect in persuading influential Conservative political figures in Britain to bow to the wind of change in Africa, and brought about a radical transformation in the attitudes of the different races in the colony towards each other.

The generals who had conducted the campaign were very different in character and method. Erskine, with extensive experience both on the staff and in command in the Second World War, made a major contribution in developing a properly organized campaign and the machinery with which to conduct it; but he was not popular with either the administration or the settlers, about whom he made some injudicious remarks. However, that was fully balanced by Hinde, an eccentric commander, popular with everyone, who relieved Erskine of the detailed planning and control of actual operations. Lathbury, an airborne soldier of less experience, came just at the right time to implement a more unconventional approach. Impatient with any hesitation or reservations on the part of the administration, he took considerable trouble to mend fences with the settlers.

*

It was fortunate for Britain that her colonial conflicts followed in succession. If they had all struck her simultaneously she would have been hard put to it to cope with them, even with two-year National Service, which provided an army of about 400,000 men from Britain. In addition the army recruited substantial numbers of soldiers overseas, Gurkhas, Malays, East Africans and others. The Mau Mau insurrection had broken out just as the situation in Malaya was being brought under control. The troubles in Cyprus erupted in the spring of 1955, just as the tide turned in Kenya.

Cyprus

The root cause of the troubles was the movement for union with Greece (*enosis*). In 1571 the Ottoman Empire had seized the island from the Frankish Lusignan family, and its sovereignty over it continued to be recognized when Britain occupied the island as a *place d'armes* in 1878, with the consent of the Sultan of Turkey, when he was threatened by Russia. However, when Turkey allied herself with Germany in 1914 Britain declared it a colony, that status being recognized in the Treaty of Lausanne in 1923. Ever since Greece had secured her independence from the Ottoman Empire in 1832, hopes had existed in Cyprus that the island could achieve the same, and join hands with Greece. At various times these hopes appeared to be near fulfilment. They had been raised when Labour came to power in 1945, and when the British withdrew from Palestine and from the rest of Egypt into the Suez Canal Zone.

In 1950 the thirty-seven-year-old Michael Mouskos was elected Archbishop of the Cypriot Orthodox Church and Ethnarch of the Greek Cypriot people, who formed 82 per cent of the island's population, assuming the name Makarios. Before that, he had been a priest at a church in Athens, where he had met a retired Greek army colonel, George Grivas, who came from Cyprus. The latter had led an unsavoury extreme right-wing private army fighting against the Greek Communists, and was embittered at not being accepted into the post-war Greek army. In 1951 he and Makarios began plotting an insurgent movement in Cyprus, designed to exert pressure on Britain to accept *enosis*. Grivas envisaged a guerrilla movement, based in the mountainous countryside, while Makarios thought more in terms of political action, strikes and sabotage in the towns. Initially they received no encouragement from the Greek Prime Minister, Sophocles Venizelos, nor initially from Field Marshal Papagos, who succeeded him in November 1952; but, two years later, the latter changed his line, after Anthony Eden, British Foreign

Secretary, appeared to rule out *enosis* in any circumstances. One of the principal reasons for this was the announcement in June 1954 that, as a result of negotiations with Egypt, the British army and air force head-quarters in the Suez Canal Zone would be transferred to Cyprus, while the Zone base was to be converted into a civilianized organization.

Grivas moved to Cyprus in November 1954 and began building up a resistance movement called EOKA (Ethniki Organosis Kuprion Agoniston: National Organization of Cypriot Fighters). While he was organizing it, he fomented agitation by students and others, leading to violent street protests.

Captain John Elderkin, whose 16th Field Squadron Royal Engineers was engaged in the construction of the Episkopi base, describes being called out to help deal with one of these at Limassol on 18 December, employing the classic methods of 'Aid to the Civil Power', as had been taught in the army's manuals for most of the century.

1330 hrs.

The crowd was now about 300 strong and were calling for the Union Jack on the hospital to be lowered. Shouting EEE-NO-SIS and other slogans was almost continuous and when a vehicle from the camp arrived with the Squadron's lunch they all became very excited. The numbers were still increasing, and at this stage a knife rest was placed across the entrance to the compound and the Sappers concerned were the target for the first stones. The police again addressed the crowd with a loudspeaker, but to no avail, and the intensity of the stoning increased. The Squadron and its vehicles were showered with missiles, some of them rocks weighing three or four pounds lobbed like hand grenades. Vehicle windscreens were shattered and canopies torn. Some Sappers were struck, but none seriously.

1400 hrs.

The Commissioner sent his striking force of two police riot squads to the hospital. One was armed with rifles, the other with batons and shields and they had a small number of tear gas bombs between them. Their success was immediate and using the tear gas they drove the crowd away from the hospital and established cordons at three points [controlling the roads leading to the hospital, 'A' on the road coming from the north, 'B' on the road immediately north of the hospital and 'C' across the road at the south-east corner of the hospital compound]. Some Sappers were caught without their respirators.

1415 hrs.

By this time the crowds had regrouped and were stoning the police cordons. The Field Squadron was deployed with one troop to the rear of the hospital and one to the front, both being readily available as striking forces. At the Command Post in the police station it was clear to the Commissioner and the Acting C.O. that the situation was deteriorating and at about 1425 hrs the command party reached the hospital. When they arrived the situation was as follows:—

(a) The armed police party was at 'C' and although there was some stoning the situation was under control.

(b) At 'B' a police baton party had a small crowd under control.

(c) At point 'A' the situation looked rather ugly. The crowd was very large and extended into the roads radiating from the cross roads. The A/C.O. estimated that 500 people were visible. The twenty odd police, equipped only with batons and shields, were being stoned continuously.

A few minutes after he arrived the Commissioner asked the Superintendent of Police to relieve some of the rifle party at 'C' with men from 'B', and to reinforce 'A' with the riflemen. However, before this could be carried out the police at 'A' started to withdraw. The movement began in an orderly way, but ended in disorder. The mob, stoning heavily, followed at about fifty yards range. The police fell back to the hospital gateway where both they and the Squadron area were again in range of the rioters. At this point the Commissioner formally requested the A/C.O. to take over the situation; the request was verbal and confirmed shortly afterwards in writing; the time was 1440 hrs. This procedure was in complete accordance with official doctrine. (The Commissioner did in fact write his request on the back of a bill which is now in the R.E. Museum).

The A/C.O. considered that the crowd could only be dispersed by fire. A banner was unfurled across the road and the crowd to the north were warned by the Police Superintendent that fire would be opened on them if they did not disperse. They were then massed in the road about fifty yards from the hospital entrance. An N.C.O. and three selected Sappers were formed up beneath the banner; magazines were charged, but the rifles were not cocked. The N.C.O. was then ordered to load and fire, but the round was obviously wildly aimed and went over the heads of the crowd without producing any noticeable reaction. The first Sapper was then given a similar order and this time, although no one in the crowd was seen to fall, the mob withdrew some yards and thinned. Stones were falling around the small party under the banner, and all were suffering from the effects of tear gas, masks having been removed in order to see more clearly.

At this stage the A/C.O. decided a further round was necessary and the N.C.O. was ordered to fire at a man in the front of the crowd, who besides wearing a distinctive shirt was also an active and accurate stone thrower. He fell. Almost magically the crowd scattered. Four of the mob carried the wounded man to the hospital entrance and troops assisted them to the casualty station.

The street was now almost clear. Sappers were formed up in line abreast and with fixed bayonets moved down the main road and the lane on the north side of the hospital. Side alleys were picketed and after reaching the cross-roads attention was turned to the small square to the east. Here a pillar of smoke, seen earlier, turned out to be coming from a bus which the rioters had overturned and burned. The area had to be physically cleared and as no police were available the troops carried out the task; inevitably they came into close contact with the crowd and the sight of their fixed bayonets had a very sobering effect. Cordons were finally established [at the original points].

By about 1515 hrs crowds had collected in front of all the cordons, and although there was no stone throwing, they would not disperse. Any gap between the troops and the crowd was only preserved with the greatest difficulty. At 1530 hrs a second Field Squadron arrived on foot and gave assistance by thickening the cordons and providing a reserve.

1630 hrs.

The mayor of Limassol (a Communist) and other leading citizens arrived at a cordon by car and asked to speak to the Commissioner. The Troop Commander marched the mayor up the street. The Commissioner allowed the party to address the crowd over the police loudspeakers, and they made every effort to persuade the people to go home. Some of the older people seemed to take the advice, but it had no effect on the youths and children.

1720 hrs.

Dusk was falling and the Commissioner and the A/C.O. agreed that the troops should withdraw to the outskirts of the town. The crowds were told that the troops were going, but must not be followed. Sappers from the first Squadron were rapidly marched back to their vehicles in the compound, and the second Squadron marched out of the town in close order. The vehicles drove away under a shower of stones and the police who came behind them had a very hot time. In some ways the situation looked as bad as it had done four hours earlier, but the provocation was gone and it did not develop. When the Commissioner got back to the police station he agreed that the police should resume control; the troops remained at readiness.

Later on in the evening the police dealt energetically with groups of rioters roaming the town, but apart from broken windows in a British-owned hotel no serious damage was done; a heavy downpour finally cleared the streets at about 2100 hrs, to the considerable relief of the civil and military authorities.

These methods were not to prove appropriate to deal with the type of terrorist action which Grivas and Makarios agreed should start on 31 March 1955, the Archbishop insisting that action should be limited to sabotage of military installations which would not cause casualties. The first bombs went off at midnight in Nicosia and elsewhere, causing some damage. In May the Governor, Sir Robert Armitage, was lucky to escape when a charity film performance ended early, a bomb exploding after he had left. Grivas told Makarios that his aim was to disperse, fatigue and irritate the British in order to force them to concede *enosis* at the United Nations General Assembly meeting in October.

Action to deal with EOKA was initially weak and ill coordinated. The Police Special Branch had only thirty-seven men, their attention centred on the island's Communist party, AKEL. The army had only two infantry battalions and a field artillery and an engineer regiment, the last, with one of the battalions, engaged in the construction of the new bases at Dhekelia and Episkopi for the transferred headquarters. The army one, of which General Sir Charles Keightley was Commander-in-Chief, had already been temporarily installed in a barracks in Nicosia, where it was more of a liability than an asset, as far as conduct of the campaign against EOKA was concerned. The situation deteriorated throughout the summer, detention of suspected members of EOKA being introduced, with a ban on persons under twenty-one carrying firearms. Reinforcement by two Royal Marine Commandos from Malta and two infantry battalions from Egypt arrived in September, a month before the first British soldier was killed, by a grenade thrown at his vehicle.

Meanwhile a Tripartite Anglo-Greek-Turkish Conference had been held, at which Harold Macmillan, now Foreign Secretary, proposed a study of how to make gradual progress towards self-government. When a constitution had been agreed and Cypriot representatives elected, they would participate in Government, but Britain would retain sovereignty 'for the foreseeable future'. The UN General Assembly in September, under pressure from the USA, Britain and Turkey, rejected Greece's appeal for discussion of the Cyprus problem. Eden, anxious to show himself a worthy successor to Churchill as Prime Minister, was in no mood for concessions, and in October he appointed Field Marshal Sir John Harding, who was retiring as CIGS, Governor and Commander-in-Chief on the pattern of Templer in Malaya. Harding introduced his version of the Briggs Plan, welding together army, police and administration, improving the organization, strength and training of all three, with high priority being given to intelligence, and infusing them all with a sense of urgency and clear direction through his two principal deputies, Brigadier George Baker for operations and George Sinclair, a provincial commissioner from the Gold Coast, on the civil side. On the political front he immediately began negotiations with Makarios, but these reached deadlock when it became clear that Harding had no authority to concede any promise of self-determination (*autodiathesis*). In reaction Grivas set off another round of explosions and attacks on service personnel and installations, including a successful raid on a store in Famagusta harbour containing arms and ammunition. Harding was reinforced with a complete infantry brigade, bringing the army strength to 12,000, the RAF numbering 2,000.

Soon after their arrival, a major operation took place in the hills south and east of Kyrenia, in which 1,700 men from five units took part, leading to the capture of a number of EOKA activists and some arms finds. Towards the end of November Grivas stepped up activity in Famagusta and Nicosia and in the mountains. After a number of serious incidents, Harding declared a state of emergency, introducing very severe penalties for offences connected with the emergency, conferring wide powers of arrest and search on the security forces, widening the causes for which people could be detained and tightening control of the press. EOKA kept up the tempo in December, prompting Baker into organizing a major operation in the mountains to catch Grivas himself, named FOXHUNTER, which was preceded by a search of all monasteries. Although a small quantity of arms and ammunition was found, EOKA had been tipped off by their friends in the police and the large amount kept at Kykko monastery and elsewhere had been removed and distributed to safe houses. Grivas was forced to abandon his hideout above Spilia and move over the mountains to another near Kakopetria.

January 1956 saw the arrival of five more battalions, followed in February by the armoured cars of the Royal Horse Guards (The Blues), bringing the number of units engaged in operations to fourteen. They were organized into four brigades, the 50th, 51st, 3rd Commando and 16th (Parachute), the last sent as general reserve for the Middle East but available to Harding when not needed for operations elsewhere. This added up to about 17,000 troops. At the same time the RAF sent more helicopters to supplement the few they had reluctantly allowed to be diverted from their search and rescue task.

Although the measures which Harding had taken were beginning to get into gear and he now had a considerable force at his disposal, his campaign was still at an embryo stage, while that of Grivas was coming to full fruition. Harding's plan had been to give priority to the security of towns and the communications between them. Clearing up EOKA in the countryside would have to wait until life could be lived normally and Government authority reigned unchallenged in and between the centres of population. He warned the Colonial Office that he was satisfied that he was working on the right lines, but that it would take time and a great deal of effort both in Cyprus and in Britain to establish a fully effective organization. Few of the routine operations designed either to inflict casualties on EOKA or to find arms and ammunition produced significant results, and the troops involved often felt frustrated.

An account of a fruitful search operation is given by Major David Wood of the 1st Oxfordshire and Buckinghamshire Light Infantry:

Ayia Phyla is a typical Greek Cypriot village within a stone's throw of Buckingham Camp where the Regiment is stationed. It boasts a population of about six hundred people and consists of the usual collection of mud and stone houses, two coffee shops and a church with a bell which everyone swears sounds to a chant of E-O-K-A whenever it is rung.

Some time ago an informer led a party of police and soldiers to a number of arms caches outside the village where, very cunningly concealed, were found both arms and ammunition in carefully preserved condition. In this way the village had earned itself a bad name, which, like the proverbial dog, it was finding hard to lose.

Information was received that the walls surrounding the village concealed quantities of hidden arms and ammunition and that a thorough search would reveal caches of various kinds.

Support Company was given the task of searching all the walls with the aid of two sections of the Turkish Mobile Reserve (tough little men in zip-fronted brown overall suits who have already gained a reputation for the thoroughness with which they tackle any job from dispersing a riot mob to searching a bus load of Cypriot workers), two mine detecting dogs with their handlers and a couple of Sappers who were bringing along a mine detector in case of buried hides. Various equipment was issued for the job, including picks, shovels, torches, 88 sets for communicating between platoons, and some beautifully designed and almost engine-turned prodders which were borrowed from the Sappers next door and were never intended to be used for anything but prodding the softest School of Military Engineering demonstration minefield.

With the help of a map and a good aerial photograph, the plan for the search was made. The area of fields and walls around the village was split up into sectors and each platoon was given a sector to search. There were to be no holds barred outside the village and searchers were encouraged to pull down walls to try and find the arms and explosives hidden in them. Perhaps, rather unwisely, but obviously convinced his money would be safe, the Company Commander offered a pound for every major find made during the search; fortunately remembering, at the last minute, to place a ceiling of ten pounds on the amount he was prepared [to provide] out of the Company fund.

The whole force rendezvous'd on time at the entrance of the village and having attached sections of the Mobile Reserve to each platoon and allotted the dogs, the search began. Luckily, the first find was made very quickly – it was a detonator packed in wadding in a small sweet bottle hidden in a dry stone wall running down the main street in the village – the news was passed round and walls were demolished with enthusiasm all round the Eastern and Southern sides of the village. Fortune was with the searchers and reports came in at intervals over the wireless of further finds of blasting powder in bottles, sticks of dynamite, slabs of guncotton and cartridge-filling machines (innocent enough in peace time but outlawed since the emergency).

The Company Commander, anxious to avoid wanton damage and a 'mention' in the *Times* of Cyprus sought out the village priest and took him to the coffee shop where several oldish men were doing what they always appear to do throughout the day – drinking coffee. In a short speech the Company Commander, remembering the well-thumbed pamphlet on internal security, pointed out that he wished to avoid doing further damage to the villagers' property but that he now knew arms and ammunition were hidden round the village and his orders were clear, that he had to find them. If the villagers would only tell him where the arms were hidden they could avoid much damage to their property. Alas! They were old men and did not know these things; it was the young men who were by now all at work in Limassol who knew the answers. A time limit was set for the information to be produced and the elders left alone to make up their minds about producing it. Nothing was gained, however, by this approach as the second visit produced no more information than the first and another attempt at exhortation was quickly cut short by a very friendly invitation to sit down and enjoy a glass of orangeade.

Apart from a short break for tea and later for tiffin, the search went on all day. Walls were pulled down, carob trees searched and every likely nook and cranny probed, sniffed out by dogs or swept with mine detectors. Finds varied from a really useful .32 automatic in what the auctioneers call mint condition and two other rusty pistols of no value to six brand new NAAFI cups and saucers hidden in a basket in a wall – these were presented to the Mobile Reserve for their Serjeants' Mess. Wherever possible, finds were blown up on the spot by an expert who was summoned from Limassol and arrived complete with a most dangerous looking box of detonators, cordex, primers and other paraphernalia. He made a very satisfying bang out of a quantity of Nescafe tin bombs, blasting powder and sulphur which one of the platoons found.

The search was called off before dark but the Commanding Officer decided that it was worth pursuing it for one more day as there were still areas to be searched and so much had been found. A guard was mounted in the fields around the village and the villagers warned not to venture too far afield during the night. Illuminating mortar bombs and a quite unauthorized curfew imposed by the Corporal commanding the guard ensured that there was no interference with any stuff which might still be hidden.

Next day, overjoyed at missing the Regimental Serjeant-Major's drill parade, the Company continued the search with only small success. Ayia Phyla appeared to have been sucked dry the day before. The Company Commander and his 'tame' police officer were asked by an old crone who spoke excellent English, but could neither read nor write, to come with her to see the damage his men had caused to her daughter's ornate mirror and sideboard. A soldier had thrust his delicate probe through the side of a house and smashed a mirror which ran the length of the sideboard in the one and only room furnished with a large and comfortable bed and the daughter's wedding dowry. The situation was discussed, sweet and sickly preserved orange peel was wisely declined by the policeman (who had met it before) and less wisely eaten by the Company Commander who suffered as a result for some time to come. The damage was admitted and the clearance certificate written in Turkish, Greek and English to suit all occasions was duly signed with the houseowner's thumb print. The operation was completed, stores checked, soldiers searched to ensure that they had not looted any of the villagers' property and the Company embussed for the return to Camp.

A couple of days later the Company Commander was asked to report to the Commissioner's office, to say exactly where the hundred and one items unearthed had been discovered, as it had been decided to recompense those villagers whose walls had been damaged and in which nothing had been found. It was not easy to pinpoint the exact spot where each item was found but with the aid of a chinagraph pencil and an aerial photograph justice at last appeared to be done.

Later the same month, a Public Relations photographer arrived in the Company lines and asked if he might photograph a couple of soldiers searching the walls of Ayia Phyla. An efficient and resourceful Company Serjeant-Major detailed two men who had never taken part in the search but happened to be in Camp to accompany the photographer to the village. On arrival, the photographer asked the men to pose near a bit of broken down wall and to look as if they were pushing down the stones during the search. One of the men leaned rather heavily on a pile of stones which gave way under his weight revealing three sticks of dynamite which were hidden there – it is not recorded who was the more surprised, the soldier or the photographer.

Many similar searches have been carried out before and since the one at Ayia Phyla but rarely has good fortune, and ten pounds from the Company funds, rewarded the searchers' efforts so handsomely.

During January 1956 Harding held a series of secret meetings with Makarios, based on a formula worked out between the British and Greek Governments. Under it Britain would 'work for a solution which will satisfy the people of Cyprus within the framework of the Treaties and Alliances to which the countries concerned in the defence of the Eastern Mediterranean are parties'. She would be prepared to discuss the future of the island with representatives of the people of Cyprus 'when self-government had proved itself a workable proposition and capable of safeguarding the interests of all sections of the community'. Grivas was getting sufficiently concerned that Makarios would give way that he stepped up his activities, adding violent and widespread rioting by students and schoolchildren to explosions and shooting, as a result of which many of the schools were closed.

Makarios persuaded him to desist while he was engaged in negotiations, but on the eve of a meeting he was due to hold with Harding and Alan Lennox-Boyd, the Colonial Secretary, Grivas set off nineteen bombs at various places in the island. Makarios was furious, but refused to condemn violence in writing unless an unconditional amnesty was granted for all EOKA men and women imprisoned or detained. As a result, with the Bishop of Kyrenia, he was arrested on 9 March and sent to 'restricted residence' in the Seychelles.

Everyone expected a violent reaction to his deportation, but it was slow in coming, perhaps because Grivas feared that widespread activity at this time could cause him losses he could not afford. Opposing Harding's 17,000 troops, EOKA had a very small force of armed men. According to Grivas's own account, he had seven groups totalling 53 men in the mountains, forty-seven groups totalling 220 men in the main towns, two groups within the British base areas, and seventy-four groups of part-time terrorists totalling 750 men, armed only with shotguns, in villages all over the island. He had to consider his future strategy and conserve the resources to implement it. There had been one incident four days before Makarios was deported which would have caused a severe reaction if it had been successful: a time bomb was placed in an RAF transport aircraft due to fly servicemen and their families to England, which was discovered and defused. One sign of a resumption of activity was an attempt on Harding's life on 20 March by the placing of a bomb under the mattress of his bed by one of the Government House servants. It was temperature-controlled, but failed to explode and was found when the servant failed to turn up for work next day. A number of serious incidents followed, including the murder of prominent police officers and the hanging of two British army deserters in retaliation for the execution of two EOKA convicted terrorists. By May the number of British soldiers killed had risen to thirty.

In July the attention of the British Government was diverted by Nasser's announcement that Egypt was nationalizing the Suez Canal. The Royal Marine Commandos returned to Malta. The Parachute Brigade commander, Brigadier M. A. H. Butler, directed two major operations aimed at the capture of Grivas and his principal lieutenants. It nearly succeeded, Grivas narrowly avoiding capture and being forced to take refuge in the town of Limassol. Under pressure from the Greek Prime Minister, Constantine Karamanlis, Grivas reluctantly agreed to call a truce to facilitate diplomatic activity. On 17 August EOKA announced that it was suspending operations in order that Cypriot demands, as set out by Makarios, could be discussed. The British Government's response was to offer surrender terms, under which EOKA members could give up their arms and choose between deportation to Greece or detention in Cyprus, at the same time publishing captured diaries of Grivas, exposing the complicity of Makarios and the involvement of Grivas and his lieutenants in brutal crimes. Not surprisingly EOKA rejected them and intensified their activity. Further operations, directed by the Parachute Brigade, were launched in reply to this, but had not produced very fruitful results when the brigade was removed from operations in October to brush up its parachute training in preparation for the ill-fated Suez operation.

However, after its return, the tide began to turn dramatically. In two major operations early in 1957 Drakos and Afxentiou were killed, their gangs broken up and Georgadjis recaptured. Nicos Sampson and other important EOKA leaders in Nicosia were picked up, and the ring broken of customs officials in Limassol implicated in smuggling arms dispatched from Greece by Azinas.

The operation in January which resulted in the death of Drakos is described by Major Arthur Campbell of the 1st Suffolks, who carried it out:

A section of men toiled up the mountain track. Though there was snow on the hills above them to their left the sun shone hot on their backs as they walked, so that the sweat rolled down their backs inside their wind-proof smocks. The ground was steep, hard, unyielding, and the men at the back grumbled as they went.

'What the hell does he want to flog us up here for just to practise ambush laying – daft I call it.'

'Yeah, – I don't know what he thinks he can teach us. Night after night we've done these things, laying out in the freezing cold waiting for some "so and so" to come along. They never come, or if they do they "scarper" before we can get a shot at them.'

'Reckon I've ambushed every bloody track in the area. They can't teach me nothing.'

One man, an older soldier than the rest, he has a year's service in, said 'Stop your moaning, it'll pay off, you'll see.'

Cpl. King halted his section and called them round him. He said 'Stop your nattering you blokes. Remember what the Company Commander said, "No talking on ops." If I hear another word out of you, I'll impose a week's silence in barracks and see how you like that. Anyone talking will get a damn good clip over the ear-hole.' Cpl. King was a big man who had a mind of his own, so the section trudged on in silence, while the Corporal ran over in his mind the points he had been told to teach the men concerning the laying of night ambushes. Very soon he found the right place and took them through the drill in meticulous detail.

Four hours later Cpl. King's section were climbing another mountain on the opposite side of the valley. On returning from his training the Corporal had been met by his Platoon Commander. He was told that a large operation was being mounted in the valley beyond. He had seen something of the start of this operation as early that morning helicopters flew in a continuous stream from the football ground adjoining his billets, putting men in position along the mountain tops. Streams of transport had been passing up the road all day, through Evrychou, through Kakopetria, down the Spilia track to disappear, with their loads of troops, into the Adelphi Forest.

His Platoon Commander told him that any enemy escaping from the operational area would move over the ridge and into the Solea Valley. He was given an area to search, was told to find the route leading through the area and to kill any enemy moving down that route into the valley.

It was three o'clock in the afternoon when he started his search, moving round the edge of the forest, across the grain of the rock-hard country, up and down the steep ridges, across the narrow valley. He moved near the edge of the forest because the forest was 'prohibited' and he could be sure that only the terrorists walked there at night; he would not have to challenge, he could shoot at sight.

At half-past four he found the track he was looking for, a tiny footpath, running down the top of a ridge to the main road just outside Evrychou. He moved up it, into the forest, until he found a good site. Here the ground fell away sharply to the right, while on the left of the track was a small shelf. At one end of the chosen site the track ran over a small saddle; at the other end it rose steeply and loose stones lay on it. Cpl. King thought these stones might give warning of the enemy's approach.

He halted his section and each man dropped his load, sleeping bag, poncho, a few tins of compo,* all rolled into one bundle. Cpl. King selected his 'rest' area, one hundred and fifty yards away from the site, and sent three men under L/Cpl. Fowler to erect bivouacs and prepare the evening meal. Meanwhile he laid out the ambush in detail. He placed himself and Pte. Woods, four yards apart, on the small shelf. Pte. Brasser he put just below the lip of the saddle, looking upwards; Pte. Cooper was sent twenty yards up the track, opposite the loose stones, to lend a little depth to the ambush. While Cpl. King supervised the laying of each position, the sun left the sky, the damp mist came down the valley, the evening chill descended on the hills, a chill soon to be replaced by an icy breeze from the snow-clad mountain above. Soon it was dark, and bitter cold, and four men lay in their ponchos, with sleeping bags drawn over them, staring out into the darkness, waiting; four more slept intermittently in their bivouacs in the rest area.

* Composite rations.

At seven o'clock, when the first relief took place, thunder and lightning boomed and flickered round the valleys, while rain fell in torrents, soaking each man. In the middle of the storm they heard firing along the hills to their right, where they knew other ambushes lay. Cpl. King felt expectancy run through his own body and felt it spread through all his men. The enemy were on the move, perhaps they would move down his track.

At nine o'clock the ambush was relieved again. Two hours is long enough to lie on watch in the winter's cold. After that time your body numbs, you shift this way and that, you breathe on your frozen hands, alertness goes. It is better to go back to the rest area and crawl into a sleeping bag to snatch an hour's sleep or so before the next 'stag'.

At 11 o'clock Cpl. King gave a low whistle which told Pte. Cooper to go and fetch L/Cpl. Fowler with his relief party. At this time a thin moon was shining through the racing clouds, just enough to cast a faint glimmer on the ground. Fowler brought his men up in complete silence. Pte. Woods found Sells lying beside him even before he was aware of his coming; Wilson, just out from home, touched Brasser's back to report his arrival; Brown and Cooper were sneaking round the back of the ambush to Cooper's original position; L/Cpl. Fowler stepped up on the shelf to relieve Cpl. King.

As Woods rose to his feet he took one last look up the track, where he had been staring for so long. Standing there, only seven yards away, was the slim figure of a man. Woods's reaction was immediate; he fired at the standing figure through the poncho draped round his shoulders. The din of Woods's Sterling, and of the enemy's Sten fired in reply, shattered the still silence of the night, electrifying the men in and around the ambush. Brasser and Wilson lay side-by-side, tensely waiting for a target to show; Brown and Cooper faced outward, peering eagerly into the gloom; Fowler hurled himself on his belly and, with Cpl. King, fired back at point-blank range at the flames spurting from the Sten. The single rounds from the F.N. rifles, repeating, sharp across the lower stutter of the automatics. In a pause in the firing, Woods heard a second man scrambling up the steep stony ground ahead. He fired the rest of his Sterling magazine at the noise and a cry of pain resulted. Then silence. The whole action had lasted less than two minutes.

Cpl. King shouted at his men 'Stay where you are'; there followed ten minutes of bleak silence. He then crawled forward with Fowler to examine the body. It was dead; very dead. He felt no heart-beat, blood trickled on to his fingers from a head which had been half shot away; the body lay huddled on the track. He dragged it to one side, covered it with Woods's poncho, saw to the relief of his ambush and went back to his bivouac to sleep. But there was little sleep for him, or for the rest of his section as the long night passed in waiting for another enemy to enter the trap. They were all too elated. At last, after so many nights of fruitless waiting, they had drawn blood.

At first light Cpl. King collected his half-frozen men. He set them on to searching the area for the man they may have wounded. They failed to find him. They tied their victim to a stake and carried him down the mountainside. A truck waited for them at the road and throughout the journey they spread the news among the parties of soldiers scattered along the roadside. Everywhere was jubilation.

They laid the body outside the company headquarters in Kako-petria. There it was identified as Markos Drakos, third in the EOKA hierarchy, a deputy of the maestro George Grivas. There followed a lunatic day of triumph. Top brass descended from the skies in helicopters to view the victim and congratulate the victors; there was a champagne luncheon with the Press; messages came in from all over the island. But throughout, Cpl. King had only one thought. His men had given an example of good soldiering; they had vindicated the training he had given them.

At the end of February information reached the 3rd Brigade that Afxentiou was hiding near the Monastery of Makhairas in the mountains south-west of Nicosia, the area for which the 1st Duke of Wellington's Regiment were responsible. Their regimental journal describes the critical part of the operation which led to his death; from 0600 hrs 3 March onwards:

At this point Petros [the informer] stated that he was unable to point out the exact location of the hide but gave the approximate area. It was therefore decided to search this general area and almost immedi-ately Cpl. Trinder of 'B' party noticed a small track running up the hill from the lower path. Cpl. Trinder followed this track and after about 10 yards noticed some footprints. He looked more closely and discovered that some of the branches of the bushes to the right of the path had been tied down to form what looked like an archway about 4 ft. high. He went inside the archway to investigate and then noticed some large stones lying on the ground. He removed these and disclosed the mouth of a 40-gal. drum lying on its side and buried in the slope of the hill. On looking inside he found a 2-inch mortar wrapped up in brown paper; it was undoubtedly this discovery of Cpl. Trinder's, due to his keen observation and perseverance, that confirmed that terrorists were, or had been, in the immediate area, and led to the next stage, which was the discovery of the hide.

At this time the helicopter was circling the area and this was signalled down and a request sent back for a platoon to cordon off the area while a thorough search was being made.

The time was now approximately 0615 hrs, and Captain Newton, following up the small track from the arms cache, noticed that the ground under his feet was seemingly hollow. He thereupon called up Cpl. Trinder, who confirmed this, and they noticed some unusual-looking stones, which on removal proved to be the entrance to a hide. Captain Newton looked inside and saw some clothing and concluded that the hide was empty. By this time the rest of the party had concentrated at the entrance and voices were suddenly heard from inside the hide.

The interpreter then called to the inmates to come out without arms, and four men crawled out slowly, offering no resistance. The entrance was a tunnel, approximately 18 in. × 18 in. The four who came out were asked how many were inside and they stated five and that Afxentiou was still there. He was called upon to come out and the answer was a short burst of fire, which hit Cpl. Brown, who was standing in front of the entrance, and knocked him backwards down the hill, badly wounded. Captain Newton then threw a grenade in the entrance. After the explosion, which was clearly inside the hide by the sound and the fact that smoke came out of the roof, there was a short silence. It was therefore decided to put one of the terrorists already taken prisoner back into the hide to see if Afxentiou was dead, or if wounded bring him out, rather than risk the life of one of our own men.

After this had been done, Afxentiou shouted out in English and with great defiance: 'Now we are two. Come and get us.' He thereupon fired one shot out of the hide. The entrance was kept covered and shortly afterwards a phosphorous grenade was thrown out of the hide. On its explosion fire was immediately opened on the entrance by Major Rodick and Cpl. Trinder and L/Cpl. Martin and this was maintained until the smoke dispersed and it was considered virtually impossible for anyone to have escaped during this time.

At about this time L/Cpl. Dowdall attempted to drag Cpl. Brown away from the entrance of the hide, but after moving him a short distance was heavily fired upon and had to abandon the attempt. The two Bren gunners were now called forward and put into position, approximately 30 to 40 yards above the hide, covering the entrance.

The following appreciation was made. First, the terrorists already captured stated that Afxentiou had two machine-guns, with a quantity of ammunition, three pistols and a number of bombs in the hide with him. Secondly, previous information, and his present actions, indicated that he was likely to make a suicidal last stand with the object of killing as many as possible. Furthermore, it would have been quite possible for him to throw a grenade just out of the entrance, which would undoubtedly have caused severe casualties to anyone standing on top of or above the hide, while doing little or no damage to those inside. Thirdly, the hide was surrounded and escape virtually impossible. It was therefore decided that it was an unacceptable risk to remain standing on the roof of the hide (bombs of unknown type within) and the party accordingly withdrew to the upper track, and it was decided that some other means would have to be found to get him out. This decision was confirmed by the Commander, 3rd Infantry Brigade, and the Commanding Officer, who arrived by helicopter at this stage and gave direct orders that Afxentiou was to be killed before any further casualties were suffered. The time was now 0715 hrs.

It was then decided that the two best means of accomplishing this were:

(a) To burn him out.

(b) To explode a heavy charge on top of the hide.

An Engineer officer arrived at 0915 hrs. and tried the second method, which proved ineffective. Three hours later petrol was thrown over the hide and set alight. The account continues:

As soon as the petrol was ignited screams were heard from the hide and a figure was seen to crawl from the exit into a neighbouring clump of bushes. Fire was immediately opened by the four covering Bren guns and all escape routes were covered. Some few minutes later ammunition was heard exploding inside the hide, followed by an explosion and smoke coming from the area of the hide. It was therefore deduced that the fire had been effective but to make sure it was decided to explode a further charge on top of the hide. This was done at approximately 1330 hrs. and immediately followed up by a small party armed with Sten guns under the command of Captain Shuttleworth, who moved down from the path to the hide. Capt. Newton was in this party and was able to point out the entrance of the hide.

A tear-gas bomb was thrown into the hide, also, shots were fired into the entrance. Remembering at this time that a figure had crawled out of the hide, a search was made of the surrounding area, discovering the terrorist who had been put back into the hide in the initial stages of the operation. He was extremely frightened and shouting: 'Do not shoot, I surrender.' He also stated that Afxentiou was dead but to make certain he was put back in the hide and told to pull out Afxentiou's body. This he could not do but provided sufficient evidence to prove that Afxentiou was dead.

While the army had been vigorously chasing EOKA, the British Government had commissioned Lord Radcliffe to recommend a constitution. His proposals had been published and had received a favourable response from the British and Turkish Governments. Neither Greece nor the Greek Cypriots were prepared to show their hand in the absence of comment from Makarios, who took the line that, being out of touch with Cyprus, he could not express any views. The United Nations debated Cyprus again in February 1957 and passed a resolution calling for a renewal of discussions. Under political pressure from Greece and military pressure from the security forces, Grivas, still undiscovered in his hideout in Limassol, distributed a pamphlet on 14 March stating that 'in compliance with the spirit of the UN resolution and in order to facilitate the resumption of negotiations between Britain and the real representative of the Cypriot people, Archbishop Makarios, EOKA declares that it is ready to order the suspension of operations at once, if the Ethnarch Makarios is released'. After a week's delay while argument raged in the Cabinet it was decided to release him, but not to allow him to return to the island until Radcliffe's constitution had been implemented.

The war against EOKA was effectively over, although operations to track down its leaders continued. In the two years it had lasted, EOKA had killed 203 people, of whom seventy-eight were British servicemen, nine British police officers, sixteen British civilians, twelve Cypriot policemen and four Turkish civilians. They had set off 1,382 bomb explosions. Fifty-one of their members had been killed, twenty-seven imprisoned and 1,500 detained.

Makarios went to Athens, and in November Harding was replaced by Sir Hugh Foot. Harding's contribution to progress in Cyprus had been as significant as had been that of Templer in Malaya, and for much the same reasons. His clarity and openness of mind, his personal example of energy, determination and moral and physical courage, and his obvious warmth of character and integrity had gained him the admiration, affection and respect of all who served under him and whom he met. Makarios himself, as he personally told the author, held him in high regard. Hugh Foot was a very different character and set about his task in a different way.

Unfortunately little progress was made in the search for an agreed political solution, the Turks insisting that if the island were to be granted independence it should be partitioned. In March 1958 Grivas decided to renew action and gave orders for an economic boycott against Britain and a general strike. This was followed by the murder of a British Special Branch interrogator and a spate of bomb attacks of which Makarios disapproved. June saw a major advance in the political field. Macmillan, now Prime Minister, reduced the size of the 'sovereign base areas' it was proposed Britain should retain after independence and produced a plan which associated the Greek and Turkish Governments with the British, and with Cypriot Ministers, in the Government of the island, which would have separate Greek and Turkish Cypriot Assemblies. Turkey at first rejected this and inter-communal tension ensued, with EOKA attacks on British soldiers; but the Turkish Prime Minister, Adnan Menderes, changed his mind, and Macmillan decided to go ahead. Makarios, fearing that he would be left out, announced in September that he abandoned his demand for *enosis* and would accept self-determination, which infuriated Grivas, causing a rift between them which never healed. The Archbishop returned to the island on 1 March 1959 to a delirious welcome. Eight days later he met Grivas and on 13 March EOKA handed in a sufficient number of arms to satisfy the authorities, Grivas being flown by the Greek air force to Athens, where he was granted the rank of General. The EOKA campaign really was now at an end, but the troubles of Cyprus were not.

Suez

While these colonial campaigns were in progress, decisions had been taken by the Conservative administrations under Churchill and Eden which had far-reaching effects on the army. The first was the promise, made by Eden as Foreign Secretary, that Britain would maintain on the Continent of Europe the effective strength of forces then assigned to NATO, four divisions and a tactical air force, or whatever the Supreme Commander Europe regarded as having equivalent fighting capacity; and that she would not withdraw these forces against the wishes of a majority of the Brussels Treaty powers. At that time the British Army of the Rhine numbered 80,000. Eden gave this undertaking in order to persuade the French, Dutch and Belgians to accept German rearmament and member-ship of NATO. While making this important commitment, the Govern-ment was nevertheless greatly concerned at the economic effects of maintaining such large forces all over the world, and at the prospect of the increasing cost of equipping them, as Second World War stocks evaporated. When Eden succeeded Churchill in 1955 he addressed himself to the problem of how to reduce the burden. As Foreign Secretary he had played a major part in laying the foundation both of the Central Treaty Organization (CENTO), which had its origins in the Baghdad Pact in January 1955 between Iraq and Turkey, and of the South-East Asia Treaty Organization (SEATO), formed in July 1954. Although both could be regarded as adding to Britain's military commit-ments, Eden saw them in the opposite light – as taking the place of the large purely British military bases and establishments maintained in the Middle and Far East.

The continuance of the former, which housed 83,000 soldiers, was the subject of negotiations with Nasser, who had come to power in Egypt in 1954. The 1936 Anglo-Egyptian Treaty, under which Britain stationed troops in the Suez Canal Zone, terminated in 1956. In any case it imposed limits which were far exceeded by the current garrison. The negotiations became entangled both with Nasser's demand for a loan to heighten the Aswan Dam on the Nile and with restrictions imposed by Britain, France and the USA on the sale of arms to Arab countries, neighbours of Israel, and to Israel herself, with whom the Arabs were technically at war. Agreement had been reached in October 1954 that British troops would be withdrawn within twenty months and that the installations of the base would be preserved as British property by a British civilian organization. Eden had failed to persuade Egypt to join a Middle Eastern alliance, which would have guaranteed Britain's use of the base in an emergency.

The last troops left on 13 June 1956. Six weeks later Eden told the Chiefs of Staff to prepare plans to return. This volte-face was brought about by Nasser's proclamation that he had nationalized the Suez Canal as a means of funding the Aswan Dam project. While various ways of countering Nasser's move were bandied about, including the formation of a Suez Canal Users' Association, France and Britain agreed that if no progress were made in negotiations they would use military force to occupy the Canal, and even go further and topple Nasser from power. Not surprisingly, there was no contingency plan already prepared for such an operation, and it was soon discovered that means of transport and assault by both sea and air were sadly lacking, as was the army's ability to provide the necessary logistic support. It was largely to provide the latter that 23,000 reservists were called up. With the recent withdrawal of 1st and 3rd Divisions from Egypt, there was no shortage of infantry; but the 10th Armoured Division, based in Libya, could not be used, owing to the objections of the country's ruler, King Idris. Shipping to move the few tanks available in England was hard to find. Lieutenant-General Sir Hugh Stockwell's 2nd Corps Headquarters was withdrawn from Germany to command the assault, in cooperation with the French General André Beaufre, both being subordinate to General Keightley in Cyprus.

The original plan had been to land at Alexandria and thrust an armoured column up the desert road to Cairo, from which columns would make for the Canal at Port Said, Ismailia and Suez. The assault was to be made on 15 September, if Nasser had not by then accepted the Canal Users' Association proposal, and Stockwell assumed that the whole operation would last only eight days. For a number of reasons, partly realization of the limitations imposed by the paucity of amphibious craft, the plan was changed to an assault on Port Said, followed by a swift dash down the length of the Canal. Britain and France had found little support for their idea of the use of force, to which Eisenhower, with a Presidential election looming, was opposed. The French and Israelis were in collusion over the possibility of joint action, and the former drew the British also into the plot. A plan was concocted by which the Israelis would invade Sinai, while Britain and France would pose as peacemakers between them and Egypt, occupying the Canal in that guise. 31 October was agreed as D-Day. The Israelis began the operation on the 29th with a parachute drop on the Mitla Pass, and by the time that the 668 British and 487 French parachutists dropped behind Port Said at dawn on 5 November, Israel had completed the conquest of Sinai.

The main body of the airdropped British force was the 3rd Battalion of the Parachute Regiment. The *Airborne Forces Journal* tells their story:

> At very short notice the Battalion was warned to stand by for possible operations, and on Sunday, 4th November, all ranks were sealed in the camp and we knew we were to undertake a parachute landing in Egypt – the first airborne operation of battalion size to be mounted by British airborne forces since 1945.
>
> At 0400 hrs. we emplaned at Nicosia and by 0700 hrs. we were over the Egyptian coast and heading for our objective. The scene below, as the long stream of Valettas and Hastings flew in, was peaceful and familiar to many of us – the long line of breakers rolling towards the sandy coast of the Nile Delta, the scores of feluccas moving up the Manzala Canal and the waterways about Port Said. Then as we stood in the door we saw the airfield, just as it looked in the photos – a building burning fiercely near the control tower and the lines of barrels put out as an obstacle by the Egyptians which had puzzled us the day before. There were the jolts as the heavy drop and container loads went away, and then it was our turn to go.
>
> Once outside there was plenty to catch the eye. Flak from 3.7-in. H.A.A. guns was bursting uncomfortably close and caused some casualties, and our opponents were clearly showing a lively interest in our arrival. Shells and mortar bombs were landing on the D.Z., and unfriendly little men with rifles and machine guns were adding to the din.
>
> On the ground groups of airborne soldiers were cheerfully emp-

tying their personal weapons containers and moving to their appointed tasks.

One or two had remarkable adventures, such as Pte. Looker of 'B' Company, who landed in an Egyptian slit trench. He realized while he was still 200 feet up that this was highly probable. The same thought appeared to have occurred to its oriental occupant, who got out and took up a threatening attitude with his musket on the edge of the trench, evidently waiting for a suitable moment to dispatch Looker for good. At this point fate intervened on Looker's side as a late oscillation sent his 80-lb. weapons container crashing against the Egyptian soldier and bowling him smartly into the trench. Looker himself landed seconds later and in the ensuing struggle came out on top.

First to reach the control tower was Pte. Frank Eccles of 'A' Company, who just missed landing on the roof and in the event got caught up in the top of a palm tree outside the main entrance.

A story with a happy ending was told by Pte. Peter Lamph of 'B' Company. He was No. 20 in a Valetta and as a result of having got his strap wrapped round his leg crossing the spar he was late away and the plane was already over the sea heading for home when he jumped. As he came down well beyond the DZ he came under heavy small-arms fire and his personal weapons container was hit several times. Landing in the sea, he feigned dead and as time passed and 'B' Company began attacking he made his way towards the beach, recovered his rifle and some of his equipment and was picked up later in the day. The happy ending came when Group Captain McNamara sent him a crate of beer with the compliments of Transport Command to compensate him for his wetting.

At the west end of the airfield 'A' Company, under Major Mike Walsh, went into action and cleared the control tower and surrounding buildings, while 2/Lieut. Peter Coates and his platoon destroyed a machine-gun post in a pillbox, killing the crew and taking eight prisoners of war. Pte. Clements contributed by a direct hit on the pill box with the rocket launcher.

Meanwhile at the opposite end, 'B' Company, under Major Dick Stevens, who had been wounded in the hand on landing, destroyed another machine-gun post in a pillbox, clearing the enemy from a group of buildings on the coast, and killed a group who were entrenched at the end of the runway. Without wasting further time they reorganized and, supported by mortars and machine-guns now coming into action, they began their task of clearing the sewage farm, a boggy stretch intersected with thick reeds. It was at once apparent that the enemy was in some strength in prepared positions in the cemetery beyond the sewage farm. This ground was slightly higher than that over which 'B' Company had to advance, and they came under heavy mortar and machine-gun fire which caused casualties and made progress difficult. In the course of this advance Major Stevens was again wounded, this time in the leg, having refused to stop for his first wound.

And now, when it was particularly welcome, support was at hand from rocket-firing aircraft of the Fleet Air Arm ably directed by two Parachute Regiment officers, Major Tony Stevens and Capt. Bill Hancock, who provided the Air Contact Team. The air-strike was made only 400 yards in front of our own troops and at once established confidence between the men of the Battalion and the naval pilots. Thereafter throughout the day this close air support was a feature of the operation and a battle-winning factor of the first order. In the first twenty-four hours over 400 sorties were flown in support of the Battalion, and that evening the Commanding Officer sent the following signal to the Royal Navy;

Many thanks for your magnificent support to us this day which thrilled all ranks. Its timely effectiveness and accuracy were beyond praise and undoubtedly saved us many casualties.

Please convey gratitude to all ranks.

The air-strike now enabled 'B' Company, by this time under Capt. Beale, to complete its attack and consolidate its position, but in justice to the enemy it must be said that one or two well-dug-in machine-guns continued firing in spite of the air attack.

It was now the turn of 'C' Company, under Major Ron Norman, and they came forward through some unpleasant mortar defensive fire to attack the strong-point in the cemetery. With the aid of further air-strikes and a carefully made fire plan, they went into the attack and by mid-afternoon had cleared the whole area, killing over twenty of the enemy and capturing or destroying three Russian S.P. guns, two 3.7-in A.A. guns, four 81-mm mortars, three medium machine-guns, one Bren-gun carrier, and a quantity of rifles and machine-guns. In the course of this attack Pte. David Beech of 'C' Company was about to engage two of the enemy with his Bren gun when he heard a noise behind him and, swinging round, he found himself covered by an Egyptian with a rocket-launcher. Fortunately for him, the mechanism of the rocket-launcher failed and he was able to dispatch his enemy with a short burst.

At this stage the C.O. was ordered to halt his advance and regroup for the night, as the seaborne landings were due to take place the following morning and it was undesirable to enter the target area of naval guns and strike aircraft operating in support of the Royal Marines.

The Battalion group were not the only British troops in the airdrop. A small party from the Guards Independent Parachute Company and 9th Parachute Squadron Royal Engineers dropped with the French. Captain Murray de Klee of the Scots Guards was in command and describes their experience:

At about five o'clock on the afternoon of Saturday, 3rd November, the door-bell rang and I got out of bed to let Kemmis in. He was in great humour and greeted me with: 'The Brigadier has really been most kind; he has given the Company a special job and you are to do it; a small party are to jump with the French south of Port Said.' I managed a somewhat sickly grin, but said nothing as I got him a drink. 'You will only have eight Guardsmen and six Sappers; I came to tell you straight away so that you can decide who you want to take and warn them tonight as you may go some time before the sea landing.' His grin reached his ears and my sickly smile died a natural death. I had only said a few hours earlier to A. that 'I think we are going by sea and 3 Para are going to jump – poor devils!'

I went back to camp with Kemmis. Choosing my little party was not easy. In the end I took Sergeant Longstaff (Coldstream Guards); my Stick Sergeant, Lance-Sergeant White, and Lance-Corporal Williams (Welsh Guards); Lance-Corporal Kent, an old soldier, Melville, my orderly, and Fletcher, all in my own Regiment; Murphy of the Irish Guards; and McNab, an irrepressible trooper in the Life Guards. I told them that we were going to drop with the French, to draw up weapon containers and to reorganize their kit with this in mind. I was showered with questions to which I could give no answers as I was only briefed the next day, but I think that the thought of jumping from a strange aircraft with strange parachutes and aircraft drill, none of which we had ever seen, was very much more on our minds than anything else. Would they say 'Allez' or 'Go'? What height would we jump from? What were the aircraft like – and where were the doors? How careful were the French parachute packers? and many other thoughts besides.

Over the next twenty-four hours de Klee learnt that their task was to patrol down the Canal and Treaty Roads to the eight-kilometre point to see if they were mined, blocked or defended in any way, meeting 2nd Para, with a squadron of 6th Royal Tanks, as they came through after landing by sea, the Sappers having cleared the bridges of any mines or explosive charges. He was impressed with the professionalism of the French, as they familiarized themselves with the French equipment and methods. He takes up the story as they fly towards their objective:

I woke up to find the sun shining through the windows and the dispatchers taking off the doors. We were still well out over the sea and down below us we could see a small convoy heading in the same direction as ourselves. Out through the starboard window was another Nordatlas aircraft, and behind us to port was a solitary fighter aircraft – rather comforting. Over the coast and southwards for ten minutes and then we banked sharply, saw a stream of Nordatlas aircraft heading in the opposite direction through the starboard door and fell into position behind them. There was no aircraft drill; we stood up, put on our helmets, hooked on our containers and hooked up ourselves and shuffled towards the door. Red light on. Five minutes to go. I had two Frenchmen jumping in front of me and the rest of my party behind me, all from the port side. The Canal and roads came into sight below us. It could only be a matter of seconds.

On went the klaxon horn, a second of buffeting and blankness and then the gentle swaying accompanied by the sigh of relief, slow twists and my helmet as usual jammed down over my eyes. Twists cleared, container away and helmet pushed back. The sun was still shining, but something had gone wrong with the 'practice' jump. The air was full of the sound of small-arms fire. Anti-aircraft shells were bursting above us, the Nordatlas aircraft were weaving and jinking all over the sky to the north, and the Frenchmen drifting down around me were firing from their parachute harness. The D.Z. was an area of very uneven soft sand. I landed and rolled into a dip with my container. Sweating and cursing, I pulled off my helmet, tore my rifle out of the container, put on my beret and, leaving the rest of my kit in the friendly little hollow, set off up the line of the stick to the rallying point. The D.Z. might well have been a battle scene from an American film, littered with parachutes and abandoned equipment, dead Egyptians, and wounded Frenchmen, spurts of sand and earth with all the accompanying noise. I met Lance-Sergeant White, Lance-Corporal Kent, Fletcher and Melville, but as our rallying point, a number of mud huts surrounded by reeds on the edge of the D.Z., was still being contested for, I sent them over to a collection of oil drums by the Treaty Road. Lance-Corporal Williams joined us with the news that Murphy was hit, but that McNab was with him; Lance-Corporal Kent and I went and carried him over. He had landed beside an Egyptian slit trench and had been shot in the stomach before he could defend himself; his assailant had been promptly killed by a French officer. I do not know whether the Egyptians had been expecting us or not, but about forty had been dug-in on and around the D.Z. and were in the middle of their breakfast when we arrived. Sergeant Longstaff joined us; he had landed in the telephone wires and though he had provided an easy target hanging down on one side of the wires with his container on the other, he only suffered a shaking when he cut himself down and landed on his back on the railway line fifteen feet below. He had seen nothing of the Sappers who jumped directly behind him, so with Lance-Sergeant White and Fletcher I set off to find them. By now the Egyptians had been cleared off the D.Z., but spasmodic 3-inch mortar fire was coming down, which was unpleasant, and three bombs landed within thirty yards of where Lance-Corporal Williams was attending to Murphy, but luckily none of these exploded.

We soon found Sapper Coggen near the railway line; he had been hit in the face by a shell splinter but nevertheless was quite cheerful. He had not seen the other two Sappers either, and though we looked for some time we found no trace of them. I went over to Regimental Headquarters, told them that we had two wounded and two missing; then after collecting our equipment, set off down the Treaty Road with what was left of my party, leaving Lance-Corporal Kent with Murphy, who was now being attended to by a French doctor. By now the sky was full of allied aircraft attacking targets in Port Said with machine-guns and rockets (in support of the French) and though the landing had not been given close support, for the rest of the time we were in the area there never seemed to be less than a dozen aircraft overhead ready to take on opportunity targets.

For the rest of that day de Klee's party remained within the French perimeter, but on the following day they set off down the Treaty Road and got as far as Ras-el-Ish, fifteen kilometres away. He takes up the story again, following a number of incidents when they stopped various vehicles there:

Little happened for the next hour or so, but suddenly Sergeant Black, who was in our O.P., sixty feet up in the Canal Station signal mast, cried out, 'Here comes the Egyptian Army.' Mugs, razors and cleaning rags were dropped, Lance-Corporal Williams and McNab shot out of the Canal where they had been swimming, and we stood to. Down the Canal road, evenly spaced out in parties of two or three, were coming about forty people. In the heat haze, even through field glasses, it was impossible to make out who they were. Soon there was no doubt – they were refugees from the villages to our south, though why they were heading for Port Said, which from this distance appeared to be a blazing inferno, we were unable to understand. Three were soldiers, obviously deserters, as they had thrown away all their equipment except for belts, bayonets and water-bottles and were wearing galabirs* over their uniforms. They joined our other prisoners. One couple, a man and a woman, had their six-year-old daughter with them. The child had a gaping hole in her cheek bone and a deep gash above one eye. McNab gave her all his sweets, which she managed to eat while I and an Egyptian soldier washed her face. We had used all our dressings, so I indicated to her father that I needed his shirt to bandage his daughter. He shook his head. More explanations. Even more violent protestations and head shaking. I hardly had to look at the Guardsmen near me. I nodded and in a matter of seconds I had sufficient blue cotton bandages to finish my job. The little family left us, the father in his singlet, the mother evidently grateful, and the child, mouth, hands and pockets stuffed with sweets. Except for these two all the refugees we saw were able-bodied men. A taxi was halted and out got fourteen civilians; we kept the taxi and its owner and sent the others on

_____
* White gowns.

towards Port Said, telling them that the next troops they would meet would be paratroops from the French Foreign Legion. They did not appear very enthusiastic about continuing their journey, and we later discovered that they stopped half a mile farther on and were still there when we left next day. The taxi had come from Cairo; they confirmed earlier refugees' reports that El Qantara, the Egyptian Army headquarters, was completely deserted, and that they had seen no sign of military life in Ismailia either. I sent Sergeant Black and McNab back on the motor-bike with the news for what it was worth.

A shout from the O.P., 'Egyptian soldiers coming up the railway line.' Two in front and one behind, well spread out and all armed: it looked like a recce patrol. We let the leaders come to within thirty yards before Lance-Corporal Kent and I stepped out of cover and challenged them. They turned and ran. Our final capture was an Egyptian, complete with steel helmet, medal ribbons and brand new Russian rifle and bayonet, who somehow had escaped from Port Said. He was caught slinking past the back of the Canal Station by Sergeant White and Lance-Corporal Kent and was overpowered before he could do any harm. He was an unpleasant character and made it quite obvious that he had no intention of staying with us if he could help it. However, he was given no chance and went with the others into the P.O.W. cage the next day.

At about half past four we heard the rumble of tanks and down both roads from Port Said came the leading troops of the 6th Royal Tanks. Though we tried to stop them they went straight past us without even a wave. Out of each steel hull protruded a steel helmet, looking neither right nor left. I was unable to give them the little information I had nor find out any news of the Company, when 2 Para were due to arrive and many other things besides, so I got our motor-bike and gave chase, but it was wasted effort, for however much I waved or shouted they would not stop and all I achieved was to amuse some French paratroopers who were sitting on the back of the rear tanks. However, on getting back to the Canal Station we had the satisfaction of watching them fight a completely futile battle with an empty pill-box half a mile south of us. If they had stopped we could have saved them the waste of both time and shells as we had been to the pill-box earlier. Shortly afterwards the Company and 2 Para came through and, after they had heard a brief account of our doings, went on southwards, telling us to catch them up next day.

While this was going on the I.O. cunningly pinched our highly prized
Russian rifle, but it was quickly recovered when we joined them later.

That evening we had a terrific meal of chicken and duck and all
of us managed to get our fair share of sleep. The next morning we
bundled our prisoners into the taxi and took them back to Brigade
Headquarters. Later we rejoined the Company who were dug in
south of El Cap, and spent the next few days sitting, waiting and
wondering. We did not have to wait long: we were relieved by the
Royal West Kents, and after one meal in Port Said, we were on board
the *New Australia* and four days later back in Cyprus. We had only
been away twelve days, though it felt like an age, but, looking back, I
do not think that I or those who went with me would have missed it
for anything.

Twenty-four hours after the parachute drop the first Buffalo tracked
amphibious craft had landed with men of 40th and 42nd Royal Marine
Commandos. The 45th came ashore by helicopter, the first occasion on
which this form of assault had been used. Next to land – from the sea –
were the rest of 16th Parachute Brigade. Fighting in Port Said was
sporadic, and Stockwell planned that General Massu's French parachutists should launch a combined air- and canal-borne attack on Ismailia,
while Butler's brigade broke out of Port Said to join them. But international pressure, principally from the USA, intervened, and a ceasefire
was ordered from midnight. It came as a frustrating anti-climax to the
3rd Commando and 16th (Parachute) Brigades, as it did to the large
numbers of troops earmarked for the operation, who had not even been
landed. British casualties were twenty-two killed and ninety-seven
wounded; French ten and thirty.

7

THE WIND OF CHANGE
1960–1997

The Suez fiasco reinforced the determination of Macmillan, who succeeded Eden as Prime Minister in January 1957, having been in succession Minister of Defence, Foreign Secretary and Chancellor of the Exchequer, to reduce the size and expense of the armed forces and abolish National Service. Major overseas bases were to be done away with and reliance based on a central strategic reserve, transported by air. The introduction of tactical atomic weapons would make a reduction in other forms of firepower possible and make it unnecessary to plan for protracted campaigns. Forces raised in the colonies, then numbering 60,000, would be increased. The 1957 Defence White Paper stated that National Service would end in 1960 and set a target for the reduction of all three services from 690,000, of whom 300,000 were National Servicemen, to 375,000, all regular, by the end of 1962. The army's share of this was a subject of fierce argument. Its strength at that time, excluding 6,000 women and 4,000 boys, stood at 373,000, of whom 164,000 were regular, although half of them only on a three-year engagement. Anticipating the end of National Service, the War Office had set up a committee to examine the strength that a wholly regular army would need. The answer given was 220,000, but the Army Council decided to lower its sights to 200,000. Macmillan's Defence Minister, Duncan Sandys, did not believe that the army could recruit that number and insisted that plans should be based on 165,000, a figure which Templer, the CIGS, continued to argue was insufficient, as was proved to be the case.

Reliance on a central reserve, to be deployed and supplied by air, soon proved an illusion. Commitments in southern Arabia increased, as Nasser fomented Arab opposition to British influence in the Middle East, and air transport proved pitifully inadequate. The few transport aircraft that the RAF possessed had insufficient range and load-carrying capacity. Transport Command's fleet improved year by year, but always had to face the difficulty of finding a route to the Indian Ocean which was not subject to diplomatic clearance. The need to have troops immediately available, with the ability to support them in operations, led in practice to the creation of new bases east of Suez, in Kenya, Aden and the Persian Gulf, the development of a new one in Malaya, and the dispersion of the intended central strategic reserve. The demands on manpower, and the difficulties of regular recruiting as long as conscripts were still serving, led to a further reduction of the British Army of the Rhine to 55,000 in 1959, while the overall regular manpower target was raised to 180,000, a figure which was not reached for some time: by 1965 it had risen to 176,000.

The severe shrinkage in the army which this caused forced a major reorganization. In 1951 British infantry battalions had numbered eighty-five: by 1957 the number had been reduced to seventy-seven, and was to come down to sixty. The Royal Armoured Corps lost seven of its thirty regiments, and the Royal Artillery, which had already lost fourteen regiments as a result of the abolition of Anti-Aircraft Command, lost another twenty: the Royal Engineers only four. Wholesale amalgamations took place, involving the disappearance of many famous regimental titles. The Army Council, faced with intense lobbying by regimental colonels and retired officers, stuck to a policy of seniority, determined by the date on which a regiment was raised, amalgamations being influenced by historic links and similar historic roles – e.g. Fusiliers, Light Infantry, Hussars, Lancers – or territorial proximity. Infantry regimental depots were abolished, regiments being 'brigaded' and sharing a depot. The reorganization took five years to complete, and while it was going on the army was almost as heavily involved as it had been before Suez.

One of the problems that had to be faced in this reorganization was the future of army aviation. During and since the Second World War, the Royal Artillery had manned light fixed-wing aircraft as Air Observation Posts, directing artillery fire from behind our own lines. The army in Malaya had begun to appreciate the potentialities of the helicopter, not only for artillery observation, but also for other forms of reconnaissance, casualty evacuation, and the transport of commanders, staff officers and urgent items of many kinds. Royal Navy helicopters had given valuable support there. The decision was taken to form an Army Air Corps in 1957, but for much of its first decade most of the aircrew were seconded from their parent regiments, as they had been in the original Royal Flying Corps. By 1967 the corps had become established as an essential arm of the service, and ten years later was considering extending its role into that of attack with missiles.

The political defeat in the Suez operation of the old imperial powers with links to the Middle East had encouraged Arab nationalists in opposition to the sheikly regimes which Britain and France had supported. 1957 saw British troops from Aden in action in support of the Sultan of Muscat and Oman to suppress a rebellion, aided by Saudi Arabia, which maintained a claim to the Buraimi Oasis. The rebels occupied a mountain stronghold in a remote desert area, and were defeated in January 1958 in a skilful operation in which the 22nd SAS Regiment played a major part, the army having to revert to animal transport with 200 donkeys hastily bought in Somaliland.

July 1958 was a crisis month in the Middle East. The young King Hussein of Jordan faced a rebellion, and his cousin, King Feisal of Iraq, and the latter's pro-British elder statesman, Nuri-es-Said, were murdered. At Hussein's request 16th Parachute Brigade was flown from Britain into Amman, the capital, Israel agreeing to the use of her airspace, while US Marines landed in Lebanon to pre-empt trouble there. Calm was restored without the need for action by the paratroops, and they were withdrawn in October.

The next threat came from the new regime in Iraq. In June 1961 its President, Kassem, announced that Kuwait formed part of his country and that he proposed to take it over. The ruler of Kuwait appealed to Britain to implement the newly signed defence agreement. Within three days a brigade had been deployed, one Royal Marine Commando from its carrier, which happened to be carrying out hot-weather trials off Karachi, one flown from Aden, and the 2nd Coldstream Guards, who happened to be in Bahrain on detachment from 24th Infantry Brigade in Kenya. A squadron of tanks of the 3rd Carabiniers, kept permanently on landing craft in the Gulf, was put ashore, and four days later the rest of 24th Brigade was flown in from Kenya, joined by the other squadrons of the Carabiniers, flown from Britain, who manned tanks stockpiled in Kuwait. Iraq was successfully deterred and the force was withdrawn in October, replaced by one from the Arab League.

Cyprus Peacekeeping

In 1963 Cyprus was once more the scene of action. At the end of December Greek Cypriot fighters attacked Turkish Cypriot areas, the origin of the fighting being the different interpretations placed on the constitution under which the island became independent in 1960. The Turkish Cypriots, egged on by Ankara, resisted attempts by the Greek Cypriots to regard the island as a unitary state. Makarios, the President, had tried to introduce some constitutional amendments to overcome Turkish obstruction and insistence on separation. The fighting was a threat to the security of British families living outside the sovereign base areas of Episkopi and Dhekelia, many in Limassol and Larnaca. There were also service and civilian families in Nicosia, where the airfield was still an RAF station. Duncan Sandys, then Commonwealth Secretary, brought pressure to bear on Makarios and the Turkish Cypriot Vice-President, Dr Kutchuk, to accept the intervention of a peacekeeping force from the garrison of the base areas.

Although the force succeeded in restricting the fighting in Nicosia, it was unable to prevent serious attacks by organized bodies of Greek Cypriots on the Turkish areas of Limassol, Larnaca, Ktima and Polis, as well as in villages all over the island. The 3rd Division, the strategic reserve in Britain, was dispatched by air in February 1964 to relieve the overstretched garrison and try to suppress the fighting. In March the United Nations Organisation assumed responsibility for peacekeeping, and the division put on its light blue beret and came under its control, gradually reducing its strength as contingents from other nations arrived over the following two months, until the British contribution stabilized at the level of a brigade. The original Security Council mandate was for three months: at the time of writing, thirty-four years later, it is still there, the British contribution having been reduced to the equivalent of a battalion.

Aden

In the same year trouble was brewing in Aden and its hinterland, the sheikly rulers of which had recently been brought together in a rather precarious Federation, into which, in January 1963, was merged the colony of Aden itself. Four months before, Imam Ahmed, the ruler of the Yemen, which maintained a long-standing claim to the area, had died. His son was overthrown by Colonel Sallal, who was supported by Egypt, and his rebellion was welcomed by Abdullah al-Asnag, leader of the People's Socialist Party in Aden, which favoured integration of Aden and its hinterland with the Yemen. Nasser sent troops to the Yemen to support Sallal against the Royalists, who were helped by Saudi Arabia and were concentrated north of the capital, Sana'a. Rioting, agitation and terrorist acts in Aden were combined with incidents up-country, notably in the mountainous Radfan area astride the road to Dhala, by which posts guarding the Yemen frontier were maintained.

In January 1964 General Sir Charles Harington, the newly appointed Joint Service Commander-in-Chief, dispatched a punitive expedition, the core of which was three battalions of the Federal army, which occupied the area while a new road was being built. The force was then withdrawn in March. Operations were resumed at the end of April with 45th Royal Marine Commando, 3rd Parachute Regiment and 1st East Anglian, supported by the RAF and naval helicopters. The headquarters of 39th Brigade (Brigadier C. H. Blacker) was flown from Northern Ireland to command this force. At the end of May, Blacker had seven battalions, two more British and two from the Federal army having been added. In operations lasting from 17 May to 11 June the rebels were defeated, and although troops were kept in the Radfan thereafter it was not again the scene of major operations. Casualties were five killed and thirteen wounded.

3 Para's operation is described in their regimental journal:

The first task was to secure a base and airstrip adjacent to the area selected for operations. Thumair, a small fortress area just east of the Dhala road was chosen and made firm. All was now ready for a sortie into the tribal areas. 45 Commando, Royal Marines, and B Company Group, 3rd Battalion, The Parachute Regiment, set off through the mountains on a long night march; the former picking their way along crests to make a frontal attack at dawn; the latter making a wide circuit to come up in rear of the enemy's positions along the northern edge of the Wadi Taym.

It was dark; the ground was unknown; the maps were poor. Parachutists and Royal Marines lost their way several times but skilfully recovered. It was hot. The route lay amongst stones and boulders. When daylight came, each group was still some way from its target, marked for B Company Group by a number of watch towers and a village below broken cliffs. As the leading platoon approached, they came under heavy small arms fire.

Major Peter Walker, the company commander, led a dash forward with most of the leading platoon to clear the closest enemy positions in and around the central watchtowers. The remainder of the two forward platoons began to clear the village. Meantime, Captain Barry Jewkes was coming up some way in the rear with the remainder of the group. The tribesmen also had a party lying back and, seeing Major Walker's advanced elements passed, they thought themselves clear to come up to attack from behind. As they dashed forward to do so, Captain Jewkes laid an ambush with great success; all the enemy were killed.

The attention of the majority of the enemy was now concentrated on Major Walker and B Company Group as it closed on the area of the village and watchtowers. Throughout a hot and anxious day, they held on to their positions under almost continuous fire, the only heavy support for the parachutists being the Hunter aircraft. These returned frequently to strike the enemy positions among crevices and rock tunnels across the cliffs. Despite their help, casualties began to mount. Captain Jewkes was killed while giving medical aid to Sergeant Baxter, seriously wounded in the lung. Private Davies was killed while dodging through bullet swept ground to fetch water. Privates Thornton and Cassidy were in serious need of attention. Lance-Corporals Bright and McKenzie and Letham and Private Clark were all awaiting evacuation as wounded. Late in the afternoon, as the Royal Marines pushed the tribesmen off the heights above, Padre Preston arrived in a Belvedere helicopter to organise the removal of the wounded. He stayed himself to give a temporary burial to Captain

Jewkes and Private Davies before climbing the cliffs with B Company Group into their night positions.

For a little while, the Company Group remained in the Wadi Taym area, patrolling to find the tribesmen who had by now disappeared. 45 Commando were then relieved and B Company Group with its Support Company elements returned to Bahrain, leaving Sgt Blyth's platoon of C, which had fought with it, in Aden.

It was now the turn of the remainder of the battalion group. A Company, C – which took Sergeant Blyth's party back into its own ranks – 3 Para Troop RE, the RAMC section and a rifle platoon found by the Heavy Drop Platoon and elements of B Platoon, 63 Company RASC, concentrated in Aden transit camp. One troop of 1 (Bull's Troop) Para Light Battery RHA were already firing in the Radfan; and the Battery Commander, Major David Drew, was much relieved to be close enough to be their master once more, despite excellent reports of their work with J Battery, whom they had temporarily joined.

The ensuing operations were divided into two phases – the first from the 17th to 20th May. Commander 39 Brigade, Brigadier C. H. Blacker, ordered 3 Para Group to move from their reserve position in the Wadi Rabwa to clear the ridge on which the Bakri villages lay. The Commanding Officer, Lieutenant-Colonel Farrar-Hockley, was told that there would be no helicopter lift available from the Belvederes, however; only the Scouts of 653 Squadron AAC could be counted on for a few light loads and reconnaissance. Rather than delay operations, Colonel Farrar-Hockley decided to divide the force into fighting elements and fighting porters, the latter carrying the ammunition and water that would be needed forward. On the night 16th/17th May, the anti-tank platoon, under command of CSM 'Nobby' Arnold, secured the village of Shab Tem between the Wadis Taym and Rabwa and, from this area, three patrols went forward in bright moonlight to seek routes up on to the Bakri Ridge.

The next task was to move forward by Land-Rover the battalion group's ammunition, food and water to Shab Tem. Unfortunately the tenuous track between the two wadis could not take the traffic of guns and vehicles. The Quartermaster and MTO* had to arrange handling parties between one vehicle point and another where the

---

* Motor Transport Officer.

track was broken, and the operation was thus set back for 24 hours. On the night 18th/19th, enough had come forward to make a start. Preceded by a reconnaissance party, the column set off – A Company, the fighting element, with mortars and machine guns; battalion headquarters and Battery Commander's party; C Company and 3 Para Troop RE in rear bearing heavy loads as fighting porters. By first light on the 19th, 3 Para Group were well established on the Bakri Ridge, while the fighting porters had marched back, minus loads, to Shab Tem. The Scouts of 653 Squadron were well to the fore giving devoted support. Next night, the roles were reversed with C Company leading and A joining the porters; the only exception being a fighting patrol of A Company under 2nd Lieutenant Hew Pike which set off at last light to get behind the enemy.

Of the tribesmen, little had been seen, minor brushes apart. But now the A Company patrol discovered a party moving back, with whom a running fight followed. After a long and wearying series of climbs and descents, the battalion group, most of whose members were carrying loads of 80–90 pounds, reached their objective above the vast gorges of Hajib escarpment where forces were joined with the Pike patrol.

There was now a pause while RAF Hunters struck at villages in the districts to the east. 3 Para Group patrols searched out the enemy ammunition and food reserves, finding a wide assortment of weapons ranging from British SMLE No 1 and No 4 to antique French Lebel rifles. There were several clashes with the enemy, CSM Arnold cleared 'Arnold's Ridge' with the anti-tank platoon, closely supported by the Hunters, and took the only live prisoners captured under arms in the campaign. 3 Para Troop RE laboured hard to cut a road forward from Shab Tem to advance the guns. In the rear, the Adjutant fed forward men and supplies, while the MTO, Lieutenant Duffy, extricated men and vehicles from the Wadi Rabwa, now flooded by the afternoon spate of seasonal rain. Captain Crane, the Quartermaster, built up forward stocks. The Regimental Sergeant Major curbed the enthusiasm of the Drum Major at being under fire when snipers returned. The doctor – Captain Callum – and Padre Preston established a sort of medical club near the Scout landing pad.

With the ending of the nearby air operations, it became possible to plan further advances, the aim being to show the tribesmen that nowhere were they safe from military action if they continued their attacks: they were to learn that they could be found in the most remote wadis and on the highest mountains. A Company were ordered to secure the tip of 'Arnold's Spur', a feature running south east from the tip of 'Arnold's Ridge'. But en route lay two village positions which required searching out in daylight.

Despite earlier action by CSM Arnold's patrol it was obvious that these villages were occupied by enemy. No sooner did C Company approach than they were fired on by rifles and automatic weapons. Supported by elements of I and J Batteries and the mortar platoon, they were able to clear the first two villages but they were held up by an open saddle on the far side of which there were a number of watch towers built of thick dry stone. The action soon became a Battalion battle and, supported by RAF Hunters, the enemy were cleared, leaving several dead in the area.

On examining the area a vast profusion of escape tunnels were found – these obviously built decades and perhaps centuries ago. The tunnels had been mined through the rock from the towers to the dead ground beyond. On one wall of a watch tower a bloodstain – some 12 feet in length – was found, confirming the fact that the enemy must have suffered a considerable number of casualties.

The possession of 'Arnold's Spur' enabled the force to observe the enemy stronghold along the Wadi Dhubsan, an area hitherto remote. Prior to this, traffic in arms and men in this area had been free but now plans were able to be made for the Radfan force temporarily to occupy the area. Due to rainstorms, this was postponed, but from the 24th preparations were put in hand to descend the 3,200 feet into the Dhubsan.

The operation was scheduled for two days, and during the 24/25th May routes were recced and stores brought in by helicopters. On the night 24th/25th patrols investigated the possible routes down from 'Arnold's Spur'. One narrow but adequate track beneath Jebel Haqla was discovered and the head of the Wadi Dhubsan was found to be passable despite an initial descent of a 30 ft. rock face, and a subsequent boulder strewn course. On the evening of the 25th C Company less one platoon established a picket line across to Jebel Haqla. At the same time the machine gun platoon and the CO's party started to rope down the cliff. At first light the machine guns were in position after a slow precipitous descent of the cliff and A Company were ready to enter the first area, the village of Bayn Al Gudr.

X Company, Royal Marines, who had come under command for the operation, now advanced further into the Wadi, which was not to remain quiet for long. Some fifty minutes later numerous reports were received that the enemy were re-entering the area in small groups of 7–12 men from the south, where they had been lying in ambush on another easier route into the area. Shortly X Company and elements from Bn HQ came under heavy small arms fire. At the same time the Scout aircraft – which had been moving the CO's 'R' Group forward into the Royal Marines position – was sniped at and forced to land some 500 yards ahead of X Company's position. The Intelligence Officer was wounded and all were forced to abandon the plane under fire.

It was found that the number of dissidents were in the region of fifty with light automatic weapons, six being noted firing simultaneously. X Company was unable to progress more than 600 yards further into the wadi. A Company passed round on their left whilst a reinforced platoon of C Company began to clear down from Jebel Haqla. This action, with the support of the RAF, a section of medium guns and battalion mortars, drove the enemy from the area.

Two REME NCOs of the AAC worked throughout the evening and successfully repaired the Scout and Major Jackson, the pilot, was able to fly it out. The Battalion Group was then withdrawn from the area by Royal Navy Wessex Helicopters.

Meanwhile Aden town itself had been quiet since December 1963, when a serious incident had taken place at the airport, from which the British High Commissioner, Sir Kennedy Trevaskis, narrowly escaped. Following it, a state of emergency had been declared throughout the Federation, 57 members of Asnag's party had been arrested and 280 Yemeni subjects deported. Two events in 1964 precipitated the outbreak of further trouble. The first was the announcement by Alec Douglas-Home's Conservative Government that Britain intended to grant independence to the Federation not later than 1968, but would maintain her base in Aden, to the extension of which, in Little Aden, 24th Brigade was to be transferred by the end of 1964 from Kenya, which would then become independent. The second was the advent to power in October of Wilson's Labour Government, which was expected to be less keen to keep the base and to support the traditional rulers.

From then on, a struggle was waged between the various factions which hoped to inherit power. Prominent among them was the National Liberation Front (NLF) which aimed at the removal of the British, the break-up of the Federation and the establishment of a Marxist-orientated state in league with Egypt and the Yemen. It had no inhibitions about the use of force to achieve its aims. November saw a serious outbreak of violence, which continued throughout 1965, in which there were 286 terrorist incidents, causing 237 casualties, one of the most unpleasant on 17 September, when a grenade was thrown at a party of seventy-three British schoolchildren about to fly back to Britain after the holidays, five of them being injured. Operations continued up-country, in which ten British soldiers were killed and sixty-one wounded.

1966 was the decisive year. In February Wilson's Government announced that it no longer intended to maintain defence facilities in the Federation after independence in 1968. Not surprisingly this intensi-fied the internal struggle and undermined the authority and confidence of the Federation's rulers, who knew that Egypt had 60,000 troops in the Yemen at that time. There were 480 terrorist incidents in the year, causing a total of 573 casualties, of whom 5 dead and 218 wounded were British servicemen. 1967 was even worse, exacerbated by the Six Day War between Israel and Egypt, in which accusations were made that Britain had helped the former.

Corporal John Valentine of the 3rd Royal Anglian describes a typical incident, which followed the arrival in the colony of a UN Mission, instructed by the General Assembly to 'Recommend practical steps for implementing previous UN Resolutions on South Arabia':

'Grenade', the shout that had so many times sent men of the 3rd Battalion diving to the ground was now pounding in my ears. I turned quickly to see Pte. Anderson appear from the smoke of the explosion and the grenadier making his bid for escape towards the Main Mosque. My mind racing, I let off two quick shots and yelled for pursuit. Before the section had gone 50 yards I was shouting at them to take cover from the heavy automatic fire from roof tops across the street. The firing stopped, we had silenced the guns, or more likely they had served their purpose. Our wounded grenadier had escaped to the Mosque, which we were forbidden to enter.

The date – 6th April 1967, Aden was in the grip of a General Strike, specially laid on to greet the UN Mission. The time – 0900 hrs, and 13 Platoon, 'D' Company, commanded by Lt. Harrington-

Spier, was moving into Section 'B' of Sheikh Othman in two patrols. Mission – to detect terrorist activity – mines, mortars, and generally to get a feeling of the strike-bound town. In the preceding two days there had been many shootings, energa* and hand grenade attacks, but no riots.

I quickly checked Pte. Anderson and found him to be only slightly injured from grenade splinters. The order 'continue the patrol' followed my sitrep. Once again the section pushed forward, moving steadily and slowly, each man covering the next as he slipped from doorway to doorway right along the front of the Mosque and then across the road into Street 5. Only half of the section were across the road when all hell broke loose from terrorist positions at the end of the street, in the Mosque itself and from tall buildings on either side of us. I heard a heavy exchange of fire from the Mosque behind me and realised that my 2IC, L/Cpl. Jarvis, and Ptes. Donald, Theophile and Butcher had been pinned down. Further back the platoon commander and his patrol had come under fire from the positions we had encountered earlier in the grenade incident. Fire was also coming from the streets to my left as Sgt. Green's patrol tried to work their way round to lend us support. Pte. Lanaghan and I covered each other as we moved in short dashes to the end of the street, searching for a way out. There seemed little hope at present, for on rounding the corner Lanaghan hurriedly dived back, as if blown by a mighty gust of wind.

Returning along the street, I checked on ammunition and casualties ready for the next move. The fire had not lessened. It seemed that the terrorists had plenty of ammunition for their Russian-made automatic rifles.

'Reorg. on street 10.' The order came from the platoon commander, with the news that a Saracen APC† and Saladin armoured car would be covering our move. We regrouped at the end of street 5. Counting the men, I found two were missing, Theophile and Butcher. Lt. Harrington-Spier, with Lanaghan, McCormick and Anderson moved back down the street to help them. They were still pinned down opposite the Mosque. A grenade came from the top of one of the tall buildings and landed not three feet from McCormick, giving

* Rifle-fired grenade.
† Armoured Personnel Carrier.

him a chance to exercise his lungs. He carried on shouting 'grenade' until it did what was expected and went off! Luckily – no casualties. Theophile and Butcher were retrieved and we started to move out step by step, from doorway to doorway, corner to corner, down to Street 11 to behind the cattle sheds where Company HQ and 14 Platoon were in position. We dashed the last 200 metres across open ground, and the patrol was out. It was over. We could relax a little.

Soon the men were resting their sweat-drenched bodies, swopping stories and laughing at one another's recent misfortunes. Who was it that had commented they had just been handed their lives on a golden platter?

They were unconcerned. Because of the strike, they had another problem – no mail again today!

The Six Day Arab–Israel War in June 1967 had decisively undermined the hopes of the Foreign Secretary, George Brown, of finding a peaceful solution to the Federation's future by improving relations with Egypt, and trouble brewed in the Federal army, as its officers began to be concerned about their future. The rulers' choice of the Arab officer to succeed the British commander, Brigadier J. B. Dye, sparked off a mutiny, which spread to the police. Rumours that the British were shooting Arab mutineers led, on 16 June, to an ambush in Aden's Crater town of British soldiers by police mutineers, in which four of the soldiers were killed. The High Commissioner, Sir Humphrey Trevelyan, and the Commander-in-Chief, Admiral Sir Michael Le Fanu, faced a difficult decision. If they ordered more troops into the city to rescue the bodies and deal with the police, they would put the lives of at least a hundred Britons all over the Federation at risk. To the anger of Lieutenant-Colonel Colin Mitchell, the commanding officer of the Argyll and Sutherland Highlanders, to which three of the dead men belonged, they stayed their hand. Two weeks later, after the affair had simmered down, the Highlanders re-entered the Crater in a skilful operation in which hardly a shot was fired. From then until the last left at the end of November 1967, British troops stood aside while the rival factions, the NLF, no longer supported by Egypt, and FLOSY (Front for the Liberation of Occupied South Yemen), which was, fought it out between them, the NLF gaining the upper hand.

Supported by a strong naval task force from the Far East, the remaining garrison of 3,500 men was evacuated between 24 and 29

November, feeling a guilty conscience at abandoning the rulers, and the Federation army soldiers with whom they had fought side by side up-country, and resentment at the political decisions which had made their efforts all in vain. In the eleven months of 1967 there had been over 3,000 incidents, in which the casualty list totalled 1,248, the British forces having suffered 44 killed and 325 wounded. The Aden garrison was replaced by a smaller body of troops stationed at Sharjah and Bahrain in the Persian Gulf, the army element of which numbered 900.

Borneo

While Aden's troubles had been brewing, the army was engaged in a more satisfactory campaign further east. This started in December 1962 with a rebellion against the Sultan of Brunei, supported from across the border by Indonesia, whose pro-Communist dictator, Achmed Sukarno, objected to the incorporation of the territories of northern Borneo, Sarawak and Sabah (North Borneo), into the Federation of Malaysia, due to come into existence in September 1963. It had been hoped that Brunei would also accede to it. Sukarno wished to add all these territories to the rest of Kalimantan, the Indonesian name for their four-fifths of the huge island. The prompt dispatch of 1/2nd Gurkha Rifles and the Queen's Own Highlanders from Singapore, followed by the 1st Green Jackets and two Royal Marine Commandos, snuffed out the rebellion in eleven days, 40 rebels being killed and nearly 2,000 detained. The only British casualties were five Royal Marines killed and several more wounded in an amphibious assault on Limbang.

The regimental journal of the Highlanders describes a critical period of their defeat of the rebels in Seria, site of the important Shell Oil Company's installation, into the airstrip of which they had been flown early in the morning of 10 December.

At 0930 hrs. the C.O.* ordered O.C. 'A' Company to establish a firm road block in the area of the Brunei Police Mobile Reserve Unit

* Lieutenant-Colonel W. G. McHardy.

Barracks at the extreme West end of Seria. As the Police were
reluctant to operate alone, O.C. 'A' Coy. decided to move 2 Platoon
from the road block about ¾ mile East of Panaga Police Station and
to command the mixed force personally until it was established.

At 1100 hrs. 2 Platoon and two sections of Brunei Police, under
the command of O.C. 'A' Coy, left Panaga Police Station in transport.
Shortly after moving off, a jeep/land-rover appeared in the far
distance, turned round and disappeared. Taking no chances, Major
Cameron gave the order to debus. 2 Platoon took up the lead with
Cpl. McGovern's section in front moving in broken arrowhead
formation on either side of the road. There was a halt after the first
½ mile as the Company Commander realised that the Police had not
followed – they were quickly brought to heel and followed on.
Moving quickly, 2 Platoon reached the roundabout without incident.
The leading section doubled across the roundabout and started down
the Kuala Belait road, but when they were 100 yards short of the
Istana Kota Menggalela (The Sultan's country palace) a car suddenly
appeared from the Palace grounds.

The Company Commander ordered Cpl. McGovern's section to
open fire. The car was hit several times and rolled into the ditch –
the driver, obviously seriously wounded, fell out of the door but got
away during the ensuing battle. As the leading section fired at the
car, heavy fire came from the Palace – there was obviously one
L.M.G. there and a number of rifles. Fortunately no one was hit and
Cpl. McGovern quickly got his section down and returned the fire.
The Company Commander ordered the two rear sections of 2
Platoon to fan out on the right flank with Cpl. Hoddinott's section
on the left and L/Cpl. Turner's section on the right. The Police were
given the task of watching the beach.

Cpl. Hoddinott and L/Cpl. Turner got their sections leapfrogging
towards the Palace until they were in a position at the forward edge
of the jungle strip in fire positions. This movement was made under
fire of the rebels' L.M.G. which was then covering that approach
along a track which divided L/Cpl. Turner's section and it was very
lucky that no one was hit. The order was given to watch and shoot,
and Cpl. McGovern's section was ordered to leapfrog into a better
position which they did quickly. Fire control was bad to start with,
but after a short time it became very good and the shooting in many
cases was excellent. Under covering fire from L/Cpl. Turner's section,

Major Cameron, Lt. McCall, Ptes. Cowie and Firmstone, all armed with tear gas grenades, doubled forward to the edge of the building. Major Cameron and Lt. McCall threw their grenades through ground floor windows. Lt. McCall, moving round the corner, saw a rebel who was holding a No. 4 rifle and shot him in the centre of his body. After this brief action, the party returned to the jungle strip as it was hoped that the tear gas would persuade the rebels to surrender. After about 5 minutes, it was obvious that they were determined to stay, and they increased their fire. Cpl. Hoddinott's section, under covering fire from L/Cpl. Turner's section, then moved out parallel to the sea along a line of trees. From there they doubled forward to the bay windows and threw one tear gas grenade and one irritant grenade and then returned to their original position.

Still the rebels continued firing. Major Cameron, Lt. McCall and L/Cpl. Turner's section approached the house from the jungle strip and took up firing positions along the balcony outside the bay windows covering all the windows on their side. Lt. McCall and Major Cameron entered the large room which was empty. They then cleared the other two rooms on the ground floor finding one wounded rebel (the one Lt. McCall shot) who surrendered. Major Cameron followed by L/Cpl. Turner and his section moved upstairs. Suddenly a rebel appeared with his hands up. Major Cameron doubled up the stairs and handed him over to L/Cpl. Turner. He then entered the first room on the first floor to be confronted by five rebels. He fired a shot over their heads and they dropped their weapons and put their hands up. The rest of the house was then cleared room by room. A dead rebel sniper was found on the roof. Cpl. Hoddinott was ordered to search the rear building and one more rebel surrendered. A total of nine rebels were taken, one of whom was killed and one wounded. During the attack, five had escaped – two of whom were fired at and hit by Sgt. McLeman and three of whom were seen, but not fired at, by the Police. Eight No. 4 rifles, 1 L.M.G., 1 Sten gun, teargas, a lot of ammunition, and police uniforms were taken.

2 Pl.[,] having reorganised, then advanced to clear the Brunei Police Mobile Reserve Unit (M.R.U.) Barracks approximately ½ mile due west of the Istana. Lt. McCall and a small group moved through the scrub and jungle while Sgt. McLeman commanded the rest of the Platoon as it moved astride the road. Two rebels got up in the jungle

and ran towards the road and although both were fired at and hit, both escaped. Two L.M.Gs had failed to work during the attack on the Istana. On reaching the M.R.U, Sgt. McLeman began repairing them, and had finished the second one when a car approached. He tested the L.M.G and stopped the car with one shot through the windscreen grazing the side of the passenger's head. The driver leaped out of the car carrying a shot gun and ammunition and ran towards the Platoon. He had taken only a few steps when he was shot dead. 2 Platoon then cleared the M.R.U. Barracks which had been ransacked, and the surrounding houses. Having completed their task and pulled down the rebel flag, the Platoon moved back down the road to the roundabout and took up positions covering all three roads leading to it.

Although the rebellion within Brunei was thus rapidly and effectively quelled, proving the value of having forces available near to hand, rather than dependent on deployment half across the world, there were signs that the Indonesians were intent on subverting all three territories by infiltrating their own men across the thousand-mile long frontier, which ran through jungle-covered mountains 8,000 feet high. By this time Major-General W. C. Walker, commander of the 17th Gurkha Division, had assumed command of all forces in the three territories. When Malaysia came into being in September 1963 he became technically subordinate to the Malaysian National Operations Committee, of which the Joint Service Commander-in-Chief Far East, Admiral Sir Varyl Begg, was a member, having succeeded the first occupant of that post, Admiral Sir David Luce, in April. There were several incidents in the rest of the year before a ceasefire in January 1964, following an appeal by the UN Secretary-General; but when talks broke down in February, the Indonesian army openly assumed responsibility for operations across the border, abandoning the pretence that the soldiers and marines in their special units were volunteers, helping local insurgents. Its tactics were to send bodies of 100 or 200 men over the border to establish jungle bases, from which they would intimidate the local inhabitants, mostly Dyak tribesmen, and gradually bring about a de facto extension of Indonesian authority.

Hitherto Walker had held his troops well away from the frontier, relying for information on small patrols, many from the SAS, in contact with the tribesmen. To counter the Indonesian tactic he had to set up bases of his own near the frontier, strong enough to resist attack by Indonesian forces of 100 or more. These were established at company strength, dependent for their supply and reinforcement on helicopters, of which there were never enough. The majority of the heavier lift ones were the naval Wessex, detached from the commando-carrier. Further talks in Tokyo in June 1964 between Tunku Abdul Rahman for Malaysia and Sukarno, under the chairmanship of President Macapagal of the Philippines, proved fruitless, and were soon followed by further Indonesian incursions into Sarawak, of which there were thirteen in July, and an unsuccessful attempt to land 100 men from the sea and 200 from the air in southern Malaya. Walker viewed with concern the increase in Indonesian activity, combined with the internal security problem posed by Communist penetration of the Chinese community in Sarawak, and asked for reinforcements, which he received. By the end of the year he had 14,000 men in three Malay and eighteen British battalions, of which eight were Gurkha and two Royal Marine Commandos, supported by five batteries of light artillery, two squadrons of armoured cars, sixty RAF and Royal Naval helicopters and forty army ones, manned by the Army Air Corps, which also manned light fixed-wing aircraft, for which landing strips were made at company bases.

Captain M. O. St Martin of the 10th Gurkha Rifles recounts his clash with a party of Indonesians in this period:

At 0845 hrs. on 2nd October 1964 began the ten most uncomfortable minutes in the lives of one British Officer, two QGOs* and four Gurkhas of 2nd 10th Gurkhas; seven men all told were ambushed by between 80 and 100 Indonesians while on a recce for ambush positions near the border. In recent weeks the enemy had been firing at night from the top of a hill inside Sarawak to intimidate the local Dyaks. I had been ordered to ambush the approaches to this hill. I left my base about 3,000 yards from the border with a recce party comprising two platoon commanders and two GORs.†

As we approached the area of the proposed ambush we found on the track an OG‡ cap, as worn by Indonesians and, nearby, the imprints of Indonesian boots.

* Queen's Gurkha officers.
† Gurkha other ranks.
‡ Olive green.

Nearing the top of a small rise the leading scout, who was crouched down, looked to his left and then turned, saying 'Dushman, Dushman', stepped back and in doing so pushed me backwards. At that very moment an Indonesian on the left fired and the round struck a tree to my right in direct line with where my head had been a second before. The enemy were about five yards off the track.

Firing broke out from all sides at point blank range. I saw four men charging from my left and as the leading scout passed back behind me, I fired four shots; the Indonesian on the right of the line five yards away and nearest the path screamed after the fourth round. Capt. (QGO) Manbahadur Rai now gave covering fire from behind, vicious bursts from his rifle on automatic, and I and the leading scout raced back down the path past him. Manbahadur's prompt reaction kept the enemy's heads down for precious seconds.

The remainder of the patrol now sought a good position from which to fight back, but we were still in the middle of the ambush and fire was coming from both sides and down the path. The enemy had at least one LMG (Bren) and several Browning machine guns. They threw grenades, but none did any damage, and opened fire with 50mm mortars, the bombs falling to the left and right further down the path behind us.

Our patrol found a slight rise and gave covering fire to allow Capt. Manbahadur to rejoin. A check was made; amazingly all were safe and sound. A shot had whipped off Sgt. Narsingbahadur Limbu's jungle hat. More firing and the enemy were again on both sides. Another move. Fire was again returned and the enemy became more cautious, moving forward using fire and movement in rushes.

Our seven men set off back down the track and quickly reached the main path at the bottom of the rise. From then on the enemy lost contact, although they hurried us on our way by a long burst of automatic fire whilst crossing a clearing.

Fifteen minutes later, we were relieved to meet 15 Platoon coming forward up the track to our aid.

Safe at last, first reactions were surprise at being still alive. For this we must thank the alertness and quick reaction of the leading scout; the immediate returning of the enemy fire by Captain Manbahadur; our continued use of fire and movement during the fighting withdrawal. One must also not forget fleetness of foot and the shocking musketry of the enemy.

We learnt (Re-learnt?) two lessons:—

First: Don't continue directly up a track on which you have just found such obvious traces of the enemy as jungle hat and recent footmarks.

Second: Small recce patrols of VIPs should not normally be sent out more than a map square or two from their platoon base.

If the Indonesians had been 'on target' that morning there would have been a lot of promotion in the Second Tenth.

Neither Britain nor Malaysia was technically at war with Indonesia and the conflict was referred to by both sides as 'confrontation'. It did not suit either side to extend hostilities to the sea nor to air attacks against targets on the mainland territory of the other. Walker, however, obtained authority to operate across the border into Kalimantan, provided that the fact that he did so was kept strictly secret. Acting on interception of Indonesian radio communications, these operations proved highly effective. By the time Walker handed over command to Major-General G. H. Lea in March 1965, the tide had turned clearly in favour of Britain and Malaysia, although Indonesian attacks across the border continued. Their effort virtually ceased after the internal coup in Indonesia in October, which led to a struggle between pro- and anti-Communist factions. The victor was the anti-Communist General Thojib Suharto, who ousted Sukarno in March 1966, and remained in power for the next thirty-two years.

Five months later 'confrontation' came to an end. It had been a satisfactory and successful campaign, skilfully and economically conducted. At its peak 17,000 servicemen, including Australians and New Zealanders from the Commonwealth Brigade in Malaya, had taken part. Of them 114 had been killed and 181 wounded, a high proportion Gurkha; 36 civilians had been killed, 53 wounded and 4 captured, almost all local inhabitants. It was estimated that 590 Indonesians had been killed, 222 wounded and 771 captured. The 'confrontation' had lasted four years and triumphantly achieved its aim of establishing the Federation of Malaysia, although Brunei never joined and Singapore withdrew from it in August 1965.

The army in Borneo was fortunate in its commanders, who were as different from each other as chalk from cheese. Walker brought with him the experience of jungle warfare that he had gained fighting the

Japanese in Burma and more recently the terrorists in Malaya, and his knowledge of the Gurkha soldier, with whom he had always served. He was a professional to his fingertips in that type of warfare, and did not conceal his contempt for those who were not, whether his subordinates or superiors. Determined, inflexible and abrupt, he set an example of determination and thoroughness. Lea brought his experience of Malaya in the SAS, accompanied by a charm and flair for handling people of all kinds which drew the best out of them, as well as a clarity of mind and shrewd judgement.

*

When the Borneo campaign finished, Harold Wilson's Labour Government faced severe economic difficulties and was determined to reduce defence expenditure to £2,000 million a year by major cuts, especially in the forces stationed east of Suez. Within six months of the end of 'confrontation', British troops in northern Borneo were to be reduced to one infantry battalion and one engineer squadron, both preferably Gurkha, and in Singapore and Malaysia to the Royal Marine Commando Brigade and the British contribution to 28th Commonwealth Brigade in Malaya. The Gurkhas were to be reduced from 15,000 to 10,000, the figure which had been agreed in 1947 with India and Nepal.

The army's 'UK adult male' strength was to be reduced by 15,000 from the 196,000 to which it had grown. The total reduction in all three services was to be continued after 1971 until it reached 75,000, when the army's strength would be reduced to only 1,100 above Duncan Sandys's 1957 figure of 165,000. The initial reduction meant the loss of four regiments each in the Royal Armoured Corps and the Royal Artillery, and three squadrons in the Royal Engineers. The infantry was reduced by eight battalions, some preferring disbandment to amalgamation. The Fusiliers, Green Jackets, Light Infantry and the remaining Irish regiments each formed a 'large regiment', that is, an amalgamation of several (usually three) regiments, which shared some territorial or historic link, into one new one, in which officers and men could be transferred and promoted freely between battalions. The Army Council followed the principle that each infantry 'brigade' (in its organizational, not its operational sense), whether or not it chose to form a large regiment, should lose one battalion, normally the junior one.

Less than six months later, the deepening economic crisis led the

Government to decide on more drastic measures. Withdrawal from Singapore and Malaysia, and also from the Persian Gulf, was to be total and completed by 1971, the Gurkhas being further reduced to 6,000, most of them in Hong Kong. Britain's defence effort was to be 'concentrated mainly in Europe and the North Atlantic area' and 'no special capability for use outside Europe' would be maintained when withdrawal from the Far East and the Gulf was completed. The navy's aircraft carriers were to be phased out and the total manpower reduction of 75,000 accelerated.

The result was that when Edward Heath's Conservative Government came to power in 1970 the Household Division had been reduced to two cavalry regiments, each of which contributed one mounted ceremonial squadron, and seven battalions of Foot Guards, the Scots Guards losing their 2nd Battalion, which was soon restored; the Royal Armoured Corps was reduced to thirteen regiments of cavalry and four of the Royal Tank Regiment; the Royal Artillery to twenty-one regiments, and the infantry, including the SAS and the Parachute Regiment, to forty-one battalions. Two regiments, reduced to company strength, were restored to full battalion strength shortly afterwards, raising the total to forty-three, while the Gurkhas had been reduced to five.

The Territorial Army

Earlier in its term of office, Wilson's Government, with Denis Healey as Defence Secretary, had effected a major reorganization of the Territorial Army, merging it with the army's other volunteer reserve, the Army Emergency Reserve. The latter was generally a reserve of individuals, rather than of units with a local territorial connection. It was a valuable and economic reserve which provided the army with a reserve of skilled men, who could be called up under the same conditions as the regular reserve. It was closely tied to the regular army and not protected by the hierarchy of the Territorial Army Associations. It was unfortunate that, when it was merged with the latter, it practically disappeared, although, thirty years later, it was generally recognized that reinforcement by individual volunteers was the primary requirement and that the likelihood of Territorial Army units being employed as such was very small.

Macmillan's Conservative administration had recognized that, as Territorial Army formations could not be made ready for operations in less than at least three months, they were only suited to home defence, which was generally taken to mean assistance to civil defence in dealing with the aftermath of a nuclear attack. The Territorial Army had relied heavily on using stocks of equipment left over from the Second World War, which by then were worn out and obsolete. It was clearly impossible to provide modern equipment, even for training, for a force which, in theory, was organized to provide eleven divisions. It was in any case becoming difficult to recruit enough men for each unit to give them any sort of interesting or meaningful training. That in itself discouraged volunteers. These inescapable realities persuaded the Army Council to approve a major reduction in the size of the two reserves combined, and to alter the emphasis to that of filling gaps in the regular army's organization required for major war, with a new and clumsy title, the Territorial and Army Volunteer Reserve (T&AVR), which a subsequent Conservative administration reverted to Territorial Army. Such a smaller reserve could be adequately provided with modern equipment and uniform, and be given realistic training. The plan was fought tooth and nail by the county Territorial Associations and the hierarchy of the Territorial Army, led by the Duke of Norfolk, as they saw their local units disappearing. Reductions in those arms which required heavy equipment were especially severe, the Yeomanry being cut to one armoured car regiment, although a second one was formed some years later. Some Yeomanry maintained their existence in name by conversion to infantry. The latter was reduced to thirty-seven battalions.

Northern Ireland

1968 was a unique year, being the only one since 1660, it is believed, in which the British army was not actively engaged in some form of operation, unless its presence in the UN Force in Cyprus is counted as such. But 1969 was to see an old sore reopened – that of the Irish troubles.

By August the Royal Ulster Constabulary (RUC) had become unable to cope with the disorders in Belfast and Londonderry, which arose from the activity of the Catholic-based Northern Ireland Civil Rights Association (NICRA), the reaction of the hardline Protestants, led by Ian Paisley, and the hostility of the Catholic population to the RUC's intervention. This persuaded Wilson's Government to order the intervention of troops to maintain order and, hopefully, to act as a peacekeeping force more acceptable to the Catholics. The normal garrison, under the command of Lieutenant-General Sir Ian Freeland, consisted of the 39th Brigade with two infantry battalions and an armoured car regiment. This did not suffice to deal with the rioting crowds, especially in Belfast, and it was soon reinforced by six more units. By the end of the year it had been increased to ten, by which time its task had changed. It was no longer just one of keeping the Protestants and Catholics apart, nor of replacing the police in Catholic areas, for the Irish Republican Army (IRA), which had had a hand in instigating the agitation of NICRA, had exploited the situation to turn the Catholic population against the army and had itself entered the fray. Whatever may have been the original intention, it was not prepared to tolerate a situation in which the British army, the traditional target, could be accepted as the protectors of the Catholic population, a role it claimed for itself.

1970 was a year of major rioting on both sides of the sectarian fence, combined with the occasional armed attack on police stations, individual members of the RUC, particularly of the Special Branch, and on army patrols. The RUC had ceased to operate in the predominantly Catholic areas of Belfast and Londonderry, and the army operated out of company and platoon bases that more and more resembled fortresses, as did police stations in adjacent areas. To cover the sensitive period of traditional Protestant marches, commemorating the battles of the Boyne and of the Somme in July in Belfast, and the resistance, in James II's siege of Londonderry of the Apprentice Boys from London, who added the name of England's capital to the town of Derry, the garrison was increased to fifteen units, and reduced again by the end of the year to eight. In June Heath's Conservative administration replaced Wilson's, Lord Carrington taking Healey's place as Defence Secretary, and Reginald Maudling, as Home Secretary, assuming responsibility for Northern

Ireland from James Callaghan. In 1970 also an addition was made to the
army's organization in the form of the Ulster Defence Regiment, a part-
time volunteer body, intended to replace the RUC's 'B Special' Reserve,
which had been accused of being a purely Protestant force, oppressing
the Catholics.

The situation did not improve in the new year. The IRA increased its
activity, and armed attacks on the security forces became more frequent,
the worst one being the brutal murder of three young soldiers of the
Royal Highland Fusiliers in March. Pressure from the Protestant right
wing, indignant at what it saw as the weakness of the Northern Ireland
Government at Stormont, which it attributed to its deference to Westminster, ousted James Chichester-Clark as Prime Minister and replaced
him with Brian Faulkner, a tough and astute businessman and politician,
who exploited Heath's reluctance to involve the Westminster Government in direct responsibility for the affairs of the province. Lieutenant-
General Sir Harry Tuzo, who had taken over command after the death
of Lieutenant-General Vernon Erskine-Crum immediately after he had
replaced Freeland, was in a difficult position. Faulkner's Northern Ireland
Government was responsible for the affairs of the province, including
the RUC, although, like other police forces in the United Kingdom, they
maintained that they were responsible only to the law. Tuzo and the
armed forces in the province were responsible to the Secretary of State
for Defence in London. He therefore had to walk delicately, like Agag,
between Stormont and Westminster.

Trouble escalated in June 1971 when two men in Londonderry were
shot dead by the army when seen to be about to fire weapons. Tuzo had
been persuaded to let the local Catholic community attempt to convince
the inhabitants of the Bogside and Creggan to bring things back to
normal, but after this incident it was clear that that policy was not
effective. By mid-July the situation both there and in Belfast had
deteriorated; rioting was frequent, petrol- and nail-bombs often being
thrown at the troops. Pressure on Faulkner from Paisley and the other
hardline Protestants to introduce internment of suspected IRA members
increased, and the annual Apprentice Boys' march in August became a
test case. Paisley insisted that it must take place, demanding internment
as a quid pro quo if it was cancelled or restricted. The possibility of
introducing internment had been under consideration in Whitehall for
some time and preparations put in hand in case it was decided upon,

but they would not be complete before November. A week before the march was due, Faulkner faced Heath with the challenge of either agreeing to internment or assuming responsibility from Stormont. The decision was for the former.

Tuzo was reinforced with three battalions to assist in the operation which, on 9 August, picked up 326 out of a list of 520 names provided by the RUC Special Branch, the accuracy of which was open to considerable doubt. It had always been hoped that a by-product of the pick-up would be the information obtained from interrogating a select few of the more important IRA personalities, and the army's intelligence experts had given instruction and administrative help to the RUC Special Branch to implement it. Procedures were based on those which had been used in Aden and had been developed as a result of the experience of British troops taken prisoner in the Korean War, in order to train men to resist such interrogation. Their use in this case caused the Government considerable embarrassment.

In spite of the introduction of internment, violence and terrorism increased, incidents escalating from an average of sixty a month to over a hundred. The predominantly Catholic housing areas of Londonderry and Belfast became IRA strongholds, in which the authority of both the Stormont and the Westminster Governments was flouted. In Londonderry gangs of rioting youths were gradually reducing the streets on the borders of the Bogside to rubble. NICRA planned a protest march there on Sunday 30 January 1972, and it was decided that if it resulted in further rioting an attempt was to be made to 'snatch' a number of the rioters and bring them to court. Two additional battalions were sent to Londonderry to man twenty-six roadblocks in order to prevent the marchers from penetrating into the Protestant area of the city. When the snatch operation was ordered, the troops involved, from 1st Battalion The Parachute Regiment, came under fire, or at least thought they had, and returned it, killing thirteen and injuring the same number. The IRA quickly named it 'Bloody Sunday', and although Lord Widgery's tribunal, which investigated the affair, concluded that 'The soldiers acted as they did because they thought their orders required it', he described the action of some of them as 'bordering on the reckless' and stated that the brigade commander might have underestimated the hazard to civilians in employing an arrest force in circumstances under which the troops were liable to come under fire.

Whatever the rights or wrongs, it set back current hopes of a possible political solution. An account of an earlier operation by A Company of that battalion in Belfast illustrates the sort of thing that the soldiers were having to face at that time:

The company had taken over as first reserve standby for Belfast at 0900 hours on the Friday. The morning began quietly by preparing men, equipment, weapons and vehicles for deployment. The company was put on State 1 (ten minutes notice to move) to assist in countering the threat of disturbances around the Law Courts. At 1130 hours a request for one search team from the company was made. Their task was to search a house in Vancouver Street in the north of Belfast.

Just before midday the company was placed on immediate notice to move to come under command of a battalion in the Falls area. At 1440 hours the order was given for the company to deploy to Paisley Park. Trouble had broken out in the area of Leeson Street. Riotous crowds had stolen buses and articulated vehicles to block off the streets. A fuel tanker had also been stolen.

Just before 1600 hours the company was ordered into the Falls to the Panton/Falls junction. When the company arrived it was ordered to go on foot down Panton Street to clear crowds forming in Leeson Street. This they did but with limited success in arresting rioters who ran away and hid, some of them behind the burning vehicles. The locals were very hostile to all Security Forces in the area.

Troops were widely dispersed in maintaining control in the streets. The locals mobbed up pairs of soldiers stretched along Leeson Street. The most hostile groups were the women, most of them teenage girls, who poured insults on 'The Army of Occupation'. Some arrests were made. In the end the barricades (burnt out double decker buses and lorries) were dragged away by Army tractors and recovery vehicles. At 1800 hours the company was ordered to the junction of Cupar Street/Falls Road. On arrival it was given the task of arresting rioters in the Balaklava and Millinkin Street area. Raglan Street runs parallel to the Falls Road and both streets are joined by numerous small ones. The rioters' tactics were to use Raglan Street for movement, then create disturbances by throwing stones, missiles or bottles with the occasional bomb from an adjoining street on to the Falls Road. They attempted to draw troops into ambush.

The direct approach of snatch squads is rarely effective or successful. A useful tactic was to set up a decoy target in one street, then infiltrate quietly along a parallel street and try to take the rioters by surprise from a flank or in the rear. This needed to be done quickly because rioters have their lookouts to warn the main body. We employed these tactics with success in the Balaklava Street area. When the gangs found their numbers depleting, they escalated the situation to bomb throwing. Petrol bombs with a mixture of nail bombs and some gelignite were used.

We penetrated Balaklava Street and more petrol and nail bombs were thrown. One Ferret* was set on fire. The CO decided that if the bomb attacks continued we would have to fire at identified bombers. The rioters were warned twice that this would happen. Some good snipers were placed behind three Ferrets which then nosed into Balaklava Street. Further bomb attacks came from Inkerman Street corner. A soldier fired and one bomber was reported hit. The company then moved up to the corner of Inkerman and snipers were positioned to cover Inkerman Street, down Balaklava and Ross Street. More petrol and nail bombs were thrown. Fire was again ordered, two hits were reported. We then moved down to Ross Street, both sides of Balaklava to Raglan Street and to our rear down Inkerman. Two Ferrets and a searchlight Land Rover illuminated Ross and Balaklava Street. One Ferret was moved down Balaklava Street and was attacked by a gelignite bomber. Two further attacks came from the Raglan Street corners of Balaklava, petrol and nail bombs were thrown. There was more shooting and two more hits reported. After each engagement we rushed to the street corners hoping to arrest the bombers and capture the wounded rioters but they had been dragged away.

The area was quiet by 0100 hours. A civilian doctor and his stretcher party were seen in Raglan Street. Two rioters, those most seriously wounded, were evacuated to the Royal Victoria Hospital. One was dead and one seriously injured in the head and shoulders. The remainder were evacuated by the rioters themselves. Company patrols found several unused petrol bombs and two nail bombs on window sills and street corners. We were relieved at 0500 hours to

* Scout car.

return to Paisley Park where we went back into reserve. Seven arrests
had been made.

The company search team had been hard at it as well. The
deployed search team under Cpl. Butler rejoined the company before
we went into Balaklava Street. He brought the good news of an
excellent find in Vancouver Street. L/Cpl. Maddocks had removed
some flooring in a garage and found: M1 carbine, two shot guns,
$6 \times 7,000$ of SA ammo, explosives, two bombs and electric detonators and various detonators and fuses.

One clear result of Bloody Sunday was Heath's decision no longer to
carry the can for decisions and policies made at Stormont. On 24 March
Faulkner and his Government resigned rather than accept that full
responsibility for security should pass to Westminster, with the result
that it did. Direct Rule became the order of the day. The Home
Secretary's rather vague responsibility for it was transferred to a Secretary
of State for Northern Ireland, to which position William Whitelaw was
appointed. This eased Tuzo's problems, although he still had a dual
responsibility: to Whitelaw and, through the Chief of the General Staff,*
to Carrington.

The new regime, hoping to be more popular with the Catholic
community than the Protestant-dominated Stormont, ushered in a new
policy of low profile in the hope that the 'hearts and minds' of the
Catholic population could be weaned away from the IRA, but both the
IRA and the Protestant hardliners had a vested interest in seeing that it
did not work. Any concession to Catholic sensitivities roused Protestant
anger and suspicion, while failure to deal with acts of violence or
defiance of authority by Protestant organizations brought Catholic accusations that the authorities were in league with them.

One example of this was the attempt by the Ulster Defence Association (UDA) to establish 'no-go' areas, equivalent to those in the Catholic
areas, such as the Bogside and Creggan in Londonderry and Anderstown
in Belfast. Because the latter were both a challenge to the Government's
authority and a provocation to the Protestants, planning started for a
major operation in which the army would clear away the barricades and
establish its presence and authority within them. Any hesitation over the
possibility of something bloodier than Bloody Sunday was dispelled by

---

* He had ceased to be 'Imperial' in 1964.

the events of 21 July, when twenty bombs were exploded simultaneously in Belfast, killing 10 and injuring 130, most of them in the main bus station. For Operation MOTORMAN, which took place on 31 July, Tuzo was reinforced to a strength of twenty-seven battalions, giving him 21,000 men, and 9,000 UDR were also called up. It was not resisted by the IRA and was entirely successful in its aim.

By the end of 1972 the garrison had been reduced again to eighteen battalions. Royal Armoured Corps and Royal Artillery units were called upon to serve four-month tours as infantry. C Squadron of the 4th/7th Royal Dragoon Guards, commanded by Major Raymond Layard, was attached to the Life Guards in that role in the autumn of 1972. In their journal he describes their experience:

Throughout September the Squadron was detached from The Life Guards and placed under command of the Welsh Guards for duty in the city centre on Operation 'Segment'. The main object of this is to prevent bombing by dividing the city into chunks or segments through which traffic may flow. Cars are not allowed to park unattended and passes are needed for drivers with vehicles wishing to go into a segment. In addition, as many pedestrians as possible were frisked. No: women were not searched! Twenty-four hours a day the Squadron provided up to 40 men in four-hour shifts. Good for watching life, and Belfast gradually recover its nerve after 'Bloody Friday' but much of the time it was very dull. As an operation, 'Segment' has succeeded, although it takes a large number of men. No bombs have been detonated within the area since the operation started but some have been very close to the edges of it.

Meanwhile, back in east Belfast . . . 'You have 20 minutes to get out'. An anonymous telephone call gives a bomb warning; police and army are called in. Once on the scene a mobile patrol helps clear the area around the threatened spot. Time is up and there is either a shattering explosion followed by the tinkle of falling glass and thudding of masonry or – nothing. It is a scare and the locals with their nerves already frayed are left to themselves. Sometimes, of course, there is no warning and it is no scare!

'Hello 33 Foxtrot: This is 3, move to . . . and investigate report of Tartans ("youths" of various ages) breaking windows and making a nuisance of themselves.' Off goes 33F with other patrols moving towards the spot. Their job is to try to catch the culprits red-handed and this is very difficult at night. More often than not it ends in a cat-and-mouse chase through the streets of the district without any arrests. Sometimes such louts are picked up; one lately with a great lump of metal still in his hand. It is remarkable how good the intelligence of these gangs is for they never hit a Protestant property; only Catholic.

Then came the troubles in east Belfast in mid-October beside which all our other experiences paled. After the desecration of the Willowfield RC Church, trouble which had been expected for several nights broke out on Sunday evening.

We were called out to reinforce 2 Squadron who had been stretched by several gangs of Tartans. On arrival we posted sentries and all seemed quiet for a short time until four or six shots rang out. Out of the 'pigs' (Humber 1-ton armoured*) we dived, cocking our SLRs† at the same time as we hit the deck. The Troop Leader ran up the street to investigate followed by one or two others, including me. We searched a few of the bystanders on the street corners but found no trace of the gunman so we returned to the vehicles. The next thing was smoke and flames coming from a car not far away. A half section (five men) went to investigate and was met by a crowd of about 50 Tartans but, with no riot kit, we were forced to withdraw, firing rubber bullets as we did so. The vehicles now moved up to us and about this time one of our men was hit by a bottle in the face and carted off to hospital. With the riot kit, shields, helmets and more rubber bullet guns we pushed the Tartans back and up towards 2 Squadron. This was seen by the Tartans and rather than get caught in the middle they melted away.

One or two of the rioters had Army-type short shields which they had picked up in an earlier scrap. After that we returned to the vehicles and that was that. One casualty and thirty or so rubber bullets fired.

On Monday night we dismounted and with small rushes up Albertbridge Road moved a crowd of 150 or so East. The Life Guards were coming towards us and the rioters rather than be caught in the middle disappeared down a side street behind two lorries. Up to that point we had only had bricks, bottles and firecrackers thrown at us,

---

* Wheeled armoured personnel carriers.
† Self-loading rifles.

but now shooting started. A soldier was hit by a bullet in the head and evacuated, the Troop Leader returned fire. The next thing that happened; two dust carts were started up and set off towards us. One of our men was pinned underneath one dust cart and we were getting him clear when a burst of Thompson* was fired at us. We took cover in the gardens and returned the fire which quickly dispersed the riot. We shot a street light out; stayed where we were until Maj. Cooper (2 Sqn Leader) took over and then only adjusted our positions to act as stops for an operation which a company of Green Jackets was doing. That was it, really; we had no more contact and returned to camp half an hour later.

Much more has, of course, happened; the Albert Bridge VCP† where 2,000 vehicles were searched in 36 hours; Sirocco works and the confrontation with Billy Hull and his men from Harland and Wolff; dealings with the UDA; the Squadron search team at work; waiting for action which never came on operation 'Motorman'; the frightful language from the women and children contrasted with Protestant and Catholic children enjoying themselves at the hut near Donaghadee.

During this time an attempt to find a political solution was made at the Darlington Conference in September, the outcome of which was a proposal that after a plebiscite to obtain the views of the population of the province as to whether or not the border with the Republic should be maintained, a Northern Ireland Government should be reinstated at Stormont on a power-sharing basis. At the same time the possibility of some link with the Republic would be pursued. The plebiscite was postponed until March 1973, by which time Lieutenant-General Sir Frank King had replaced Tuzo. It passed off without incident and gave the answer expected, a majority against Union with the Republic. The elections to the new Northern Ireland Assembly also passed off quietly at the end of June, Faulkner's Official Unionists gaining the highest number of seats – twenty-three out of seventy-eight; but other Unionists came close. Without their cooperation, Faulkner formed an Executive with five of his own supporters, four of Fitt's Catholic SDLP and one from the middle of the road Alliance Party. Violent incidents of all kinds

---

* Thompson sub-machine-gun.
† Vehicle Control Point.

continued, but at a reduced level. In 1972 there had been 10,628 shooting and 1,853 bomb incidents: 239 civilians, and 103 regular army, 20 UDR and 17 RUC men had been killed. In 1973 the figures fell to 5,018 shooting and 1,520 bomb incidents: 127 civilians, 58 regular army, 8 UDR and 12 RUC killed.

The hopes raised by these constitutional changes were dashed in 1974. The first General Election in Britain in that year came at a critical time for Faulkner's delicately poised Executive. The Sunningdale Conference in December 1973 about methods of pursuing the 'Irish Dimension' had aroused Protestant suspicions, giving a handle to Paisley and Faulkner's other critics. The election result showed that Faulkner did not have the support of the majority of the Protestant electorate, and a general strike brought him, and Whitelaw's constitutional experiment, down. Wilson, whose party had won the election, accepted that direct rule was, at least for the present, the only solution. No further moves in that direction were made until November 1985, when Mrs Thatcher and the Irish Prime Minister, Garrett Fitzgerald, met and agreed that there would be no change in the status of Northern Ireland unless a majority in the province voted for it, and to establish a standing Anglo-Irish Conference to foster talks on political progress both in restoring democracy to Northern Ireland and in improving cooperation between North and South. The Unionists remained, as ever, highly suspicious of the latter, fearing that it would prove to be the thin end of a wedge which would inexorably lead to the province's submission to Dublin. Talks initiated by this meeting got nowhere and gradually petered out, although the contacts established between London and Dublin were maintained.

Meanwhile the army continued to carry out much the same role, although it progressively took second place to the RUC, which assumed more and more responsibility for maintaining order and pursuing the IRA. The latter reduced its activity in the province and began to plot and carry out terrorist attacks against British military personnel and installations both on the mainland, including on army recruiting offices, and abroad, in Germany and elsewhere. It was forestalled in Gibraltar, resulting in the death of the IRA personnel involved at the hands of the SAS, provoking an outcry in sympathetic circles. In the late 1980s and 1990s it switched its effort to attacks on civilian targets in England. By 1983 the number of battalions or their equivalents in the province had been reduced to nine, but later rose again and was maintained at eleven. In the major reorganization of the army which took place in 1991, which will be referred to later, the UDR was merged with the sole remaining Irish infantry regiment, the Royal Irish Rangers, to form the Royal Irish Regiment, which had one regular and five part-time volunteer battalions.

Clashes with the IRA tended to take place more in the countryside than in the towns. South Armagh was always regarded as 'bandit country', and in December 1989 the King's Own Scottish Borderers were involved in a serious incident there, described in their journal:

On 13 December 1989 PVCP* Derryard, North of Rosslea, 2 kilometres from the Fermanagh/Monaghan border, was manned by two teams of Sp Coy 1 KOSB. The commander was Cpl R. B. Duncan, the 2IC was L/Cpl M. J. Paterson, and the other members of the teams were Ptes C. G. Gray, H. Harvey, J. Houston, D. Landsell, J. Sloan and K. P. Whitelaw. That day, as the result of an unspecified threat to all border locations the PCVP had been reinforced by an additional Sp Coy team commanded by Cpl I. B. Harvey with Ptes S. R. Dunn, W. Common and W. R. G. Maxwell as team members. As normal the PVCP was operated by four men: Cpl Duncan in the Command Sangar, Pte Whitelaw in the rear Observation Sangar, Pte Houston the roadman checking vehicles and Pte Harvey was the runner. A visitor, S/Sgt† S. M. Bradley RE, a NISS‡ SNCO, was in the Command Sangar carrying out maintenance work. L/Cpl Paterson and his team were off duty and asleep in one of the three small portakabins. Cpl Harvey's team were on an external security patrol.

At 1620 hours PIRA§ attacked the checkpoint in considerable force. It is clear the enemy had good knowledge of the layout, manning levels and routine of the PVCP, undoubtedly built up over many months of reconnaissance. For the terrorist it was a 'soft target', being tactically indefensible, poorly protected and manned with the minimum of weaponry. PIRA brought with them the manpower, weapons, vehicle and explosive devices to destroy the base, which was their intent. They had not counted on the fighting

---

* Personnel and Vehicle Control Point.
† Staff sergeant.
‡ Northern Ireland Security Service.
§ Provisional IRA.

spirit, training and natural aggression of the Jocks and did not know Cpl Harvey's team were in the area of the base. The enemy failed in their mission. At least 12 terrorists were concealed under a tarpaulin in the back of a Hino flatbed lorry. The sides of the lorry had been built up and protected with spaced compressed sand. A crash bar had been fitted, as had mountings for two machine gun stands and external armour plates. A second vehicle, an Isuzu van, contained a 240 kilogram bomb. The terrorists were armed with six RPG-7* rockets, a flamethrower, six Armalite and AK47 rifles, two MGs and several fragmentation grenades.

The lorry approached from the direction of the border and stopped in the PVCP road area. It was seen and reported by Pte Whitelaw and Cpl Harvey's team who were on high ground to the north. Cpl Duncan instructed Pte Houston to check the back of the vehicle. The lorry sounded its horn, at which point Pte Whitelaw, who was observing his other arc, turned around to see the enemy attack launched. Simultaneous automatic gunfire killed Pte Houston, suppressed the Command and Observation Sangars and sprayed the thinly protected walls of the base. Grenades were thrown into the base. Flame was fired at the Command Sangar. Two RPG-7s were fired at the Observation Sangar, both hit and the sangar was destroyed. Heavy suppressive fire continued as the lorry was reversed and was then driven out of the base. The Isuzu van was driven in and the bomb primed. At least three terrorists dismounted and, with flame, gunfire and grenades, systematically set about clearing the portakabins.

As the enemy attack started Cpl Duncan immediately returned fire from the Command Sangar. He continued to do so until forced to withdraw by the weight of fire and flame that was splintering the sangar walls and penetrating inside the sangar through the observation ports. He ordered S/Sgt Bradley to move under cover to the rear of the base. Pte Whitelaw was thrown to the ground inside the Observation Sangar as the structure broke apart and the upper floor collapsed. He suffered minor blast burns from the exploding rockets. As he recovered his senses, he saw an unexploded grenade at his feet. He kicked it away. The grenade exploded harmlessly. A second grenade exploded causing him multiple minor fragmentation injuries

---

* Rocket-propelled grenade.

in his side and back. As the enemy sprayed the base with gunfire and grenades and smashed the lorry into the compound, Cpl Duncan, still firing, crossed through the fire to check all the portakabins and to order his men to regroup behind cover at the rear of the base. He checked the Observation Sangar but Pte Whitelaw was not there. He moved to the rear gate. Inside the kitchen portakabin Pte Harvey was pinned down. Inside the accomodation portakabin L/Cpl Paterson and his team awoke as the attack started. He ordered his men to put on their helmets and flak jackets, grab their weapons and stay under cover. L/Cpl Paterson left by the rear door. He moved to the Observation Sangar where he found S/Sgt Bradley helping the injured Pte Whitelaw. The two NCOs moved him back into the accomodation. L/Cpl Paterson left the accomodation again and moved round into the compound where he was killed by gunfire. By this time Cpl Duncan was fighting his way to the Observation Sangar and back to the rear gate. Finding no one there, he moved into the compound to discover the body of L/Cpl Paterson. The terrorists had just withdrawn, still firing automatic weapons and another RPG-7 at the base. He ordered his soldiers to give first aid, check for casualties and get to the radio in the Command Sangar. He moved to the front of the base to check for Pte Houston.

Following the sighting of the Hino lorry Cpl Harvey and his team were moving down towards the PVCP from the north when the attack began. Cpl Harvey's contact report at that time was critical. It was the only message received by Battalion HQ until after the action. It allowed the essential re-deployment of reserves and follow-up agencies. The team rapidly made their way to the PVCP, halting on the road some 75–100 metres to the north. The rear of the lorry was visible outside the base. The terrorists were clearly identified firing into the compound. Cpl Harvey and his men opened fire hitting the rear of the lorry five times. The enemy immediately switched the bulk of their fire on to the patrol forcing them to dive for cover into the hedgerows to the west of the road. By skilful fire and manoeuvre, the patrol worked its way to a position adjacent to the PVCP, continuing to draw heavy fire and forcing the enemy to withdraw. The lorry was found abandoned at the border with a 210 kilogram bomb on board. Cpl Harvey and his men came on to the road just as the lorry was disappearing and as Cpl Duncan was trying to revive Pte Houston. The two corporals, recognising that the Isuzu van was a bomb, evacuated the base and established the cordon. As the booster charge of the bomb exploded the first helicopter arrived bringing reserves. The casualties were rapidly evacuated and the follow-up began.

This was a terrifying close quarter action which lasted some 10 minutes. It was a fight for existence, in which every man involved acted with exemplary courage and the determination to defeat the enemy.

Corporals Duncan and Harvey were both awarded the Distinguished Conduct Medal and Lance-Corporal Paterson was posthumously mentioned in dispatches.

*

In 1993 a fresh attempt was made to make political progress. John Hume of the Northern Ireland Social Democratic and Labour Party worked hard behind the scenes, backed by Albert Reynolds, the Irish Prime Minister, to persuade Sinn Fein to abjure violence and adopt a more flexible attitude. Talks between the British and Irish Governments in that year resulted in a meeting between John Major and Albert Reynolds, at which they agreed what was known as the Downing Street Declaration. It repeated the usual formula about no change in the status of Northern Ireland unless a majority of the population voted for it, but included an assurance by the British Government that, if they did so, it would not oppose it as Britain 'had no strategic interest' in Ireland. It proposed all-party talks, at which representatives of the British and Irish Governments would be present, attendance by parties requiring a clear rejection by them of violence and adherence to democratic methods of achieving political ends. There was also the customary emphasis on creating better methods of cross-border cooperation. The Ulster Unionists insisted that the IRA must observe a genuine ceasefire before Sinn Fein could participate, while the latter constantly insisted on talks without conditions. After months of pressure from various sources, including the US President Clinton, who visited the island, the IRA declared a ceasefire in August 1994. The British Government, pressed by the Unionists, insisted that firearms and explosives must be 'decommissioned' before Sinn Fein could join the talks. The latter insisted that decommissioning must apply also to the RUC and the British army. The army ceased patrolling the streets, replaced helmets and bullet-proof vests with normal combat uniform, and left the maintenance of order firmly to the RUC. Some reduction in numbers was made, but there was no significant lowering of force levels. In April 1997 there were still 13,364 regular soldiers there.

Eventually talks about how such decommissioning might be initiated started under the chairmanship of the US Senator George Mitchell, but had not got beyond the stage of discussing procedures when the IRA set off a huge explosion at Canary Wharf in the East End of London in February 1996. In October they managed to penetrate the high security of the army's headquarters at Lisburn outside Belfast and set off two bombs, injuring thirty soldiers, one of whom died of his wounds.

The ceasefire was re-established in July 1997 after Blair's Labour victory in the May General Election and Ahern's Fianna Fáil's in the Irish election in June had led to a fresh Anglo–Irish initative to resuscitate the all-party talks, chaired by Senator George Mitchell. The resumed talks resulted in the Good Friday agreement in April 1998, which was approved by referendums in both North and South the following month, in spite of some violent incidents in the North perpetrated by break-away Republican factions. Immediately before the British election, the IRA had carried out a number of minor explosions and hoax calls to cause maximum nuisance in England, one involving cancellation of the Grand National.

Cyprus

From 1970 onwards almost every unit of the army served in Northern Ireland, mostly on four-month tours, although from the 1980s a larger number served for two or three years, accompanied by their families. A small number of units were involved in two significant operations. One was the reinforcement of the UN Force in Cyprus in July 1974 when Turkey invaded the island after the coup against Makarios, instigated by the Government of Colonels in Greece: rapid reinforcement of the UN Force from the base at Dhekelia helped the former to deter Turkish forces from seizing Nicosia airfield.

The Dhofar

The other was a much longer drawn-out affair, the war in the Dhofar, the southern area of Oman. There the authority of the young Sultan Qaboos, who replaced his obscurantist old father in 1970, was threatened by a rebellion among the wild inhabitants of the rugged Jebel north of Salalah, where the RAF had the use of an airfield. The rebellion was actively supported by the Peoples' Democratic Republic of Yemen, the Marxist Government of which now ruled over what had been both the Western and the Eastern Aden Protectorates. British officers and non-commissioned officers served in the Sultan's forces and commanded them, and some British army units, notably Royal Engineers and SAS, served with them. The campaign resembled those fought in days gone by on the North-West Frontier of India, aircraft, helicopters, rocket-propelled projectiles and mines adding new features to a form of warfare in which the skill, courage and endurance of the man on his feet remained the decisive factor. The campaign was successfully concluded in 1975.

The Falkland Islands

The next major commitment arose when Argentina invaded the Falkland Islands on 2 April 1982 and Margaret Thatcher's Government decided to recapture them. At first it appeared that the Royal Navy thought that it would be able to complete the task with 3rd Royal Marine Commando Brigade, embarked on the passenger liner *Canberra*, to which a squadron of 22nd SAS and 3rd Battalion The Parachute Regiment had been added, to be joined later by the 2nd Battalion. But when it became clear that the Argentine force on the eastern island had been built up to at least 6,000 men, it was decided to embark also the 5th Infantry Brigade, with 2nd Scots Guards, the Welsh Guards and 1/7th Gurkhas.

The initial assault was made by the Commando Brigade at San Carlos Bay, fifty miles west of the capital Port Stanley, on 21 May. It was immediately successful, meeting little resistance on land. However, air attacks on shipping delayed the build-up of reinforcements and supplies. The Royal Marine brigade commander, Brigadier J. A. H. Thompson, wanted to await the disembarkation of 5th Brigade before he set off towards Port Stanley, which the main strength of the Argentine forces was defending; but London feared that any delay might mean that international peace efforts could force some form of truce before Port Stanley had been recaptured. Thompson was therefore urged to send off his marines and one parachute battalion trudging across the rain-soaked heathland towards Port Stanley, while the 2nd Battalion attacked the Argentine garrison of Darwin and Goose Green, fifteen miles south of San Carlos on a narrow isthmus linking East Falkland with Lafonia, the only force which could threaten his beachhead base area. This they did on 28 May in a brilliant action, in which the infantry, with little fire support, forced the surrender of the 1,400-strong garrison, after killing 250 of them. The battalion's casualties were 17 killed and 36 wounded, the dead including the adjutant and the commanding officer, Lieutenant-Colonel H. Jones, who was posthumously awarded the Victoria Cross.

Their Regimental Medical Officer, Captain S. J. Hughes, tells his story of the day:

> We set off from Camilla Creek House at about 2 a.m. tired before we started after the previous night's TAB.* On our backs the RAP (Regimental Aid Post) Medics were all carrying in excess of 80 lbs of medical kit and the uneven ground ensured that we all fell regularly.
>
> We laid up near the mortar line just north of the Darwin Peninsula whilst A and B Companies put in their first attacks. There was a steady drizzle, and those of us who had worn waterproofs were glad of them – some of us even dozed.
>
> About 2 hours after the initial H hour, Battalion Main HQ, (including the RAP), moved off and down the narrow track onto the Peninsula itself. To our left, a large area of gorse had been ignited by white phosphorous grenades and the flames lit up the night sky. The crackle of burning gorse could be heard above the reassuring crump of the naval gunfire support.

* TAB is the Parachute Regiment's faster version of 'yomping'.

We had just come level with the first cache of Argentinian prisoners, on the edge of the track, when the first salvo of the Argentinian guns bracketed the track.

We heard the distant crump and the incoming whistle and barely hit the ground before the first rounds of 'HE' hit the peat on either side of the track. We wormed our bodies in, face down to the banks on either side of the track, so that our Bergens* gave our backs some protection. The reality of the war began to sink in.

Again we were bracketted, but miraculously nothing landed on the track, and the soft, wet peat, off the track, kept the shrapnel to the minimum. We had no casualties.

A tracer round cracked 6 ins over my head from somewhere off to the right – a stray round. I buried my head further into the earth.

The first two attacks had had no casualties, but now D Coy came up against stiffer opposition and Chris Keeble, the Bn 2IC asked me to move forward up the track to deal with the first casualties. His parting words, as I led the RAP off, were: 'Watch out for the sniper on the right flank.'

I then realised where that not so stray round had come from, and was convinced that the collar of my waterproof jacket, white on the reverse, would make me a perfect target. It may well have, but nothing happened.

We ran low and fast for about 400 metres, until we came across the two D Coy wounded, both minor gunshot wounds. It was about 6 a.m. still with a further 4 hours of darkness – so, after finishing our treatment regime, all we could do was reassure them and keep them warm and sheltered from the rain until dawn, when the first choppers would fly.

The CO, 'H', appeared, with his TAC HQ and came to find out how the casualties were – 'Alright, Sir, we'll try and get them back to Camilla Creek in the captured Argie Landrover.' He and the Adjutant, one of my close friends, David Wood, were joking about a shell that had landed between them, yet left them both unscathed. 'These Argies have got some shit ammunition.' It was to be the last time I would see either of them alive again.

TAC 1 disappeared and Battalion Main moved in around us. Time drifted by and the shelling periodically came our way. As the

* Rucksacks.

sky started to brighten we lost the benefit of the naval gun support and as dawn came we found ourselves in a natural bowl of land to the north of Coronation Point.

One or two more casualties were brought in, together with our first dead. Two of my Medics had lost friends and I had lost some of my own patients – we were all affected. We improvised shelter for the wounded using a captured Argie tent until at first light helicopters came in bringing ammunition resupply. We got the casualties into the Choppers and I went back to my routine of listening in to the Battalion Command net – Reading the Battle.

There was a big battle raging ahead of us, and nothing seemed to be moving. We all began to dig in to the peat because the shelling was now more constant, our own guns becoming less vociferous.

Shortly after 1300, I heard the message over the net 'Sunray* has been hit'. The Battalion called for a helicopter to pick him up and it became obvious that there were other casualties in trouble. I rounded up my Medics and split them up into two teams – one under my command and the other under Capt. Rory Wagon, the doctor who had been attached to us from the Ajax Bay Field Hospital.

Both forward companies had casualties in locations 1½ km apart. Rory's team went out to the right flank and I moved my lads out to the left, to the hills round Darwin. As we moved forward we had to dive for cover as two Pucara aircraft appeared ahead. They roared over us and I turned in time to see them spot two scout helicopters emerge from the direction of Camilla Creek House. The Pucara swooped like hawks, and the Choppers took desperate evasive action. One Chopper disappeared up the valley whence it had come and managed to escape. The other exploded in a ball of flame. The Pucara disappeared.

We found 'A' Company on a hill 1 km to the west of Darwin, their casualties collected together at the base of the hill, amongst them the Company Medic. Again the shock of dealing with people you knew in a far from clinical environment – but we steeled ourselves and went to work.

We dealt with the casualties and I'd once more called for helicopters. Ahead of us the battle carried on. There was no sign of 'H' so I asked the Sgt. Major. 'H is dead, Sir, and Captain Wood,

---

* Radio jargon for 'commander'.

and Captain Dent' – the CO and two good friends all at once; – but there was nothing else but continue the job.*

The casualties had all had their wounds dressed and drips set up. We'd given them pain killers and filled them full of antibiotics. We tried to keep them dry and warm and kept up a steady banter to reassure them, especially a lad with a head injury, who I didn't want to go into coma.

By now we were beginning to run low on medical supplies – there's a limit to how much you can manpack. At least no more casualties had come in, although there were some wounded amongst the Argie prisoners for whom we did what we could.

Then over the hill came, what for me will always be the Seventh Cavalry – 4 scout helicopters, fitted with Casevac Pods and bringing our medical resupply. We got all the wounded away and even some of the more seriously wounded Argie prisoners. Then the shelling started again and we moved up the hill slightly, into a gully which gave natural cover against low trajectory artillery fire. It was here that we spent the rest of the day, the helicopters coming in under the cover of the hill.

We continued to treat casualties, our own, and in quiet phases Argentinians, with the smoke of the battlefield and the burning gorse at times almost fogging us out. Fatigue was setting in and we all wondered how much longer this could go on. For most of the afternoon the battle had seemed to be going against us, but, as dark set in, it swung back in our favour and as darkness fell the artillery fell silent and gunfire became sporadic. We were still holding three battle sick – twists and sprains – and though we tried for a helicopter we knew they would keep, if it didn't arrive.

We were all expecting the battle to start afresh the next day, so we set up a stag system to look after the casualties and laid down in the gorse to sleep, after I'd first sat down with the RSM and the Padre to work out who our dead were.

The day had been long and hard, tragic and frightening. The night was bitterly cold, and we none of us had sleeping bags. Some people lay down actually in burning gorse in an effort to keep warm. I lay down in a large clump of non-burning gorse and thanked my

---

* Lieutenant-Colonel Jones was posthumously awarded the Victoria Cross.

stars for the space blanket I'd bought in the UK and shoved in the back of my smock!

I managed to wrap my body in this totally non-tactical piece of foil. The silvered surface caught the flicker of gorse flames and I crinkled like a Sunday roast, but it made the temperature bearable.

Although I was exhausted I wondered whether I should sleep after the horrors of the day and as I lay in a twilight state every rustle of my foil blanket was a machine gun and every crackle of gorse was an artillery shell. I was aware of the tricks my mind was playing on me – and wondered if I was cracking up.

I slept.

I awoke in the half light of mid-morning and couldn't feel my feet. Then I could and they were painful. Around me the RAP was stirring.

Chris Keeble* happened by and told the Padre and I of his plan. He would give them the opportunity of an honourable surrender.

There followed a void; a lack of hostilities. Whilst the Battalion took the time to fly in ammunition, we took the time to fly out our casualties and do what we could for the remaining injured amongst the prisoners.

It was as we were treating the prisoners that we heard the news of the surrender. The battle was over. Although our work was not quite finished, yet at least it could not get worse.

All told we treated 33 of our own and over twice that number of Argentinians.

A number of factors, including the deteriorating weather, made it necessary to hasten the day when the assault on the hills surrounding Port Stanley should begin. The loss of heavy-lift helicopters when the ship carrying them, the *Atlantic Conveyor*, was hit by Argentine aircraft was a limiting factor, and 5th Brigade was therefore moved round from Goose Green to Bluff Cove, to the south of those hills, by sea. Two of the Landing Ships Logistic (LSLs), the *Sir Tristram* and the *Sir Galahad*, were hit by Argentine aircraft and set on fire on 8 June. The casualties were fifty-one killed and fifty-seven wounded. Of these thirty-nine dead and twenty-eight wounded were from the Welsh Guards in the *Sir Galahad*.

* Now the acting commanding officer.

The final battle for Port Stanley started on 11 June, 3rd Parachute Regiment successfully assaulting Mount Longdon, while 42nd and 45th Royal Marine Commandos captured Two Sisters and Mount Harriet to the south of them. 5th Brigade then took over, 2nd Parachute Regiment passing through their sister battalion to capture Wireless Ridge on the night of the 13th, while the Scots Guards attacked Tumbledown Mountain, the Gurkhas Mount William and the Welsh Guards Sapper Hill, to which they were lifted by helicopter. Fighting was fiercest at Tumbledown, and in the afternoon of 14 June the enemy surrendered.

Lieutenant-Colonel Michael Scott, commanding officer of the Scots Guards, describes their battle:

During the night 11/12th June, 3 Commando Brigade took Mount Longdon, Two Sisters and Mount Harriet. The 5th Infantry Brigade plan was for the Battalion to take Mount Tumbledown from the west and, when firm, to provide fire support for 1st Battalion 7th Gurkha Rifles to assault Mount William. The Welsh Guards were subsequently to be prepared to take Sapper Hill.

The Battalion plan was for a silent night attack in three phases. The fire plan was to include fighter ground attack, five batteries of 105mm light guns and naval gunfire from HMS *Active* and *Yarmouth*. The mortars of 42 Commando and 1st Battalion 7th Gurkha Rifles were also available. Each phase was to involve a company attack on a different part of the objective. Phase I was for 'G' Company to take the first part of Tumbledown. Thirty minutes before 'G' Company crossed the start line, there was to be a diversionary attack from the obvious southerly approach. Phase II involved Left Flank moving through and assaulting the main part of the mountain, while in Phase III Right Flank would secure the final part.

On the morning of 13th June, the Battalion moved by helicopter to an assembly area to the south west of Goat Ridge, well out of sight of the enemy and dug in. Enemy shell fire was sporadic and ineffective, although one casualty was taken and a spectacular phosphorous explosion occurred when a shell hit some white phosphorous grenades on a Guardsman's equipment. Detailed recces and orders took place throughout the day and rehearsals for the move into the FUP* were held. The recognition signal 'Hey Jimmy' was

* Forming-Up Point.

adopted in lieu of the standard NATO password system, for speed and in the knowledge that Argentinians are incapable of pronouncing a J! Steel helmets were carried rather than worn also for recognition in the dark, in that the Argentinians wore helmets.

The diversionary attack, led by Major Bethell, started on time and, after initial success, ran into trouble. The Argentinians were much stronger than anticipated and, sadly, D/Sgt Wight and Cpl Pashley, of the Engineers, were killed. After being mortared in a minefield, the attackers withdrew with a number of casualties. It was subsequently discovered after the battle, in an interview with the captured Argentinian battalion commander, that the diversion had the desired effect and the Argentinians did think the main attack was coming from the south and not the west.

'G' Company crossed the start line at 2100 hours (local time) with one platoon and company headquarters leading to secure the first half of the company objective, to be followed by the other two platoons to secure the second half. Progress across the open ground was slow through sporadic mortar and shell fire and the occasional star shell. The cold was intense. The company secured their objective by 2230 hours and gave supporting fire when and where they could to Left Flank who were now moving through them and coming under very heavy machine gun and sniper fire.

Left Flank advanced with Second Lieutenant Stuart's platoon taking the high crags on their left and Lieutenant Mitchell's platoon the enemy positions on the lower slopes to the right. Company Headquarters and Lieutenant Fraser's platoon were in depth. In addition to small arms fire, the company began to come under increasing mortar and artillery bombardment. Enemy sniper fire, with high grade night sights, was devastating, killing Guardsmen Stirling and Tanbini and mortally wounding Sergeant Simeon. Company Sergeant Major Nicol was also shot in the hand in the early moments of the attack. 66mm, 84mm, and M79 rounds* were used against the enemy sangars but were only partially effective. The leading sections of the left forward platoon had some success with grenades, flushing out the forward snipers and following a communication cable, located and destroyed several sangars and sniper positions despite fierce enemy resistance.

---

* 66mm and 84mm mortar and M79 rifle-grenade rounds.

At this stage the Battalion was having difficulty in getting mortar and artillery fire really accurate. At approximately 0230 hours, artillery rounds landed accurately in front of the right forward platoon, and the platoon commander, together with the company commander and company headquarters, then led an attack on the forward enemy positions. This assault was successful and the momentum of the attack was maintained. About eight enemy were killed with grenades, rifles and bayonets. The company commander himself, Major J. Kiszley, killed two and bayoneted a third. Although one section commander, Lance-Sergeant Mitchell, was killed, the assault continued up the hill, with sangars and bunkers being taken at the point of the bayonet. The demands of clearing these positions and guarding prisoners resulted in only seven men of Left Flank reaching the top of the mountain and the end of their objective. Below them were the lights of Stanley and enemy running away. Of these seven, three, including Lieutenant Mitchell, were immediately cut down by machine gun fire from Right Flank's objective.

Major Price, commanding Right Flank, came forward, assessed the situation and, leaving Second Lieutenant Lord Dalrymple's platoon to give covering fire, approached the enemy with his other two platoons from the right. The assaulting sections moved forward, firing 66mm and M79s as they went. The attack became fragmented, and groups of four to six men moved through the rocks, covering each other and destroying the enemy with grenades and bayonets. The enemy positions were well prepared and supported each other, making the assault a hazardous affair. At one point, Lieutenant Lawrence was wounded in the head and pulled back to safety by Lance-Corporal Rennie while under covering fire from two others. By about 0815 hours, the company was secure and Tumbledown Mountain was in the hands of the Battalion.

The Gurkhas were already moving through the position and by the time they reached the lower slopes of Mount William, the cease fire had been declared and the fighting ended. The Battalion prepared for another cold night on the mountain before being extracted by helicopter to the shearing sheds of Fitzroy on 15th June.

Lieutenant Mark Coreth of B Squadron of the Royal Horse Guards (The Blues and Royals) was commanding a troop of Scorpion light tanks in the operation. He tells his story:

I was attached to the Scots Guards for their Mount Tumbledown attack, and was to support the diversionary attack in the south. The 13th, and I could not but think that it was a hell of a day to have a scrap. I arranged with the locals to get some air pressure into my recuperators since both were dicey. They were fantastic, sliced their air pipes in order to fit ours and built up pressure enough to render their machine useless thereafter.

The area of our advance was littered with minefields. The enemy marked them only by piles of stones, a sign known only to their men ... at Darwin a 1000lb mine was found connected to an AP* mine. As far as worries went, mines were high on my list of priorities. The engineers told me there were three types of anti-tank mines – two of them powerful enough in theory to rip us apart like a can opener. With the above grizzly knowledge my little convoy moved along the unfinished Darwin to Stanley road ... There were engineers belly down probing for mines, a job I would never envy. I was warned of the danger of leaving the road ... I soon came across another engineer occupied culvert, uncrossable, but they cleared a track round it, finding no mines.

The plan was that I was to open fire on two enemy positions from H minus 30 to H plus 30, H Hour being 2100. We carried the infantry forward and they debussed about 1800. I planned to move in two hours, giving them time to recce and get in position. Time ticked by. I became ever more anxious as radio communications became worse and worse. Midnight passed. [?] I had word not to move but wait. I could not get hold of Richard Bethell, leading the patrol, though I could hear one section – only just.

Come 2030 and I decided the time had come. I could barely hear on the radio, but the gist was plainly that they were in trouble. I decided to move, and to lead the way myself, despite the rules which say otherwise. As we reached the forward positions, a flare skylined my vehicles in a magnificent silhouette ... Then we were under heavy DF† fire being corrected onto us. About 300 metres on, and still 1,000 metres short of my planned fire position, the road was blocked by a huge quite impassable crater. I stopped for a split second to consider my situation. I knew the likelihood of mines was

* Anti-personnel.
† Defensive.

high. But I had been told that the road was plain sailing, so thought this was probably a lucky shot from a 155mm round. The deciding factor, however, was that our patrol was ahead and was in trouble; so far as I was concerned almost anything was worth the risk. A crew that works well together is one that will trust its commander and obediently follow his instructions and trust his judgement. I decided the only decent option was a risk and thus tried to creep the wagon around the crater. We had barely moved off the road when we hit an anti-tank mine, CoH* Stretton, who was behind me, saw us rise three to four feet into the air over a blinding flash. There was a concussing explosion, and a shock wave that felt like two hammers hitting either side of your helmet. I thought we would brew up into a funeral pyre. With this in mind I shouted to the crew to get out, but found they were already on the home run. The trick when you are in a minefield is to zip back along your own tracks, as this is at least a known clear area, and that is what I did – with a head that was a battlefield of cracks, bangs, drums and bugles, but no other apparent injuries. Nor was anyone else hurt.

At this stage it was vital to provide fire support for the infantry ... From the outside of another vehicle the troop leader controlled the fire of his remaining vehicles while under artillery fire himself. A significant amount of enemy fire and attention was drawn by this diversion.

Sadly I could only have one vehicle firing at a time because the road was too narrow ... and this was the only position from which we could cover our target. It became a crazy shoot from one vehicle, sitting on the outside, reverse him, climb into another, bring him forward, fire him, and so on until the last. There was some excellent shooting by all vehicles ... There was some very dodgy fire coming down in our area but one got used to listening to them and judging just when to leap off the side and hit the dust ...

Next day the engineers found fifty-seven mines round my wagon, all about four foot apart; it was lucky we did not hit two. The theory they gave for our survival was the fact that the vehicle was relatively light, 8.5 tons, sturdy enough not to open like a can of beans, but light enough to be thrown into the air, and thus dissipate some of the blast. Also the ground was pretty soft, enough to make a hole

---

* Corporal of Horse, the Household Cavalry equivalent of sergeant.

and absorb the shock. There was actually surprisingly little damage done to the vehicle. The turret was in working order once the chaos inside was sorted out.

The white flag was over Stanley ... we joined the long and jubilant column, truly an impressive sight, going hell for leather for our prime target. We were allowed to press on up to Sapper Hill, and we were the first to the top! The thrill and jubilation was almost overpowering. We were a happy crowd.

Staff-Sergeant Victor Macdonald-Evans of the Royal Army Pay Corps took an active part in the attack on Mount Longdon, of which he gives an account:

I had been employed as Service Funds Accountant with 3rd Battalion The Parachute Regiment since 1979 and my inclusion in the Task Force did not come as a surprise, as all attached personnel serving with 3 PARA were expected to be soldiers first and military account-ants or cooks etc second, a sentiment with which I am in agreement.

June 18 [13] was to be our day for the attack on Mount Longdon. 45 Commando was to commence its attack on the Two Sisters an hour before us, thereby drawing any enemy fire away from our positions. On the line-up for the march to our Start Line we were told that Brigade thought there were about 40 Argies on Longdon and that it would be a two company job ('B' and Sp Coys). I and my section were attached to Sp Coy.

After what seemed an endless advance in the dark through a river with all our kit and extra ammunition etc we arrived at our Start Line.

'B' Coy made their way round to the Northern slope of Mt Longdon, Sp Coy stayed in position not far from the West slopes. Our orders were that 3 PARA ('B' and Sp Coys) would make a silent attack as opposed to a creeping barrage proceeding us, as was originally thought.

A short while later when all hell let loose, it was relayed that 'B' Coy were pinned down and that Sp Coy should advance up the Western slopes.

After crossing an enormous expanse of open ground (which we later learned was a minefield) we crawled our way up Mt Longdon. Everything seemed in total confusion at this point and rounds were landing all over the place. Halfway to the summit I had lost half my section killed. There was one Argy Sniper who was particularly good and had quite a number of us pinned down for a while. However, he was eventually dealt with by, I believe, a 66mm rocket launcher. On reaching the summit there were already quite a number of casualties, but to a certain extent one had to ignore this. It was at this stage that 45 Cdo seemed to be starting their attack on the Two Sisters. I remember that it was stated that they were an hour late! We were receiving heavy Browning fire from the Two Sisters on our side. At this point a Para Platoon Commander said to me that I was to take three men and work my way back down as there were Argy trenches and sangars behind us. I grabbed the 3 men nearest me and we began our task of trying to locate and clear these positions. I had cleared 3 or 4 positions with my LMG hauling out any Argies who were still alive, when I realised that the other 3 men had gone down another gully some 50 yards from me and that I was quite alone at this stage. I had with me now 5 Argy prisoners when I heard the Provost Corporal's voice to my right. Shouting across to him and receiving his acknowledgement in the semi-darkness, I pushed the prisoners over the rocks to his position, and continued to seek out a further two positions of Argies but I failed to take any further prisoners as after my bursts of fire into their positions they were all killed. The last trench/sangar, I noticed, just in time, had a booby-trap, which was a length of wire attached to an Israeli grenade. Luckily I realised without thinking that this was a booby-trap and withdrew.

When light came we counted the lost and took up positions as best we could on the hill. At this stage I reverted to the Provost role and set up a roster to guard the 52 prisoners we had taken. They had to remain with us until helicopters could ferry them back to the rear.

For the next 36 hours we came under heavy artillery and mortar fire on Mt Longdon and we waited hoping that the next shell didn't have our number on it. We received more casualties due to this shelling and from air-bursts. It was then I noticed Cpl. Jackson running up and down the hill with a stretcher, ferrying the wounded and dead to the RAP. He had done a magnificent job, coming under fire almost continuously, and I remember thinking that at least I was able to fire back and he couldn't. L/Cpl Caraher was there with the Int Section* eventually (next day) and helped out with the prisoner

* Intelligence section.

problem, as there were only 6 of us to guard them. It was discovered that instead of 40 Argies holding Mt Longdon, there were reportedly 360, of which 52 survived.

Our feet were frozen solid, as little protection was afforded by the DMS* boot and having waded through a river on our advance, there was no time to dry socks, although we managed to get on a dry pair later on. I had managed to sustain a hole in my big toe from a piece of mortar base that had been blown to pieces sent flying everywhere, one of which struck my feet, so that left me limping badly. I remember I was offered 'casevac' to the rear but felt that I wanted to be with the Battalion to the end.

I am very proud to have served with the members of my Pay Team, all of whom proved, in action, that they are soldiers fully up to any required infantry or other tasks outside the sphere of their normal duties. I was particularly impressed by our younger, less experienced soldiers in this respect.

Twenty-eight thousand men of all three services had taken part in the expedition, of whom 10,000 army and Royal Marines had landed. Casualties were 255 dead (86 Royal Navy, 27 Royal Marines, 123 army, 1 RAF, 18 Merchant Navy), and 777 wounded, of whom 464 were army. Argentine prisoners totalled 11,400 and they reported their dead as 672, of whom 386 were lost when their cruiser, the *General Belgrano*, was sunk. The landing force, under the Royal Marine Major-General J. J. Moore, had not only been outnumbered, but had had to operate in increasingly severe weather, marching long distances, carrying heavy loads, over rough, wet terrain which offered no shelter from the permanently fierce wind and no concealment. The performance of the British soldier of 1982 was fully worthy of the feats of arms emblazoned on the colours of his regiment.

* Directly Moulded Sole.

Options for Change

In the immediate aftermath of the Falklands campaign the armed forces basked in the approval of the Government and of the public. The campaign gave a boost to recruiting and to the approval of significant improvements to the army's equipment, including the Challenger II tank for eight out of the twelve tank regiments of the Royal Armoured Corps, Warrior armoured personnel carriers for thirteen infantry battalions and the Multiple-Launch Rocket System for three regiments of the Royal Artillery, whose light anti-aircraft batteries were to receive more and better Rapier missiles. The infantry was to get a new rifle and mortar, and the radio communications of the Royal Signals significantly improved. But the optimism this induced was soon to be tempered by the fundamental change in attitudes to defence caused by the advent to power in the Soviet Union in 1985 of Mikhail Gorbachev. Within the next five years, a treaty on Conventional Forces in Europe was signed, the Warsaw Pact broken up, and Germany unified. This was followed by the withdrawal of Soviet forces from Germany and the break-up of the Soviet Union itself. These changes sparked off a Ministry of Defence study called *Options for Change*, the preliminary conclusions of which were published on 25 July 1990. The army would be reduced from 156,000 to 120,000, the four divisions in Germany being reduced to one, which would be reinforced from Britain in emergency by the equivalent of another.

The Gulf War

On 2 August, only a week after this announcement, and before its impact could be assessed, Saddam Hussein invaded Kuwait, and on the 8th announced that he had annexed it. On that day President Bush announced that US forces, at the request of King Fahd, were being deployed to Saudi Arabia to help in its defence. The UN Security Council had by then adopted two resolutions, one condemning the invasion of Kuwait and demanding Iraq's unconditional withdrawal, and, when Iraq refused to comply, another imposing extensive mandatory sanctions. The immediate military need was to reinforce the defence of Saudi Arabia and the Gulf states and to impose the sanctions. For the first, the British Government's immediate reaction was to provide air forces. It was not long before pressure from the USA for larger contributions, supported by Saudi Arabia and the Gulf states who did not wish to be seen as relying solely on the US, led to an increase in the British contribution, but not yet to a land force one.

But the dispatch of another RAF squadron and an air-defence destroyer of the Royal Navy did not satisfy the Americans, who were sensitive to the problem that if it came to actual fighting GIs might be the only ones killed. After some hesitation, the Government accepted the advice of the CGS, General Sir John Chapple, that an armoured brigade group was the minimum viable tactical entity that should be sent. On 14 September it was announced that 7th Armoured Brigade, commanded by Brigadier Patrick Cordingley, would be sent from Germany, with two armoured regiments, the Royal Scots Dragoon Guards and the Queen's Royal Irish Hussars (about a hundred tanks), and one infantry battalion, 1st Staffords, in armoured personnel carriers, with the appropriate support of other arms and services. The tanks would be the new Challengers and the APCs the new Warriors. Contributions from other European members of NATO were disappointing, only France providing any significant land force, a Foreign Legion light armoured brigade (*division léger*), which initially emphasized its independence from the American effort. In contrast to that attitude, the British Government agreed that when 7th Armoured Brigade completed its deployment to the Gulf at the end of October it would operate under the command of the US Marine Division on the southern border of Kuwait.

This deployment, in addition to that of several RAF squadrons, led to the appointment of Lieutenant-General Sir Peter de la Billière to command all British forces in Saudi Arabia and the Gulf, subordinate to Air Chief Marshal Sir Patrick Hine, Commander-in-Chief of RAF Strike Command back in England, who was also NATO CINCUKAIR. He did not exercise any operational command himself, but had to approve of the subordination of specific British formations and units to American

91. West Yorkshires and 10th Gurkha Rifles advance along the Imphal–Kohima road behind Lee-Grant tanks, May 1944.

92. Kohima after the battle, June 1944. Trenches on DIS Ridge looking towards the District Commissioner's Bungalow. In the right distance is Kohima town and the beginning of Naga village.

93. ATS manning a height-finder at a mixed battery of Anti-Aircraft Command.

94. 3in. mortar crews firing their shells into Meiktila, March 1945.

95. Windermere Home Guard on boat patrol with Vickers machine-gun.

96. ATS anti-aircraft gunners march past their 3.7in. gun.

97. Home Guard armoured train, February 1944.

98. Palestine. A wounded soldier is carried out from the ruins of the King David Hotel on a stretcher, after being hauled out from under the wreckage on 23 July 1946.

99. Palestine. A British officer checks the illegal Jewish immigrants boarding the British troopship *Empire Rival* en route to Cyprus in August 1946. Care was taken to avoid terrorists, who had been operating in the area, escaping with the immigrants.

100. Korea –
front line. Winter.

101. Korea.
Royal Ulster
Rifles and a tank
of the 8th
Hussars near the
Imjin River,
April 1951.

102. Malaya.
A British patrol in the
jungle, *c.* 1952.

103. Malaya.
An Iban tracker
advises the patrol
commander, *c.* 1950.

104. Kenya. A British officer leads soldiers on a patrol through the dense Kenya forest. Travelling under these conditions, a patrol could only expect to cover 500 yards in an hour.

105. Kenya. Members of a British army patrol search a captured Mau Mau suspect.

106. Cyprus. Troops of the 1st Royal Ulster Rifles conduct a search at a checkpoint, 1956.

107. Cyprus. Ferret scout cars of C Squadron, The Life Guards, during a routine patrol of villages under the control of Limassol District of UNFICYP, 1964.

108. Suez 1956, Operation MUSKETEER. Last of first lift of 3 Para, dropping on
El Gamil airfield Port Said, 5 November. Men are seen making for their rendezvous.
The water tower, B Company 3 Para's objective and RV, can be seen left background,
and foreground are some of the forty-gallon drums placed across
the runway by the Egyptians to prevent aircraft landing.

109. Operation MUSKETEER. Special Company HQ 3 Para digging in on El Gamil airfield,
5 November 1956. Private Waterman standing, Colour Sergeant Graves with shovel.

110. Aden. Members of the Argyll and Sutherland Highlanders searching suspects in 1967. In June the Crater district of Aden fell into the hands of dissidents. The area was recaptured by Lieutenant-Colonel Colin Mitchell's 1st Argyll and Sutherland Highlanders on 3/4 July.

111. Aden. A member of the 2nd Battalion, Coldstream Guards, checking a donkey train in the Radfan mountains in March 1965.

112. Borneo. A four-man patrol of 2nd Battalion, The Parachute Regiment crossing a bridge made out of a tree trunk and bamboo over one of Sarawak's many jungle rivers.

113. A helicopter of the Royal Navy takes off after bringing men of the Gurkha Rifles back to their position after a patrol in Borneo.

114. Falklands, 1982. Evacuating Scots Guards wounded by helicopter.

115. Falklands, 1982. Men of 5th Infantry Brigade landing at San Carlos.

116. Gulf War, 1990–91. An MCT Spartan churns through the soft sand of the Saudi desert after a missile-firing exercise. The racks for its Milan anti-tank missiles are empty. Note the red jerboa or 'desert rat' – emblem of 7th Armoured Brigade – painted on the side of the vehicle.

117. Bosnia, UNPROFOR November 1992. Travnik market place.
Warrior APCs of 1st Cheshires.

118. Bosnia, UNPROFOR 1993. Ambulances of 4th Armoured Field Ambulance RAMC
passing a Croat checkpoint.

119. Germany. A Chieftain tank of the Blues and Royals crossing a
Royal Engineer M2 floating bridge over the River Weser.

120. Germany. Honest John missile of 24th Missile Regiment, Royal Artillery being fired.

121. Northern Ireland. Soldiers from 2nd Royal Anglian Regiment firing a baton round in the Hunger Strike riots, Easter 1981.

122. Searching shopping bags, Belfast.

operational command. He located himself and his staff alongside the joint Supreme Headquarters of the Saudi Arabian Commander-in-Chief and the US General Schwarzkopf, an arrangement which worked very smoothly, helped by the fact that he had on previous occasions worked with both Arab and US forces.

In November the emphasis changed from defence of Saudi Arabia and the Gulf states to preparations for offensive action to evict Iraqi forces from the territory of Kuwait, knowledge of which it was hoped would persuade Saddam Hussein to comply with the Security Council resolutions. Both British and American plans to prepare for the relief of their troops deployed to the Gulf were cancelled and the planned reliefs became reinforcements. When President Bush committed a further 150,000 troops, including two armoured divisions and a second Marine amphibious group, with substantial naval and air support on 8 November, Margaret Thatcher and her Government therefore decided to increase the British contribution by adding the 4th Armoured Brigade (Brigadier C. Hammerbeck), comprising one armoured regiment (14th/20th King's Hussars) and two mechanized infantry battalions (1st Royal Scots and 3rd Royal Regiment of Fusiliers) and a strong artillery brigade, which, together with 7th Armoured Brigade, would form the 1st Armoured Division (Major-General R. A. Smith). The whole force came from the British Army of the Rhine in Germany, which it virtually stripped of all its Challenger tanks and their spares, as well as most of its Warrior APCs. The units chosen to go were those who had been trained on this equipment, and had to be brought up to strength with soldiers from other units trained on them, regardless of regimental or other affiliations. The artillery brigade consisted of three field and two heavy regiments, one of the latter equipped with the new Multiple-Launch Rocket System, and an air defence regiment – a generous allocation of fire support.

The reinforcement brought British army strength in the Gulf up to 33,000, more than half of that of BAOR, and a total service strength of 45,000. Deployment of personnel was carried out almost entirely by air, while most of the equipment was shipped in chartered vessels to the extremely well-equipped Saudi Arabian port of Al Jubayl. Logistic support in a distant theatre where there were no established British military facilities posed severe problems which were overcome by drawing on the whole of the army's logistic and administrative resources, as well as on the firms which had manufactured the equipment. In the medical field, this involved the call-up of a Territorial Army General Hospital.

Before the deployment had got far under way, the political crisis over the leadership of the Conservative Party erupted, as a result of which John Major replaced Margaret Thatcher as Prime Minister on 28 November, but there was no weakening of Britain's resolve. Deployment of these reinforcements was completed early in January 1991.

On the day after John Major became Prime Minister the UN Security Council gave Saddam Hussein until 15 January to comply with its resolutions, and authorized the use of military force if he did not. President Bush had strong international backing, therefore, when he authorized Schwarzkopf to initiate Operation DESERT STORM in the early hours of 17 January. The aims of the operation were: to secure the complete and unconditional withdrawal of Iraqi forces from Kuwait; to restore its legitimate Government; to re-establish international peace and security in the area; and to uphold the authority of the United Nations.

Schwarzkopf's strategy was to destroy the Iraqi air force and Iraq's capability to deliver weapons of any kind by missile, of which they had a considerable number; when that had been done, to switch his air and missile effort against the Iraqi army, wearing it down until a land offensive could expect a fair chance of success. Before he reached that stage, which many thought would involve heavy casualties, there was a further spurt of diplomatic activity after Iraq had announced, on 15 February, that it would 'deal with Security Council Resolution 660 [the original one] with the aim of reaching an honourable and acceptable solution, including withdrawal'; but the conditions attached were unacceptable. On 22 February the coalition Governments set out conditions which Iraq had to meet by noon (New York time) on 23 February. On that day Iraq set fire to 600 oil wells in Kuwait and rejected the ultimatum. In the early hours of 24 February Schwarzkopf launched his attack.

His general plan was to pretend that his main thrust would be near the coast. There the US Marines had two divisions, sandwiched between forces of all the Arab contributors, amounting to the equivalent of some seven divisions. The Marines also posed an amphibious threat with two brigades afloat. The main thrust was in fact to be made 200 miles inland, round the western edge of the Iraqi defences, by the 7th US Corps of one infantry and three armoured divisions, one of them the British, and a 'cavalry' or light armoured division. This corps was to turn the flank of the Iraqi defences and head towards Basra to engage the Republican Guard, an elite force of armoured and mechanized divisions. Wider on the flank, the 18th US Corps of one infantry and two airborne divisions, one of them carried entirely in helicopters, and the French *division léger* were to seal off the left flank by occupying a series of positions up to the west bank of the Euphrates, aiming towards Nasiriyah. When the decision had been made to increase the British contribution from 7th Armoured Brigade to the whole of 1st Armoured Division, de la Billière had asked Schwarzkopf to employ the division with 7th US Corps in the main thrust instead of just providing tank support to the US Marines. This would exploit their training and equipment and would ensure that the British, the largest European contribution, would play a significant part in the main thrust. It would also make tactical cooperation easier, as the US Army divisions followed NATO procedures, whereas the Marines had peculiar ones of their own. Once Schwarzkopf was satisfied that the British would be able to ensure the full logistic support of their forces from the base area round Dharan and Al Jubayl – 350 miles to the start line and operations up to 200 miles beyond it – he readily agreed, although it meant that he had to switch a US Army tank formation from 7th US Corps to support the Marines.

The attack was launched in the early hours of Sunday 24 February by the Marines in the coastal sector and the 18th US Corps 250 miles inland. Both were initially so successful that Schwarzkopf decided to bring forward the attack by the 7th Corps, originally planned to start at 3 a.m. the following day, and launch it at noon that day. This meant carrying out an attack, including clearing gaps in minefields in the desert, where there is no cover to conceal what one is doing, in broad daylight, an operation nobody in their senses would have undertaken in the desert in the Second World War. But the signs that Iraqi resistance was feeble, and the availability of overwhelming fire support from aircraft and artillery, justified Schwarzkopf's bold decision. Unbelievably, the 1st US Infantry Division took only one hour and twenty minutes to break through the Iraqi defences and clear sixteen lanes for the advance of the armoured divisions. The task of the 1st (British) Armoured Division was to protect the eastern flank of the corps advance by swinging right to attack the Iraqi reserves immediately behind their forward defences, which they did during the night of 25/26 February. Enemy resistance was weak and continued to be so, leading elements of the division reaching the Kuwait–Basra road half an hour before the ceasefire came into effect at 8 a.m. (local time) on 28 February.

After all the build-up and intense training, and a certain degree of anticipatory anxiety, the actual operation came as something of an anti-climax, as becomes clear from the account in its journal by Major Austen Ramsden of the action of his B Squadron of the Royal Scots Dragoon Guards, the leading regiment of the 7th Armoured Brigade.

Once in KEYES [their staging area] we again set up the hide routine although this time there was a definite air of tension within the Sqn. In the distance the low rumble of air strikes could be heard and dim flashes illuminated the night horizon to our north. Final preparations were made here and rehearsals for breaching the border 'berm'* were carried out. Several exercises were carried out and it was at this stage that we were issued with the revolutionary GPS† satellite navigation system on a scale of three per sqn. This changed our whole *modus operandi* as we were now able in conjunction with the use of TOGS‡ to move accurately and swiftly to any given point in any weather by day or night.

Orders to move came quickly and on 25th February we found ourselves heading north along pre-arranged routes through the border obstacles and into Iraq. Having made our way through a maze of vehicles we went firm§ in our FUP on the afternoon of 25th February. It was on the move up that we saw our first Iraqi 'EPW's¶ and the odd burnt out vehicle. When firm in the FUP we used the short time that we had to refuel using the newly fitted 45 gal drums that we carried on the back of the tanks.

We broke out of the FUP at approximately 25 1530 and we headed north towards heavy storm clouds brewing on the horizon and just as it was getting dark the Sqn took its first prisoners. They were a group of ten rather pathetic looking soldiers who seemed overjoyed to see us and who made it very clear that they had absolutely no intention of fighting. By 25 1900 we had advanced 98

* An artificial bank of sand.
† Global Positioning System.
‡ Thermal Observation Gunnery Sight.
§ Consolidated their position.
¶ Enemy prisoners of war.

kms from the forward staging area and it was at this point that we had our first brief halt while we waited for enough satellites to appear above the horizon to enable our GPS systems to work.

The Sqn basically went firm that night in a position covering the movements of the battle groups to our south. The SCOTS DG BG* had been having a small action in the area of what was to become known as the 'comcen'. The only action that we saw that night was the clearance of the northern parts of the objectives 'Copper' and 'Zinc'. Up to that point the only sightings that we had experienced were of what turned out to be elements of 16/5 L† who were extremely lucky not to have been engaged on each occasion. It is a credit to all those involved and especially the Sqn Ldr that none of the 16/5 L were engaged even though they were in completely the wrong place as far as we were aware.

Having cleared 'Zinc' we were told to go firm in a counter penetration position covering the northern flank as we had been warned of enemy armour moving in that area. Fortunately nothing came of those reports and we received orders on the morning of 'G'+2 to take on 'Platinum'. This basically meant moving south east past a minefield where we would line up with 'C' Sqn QRIH‡ and one of the Staffords Coys. By mid day that Tuesday we were holding just north of that start line while the immediate area was cleared. The rain and drizzle of the night before had given way to strong winds and consequently visibility was reduced to as little as 50m as the sand swirled about. Eventually we were given the 'all clear' and we advanced to join up with 'C' Sqn on the start line. After having overcome the initial difficulties of marrying up in the sandstorm we were eventually set. Just as H hour came the wind miraculously subsided and visibility was restored. In the early stages of the following assault several 'hard' targets were engaged but all proved to have been abandoned. Having advanced about six km we came across our first significant position. To our astonishment there were literally hundreds of Iraqi soldiers just milling about on top of their trenches apparently oblivious to the ordnance falling all around them. Having reached our limit of exploitation we went firm and awaited fresh

* Battle Group.
† 16th/5th Lancers.
‡ Queen's Royal Irish Hussars.

orders. 'Platinum' was supposed to have been occupied by elements of 52 Bde, 12 Armd Div: we had seen little of them other than the odd destroyed vehicle and a large number of abandoned positions.

As dusk fell we moved north east into a hide location again to await new orders and cover any threat from that direction. Meanwhile the remaining elements of 7 Bde were taking on 'Lead'. The move into this supposed 'hide location' proved more difficult than anyone had imagined. No detailed recce had been carried out and it turned out that as night fell the leading elements of the BG were debussing on what was later discovered to be a battalion sized enemy position. After a short exchange of fire the Staffords cleared the position, and we went firm in a box leaguer ready to replen[ish] later that night.

At first light the next day we received orders to advance east to objective 'Varsity' and from there on into Kuwait. The Staffords BG was now on the southern flank and again we advanced with little opposition. Every so often we would encounter small pockets of enemy however their only desire appeared to be to want to give themselves up. In the end we just had to ignore them as even if we had wanted to we didn't have enough of the correct assets to be able to handle them.

We crossed the Wadi-al-Batin at about 27 0900 and continued the advance into Kuwait at breakneck speed. When approximately 20 km into Kuwait we received orders to go firm and again we went into a counter penetration this time facing east. We were the Bde reserve at this stage and so expected little action in this new position. We were to remain there until the early hours of the following morning when again we were to receive orders to move. This time the objective was to be known as 'Denver' and it was situated on the Kuwait City to Basra highway just north of Kuwait City itself. The Sqn Ldr returned from his 'O' group at 28 0600 and then began one of the fastest advances in the history of armoured warfare. The Sqn found itself again leading the BG and once more we found the visibility appalling; this time due to our proximity to the burning oil wells. Having lost count of the number of abandoned positions that we had driven through we eventually went firm at 28 0850. Just prior to that we had been informed that a temporary cease-fire had been implemented as of 28 0800 which explained the orders that we had received earlier that morning which stated that we were effectively not allowed to engage unless we were ourselves first engaged.

The advance to Denver had again fortunately been uneventful although you could see that the enemy had left in a hurry. Equipment, most of it untouched, was left strewn everywhere. Having had time to digest the news that the war was effectively over we then regrouped back under command SCOTS DG and by late afternoon we were once more back in 'the fold'.

In the land campaign of 100 hours, the division advanced 180 miles, destroying almost three Iraqi armoured divisions and capturing over 7,000 prisoners, including several senior commanders, at a cost to itself of nineteen men killed, nine of them when two US Air Force aircraft fired on an armoured personnel carrier of the 3rd Royal Fusiliers.

They tell the story of their experiences in the other armoured brigade, the 4th:

As dawn broke on Tuesday 26th of February (G+2) the Bn had reached the area of Objective COPPER. The area was littered with burning and destroyed tanks. The whole area was covered in a pall of smoke. In many respects it was a bit like a scene out of a Hollywood film, but only this time it was for real.

The Bn continued to move eastwards, collecting groups of prisoners who literally appeared from nowhere to surrender. Meanwhile Capt Guy Briselden with elements of the Recce Group had successfully completed a short sharp action which involved debussing of a Milan* ground section to act as normal infantry and clear several trenches. This incident started when an Iraqi soldier changed his mind about surrendering and began firing with an AK47 at the NCOs who had already accepted his surrender. With great presence of mind, Fus Casser who was driving a MCT(S)† took his rifle and shot the Iraqi in the head, killing him instantly. (This is the only officially documented case of an enemy soldier in the theatre being shot by an SA80.)‡ Other enemy positions then opened fire which

---

* Milan is the infantry's anti-tank missile, normally hand-held.
† Milan compact turret (Spartan): the Spartan is a tracked light armoured personnel carrier, and the MCT(S) a version from which a Milan could be fired from a turret.
‡ The British L85A1 rifle.

were finally subdued by the Milan ground section as previously mentioned.

The attack against objective BRASS was the next brigade task and it was to be done in three phases. Commander 4 Brigade's plan was for the sequential committal of the Battle Group at this stage, thereby ensuring maximum indirect fire support for each phase. The Fusiliers were to conduct the final phase of the Brigade attack, having a squadron of armour from 14/20 Hussars grouped with us. The Bn moved up to the line of departure, just North/West of the enemy objective and was secure in the area just before 1300 hours. The rain had now stopped, but it was very windy, with great clouds of dust obscuring the area. Visibility dropped to less than 50 metres at one stage and concern was expressed by the Battery Commander as to the difficulty in adjusting the artillery fire plan. However, there was a delay in the operation as the tank squadron (D Sqn 14/20 Hussars commanded by Maj Alistair Wicks) was not immediately available to be re-grouped. The tanks appeared out of the murk at 1350. H hour was then confirmed as 1400 by which time all targets had been adjusted.

The plan was that C Coy (Maj Alex Bain) would attack the Northerly positions, with A Coy (Maj Patrick Vyvyan-Robinson) attacking the centre ones. Immediately afterwards No 2 Coy (Maj Andrew Ford) would move round to the south of A Coy to clear away any extra positions that may be encountered and then exploit onto objective STEEL. C Coy as the final phase of the attack would exploit from their initial objective in BRASS onto the Northern edge of objective STEEL. Just before H hour, a convoy of soft skinned vehicles drove past A Coy in the direction of the objective. Having no way of contacting them and pointing out the danger they were in, the Coy Commander dispatched the Milan Section Commander, Sgt Shrowder, to stop the convoy. It later transpired that they were the Echelon from another Brigade unit which had become disorientated in the sandstorm.

The attack commenced at 1400 preceded by a massive artillery bombardment, delivered by six batteries plus some MRLS salvos. The noise was fantastic and even in the Warriors one could feel the ground trembling with the concussions of the explosions. C Coy advanced quickly onto the northern objectives and met limited resistance. A few well placed rounds of 30mm HE put paid to any thoughts of resistance by the enemy. C Coy quickly cleared its objectives and fired upon numerous bunker positions. Many of the guns had been disabled by the artillery barrage, but the destruction was completed by 30mm rounds and an attached Engineer squadron which followed the main assault.

A Coy's attack followed a similar pattern, with the Coy advancing quickly through the position destroying any enemy equipment that was in its way. Again resistance was very light, the enemy having been subdued by the artillery bombardment and then totally surprised by the speed and momentum of the advance, appearing as if by magic out of a sandstorm from a totally unexpected direction.

After a few moments of re-grouping No 2 Coy assaulted its objective STEEL. Again the speed of the assault appeared to demoralise the enemy who put up limited resistance and surrendered in droves. No 2 Coy cleared several positions on the south of the objective and then began to reorganise. In the north of objective STEEL, C Coy was completing the final clearance operations and the whole position was secured by 1500 hours.

There then occurred the major tragedy of the campaign. C Coy was reorganizing in the Northern part of Objective STEEL when at 1502 two Warriors were destroyed. Initially it was not clear whether they had hit mines or come under fire from in depth enemy positions. C/S* 22 and 23 were destroyed with nine soldiers being killed and 11 injured. The RAP immediately went to the Coy's assistance deploying several ambulances to the scene. Unfortunately nothing could be done for the dead other than retrieve them from the Warriors. It was here that the excellent preparation of the RAP, including the Duke of Kent's Band, was put to the test. The injured were quickly and effectively treated, then evacuated through the dressing station.

This was a cruel blow; to be so severely hit at a time when the action had gone so well. Doubts were raised as to the cause of the incident and prisoners were questioned as to the position of minefields. Gradually the awful truth dawned and it seemed possible that these casualties were inflicted by friendly US A10 aircraft mistakenly attacking the Warriors. That all of the casualties came from No 8

* Call sign.

platoon concentrated the anguish and made it even more difficult to bear.

The Battle Group did not have time to dwell on the tragedy as another objective to the East (TUNGSTEN) had to be seized. It was apparent that the enemy was stunned by the speed of the advance and it was therefore vital to maintain the momentum of the assault. (News was coming in that Hussein had ordered his forces out of Kuwait; President Bush rejected this situation).

The Battle Group stopped on the northern edge of STEEL and replen[ish]ed from A1 Echelon which had followed up behind the Coys. No 2 Coy was re-grouped to the 14/20 Hussars and we received another squadron of tanks (B Squadron, Maj Richard Shereff) for the following operation. This operation involved a preliminary phase in crossing an oil pipe line which ran approximately north/south in front of objective TUNGSTEN.

The recce group under Maj Cortin Pearce, moved forward to mark the route and discovered a suitable crossing point over the oil pipe line which was improved by Mr Lobb and his engineers. The attack was officially due to start at 2330 hours but there were some skirmishes as the recce group crossed the pipeline when enemy infantry appeared at an extremely large oil installation which was just north of the crossing site. They were immediately fired upon by Rarden cannon and even Milan missiles from the recce group. Soon all resistance there had ceased, leaving the installations burning and many Iraqis waving white flags. Meanwhile the artillery put down a constant barrage onto the enemy. Particularly impressive was the use of the 8 inch batteries and the MLRS, which caused a really spectacular explosion in the enemy position as an ammunition dump exploded in a massive orange fireball.

The Brigade attacked onto TUNGSTEN from the South with the Royal Scots on the left and the Fusiliers on the right. The armoured squadrons made an excellent use of their thermal night sights to destroy enemy at long range. Again more gun emplacements were destroyed by the Fusiliers and many prisoners taken. The night battle was fast and furious with C Coy having to take rapid evasive action to avoid being caught in an artillery barrage. The position was cleared by 0400 hours on the 27th February (G+3) and the Bn moved slightly further north and west into the area of the Wadi Al Batin to reorganise. Everyone by this stage was tired after two sleepless nights and most people took the opportunity to snatch a couple of hours rest. Immediately after first light, the Bn was put on immediate notice to move for a possible counter penetration task to the North, to act as a counter movement force blocking the vital routes that traversed the Wadi Al Batin.

Most of the morning passed quietly, with the Bn collecting significant numbers of prisoners. Included among these was the Commander of the Iraqi's 27th Infantry Division and his staff. He emerged from his bunker in the desert looking in pristine condition as if he had just been shopping in Harrods, in complete contrast to the ragged condition of his soldiers. His arrogance was somewhat dented when he learned that the Americans were now on the outskirts of Basra. He had further lessons in humility when dealt with by the RSM who was in charge of all prisoner handling.

Just before lunch the Padre conducted an impromptu memorial service for those who had died and in a short but moving ceremony the Bn remembered its fallen comrades. The service was carried out in a cloudburst, the grey sky and rain set a melancholy tone to the proceedings.

Entirely separate from the operations of 1st Armoured Division, the SAS had been employed from 20 January onwards on patrols well behind the Iraqi lines to locate their mobile missile launchers and report them to the US Air Force, which would then attack them. This became of increased importance after 22 January, when Iraq launched missile attacks on Israel in the hope of involving her and splitting the Arab members of the coalition away from the USA. The SAS not only destroyed some of the Scud transporters themselves, but, in cooperation with the air forces, forced them to move out of range of their targets in Israel and Saudi Arabia.

The decision to halt operations on 28 February, when Schwarzkopf's forces were close to Basra and had reached the Euphrates near Nasiriyah, was controversial then and became more so later, Saddam Hussein and his cronies having remained in power contrary to expectations that overwhelming defeat would lead to his overthrow. But none of the coalition partners wished to step into the politico-military morass which an attempt to occupy Iraq and support an alternative regime would undoubtedly have involved. World opinion was also withdrawing its support as the coalition forces appeared to be inflicting heavy casualties on Iraqi forces only intent on escape. Some air force pilots appear to have shared that view. The British Government was certainly no keener than the American to take a step into that bog, although it was instrumental in forcing America to join Britain and France in responding to the popular demand for intervention in Kurdistan to relieve the plight of the Kurds, fleeing from Iraqi forces but denied entry into Turkey.

The Gulf War gave a considerable fillip to the self-confidence and morale of all three services at a time when their future seemed uncertain. The strong popular support which had been shown to them and their activities had been reassuring, and many hoped that it would temper the severity of the reductions which had been forecast just before Iraq invaded Kuwait.

Application of *Options for Change*

They were to be disappointed. The Government confirmed the decisions of the *Options for Change* review, reducing the army's manpower target further to 116,000, including men and women under training. The actual number of trained adults in the army in 1991 was 135,500, of whom 6,300 were women: by 1997 that was to be reduced to 104,000, while the strength of the army in Germany was to be reduced from 55,000 to 23,000. This would involve the disbandment of six regiments of the Royal Artillery, leaving sixteen, the equivalent of four regiments of the Royal Engineers, leaving ten, amalgamations in the Royal Armoured Corps which reduced the number of regiments from nineteen to twelve, two of which would be training regiments, and amalgamations in the infantry which would reduce the number of battalions, including Guards and Gurkhas, from fifty-five to thirty-six, bringing the number of Gurkha battalions down from five to two by the time Hong Kong was to be returned to China in 1997. All the large regiments would be reduced to two battalions, except for the Parachute Regiment, which was to keep three, only two of which would be fully trained in the parachute role, while the Guards regiments were to be reduced to one battalion each.

The Army Air Corps would retain six regiments, losing the equivalent of one after 1997.

There was to be a major reorganization of the army's 'tail'. A new Adjutant-General's Corps was to absorb the Women's Royal Army Corps, the Royal Army Pay Corps, the Royal Military Police, the Royal Army Educational Corps, the Military Provost Staff Corps (the army's prison service) and the Army Legal Corps. It would also include all clerks, both on the staff and in units, and would 'support' the Royal Army Chaplains' Department. In future women were to join the corps 'appropriate to their specialization and serve alongside their male colleagues'. The logistic services were to be reorganized into only two corps: one, for equipment support, based on the Royal Electrical and Mechanical Engineers, which would assume from the Royal Army Ordnance Corps responsibility for provision and distribution of all stores, including spares, concerned with equipment; the other, the Royal Logistic Corps, for 'service support', absorbing the remaining responsibilities of the RAOC, as well as those of the Royal Corps of Transport, the Army Catering Corps, the postal and courier functions of the Royal Engineers, and some of the supply functions of the Royal Army Medical Corps. This reorganization was almost a reversion to the pre-Second World War pattern before the REME was hived off the RAOC and when the Royal Army Service Corps was responsible for almost all other supply and transport services.

The army's operational organization was to be based on a NATO agreement that Britain's contribution to Allied Command Europe should be made to an ACE Rapid Reaction Corps (ARRC), which was to be commanded by a British lieutenant-general with a multinational staff. The corps was to have four divisions, two of them British and two multinational. The British would be the 1st Armoured Division of three strong armoured brigades, stationed in Germany, and the 3rd Division, stationed in Britain, of two mechanized brigades, an airborne brigade and, if required, also the Royal Marine Commando Brigade. Of the two multinational divisions, one would be formed from the Central Region, with a brigade each from Britain, Germany, the Netherlands and Belgium, the other division from the Southern Region. Outside the ARRC, the army would have fifteen infantry battalions with Engineer, Signals and Aviation support in Britain, five, mostly Gurkha, in overseas garrisons, and one in the Allied Command Europe Mobile Force. Army

Districts in Great Britain would be renamed Divisions. Five years later the reorganization of the Territorial Army was undertaken, emphasis being laid on methods by which individuals, or sub-units, could more readily reinforce the regular army in operations short of major war, preferably voluntarily. It was at last recognized that the chances of complete units being either required or able to be employed as such, other than medical or specialist ones, was increasingly improbable.

In 1992 a slight concession was made by allowing the army to recruit up to a manpower target of 120,000 and reprieving two infantry battalions from amalgamation; but the second thought came too late, as drastic cuts had been made in the recruiting organization, which some years later had to be reversed. They included the decision to abolish army recruiting offices and the teams which operated from them, relying instead on civilian Job Centres, and also do away with Junior (16–18) recruitment, both of which proved disastrous. In April 1997 the regular army, excluding Gurkhas, numbered only 111,572 soldiers, of whom 6,932 were women.

Bosnia

The army owed the manpower target concession largely to a new commitment, a contribution to the UN peacekeeping force in the former Yugoslavia. The danger had always existed that once Tito died, Yugoslavia, a product of Allied support for Serbia in the First World War, would disintegrate into its different racial elements, Slovenes, Croats, Bosnians, Montenegrins, Macedonians and Serbs, held together in Tito's lifetime by the common bond of a weak form of Communism. After Tito's death in 1980 and the later collapse of Communist regimes in Central and Eastern Europe, the Serbs turned to banging the nationalist drum as a means of retaining popular support. Slobodan Milosevic, the Serbian President of Yugoslavia, did that, arousing the antagonism of the other racial elements, who had always resented the domination of Yugoslavia between the wars by the Serbian Karadjordjevic dynasty. Slovenia was the first to break away, backed by a plebiscite in December

1990 which resulted in a vote of 88 per cent in favour. Milosevic firmly opposed this as setting an example which threatened the one-third of the Serbian population which lived outside the province of Serbia itself. He was supported in his attitude by both the European Community and the USA, who did not want to see Yugoslavia break up and were preoccupied, respectively, by negotiations about the Community's future, which culminated in the Maastricht Treaty, and by the Gulf War. Milosevic employed the Yugoslav army, dominated by Serbs, to try to suppress Slovenia's action, moving it into the province in June 1991, fighting spreading into Croatia in July. By September Milosevic saw that it was hopeless to try and hang on to Slovenia, where in any case there were hardly any Serbs, while Croatia, where there was a substantial number, especially in the Krajina area, followed Slovenia's example.

President Tudjman of Croatia, another Communist turned nationalist, held his own referendum and demanded the international recognition which had been given to Slovenia. Under intense pressure from Germany, which was struggling with the problems of its own reunification, the European Union (as it was now called) granted this, although he did not fulfil the conditions which insisted on equal treatment of minorities. This inevitably led to the same demand from Bosnia-Herzegovina, the population of which was 44 per cent Muslim, 32 per cent Serb and 17 per cent Croat, and had little chance of ever being able to form a viable state on its own. Nevertheless that was granted in April 1992 after a referendum boycotted by the Serbs, who were now fighting the Croats in most parts of Croatia and Bosnia. The fighting was accompanied by widespread inter-communal brutality, including 'ethnic cleansing', resulting in a massive refugee problem.

At first the European Union tried to deal with the situation itself by political and diplomatic action, but by the end of 1991 the United Nations was also involved, and in June 1992 a UN Protection Force (UNPROFOR) was established in order to protect minorities, ensure the withdrawal of the Yugoslav army to Serbia proper, and demilitarize the other various bodies of armed men. In August Britain sent 24th Field Ambulance, Royal Army Medical Corps, to join the force in Croatia, where UNPROFOR was supposed to be 'demilitarizing' the Serb enclave in the Krajina area. At the same time a mechanized infantry battalion, 1st Cheshires, was sent to Bosnia, accompanied by an armoured reconnaissance squadron from 9th/12th Lancers, their principal task being to ensure the safe passage of humanitarian aid. In October they were joined by a Royal Engineer field squadron from 35th Engineer Regiment, bringing the British contribution to UNPROFOR to a strength of 3,000 men and women. A base was established at the Bosnian port of Split.

The combined diplomatic efforts of the European Union and the United Nations met with no success, constantly frustrated by one side or the other, while more active peacekeeping in its usual form of keeping the armed forces of the warring sides apart and restraining them from fighting each other was added to that of escorting humanitarian aid.

The Prince of Wales's Own Regiment of Yorkshire (PWO) had relieved the Cheshires in May 1993 and was based at Gornji Vakuf during this period. B Company describes its experience:

> There was only one secure supply route in Central Bosnia. It bisects Gornji Vakuf and transits the front lines. Our primary task was to escort both military and aid convoys as they travelled along 40 km of vulnerable route. In places the road is nothing more than an old logger's trail. The route was prone to closure for extended periods at short notice due to shelling, shooting and drunken soldiers manning check points. But perhaps the greatest danger was posed by the cows whose owners had vacated the area leaving them to forage by the side of the road. They seemed to regard our presence as something of a threat. Despite the fighting there were very few delays to aid convoys.
>
> The Militia Armies fighting this civil war do not have the capacity to care for their wounded. Visions of children without legs being transported in wheelbarrows, stretchers being loaded into makeshift ambulances, amputations being conducted by candlelight, seeing people literally blown apart by high explosive are images that will remain with us for ever. We assisted wherever and whenever we could. In all we must have evacuated nearly 500 people during the midst of the fighting. There were some horrible choices to be made. Should we have stopped during the middle of an artillery barrage to pick up a young girl lying seriously injured by the side of the road? Was it worth risking the crew of a Warrior in order to recover a man who would have bled to death in a minefield? Decisions that no amount of training could have prepared us for. Decisions that had to be made on a daily basis.

Our base was caught in the cross fire on numerous occasions. A round hit the liaison officer's bedside light. A mortar shell came through the roof of 4 Pl's accommodation, shrapnel destroyed our water purification unit and damaged several of our vehicles. The guardroom and rear sanger* were hit by small arms fire almost every night. Sgt Williamson was shot in the chest whilst on patrol. It was difficult to believe that we were not being deliberately targeted by some rebel factions of the local militia. We fired back whenever the situation warranted it. 6 Pl went mine hunting. We became experts at judging the crack and thump of high velocity rounds and learned to live with things going crummph in the night. It was always a pleasure to watch the reactions of those who were new to Gornji Vakuf or just passing through.

There seemed to be an almost insane desire to retain the rituals of Regimental life, despite the circumstances. Area sweeps were conducted in flak jackets and helmets. Orders and interviews proceeded despite the flash of tracer rounds outside the office. Soldiers sunbathed behind sandbags in order to achieve a healthy glow prior to R and R.† Company HQ paraded for PT at 0700 hours daily, and as usual the CQMS's crew never attended. Things were painted maroon and old gold. Our forbears would have been proud – we hope.

In 1994, the year during which Lieutenant-General Sir Michael Rose commanded the UNPROFOR troops in Bosnia, the British contribution was reinforced by another infantry battalion and armoured reconnaissance squadron, bringing the total to 3,500. The battalions by then were the 1st Coldstream Guards, relieved in May by 2nd Royal Anglian, and the 1st Duke of Wellington's: both reconnaissance squadrons came from the Light Dragoons, formed in December 1992 by the amalgamation of the 13th/18th and 15th/19th Hussars.

It was during this period that in response to attacks by the Bosnian Serb militia on Muslim-inhabited towns on the River Drina, east of Sarajevo, some were declared UN Safe Areas. The Duke of Wellington's Regiment found itself responsible for that of Gorazde. A Company describes its experience there:

* Sangar: fortified look-out post.
† Rest and recreation.

By the beginning of June Alma Company had developed an uneasy understanding with the Serbs remaining on the East Bank overlooking Gorazde. Serb armed 'police' had been substituted for armed 'civilians'. These were clearly soldiers under military orders, with service weapons, occupying tactical positions overlooking the town. Their presence within the 3 km zone was unacceptable but our mandate made the pre-emptive use of force to move them out impossible. Events in Geneva where peace talks were in danger of stalling, provided the catalyst to dramatically reduce the number of Serbs in the zone. The Bosnian delegation refused to negotiate until guarantees could be made that Serbs were out of the 3 km zone around Gorazde. The main area of concern was the East Bank. Alma Company patrols had, over the preceding six weeks, identified and monitored precise locations of Serb concentrations. This meant that we were ready to take action against them should it be required. The Bosnian delegation in Geneva refused to continue peace talks unless the Serbs were withdrawn from the East Bank. A deadline was imposed and General Rose was on the direct satellite link with the Commanding Officer and Operations Officer while the operation to move the Serbs was conducted. The Commanding Officer* and OC Alma† patrolled the hills with the local Serb commanders, Captain Ivanovic and Colonel Luka. The first positions visited proved the sticking point, with the Serbs steadfastly refusing to move from houses overlooking the town on Pargani Ridge. With the deadline of 1100 hrs drawing closer a robust insistence of a Serb withdrawal finally produced results. At 1055 hrs we were able to report to General Rose that the Serbs were on the move and the Geneva talks were back on – in the proverbial 'nick of time'! Once this first position had been cleared the momentum for a withdrawal grew, but we had to keep the pressure on, seizing concealed weapons and ensuring that the Serbs did not try to return to positions first vacated. With only two minor exceptions the Serbs withdrew from all their positions overlooking the town although many remained in dead ground within the 3 km zone.

Over the next fortnight, from 11 to 25 June, Alma Company kept the pressure up on the Serbs, searching for weapons, confiscating

* Lieutenant-Colonel D. M. Santa-Olalla.
† Major N. G. Borwell.

them and moving on all men in uniform. Over this period Alma Company took a platoon of Princess Patricia's Canadian Light Infantry (PPCLI) under command for about ten days. Their professionalism and good humour were much appreciated by all of us and their ability to integrate with Alma Company's operations was most impressive. On one occasion armed Serb 'civilians' had reinforced the area of the Pargani Ridge and a company operation was mounted to remove their weapons. At 0600 hrs Sergeant Ness and 1 Platoon moved down from OP4 overlooking Pargani Ridge. The PPCLI Platoon moved up the ridge from the river. The Serbs had a rude awakening as the Canadians and Dukes moved in from either end covered by GPMGs* from OP4. Bleary-eyed Serbs tried to prevent Sergeant Ness and his team entering the house they were occupying. Their commander attempted to bring his rifle into action but was dissuaded from this option by Sergeant Ness. Meanwhile, at the other end of the feature the Canadians were obstructed by Serbs claiming that the UN did not have the mandate to search for weapons. Technically they may have been correct but the OC told them that we did have the mandate and were going in. The Serbs gave way and the Canadians started their search. A total of sixteen rifles and machine guns were recovered, Corporal Foster and his team did particularly well in finding some cunningly concealed AK47s in a building already searched by the Canadians; Northern Ireland search training was still paying off! The aim of this operation was to deter the Serbs from openly moving around with weapons in the 3 km zone – to prevent them totally would have been impossible. To this end the next part of the plan was executed. Twenty French engineers armed with chainsaws moved in and cut down all the trees around the Serb positions. The faces of the Serbs was a study in disbelief as the cover from view disappeared allowing domination of their positions from OP4. Following this operation the Serbs were more willing to comply with the restrictions of the 3 km zone and even saw the funny side of what was a fairly liberal interpretation by us of our mandate. This showed, once again, that the Serbs respect strength and will normally back down when confronted.

Whilst the Muslim commander, Buljabasic, was prepared to assert

---

* General Purpose Machine-Guns.

that the Serbs had moved out of military positions around the town, many Muslim civilians were less convinced.

On 13 June members of 2 Platoon were manning Checkpoint 1 between the Serb and Muslim lines. They were in 'dead' ground until about 200 metres from the checkpoint and, even though the crowd comprised mostly women and children, this distance was covered rapidly. Sergeant Wilson and his men realised the gravity of the situation. Once through the checkpoint the crowd would have only about 150 metres until they reached the Serb line. The Serbs, Sergeant Wilson knew, would mow down the crowd rather than allow the people through to reach their houses. He and his men, with the river on one side and a steep hillside on the other, linked arms to prevent the rush, but to no avail. The crowd was checked briefly and the half-dozen Dukes were swept aside. Meanwhile, the Commanding Officer, standing in the Battalion operations room, heard the commotion over the radio net. He grabbed the nearest interpreter and sped down to the scene in his Land Rover with OC Alma in hot pursuit.

By this time reinforcements from 2 Platoon had started to bolster Sergeant Wilson's beleaguered team. The CO ran ahead of the crowd, stopping them with oustretched arms at the moment the Serbs manning their checkpoint cocked their weapons. The crowd halted ten metres from the Serbs, intent on going forward but hesitant now that their ringleaders had been halted by the Colonel. A tense stand-off developed with Sergeant Summersgill, Corporal Hind and their men out-flanking the Serbs from the ridge above and members of 2 Platoon with the OC on the road with the CO. After about ninety minutes the Serbs were persuaded to back off and the Muslim women and children had moved back down the road. It is no exaggeration to say that the Geneva peace talks were a trigger-pressure away from disaster that morning. But for the effort of Alma Company and more particularly the CO, Muslim women and children would have been shot down with UN soldiers being accused of protecting the Muslims or standing back and doing nothing. An invidious position and one which, either way, would have cost the lives of several Dukes and led to renewed fighting in Gorazde.

Throughout June and July Alma Company continued a punishing patrol programme both inside and, more controversially, outside the zone. Ops were strengthened and our hold on the East Bank consolidated. One visiting officer from General Rose's staff commented that the Gorazde force was unique in Bosnia – we were dominating the area in the face of Serb and Muslim brinkmanship.

In January 1995 Rose was replaced by Lieutenant-General Sir Rupert Smith. In June, after the Bosnian Serb army had taken hostage some 350 UN troops (including thirty-three from the Royal Welch Fusiliers, who were protecting the so-called Safe Area of Gorazde), most of 24th Airmobile Brigade, with its regiment of light field artillery and a regiment of tanks, the Queen's Royal Hussars, formed by the amalgamation of the Queen's Own Hussars and the Queen's Royal Irish Hussars was sent to Bosnia to act as a Rapid Reaction Force for UNPROFOR, bringing the total British contribution to 8,000.

The Commanding Officer of the Royal Welch Fusiliers, Lieutenant-Colonel Jonathon Riley, records events at Gorazde:

Both locally and regionally the situation deteriorated steadily after April. Combat incidents increased in number and intensity, and restrictions by the Serbs on our re-supply tightened to a stranglehold. To save resources, and because I was concerned at their isolation, we closed OP 9 and CP 8. On the 24th and 25th May, following the Serbs' refusal to remove heavy weapons from the Sarajevo TEZ,* NATO launched air strikes against targets around Pale. The explosions could be clearly heard by our outlying OPs.

Almost immediately the Serbs began taking hostages from the UN troops around Sarajevo. That afternoon, several towns, including Gorazde, were shelled and I along with other UN Commanders was told that, by General Mladic's orders, should any further air strikes take place then our camp would be shelled.

Gorazde Force was already at a high state of alert. I was certain that I could not just sit and wait for this to happen. With General Smith's approval I stayed with a small security and command party in Gorazde Camp, and kept the OP line and a liaison and medical detachment in the town. Everyone else was moved to a hide location away from direct fire and observed indirect fire, and out of mortar range of the Serb positions. An RV, from which the hide could be re-supplied, was also established, and these positions were maintained

* Tactical Exclusion Zone.

until the threat had diminished. We also implemented another long-standing contingency – we changed the insecure command nets to Welsh speaking – I thought the chances of either the Serbs or Muslims being able to produce a Welsh speaker were slight!

The move to the hide was accomplished safely in darkness, and enough activity was maintained to give the appearance of normality. The deception worked. For the next two days, there was a strange and unreal quiet. Then, early in the afternoon of May 28th, three of the A Coy OPs on Sjenokos were surrounded by a large force of Serb soldiers. We were able to withdraw the remaining two OPs in A Coy's areas before they were attacked – both were isolated and impossible to support. There are detailed accounts of what happened to Lieutenant Hugh Nightingale, Sergeant Nick Warren and their twenty-five men of A Coy who were taken hostage; all I will say here is that they acted absolutely in accordance with my orders, and they ensured that no lives were lost among their Fusiliers.

But while A Coy OPs were being taken, there were indications that the same was about to happen across on the East Bank. I ordered OC B Coy to defend the line if attacked and to be prepared to withdraw if the position became untenable. Had the Serbs coordin-ated their actions on both sides of the river (which was, it will be recalled, an inter-corps boundary), they would have taken many more hostages. Their lack of coordination gave us the time to prepare our response. B Coy was attacked, and all that afternoon we fought the Serbs. At the end of the fight we had lost another eight hostages (Cpl Parry 43 and his section) but taken no casualties, although it is certain that we inflicted a good many.

The next twenty-six days were, for most of us, an extremely unpleasant time as the battle for Gorazde raged. Artillery fire fell at the rate of 330 to 500 rounds per day on the worst days. Serb attacks were repulsed, and Muslim counter-attacks gained ground in some areas. We maintained armed neutrality. By day, it was too dangerous to move around in the open so we remained under cover in our shelters. To keep up morale we trained on our weapons, first aid and map reading skills, observed and reported on the progress of the battle, and brewed beer! Liaison with the BiH* local commanders, civil authorities and aid agencies was conducted by night with me

* The Bosnian Government, mostly Muslim, force.

and the company commanders, but with caution, as any light, whether torch or vehicle, attracted a fearsome amount of fire.

Relations with the BiH were not that easy though. With the OP line gone and no convoys coming in, our usefulness to the Muslims disappeared. Inevitably they became more restrictive to us and even more so on the Ukrainians. They also placed guns and mortars around our base, using us as a shield against retaliatory Serb force. This had to be overcome by a mixture of blackmail, threats, and the reminder that future aid supplies would depend on us.

But by the end of June the Serb attack had failed, and the BiH had made substantial territorial gains on the East Bank, so that shelling and limited direct fire were the main threat. We were able to negotiate with the BiH to patrol their front line and confirm the Serb positions. Soon after we were able to open the main road so as to allow UNHCR* and military convoys into Gorazde. Whilst it was a hazardous platoon operation involving a minefield breach and inter-position between two active front lines, it allowed us to get vital food supplies into the town.

Finally, there was the desperate imperative to improve both the town's and our own logistic situation. We ran the force on the equivalent of two full tanks of fuel for a Volvo per day – this meant no electricity for lights, hot water, or laundry; walking everywhere; and cooking on wood. Fuel was used for essential vehicles, and to maintain communications (including those vital welfare phone calls home), refrigeration of our food and medical facilities, and water purification. Our problem now was that, around Sarajevo, fierce fighting meant that the existing supply route was impracticable. In the end, we were saved by General Janvier, the Force Commander, who went personally to see Mladic, and made an agreement for us to be supplied on the road route from Serbia. With only three days of supply left, a French convoy made it through to us. This convoy was commanded by a resourceful and determined officer called Philippe Coiffet. He was subjected to every conceivable harassment by the Serbs, but nothing deterred him. Thereafter a new route, which only required us to be on Bosnian Serb territory for 25 kms, worked wonders and we were never again in logistic difficulties. It also allowed us to recommence R and R. But the route meant a complete

* United Nations High Commission for Refugees.

reconfiguration of the logistic chain. The distances were immense but the system was in place within ten days thanks to some miracles worked by HQ BRITFOR, Captain Nick Ravenhill, Captain Des Williams and all the lads at Kiseljak.

Tension was heightened in July and August by Bosnian Serb attacks on UN Safe Areas, which eliminated two of them, and mortaring of Sarajevo market. After negotiations with General Mladic, the Royal Welch Fusiliers were evacuated eastward into Serbia. This was followed within twenty-four hours by NATO air attacks to deter further attacks on Safe Areas and to make the Bosnian Serbs move their heavy guns out of range of Sarajevo. This tough action led to a US-backed ceasefire in October and a conference in Dayton, Ohio, which resulted in an agreement, signed in Paris in December, by which all the participants accepted that Bosnia would remain a single multi-ethnic nation state. A NATO force (IFOR), including American troops, would enforce the withdrawal of armed forces into agreed areas, and preserve peace and order, while elections would be held in the autumn of 1996 to establish a Bosnian Government. NATO's British-commanded Allied Rapid Reaction Corps (Lieutenant-General Sir Michael Walker) assumed command of the land forces, consisting of three divisional areas, the northern one American, with some Scandinavian troops and a Russian brigade, the eastern one French, including Spanish and Portuguese troops, and the western one British, including a Canadian brigade in which Malaysian and Dutch troops also served. The divisional headquarters was that of the 3rd Division (Major-General M. D. Jackson) and the British combat element was not significantly increased.

Second Lieutenant T. A. Harper, commanding 7 Platoon in C Company of the 2nd Light Infantry, describes how the new regime started:

At the end of December 1995, C Company 2LI was tasked to Banja Luka to implement the Dayton Peace Agreement. With the change from the UN to IFOR came new rules of engagement and an entirely new operational requirement. C Company found itself in a not possible unique situation by being allocated an area entirely in Serbian territory. Given the vast areas to be covered and the need for an extensive and consistent liaison structure, platoons were allocated Areas of Responsibility or AORs. 7 Platoon's boundaries matched exactly those of the famous 16 Krajina Motor Rifle Brigade which included a 17 km front. 16 Brigade proudly boasts that it has never lost a square metre in battle and wherever the fighting was difficult they would be found. They were last in the area of the Posavina Corridor before moving to Banja Luka. The Commanding Officer of 16 Bde (equivalent roughly to a UK Battle Group) was Lieutenant-Colonel Dragan Vukovic, twice wounded in the conflict, who liaised directly with OC C Company Major Rex Sartain. This left the three Battalion Commanders (equivalent roughly to a UK Company Group) liaising at Platoon level with Second Lieutenant Tom Harper. 16 Brigade also provided a liaison officer, Captain Zec, who had spent 22 years in the Army and was an ex Yugoslav National Army infanteer. The Brigade quickly became renowned for its hospitality and co-operation with the Dayton Agreement.

The run up to D+30 on 19 January 1996, the date the Factions withdrew 2 km either side of the ceasefire line to form the Zone of Separation, kept the platoon busy in attempts to acquaint itself quickly with the new AOR. In fact the first patrol into the rear area of the AOR found a previously undiscovered AA Battery. There was also a large training area and camp full of 'Eastern' tanks and APCs. Being so close to the old Soviet type equipment felt very odd! Having met the three Battalion Commanders, and once again given the size of the frontage, the need to break down again further into Section AORs became apparent. The 2nd Battalion's area, covered by 1 Section under Cpl N. Lindley, was the most heavily populated with 259 civilians living in or planning to live in, the actual ZOS.* When three more Warriors, from the Corunna Platoon Milan Detachment under Serjeant Bramwell, were attached, they quickly teamed up with 1 Section to cover the whole Battalion area. The first and third Battalions were covered by Cpl Hayward commanding 3 Section and Serjeant Stewart commanding 2 Section. Having found accomodation in deserted houses, the soldiers started developing a friendly rapport with the locals. In the few days remaining until D+30, the main effort was to mark the ZOS with Orange 6 foot piquets, using satellite navigation to place them accurately on all main routes.

On D+30, the withdrawal of forces went very smoothly. It was quickly established that the civilians were very concerned about their

* Zone of Separation.

safety, now that their soldiers were no longer present to protect them. The Platoon began extensive patrolling with, due to the mine threat, unarmed VRS* guides to ensure the ZOS was clear of any military factions. This became a very intense period. With amazingly clear and warm weather, many unfinished mine clearances and other disposal tasks were able to take place. Tasks included overwatch of body exhumation; which turned out to be a sheep carcass; overwatch of minefield clearance by unarmed VRS engineers and handing out IFOR's 'newspapers' from American Psy Ops, a task which Corporal Stanley particularly enjoyed. Shortly after D+30 on 24 January an artillery Warrior OPV† attached to the Company hit an anti-tank mine seriously damaging the vehicle but thankfully injuring nobody. Lance-Corporal Butcher also had an exciting moment when he confirmed, with satellite navigation, that a manned VRS position was inside the ZOS. He confiscated four weapons and various munitions. The few days remaining until D+45 (3 February 1996) were spent preparing for the civilians, although strongly discouraged, who were expected to return to areas recently vacated by the Croatians under the Peace Agreement.

A troop of Challenger Tanks from The Queen's Royal Hussars, commanded by Lieutenant Rupert Greenwood, arrived just prior to D+45. The tanks worked closely with the Platoon by helping to provide an OP screen and check point with Lance-Corporal Judd and his vehicle on the 'Golden Mile', a main route within our area. The expected 'mass exodus' did not occur. However, a rather Right Wing Serbian Colonel initially refused to let an 'undisciplined', 'leaderless' civilian group of about 50 to pass into the Golden Mile. From D+45 the Platoon began to concentrate on verifying the clearance of all heavy weapons from the 10km zone while maintaining the integrity of the ZOS. It also roughly marked the half way point of the tour, the lads insist. Since then the Platoon have continued to develop relations with the locals, Private N. Oakley being a favourite of Mr Savanovic, Mayor of the town of Sarici. The locals also helped the Platoon with free firewood, the occasional slivovitz, and Turkish coffee.

Throughout the implementation of the Peace Agreement, the

---

* The Bosnian Serb army.

† Observation Post Vehicle.

Platoon worked off a 4 day ration and water supply and a 48 hour fuel replenishment. This along with constant demands for post, chocolate and fresh rations certainly kept Serjeant Lovell (7 Platoon's 'brand new' Platoon Serjeant) very busy indeed. The constant use of the Warriors left the drivers, Privates Shingler, Thurlow, Williams and Blewett, with few spare moments. Long days and patrols aside, everyone enjoyed the interaction with the civilians and soldiers. We all learnt a great deal about a very different culture and military organisation. Working with the VRS to see the Dayton Agreement through and also seeing civilians return to their homes has made this the most productive and rewarding part of the tour.

The original intention was that IFOR would complete its task and withdraw by the end of 1996; but as that date approached it became clear that the force could not be withdrawn without seriously prejudicing the continued viability of the Dayton Agreement. Reduced in strength, it remained in being, and in April 1997 there were still 4,822 British army soldiers in Bosnia, of whom 989 were Territorials who had volunteered for a tour there.

EPILOGUE

Near the end of the twentieth century, the British army is very different from the army it was at the beginning; but it retains much of the image that it projected then. The main changes are that, in all ranks, it is much more professional; that technology has transformed its weapons, communications and transport almost out of recognition; and that women now serve alongside men almost everywhere.

Nevertheless a pattern remains, originating in the seventeenth and eighteenth centuries, primarily in the cavalry and infantry, of a tribal regimental system, even though the names of the regiments have changed and changed again ever since they were, in both arms, known only by numbers. In spite of this devotion to the past, the army has managed, not without difficulty and resistance at times, to adapt itself to new technologies.

The first phase of the Boer War opened its eyes to the effect of improvements in the firepower of artillery and infantry weapons, sited in concealed and dug-in defences: the second phase impressed on it the value of mobility. The emphasis which that gave to the value of cavalry persisted in the minds of that arm, and of the many higher commanders who came from it, when, from 1915 onwards, the conditions of the battlefield made it virtually obsolete. Even when it could be used, as in Palestine, it could not decide whether the traditional sabre or lance or the new-fangled rifle should be used.

As previous pages have made clear, the Great War was dominated by artillery and the machine-gun covering an obstacle and fired from a well-concealed and protected defensive position. The tank helped to break the stalemate this imposed. Although its introduction was not the decisive factor in final victory, it pointed the way to the replacement of the horse by the mechanized vehicle and to a restoration of mobility to the battlefield. The aeroplane proved a useful adjunct, particularly for reconnaissance.

A major handicap was the invariable breakdown of communications, as telephone and telegraph lines were shattered by artillery bombardment. Radio communication had hardly been developed, except at the highest levels of command.

The Second World War saw these new features developed, although not to the extent they could and should have been if more effort of all kinds had been devoted to them between the wars. Although, with the exception of the Cavalry Division, the whole army was mechanized by 1939, much of the equipment was of poor quality and almost all of it insufficient in quantity, especially tanks and artillery of all kinds. This was one of the reasons for the lack of effective training in the cooperation of all arms, but not the only one. Conservatism and ingrained prejudice played a part.

A combination of these factors goes far to explain the poor performance of the army on 'the Hard Road to Alamein'; but, when those omissions were remedied, the army's traditions and training, and the inherent virtues of its members, brought about 'the Turn of the Tide' and, with the help of the United States of America and the Soviet Union, both of whom carried far larger shares of the burden, brought victory at last in 1945. Aircraft, manned by the Royal Air Force, which had absorbed the army's Royal Flying Corps in 1918, became essential for support to the army in several different roles: reconnaissance, interdiction, close support, air defence and transport, including that of parachute and air-landed troops. Both services learned the hard way how to cooperate with each other.

A major feature of the Second World War was amphibious landing, in which the army had to become as expert as the Royal Marines had always been, some serving with the latter in specially trained commandos. The war also saw the blossoming of other special forces, virtually private armies.

Since 1945, with the exceptions of Korea, Suez, the Falklands and the Gulf, the army has reverted to its familiar task of 'low intensity' operations, which now include international peacekeeping. The helicopter has come to play an essential part in several different roles. Communications have been transformed by leaps and bounds as the information technology era has affected every aspect of life. The electronic revolution has affected an even wider field. It is transforming the gathering and distribution of information of all kinds, navigation, the direction and propulsion of weapons, and the means of countering them. Electronic warfare enters into every field and brings about rapid changes, adjustment to which does not come easily to Britain's tradition-oriented army. Who, even a few years ago, would have envisaged Lance-Corporal Butcher of the 2nd Light Infantry fixing his position in Bosnia by satellite?

In spite of these changes, the task of the soldier in the front line remains much as it has always been, and the soldierly virtues and skills he needs remain remarkably unchanged. He must still be skilful in the use of his weapons and of ground: he must be alert, steadfast and brave, and must be able to endure hardship of every kind. He must be prepared to stay where he is or go forward in the face of firepower more intense than ever before, risking wounds or death, and himself be prepared to kill.

His commanders during the century have borne a great responsibility for him. At the start many were too old and unable to adapt to new conditions. Periods of peace have always tended to result in that. At the start of wars, there is always dross to be got rid of; but not all who failed then were in that category. Some, like Gort and Wavell, were unlucky to have held responsibility when the cards were stacked against them, and their successors were fortunate to enter the fray when resources were more adequate and strategic conditions more favourable. First World War generals were influenced by their experience in the Boer War, Second World War ones by that of the First, and post-1945 ones by theirs in the Second. Now few have any experience of anything but 'low intensity' operations, but the short, sharp Gulf War showed that their training for 'high intensity' in Germany had served them well. Fortunately none have had to face nuclear war, for which previous experience would have been useless. In the Gulf War the army prepared itself to meet the possibility of chemical or biological attack, but fortunately did not experience either.

Whatever the changes, a tradition has been preserved, handed down since the days of Marlborough, of friendship and loyalty to comrades, whatever their rank, in the same unit, bolstered by great pride in the latter, however ancient or recent its history. There are many examples of that in the personal accounts in the preceding pages.

In May 1997, as this book was being written, a Labour administration came to power and declared that it would embark on a strategic review to reassess the purposes for which the armed forces were required, as the Stanhope Memorandum had done for the army 106 years before. It will be interesting to compare the two. International peacekeeping has very largely taken the place of 'the number of men for India' and 'garrisons for all our fortresses and coaling stations'; 'effective support of the civil power in all parts of the United Kingdom' remains a major commitment in Northern Ireland; 'home defence' has ceased to be a real task, even for the Territorial Army; but the requirement to 'send abroad two complete Army Corps' will be as open to question as it was in Stanhope's day, and there are likely to be voices echoing his theme that 'it will be distinctly understood that the probability of the employment of an Army Corps in the field in any European war is sufficiently improbable to make it the primary duty of the military authorities to organize our forces efficiently for the defence of this country', although international peacekeeping is likely to be preferred to the latter. The history of the century, as of previous ones, illustrates the dire effects, particularly in 1940, of making that assumption.

MAPS

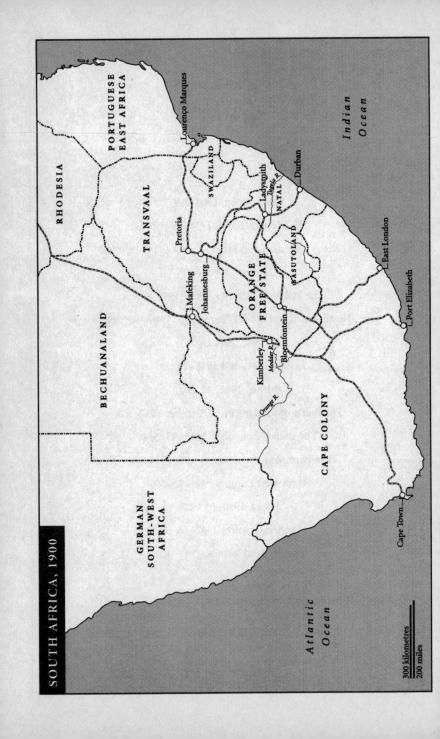

SOUTH AFRICA, 1900

RHODESIA

PORTUGUESE EAST AFRICA

Lourenço Marques

TRANSVAAL

SWAZILAND

Pretoria

Durban

Ladysmith

Tugela R.

NATAL

Mafeking

Johannesburg

ORANGE FREE STATE

BASUTOLAND

East London

BECHUANALAND

Kimberley

Modder R.

Bloemfontein

Port Elizabeth

Orange R.

GERMAN SOUTH-WEST AFRICA

CAPE COLONY

Cape Town

Indian Ocean

Atlantic Ocean

300 kilometres
200 miles

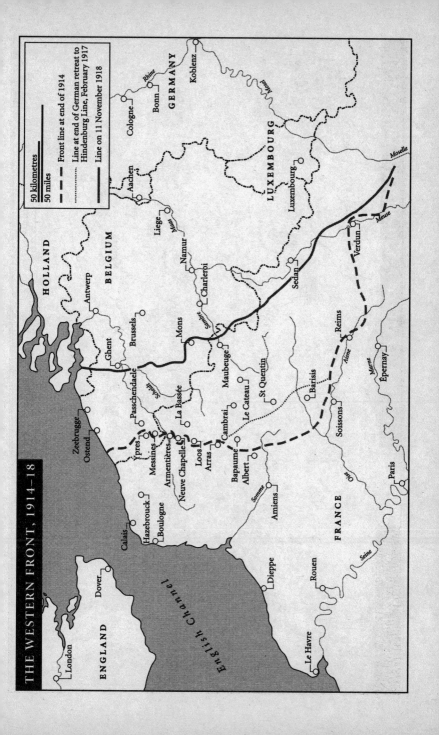

THE WESTERN FRONT, 1914–18

ENGLAND

London

Dover

English Channel

Calais
Boulogne
Hazebrouck
Dieppe
Rouen
Le Havre

HOLLAND

Antwerp
Brussels
Ghent

BELGIUM

Zeebrugge
Ostend
Ypres
Passchendaele
Messines
Armentières
Neuve Chapelle
Loos
Arras
Bapaume
Albert

Mons
La Bassée
Cambrai
Le Cateau
St Quentin
Maubeuge
Amiens

FRANCE

Paris
Soissons
Barisis
Reims
Épernay
Sedan
Charleroi
Namur
Liège

LUXEMBOURG

Luxembourg

GERMANY

Koblenz
Bonn
Cologne
Aachen
Verdun

Rhine
Maas
Mosel
Meuse
Moselle
Sambre
Schelde
Somme
Oise
Aisne
Marne
Seine

50 kilometres
50 miles

- - - Front line at end of 1914
········· Line at end of German retreat to
Hindenburg Line, February 1917
——— Line on 11 November 1918

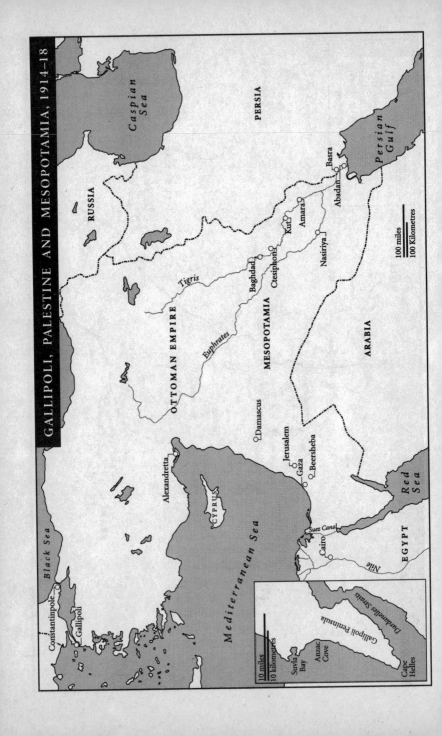

GALLIPOLI, PALESTINE AND MESOPOTAMIA, 1914–18

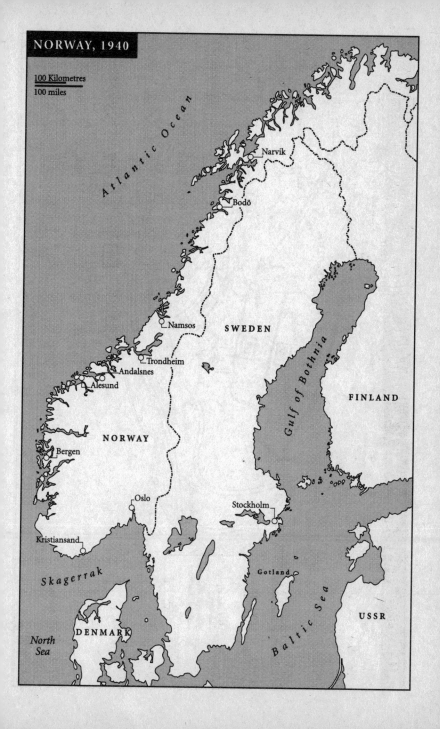

NORWAY, 1940

100 Kilometres

100 miles

Atlantic Ocean

Narvik

Bodö

Namsos

SWEDEN

Trondheim

Andalsnes

Alesund

Gulf of Bothnia

FINLAND

NORWAY

Bergen

Oslo

Stockholm

Kristiansand

Skagerrak

Gotland

Baltic Sea

North Sea

DENMARK

USSR

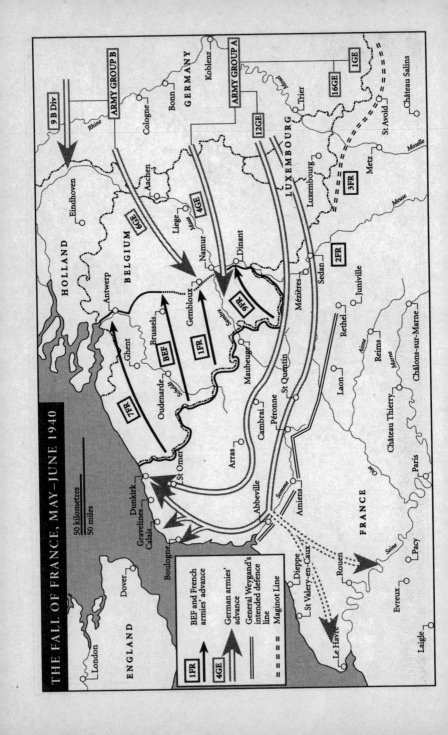

THE FALL OF FRANCE, MAY–JUNE 1940

50 kilometres
50 miles

ENGLAND

London
Dover

HOLLAND

Eindhoven

GERMANY

9 B Div
ARMY GROUP B

Rhine
Cologne
Bonn
Koblenz

Aachen

ARMY GROUP A

12GE

16GE

1GE

Mosel

Trier

St Avold

Chateau Salins

BELGIUM

Antwerp
Ghent
Brussels
Oudenarde
Schelde

6GE
Liege
Maas
Namur
4GE

Gembloux

Dinant

Sambre

9FR

Meuse

LUXEMBOURG

Luxembourg

Metz

3FR

Moselle

2FR

Sedan

Mézières

Juniville

7FR
BEF
1FR

Maubeuge

St Quentin

Rethel
Aisne
Reims

Laon

Chálons-sur-Marne

St Omer
Arras
Cambrai
Péronne

Château Thiery

Dunkirk
Gravelines
Calais
Boulogne

Abbeville
Amiens
Somme
Oise
Seine
Paris
Pacy

FRANCE

Dieppe
St Valery-en-Caux
Rouen

Marne

Evreux

Le Havre

Laigle

1FR   BEF and French
       armies' advance

4GE   German armies'
       advance

       General Weygand's
       intended defence
       line

= = = = Maginot Line

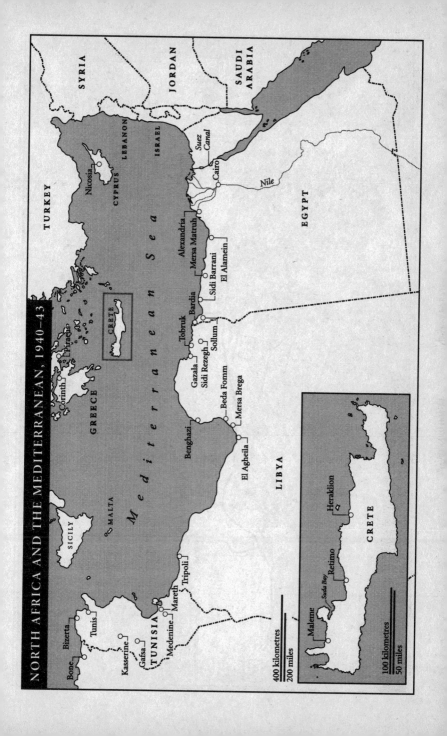

NORTH AFRICA AND THE MEDITERRANEAN, 1940–43

TURKEY

SYRIA

JORDAN

SAUDI ARABIA

LEBANON

ISRAEL

CYPRUS

Nicosia

Suez Canal

Cairo

Nile

EGYPT

Alexandria

Mersa Matruh

El Alamein

Sidi Barrani

Bardia

Tobruk

Sollum

Sidi Rezegh

Gazala

Beda Fomm

Mersa Brega

Benghazi

El Agheila

LIBYA

Mediterranean Sea

GREECE

Corinth

Piraeus

CRETE

MALTA

SICILY

Tripoli

Mareth

Medenine

Gafsa

Kasserine

Tunis

Bizerta

Bône

TUNISIA

400 kilometres
200 miles

CRETE

Maleme

Suda Bay

Retimo

Heraklion

100 kilometres
50 miles

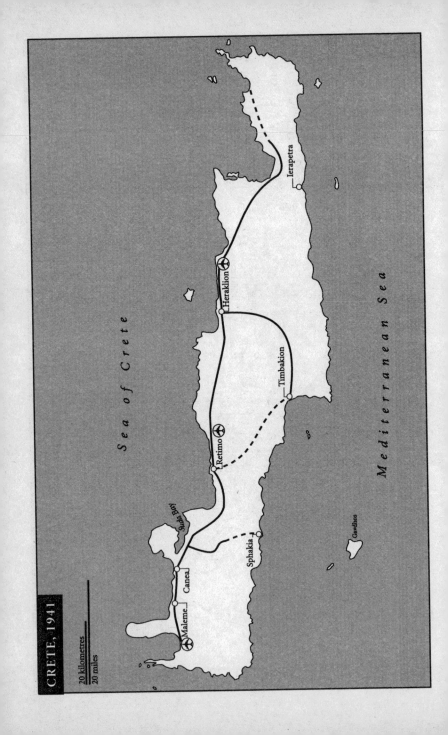

CRETE, 1941

20 kilometres
20 miles

Sea of Crete

Mediterranean Sea

Maleme
Canea
Suda Bay
Retimo
Sphakia
Timbakion
Heraklion
Ierapetra

Gavdhos

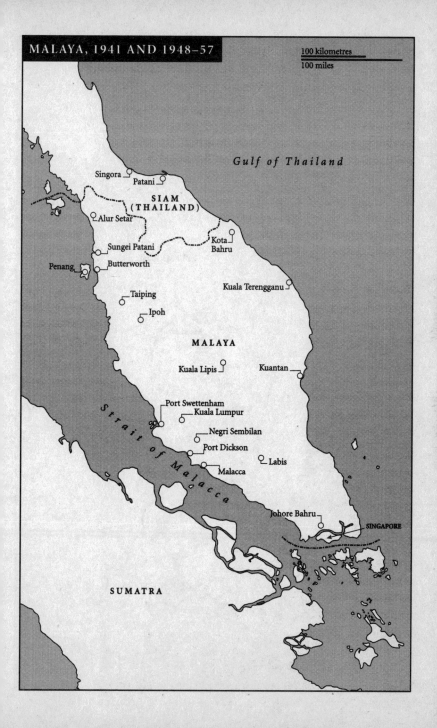

MALAYA, 1941 AND 1948–57

100 kilometres
100 miles

Gulf of Thailand

Singora
Patani
**SIAM
(THAILAND)**
Alur Setar
Sungei Patani
Kota
Bahru
Penang
Butterworth
Kuala Terengganu
Taiping
Ipoh
MALAYA
Kuala Lipis
Kuantan
Port Swettenham
Kuala Lumpur
Negri Sembilan
Port Dickson
Labis
Malacca
Strait of Malacca
Johore Bahru
SINGAPORE
SUMATRA

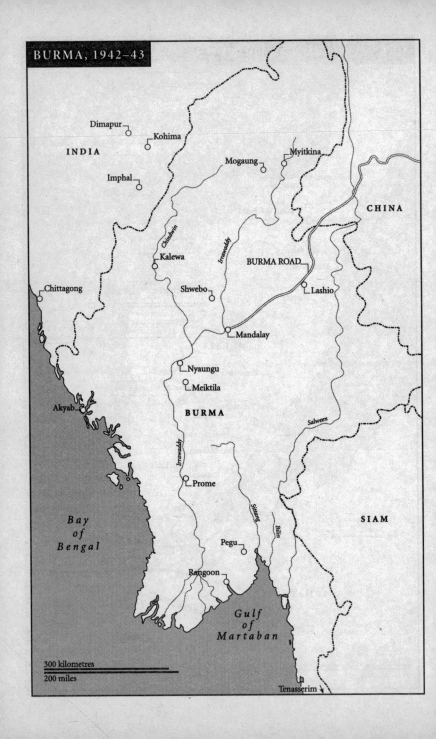

BURMA, 1942–43

INDIA

Dimapur

Kohima

Imphal

Kalewa

Chittagong

Shwebo

Akyab

Chindwin

Irrawaddy

Mogaung

Myitkina

CHINA

BURMA ROAD

Lashio

Mandalay

Nyaungu

Meiktila

BURMA

Irrawaddy

Prome

Sittang

Bilin

Salween

SIAM

*Bay
of
Bengal*

Pegu

Rangoon

*Gulf
of
Martaban*

300 kilometres

200 miles

Tenasserim

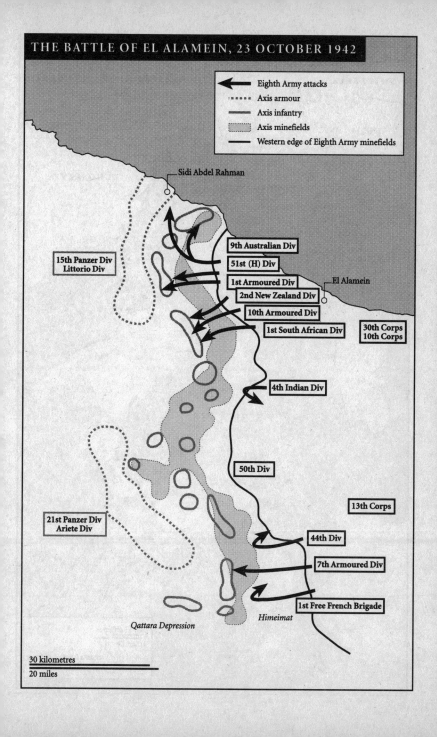

THE BATTLE OF EL ALAMEIN, 23 OCTOBER 1942

Eighth Army attacks
Axis armour
Axis infantry
Axis minefields
Western edge of Eighth Army minefields

Sidi Abdel Rahman

9th Australian Div
51st (H) Div
1st Armoured Div
2nd New Zealand Div
10th Armoured Div
1st South African Div

15th Panzer Div
Littorio Div

El Alamein

30th Corps
10th Corps

4th Indian Div

50th Div

13th Corps

21st Panzer Div
Ariete Div

44th Div

7th Armoured Div

1st Free French Brigade

Qattara Depression   Himeimat

30 kilometres
20 miles

THE ITALIAN CAMPAIGN, 1943–45

SWITZERLAND   AUSTRIA   HUNGARY

VENETIAN LINE

Ljubljana

Venice

Trieste

GOTHIC LINE

Po

Lake Comacchio

YUGOSLAVIA

Bologna

Senio

Ravenna

Florence

Rimini

Adriatic Sea

CORSICA

CAESAR LINE

Pescara   GUSTAV LINE

Rome

Garigliano

Sangro

Valmonte

Biferno

Anzio

Cassino

Foggia

Naples

Volturno

Salerno   Bari

SARDINIA

Taranto

Tyrrhenian Sea

CALABRIA

Mediterranean

Palermo   Messina

SICILY

Ionian Sea

Syracuse

Pachino

Sea

TUNISIA

100 kilometres

100 miles

········ German lines of defence

—·—·— International border

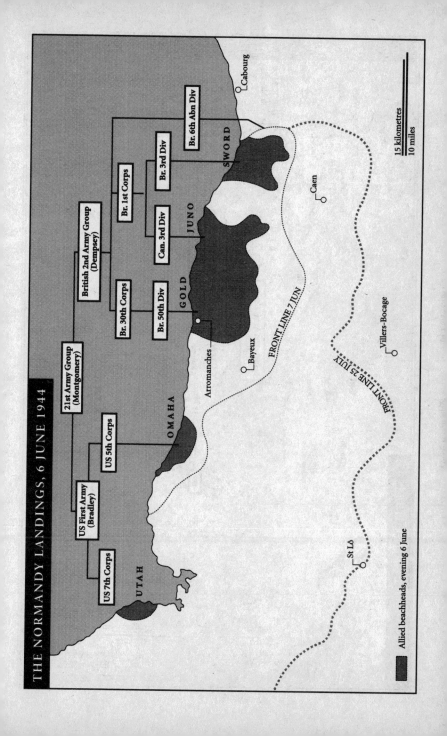

THE NORMANDY LANDINGS, 6 JUNE 1944

21st Army Group (Montgomery)

US First Army (Bradley)

British 2nd Army Group (Dempsey)

US 7th Corps

US 5th Corps

Br. 30th Corps

Br. 1st Corps

Br. 50th Div

Can. 3rd Div

Br. 3rd Div

Br. 6th Abn Div

UTAH

OMAHA

GOLD

JUNO

SWORD

Arromanches

Bayeux

Caen

Cabourg

FRONT LINE 7 JUN

FRONT LINE 25 JULY

St Lô

Villers-Bocage

15 kilometres
10 miles

Allied beachheads, evening 6 June

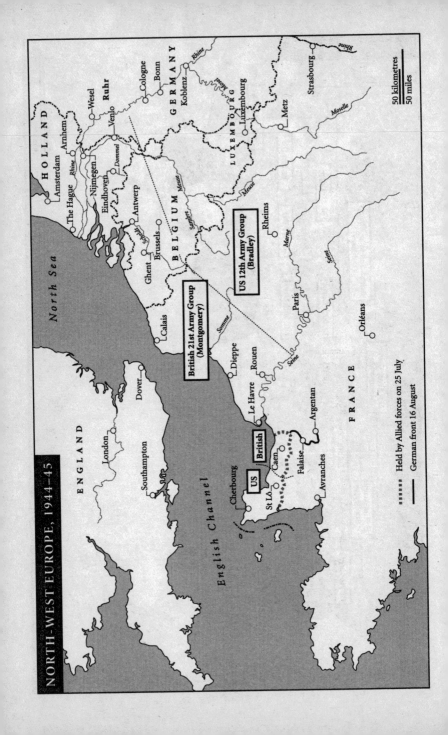

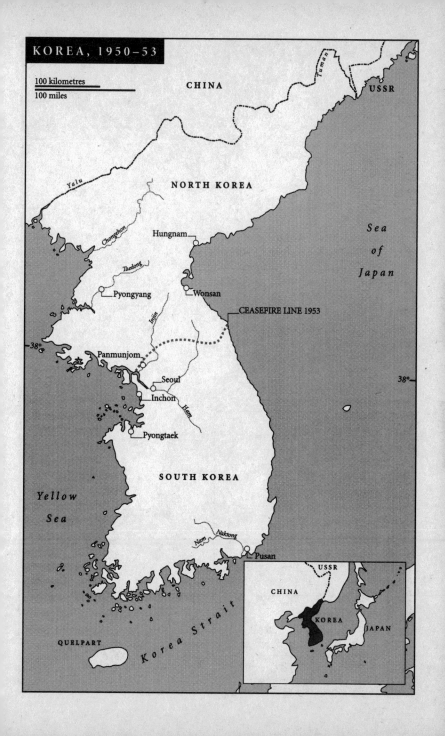

KOREA, 1950–53

100 kilometres
100 miles

CHINA

USSR

Yalu

NORTH KOREA

Tuman

Chongchon

Hungnam

Sea
of
Japan

Taedong

Pyongyang

Wonsan

CEASEFIRE LINE 1953

Imjin

–38°

Panmunjom

Seoul

38°

Inchon

Han

Pyongtaek

SOUTH KOREA

Yellow
Sea

Nam *Naktong*

Pusan

USSR

CHINA

KOREA

JAPAN

QUELPART

Korea Strait

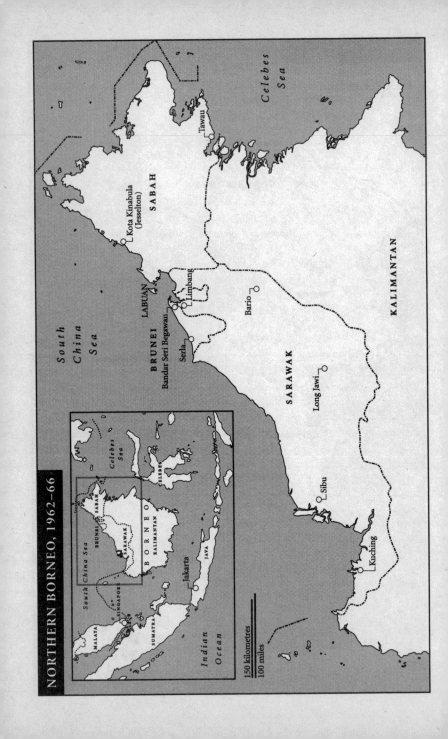

NORTHERN BORNEO, 1962–66

South
China
Sea

Celebes
Sea

SABAH

Kota Kinabula
(Jesselton)

LABUAN

Limbang

Bario

BRUNEI

Bandar Seri Begawan

Seria

SARAWAK

Long Jawi

KALIMANTAN

Sibu

Kuching

Tawau

Celebes
Sea

BORNEO

BRUNEI SABAH

SARAWAK

KALIMANTAN

Jakarta

JAVA

South China Sea

SINGAPORE

MALAYA

SUMATRA

Indian
Ocean

CELEBES

150 kilometres
100 miles

THE FALKLAND ISLANDS, 1982

South Atlantic Ocean

Port Louis
Berkeley Sound
Port Stanley
Port Salvador
Bluff Cove
Fitzroy
EAST FALKLAND
San Carlos
Darwin
Goose Green
Falkland Sound
PEBBLE ISLAND
Port Howard
Fox Bay East
Port Egmont
WEST FALKLAND
Fox Bay West

40 kilometres
25 miles

2 kilometres
1 mile
Two Sisters
Mt Longdon
Wireless Ridge
Tumbledown Mt
Government House
Mt Harriet
Mt William
Sapper Hill
Port Stanley

BIBLIOGRAPHY

Books

Place of publication is London, unless stated.

Babington, Anthony, *For the Sake of Example*, 1983.

Beckett, Ian (ed.), *The Army and the Curragh Incident*, Army Records Society Vol. II, 1986.

Belchem, David, *Victory in Normandy*, 1981.

Blacker, General Sir Cecil, *Monkey Business*, 1993.

Blake, Robert, and Louis, Roger, *Adventures with Britannia*, 1995.

Bond, Brian, *Liddell Hart: A Study of his Military Thought*, 1988.

Byford-Jones, W., *Grivas and the story of EOKA*, 1959.

Calwell, C. E., *Field Marshal Sir Henry Wilson: His Life and Diaries*, 1927.

Carver, Michael, *Second to None: The Royal Scots Greys 1918–1945*, Edinburgh, 1954.

—— *El Alamein*, 1962.

—— *Tobruk*, 1964.

—— *Harding of Petherton*, 1978.

—— *The Apostles of Mobility*, 1979.

—— *War Since 1945*, 1980 and 1990.

—— *The Seven Ages of the British Army*, 1984.

—— *Dilemmas of the Desert War*, 1986.

—— *Twentieth Century Warriors*, 1987.

—— *Tightrope Walking: British Defence Policy Since 1945*, 1992.

Chandler, David, and Beckett, Ian, *The Oxford Illustrated History of the British Army*, Oxford, 1994.

Clutterbuck, Richard, *The Long, Long War*, 1960.

Connell, John, *Wavell, Scholar and Soldier*, 1964.

Crutwell, C. R. M. F., *A History of the Great War, 1914–1918*, Oxford, 1936.

Dean, Sir Maurice, *The Royal Air Force in Two World Wars*, 1979.

Dennis, Peter, *The Territorial Army*, 1987.

D'Este, Carlo, *Decision in Normandy*, 1983.

Dunlop, Colonel John K., *The Development of the British Army 1899–1914*, 1938.

Fraser, David, *Alanbrooke*, 1982.

—— *And We Shall Shock Them*, 1983.

Grenfell, Russell, *Service Pay*, 1944.

Harris, J. P., *Men, Ideas and Tanks*, Manchester, 1995.

Hastings, Max, *Overlord*, 1984.

—— *The Korean War*, 1984.

—— with Jenkins, Simon, *The Battle for the Falklands*, 1983.

Jackson, W. G. F., *The Battle for Italy*, 1967.

—— *Withdrawal from Empire*, 1986.

Kee, Robert, *The Green Flag*, 1972.

Kersaudy, François, *Norway 1940*, 1990.

Kitson, Frank, *Gangs and Counter-gangs*, 1960.

Lewin, Ronald, *Slim*, 1976.

Liddell Hart, Basil, *Paris or the Future of War*, 1925.

—— *The British Way in Warfare*, 1932.

—— *The Tanks*, Volumes I and II, 1959.

—— *History of the First World War*, 1930.

—— *History of the Second World War*, 1970.

Mackesy, Kenneth, *Armoured Crusader*, 1962.

—— *A History of the Royal Armoured Corps, 1914–1975*, Beaminster, 1983.

Majdalany, Fred, *State of Emergency*, 1962.

Mearsheimer, John J., *Liddell Hart: A Study of his Military Thought*, 1988.

Mockaitis, Thomas R., *British counterinsurgency in the post-imperial era*, Manchester and New York, 1995.

Oatts, Lieutenant-Colonel, L. B., *Emperor's Chambermaids: The story of the 14th/20th King's Hussars*, 1973.

Official Histories of the War in South Africa, the First and the Second World Wars.

Pakenham, Thomas, *The Boer War*, 1979.

Paget, Julian, *Last Post*, 1969.

Pigott, Major-General A. F. K., *Manpower Problems: Second World War*, War Office, 1949.

Pocock, Tom, *Fighting General*, 1973.

Swinson, Arthur, *North-West Frontier*, 1967.

Thomas, Hugh, *The Suez Affair*, 1966.

Townsend, Charles, *The British Campaign in Ireland 1919–1922*, Oxford, 1975.

Trythall, A. J., *Boney Fuller*, 1977.

Wilson, R. D., *Cordon and Search*, Aldershot, 1949.

Journals

4th/7th Dragoon Guards Regimental Magazine

The Borderer's Chronicle. The King's Own Scottish Borderers.

The Castle. The Royal Anglian Regiment.

Eagle and Carbine. The Royal Scots Dragoon Guards.

The Fusilier. The Royal Regiment of Fusiliers.

The Guards Magazine (formerly *The Household Brigade Magazine*).

The Iron Duke. The Duke of Wellington's Regiment (West Riding).

Journal of The Queen's Royal Regiment.

The Journal of The Royal Army Medical Corps.

The Journal of The Royal Army Pay Corps.

The Journal of The Royal Engineers.

The Kukri. The Brigade of Gurkhas.

The Oxfordshire & Buckinghamshire Light Infantry Chronicle.

Pegasus. The Airborne Forces.

The Queen's Own Highlander.

St George's Gazette. The Royal Northumberland Fusiliers.

The Silver Bugle. The Light Infantry.

The Suffolk Regimental Gazette.

The White Rose. The Prince of Wales's Own Regiment of Yorkshire.

Y Ddraig Goch. The Royal Welch Fusiliers.

INDEX OF CONTRIBUTORS

Ranks and units are given as they were at the time of the experience described, as far as could be determined. Unless other acknowledgement is made, extracts are all from papers deposited with the Department of Documents of the Imperial War Museum. The name of the copyright holder, who has given permission, is shown in brackets, unless it is the individual himself. An asterisk denotes that it has not been possible to trace the copyright holder: the Museum would be grateful for any information which might help to trace those whose identities or addresses are not known. In the case of extracts from Regimental or Corps Journals, permission was given by the Editor, the Regimental Secretary or the Trustees in whom it was vested.

Captain J. K. **Wilson**. Tank Corps.*

Major D. J. **Wood**. 1st Bn. Oxfordshire & Buckinghamshire Light Infantry. (*The Regimental Journal*)

Lieutenant G. N. **Wood**. 1st Bn. Dorsetshire Regt.*

INDEX

Index